Street by Street

C000157580

NORTH HAMPSHIRE
PLUS CAMBERLEY, FARNHAM, HASLEMERE, NEWBURY, NORTH TIDWORTH

Enlarged Areas Aldershot, Andover, Basingstoke, Winchester

Ist edition May 2001

© Automobile Association Developments Limited 2001

This product includes map data licensed from Ordnance Survey® with the permission of the Controller of Her Majesty's Stationery Office. © Crown copyright 2000. All rights reserved. Licence No: 399221.

Published by AA Publishing (a trading name of Automobile Association Developments Limited, whose registered office is Norfolk House, Priestley Road, Basingstoke, Hampshire, RG24 9NY. Registered number 1878835).

Mapping produced by the Cartographic Department of The Automobile Association.

ISBN 0 7495 2360 3

A CIP Catalogue record for this book is available from the British Library.

Printed by G. Canale & C. s.p.a., Torino, Italy

The contents of this atlas are believed to be correct at the time of the latest revision. However, the publishers cannot be held responsible for loss occasioned to any person acting or refraining from action as a result of any material in this atlas, nor for any errors, omissions or changes in such material. The publishers would welcome information to correct any errors or omissions and to keep this atlas up to date. Please write to Publishing, The Automobile Association, Fanum House, Basing View, Basingstoke, Hampshire, RG21 4EA.

Ref: MX006

Key to map pages	ii-iii
Key to map symbols	iv-1
Enlarged scale pages	2-11
Street by Street	12-239
Index – towns & villages	240-241
Index – streets	241-258
Index – featured places	258-261

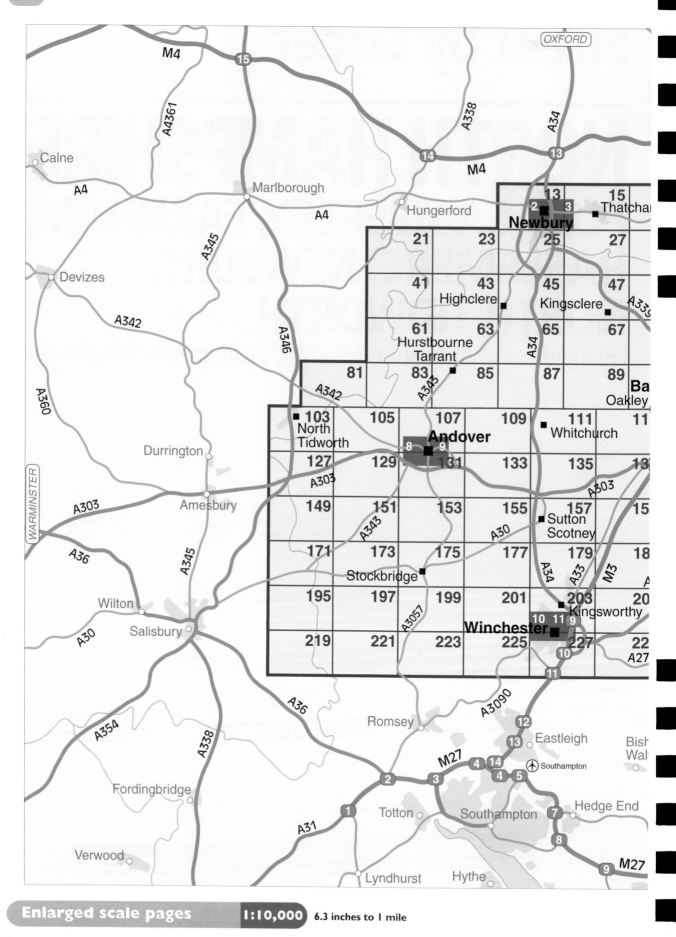

OXFORD

M4

A4361

A34

A338

Calne

A4

Marlborough

A4

Hungerford

M4

Newbury

2 **13** **3** **15** Thatchan

21 **23** **25** **27**

A345

Devizes

A342

A346

41 **43** **45** **47**

Highclere

Kingsclere

A339

61 **63** **65** **67**

Hurstbourne
Tarrant

A34

A360

A342

A343

81 **83** **85** **87** **89** **Ba**

A343

Oakley

103 **105** **107** **109** **111** **11**

North
Tidworth

8 Andover **9**

Whitchurch

WARMINSTER

Durrington

127 **129** **131** **133** **135** **13**

A303

A303

149 **151** **153** **155** **157** **15**

Amesbury

A343

Sutton
Scotney

A345

A303

A36

171 **173** **175** **177** **179** **18**

Stockbridge

A34 A33 M3

195 **197** **199** **201** **203** **20**

Kingsworthy

Wilton

10 **11** **9**

Winchester

A30

Salisbury

219 **221** **223** **225** **227** **22**

10 A27

11

A36

A354

A3090

Romsey

12

A338

13 Eastleigh

Bish
Wal

M27 **4** **14**

Fordingbridge

2 **3** **4** **5** Southampton

A31

1

Totton

Southampton **7** Hedge End

Verwood

8

M27

Lyndhurst Hythe **9** M27

A31

Enlarged scale pages 1:10,000 6.3 inches to 1 mile

0 1/4 miles 1/2 3/4

0 1/4 1/2 kilometres 3/4 1 1 1/4

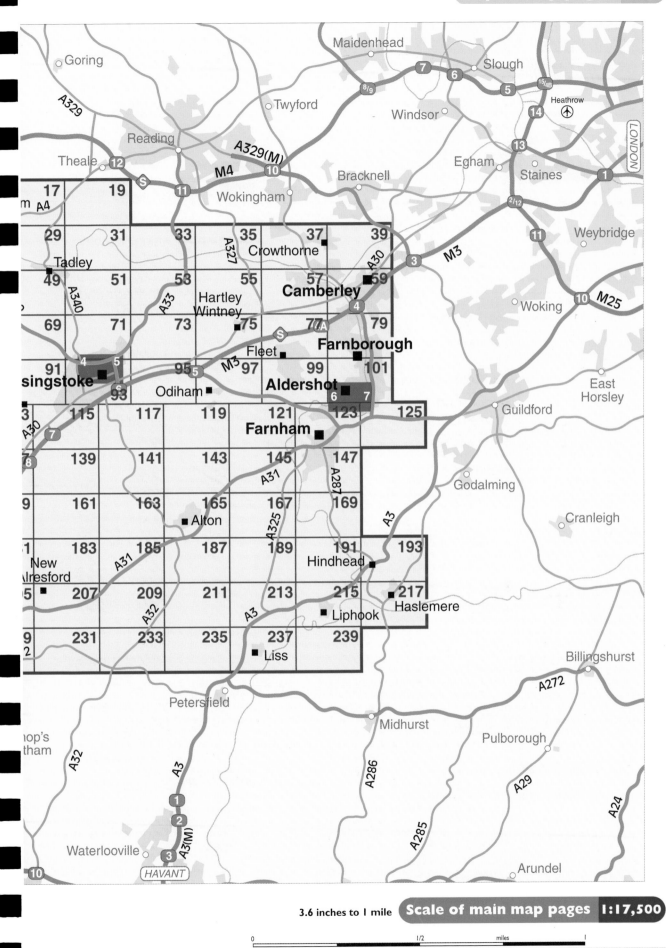

Goring

Maidenhead

Slough

7

6

8/9

15/4B

Twyford

Windsor

Heathrow

14

A329

Reading

A329(M)

13

LONDON

Theale

12

M4

10

Egham

Staines

1

11

Bracknell

2/12

| 17 | 19 | | | | | |
A4 | Wokingham | | | | **11** | Weybridge |

| 29 | 31 | 33 | 35 | 37 | | 39 |
A327 | Crowthorne | | | A30 | **3** | M3 | Woking | **10** | M25 |

Tadley

| 49 | 51 | 53 | 55 | 57 | 59 |
A340 | Hartley | **Camberley** | | |
A33 | Wintney | | **4** |

| 69 | 71 | 73 | 75 | 77A | 79 |
| | | | | **Farnborough** |
Fleet | M3 | S |

East
Horsley

| 91 | 4 | 5 | 95 | 97 | 99 | 101 |
singstoke | | 93 | Odiham | **Aldershot** | **6** | **7** |

Guildford

| 3 | 115 | 117 | 119 | 121 | 123 | 125 |
A30 | **7** | | | **Farnham** |

| 8 | 139 | 141 | 143 | 145 | 147 |
| | | | A31 | A287 |

Godalming

| 9 | 161 | 163 | 165 | 167 | 169 |
| | | Alton | A325 | A3 |

Cranleigh

| 1 | 183 | 185 | 187 | 189 | 191 | 193 |
New | A31 | | | Hindhead |
lresford |

| 5 | 207 | 209 | 211 | 213 | 215 | 217 |
| A32 | A3 | Liphook | Haslemere |

| 9 | 231 | 233 | 235 | 237 | 239 |
2 | | | | Liss |

Billingshurst

Petersfield

A272

op's
tham

A32

Midhurst

Pulborough

A3

A286

A29

A24

1

2

A3(M)

A285

Waterlooville

3

HAVANT

Arundel

10

0   1/2   miles   1

0   1/2   kilometres   1 1/2   2

Junction 9	Motorway & junction
Services	Motorway service area
	Primary road single/dual carriageway
Services	Primary road service area
	A road single/dual carriageway
	B road single/dual carriageway
	Other road single/dual carriageway
	Restricted road
	Private road
	One way street
	Pedestrian street
	Track/ footpath
	Road under construction
	Road tunnel
P	Parking

P+🚌	Park & Ride
🚌	Bus/coach station
	Railway & main railway station
	Railway & minor railway station
⊖	Underground station
⊖	Light railway & station
+++++++++++	Preserved private railway
LC	Level crossing
•—•—•—•—•	Tramway
-------------	Ferry route
·············	Airport runway
– · – · – · –	Boundaries- borough/ district
vvvvvvvvv	Mounds
93	Page continuation 1:17,500
7	Page continuation to enlarged scale 1:10,000

River/canal lake, pier		Toilet with disabled facilities
Aqueduct lock, weir		Petrol station
465 ▲ Winter Hill	Peak (with height in metres)	PH	Public house
Beach		PO	Post Office
Coniferous woodland		Public library
Broadleaved woodland		i	Tourist Information Centre
Mixed woodland		✗	Castle
Park		Historic house/ building
Cemetery		Wakehurst Place NT	National Trust property
Built-up area		M	Museum/ art gallery
Featured building		†	Church/chapel
City wall		Country park
A&E	Accident & Emergency hospital		Theatre/ performing arts
Toilet			Cinema

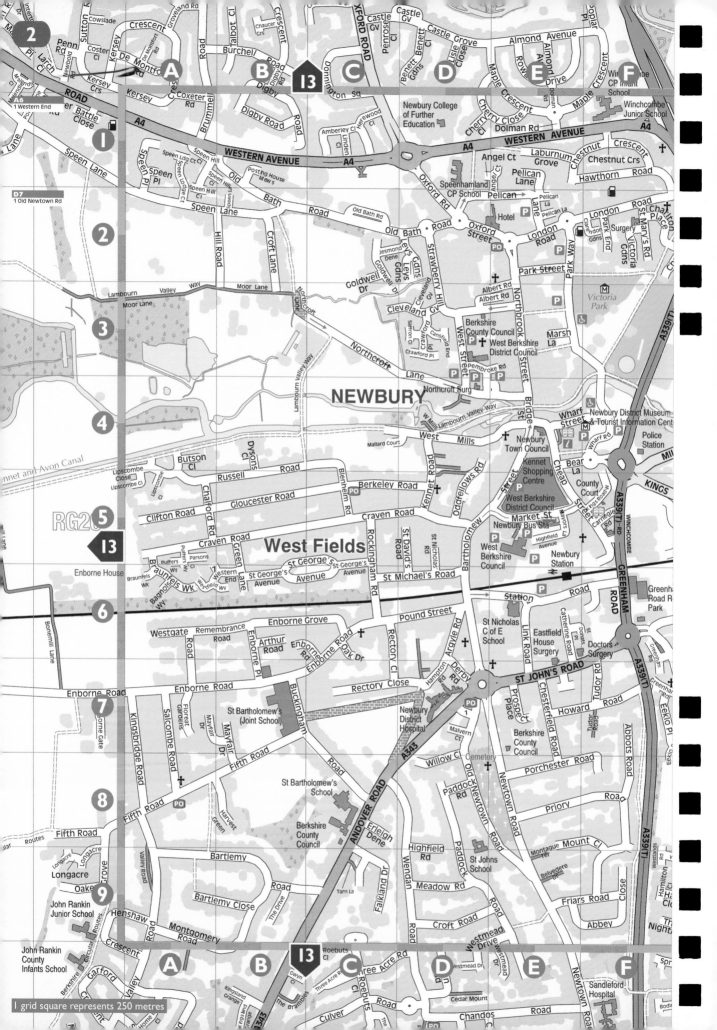

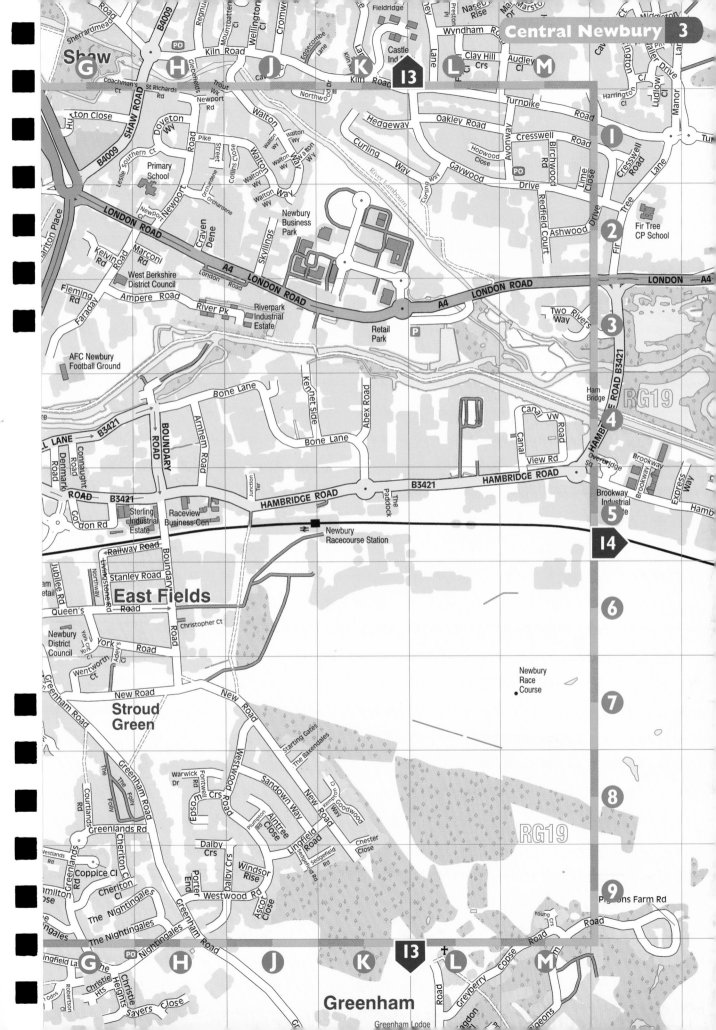

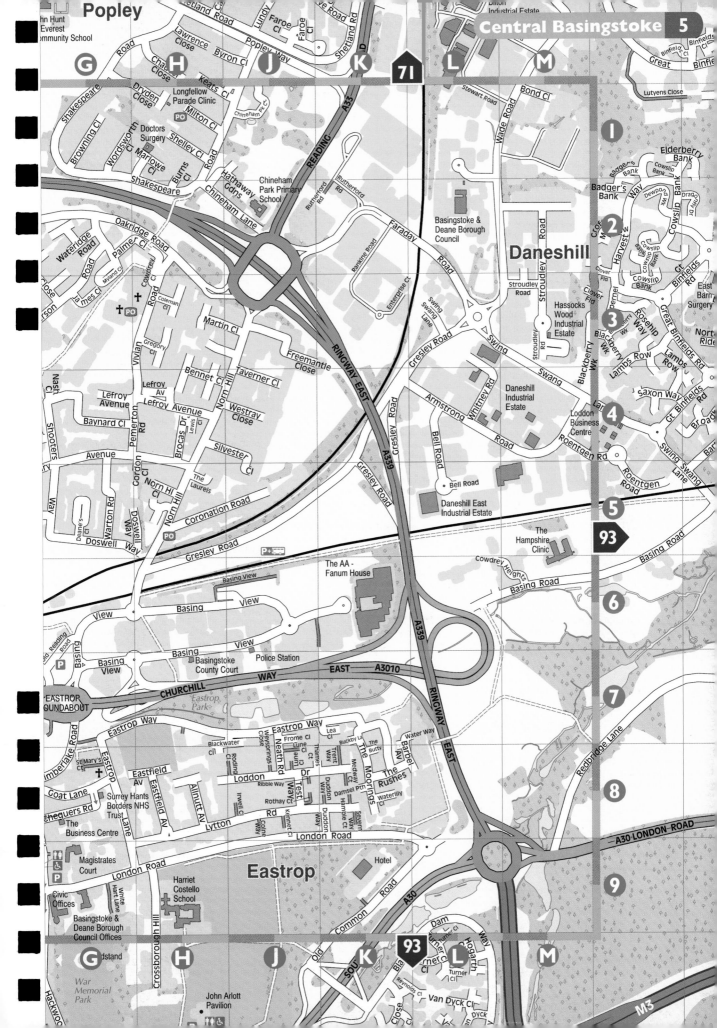

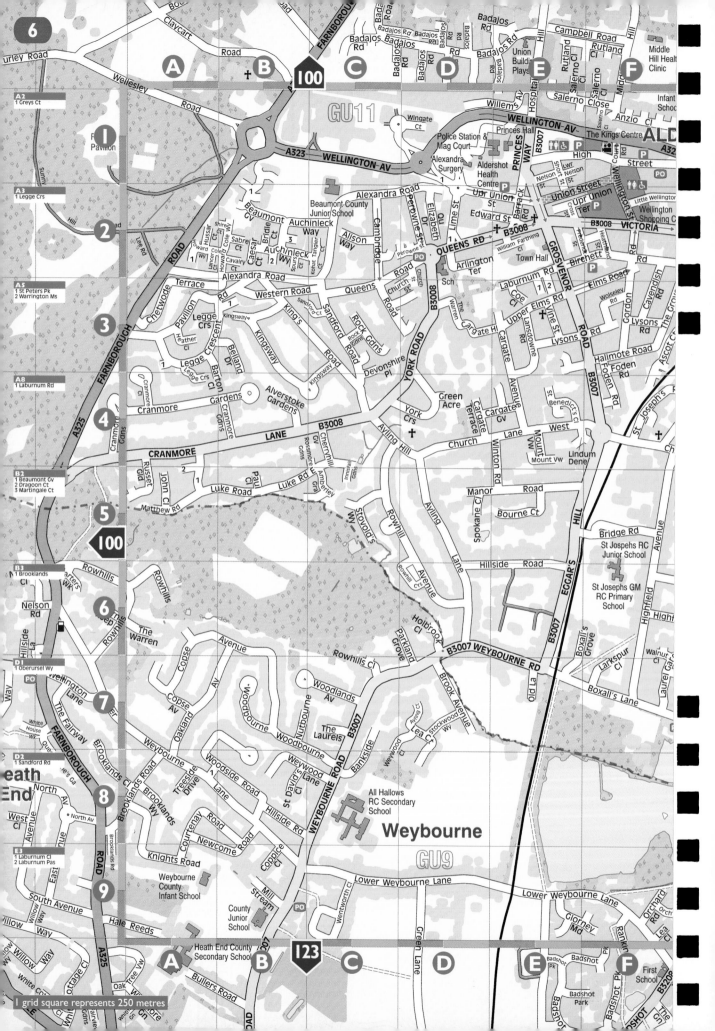

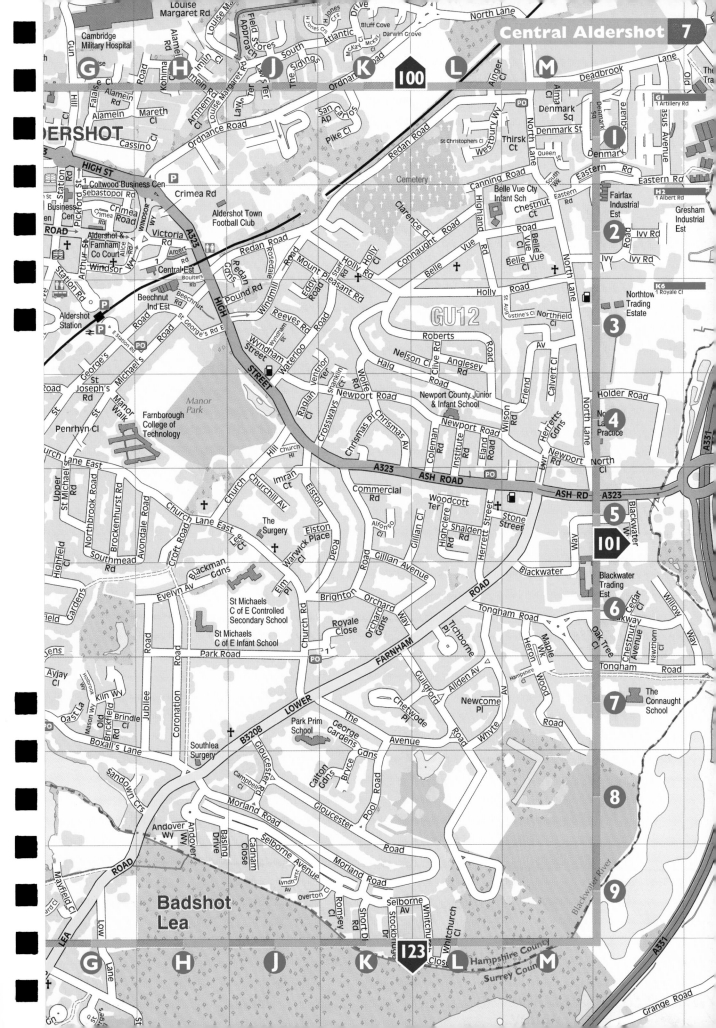

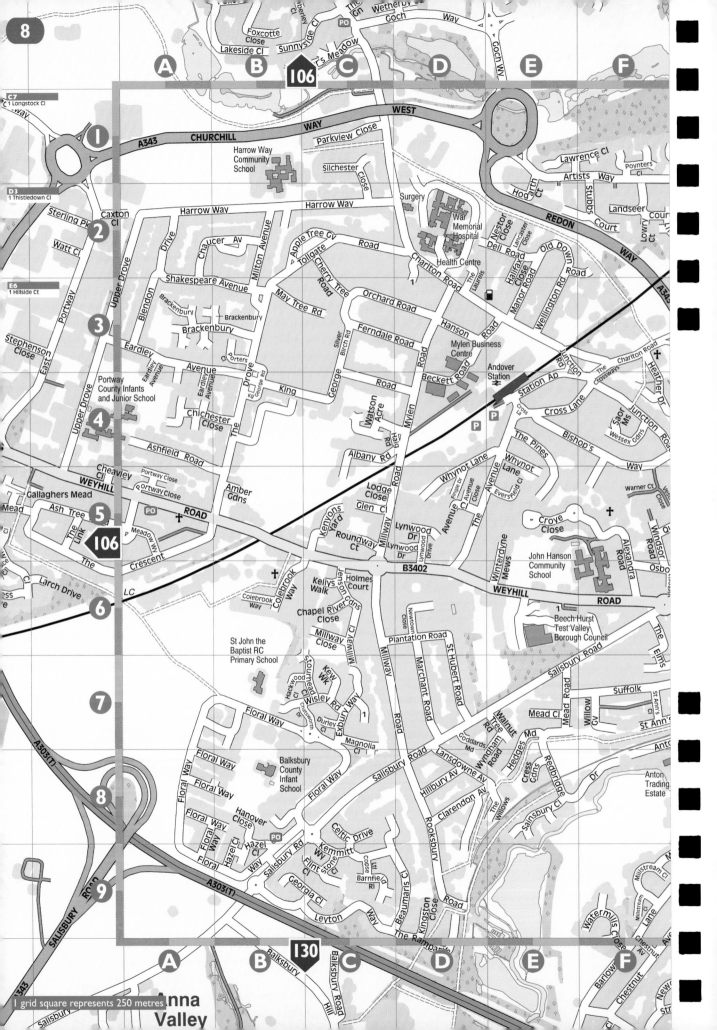

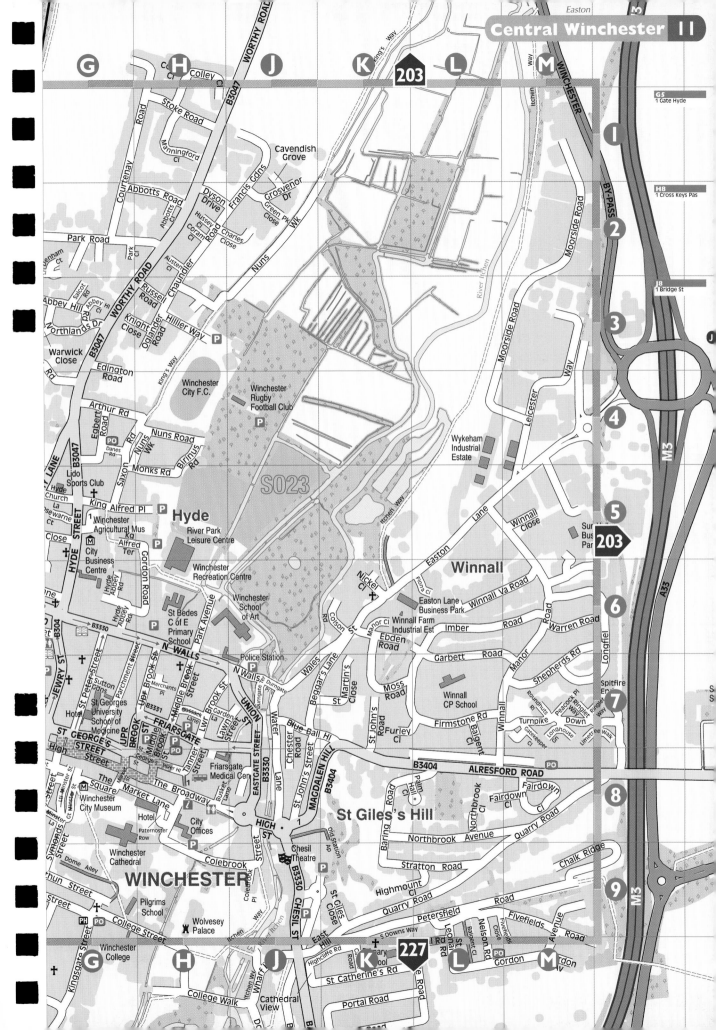

G3
1 Coster Cl
2 Cowslade
3 Majendie Cl
4 Marshalls Ct
5 Newbold Rd

G4
1 Caunter Rd

H3
1 Sylvester Cl

H4
1 Posting Ho Ms
2 Speen Hill Cl
3 Speen La
4 Speen Lodge Ct
5 Speen Pl

H6
1 Parsons Cl
2 Puffers Wy
3 Western End

I1
1 The Chase

Huntsgreen Farm

A B C D E F

Bagnor

Lambourn Valley Way

Woodspeen

Woodspeen Farm

Watermill Theatre
& Restaurant

PH

I1

RG20

B4000

Snake Lane

Cricketers

Chapel Road

Rookswood

Stockcross School

PO

Deanwood Farm

2

Church Road

Glebe Lane

†

Stockcross

A34(T)

Lambourn

B4000

Spee

3

GRAVEL HILL

Benham Cha

A4

A4

Speen House

Kinners

Milkhouse Rd

Benham Park

Elmore House

†

4

Marsh Benham

5

Benham Marsh Farm

6

Enborne Road

7

Enborne Copse

A34(T)

8

†

Church Lane

Enborne

Berkshire Circular Routes

Skinners Green

A34(T)

M7
1 Plumpton Rd

A

M6
1 Junction Ter
2 The Paddock

B

M4
1 Collins Cl

C

24

D

L7
1 Fontwell Rd
2 Wentworth Ct

L6
1 Adey's Cl

E

F

Cope Hall

M3
1 Fieldridge
2 Mountbatten Cl
3 Wellington Cl

L8
1 Coppice Cl
2 Robertson Cl

1 grid square represents 500 metres

The

Green

Miles's Green

Turner's Green

Upper Bucklebury

Colthrop

Thatcham Station

Thatcham Town Football Club

Crookham Manor

Chamberhouse Farm

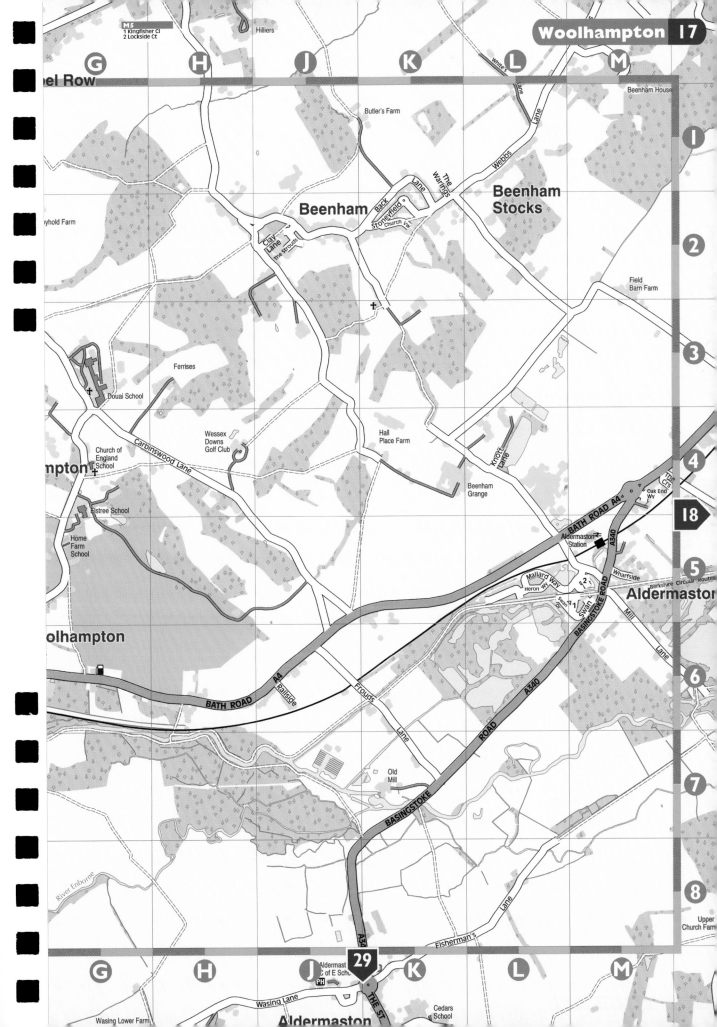

M5
1 Kingfisher Cl
2 Lockside Ct

Hilliers

Beenham House

Butler's Farm

Beenham

Beenham Stocks

Field Barn Farm

Ferrises

Douai School

Wessex Downs Golf Club

Church of England School

hpton

Hall Place Farm

Elstree School

Beenham Grange

Home Farm School

olhampton

Aldermaston Station

BATH ROAD A4

Oak End Wy

The Crs

18

A340

Wharfside

Berkshire Circular Routes

Aldermaston

Mallard Way

Heron Wy

Swan Gn

BASINGSTOKE ROAD

Mill Lane

BATH ROAD

Railside

A4

Frouds Lane

A340 ROAD

River Enborne

Old Mill

Aldermast C of E Scho

PH

29

THE ST

Wasing Lane

Cedars School

Wasing Lower Farm

Aldermaston

Carbinswood Lane

Clay Lane

The Strouds

Back Lane

Stoneyfield

Church Vw

The Warings

Webbs Lane

white's Lane

Knott Lane

Fisherman's Lane

Upper Church Farm

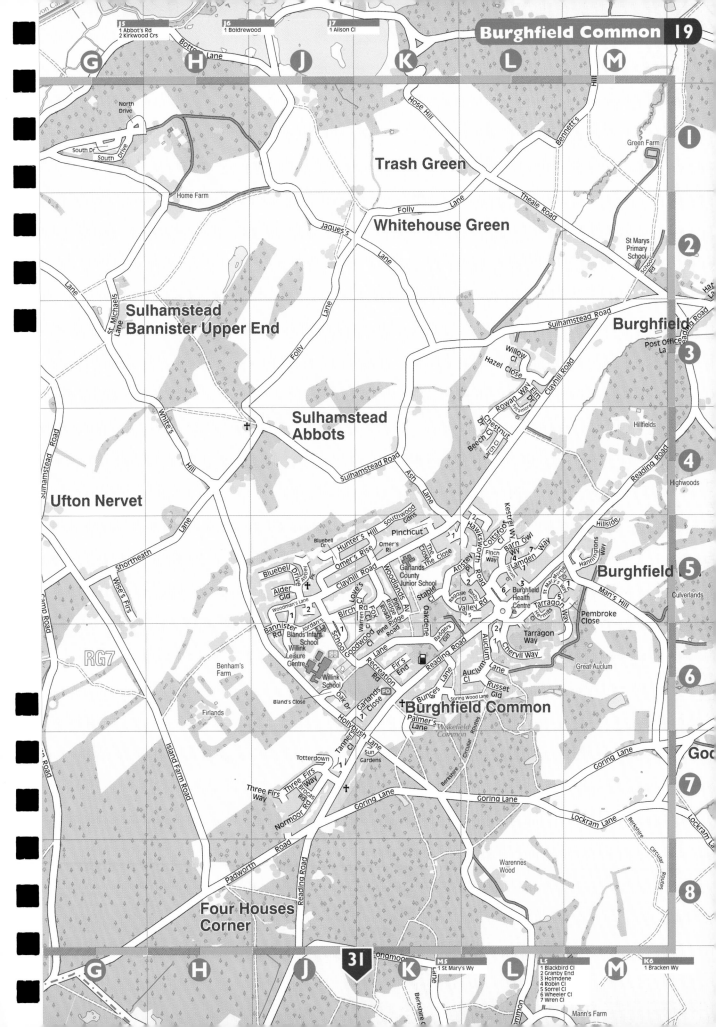

G H J K L M

J5
1 Abbot's Rd
2 Kirkwood Crs

J6
1 Boldrewood

J7
1 Alison Cl

Bottom Lane

Hose Hill

Bennett's

Green Farm

I

North Drive

South Dr
South Drive

Home Farm

Trash Green

Folly Lane

Theale Road

St Marys Primary School

School Rd

2

Jaques's Lane

Whitehouse Green

Sulhamstead Road

Burghfield

St Michaels Lane

Sulhamstead Bannister Upper End

Lane

Folly Lane

Willow Cl

Hazel Close

Post Office La

3

White's Hill

†

Sulhamstead Abbots

Rowan Way
Elm Dr
Sycamore
Clayhill Road

Chestnut Dr
Beech Cl
Larch Cl

Hillfields

Reading Road

4

Sulhamstead Road

Ash Lane

Highwoods

Shortheath

Wise's Firs

Ufton Nervet

Southwood Gdns
Pinchcut

Hunter's Hill

Omer's Rise

Omer's Ri

The Close
The Close

Hawksworth Rd

Kestrel Wy
Coltsfoot Cl

Barn Owl Way

Finch Way

Lamden Way

Hillside

Hannington's Way

Burghfield

5

Camp Road

RG7

Sulhamstead Road

Bluebell Dr

Bluebell Drive

Abbey Pk

Alder Cld

Woodman's Lane

Clayhill Road

Love's

Birch Cl

Woodlands Av

Garlands County Junior School

Stable Cl

Anstey Rd

Ragdale Cl

Finch

6

Burghfield Health Centre

St Mary's Way
Tarragon Way

Arbutus

Man's Hill

Culverlands

Pembroke Close

Bannister Rd

Jordan's La

Blands Infant School

Willink Leisure Centre

Warren Cl

Fox Cl

Pine Ridge

Pine Ridge Road

Oakdene

Badger's Cld

Valley Rd

Tarragon Way

6

Benham's Farm

Goodwood

Fir La

Recreation Rd

Fir's End

Reading Road

Auckum Cl

Chervil Way

Auckum Lane

Russet Gld

Great Auckum

Willink School

Oak Dr

Bland's Close

Garlands Close

PO

Bunges Lane

Spring Wood Lane

†**Burghfield Common**

Firlands

Hollybush Lane

Tanner's Cl

Palmer's Lane

Wakefield Common

Berkshire Circular Routes

7

Totterdown

Three Firs Way

Three Firs Way

Tyle Rd

Brocas Rd

Sun Gardens

†

Goring Lane

Goring Lane

Goring Lane

Goo

Normoor Road

Reading Road

Lockram Lane

Lockram La

Berkshire Circular Routes

8

Warennes Wood

Four Houses Corner

Padworth Road

G H J K L M

Longmoo

M5
1 St Mary's Wy

L5
1 Blackbird Cl
2 Granby End
3 Holmdene
4 Robin Cl
5 Sorrel Cl
6 Wheeler Cl
7 Wren Cl

K6
1 Bracken Wy

Mann's Farm

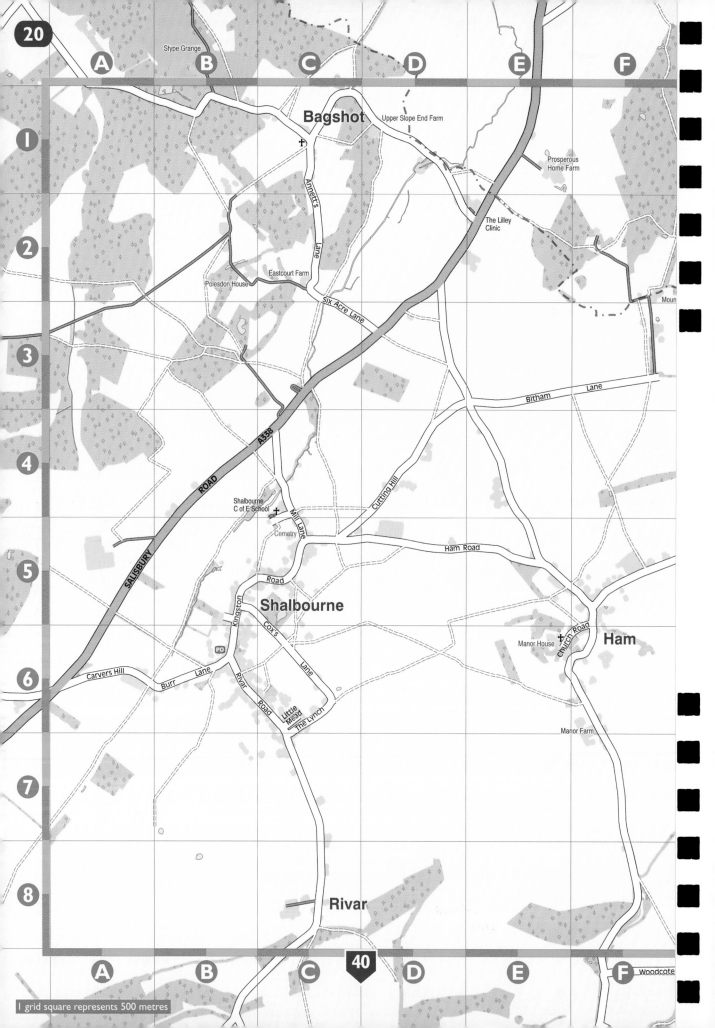

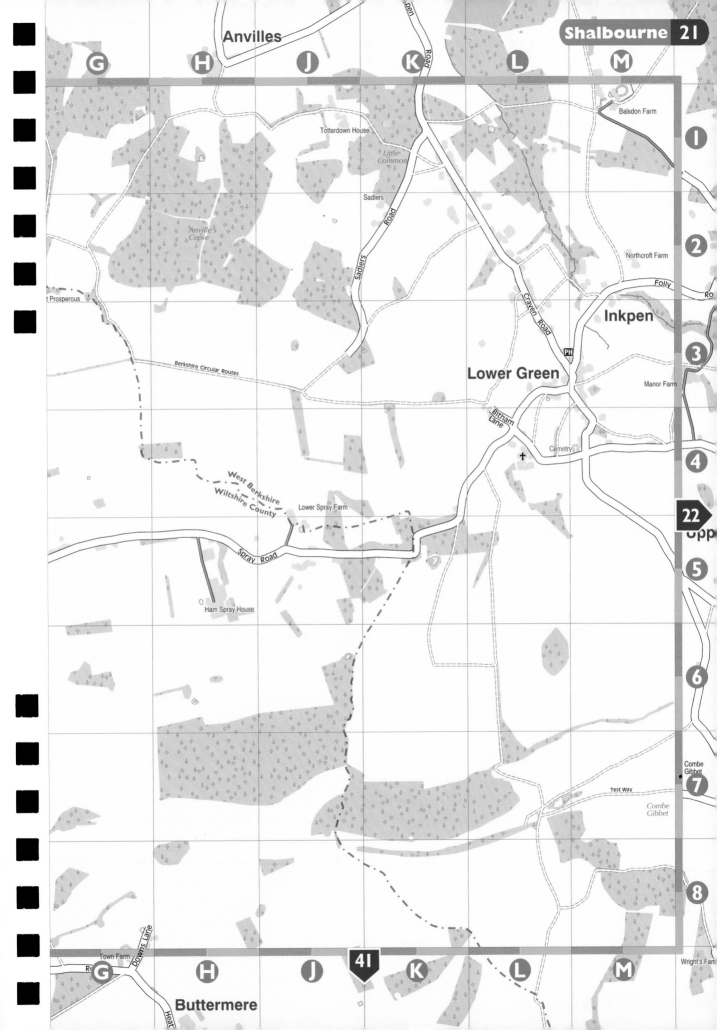

Anvilles

Balsdon Farm

Totterdown House

Little Common

Northcroft Farm

Sadlers

Anville's Copse

Folly

RO

t Prosperous

Craven Road

Inkpen

Sadlers Road

Berkshire Circular Routes

PH

Lower Green

Manor Farm

Bitham Lane

Cemetry

West Berkshire
Wiltshire County

Lower Spray Farm

22
Upp

Spray   Road

Ham Spray House

Combe Gibbet

Test Way

Combe Gibbet

Downs Lane

Town Farm

41

Wright's Far

Heat

Buttermere

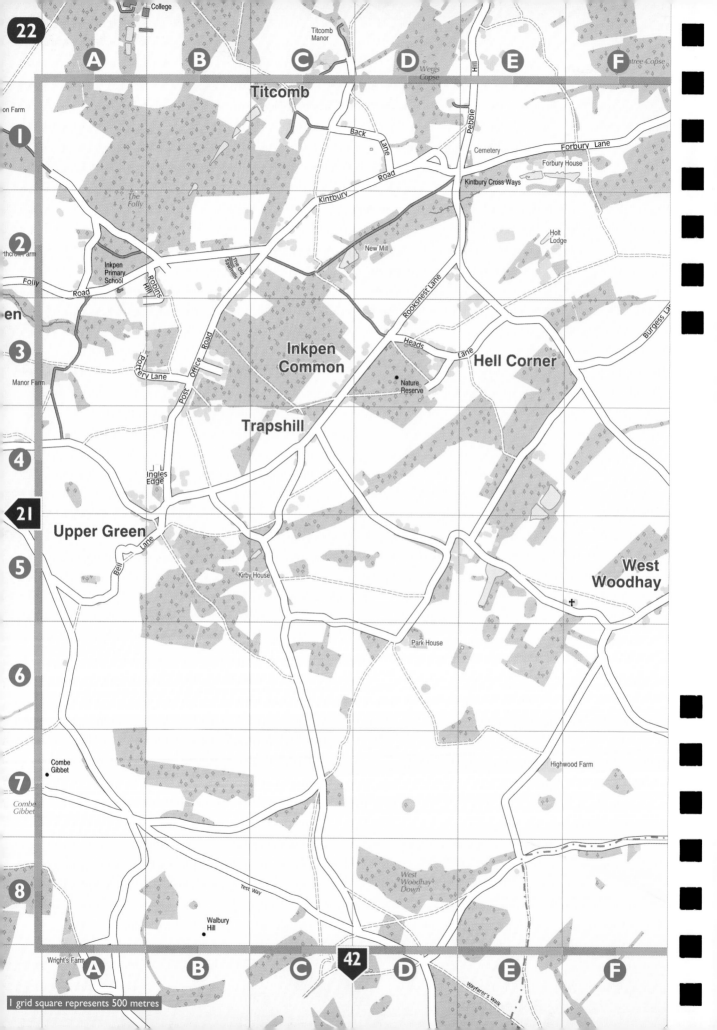

College

A B C D E F

Titcomb Manor

Wergs Copse

tree Copse

Titcomb

on Farm

1

Back Lane

Pebble Hill

Road

Cemetery

Forbury Lane

Forbury House

Kintbury Cross Ways

The Folly

New Mill

Holt Lodge

2

rthcroft Farm

Inkpen Primary School

Robins Hill

The Old Sawmills

Folly Road

en

Rooksnest Lane

3

Pottery Lane

Post Office Road

Inkpen Common

Heads Lane

Hell Corner

Manor Farm

Nature Reserve

Trapshill

4

Ingles Edge

21

5

Upper Green

Bell Lane

Kirby House

West Woodhay

†

6

Park House

Combe Gibbet

Highwood Farm

7

Combe Gibbet

8

West Woodhay Down

Test Way

Walbury Hill

Wright's Farm

A B C **42** D E F

Wayfarer's Walk

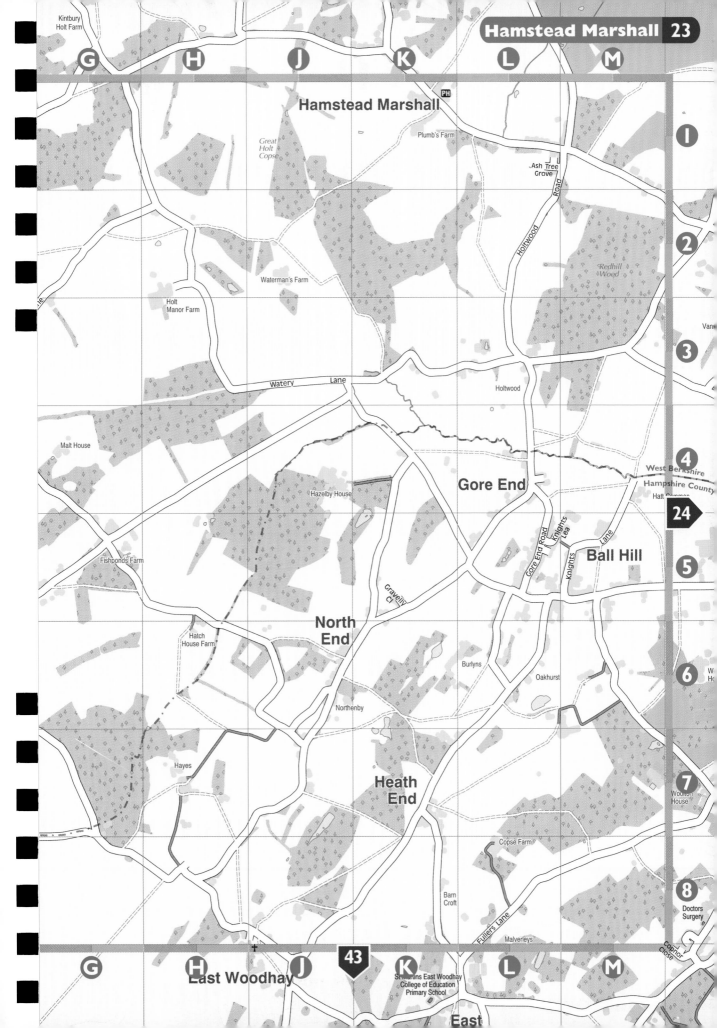

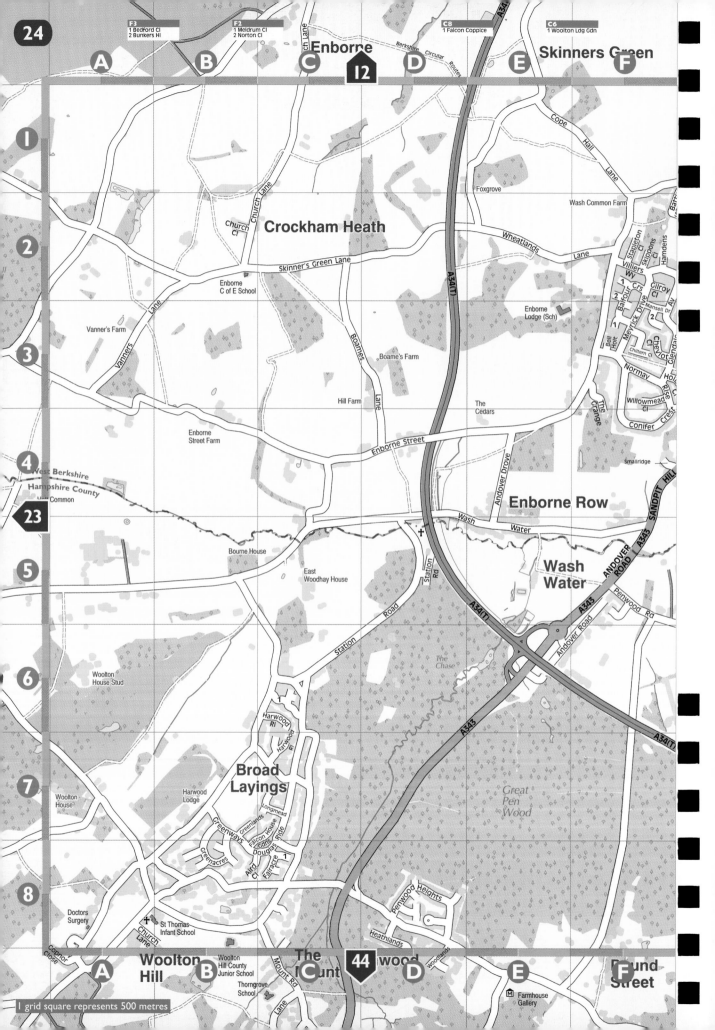

I grid square represents 500 metres

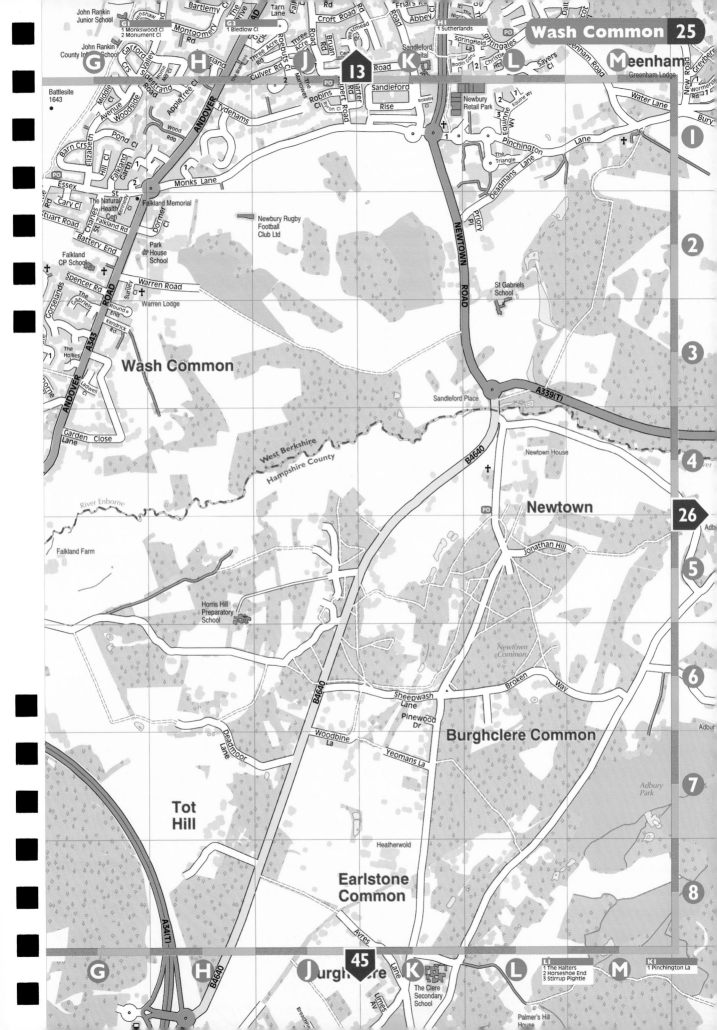

Greenham
Greenham Lodge

Young
Crs

Greyberry Copse Road

Farm Rd

New Road

Wormersley Rd

Water Lane

Pigeons Rd

Pigeon's Farm

A I
1 Marchant Cl
2 Pritchard Cl

River Kennet

Bury's Bank Road

Bury's Bank

Golf Course

Bowdown House

The Round House

Bury's Bank Road

2

Greenham Common
Airfield (disused)

3

Seventh St

Sixth St

Fifth St

Watermill Theatre

Third Street

Second street

Barracks Rd

Warehouse Rd

Third St

Main St

Second Street

Ministry Road

First St

New Greenham Park
Leisure Cen

**Goldfinch
Bottom**

Foxhold

4

A339(T)

River Enborne

Thornford Road

Adbury House

Aldern
Bridge House

Sydmonton
Common

**Bishop's
Green**

Knightsbridge
House

Knightsbridge Dr

5

6

Ash Rd

Beech Rd

Ash Rd

Willow Rd

Eagle Road

Rooksfield

A339(T)

Adbury Farm

Hyde Lane

Headley Stud

7

North
Sydmonton House

North
Ecchinswell Farm

8

Fifth Rd

**Brock's
Green**

Hyde
Farm

I grid square represents 500 metres

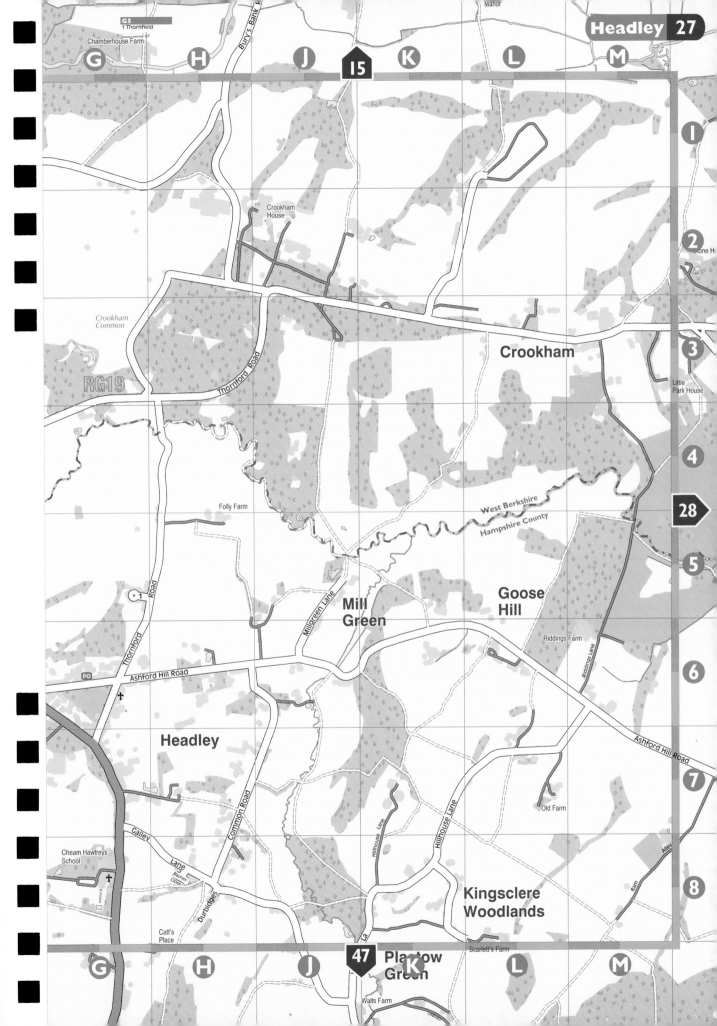

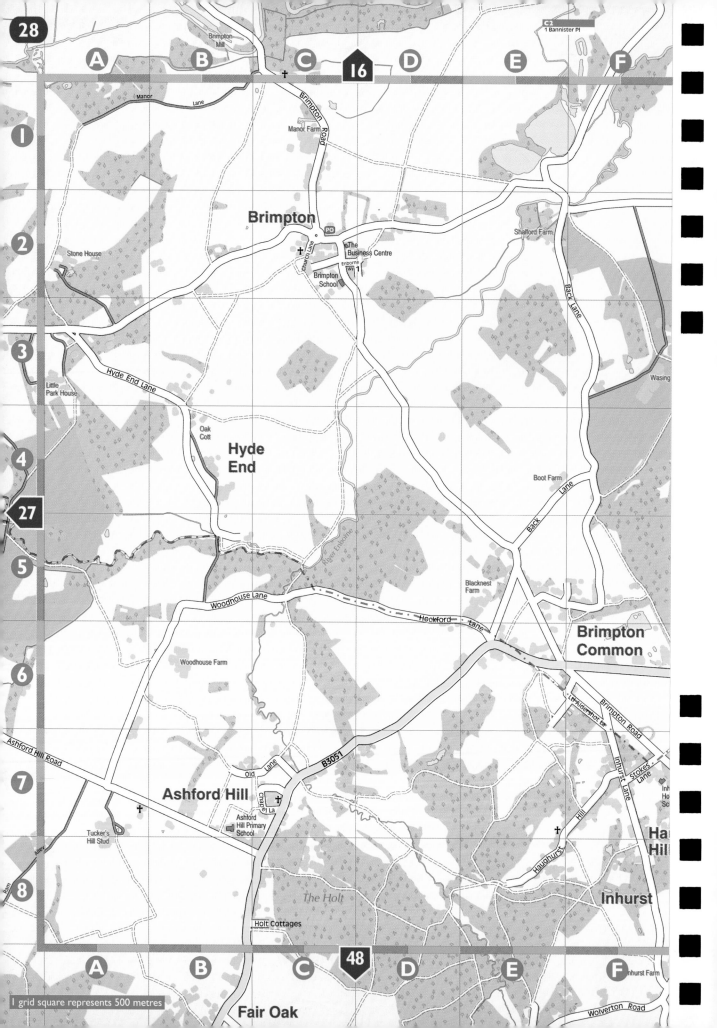

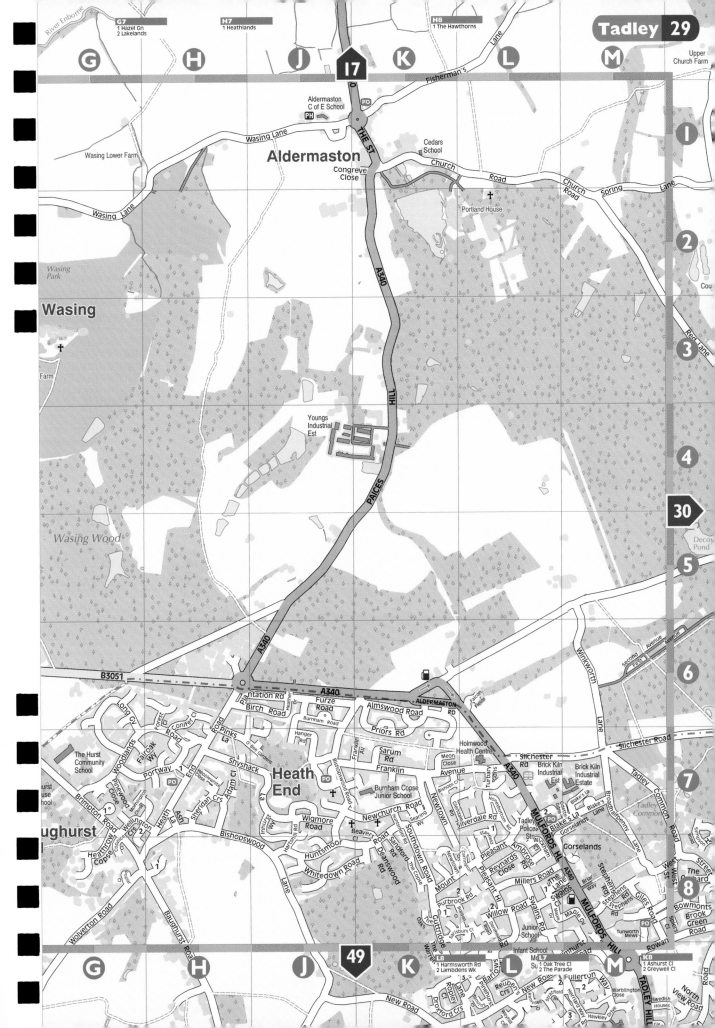

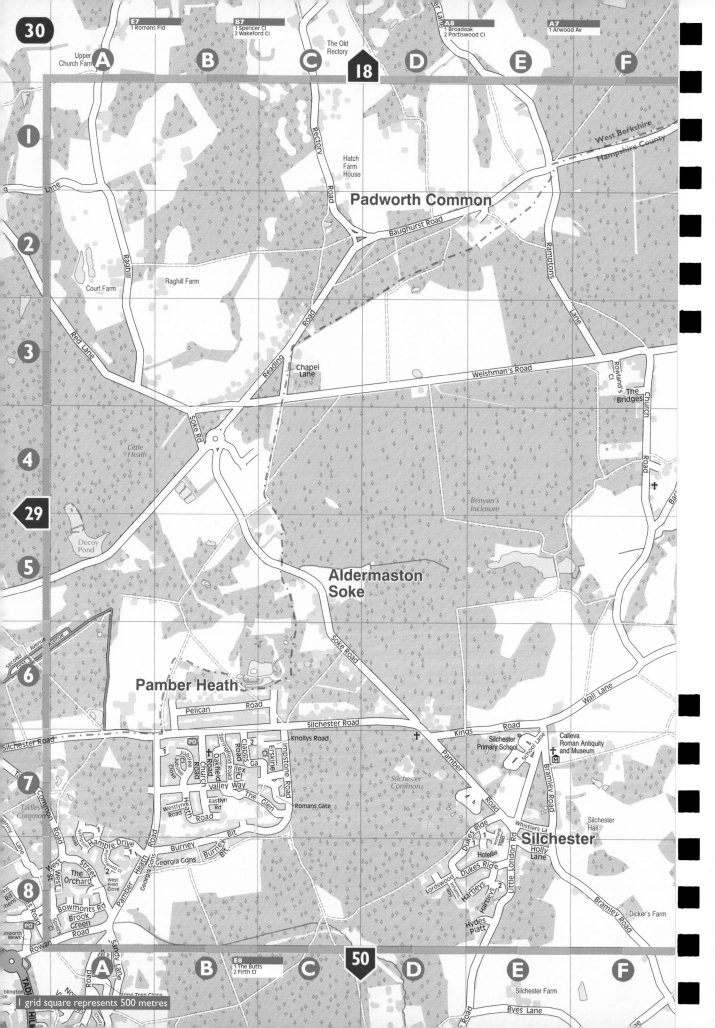

Padworth Common

Aldermaston Soke

Pamber Heath

Silchester

I grid square represents 500 metres

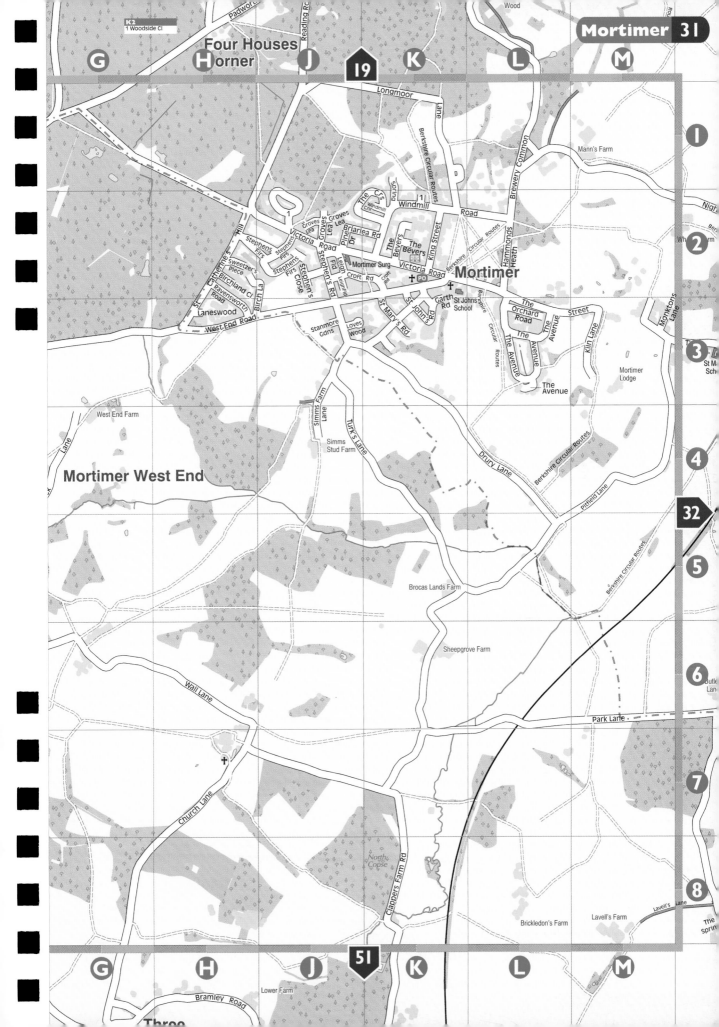

A **B** **C** **D** **E** **F**

I

Bloomfield
Hatch

Cross Lane

Cross Lane

Mortimer
Park

Wokefield
Park

Mortimer Ho

Nightingale Lane

Trunkwell
House

Be

2

Wheat's Farm

Berkshire Circular Routes

Great
Park Farm

3

The
Street

St Marys
School

Church Barns

Monktons Lane

Church Farms

**Stratfield
†Mortimer**

Mortimer
Station

Station
Road

4

The
Forehead

Perrins Farm

31

5

Little
Park Farm

Routes

6

Butlers
Lands

Park   Lane

Park   Lane

West Berkshire
Hampshire County

Home Farm

7

Wigmore Farm

Forelands

New Street

New Street

Green Lane

**Stratfield
Saye**

8

Lavell's Lane

The
Springs

Mortimer Lane

West End Green

Herriot's

Green Lane

A **B** **C** **52** **D** **E** **F**

Fair Oak Lane

Kings Farm

I grid square represents 500 metres

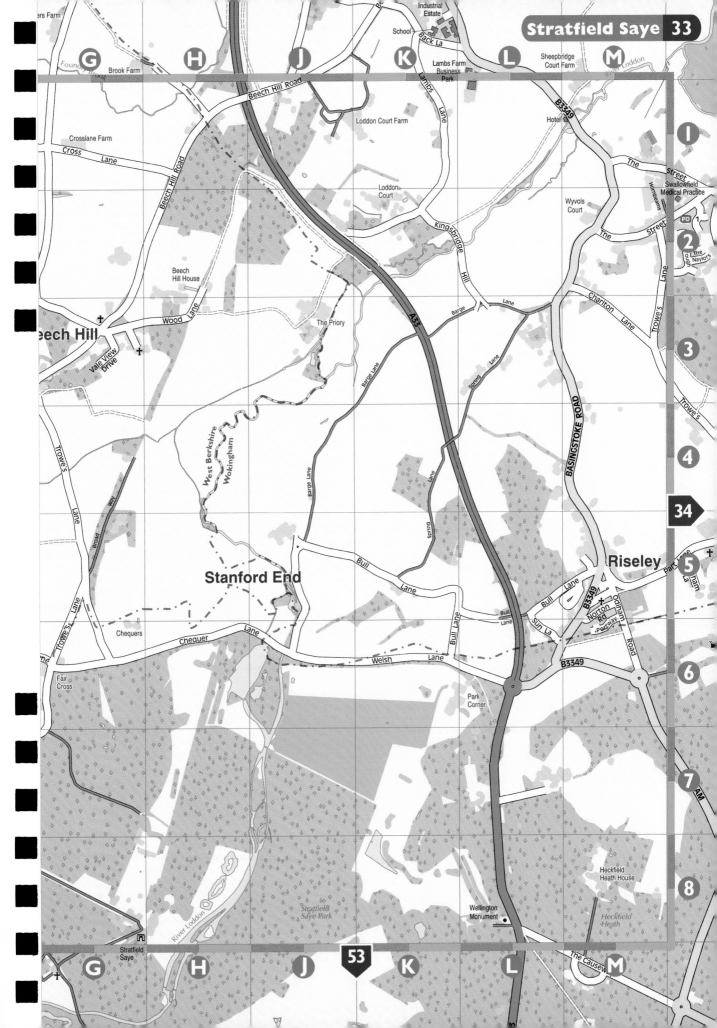

A B C D E F

1

Great
Wood

Tanner's Farm

A2
1 Curleys Wy

Swallow
Park

Swallowfield Road

Kiln Hill

Castle Hill

The
Chatters

The
Street

Swallowfield
Medical Practice

Swallowfield

Road

PO 1

The Naylors

Foxborough

Street

Trowe's Lane

Part Lane

Brookside
Business
Centre

Rowe's Farm

PH

Swallowfield

Bungler's Hill

2

Cemetery

Farley
Court

Farle
Prima
Scho

3

Nurbean Lane

Sandpi

Lane

Part Lane

The Broadwater

Riseley Farm

Ford Lane

Trowe's Lane

4

33

School Lane

School

Road

Part Lane

†

Benham La

Part Lane

Wokingham

Hampshire County

Well

House

Lane

Well
House Far

5

Road

Wellington
Country Park

Cordery's Farm

Bramshill
Plantation

6

ODIHAM

Riseley
Mill

Ford Lane

Id
House

7

ROAD

Hall's Farm

Springwater Farm

8

River Whitewater

Park Farm

1 grid square represents 500 metres

Bramshill

H1
1 Faraday Cl
2 Kelvin Cl

G   H   J   K   L   M

I

2

3

4

36

5   Finch

6

7

8

G   H   J   55   K   L   M

Arborfield Garrison

Farley Hill

Lower Common

Eversley

Parsons Farm

Church Lane

Westwood Farm

Sheerlands Road

Whitehall Baird Road

Fleming Tcr

Tyler Dr

Princess Marina Drive

Rowcroft Rd

Nuffield Road

James Watt Road

Whitworth Rd

Weller Dr

Marino Way

Ivanhoe Road

Hogwood La

Hogwood Farm

Coleshill Farm

Longs Moor

California Country Park

Nine M

White Horse Lane

Larchwood Fa

EVERSLEY

A327

READING ROAD

New Mill Road

The Leas

Bulloway's Farm

Blackwater River

New Mill

New Mill Lane

Oaklea Drive

Lower Common Road

Mud La

St Neots Preparatory School

St Neot's Road

West Court

Lea Farm

Park Lane

Park Lane

Park Lane

Wheatlands Manor

Banisters Farm

FLEET HILL

Fleet Lane

Fleethill Farm

The Rise

EVERSLEY STREET

Warbrook Lane

Warbrook

Wokingham
Hampshire County

Glaston Hill Road

B3272

Kingsley Road

Charles Kingsley School

Glaston Hill House

Three

READ

Biggs Lane

Buttenshaw Avenue

Marina
Dr

Isaac
Newton
Rd

Tope Rd

Parsons
Rd

Stephen

Joulding Lane

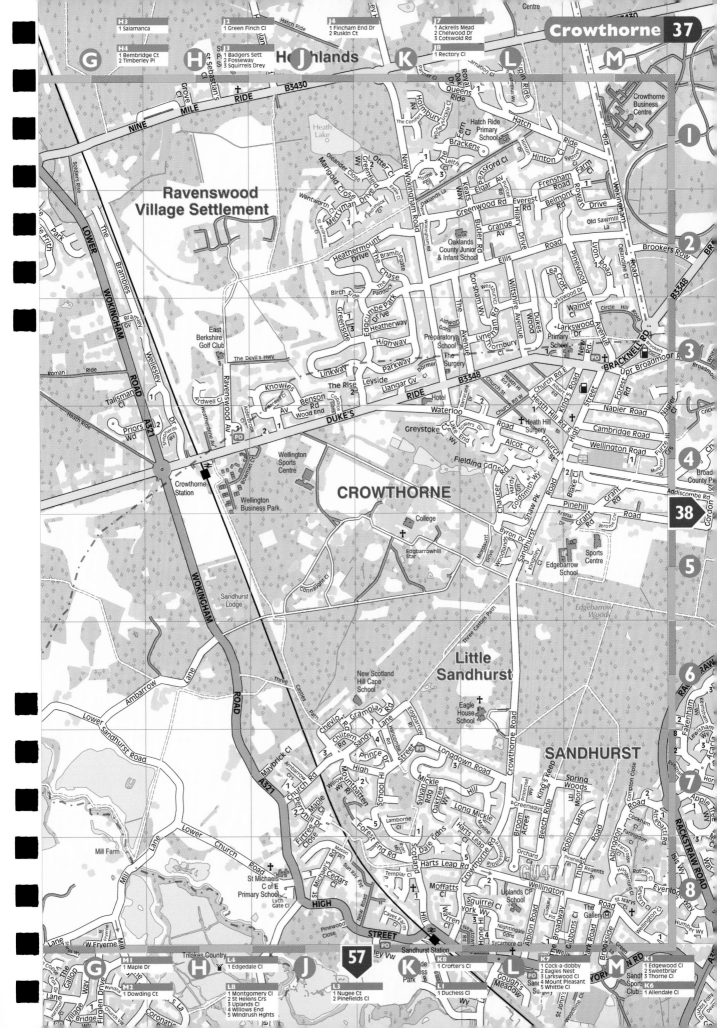

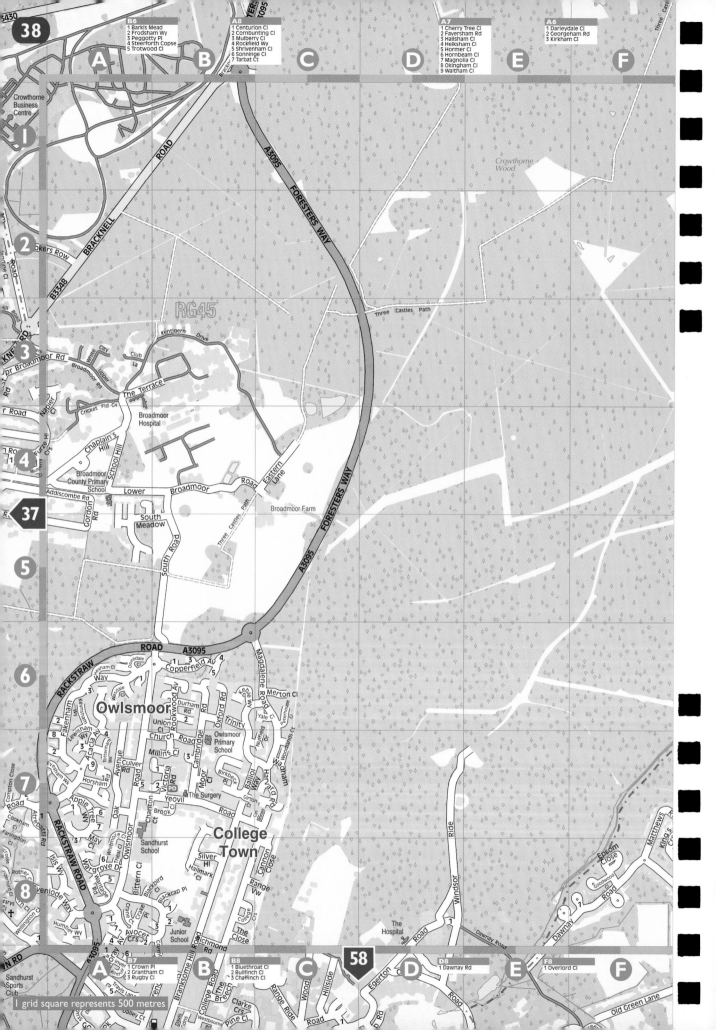

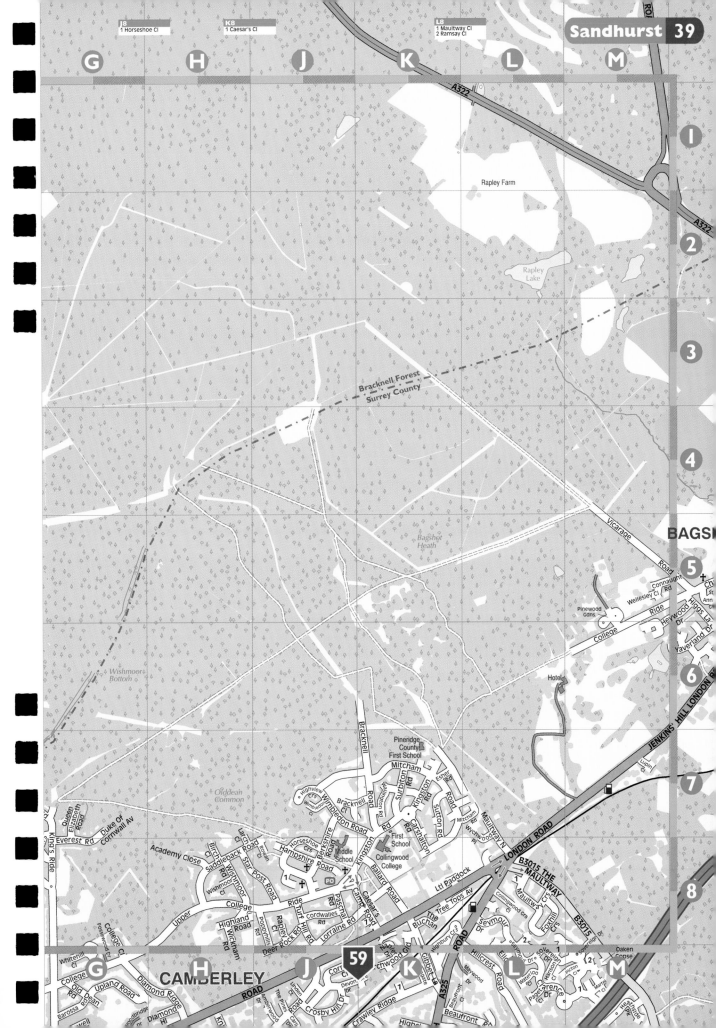

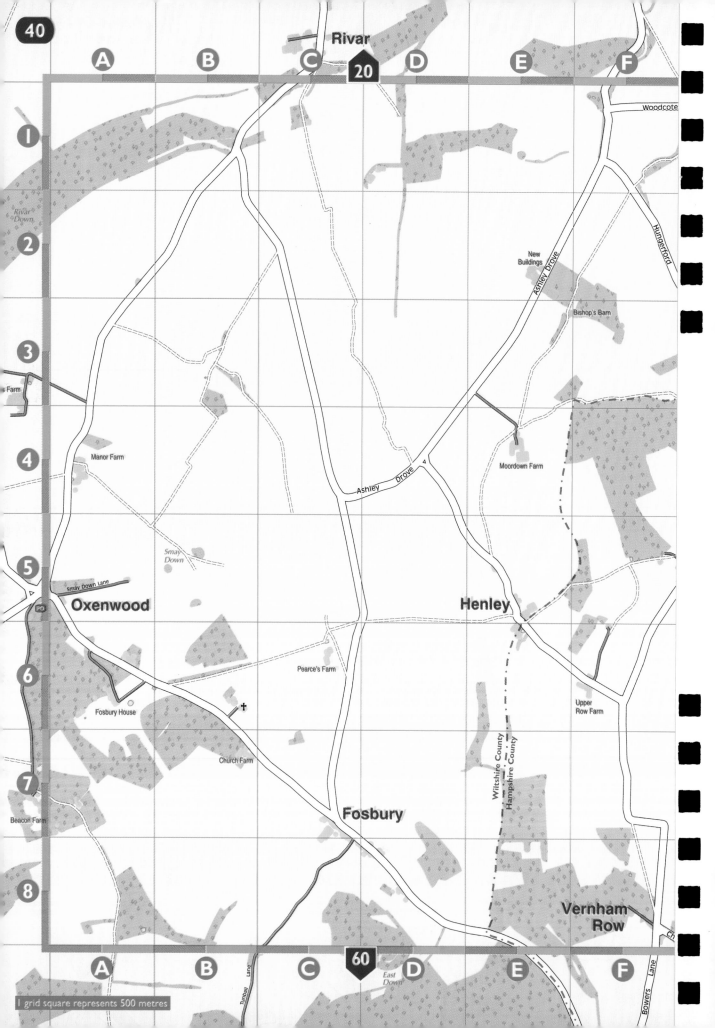

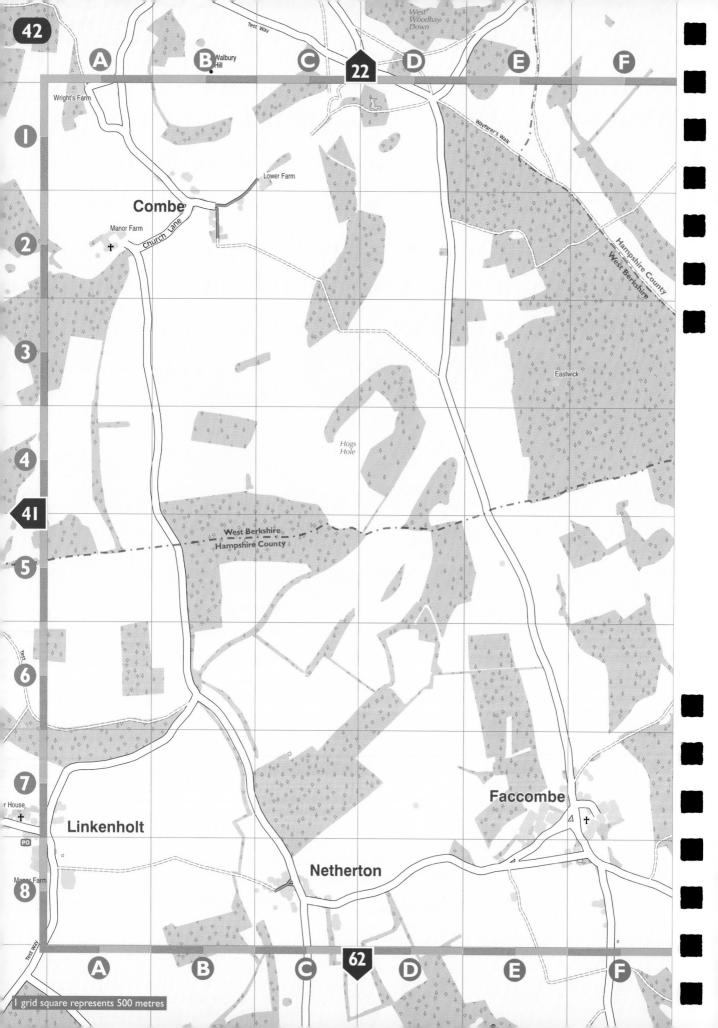

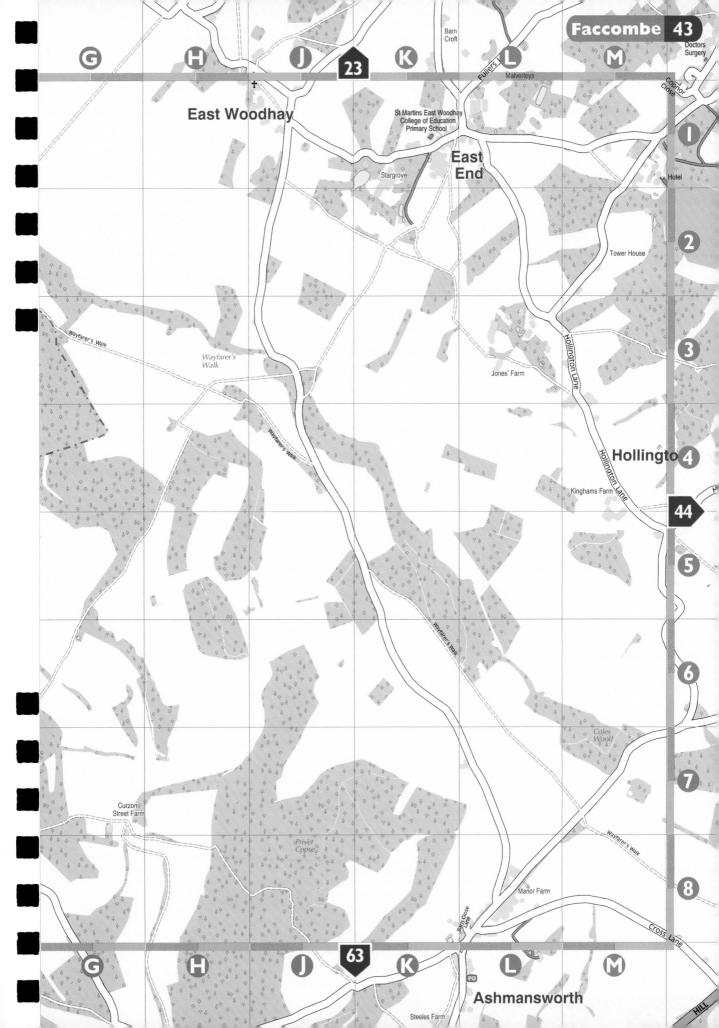

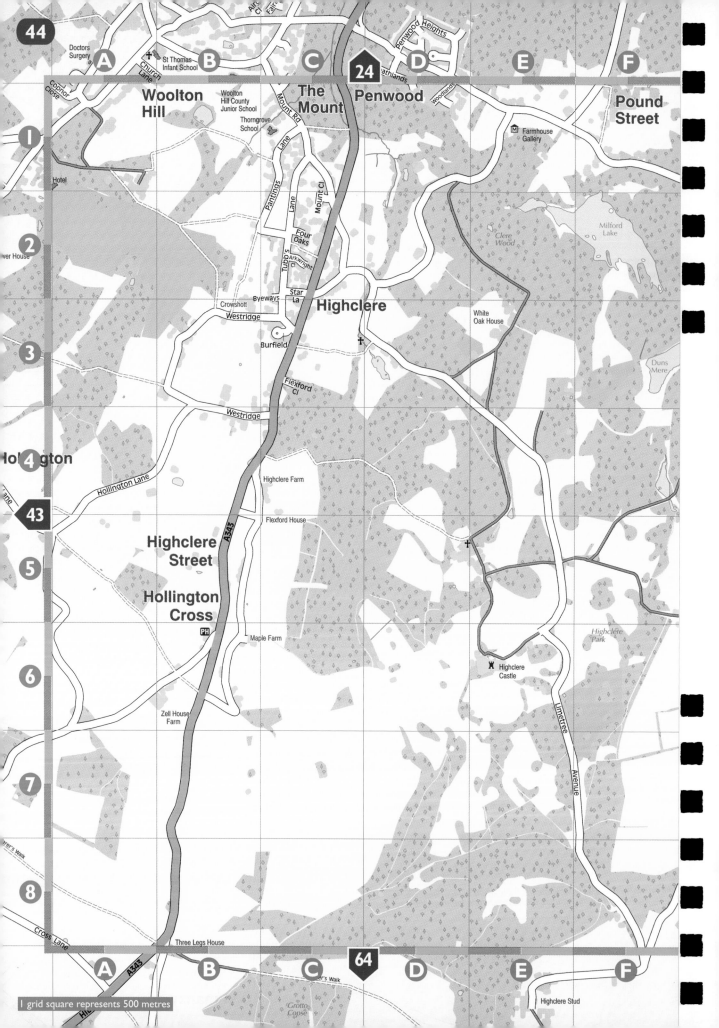

44

A — Doctors Surgery
B — St Thomas Infant School — Church Lane
C
24
D
E
F

Woolton Hill
Woolton Hill County Junior School
Thorngrove School
The Mount
Penwood
Pound Street

Farmhouse Gallery

Copnor Close

1

Hotel

ver House

2

Pantings Lane
Mount Cl
Mount Rd
Four Oaks
Tubbs La
Arkwright Cl
Star La

Clere Wood
Milford Lake

Byeways
Crowshott
Westridge

Highclere

White Oak House

Burfield

Duns Mere

3

Flexford Cl

Westridge

Ho—gton

4

Hollington Lane

Highclere Farm

43

Flexford House

Highclere Street

A343

Hollington Cross

5

PH

Maple Farm

Highclere Park

6

Highclere Castle

Zell House Farm

Limetree Avenue

7

8

arrers Walk

Cross Lane

Three Legs House

A343

A — A343
B
C — er's Walk
64
D
E
F

Highclere Stud

Grotto Copse

1 grid square represents 500 metres

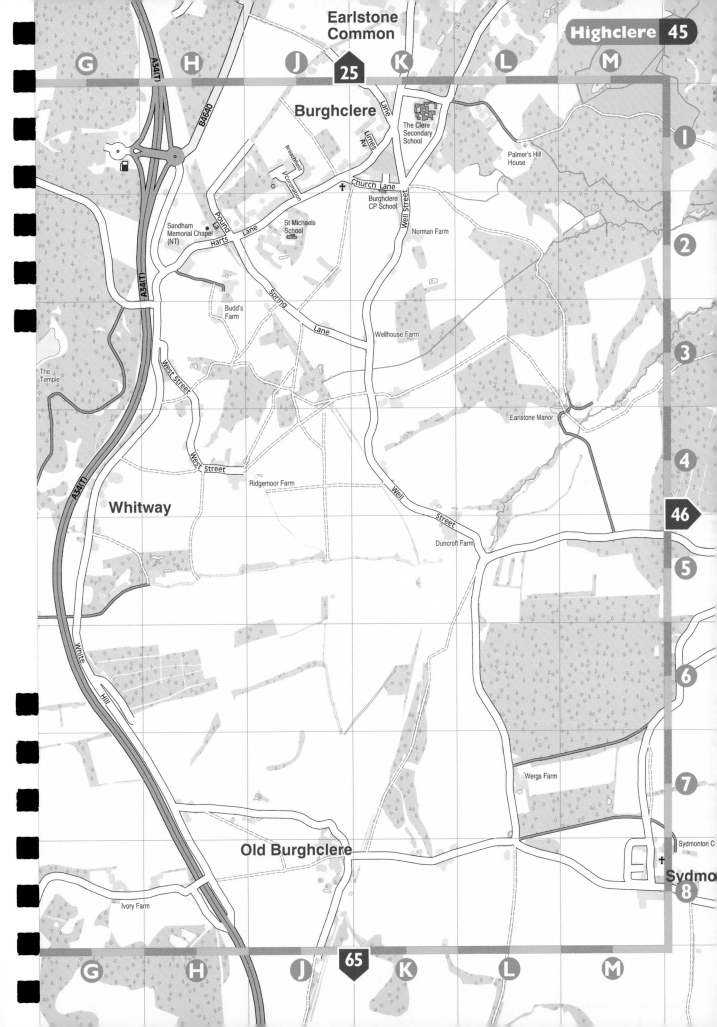

Earlstone
Common

G H J K L M

25

Burghclere

The Clere
Secondary
School

Palmer's Hill
House

I

Church Lane

Burghclere
CP School

Well Street

2

Sandham
Memorial Chapel
(NT)

Pound La

Harts Lane

St Michaels
School

Norman Farm

Breachfield

Coronation

Limes Av

Spring

Lane

Wellhouse Farm

3

West Street

The
Temple

Earlstone Manor

4

West Street

Ridgemoor Farm

Well

Street

46

Whitway

Duncroft Farm

5

A34(T)

White

Hill

6

Wergs Farm

7

Old Burghclere

Sydmonton C

Sydmo

8

Ivory Farm

G H J K L M

65

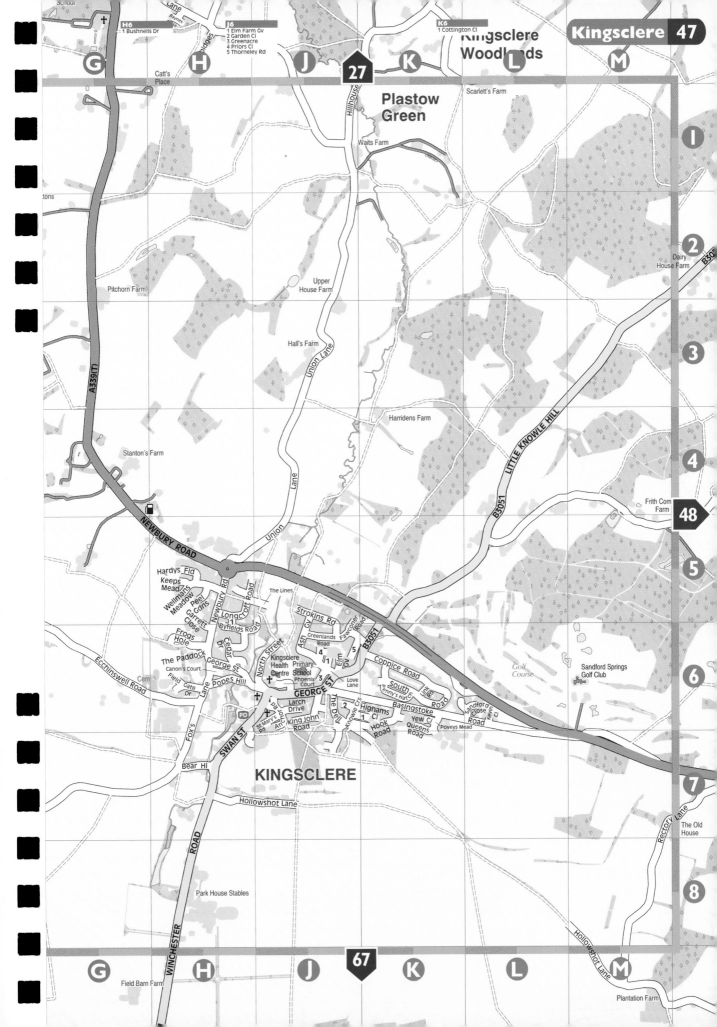

Kingsclere Woodlands

KINGSCLERE

Plastow Green

H6
1 Bushnells Dr

J6
1 Elm Farm Gv
2 Garden Cl
3 Greenacre
4 Priors Cl
5 Thorneley Rd

K6
1 Cottington Cl

Catt's Place

Scarlett's Farm

Dairy House Farm

Hillhouse Lane

Waits Farm

Upper House Farm

Pitchorn Farm

Hall's Farm

Union Lane

Harridens Farm

LITTLE KNOWLE HILL

B3051

Stanton's Farm

Union Lane

Frith Com Farm

A339(T)

NEWBURY ROAD

Hardys Fld
Keeps Mead
Wellman's Meadow
Peel Gdns
Garrett Close
Frogs Hole

Newbury Rd
Croft Road
Longc
Byfields Road
Cedar Dr

The Lines

Strokins Rd

Ash Gv
Greenlands Road
4 1

Elm Gv
Fawconer Road
5

B3051

Coppice Road

Golf Course

Sandford Springs Golf Club

The Paddock
Canon's Court
Field
Gate Dr

George St
Popes Hill

North Street

Kingsclere Health Centre

Kingsclere Primary School
Phoenix Court
3

Love Lane

Penny's Hatch

South Rd

Link Rd

Basingstoke Road

Sandford Close
Kevin Cl

Echinswell Road

Cem

Fox's Rd

St Mary's Rd

GEORGE ST

Larch Drive

The Dell

Knowle Crs

King John Road

2
Highams Cl
1

Hook Road

Yew Cl
Queens Road

Poveys Mead

Bear Hl

SWAN ST

KINGSCLERE

Hollowshot Lane

WINCHESTER ROAD

Park House Stables

Rectory Lane

The Old House

Hollowshot Lane

Field Barn Farm

Plantation Farm

27

48

67

G H J K L M

I 2 3 4 5 6 7 8

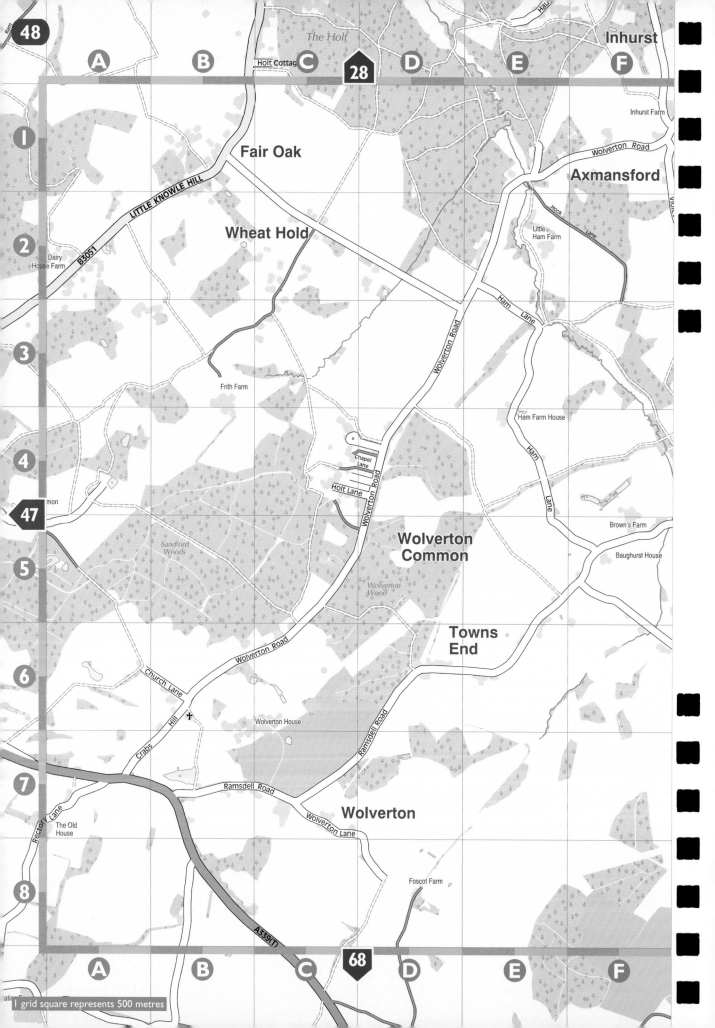

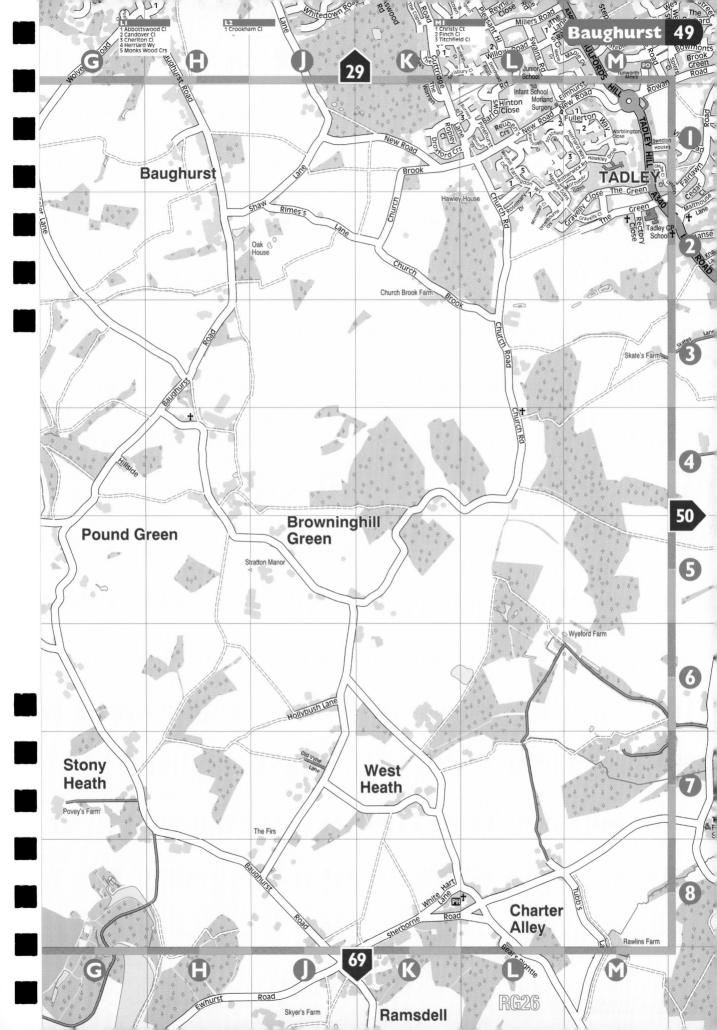

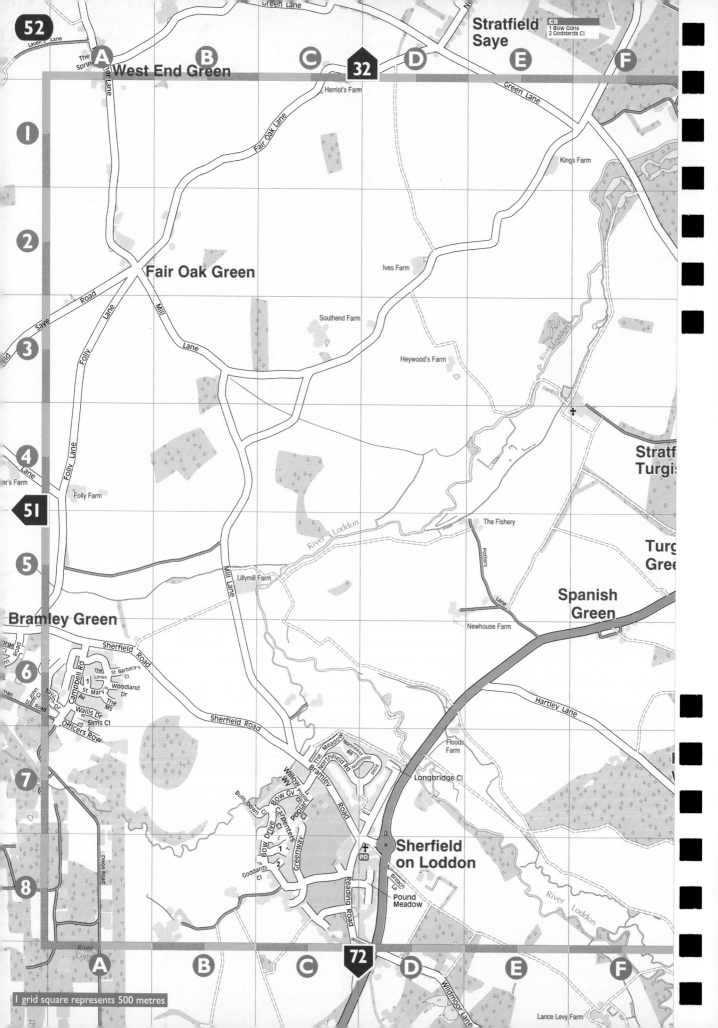

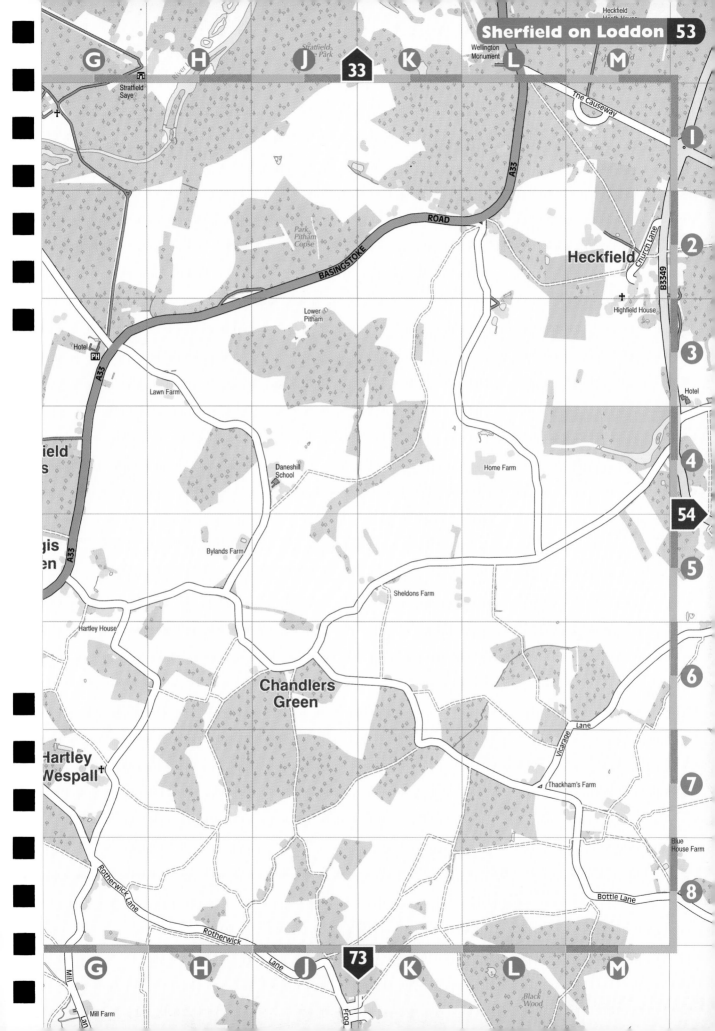

G   H   J   **33**   K   L   M

I

2

3

4

54

5

6

7

8

G   H   J   **73**   K   L   M

Stratfield
Saye

†

Park
Pitham
Copse

BASINGSTOKE   ROAD

Lower
Pitham

A33

Hotel

PH

Lawn Farm

Daneshill
School

Bylands Farm

Hartley House

**Chandlers
Green**

Hartley
Wespall †

Rotherwick Lane

Rotherwick   Lane

Mill Farm

Mill Lan

Frog

Stratfield
Park

Wellington
Monument

The causeway

Heckfield
Heath House

Church Lane

Heckfield

B3349

†
Highfield House

Hotel

Home Farm

Sheldons Farm

Lane

Vicarage

Thackham's Farm

Blue
House Farm

Bottle Lane

Black
Wood

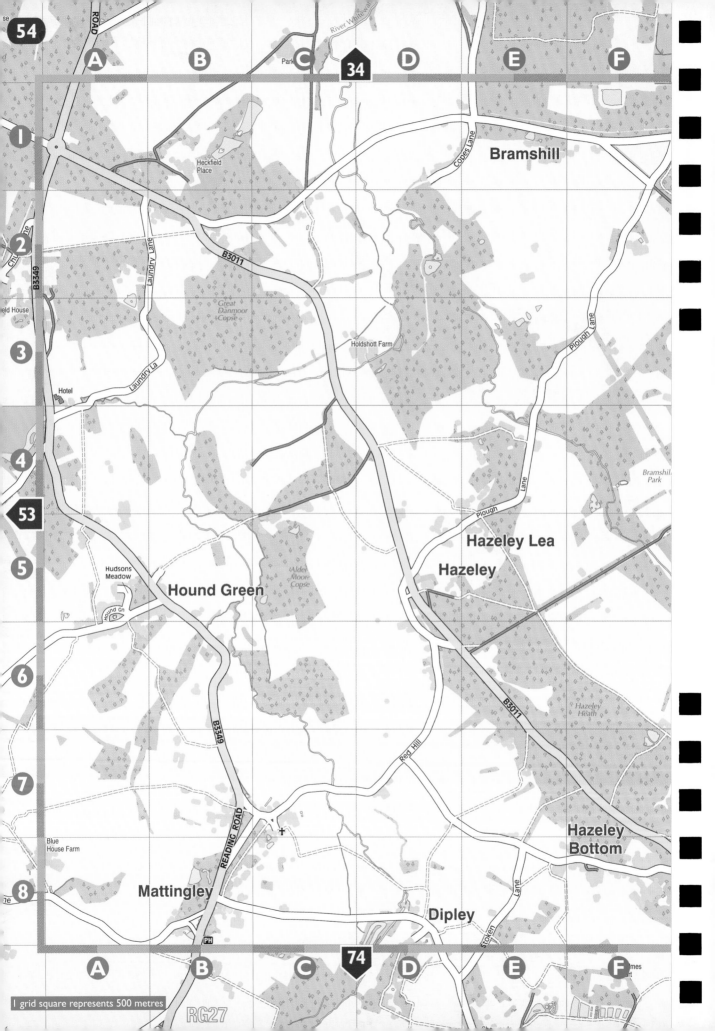

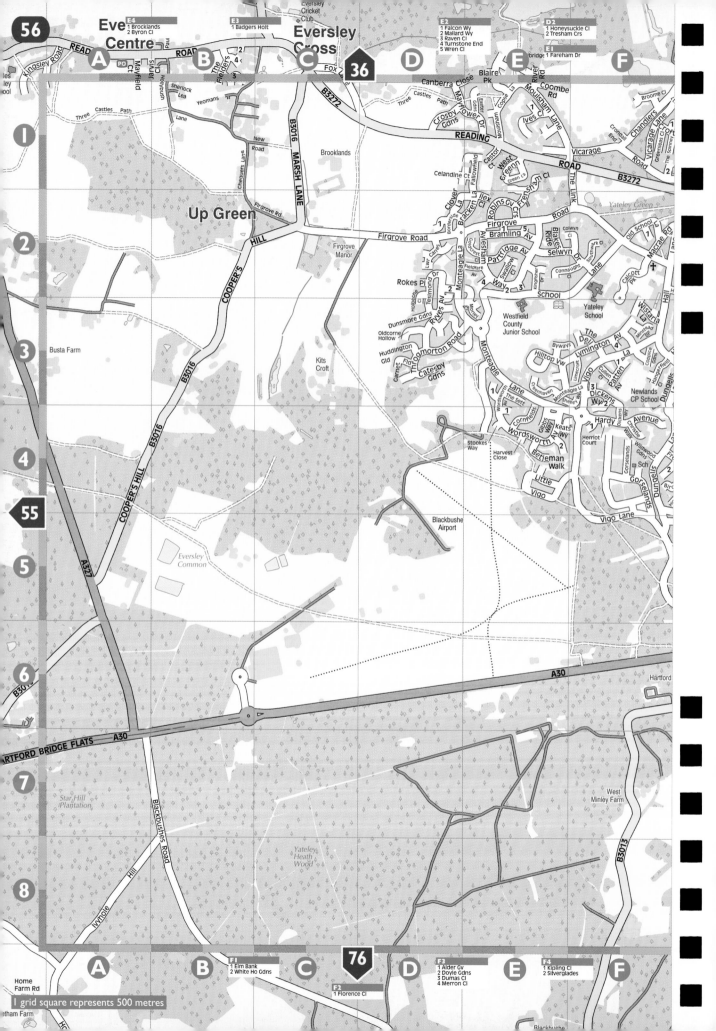

G1
1 Green End
2 Harpdon Pde
3 Heathwood Cl

G2
1 Rosary Gdns
2 Woodbourne Cl

G3
1 Barnfield
2 Brockenhurst Dr
3 Lower Moor
4 Tudor Dr
5 Wentworth Cl

K1
1 Dungells Farm Cl
2 Glenavon Gdns

M3
1 Denham Dr
2 Mason Cl

HIGH STREET

37

YATELEY

GU46

Frogmore

Darby Green

Cricket Hill

GU17

A30

A327

B3013

Yateley Common

Hornley Common

Minley Wood

Minley Manor

Hawley Common

Hawley Lake

Starve Acre

77

MINLEY ROAD

G
M3
1 Grayshot Dr
2 Salisbury Rd

H
M2
1 Ringwood Rd
2 Romsey Cl
3 Selborne Cl
4 Southampton Cl
5 Winchester Wy

J

K
M1
1 Travis La

L
L3
1 Acorn Rd
2 Brooksby Cl

M
1 Bannister Gdns
2 Caswall Ride
3 Hatherwood

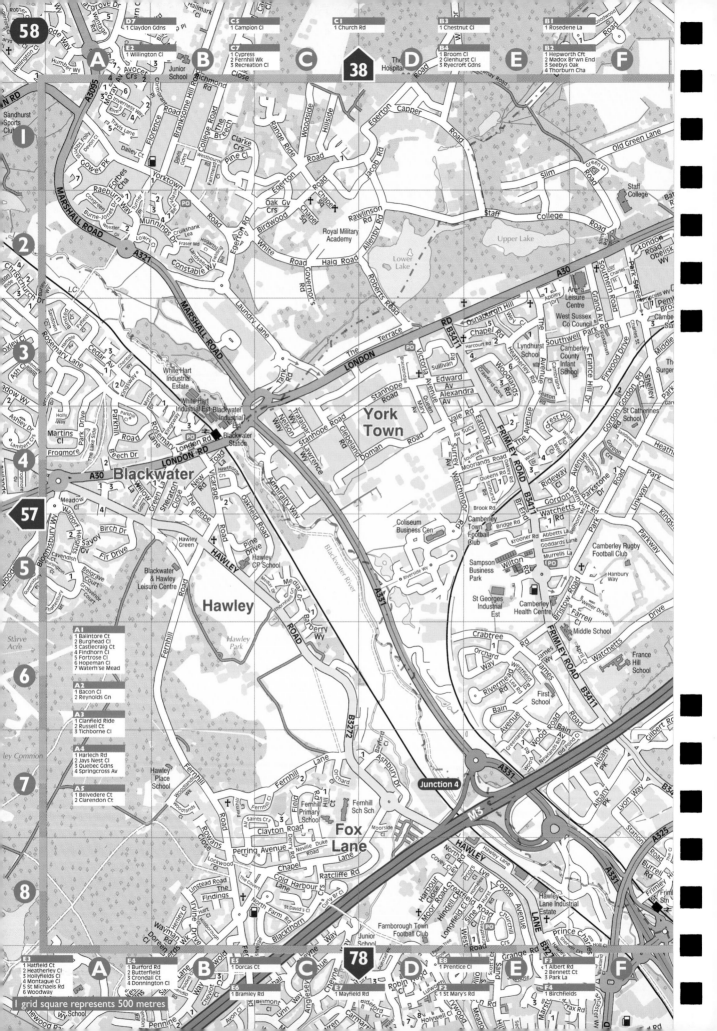

A B C **40** D E **Vernham Ro** F

1

The Slay

East Down

Oakhill Wood

Tunball Lane

Fosbury Farm

2

Vernham Bank

Bowers Lane

3

Hippenscombe

254
▲
Haydown Hill

Conholt Hill

4

Cleves Copse

5

Little Down

Chute Causeway

Middle Conholt Farm

Conholt House

6

Du Lane

Conholt Park

Hungerford Lane

7

Hampshire Gate

Wiltshire County
Hampshire County

Cathanger Wood

8

Standen House

Chute Standen

Breach La

Dummer

A B **Chute CCley** **82** D E F

Lower Chute

Dowlands Farm

Tangley

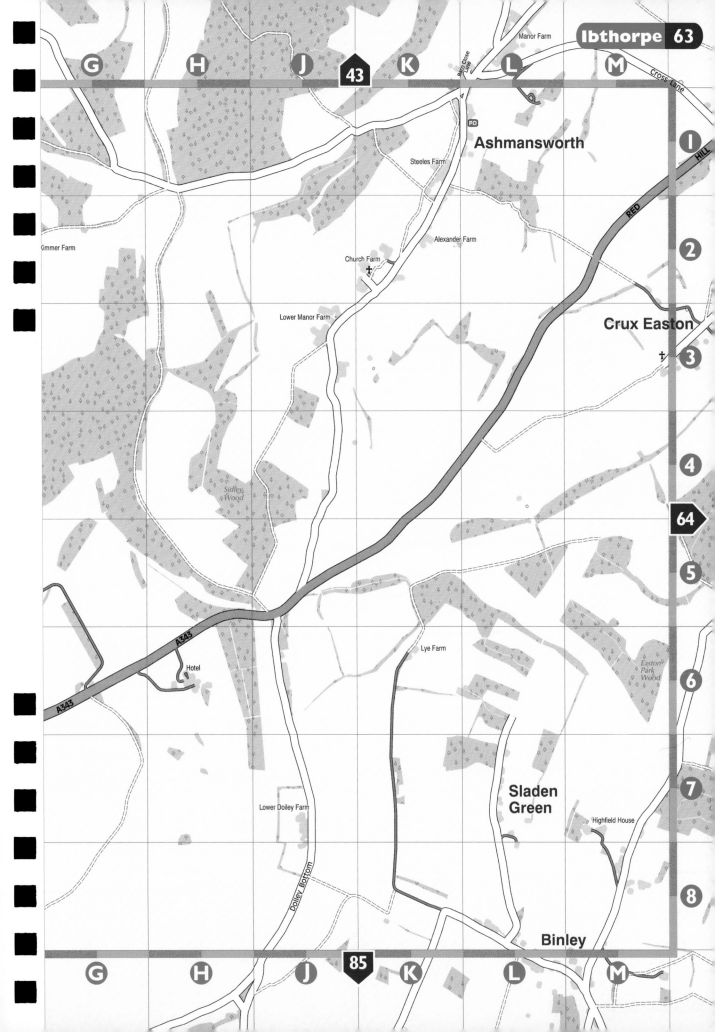

G   H   J   **43**   K   L   M

Manor Farm

Cross Lane

Bath Close Lane

PO

Ashmansworth

Steeles Farm

Kimmer Farm

Alexander Farm

Church Farm ✝

I

HILL

RED

2

Crux Easton

✝ **3**

Lower Manor Farm

4

Sidley Wood

64

5

A343

Hotel

Lye Farm

Easton Park Wood

6

Sladen Green

7

Lower Doiley Farm

Highfield House

Dolley Bottom

8

Binley

G   H   J   **85**   K   L   M

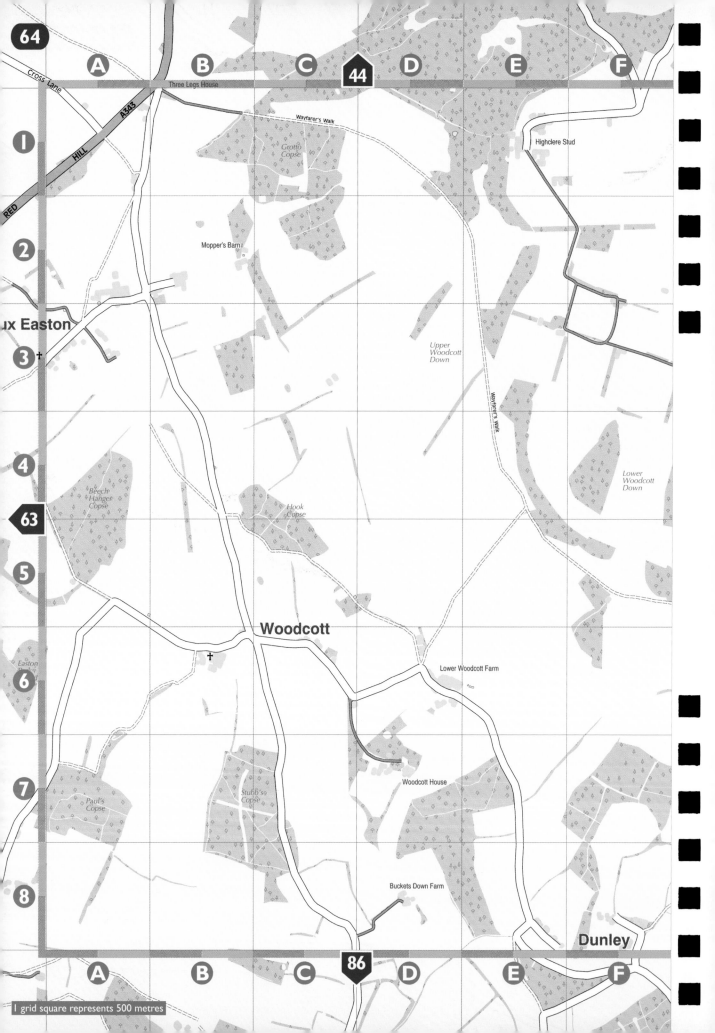

Ivory Farm

G H J **45** K L M

I

262
▲
Beacon
Hill

234
▲
Ladle
Hill

2

3

4

*Great
Litchfield
Down*

66

Wayfarer's Walk

5

6

A34(T)

7

Down Farm

8

*Wormley
Copse*

Litchfield

G H J **87** K L M

Angledown

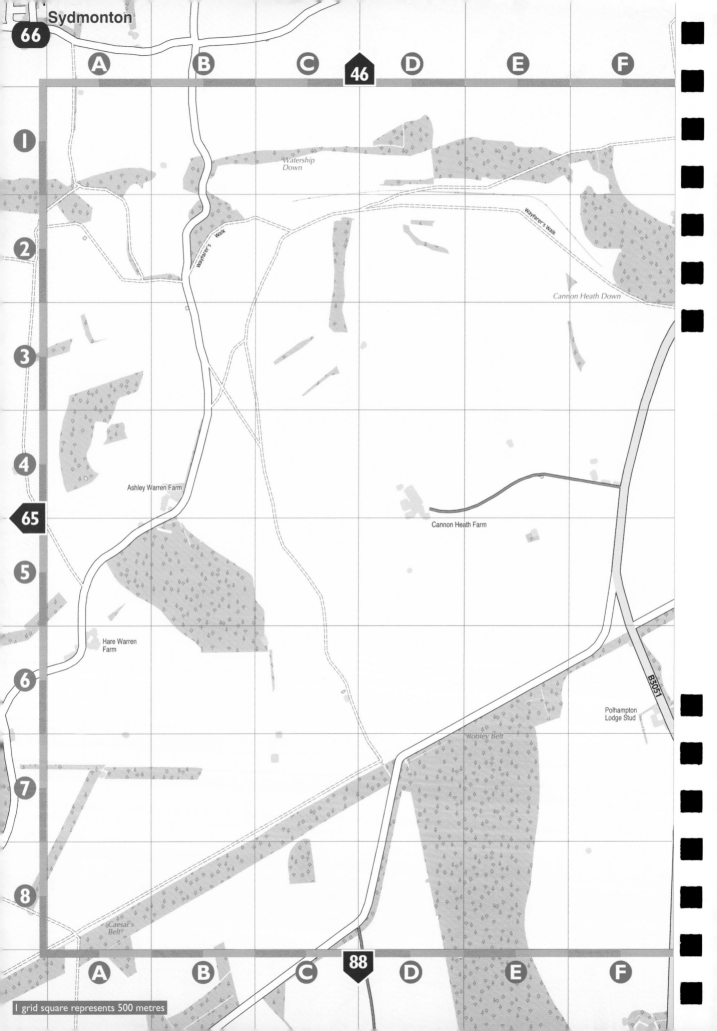

66

A   B   C   46   D   E   F

1

Watership
Down

2

Wayfarer's Walk

Wayfarer's Walk

Cannon Heath Down

3

4

Ashley Warren Farm

65

Cannon Heath Farm

5

Hare Warren
Farm

6

B3051

Polhampton
Lodge Stud

Robley Belt

7

8

Caesar's
Belt

A   B   C   88   D   E   F

1 grid square represents 500 metres

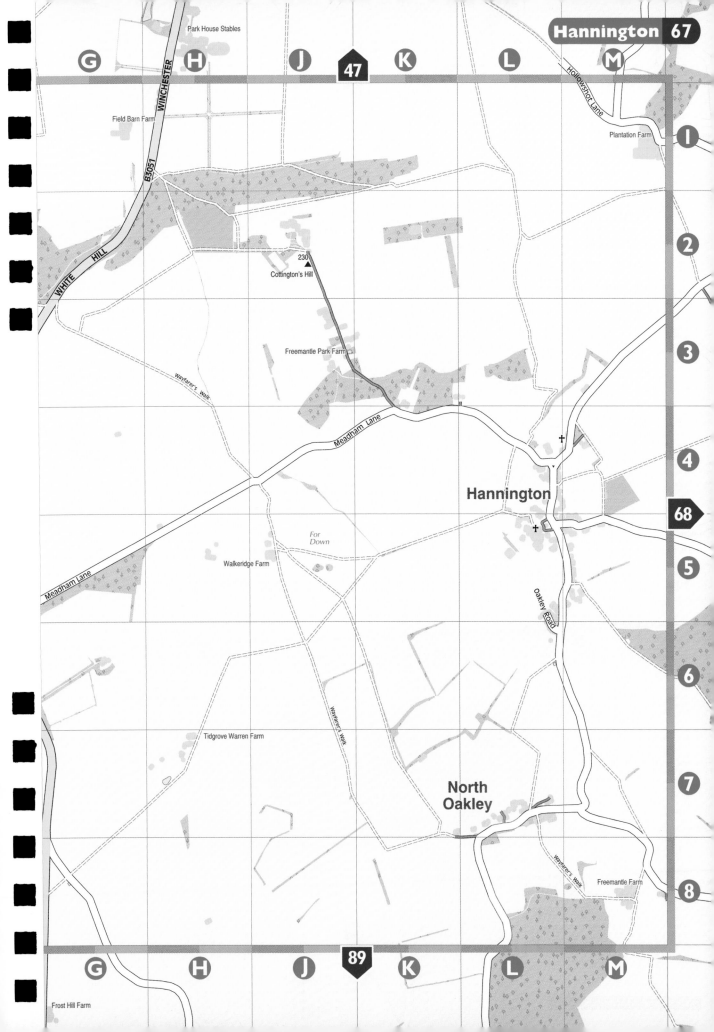

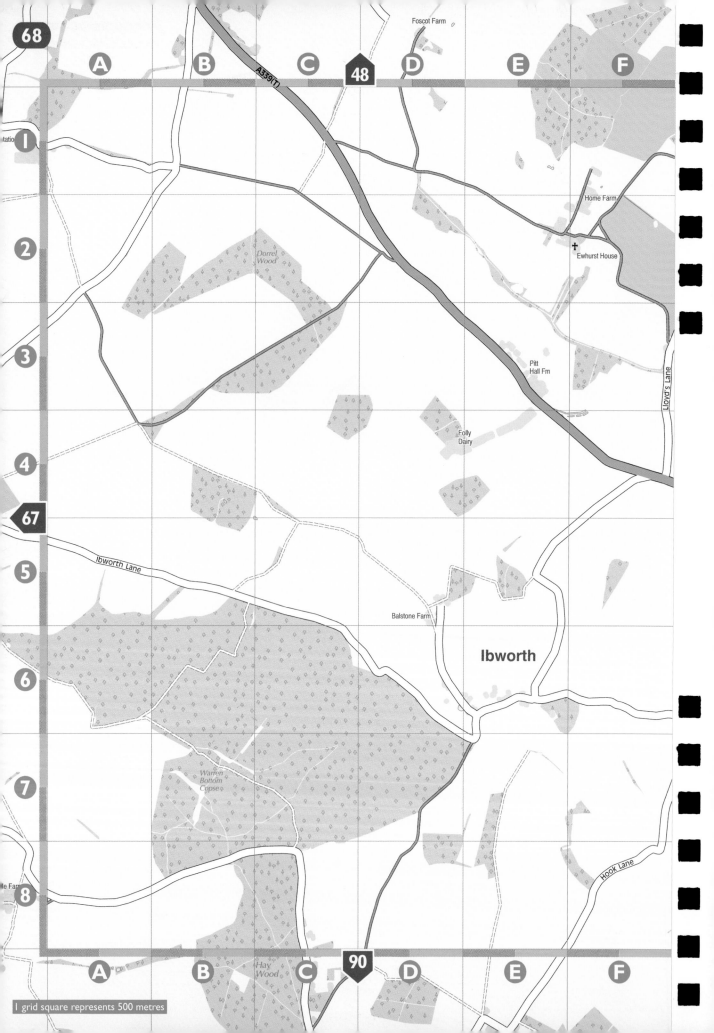

G   H   J   **49**   K   L   M

White Hart
Lane
PH ✝
Shei- Road

Charter
Lley

Rawlins Farm

Beal's Pightie

✝ Monk-

I

Ewhurst   Road

Skyer's Farm

Ramsdell

RG26

2

Ewhurst Park

Sheepwash Lane

Skyer's
Wood

Privett
Copse

Kiln
Lane

Kiln
Green

3

Basingstoke Road

Lower Farm

4

70

5

Field Barn Farm

Basingstoke Road

Woodgarston Farm

6

Upper
Wootton

A339(T)   KINGSCLERE ROAD

A339(T)

7

✝

Whitedown

KINGSCLERE

8

G   H   J   **91**   K   L   M

PO

Tangier

Wootton
St Lawrence

✝

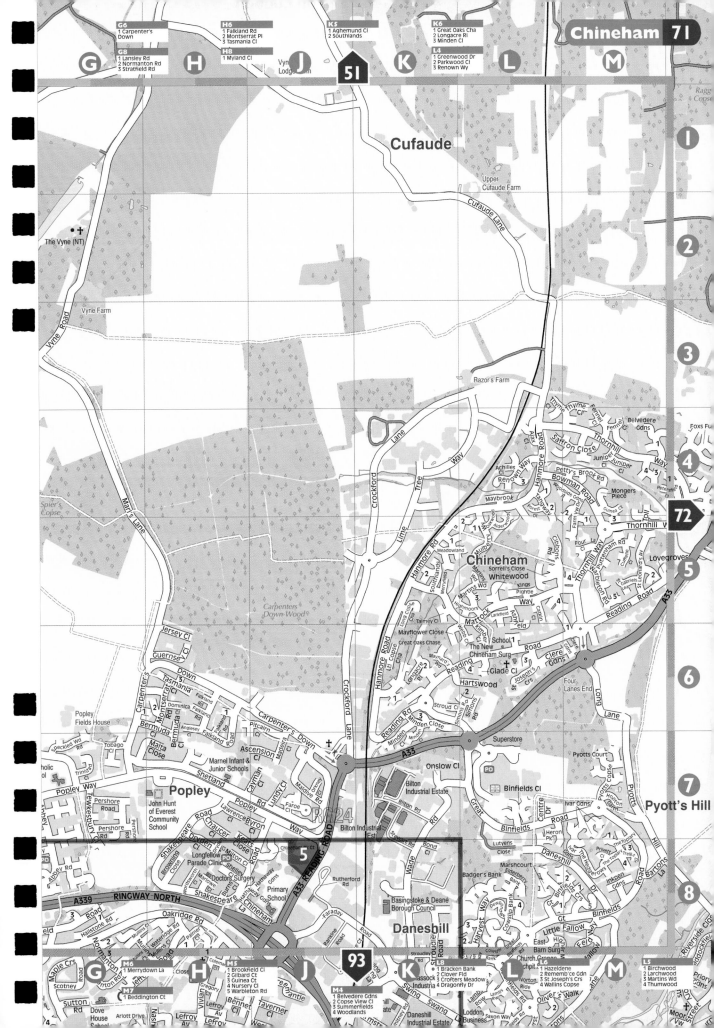

G   H   J   53   K   L   M

I
2
3
4
74
5
6
7
8

Lyde Green

Rotherwick

Cowfold Lane

Wedman's Lane

Lampards Cl

Mill Lane

Mill Farm

Mill Lane

Rotherwick Lane

Frog Lane

Black Wood

Street End Copse

Readon Pond

Reaon Pond

Whitewater
C of E (Controlled)
Primary School

The Street

Hook Road

Summerstead
Farm

Lyde River

The Old
House

Tylney Park
Golf Club

Post Horn Lane

Hotel

Tylney House

Tylney Lane

Ridge Lane

Newnham Lane

Owen's Farm

Manor Farm

Newnham

Newnham Road

Crown Lane

Crown La

Morris Street

Old School Rd

LONDON ROAD A30

HOOK COMMON

A287

B3349

Osborn Way
Industrial Est

Hook Station

Rectory Road

Memorial Road

Station Road

Reading Rd

John Morgan

John Morgan Cl

Great Sheldons Coppice

Goose Gn

Gt. Sheldons Coppice

Painters Pightle

Brown Cft

Hog Gdn

Ferrell Fld

Scures Rd

Sheldon's Rd

Sheldon's La

Carleton

New Road

Middle Mead

Middle Mead

Charles Rd

Garden Rd

Dorchester Road

Elms Road

Lynwood Gdns

Nightingale Gdns

Hazel Coppice

Alder Cl

Oak Cl

Birch Cl

Hatchgate

Goose La

95

Nately
Scures

G   H   J   95   K   L   M

Hotel

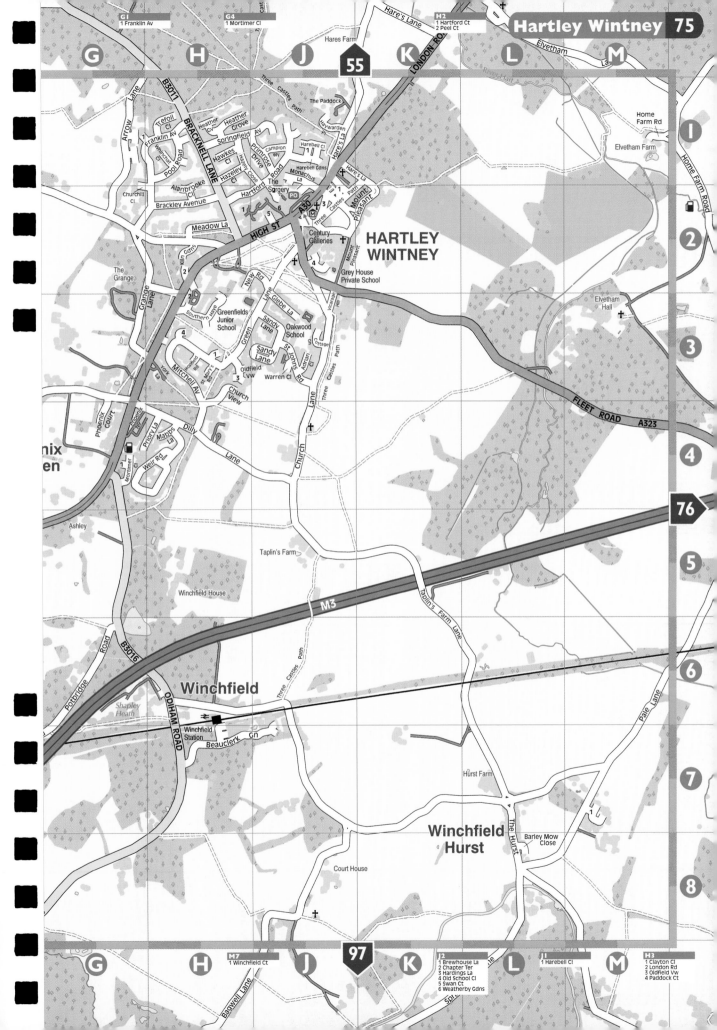

A · B · C · D · E · F

56

Home Farm Rd

I

etham Farm

2

Home Farm Road

Word Hill Farm

Turner's Green Lane

Blackbushes Road

Lichett Plain

Blackbushe Farm

B3013

3

Elvetham

Rotten Green

Broomhurst Farm

A323

Street End

Pale Lane

Turner's Green Lane

Pale Lane

Fleet Service Area

M3

4

75

Palelane Farm

5

Elvetham Pl

Elvetham Cl

Coach House Gdns

Elvetham Road

Ou Mary Cl

Waverley Avenue

Cranbrog

Darse

The Mt

6

Pale Lane

Elvetham Road

Fleet Community Hospital

Calthorpe Rd

Calthorpe Road

Church Road

Avenue Road

Pines Rd

Stockton Ave

Rose Wk

Woodlands

Stockton Park

Brick

Knoll Cl

Knoll Rd

Highdown

AV

Bramsho

Dr

READING ROAD N

Glendale Pk

Pheasant Copse

Broomrigg Road

Broomrigg

Sunnyside

Rosedene Gdns

Church

Church Av

Glebe Ct

St Nicholas

Birch

FLEET

ROAD

Pinewood Hl

Dunmow

B30

Fitzroy Road

Hagley Road

Gough

Victoria Hl

Victoria Rd

Church Grove

Branksomewood Road

Church Road

Street

Church Rd

The Laurels

Abbots Wood

7

Perry Dr

Dukes

The Oaks

Herbert Rd

Fitzroy Road

Bramblewood Place

Cemetery

The Av

Springfield

Campbell Cl

Civic Offices

Harrington Way

Victoria Road

Albert Street

Rochester Rd

Winchcombe Cl

Albany

Byron Cl

Brook Cl

Sheley

Russetts Dr

OakEy C

Woodleigh

Brinksway

F

Mead

Priory Rd

Woodcote Cl

Dukes Md

Tavistock

Tavistock Road

A3013

Upper Street

Clarence Road

Connaught

PO

8

Calthorpe Park School

Hart Sports Centre

Merivale

Tavistock County Infant School

Junior School

New Barn

Stanton Dr

Fleet Police Station

READING RD S

James Rd

Fir Cl

Glen Rd

Lawrence Rd

Glen

Avenue

A323

Kingscroft

Holland Gdns

Basingstoke Canal

ALDERSHOT

Regent St

A · B · C · D · E · F

98

Leawood Road

Frere Av

Crookham Road

Dinorben Ct

Heathvield Cl

The Lea

1 Westminster Cl

Denning

Nethermos

Richard Cl

Larmer Cl

Cemetery Rd

Dinorben Terrace

Carlo na Dr

Castle Street

Courtmoor

Lti Copse

EADING

B3

Velmead

Magnolia Way

Haywood Dr

Follit

Larch

Queen

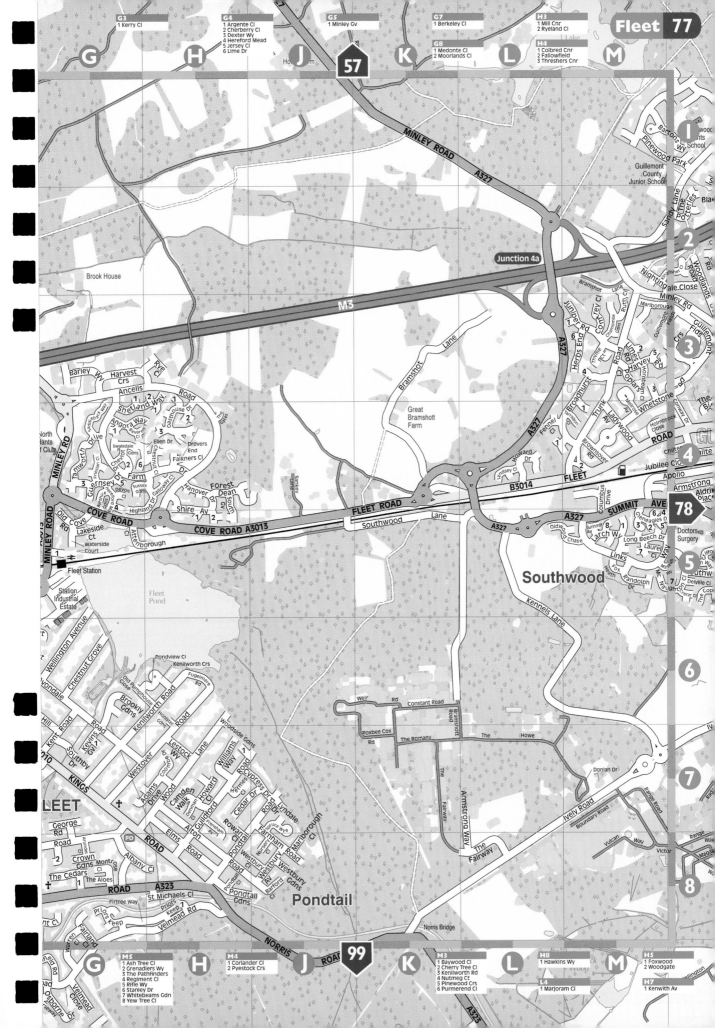

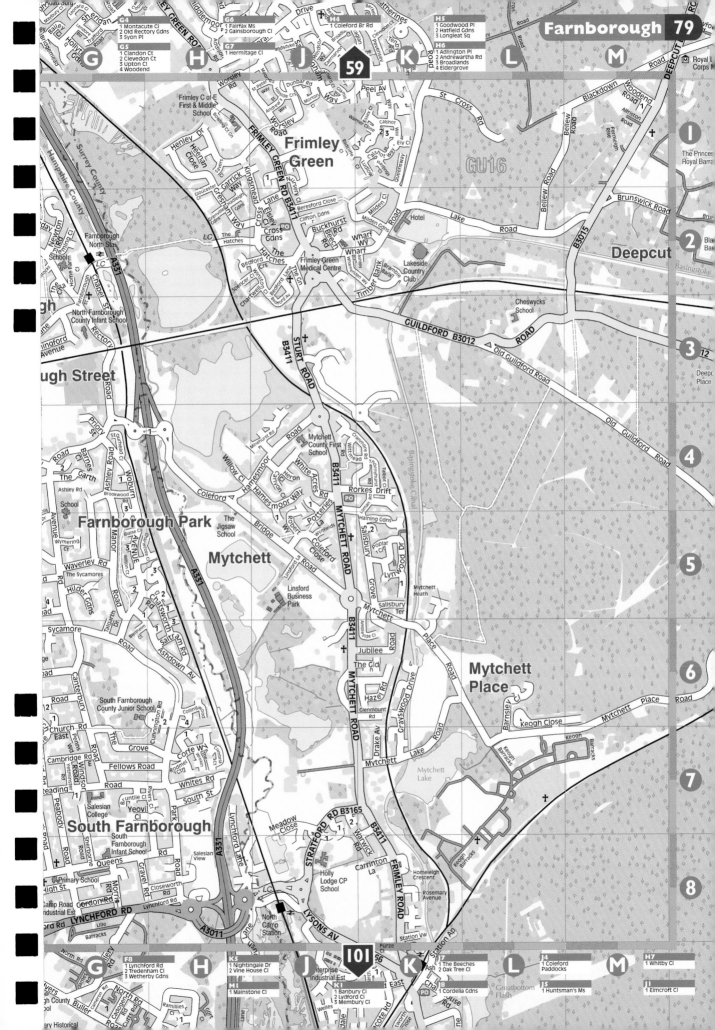

G6
1 St Nicholas Cl

G   **H**   **J**   **K**   **L**   **M**

Collingbourne Wood

Chute Down

PO

Forest Lane

Hookwood Lane

Juse Lane

1 ow

Honey Bottom

Coldridge Wood

Forest House

2 Jolly's Farm

3

Stert Copse

4

82

Coldridge Down

Long Bottom

Long Bottom   Longbottom Farm

Lodge Lane

5

Biddesden House

LL

Crawlboys Lane

Biddesden Lane

6

Close

Spray Leaze

Maple Crs

Elm Cl

Abbatt Cl

Biddesden Lane

1

Pretoria Rd

Grespan Rd

Wiltshire County

Hampshire County

Wiltshire

Hampshire

7

OVER ROAD

A342

Faberstown

ANDOVER ROAD

A342

104

Redenham House

Tilly Down

Redenham Drove

New House

8

G   **H**   **J**   **K**   **L**   **M**

Redenham

G H J **61** K L M

Holt

Whistler's Farm

Pill Heath Farm

Tangley Farm

Blagden Copse

Blagden House

Doles Farm

84

Hatherden Manor

The Avenue **Wildhern**

Hungerford Lane

Hatherden House

The Close

Plough Farm

Cemetery

Hatherden C of E Primary School

Hatchet Lane

Hungerford Lane

Hatherden

Goddards Farm

Pigeon House Farm

et Lane

Charlton Down Farm

A343 NEWBURY

I

2

3

4

5

6

7

8

Gr

Newbury Road

A B C **62** D E **The Dene** F

C8
1 Ridges Cl

B8
1 Greenfields

Bladon
Gallery

PO

**Hurstbourne
Tarrant**

Hurstbourne
Tarrant
School

B3048

The Crescent Dean Rise

River Swift

CHURCH STREET

Dines Close

Doctors Drove

Windmill Lane

Locke's Drove

Horseshoe Lane

Test Way

1 I

2

83

3

4

5

6

7

8

Windmills

Doles Wood

Test Way

Bourne Rivulet

Stokeh

A343 NEWBURY ROAD

Bourne Park

Rag Copse

Frenches Farm

Ridges Copse

Green Drove

Upper
Enham

MacCullum
Court

Weston
Court

Anthone
Close

Road

Dunhills
Lane

**Little
London**

Stoke Road

A B **107** C D E F

NEWBURY Road

Malt House

Lane

Newbury
Road

Kings Alamein Rd

PO

Enham Alamein

Smannell & Enham

1 grid square represents 500 metres

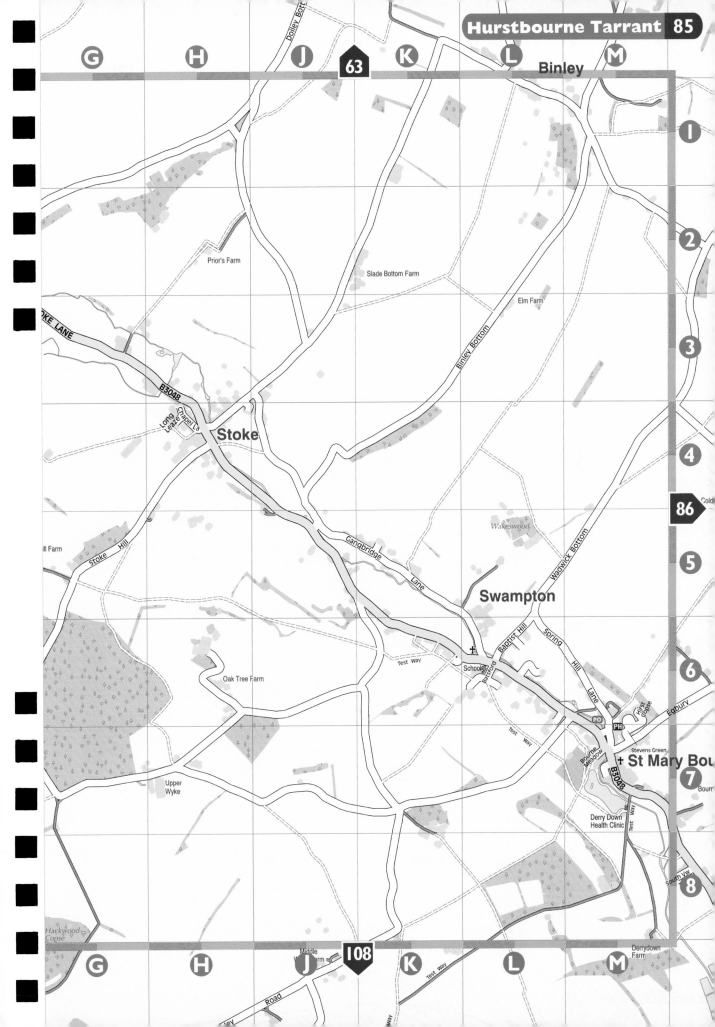

G H J **63** K L **Binley** M

I

2

3

4

86

5

Prior's Farm

Slade Bottom Farm

Elm Farm

Binley Bottom

OKE LANE

B3048

Long Leaze La

Chapel La

Stoke

Gangbridge

Lane

Wakeswood

Wadwick Bottom

Cold

Hill Farm

Stoke Hill

Swampton

Oak Tree Farm

Test Way

Baptist Hill

Batsford

Spring Hill Lane

School

Test Way

H'st Copse

Egbury

6

PO

PH

Stevens Green

Bourne Meadow

St Mary Bou

B3048

Upper Wyke

7

Bourn

Derry Down Health Clinic

Test Way

South Vw

8

Hackwood Copse

Middle Farm **108** Road Test Way Derrydown Farm

G H J K L M

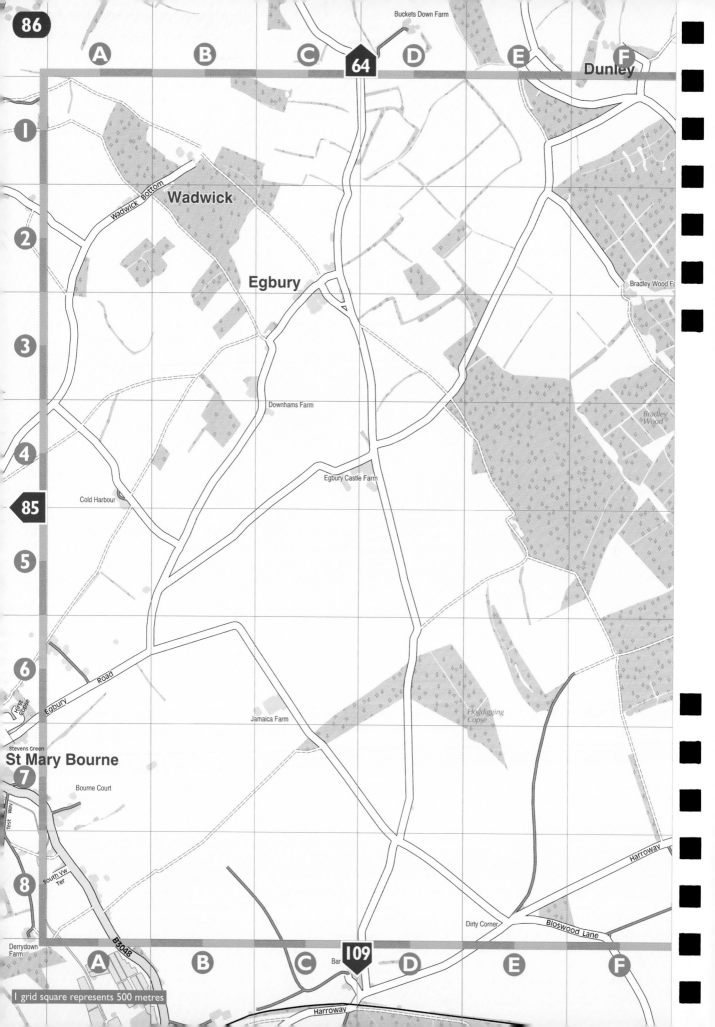

A   B   C   64   D   E   F   Dunley

Buckets Down Farm

I

Wadwick Bottom   **Wadwick**

2

Egbury

3

Bradley Wood Fa

Downhams Farm

Bradley Wood

4

85   Cold Harbour

Egbury Castle Farm

5

6

Hirst Copse

Egbury Road

Hogdigging Copse

Jamaica Farm

Stevens Green

St Mary Bourne

7   Bourne Court

Test Way

Harroway

8   South Vw Ter

Dirty Corner   Bloswood Lane

Derrydown Farm   B3048   A   B   C   **109**   D   E   F

Bar

Harroway

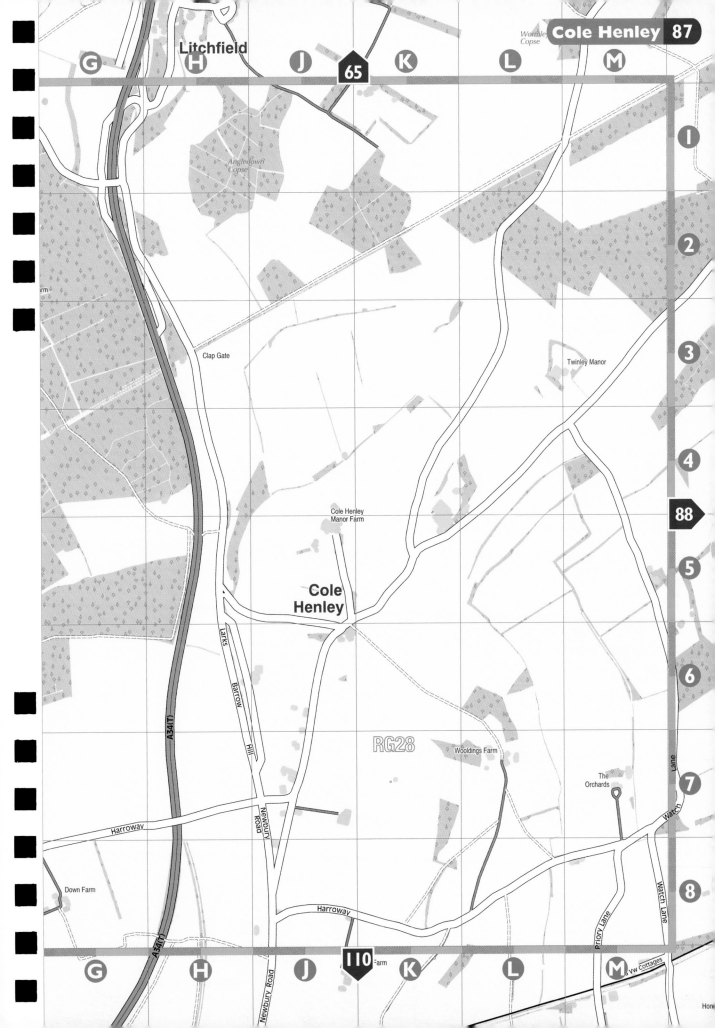

Wormle Copse

G H J **65** K L M

Litchfield

Angledown Copse

Clap Gate

Twinley Manor

Cole Henley Manor Farm

88

Cole Henley

5

Larks

Barrow

Hill

A34(T)

RG28

Wooldings Farm

6

The Orchards

7

Watch Lane

Harroway

Newbury Road

Down Farm

Harroway

8

Priory Lane

Watch Lane

1

2

3

4

G H **110** J K L M

Farm

VW Cottages

A   B   C   **66**   D   E   F

1

2

Ridgeway Farm

Willesley Warren Farm

3

4

Whitnal

87

New Barn

Court Drove

B3051

5

6

Hill Meadow

7

Watch Lane

Primary School

Court Farm

Lordsfield Gdns

Court Drove

Church Road

Overton Gallery

KINGSCLERE ROAD   B3051

8

Watch Lane

Lynch

The Lynch

Silk Mill Lane

Southington Close

Southington La

Glebe Meadow

White Hart Gallery

Mill Lane

Bridge St

HIGH ST

Red Lion Lane

Dellands Lane

A   B   C   **III**   D   E   **B3400**   Southington   F

Dellands

1 grid square represents 500 metres

G8
1 Waltham Ct

G   **H**   **J**   **67**   **K**   **L**   **M**

Frost Hill Farm

1

2

3

Ashe
Warren Ho

4

90

5

Overton
Station

6

Hilltop Road

Foxdown

Elm Rd
Beech
Cl
Station Road
Copse Road
Foxdown
Hill

Polhampton Farm

Quidhampton

Overton
Surgery
Waltham Rd
Riverside
Close

7

Deane

Source of
the River Test

Ashe

ANDOVER ROAD

B3400

B3051

8

Cheesedown Fa

LONDON ROAD B3400

Battens
Avenue
Winchester Street
The Green
Two Ga Meadow
Two Gate Lane
Alexander
Pound Road
Mede
Close
Paper m
Gingale
se

G   **H**   Berrydown Lane   **112**   **J**   **K**   **L**   **M**

OVERTON

Berrydown Court

Berrydown
Farm

Ashe
Park

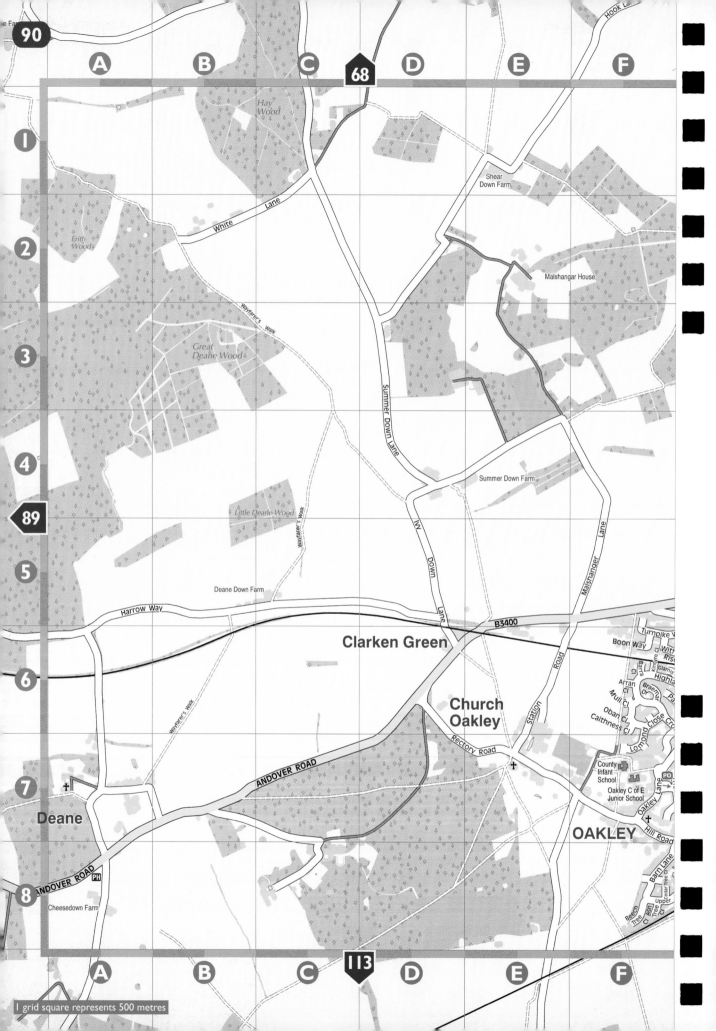

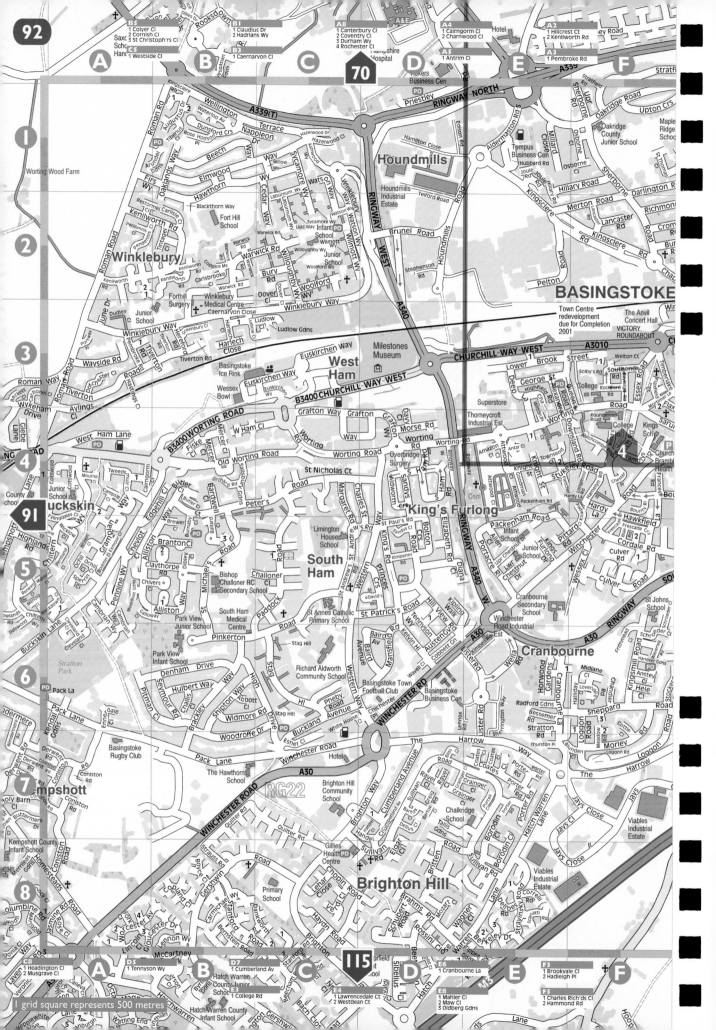

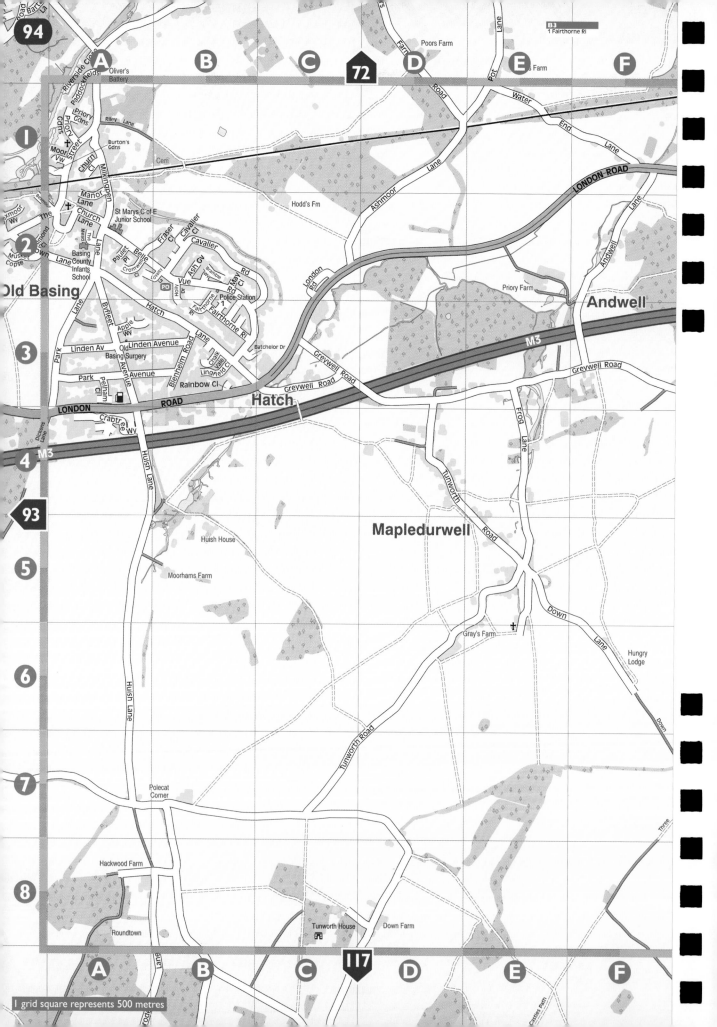

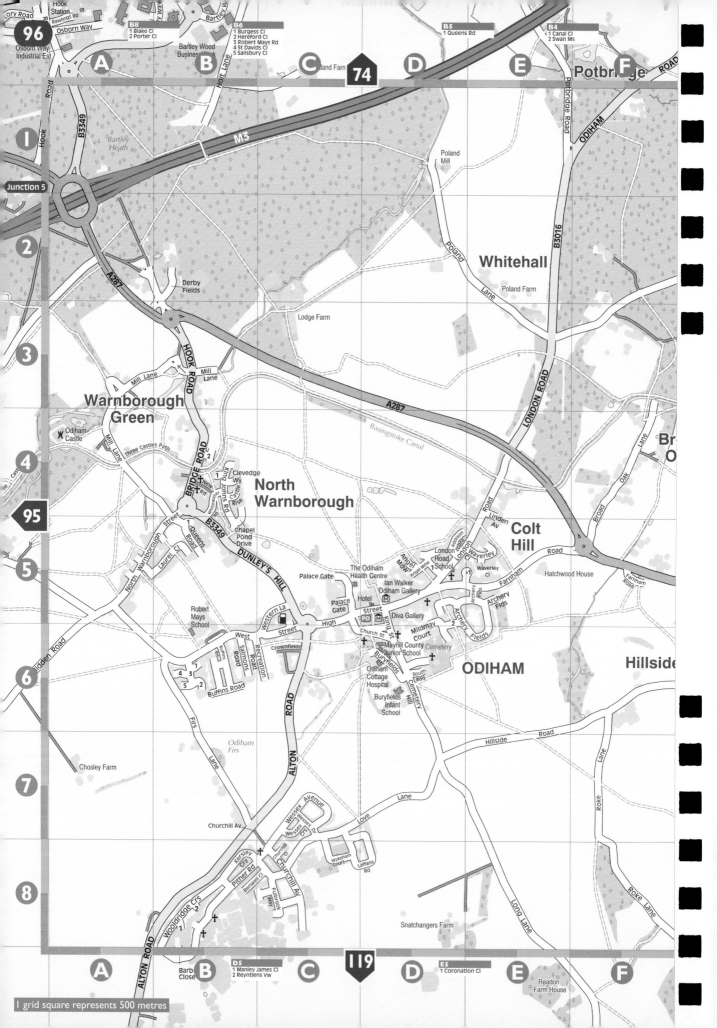

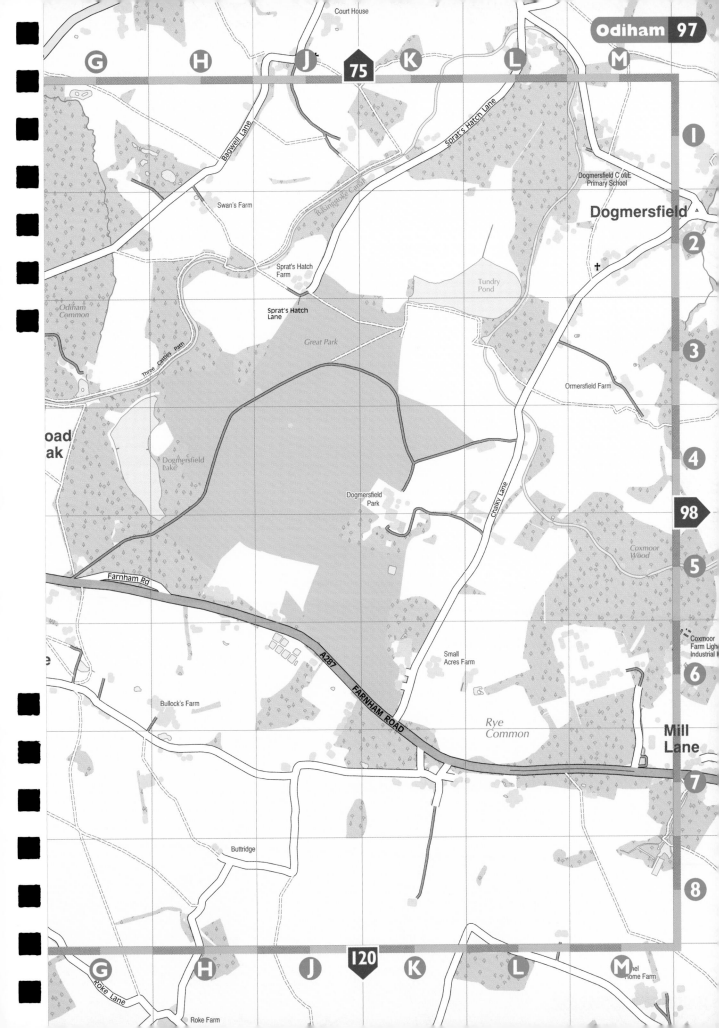

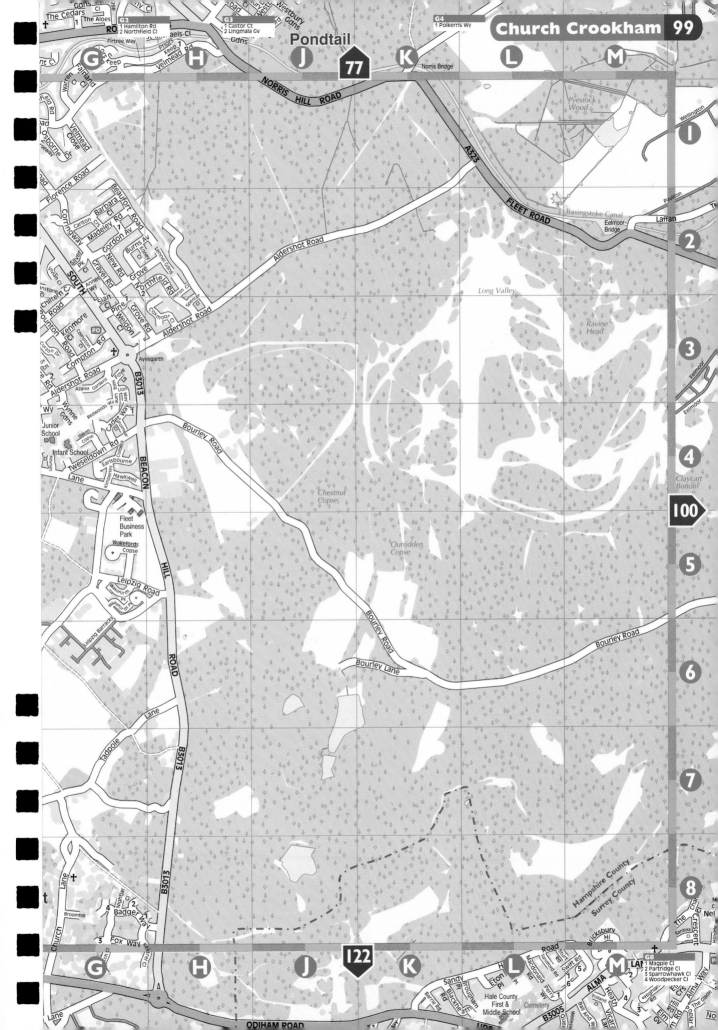

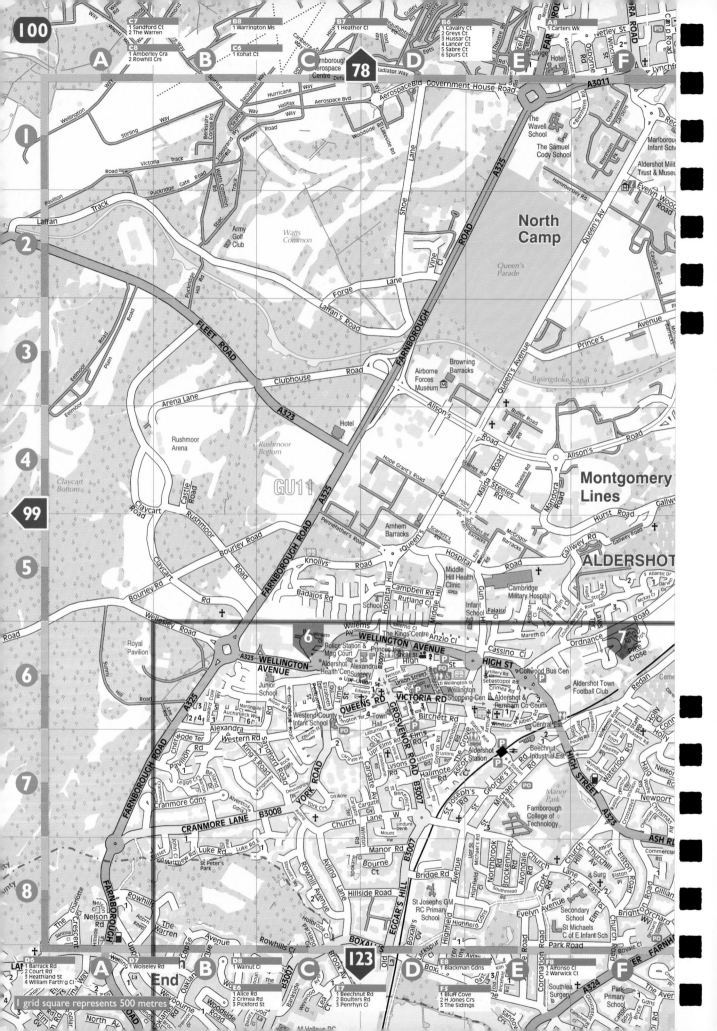

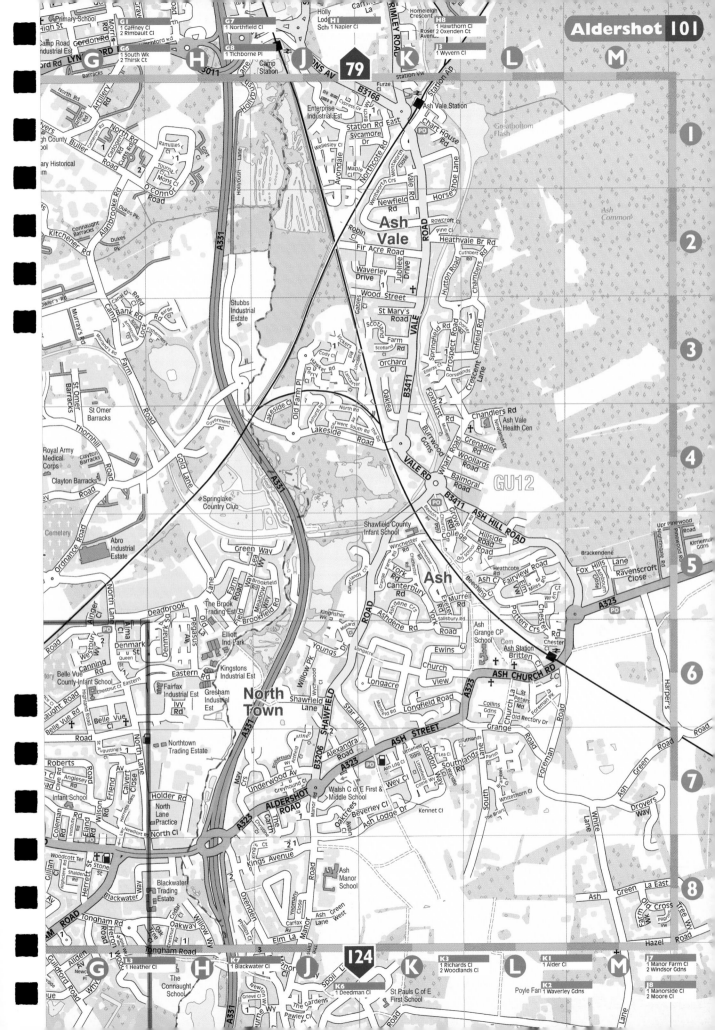

1 Brisbane Cl
2 Sydney Cl

G   H   J   80   K   L   M

TIDWORTH

Perham Down

Somme Road

Wouldham Cl

Upnor Close

Kemmel Rd

Lambdown Terrace

Lambdown Terrace

Lambdown Way

Adelaide Rd

Harton

Perth
Cl

2   1

Fyfield Way

Benintobruk Rd

Furze Dr

Appleshaw Way

Downsview Way

Lamb Down

I

Andover Lane

South Park

Great Shod sc

2

Wiltshire County

Hampshire County

Newdown Copse

3

4

104

Kimpton Down Farm

Down Road

5

Kimpton Wood

Ox Drove

6

Ox Drove

7

Old Coach Road

8

G   H   J   127   K   L   M

Shoddington

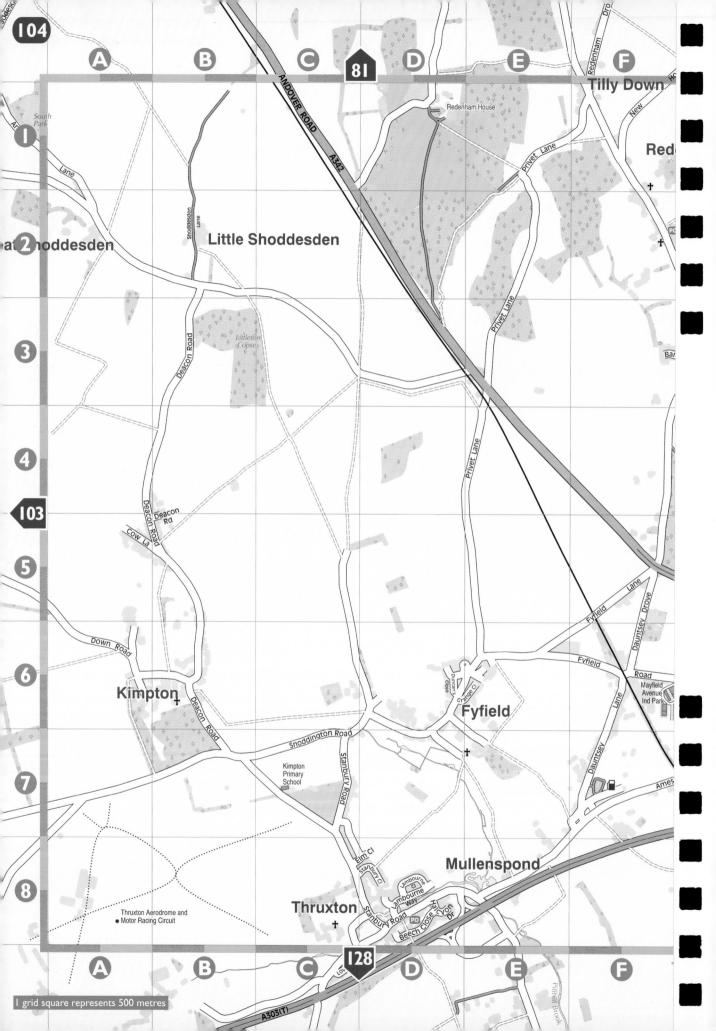

104

A B C **81** D E F

Tilly Down

1

South Park

Ar Lane

Red

2 hoddesden

Shoddesden Lane

Little Shoddesden

Redenham House

Privet Lane

ANDOVER ROAD A342

3

Deacon Road

Littleton Copse

Privet Lane

Bar

4

Privet Lane

103

Deacon Road

Deacon Rd

Cow La

5

Fyfield Lane

Down Road

Dauntsey Drove

6

Kimpton

Deacon Road

Duncan's Close

Canoe Cl

Fyfield

Fyfield Road

Lane

Mayfield Avenue Ind Park

7

Snoddington Road

Stanbury Road

Kimpton Primary School

Dauntsey

Ames

8

Thruxton Aerodrome and Motor Racing Circuit

Elm Cl

Stanbury Cl

Mullenspond

Lambourne Way

Thruxton

Stanbury Road

Beech Close

Lyon Dr

A B C **128** D E F

A303(T)

Pillhill Brook

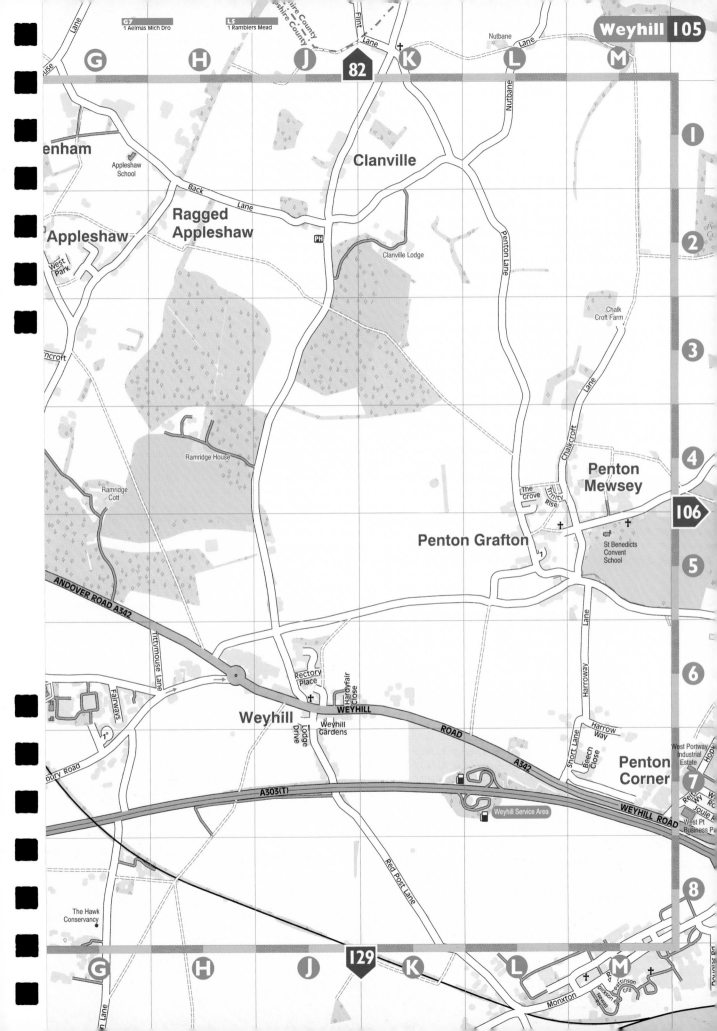

E5
1 Hamburg Cl
2 Lingen Cl
3 Minden Cl
4 Verden Wy

D8
1 Lodge Cl

E4
1 Marsum Cl

D7
1 Silver Birch Rd
2 Thistledown Cl

C6
1 Kimberley Cl

D6
1 The Green

C5
1 Augustine Wy
2 Barton Cl
3 Brancaster Av
4 Ethelbert Dr
5 Hengest Cl
6 Home Farm Gdns

A B 83 C D E F

I

2

SP11

Penton Copse

3

Cemetery

New Street
Football
Club

**Knights
Enham**

Manor Farm

Enham Lane

4

105

Foxcotte

Mercia
Mercia Avenue
Avenue

Richborough Drive

Porchester
Bede
Drive
Tower Cl

Litchfield
Cl

Saxon
Way

Rune
Drive

Saxon
Way

Enham
Lane

Aldrin Cl
Armstrong
Collins

Elbe Way
Holland Dr
Cuxhaven

Emden Rd
Altona
Flensburg

Lubeck Drive

River Anton

Caerleon Dr
Ryon Cl
Mervin Close

Tintagel
Junior School
Launcelot

Galahad Close

Camelot
Cl

Atholl Cl

5

Foxcotte Lane

St Thomas

Wetherby Gdns
Goch Way

Bremen
Gdns

Charlton

Goch
Way

Greenwich

6

Andover
Football Club

West Portway

Lakeside
Close
Sunnyside Cl

Carter's
Meadow

8 A343

War
Memorial
Hospital

Poynters
Close
Artists

Ward Cl

7

West Portway
Industrial
Estate

Hopkinson
Smeaton Rd
Mitchell
Cl
Watt
Cl
Caxton
Cl

Sterling
Pk

Portway
Drive
Blendon Drive

Harrow
Way

CHURCHILL WAY WEST

Parkview

Silchester
Cl

Harrow Way
Community
School

Chaucer Av
Milton Av
Shakespeare Av
Brackenbury

Charlton
Hill Surgery

Tollgate Rd
Apple Tree
Grove
Cherry
Tree Rd

Charlton
Health
Centre

Dell

Lawrence Cl
Hogan
Stubbs Ct
Landseer

A343 REDON WAY

Moore

Constable

Artists

NORTHERN AVENUE

enton
Corner

Reith Wy
Whittle Rd
Macadam
Royce Close
Joule Road

A343
Stephenson
Close

East
Portway

Upper
Drove

Eardley Av
King George

Chichester

Porters

Ferndale
Road

Orchard Rd
Hanson
Road

Beckett Rd

Wellington
Rd
Manor
Rd
Old
Down
Rd

Andover
Stn

Station
Rd

Cross Lane
Junction

Charlton Road

Heather Dr

Western Av

SP10
Cricklade

Leisure
Cen

7

West Pt
Business Park

WEYHILL

WEYHILL ROAD

Monxton
Rd

Callaghers Mead

Danehurst Pl

Portway County
Infants and
Junior Schools

Cheaviers Cl

Ashfield
Road

PORTWAY
ROAD

Haig Rd

Amber
Gdns

Mylen
Rd

Winnot

Mylen Business
Cen

Albany
Rd

Glen Cl

The Pines

The
Avenue

Bishop's
Way

Queens
Rd

Chantry
Centre
Shopping
Precinct

8

Salmond Road

Ellington Cl

Portal

Ash Tree Road
Shaw Larch
The
Link

Crescent

Meadow

B3402

Roundway

Winterdyne
Mews

John Hanson
Community
School

Warner
Ct

Verity
Ct

HILL

Osborne Rd

A343

ERN RD

WESTERN AV

E6
1 Hattem Pl

E7
1 Lancaster Cl
2 Lowry Ct

E8
1 The Crossways
2 Saor Ms

F4
1 Gawaine Cl

A B 130 C D E F

F7
1 Landseer Ct

F8
1 Portland Gv
2 West St

St John the B
RC Primary School

1 Agravaine Cl

Beech Hurst
Test Valley
Borough
Council

Suffolk

1 grid square represents 500 metres

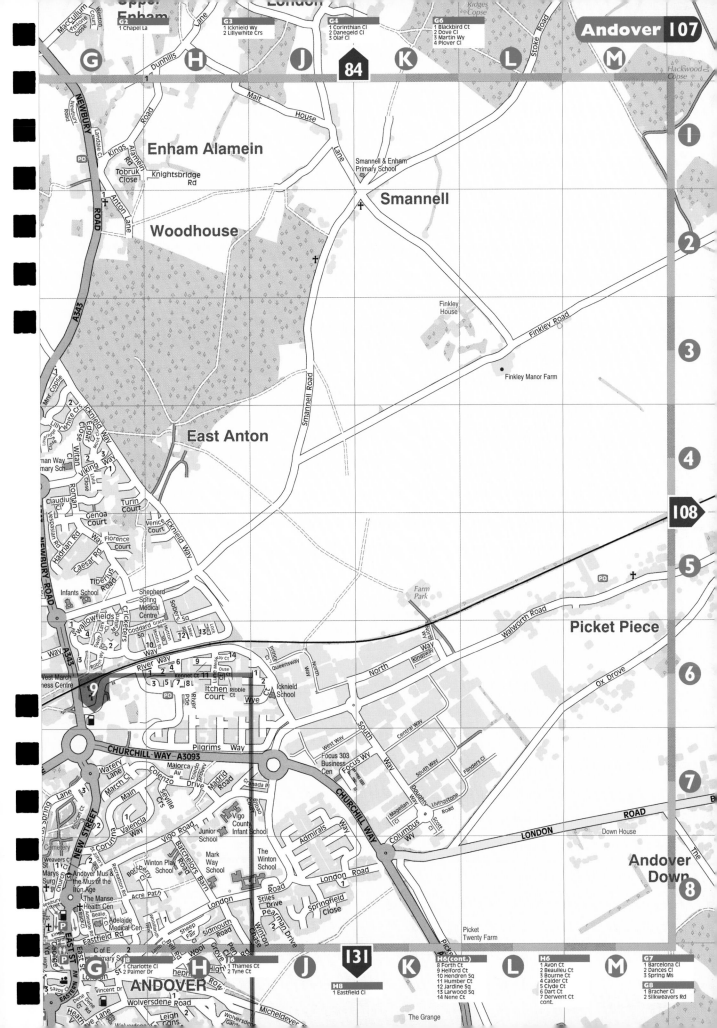

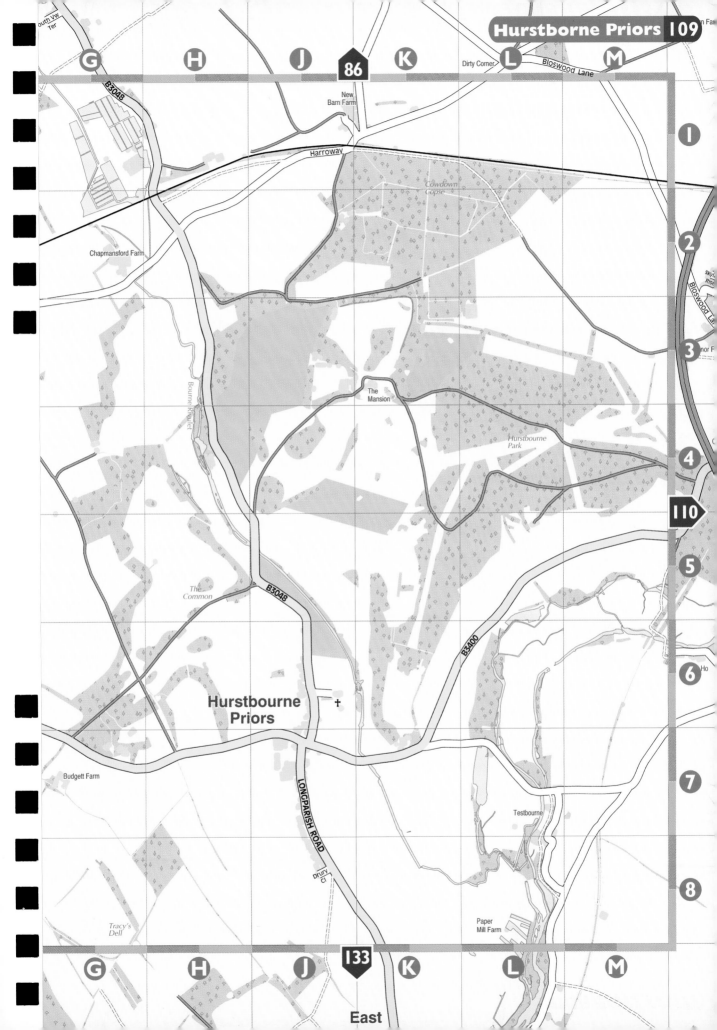

G H J **86** K **Dirty Corner** L Bloswood Lane M

I

New
Barn Farm

Harroway

Cowdown
Copse

Chapmansford Farm

2

SKYL
RISE

Bloswood Lan

nor F

3

Bourne Rivulet

The
Mansion

Hurstbourne
Park

4

110

5

The
Common

B3048

B3400

6 Ho

**Hurstbourne
Priors**

7

Budgett Farm

Testbourne

LONGPARISH ROAD

Drury
Cl

8

Tracy's
Dell

Paper
Mill Farm

G H J **133** K L M

East

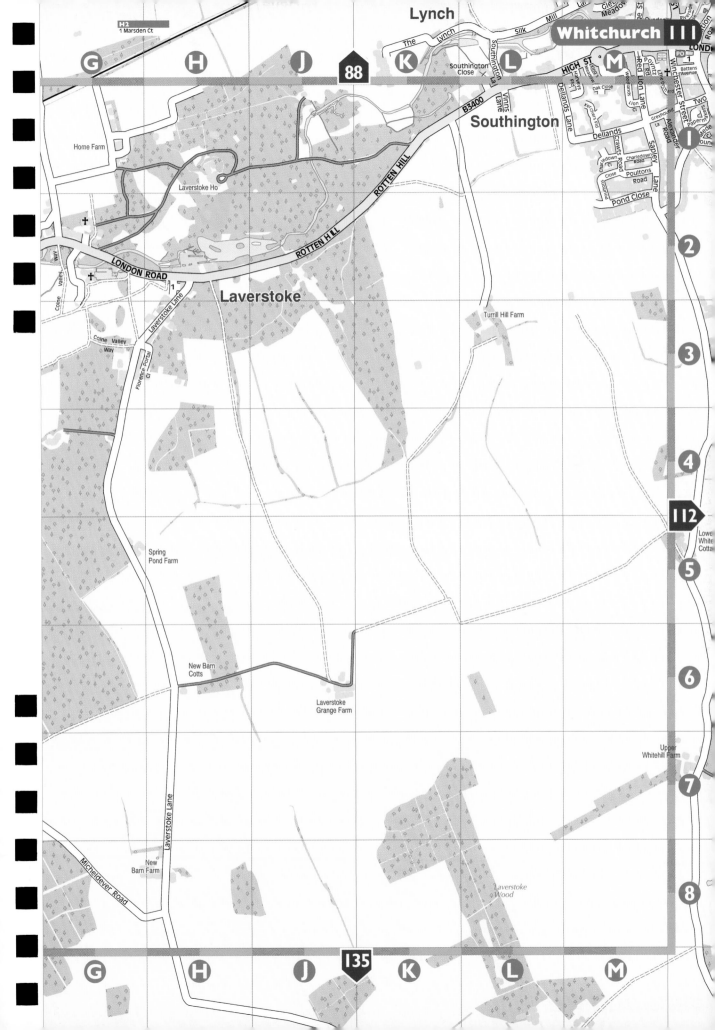

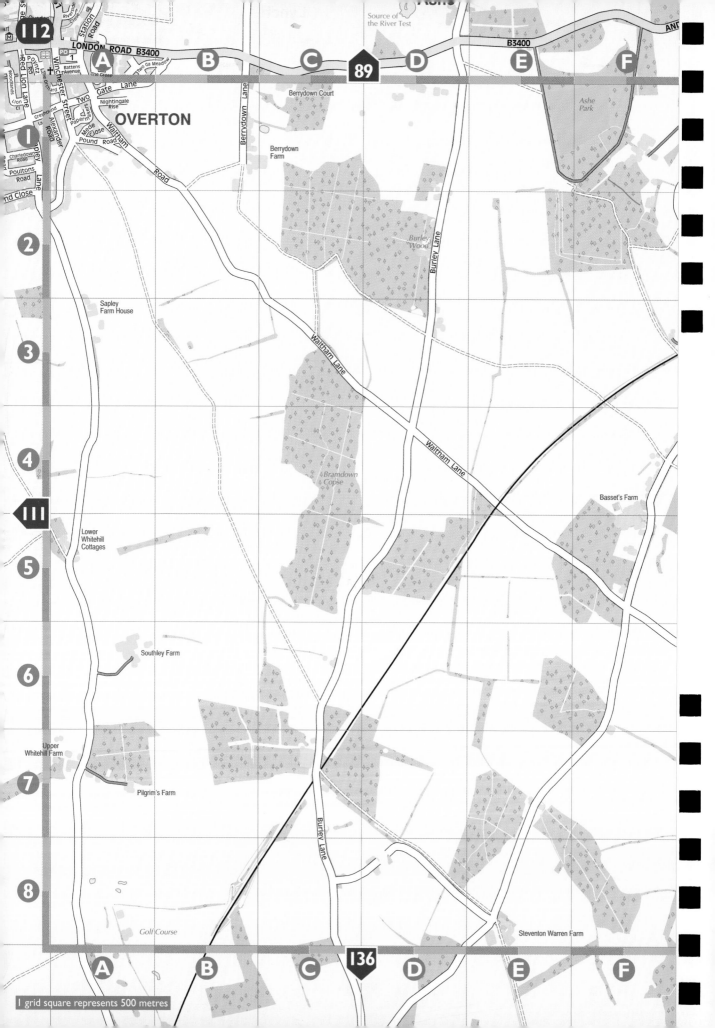

K7
1 Old Barn Cl
2 Ramsholt Cl

L7
1 Burydown Cl
2 Meadow Ri

G **H** **J** **90** **K** **L** **M**

Fairview
Meadow
Th

1

Pard

2

Bull's
Bushes
Copse

Wayfarer's Walk

Wayfarer's Walk

Bull's Bushes F.

3

Dean
Heath
Copse

4

Steventon

Stubb's
Copse

114

5

West
Wood

Village Farm

6

North Waltham

Waltham

Manor Farm

Mary Lane

Smith's Md

Lane

Steventon Rd

North
Waltham
School

Elizabethan Rise

Longfield

Home
Md

Well
Close

Chapel St

Cuckoo Cl

Maidenthorn
Lane

7

Folly Farm

St Michael's Close

Church Road

Cuckoo
Lane

Yew Tree
Lane

Up St

Coldharbour

Popham

PH

Lane

A30

M3

8

G **H** **J** **137** **K** **L** **M**

A30

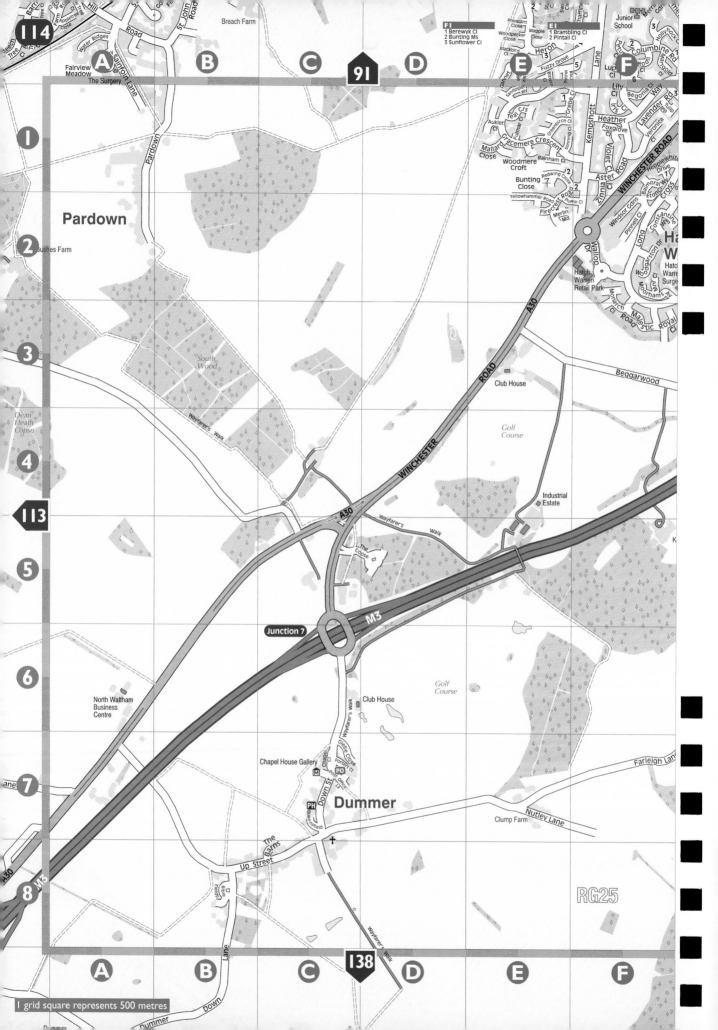

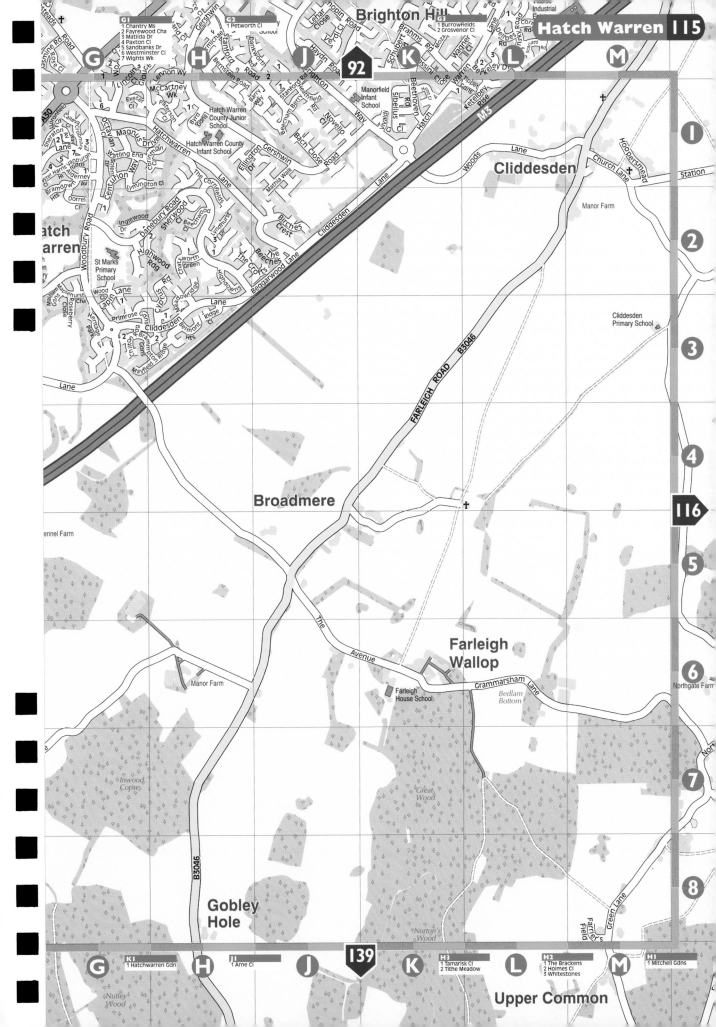

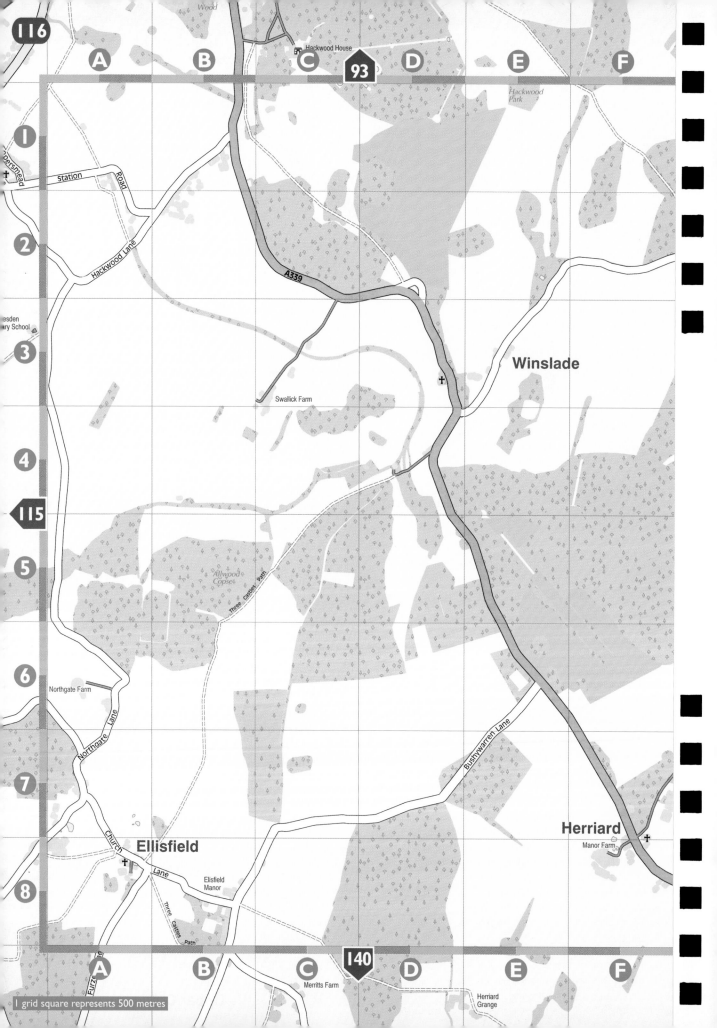

G Roundtown
H
J unworth Down
94
K
L
M

Longroden Lane

Three Castles Path

1

Cleves

2

Upton Grey House

Upton Grey

3

Tunworth

✝

The Dower House

4

Weston Road

118

5

Hen Wood

Weston
Corbett

✝ Weston Patrick

6

Herriard
Park

7

Herriard House

Park Farm

8

A339

G
H
J Lee Farm
141
K
L Wood
M New Farm

Nash's Green

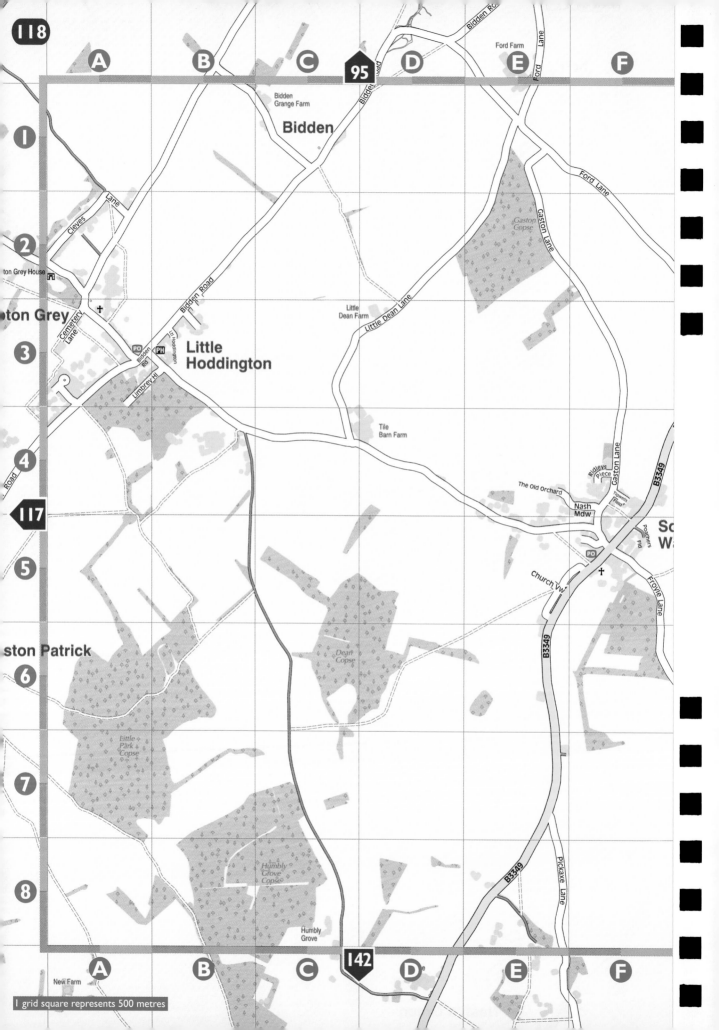

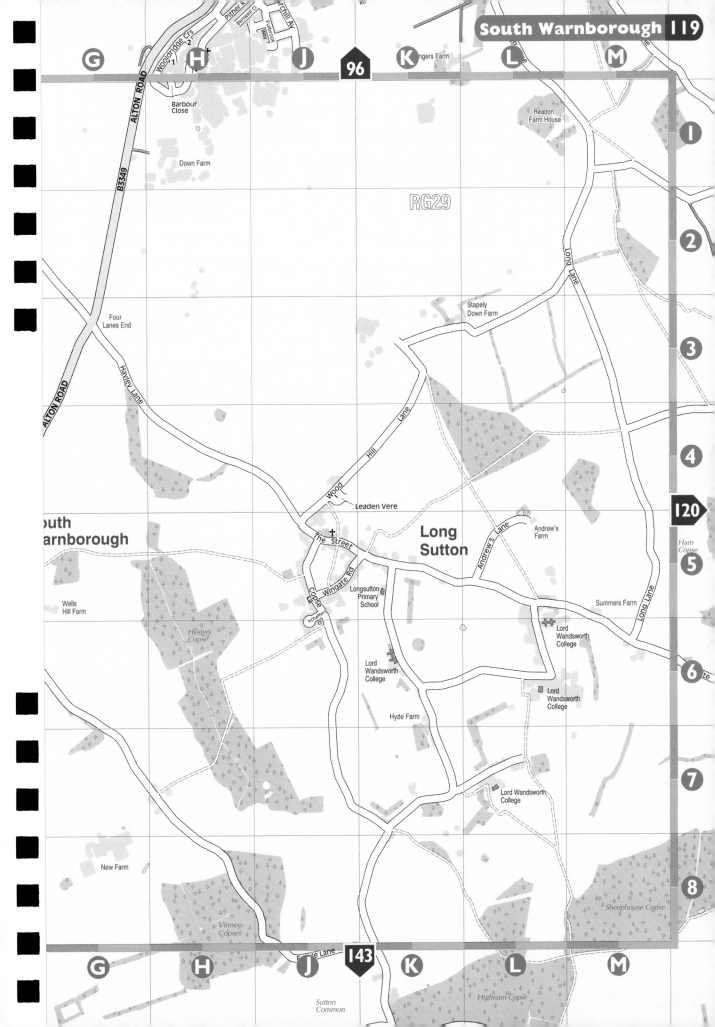

G H J 96 K L M

I

2

3

4

120

5

6

7

8

Woolridge Crs
Pither R
Benwell Cl
Churchill Av
Fulbrook Way

Barbour
Close

ALTON ROAD

B3349

Down Farm

Four
Lanes End

Havley Lane

ALTON ROAD

RG29

Rangers Farm

Readon
Farm House

Long Lane

Stapely
Down Farm

Wood Hill Lane

Leaden Vere

South
Warnborough

Long
Sutton

Andrew's Lane

Andrew's
Farm

Ham
Copse

Summers Farm

The Street

Copse Lane

Wingate Rd

Chaffers Cl

Longsutton
Primary
School

Lord
Wandsworth
College

Long Lane

Wells
Hill Farm

Hesters
Copse

Lord
Wandsworth
College

Lord
Wandsworth
College

Hyde Farm

Lord
Wandsworth
College

New Farm

Lord Wandsworth
College

Sheephouse Copse

Vinney
Copse

G H J 143 K L M

Sutton
Common

Highnam Copse

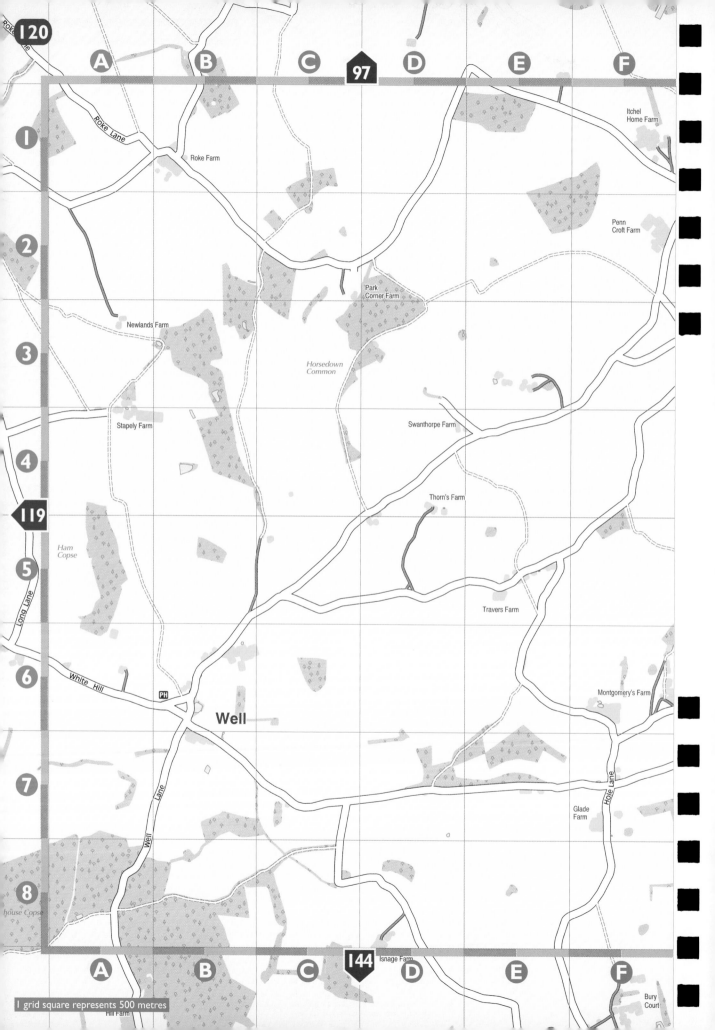

A   B   C   D   E   F

119

1

2

3

4

5

6

7

8

Roke Lane

Roke Farm

Itchel
Home Farm

Penn
Croft Farm

Newlands Farm

Park
Corner Farm

Horsedown
Common

Stapely Farm

Swanthorpe Farm

Thorn's Farm

Ham
Copse

Long Lane

Travers Farm

Montgomery's Farm

White Hill

PH

Well

Well Lane

Hole Lane

Glade
Farm

house Copse

Isnage Farm

Bury
Court

A   B   C   D   E   F

Hill Farm

1 grid square represents 500 metres

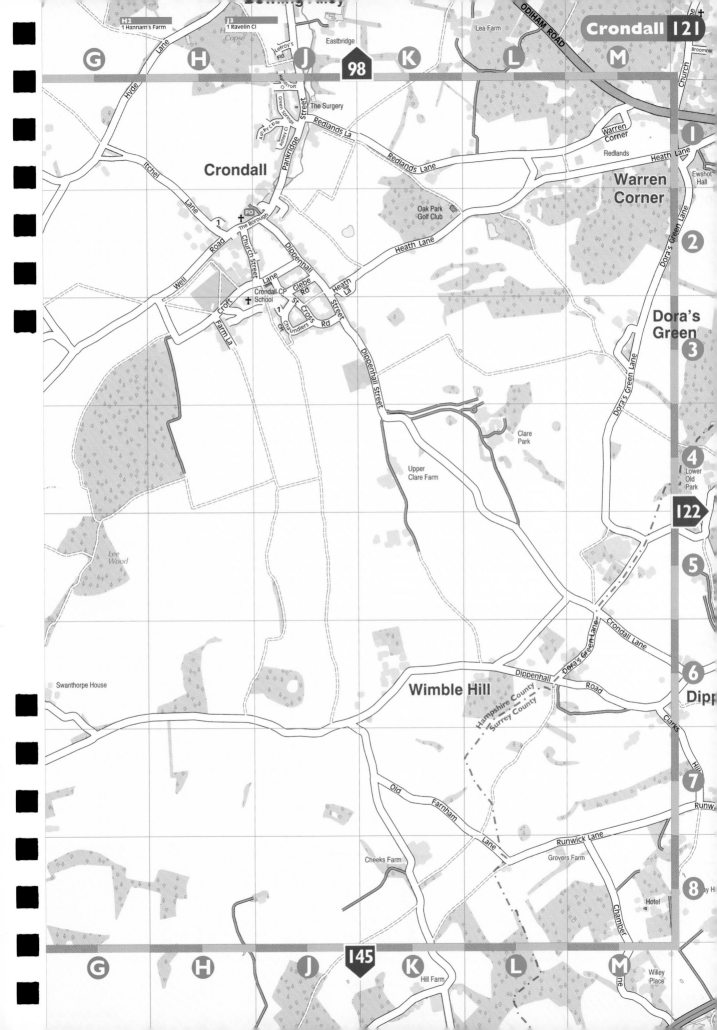

99
121
146

E6
1 College Gdns
2 Fox Yd
3 Long Garden Wk
4 Long Gdn Wk E
5 Long Gdn Wk W
6 Lower Church La
7 Middle Church La
8 Penns Yd
9 Upper Church La

E1
1 St Marks Pl

E2
1 Balmoral Crs
2 Chatsworth Gv
3 Oaktrees
4 Wings Cl

D6
1 Chantry Cl

D2
1 Ambleside Crs
2 Beck Gdns
3 Dukes Cl
4 Folly La South
5 Trinity Flds
6 Ullswater Cl

D1
1 Lawday Pl

Ewshot Lane

Church Lane
Broomhill
Ba
Nums Mountferret Cl
Fox Way
3

Heath Lane

Warren
orner

Ewshot
Hall

Dora's
Green

Dora's Green Lane

Green Lane

Middle
Old Park

Lower
Old Park

Dippenhall

Clarks Hill

Crondall Lane

Three Stiles Rd

Larkfield Rd

Byworth Rd
Byworth Cl
Tor Rd
Wavnflete Lane
Marston Rd
Hazell Rd

Beavers
Hl

Beavers
Close

Parfitts Cl
W End Gv
Mt Pleasant

The Chantrys

Coxbridge
Dr
Mdw

Runwick Lane

Ridgway House

Runwick House

WRECCLESHAM RD
Wrecclesham ROAD

River

ODIHAM ROAD

Old Park Lane

Heathfields Road

Hog
Hatch

Upper Old Park Lane

Upper
Old Park

Old Park Lane

Middle Old Park

Knowle Farm

Folly
Hill

FOLLY HILL

CASTLE HILL

Golf
Course

The Grange

Sandy Hill Rd
Barrie Rd
Blackheath
Brougham

Lawday
Link
Lawday
La
Spring La
Folly La North
Bishops Rd
Grasmere
Rd
Windermere
Wy
PO
Ennerdale Cl
Hoghatch La
Derwent Cl
Infant
School
Coniston
Dr
Drovers Way
Hampton Road
Blenheim
Crs
Winder Crs

Hillbrook Rd
Hereford Rd
Hope Rd
Trinity Hill
Farnham
Pk Cl
Shady Nook

Hale County
First &
Middle School

Cemetery

UPPER HALE ROAD

B3005
Queens Con
Wellesley Rd

Macdonald Rd
Eton Pl
Lyall Pl
Sandford Rd
Swift Cl
Perry
Bill and Wicket La

Yolland
Heath
eHighlands

ALMA
LANE
Vicarage Lane
Elm Gv
Wood Rd

Fernhill Dr
Fernhill La
Parkside

The Green
Nutshell
Bricksbury Hl

Upper
Hale

Farnham
Park

GU9

Farnham
Castle

Stoke
Hills

St James
Ter
Summer Rd
Beaufort Rd

East Hill
EAST ST
DOGFLUD WK

CASTLE ST
THE BOROUGH

Park Row
High
Lower So

Long Gdn
Lion Wy
Lamb Wy
The Hart
Lion La
Potters Gate

SOUTH ST
DOWNING ST

Bear La
Victoria Rd
UNION RD
Bishops Md
Farnham
Museum

Falkner Rd
Beavers Rd

Primary
School

Bags Ct
Crosby Wy

Mead La
Pengilly

Red Lion Lane

Global
Adventure
Sailing Club
Hotel
New
Ashgate
Gallery

ABBEY ST
LONG BR

Approach Rd
Southern Wy
Farnham
Station

P
Health
Cen
The
Clinic
Sports
Cen

FARNHAM
STATION HILL

Wessex Rd

Trafalgar Ct

Farnham
College

FIRGROVE HILL

WEST STREET

FARNHAM   BY-PASS

A31
Weydon Mill La
Hookstile La

Cemetery

Farnham Business
Park

The
Hatches

Farnham
Business
Centre

Pilgrims Way
Infants' School

Weydon Lane

Weydon
Way

Talbot Road

Pilgrims Way

St Johns' Rd

Arthur Rd
Avon Rd

Searle Road

Ryle Rd

The
Hop-Kiln

Grove End Road

Upper
Bourne
Green

St Cross Rd

Bramble
 Av

St Johns' Rd

Ridgeway Pl

Old
Farnham
La

Sheephouse

Bourne
Tennis
Club

RIDGEWAY ROAD

The Drive

Middle Bo

E7
1 Arthur Cl
2 Whitlet Cl

Place

E8
1 Hillary Cl
2 Weydon Hill Cl

F1
1 Alwin Pl
2 Beam Hollow
3 Heath Cl
4 Old Heath Wy
5 Topiady Pl
6 Trimmers Cl

Second
School

F2
1 Bishop Sumn'r Dr
2 Brookside
3 Levern Dr
4 Queens Rd

Cemetery

E6
1 Mike Hawth'rn Dr
2 St Cross Rd
3 Thorold Rd
4 Weybank Cl
5 Wykeham Rd

F6
1 Brightwells Rd

F5
1 Barncroft
2 Fairholme Gdns
3 Firgrove Ct
4 Merlins Cl
5 Saxon Cft

Ridgeway
School

1 grid square represents 500 metres

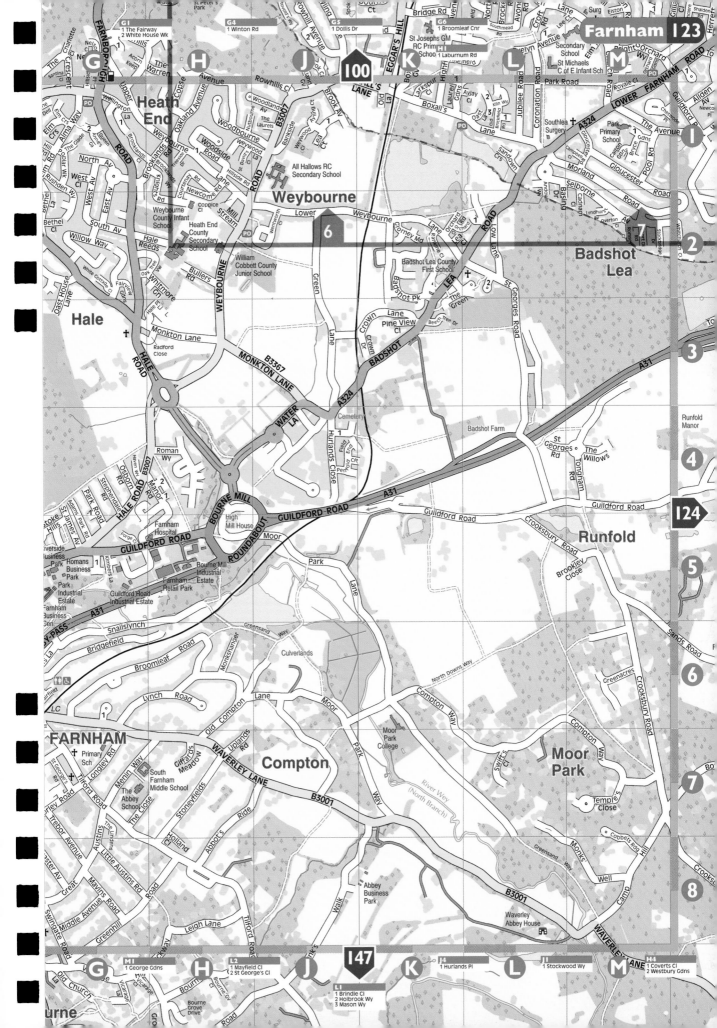

G H J **100** K L M I

G1 1 The Fairway
2 White House Wk
G4 1 Winton Rd
G5 1 Dollis Dr
G6 1 Broomleaf Cnr

Heath End

St Josephs GM
RC Prim
School
St Michaels
C of E Infant Sch
1 Laburnum Rd

Secondary
School

Woodbourne
Woodland Av
The Laurels

Park
Primary
School

Woodside
Road

Southlea
Surgery

Lower Farnham Road

All Hallows RC
Secondary School

Weybourne
County Infant
School

Weybourne

Morland

Weybourne

Heath End
County
Secondary
School

Lower   Weybourne

**Badshot
Lea** 2

Hale Reeds

William
Cobbett County
Junior School

Badshot Lea County
First School

Badshot PK

The Green

Hale

Monkton Lane

Pine View
Cl

Crown Lane

3

Radford
Close

MONKTON LANE

B3367

Badshot Farm

Runfold
Manor

WATER
LA

Cemetery

Badshot Farm

St
Georges
Rd

The
Willows

4

Roman
Wy

Hurlands Close

124

High
Mill House

BOURNE MILL
ROUNDABOUT

GUILDFORD ROAD

A31

Guildford Road

Runfold

Farnham
Hospital

Moor

Crooksbury Road

Riverside
Business
Park

Romans
Business
Park

Bourne Mill
Industrial
Estate

Park

Brookley
Close

5

Park
Industrial
Estate

Farnham
Retail Park

Farnham
Business
Cen

Guildford Road
Industrial Estate

BY PASS   A31

Snailslynch

Bridgefield

Greensand
Way

North Downs Way

Greenacres

Crooksbury Road

6

Broomleaf Road

Lynch   Road

Culverlands

Lane

Moor

Compton Way

Moor Park
College

**Moor
Park**

7

FARNHAM

Primary
Sch

South
Farnham
Middle School

Gifford's
Meadow

WAVERLEY LANE

Compton

River Wey
(North Branch)

Swift's

Temple
Close

The Abbey
School

The Close

Stoneyfields

Ride

B3001

Park   Way

Holland
Cl

Abbot's

Walk

Abbey
Business
Park

Waverley
Abbey House

Cobbets Rd

8

Leigh Lane

B3001

Monks
Well

Greensand Way

WAVERLEY LANE

G H **147** J K L M

1 George Gdns
L2 1 Mayfield Cl
2 St George's Cl
J4 1 Hurlands Pl
J1 1 Stockwood Wy
H4 1 Coverts Cl
2 Westbury Gdns
1 Brindle Cl
2 Holbrook Wy
3 Mason Wy

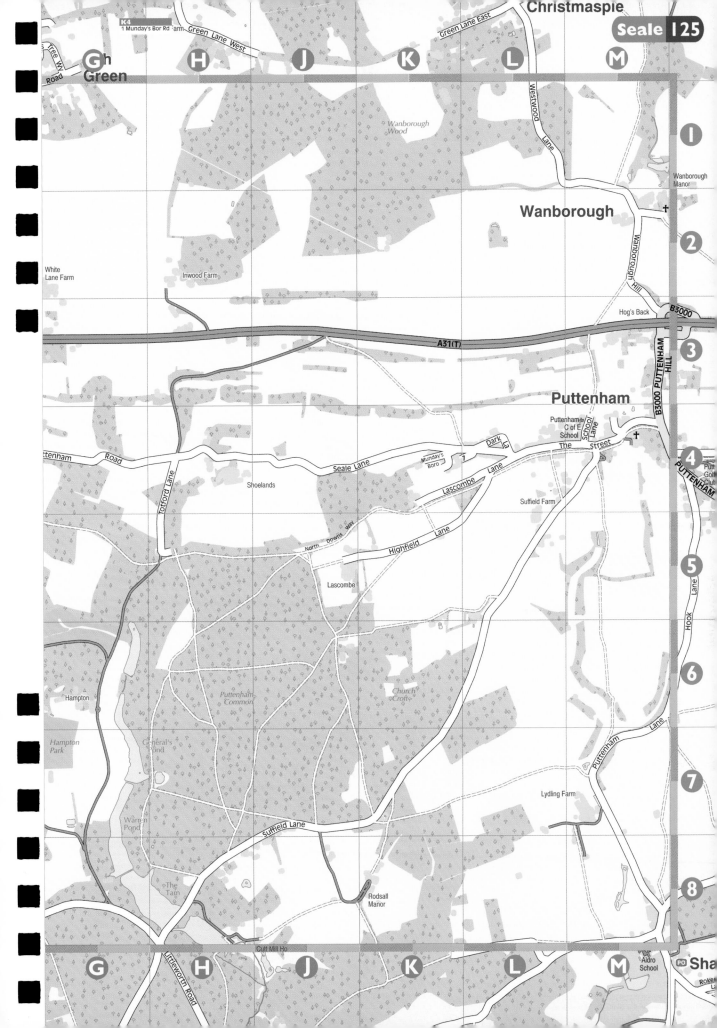

A   B   C   **102**   D   E   F

1

**Shipton
Bellinger**

Bulford Road

High Street

St. Peters

Bourne La

Muscott Close

Primary School

Threadgill Way

Parkhouse

Mayfe HCl

Scrum cl

Close

Hedges Road

Gardener's Green

2 Kingfishers

Manor Cl

1

2

Muscott

PO

2

I

2 Snoddington
Manor

Hampshire County
Wiltshire County

A338

SALISBURY ROAD

Althorne

3

4 Thruxton Farm

Park House

A338

A303(T)

5

River Bourne

A338

Home Farm

6 B3084

Cholderton House

Choldertn
Lodge

Cholderton

nesbury Road

Beech
Hanger

Grateley   Road

Cholderton Road

7

Quarley
Down Farm

8

A   B   **148**   C   D   E   F

Wilbury House

Pit   UK

1 grid square represents 500 metres

G   H   J   **103**   K   L   M

I

2

Snoddington Road

Snoddington Down Farm

3

Racedown

A303(T)

Lains Farm

†

Park Lane

Etwall

Quarley

4

128

ew Ro

Middlecot House

5

Cholderton Road

Quarley
Manor Farm

6

•Quarley
Hill

7

Grateley Drove

Grateley

High

Lawren

Street

†

Grateley Junior
& Infant School

8

Portway
Farm

CHOLDERTON

149

ROAD

K   L

St   Road

Grateley
Station

G   H   J   **149**   K   L   M

Grateley
Business
Park

Station
Ap

Campbell   B308A

128

A
Thruxton Aerodrome and
● Motor Racing Circuit
B

C †
Thruxton
104

Mullenspond

Stanbury Cl
Lambourne Way
D

Becker Close Park
Cyon
Dr

A8
1 Hawthorne Cl

A7
1 St Leonards

E

F

Lovell Cl

1

A303(T)

Pillhill Brook

2

Bush Farm

East
Cholderton

Wiremead
Lane

3

Hay Down Lane

†
Amport

Amport C of E
Primary Sch

Furzedown
Lane

Amport House

Keeper's Hill

4

Amport
Wood

127

Skew Road

Fox Farm

5

Grateley Drove

Georgia Lane

Sarson
Wood

Quarley
Manor Farm

6

Monxton Road

The Dell

ateley

High
Street

Lawrence Houses
7
PO
Hawthorne
Cl
7

Chapel
Lane †

Grateley Junior
& Infant School †

Gollard Farm

Georgia Farm

7

Hurst
Copse

8

Wa

A

B

C
150

D

E

F

1 grid square represents 500 metres

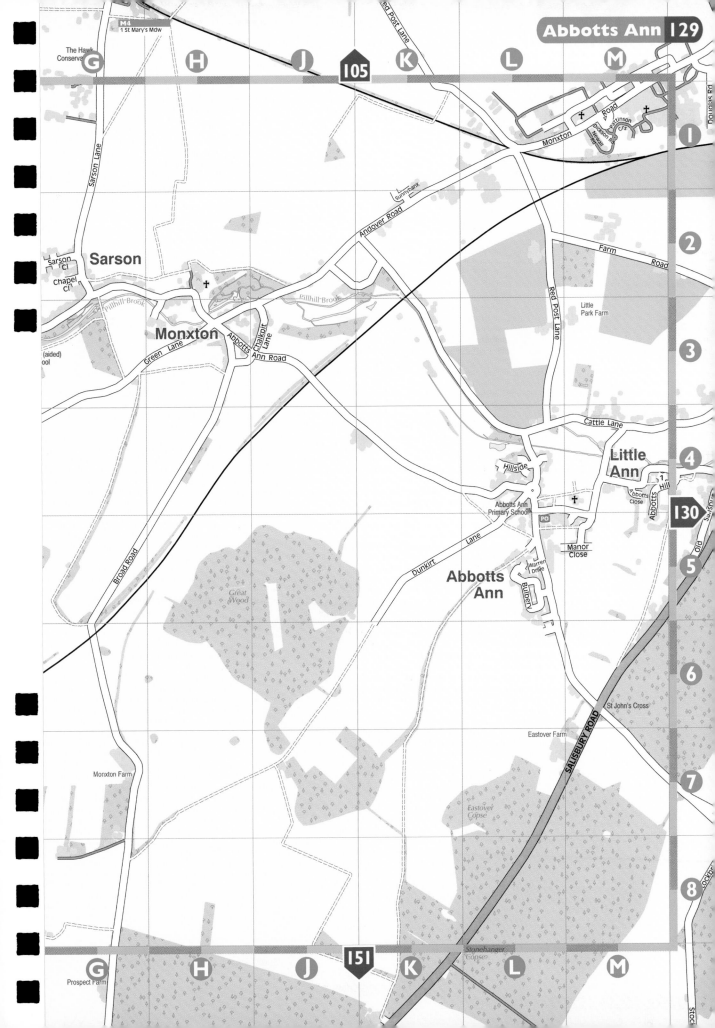

A B C 108 D E F

131

I

2

3

4

5

6

7

8

A B C 154 D E F

Old
Micheldever Road

Old Pound

Harewood Forest

Balls Cottages

Middleton Farm

Test Way

The Middleway

Middl

Forton

A303(T)

B3048

Test Way

Test Way

Pachington Farm

Gavelacre

Test Way

Park Farm

Test Way

LONGPARISH ROAD

Bransb

Bransbury Common

B3048

River Test

B3048

LONGPARISH ROAD

Dublin Farm

Wherwell School

1 grid square represents 500 metres

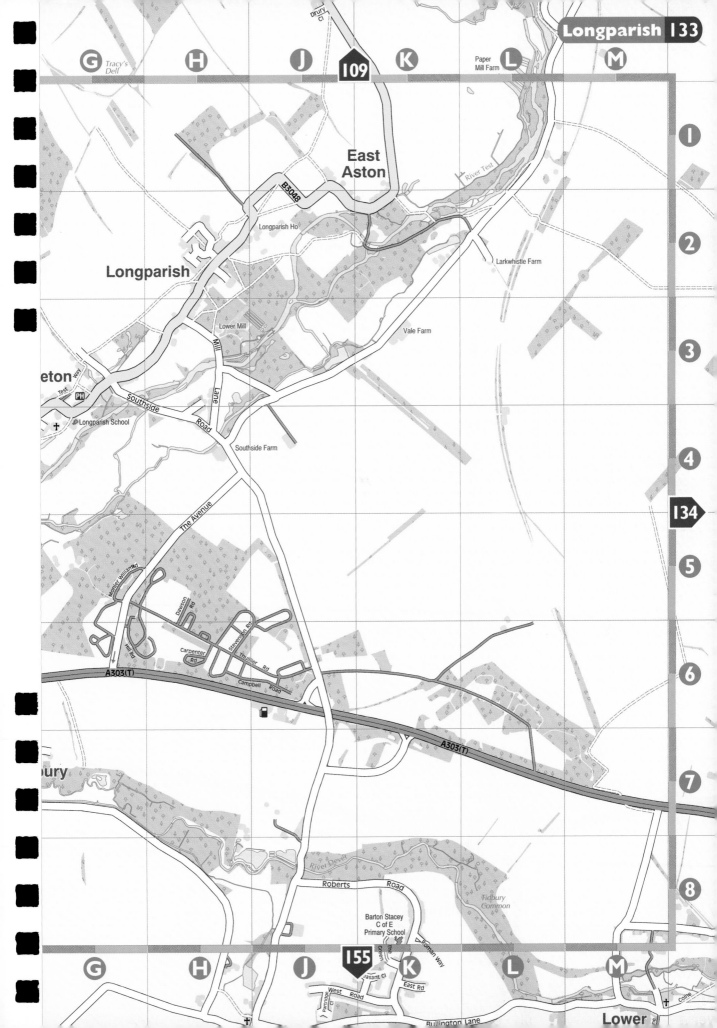

G H J **109** K Paper Mill Farm L M

I

East Aston

River Test

2

Longparish Ho

B3048

Larkwhistle Farm

Longparish

Lower Mill

3

Vale Farm

eton Way

Test

PH

Southside

Longparish School

Mill Lane

Road

Southside Farm

4

134

The Avenue

5

Moller William Rd

Dawson Rd

Stevenson Rd

Carpenter Rd

Thullier Rd

Hill Rd

A303(T)

Campbell Road

6

A303(T)

7

bury

River Dever

Roberts Road

Tidbury Common

8

Barton Stacey C of E Primary School

G H J **155** The Green K East Rd Roman Way L M

West Road

Partridge Cl

Pheasant Cl

East Rd

Colne

Bullington Lane

Lower

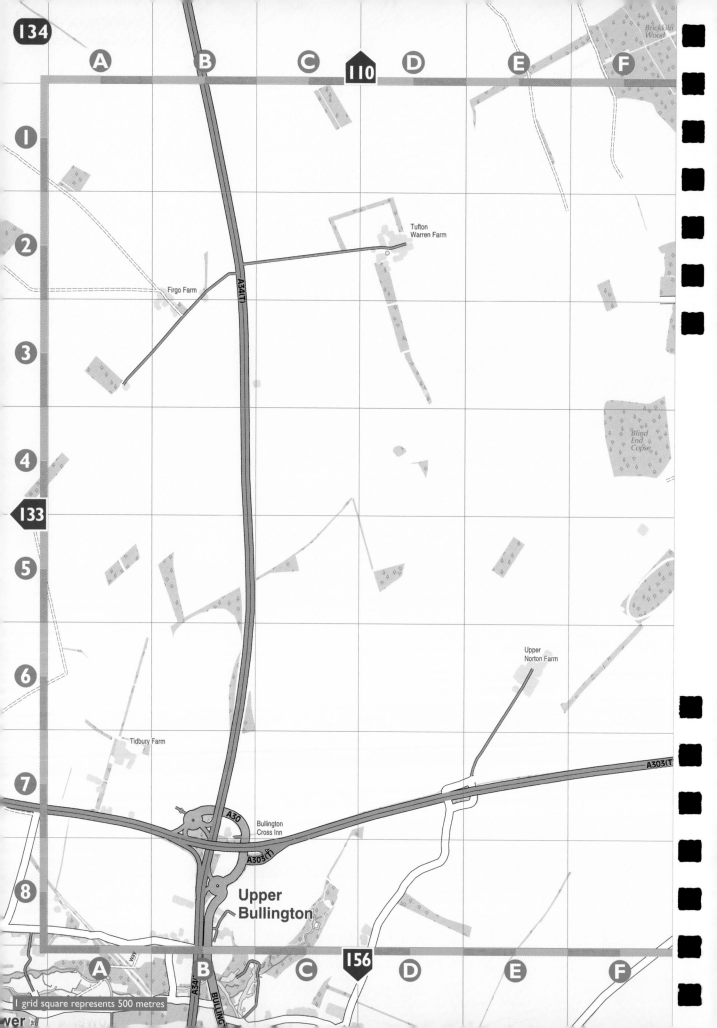

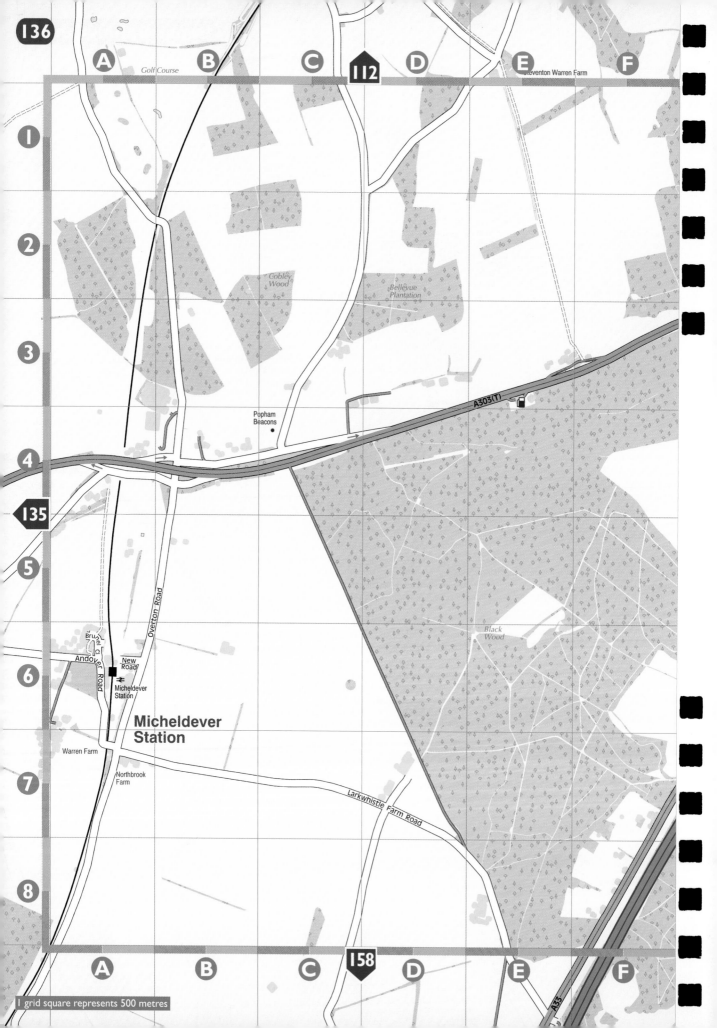

136

A B C **112** D E F

Golf Course

Reventon Warren Farm

1

2

Cobley Wood

Bellevue Plantation

A303(T)

3

Popham Beacons

4

135

5

Overton Road

Black Wood

Bru... el over Road

Andover Road

New Road

Micheldever Station

6

Micheldever Station

Warren Farm

Northbrook Farm

Larkwhistle Farm Road

7

8

A B C **158** D E F

A33

1 grid square represents 500 metres

G H J **113** K L M

I
2
3
4
138
5
6
7
8

A30

Junction 8

Dummer
Down Farm

Waltham
Trinleys

West Farm

Popham

Popham
Court Farm

A33

College
Wood

Bradley Farm

M3

Rownest
Wood

Woodmancott

Embley
Wood

PH

G H J **159** K L M

Lone Farm

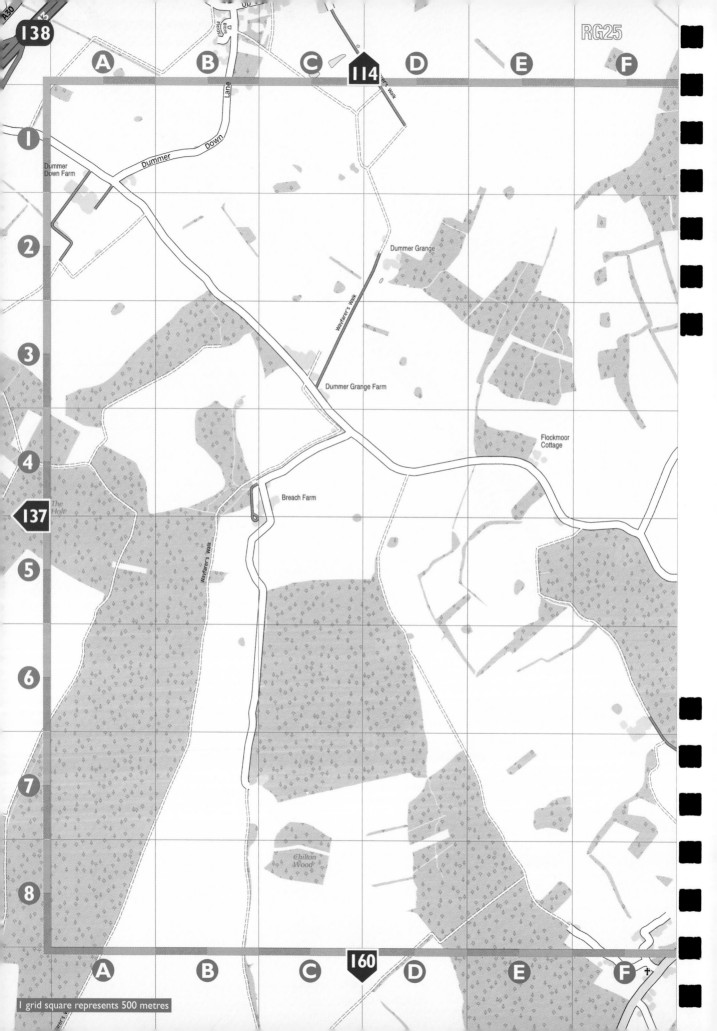

A   B   C   114   D   E   F

1

Dummer Down Farm

Dummer Down

Dummer Lane

2

Dummer Grange

Wayfarer's Walk

3

Dummer Grange Farm

Flockmoor Cottage

4

137 The Holt

Breach Farm

Wayfarer's Walk

5

6

7

8

Chilton Wood

A   B   C   160   D   E   F

1 grid square represents 500 metres

140

A   B   C   **116**   D   E   F

I

Furzen Lane

Elisfield Manor

Three Castles Path

Lane

Merritts Farm

Herriard Grange

Oxlease Lane

Hurst Farm

Bagmo

2

Lower Common

College Farm

College Lane

Three Castles Path

Bell Lane

Bagmore Lane

3

Berrydown Lane

Great Matt's Copse

4

Preston Oak Hills

Red Lane

Herriard Common

139

5

Spain Lane

wood Farm

6

Three Castles Path

Burkham House

A339

7

8

Bradley

Oxdrove Way

A   B   C   **162**   D   E   F

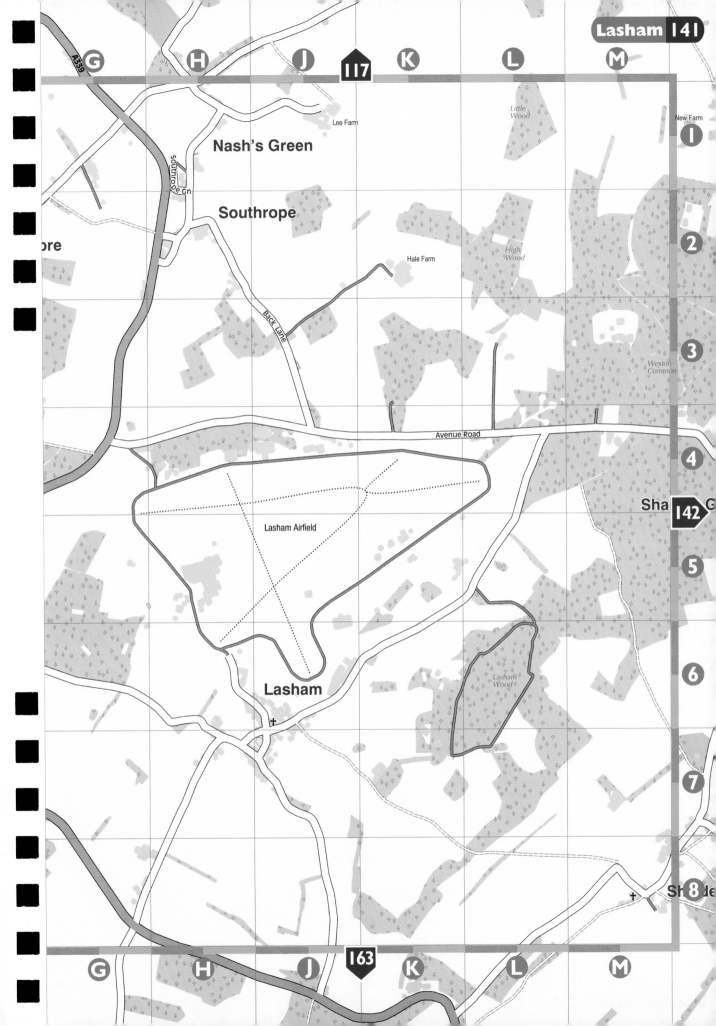

A339

G H J **117** K L M

1

Little Wood

New Farm

1

Lee Farm

Nash's Green

2

High Wood

Hale Farm

Southrope Gn

Southrope

3

Weston Common

Back Lane

Avenue Road

4

Sha **142** G

Lasham Airfield

5

Lasham Wood

6

Lasham

†

7

8 **8** Sh de

†

G H J **163** K L M

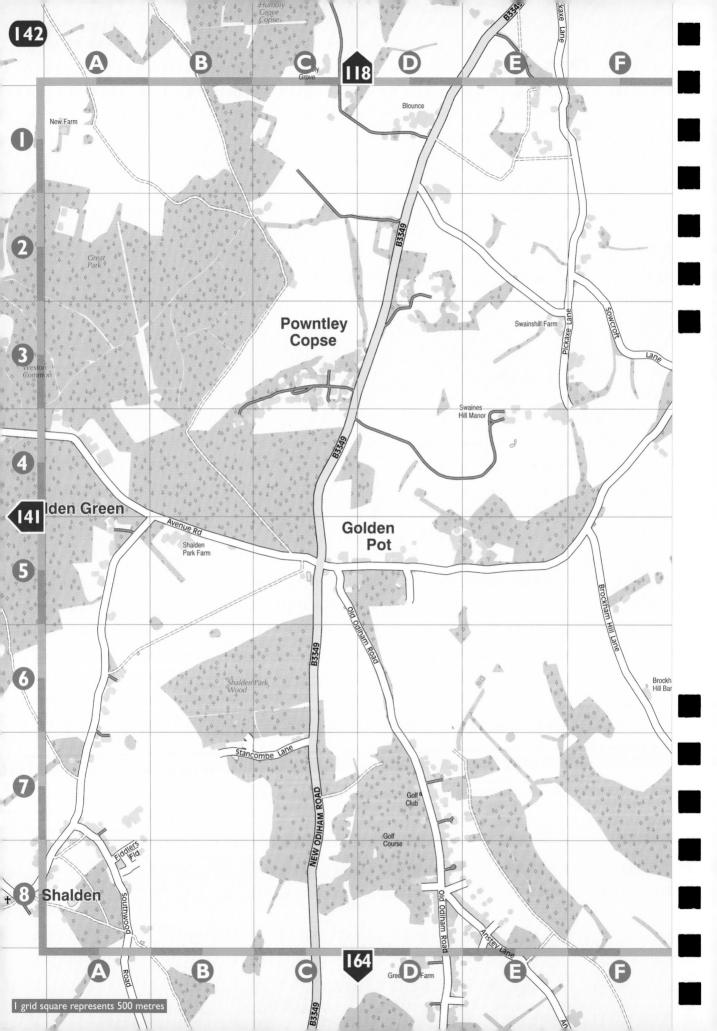

A   B   C **120** D   E   F

I

2

3

Lower Froyle

143

5

6

7

8

A   B   C **166** D   E   F

120

Isnage Farm

B4
1 Barnfield Cl

Bury Court

Crest Hill Farm

Well Lane

Hussey's Lane

Husseys Farm

Pax Hill

Jenkyn Place

Bentley

Church Lane

Hole

Longcroft Lane

Hole

Babs Flds

Bonner's Fld

Oakway

Park Lane

Westburn

Bamber Lane

Pax Hl

A31

Station

Bentley Green Farm

Highway Home

Gid Lane

Froyle Mill

Isington Lane

A31

Lord Mayor Treloar College Lower School

River Wey

Isington Road

Isington Close

Isington

LC

PH

Mill Court

166

Binstead

Broadview

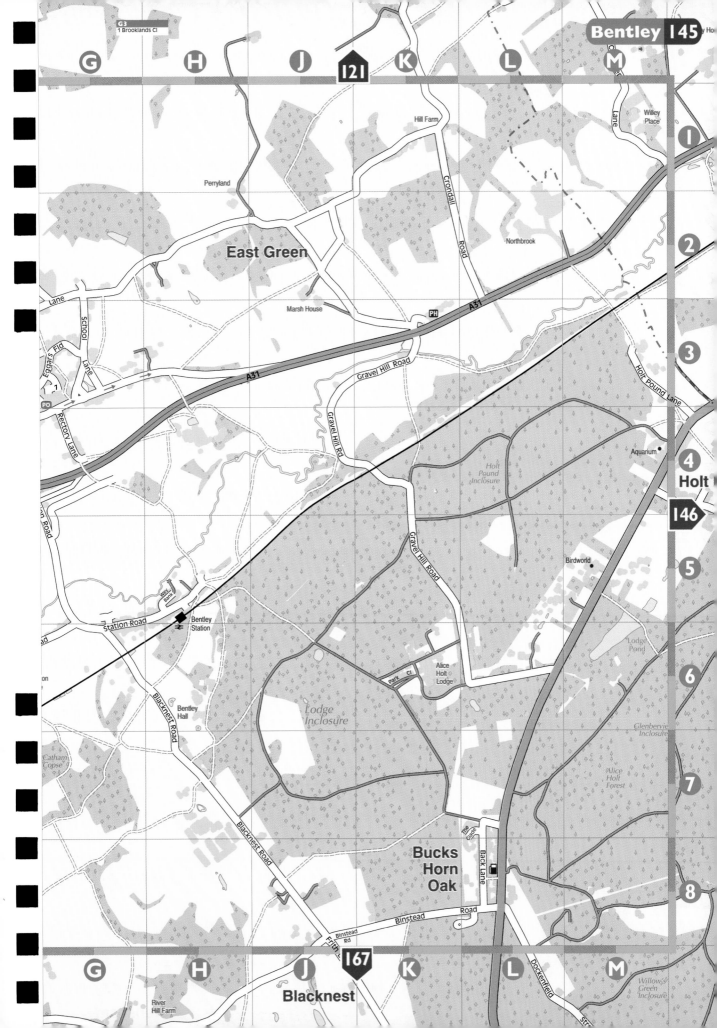

G H J 121 K L M

I
2
3
4 Holt
146
5
6
7
8

G H J 167 K L M

G3
1 Brooklands Cl

Willey Place

Hill Farm

Perryland

Crondall Road

Northbrook

East Green

Marsh House

PH

A31

Gravel Hill Road

A31

Holt Pound Lane

Gravel Hill Rd

Holt Pound Inclosure

Aquarium

Gravel Hill Road

Birdworld

Lodge Pond

Bentley Station

Station Road

Way Barn

Park Cl

Alice Holt Lodge

Glenbervie Inclosure

Blacknest Road

Bentley Hall

Lodge Inclosure

Alice Holt Forest

Catham Copse

Bucks Horn Oak

The Glade

Back Lane

Binstead Road

Binstead Rd

Friday

Blacknest

Dockenfield

River Hill Farm

Willow's Green Inclosure

Eggar's Fld

School Lane

Rectory Lane

PO

1

A   B   C   126   D   E   F

Quarley
Down Farm

I

Road

Cemetery

Wilbury House

Pit   Walk

River Bourne

Three
Corner Hat

Beechfield

2

PO

Newton Tony

The Cart

Newton
Tony
School

3

St Just Cl

Hampshire County
Wiltshire County

4

5

6

Allington Farm

7

8

A   B   C   170   D   E   F

Boscombe
Down
East

1 grid square represents 500 metres

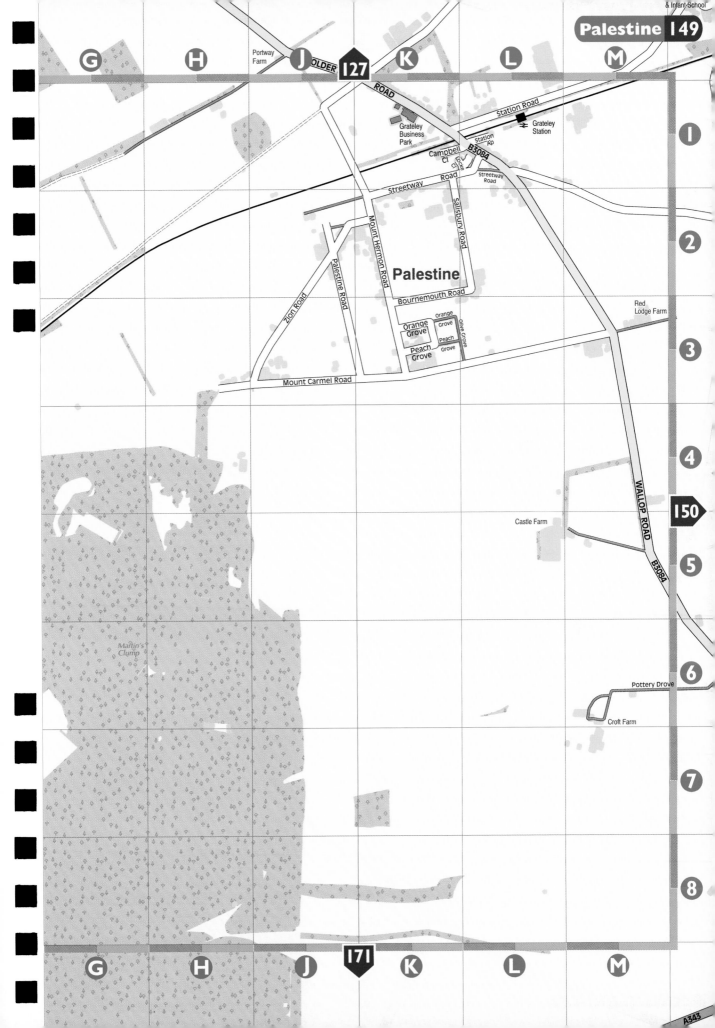

& Infant School

G   H   J   **127**   K   L   M

Portway Farm

OLDER ROAD

Station Road

Grateley Business Park

Grateley Station

Campbell Cl

Station Ap

Streetway Road

B3084

Streetway Road

Salisbury Road

Mount Hermon Road

Palestine

Bournemouth Road

Red Lodge Farm

Palestine Road

Zion Road

Orange Grove

Orange Grove

Olive Grove

Peach Grove

Peach Grove

Mount Carmel Road

Castle Farm

WALLOP ROAD

150

B3084

Martin's Clump

Pottery Drove

Croft Farm

G   H   J   **171**   K   L   M

A343

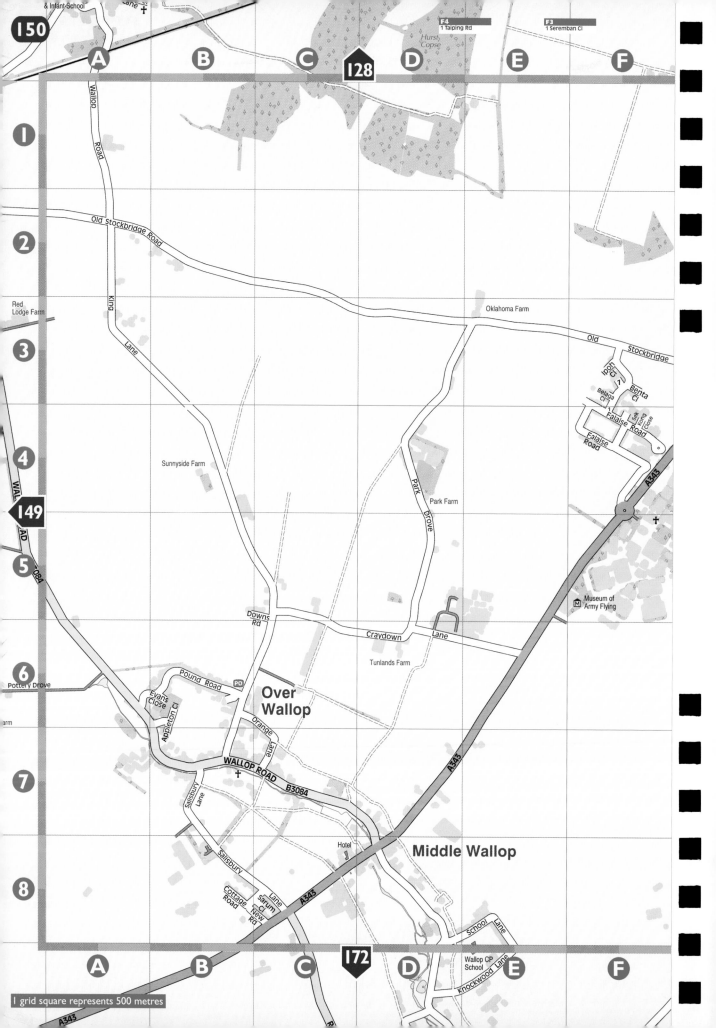

A · B · C · **128** · D · E · F

F4 1 Taiping Rd   F3 1 Seremban Ci

Hurst Copse

1

2

Old Stockbridge Road

Red Lodge Farm

3

Oklahoma Farm

Old Stockbridge

Ipoh Ci
Benta Ci
Belaga Ci
Falaise Road
Sak kong Close
Falaise Road

King Lane

4

Sunnyside Farm

149

WALLOP ROAD

B3084

Park Drove

Park Farm

A343

Museum of Army Flying

5

Downs Rd

Craydown Lane

6

Pottery Drove

Evans Close

Pound Road

PO

Appleton Ci

Tunlands Farm

Over Wallop

Orange Lane

Farm

7

Salisbury Lane

WALLOP ROAD

B3084

A343

Salisbury Lane

Hotel

Middle Wallop

8

Cottage Road

Sarum New Rd

A343

School Lane

Wallop CP School

Knockwood Lane

A · B · C · **172** · D · E · F

A343

A343

1 grid square represents 500 metres

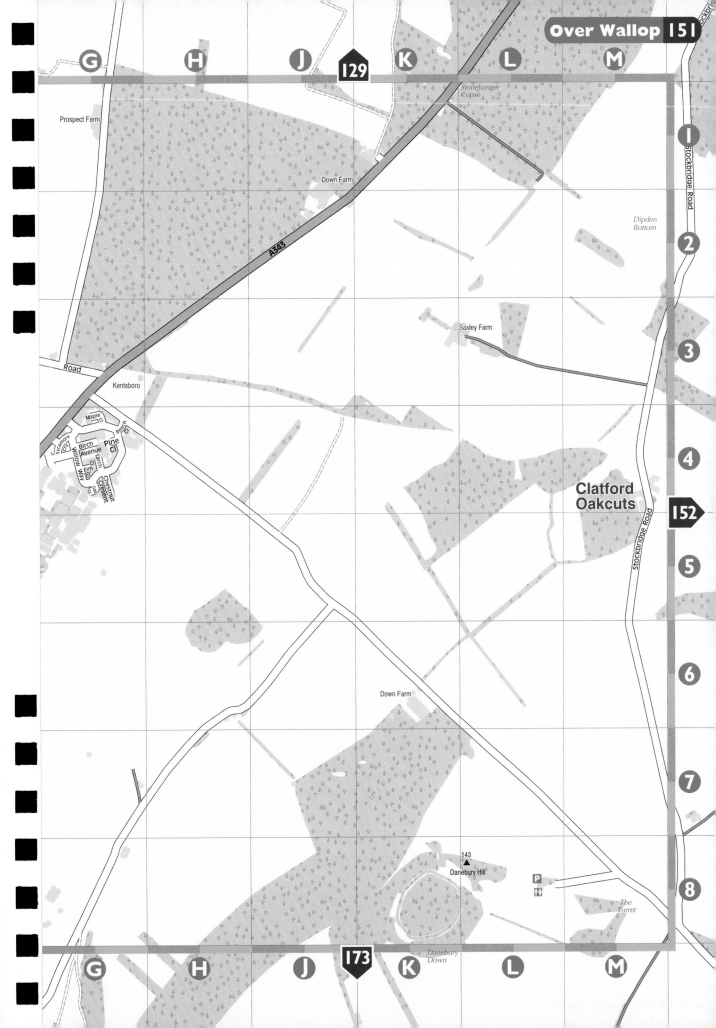

G

H

J

129

K

L

M

Stonehanger Copse

Prospect Farm

Down Farm

A343

Dipden Bottom

Saxley Farm

Road

Kentsboro

Maple Cl

Beech Cl

Sycamore Cl

Birch Avenue

Larch Cl

Willow Way

Elm Cl

Oak Cl

Pine Cl

Chestnut Crescent

Clatford Oakcuts

Stockbridge Road

Stockbridge Road

Down Farm

143

Danebury Hill

P

The Turret

G

H

J

173

K

Danebury Down

L

M

I

2

3

4

152

5

6

7

8

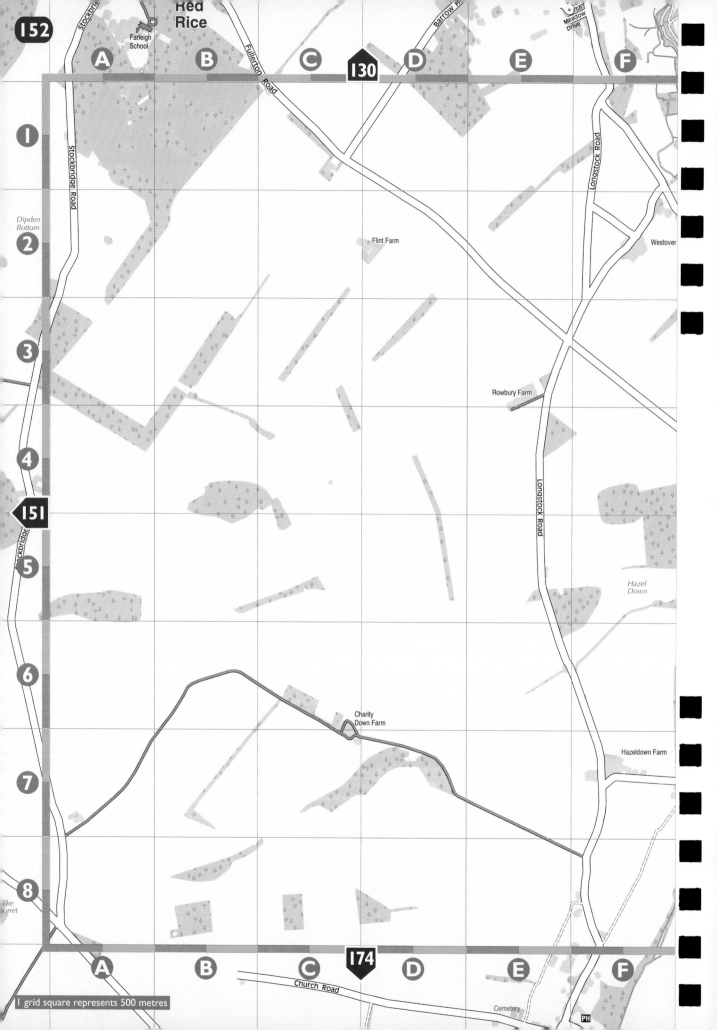

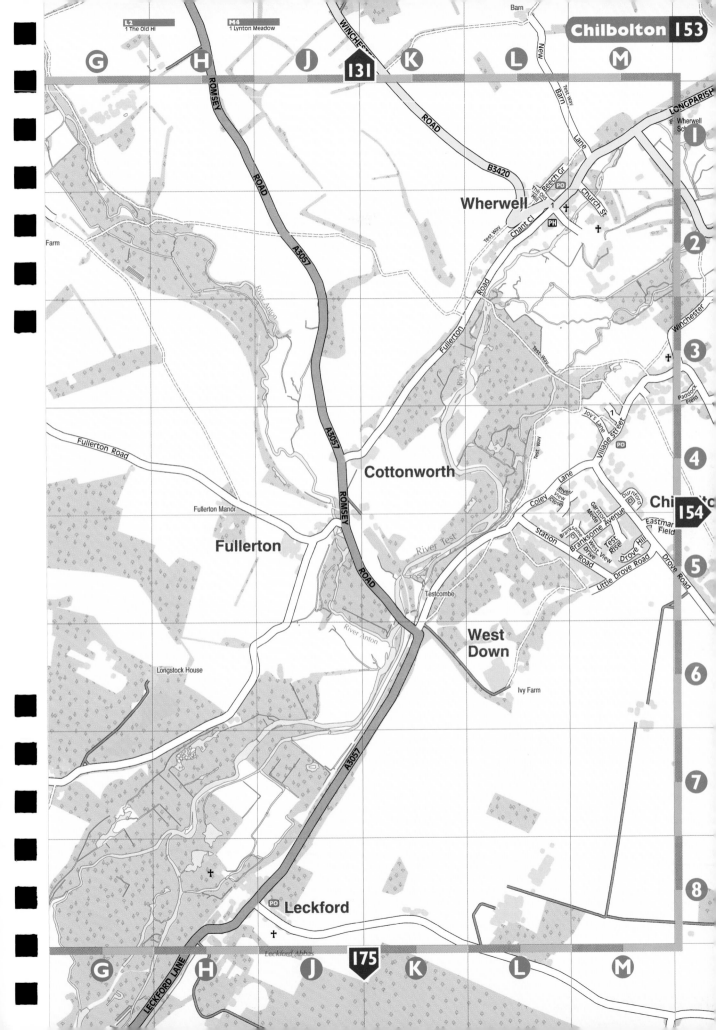

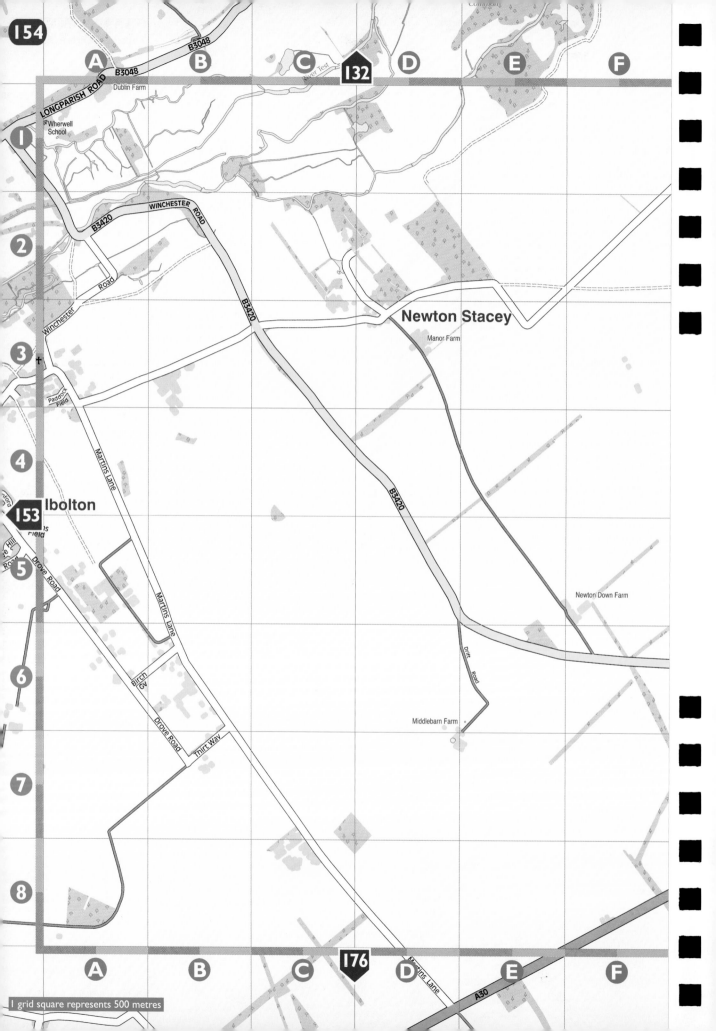

A B C 132 D E F

LONGPARISH ROAD
B3048
B3048
Dublin Farm

Wherwell
School

1

WINCHESTER ROAD
B3420
B3420

Winchester Road

2

River Test

Newton Stacey

Manor Farm

3

Paddock
Field

Martins Lane

4

153 Ibolton

Field

5 Drove Road

Newton Down Farm

Martins Lane

6

Birch
Gv

Drift Road

Drove Road

Middlebarn Farm

Thirt Way

7

8

A B 176 C D E F

Martins Lane

A30

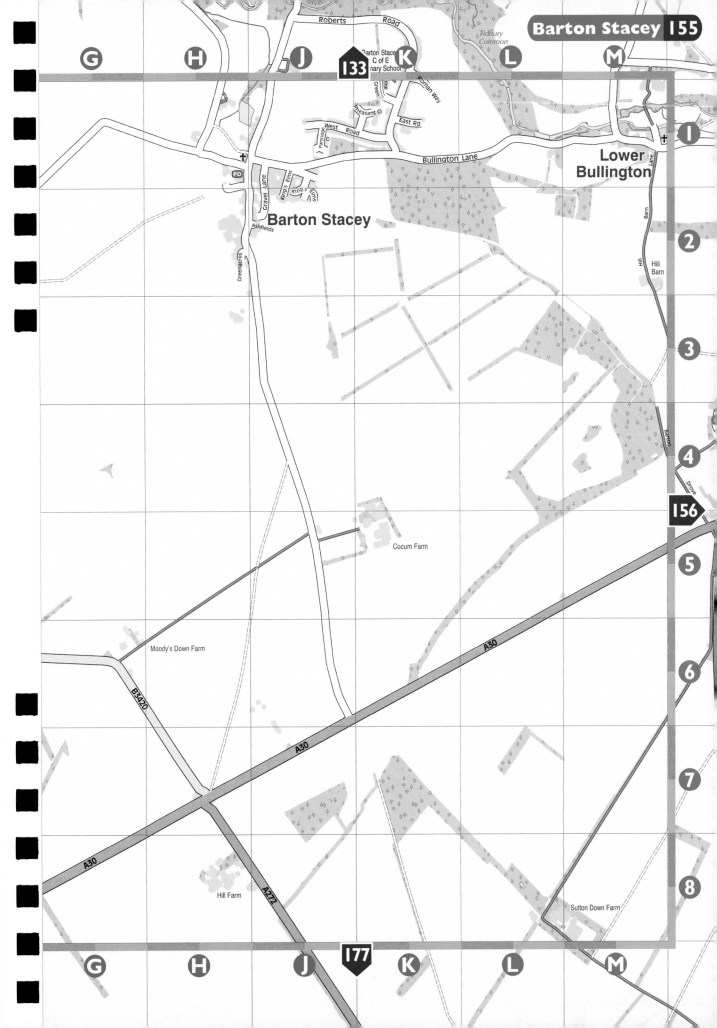

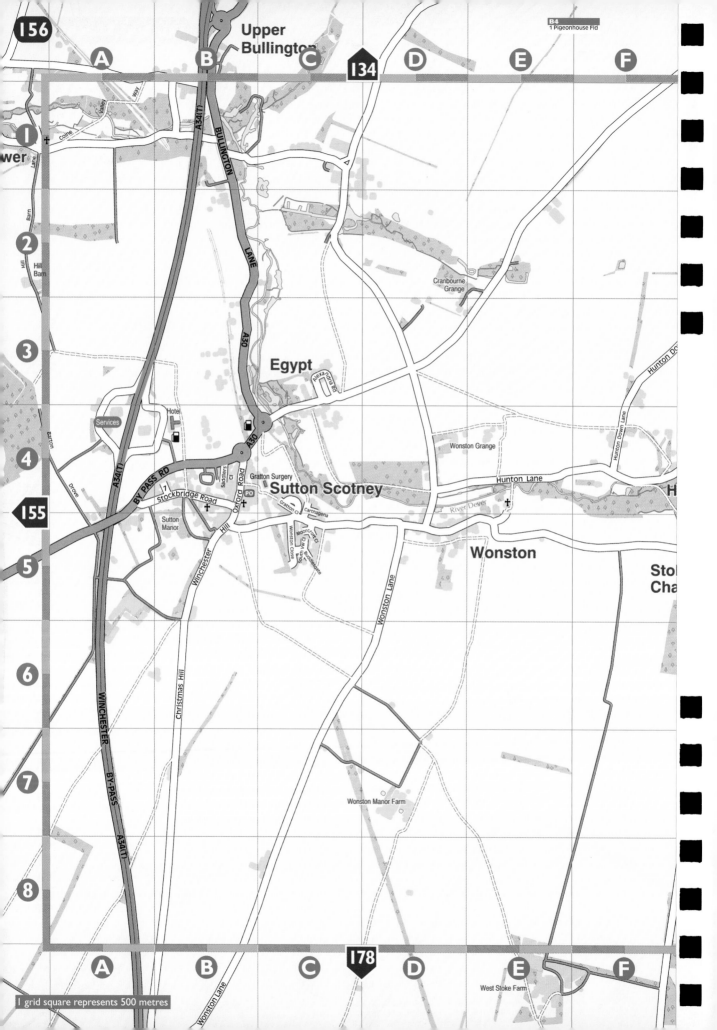

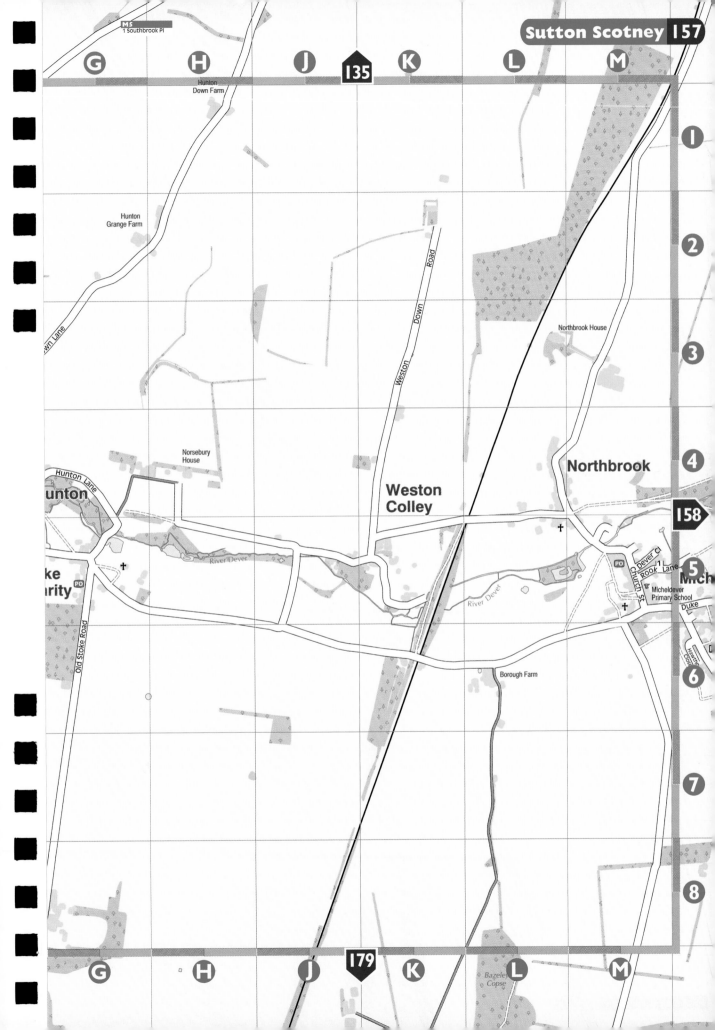

M5
1 Southbrook Pl

G　　H　　J　**135**　K　　L　　M

Hunton
Down Farm

Hunton
Grange Farm

Weston Down Road

Northbrook House

Norsebury
House

Hunton Lane

Northbrook

unton

Weston
Colley

158

Michel

PO

Micheldever
Primary School

Duke

River Dever

ke
arity

PO

Old Stoke Road

River Dever

Dever Cl

Rook Lane

Church St

Hawthorn Close

Borough Farm

G　　H　　J　**179**　K　　L　　M

Bazeley
Copse

1
2
3
4
5
6
7
8

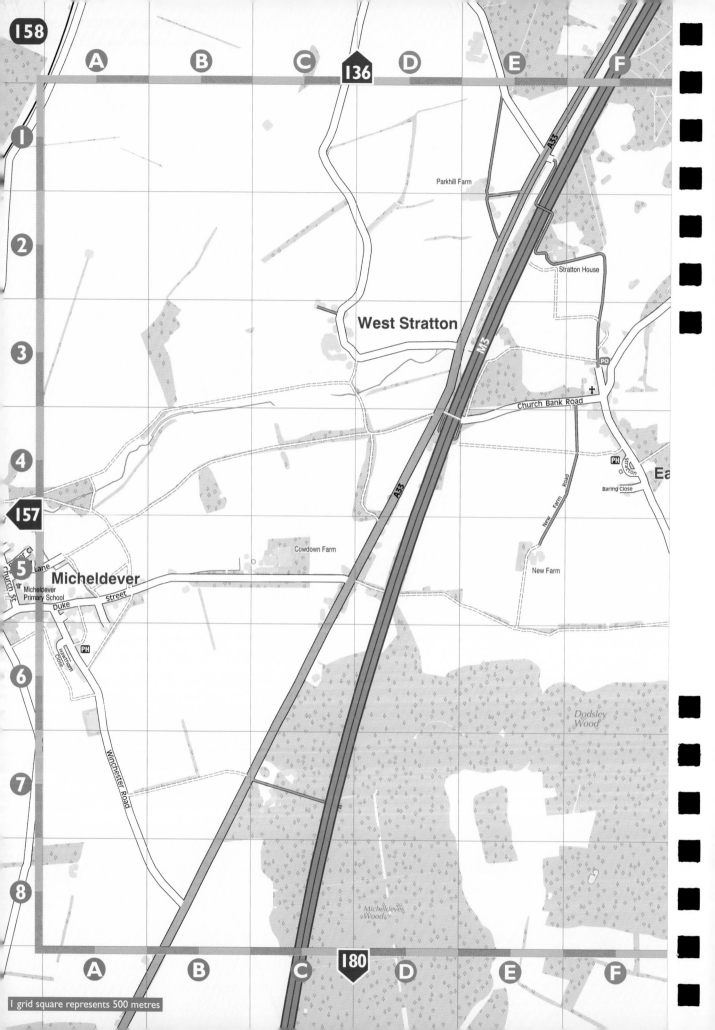

Embley Wood

G   H   J   **137**   K   L   M

Lone Farm

I

Wayfarer's W.

Whiteway Farm

Lone Barn

2

Gunners Lane

3

Candover Copse

Thorny Down Wood

Foxhill

4

st Stratton

160

Copse Lane

5

Copse Lane

Bryces Lane

6

Burcot Farm

Totford Farm

7

Stratton Lane

Totford

8

Northington Down Farm

Northington

G   H   J   **181**   K   +   L   M

Swewater

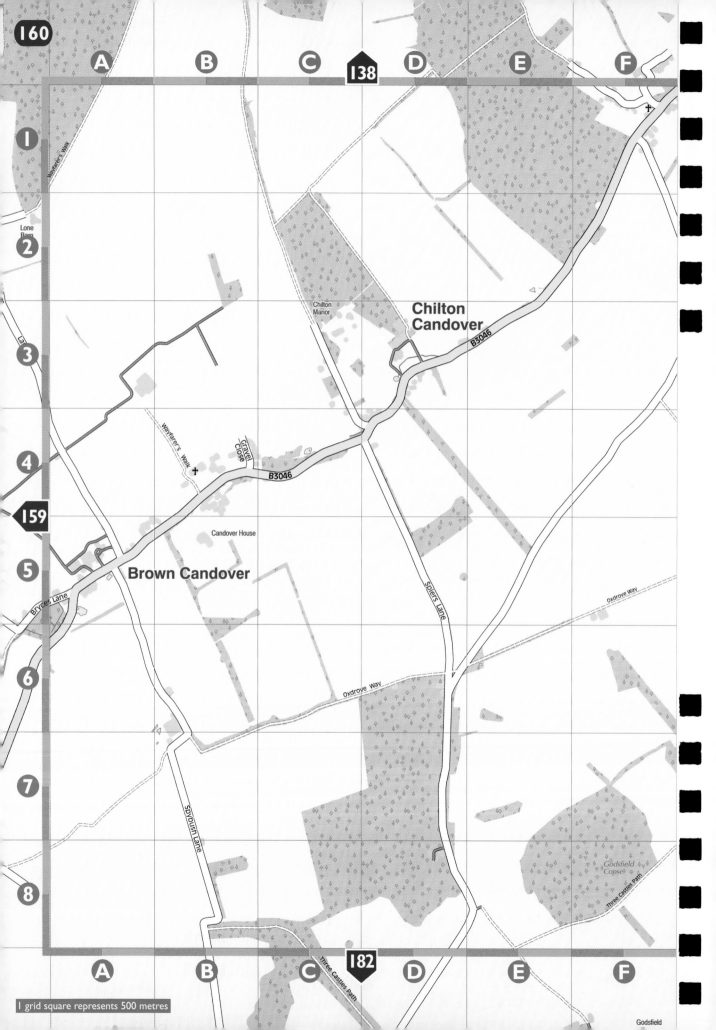

138

A **B** **C** **D** **E** **F**

I

Wayfarer's Walk

Lone
Barn

2

3

La

Chilton
Manor

**Chilton
Candover**

B3046

4

Wayfarer's Walk

Gravel
Close

+

B3046

159

Candover House

5

Brown Candover

Spiers Lane

Oxdrove Way

Bryces Lane

6

Oxdrove Way

7

Spybush Lane

8

Godsfield
Copse

Three Castles Path

A **B** **C** **D** **E** **F**

182

Three Castles Path

Godsfield

Candover

Candover
Primary School

Stenbury
Drive

G   H   J   **139**   K   L   M

Preston
Down

Three Castles Path

Preston
Grange

Down Farm

Oxdrove Way

Oxdrove Way

Wield
Wood

Three Castles Path

Three Castles Path

Upper Wield

PO

Home Close

Pound
Cl

Barton
Copse

Armsworth
Hill Farm

Barton
Industrial
Estate

Ferney Lane

Newmer Farm

Armsworth Ho

Ferney   Lane

G   H   J   **183**   K   L   M

Hoggs
Lodge

Heath

Bradle

Bern—od

Lane

1

2

3

4

Pi

162

5

6

7

8

Heath Green Lane

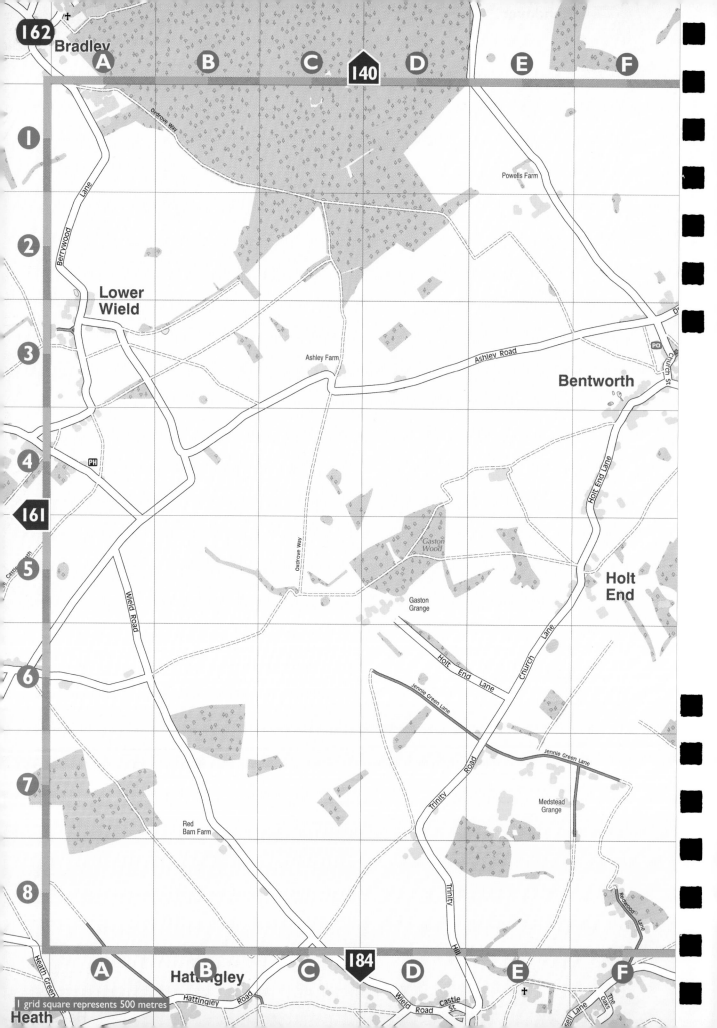

G H J K L M

141

I
2
3
4
164
5
6
7
8

Wadgett's Copse

Warren Farm

Bentworth Lodge

Thedden Copse

BASI... OKE ROAD

Curv Lane
Glebe
Cl
Glebe Rds

Summerley
PH

St Marys Primary School

Village Street

Childer Hill Farm

Heathcroft Farm

Thedden Grange

Snode Hill

Wivelrod Road

Medstead Road

Bentworth Hall

Wellhouse Road

Cranford

Beech

Ackender Wood

Wivelrod

Wivelrod Road

Bushy Leaze Wood

Medstead Road

King's Hill

The Abbey

Cem

Abbey Road

Old Park Farm

Chawton Park Farm

Jennie Green Lane

Hussell Lan...

G H J K L M

185

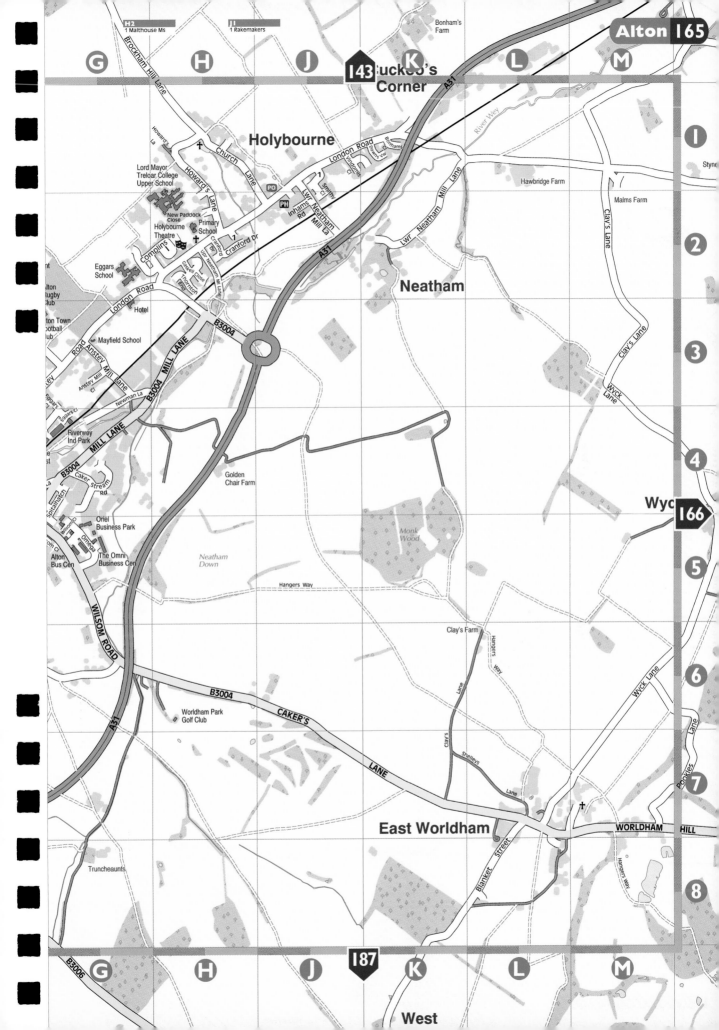

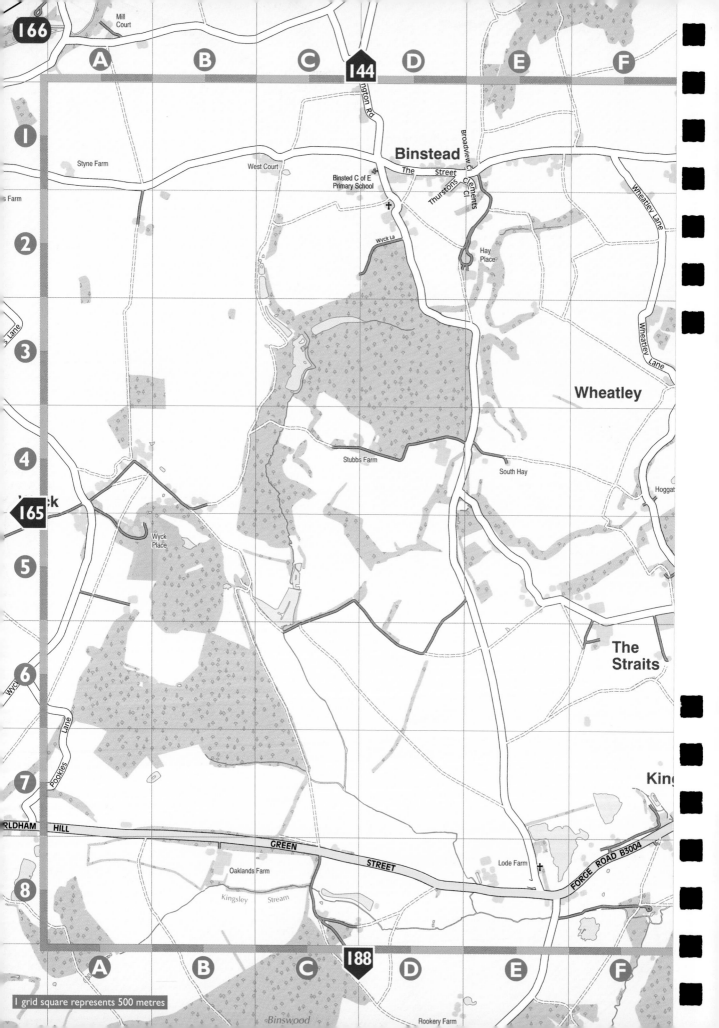

166

A B C 144 D E F

1

Mill Court

Styne Farm

West Court

Binstead

Broadview Cl

The Street

Clements

Binsted C of E
Primary School

Thurstons

Wheatley Lane

2

s Farm

Wyck La

Hay
Place

3

Lane

Wheatley

Wheatley
Lane

4

Stubbs Farm

South Hay

Hoggat

165

Wyck
Place

5

6

The
Straits

Wyck

Lane

Pookes

7

King

RLDHAM   HILL

GREEN

STREET

Lode Farm

FORGE   ROAD B3004

8

Oaklands Farm

Kingsley   Stream

A B C 188 D E F

Binswood

Rookery Farm

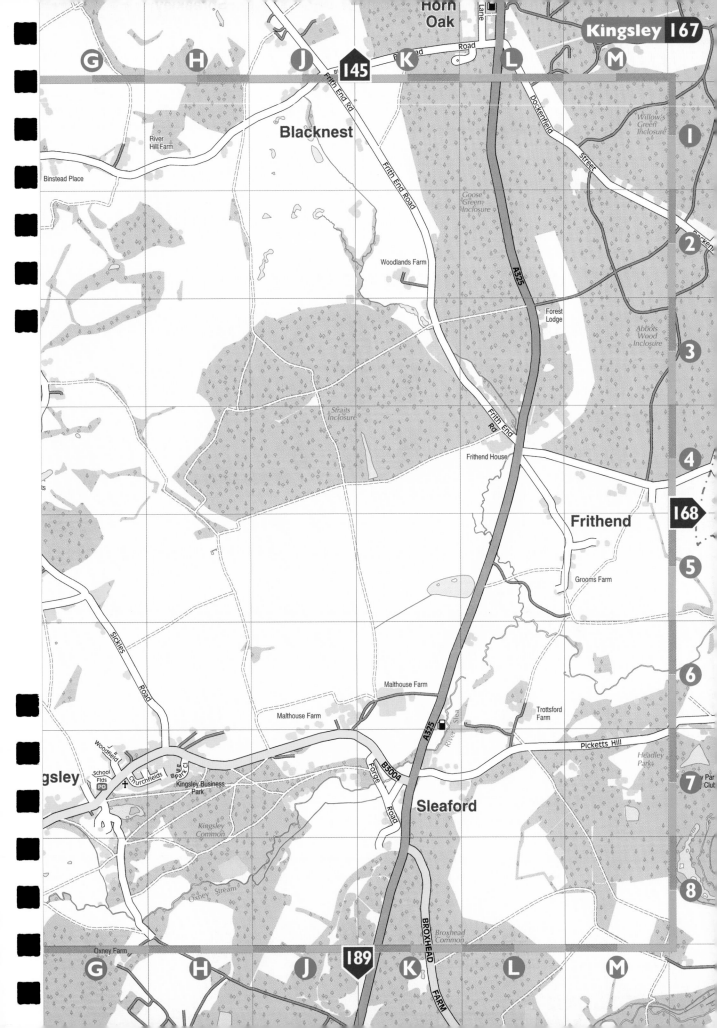

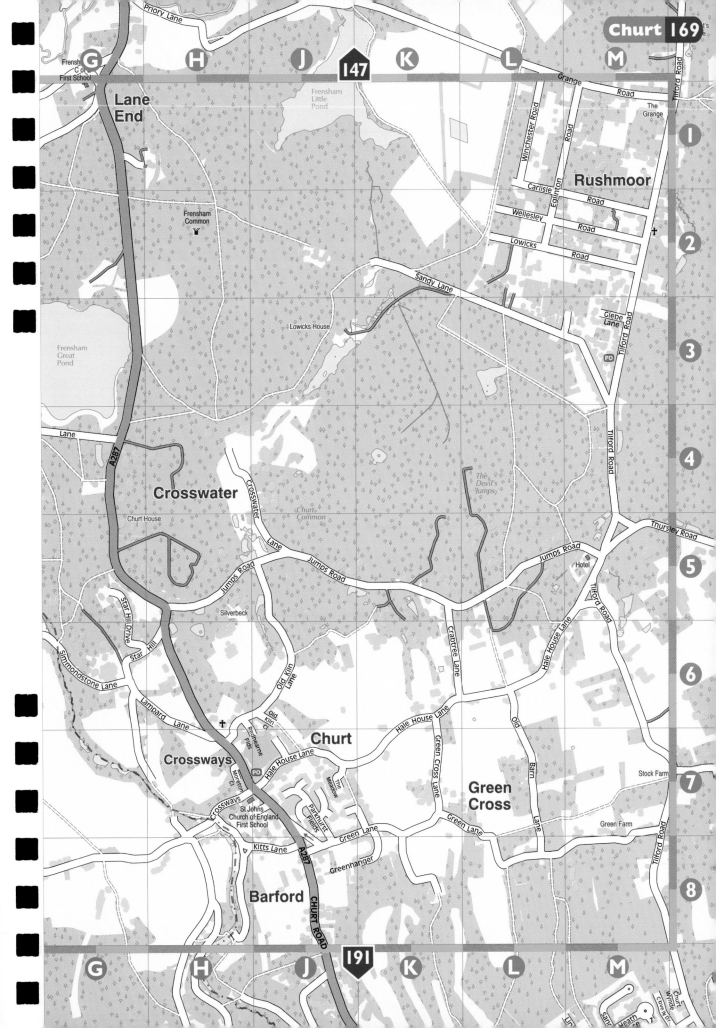

Priory Lane

147

G H J K L M

Frensh C of
First School

Lane
End

Frensham
Little
Pond

Grange
Road

The
Grange

Tilford Road

I

Frensham
Common

Winchester Road

Eglinton
Road

Carlisle Road

Rushmoor

Wellesley Road

†

2

Lowicks Road

Frensham
Great
Pond

Lowicks House

Sandy Lane

Glebe
Lane

PO

Tilford Road

3

Lane

A287

Tilford Road

4

Crosswater

Crosswater Lane

Churt
Common

The
Devil's
Jumps

Thursley Road

Churt House

Jumps Road

Jumps Road

Jumps Road

Hotel

5

Silverbeck

Star Hill Drive

Star Hill

Crabtree Lane

Hale House Lane

Tilford Road

Simmondstone Lane

Old Kiln Lane

6

Lampard Lane

Old
Kiln
Cl

Hale House Lane

Old
Barn
Lane

Churt

†

Rectrearne
Flds

Stock Farm

7

Crossways

PO

Hale House Lane

Green Cross Lane

**Green
Cross**

Moreton

The
Meadow

Parkhurst
Fields

St Johns
Church of England
First School

Green Lane

Green Lane

Green Farm

Crossways

Kitts Lane

A287

Green Lane

Greenhanger

Tilford Road

8

Barford

CHURT ROAD

191

G H J K L M

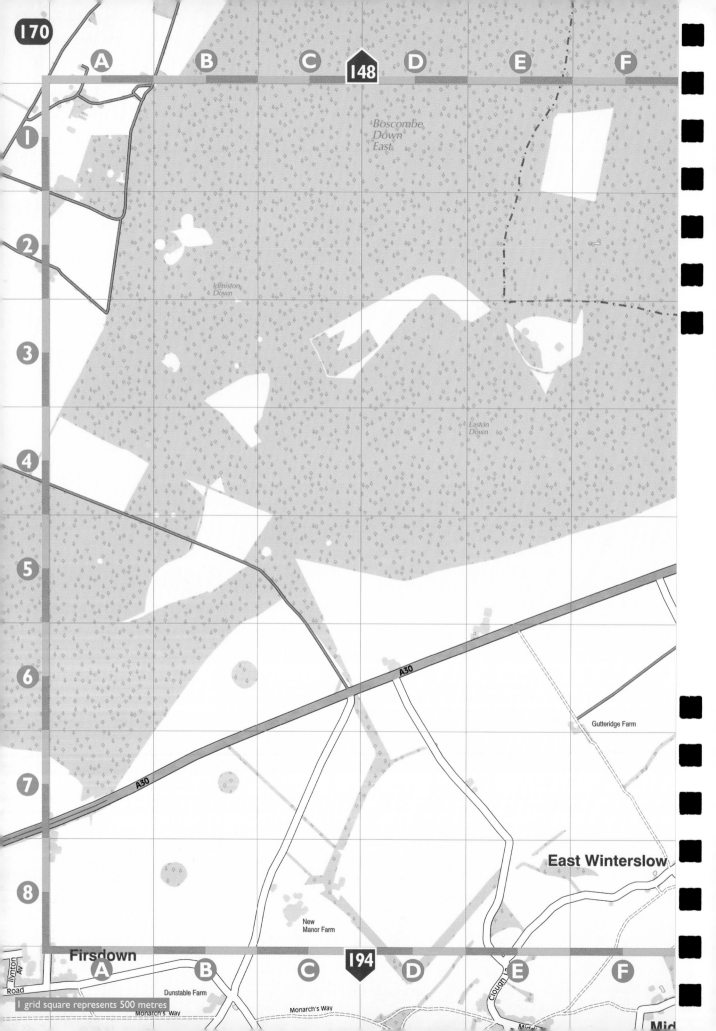

A   B   148   C   D   E   F

1

Boscombe
Down
East

2

Idmiston
Down

3

Easton
Down

4

5

A30

6

Gutteridge Farm

A30

7

East Winterslow

8

New
Manor Farm

Firsdown

Ilynton
Av

Road

Dunstable Farm

A   B   C   194   D   E   F

Monarch's Way

Monarch's Way

Clough

Mid

1 grid square represents 500 metres

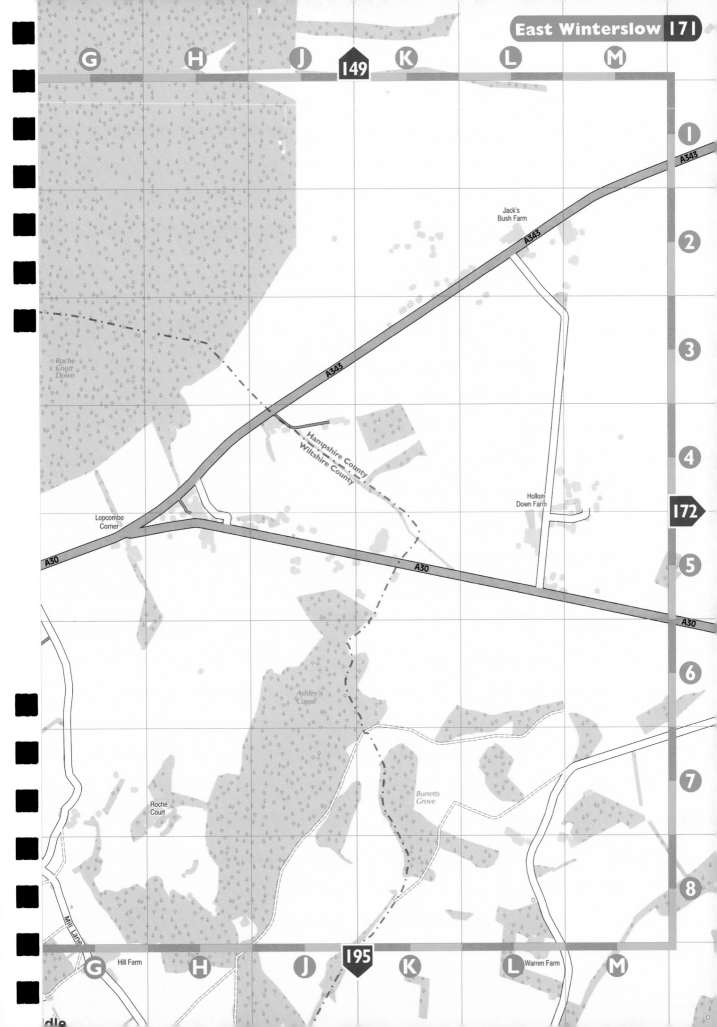

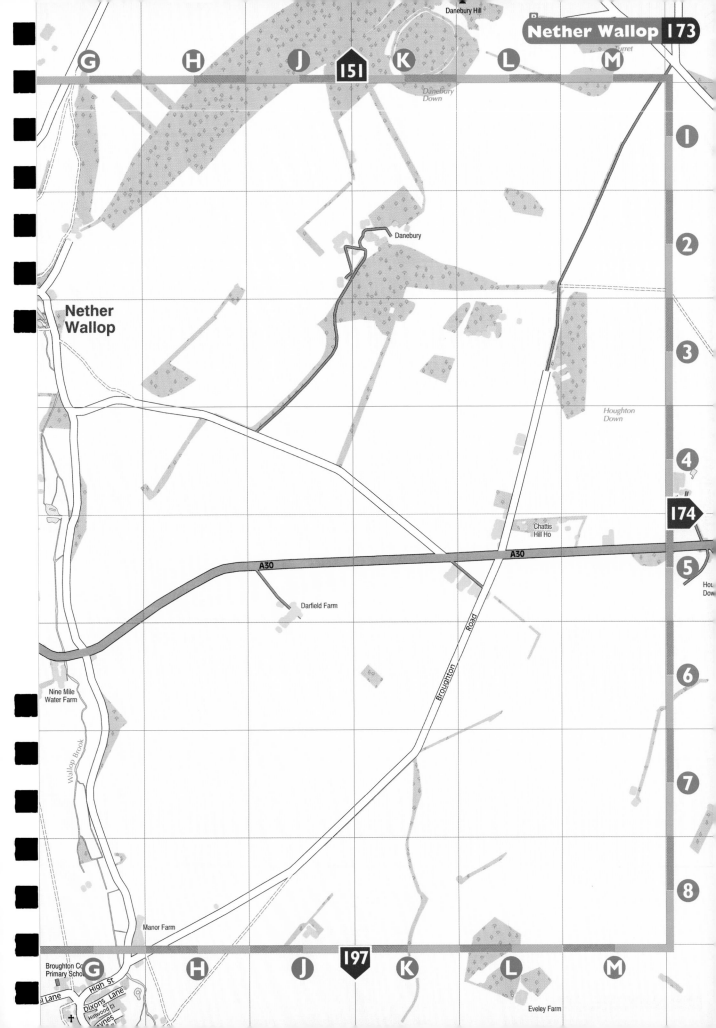

G H J **151** K L M

I

2

3

4

174

5

Danebury Hill

Danebury Down

Danebury

Houghton Down

Chattis Hill Ho

A30 A30

Darfield Farm

Turret

Nether Wallop

Nine Mile Water Farm

Wallop Brook

Broughton Road

6

7

8

Manor Farm

Broughton Co Primary Scho

High St

Dixons Lane

Hinwood Cl

l Lane

G H J **197** K L M

Eveley Farm

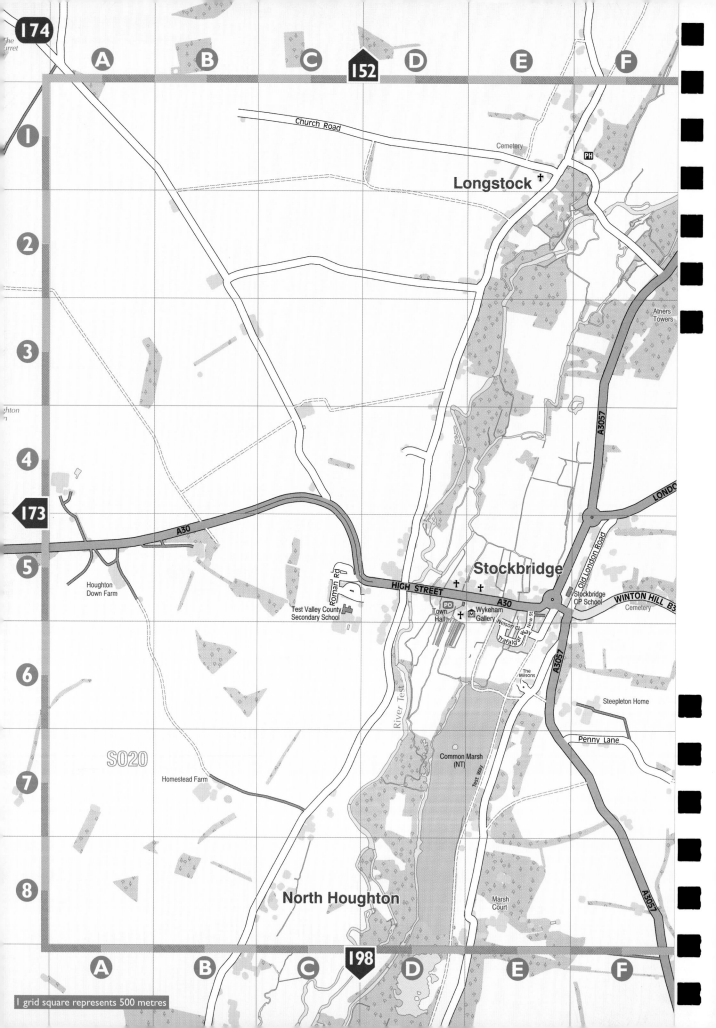

174

A   B   C   **152**   D   E   F

1   Church Road   Cemetery
    Longstock ✝
    PH

2   Atners Towers

3

4   A3057   LONDO

173

5   A30   Houghton Down Farm   Roman Rd   **Stockbridge**   Old London Road   WINTON HILL B3   Cemetery
    HIGH STREET   A30
    Test Valley County Secondary School   PO   Wykeham Gallery   Stockbridge CP School
    Town Hall   Nelson Cl   New St
    Trafalg   A3057

6   SO20   The Milsons   Steepleton Home
    Penny Lane

7   Homestead Farm   River Test   Common Marsh (NT)   Test Way

8   North Houghton   Marsh Court   A3057

A   B   C   **198**   D   E   F

I grid square represents 500 metres

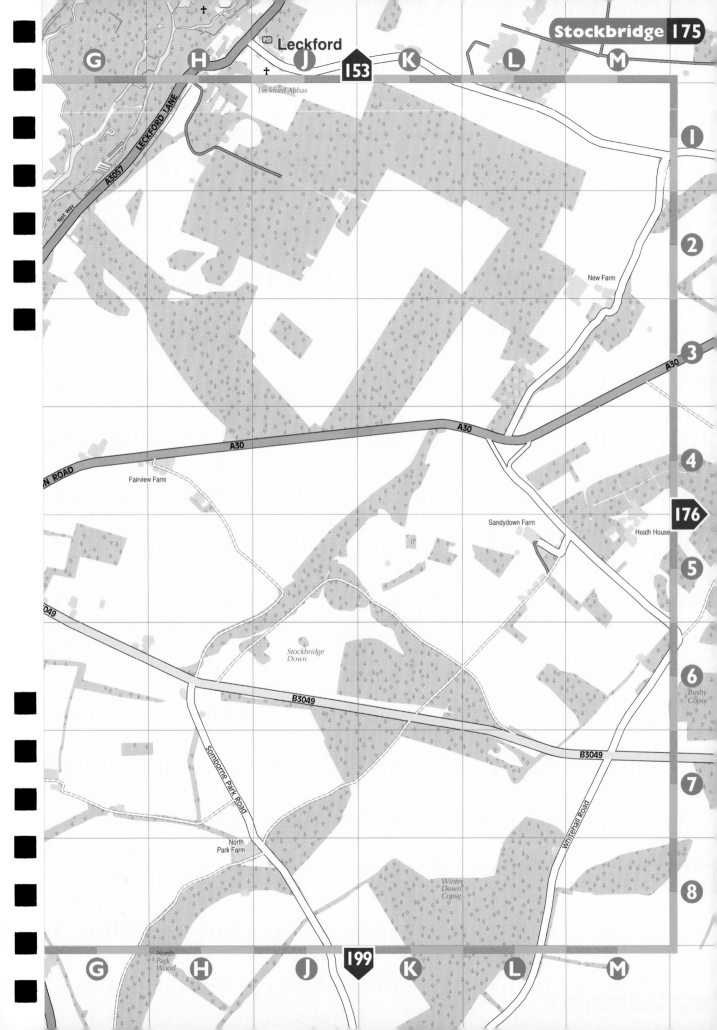

G H J K L M

Leckford

PO

153

Leckford Abbas

LECKFORD LANE

A3057

Test Way

New Farm

I

2

A30

3

N ROAD

A30

Fairview Farm

Sandydown Farm

4

176

Heath House

5

B3049

Stockbridge
Down

6

Bushy
Copse

B3049

Somborne Park Road

Whitehall Road

7

North
Park Farm

Winter
Down
Copse

8

North
Park
Wood

G H J K L M

199

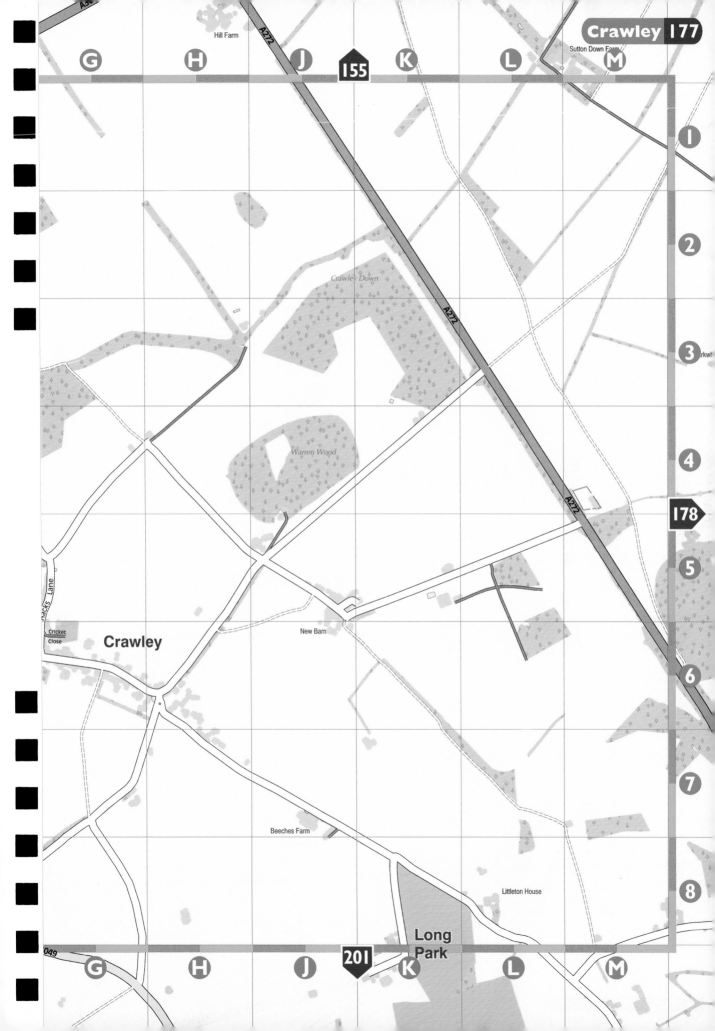

G H J 155 K L M

1

2

3 Parkwh

4

178

5

6

7

8

A272

Hill Farm

Sutton Down Farm

Crawley Down

Warren Wood

Cricket
Close

Crawley

New Barn

Beeches Farm

Littleton House

Long
Park

201

049

G H J K L M

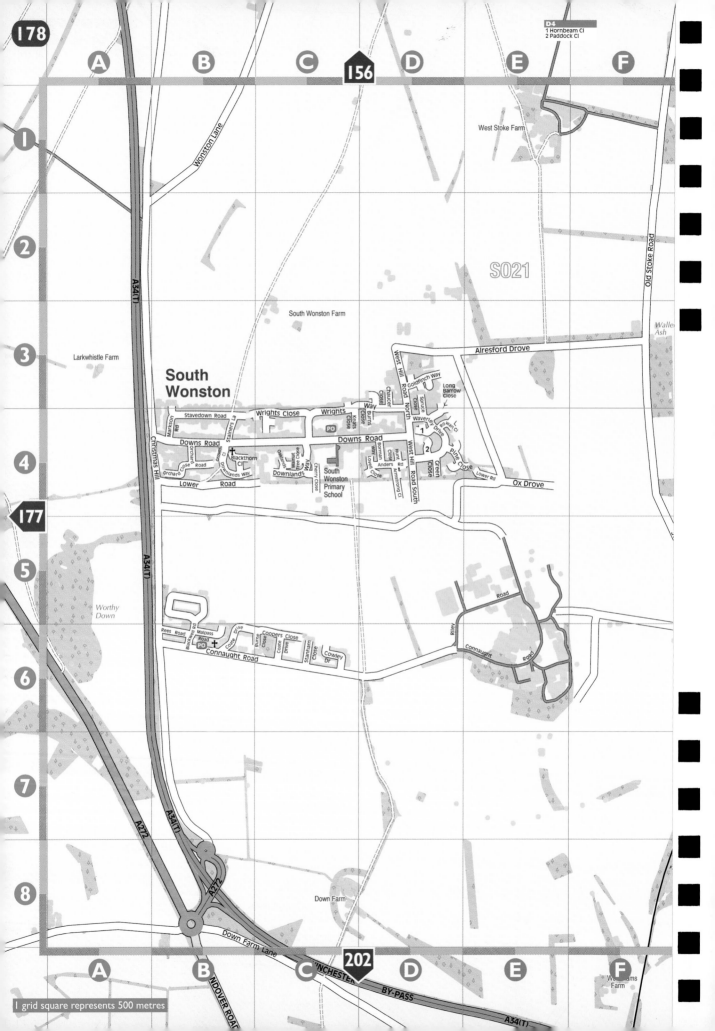

D4
1 Hornbeam Cl
2 Paddock Cl

156

A B C D E F

West Stoke Farm

S021

Wallers
Ash

1

2

Old Stoke Road

Alresford Drove

South Wonston Farm

3

Larkwhistle Farm

**South
Wonston**

West Hill Road North

Goldfinch Way

Long
Barrow
Close

Chaucer Close

Spruce Close

Rowan Cl

Waverley Drive

Stavedown Road

Wrights Close

Wrights

Keats Close

Burns Way

Markson Rd

Stainer La

PO

Downs Road

Downs Road

West Hill Road South

Pine Close

Green Close

Lower Rd

4

Orchard

Close

Downlands Way

Blackthorn Cl

Oaklands

Walnut Tree Close

Downlands

Cherry Close

**South
Wonston
Primary
School**

Borman Way

Lovell Close

Anders

Hunt Rd

Armstrong Cl

Ox Drove

Lower   Road

Orchard Road

5

Worthy
Down

A34(T)

Christmas Hill

Road

Riley

6

Rees Road

Blackwell Rd

Malpass Road

PO

Coxe Drive

Connaught Road

Burne Close

Coopers Close

Coate Drive

Stanham Close

Cowley Dr

Connaught   Road

7

A272

A34(T)

8

Down Farm

A272

Down Farm Lane

WINCHESTER

202

BY-PASS

Williams
Farm

A B C D E F

A34(T)

1 grid square represents 500 metres

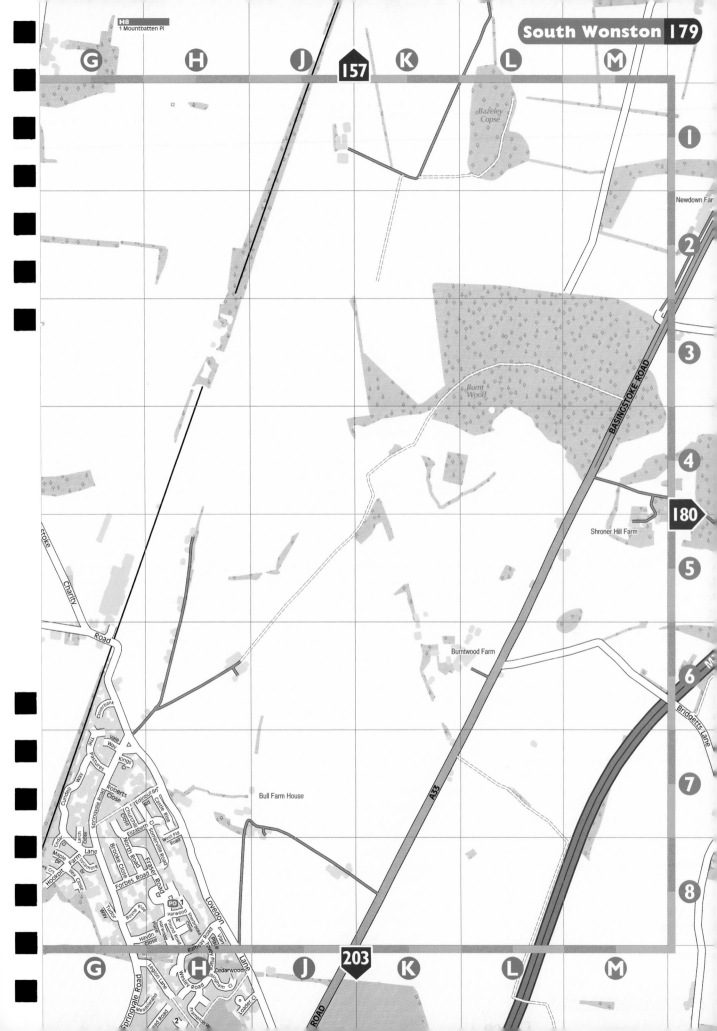

H8
1 Mountbatten Pl

G   H   J   **157**   K   L   M

I

Newdown Far

2

Bazeley
Copse

3

Burnt
Wood

4

BASINGSTOKE ROAD

180

Shroner Hill Farm

5

Charity

Road

Burntwood Farm

6

Bridgetts Lane

Coverbank

Vale
Way

The
Pastures

Cundell Way

Kings
Cl

Springvale Road

Roberts
Close

Edinburgh
Rd

Churchill
Close

Castle Rise

West Fld

7

Bull Farm House

Cedar
Farm
Lane

Maple
Dr

Larch
Close

Sycamore
Close

Brooke Close

North Road

Elizabeth
Cl

Somerville Road

Road

Fraser Road

A33

Hookpit

Crs

Forbes Road

Tudor
Way

Boyne Rise

PO

Harwood

Pound Road

Loveden

8

Haydn
Close

Hazelwood Cl

Power Place

Vian

Ram

Wesley
Road

Cedarwood

Rougham Cl

Lane

Lower Cl

Springvale Road

Legion Lane

Meadowland

ad Road

Framptom W

G   H   **203**   J   K   L   M

ROAD

158

204

179

179

Newdown Farm

STOKE ROAD

M3

Shroner Wood

Micheldever Wood

Itchen Wood

Chillandham Lane

Chillandham Lane

Oxdrove Way

Oxdrove Way

Oxdrove Way

M3

Bridgetts Lane

Bridgets Farm

Lone Farm

Itch Down Fa

Rectory Lane

Baring Cl

Old Station Road

Couch

A B C D E F

A B C D E F

I 2 3 4 5 6 7 8

1 grid square represents 500 metres

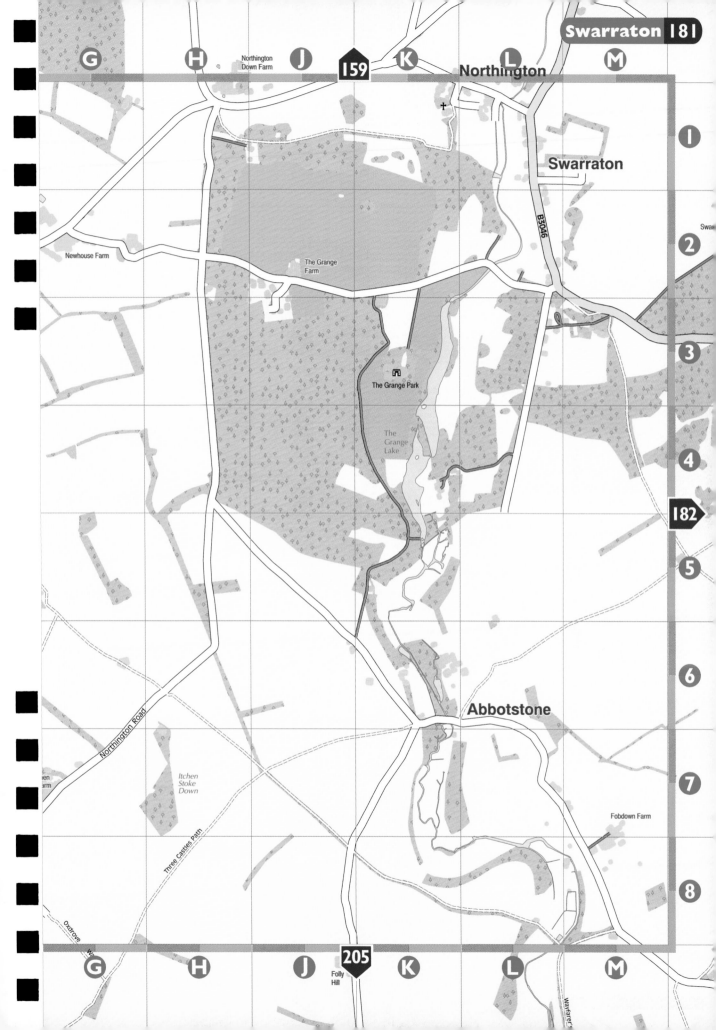

G H J 159 K L M

Northington Down Farm

Northington

†

Swarraton

B3046

Newhouse Farm

The Grange Farm

The Grange Park

The Grange Lake

182

Northington Road

Itchen Stoke Down

...en Farm

Three Castles Path

Abbotstone

Fobdown Farm

Oxdrove...

G H J 205 K L M

Folly Hill

Wayfarer's...

I

2

3

4

5

6

7

8

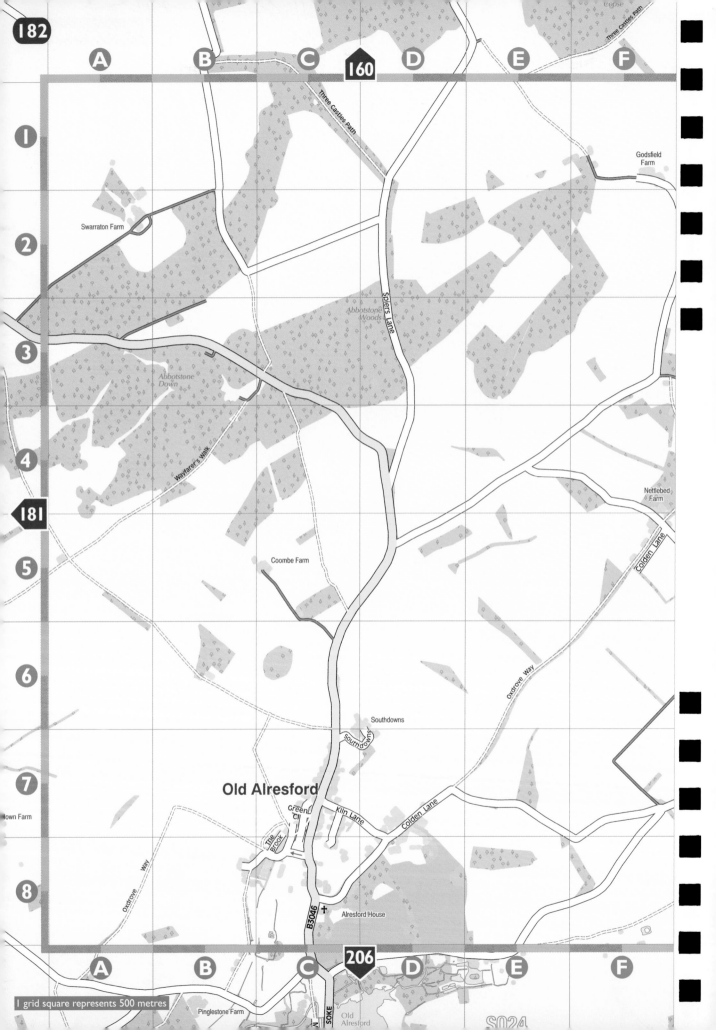

160

181

206

Old Alresford

A B C D E F

I
2
3
4
5
6
7
8

Swarraton Farm

Abbotstone Woods

Abbotstone Down

Wayfarer's Walk

Spiers Lane

Three Castles Path

Godsfield Farm

Nettlebed Farm

Colden Lane

Coombe Farm

Oxdrove Way

Southdowns

Southdowns

Kiln Lane

Colden Lane

Green Cl

The Brook

Oxdrove Way

lown Farm

B3046

Alresford House

Pinglestone Farm

SOKE

Old Alresford

SO24

1 grid square represents 500 metres

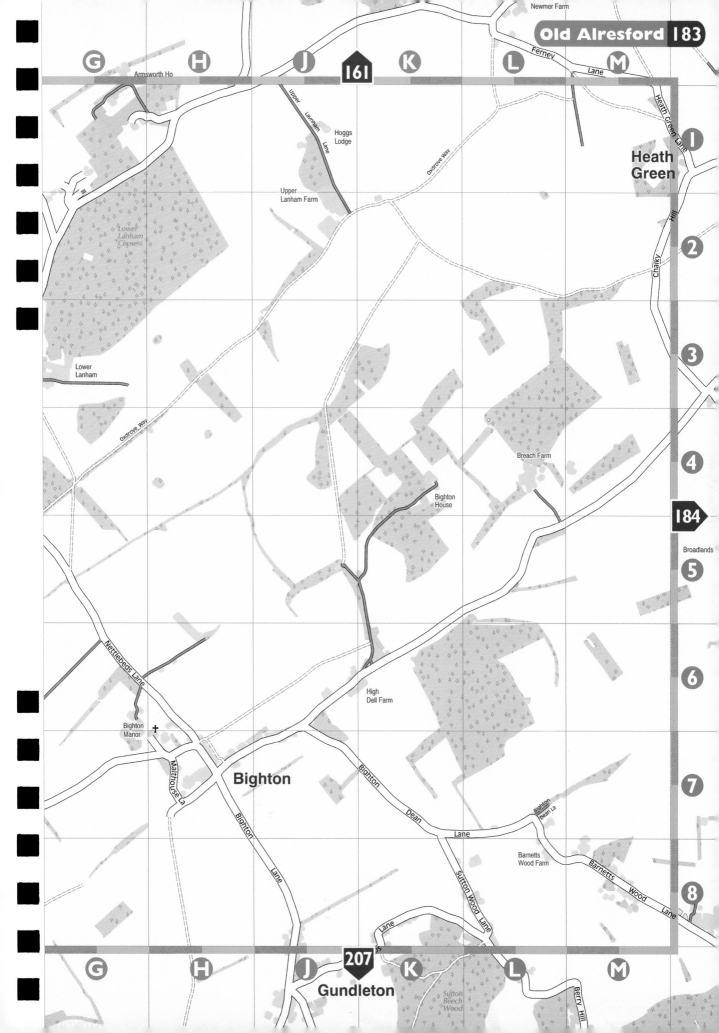

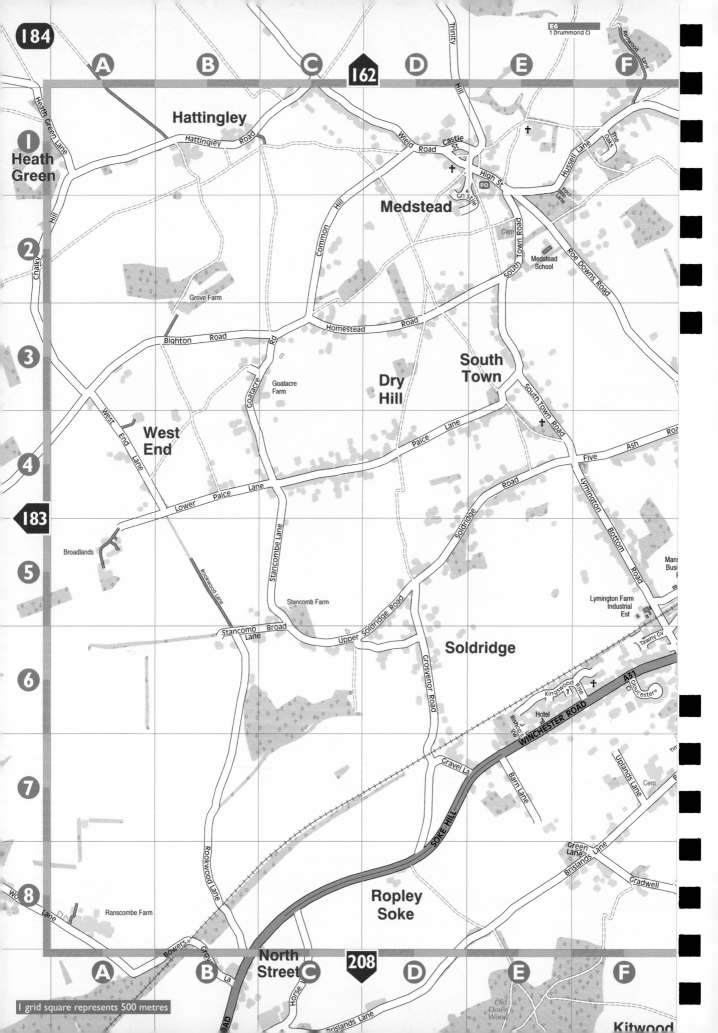

184

I84

A B C 162 D E F

I
Heath
Green

Heath Green Lane

Hattingley

Hattingley Road

Wield Road

Trinity

Hill

Castle St

†

Castle

High St

PO

Gri Stile

Medstead

†

E6
1 Drummond Cl

The Oaks

Redwood Lane

Hussell Lane

Roul Lane

Cem

Medstead School

2

Chalky Hill

Common Hill

South Town Road

Roe Downs Road

3

Bighton   Road

Goatacre Rd

Grove Farm

Homestead   Road

Dry
Hill

South
Town

4
183

West
End

West End Lane

Goatacre Farm

Paice   Lane

South Town Road

†

Five   Ash   Road

Lower   Paice   Lane

Stancombe Lane

Rockwood Lane

Soldridge   Road

Lymington   Bottom   Road

5

Broadlands

Stancomb Farm

Upper Soldridge Road

Lymington Farm Industrial Est

Mans
Busi

Tawny GV

6

Stancomb   Broad
Lane

Grosvenor Road

Soldridge

A31

Kingswood Rise

7

†

Gloucester

Hotel

Bishops VW

WINCHESTER ROAD

7

Rookwood Lane

Gravel La

Barn Lane

SOKE HILL

Cem

Uplands Lane

8
Wo   Lane

Ranscombe Farm

Bowers

Grov La

North
Street

Horse La

Ropley
Soke

Green
Lane

Brislands Lane

Gradwell

A B C 208 D E F

Brislands Lane

Old
Down
Woo

Kitwood

1 grid square represents 500 metres

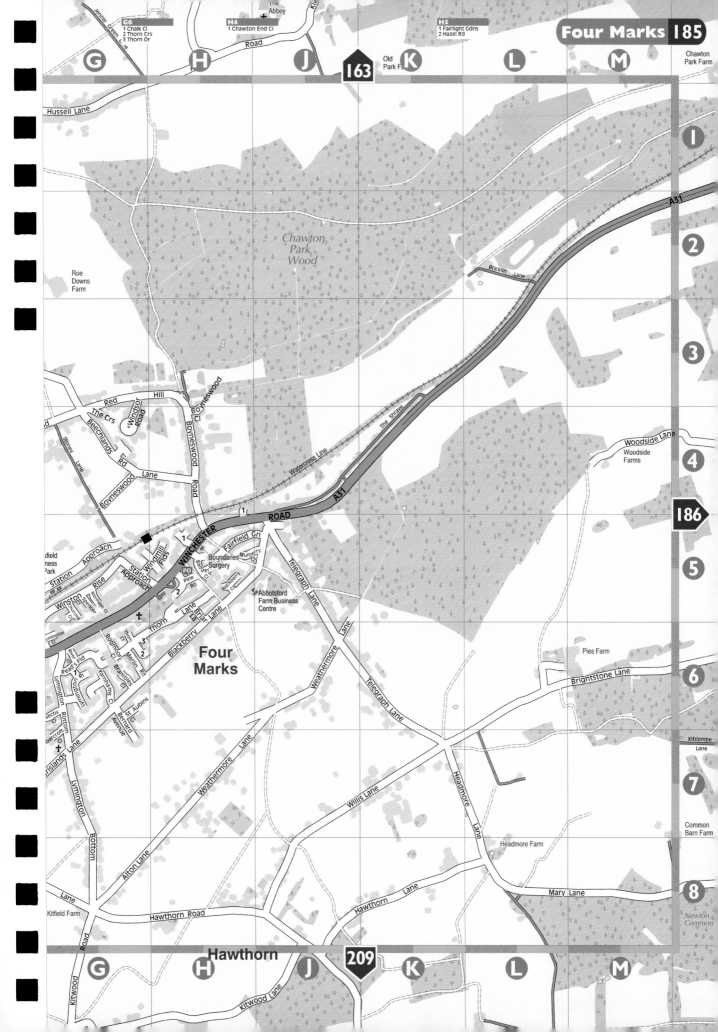

G6
1 Chalk Cl
2 Thorn Crs
3 Thorn Dr

H4
1 Chawton End Cl

H5
1 Fairlight Gdns
2 Hazel Rd

The Abbey

G H J **163** K L M Chawton Park Farm

Old Park Fa

I

2

A31

Hussell Lane

Chawton Park Wood

Roe Downs Farm

Bricklin Lane

3

Woodside Lane
Woodside Farms

4

The shrave

Red Hill Windsor Road The Crs
Beechlands Rd
Boyneswood Cl
Boyneswood Lane
Stoney Lane

Watercress Line

A31

186

1 ROAD
7 WINCHESTER

Fairfield Gn

Mulberry

5

Approach
sfield ness Park
Station
Windmill Flds
Boundaries Surgery
Telegraph Lane
Badger Cl
PO
Pine Rd
Winston Rise
Spencer
2 Blenheim
Blackberry
Abbotsford Farm Business Centre

Pies Farm

Thorn Lane
Briar Lane
Blackberry Lane
Boamoor Cl
Merlin Rd
Bramoles
Brightstone Lane

6

Four Marks

Weathermore Lane
Telegraph Lane

Read's Fld
Yarnams Cl
Vectis Cl
Bottom
Bernard Avenue
St. Aubins

Kitcombe Lane

7

risland's Lane
Lymington Bottom
Weathermore Lane
Willis Lane
Headmore Lane

Common Barn Farm

Alton Lane
Headmore Farm

Mary Lane

8

Kitfield Farm
Hawthorn Road
Hawthorn Lane
Newton Common

Lane

Hawthorn

Kitwood Road
Kitwood Lane
G H **209** J K L M

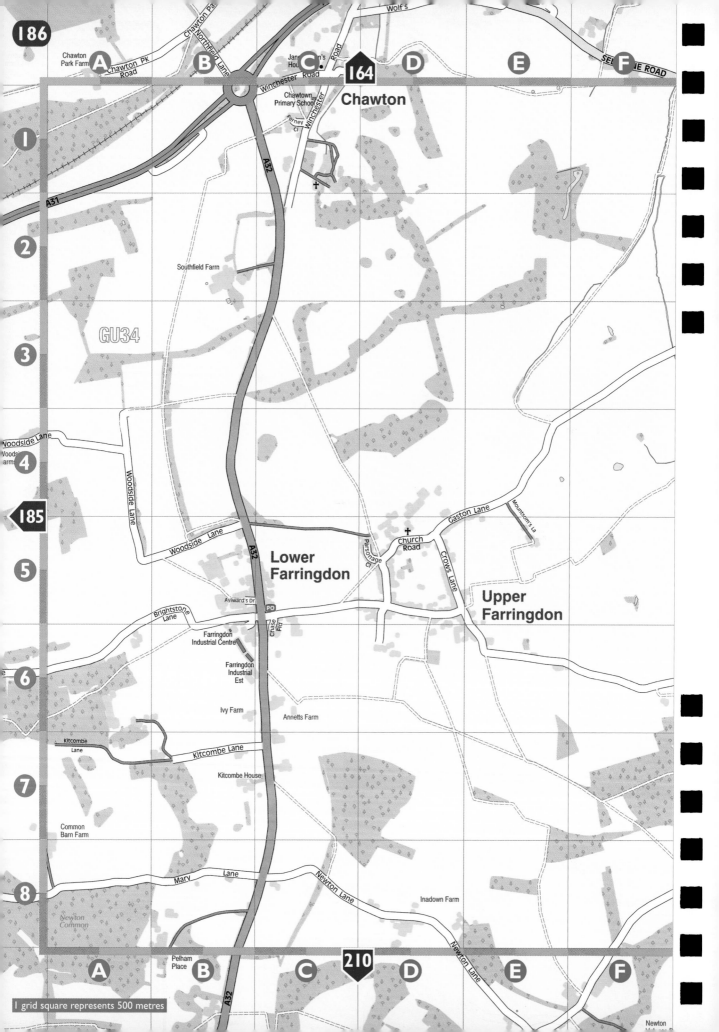

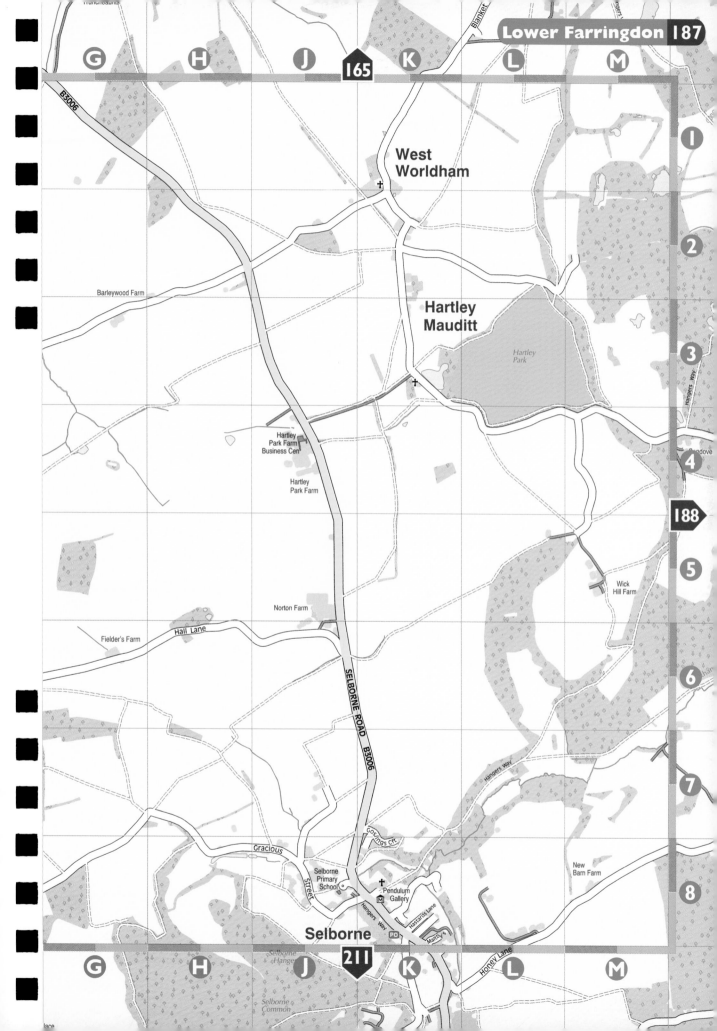

G   H   J   165   K   L   M

West
Worldham

Hartley
Mauditt

Hartley
Park

B3006

Barleywood Farm

Hartley
Park Farm
Business Cen

Hartley
Park Farm

188

Wick
Hill Farm

Norton Farm

Fielder's Farm

Hall Lane

SELBORNE ROAD B3006

Hangers Way

New
Barn Farm

Gracious

Gosings Cft

Selborne
Primary
School

Pendulum
Gallery

Hangers Way

Honey Lane

Street

Hascards Lane

Martby's

PO

Selborne

211

Selborne
Hanger

Selborne
Common

G   H   J   211   K   L   M

1   2   3   4   5   6   7   8

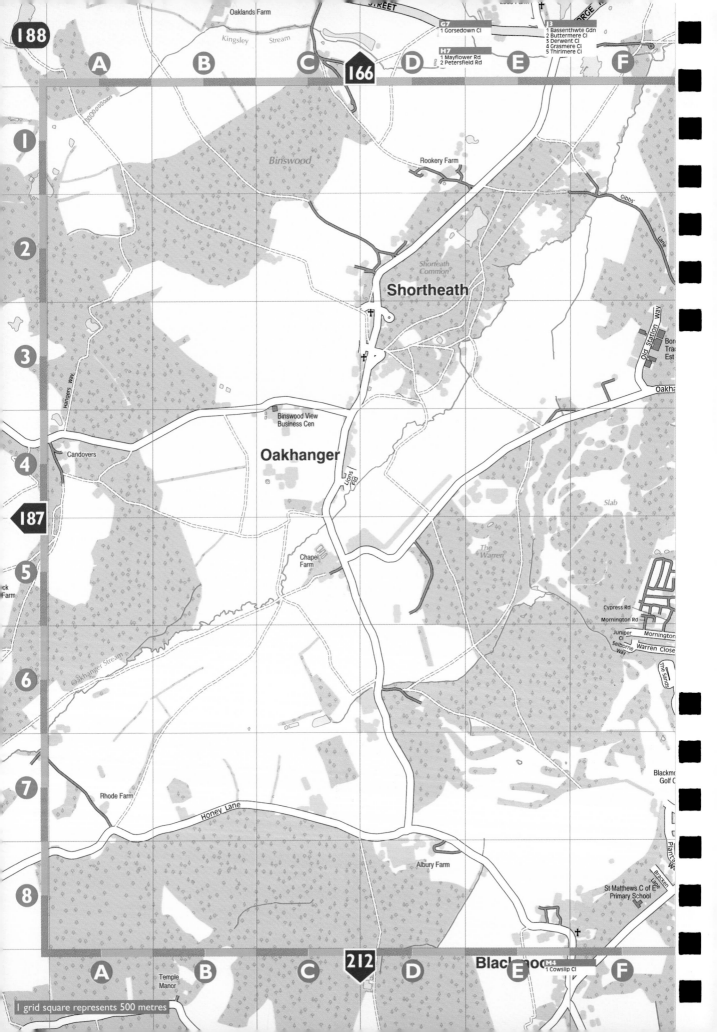

A   B   C   166   D   E   F

1

Kingsley   Stream
Oaklands Farm

G7
1 Gorsedown Cl

J3
1 Bassenthwte Gdn
2 Buttermere Cl
3 Derwent Cl
4 Grasmere Cl
5 Thirlmere Cl

H7
1 Mayflower Rd
2 Petersfield Rd

Binswood

Rookery Farm

2   Shortheath Common   Shortheath

Gibbs'   Lane

3   Old Station Way   Bord Trad Est

Hangers Way   Oakha

4   Candovers   Binswood View Business Cen   Oakhanger   Slab

187

Chapel Farm   The Warren

5   Cypress Rd   Mornington Rd

Juniper Cl
Selborne Way   Warren Close   Mornington

6   Oakhanger Stream   The Sands

7   Rhode Farm   Honey Lane   Blackmo Golf C

Albury Farm

8   St Matthews C of E Primary School

A   B   212   C   D   Blackmoo   E   F

M4
1 Cowslip Cl

Temple Manor

1 grid square represents 500 metres

G5
1 Lavender Gdns
2 Manica Cl
3 Tilbury's Cl
4 Woodside Crs

J6
1 Connaught Cl
2 Dene Cl
3 Melrose Cl
4 Nutley Cl

J7
1 Bedford Cl
2 Nthumberld Rd
3 Richmond Cl

K4
1 Beavers Ms

167

190

213

M3
1 Buttercup Cl
2 Colts Foot Rd
3 Grayshott Laurels
4 Lynwood Cl
5 Mallow Cl
6 Periwinkle Cl
7 Torrington Cl

L4
1 Greenacres

L5
1 Britannia Cl
2 Mercury Cl

L3
1 Cricket Lea
2 Five Acres Cl

K6(cont.)
6 Hibiscus Gv
7 Jasmine Wy
8 Kingfisher Cl
9 Magpie Cl
10 Neptune Rd
11 Nightingale Rd

K6
1 Amber Cl
2 Chestnut Ct
3 Ducklands
4 Foxglove Dr
5 Hendon Rd
cont.

K5
1 Blackthorne Rd
2 Ferncote Rd
3 Norman Cl
4 Primula Rd

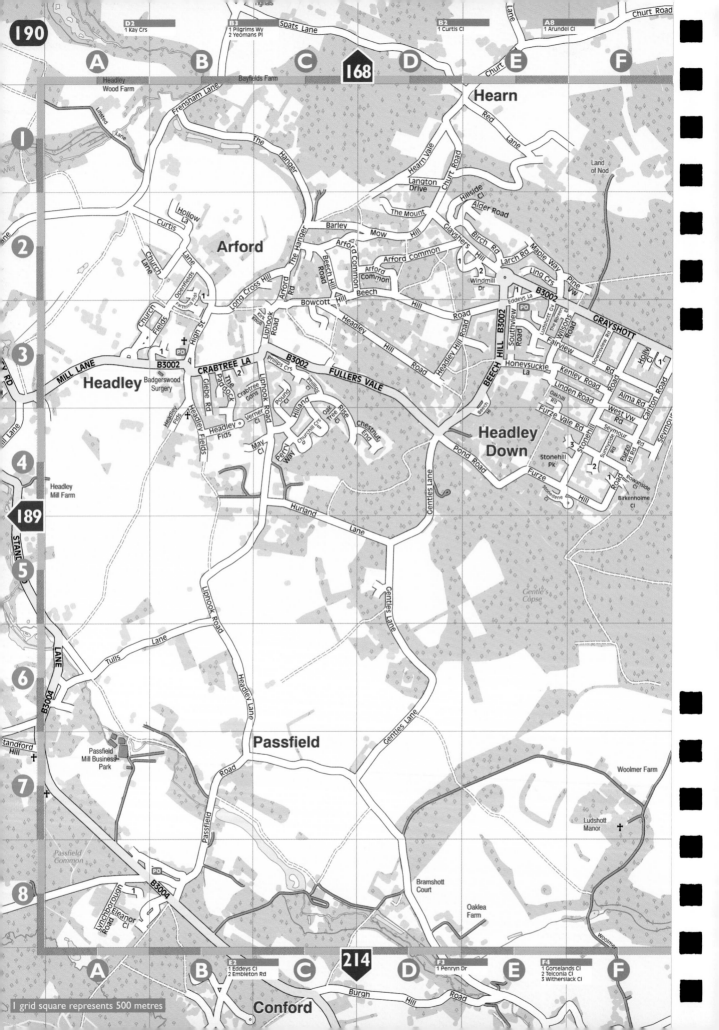

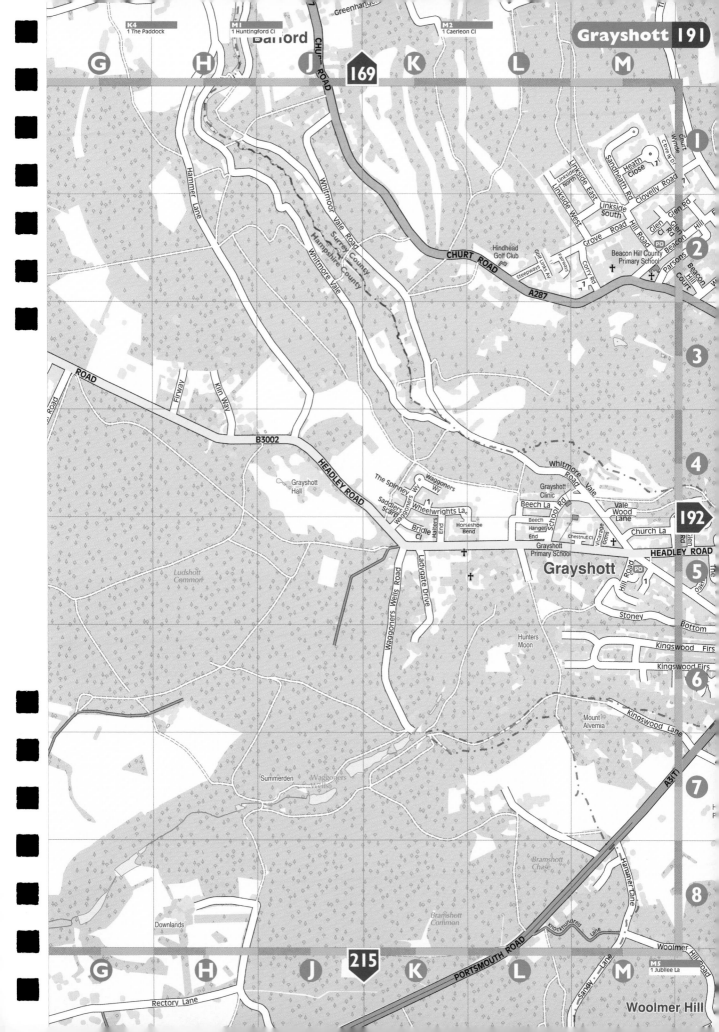

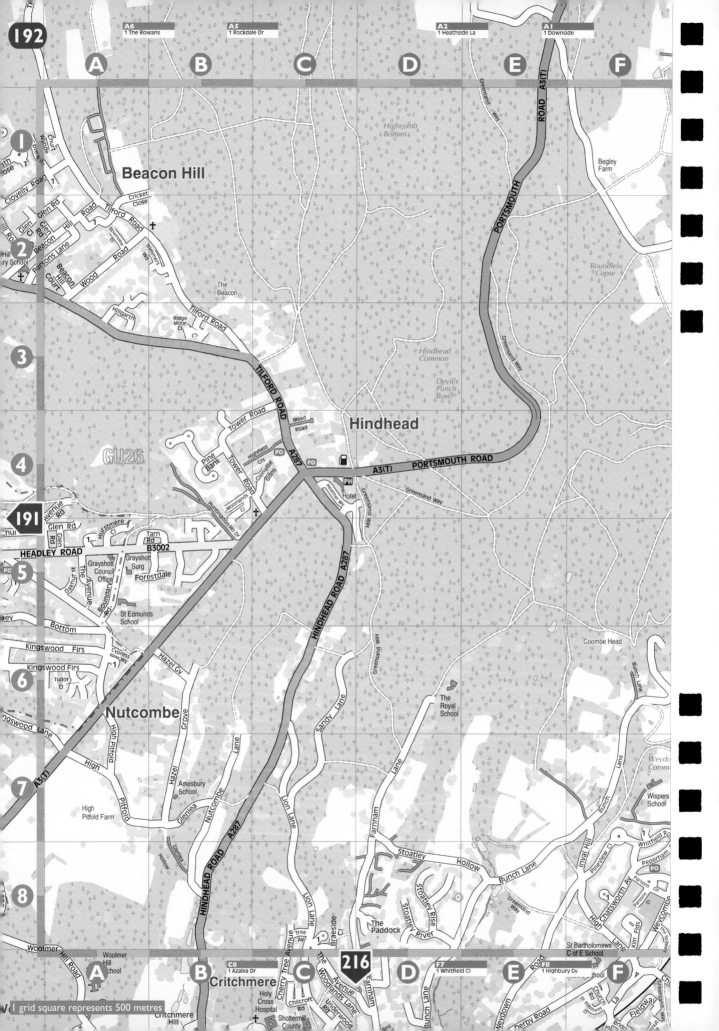

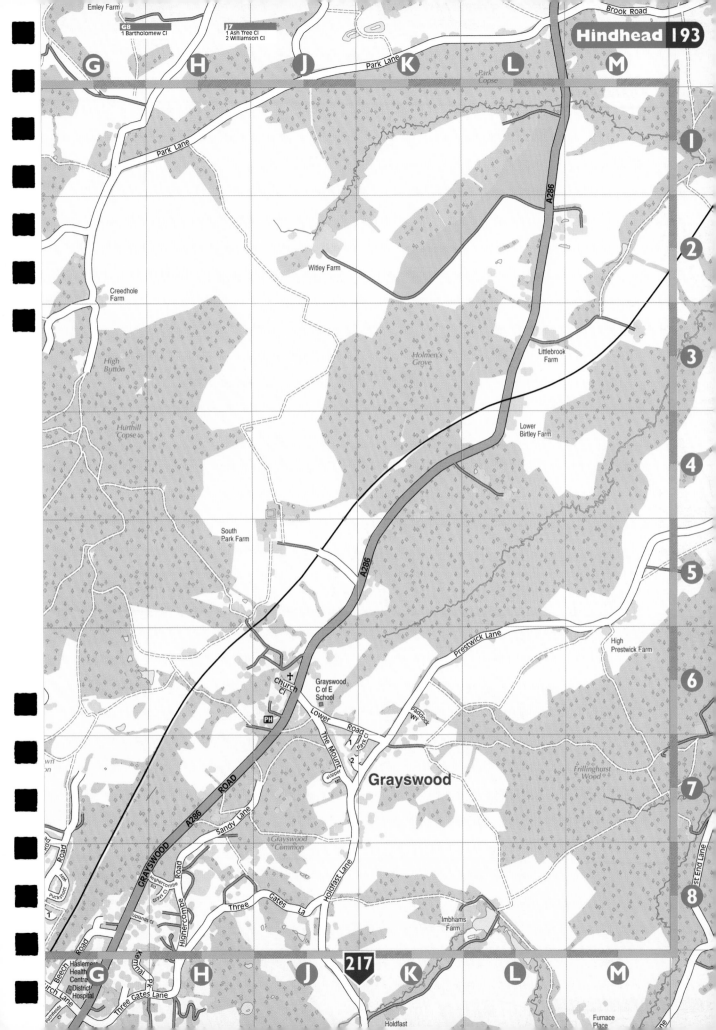

G H J K L M

Emley Farm

G8
1 Bartholomew Cl

J7
1 Ash Tree Cl
2 Williamson Cl

Brook Road

Park Lane

Park Copse

1

Park Lane

2

Witley Farm

Creedhole Farm

A286

Littlebrook Farm

3

High Button

Holmen's Grove

Lower Birtley Farm

Hurthill Copse

4

South Park Farm

A286

5

Prestwick Lane

High Prestwick Farm

6

Church Cl

Grayswood C of E School

Paddock Wy

PH

Lower Road

The Mount

Park Cl

Frillinghurst Wood

7

Copper Ms

Grayswood

GRAYSWOOD ROAD

A286

Sandy Lane

Grayswood Common

Holdfast Lane

St End Lane

8

Road

Puck's Oreft

Highercombe Rd

Grays Cl

Highercombe Road

Three Gates La

Imbhams Farm

Uplands Cl

Haslemere Health Centre & District Hospital

Beech Road

Kemnal Pk

Three Gates Lane

G H J K L M

Holdfast

Furnace Place

Church Lane

Parkfields Cl

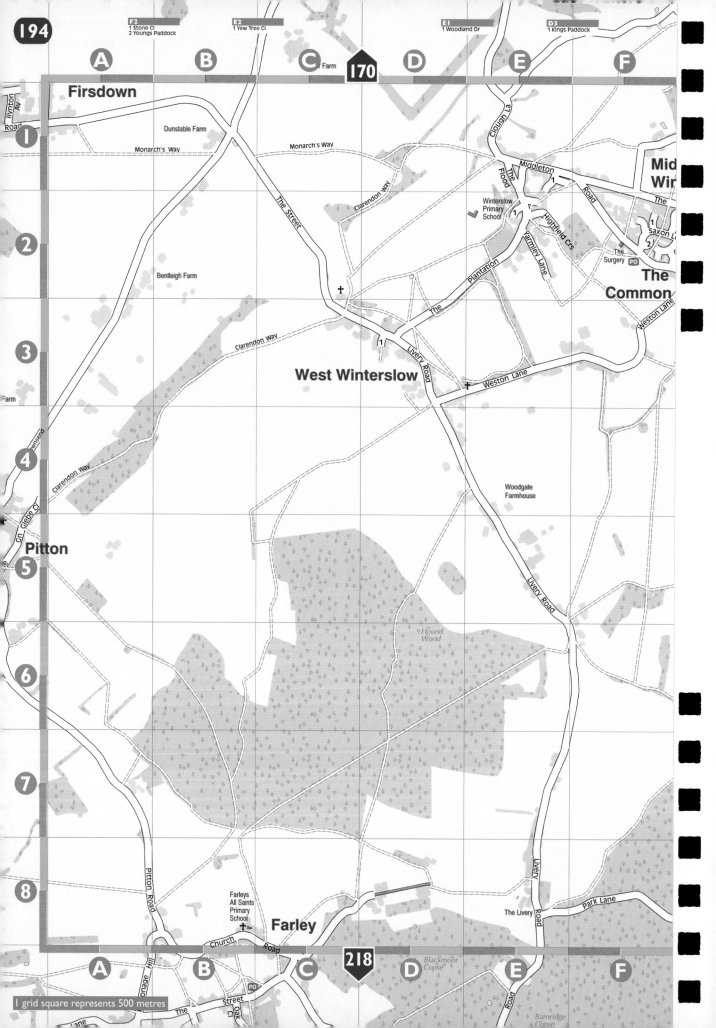

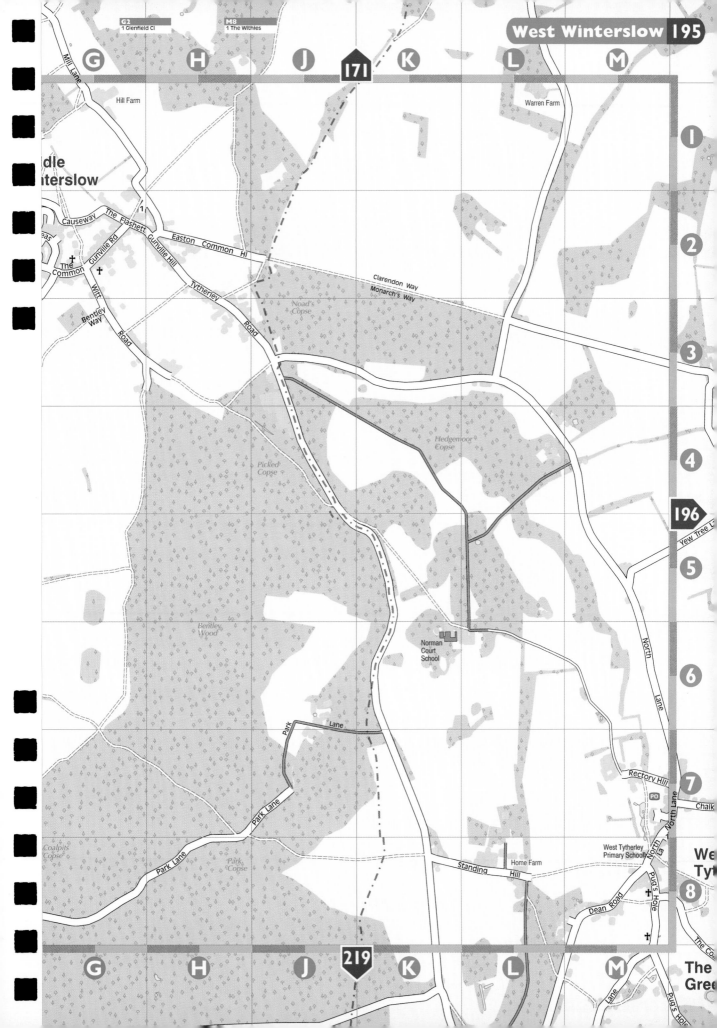

G2
1 Glenfield Cl

M8
1 The Withies

171

G H J K L M

1

2

3

4

196

5

6

7

8

219

G H J K L M

Hill Farm

Warren Farm

dle
nterslow

Causeway
The Flashett
Gunville Rd
Gunville Hill
Easton Common Hl

The Common

Witt

Bentley Way

Road

Tytherley Road

Clarendon Way
Monarch's Way

Noad's Copse

Picked Copse

Bentley Wood

Hedgemoor Copse

Norman Court School

Park Lane

Park Lane

Park Lane

Coalpits Copse

Park Copse

Lane

Standing Hill

Home Farm

Yew Tree L

North Lane

Rectory Hill

PO

Chalk

West Tytherley Primary School

North La
North Lane

Pug's Hole

Dean Road

We
Tyt

We
Gree

The Co

Pug's Hol

The Green

Broughton
Down Farm

B3084

A B Broughton
Down C **172** D E F

SALISBURY

ROAD

School

I

2 Church Farm

Clarendon Way

Monarch's Way Buckholt Road

Clarendon Way

Monarch's Way

3

Buckholt Farm

4

195

Yew Tree Lane

5

Queenwood Farm

North

6

Lane

Reddish Hill

7 PO

Chalk Pit Lane

North Lane

**West
Tytherley** **Stony Batter**

...therley
School

North La

Stride's Farm

8

Pound Hole

Manor Farm

The Coach Road

The Coach Road

**The A
Green** **B** **C** **220** **D** Manor
Rd **E** **F**

**East
Tytherley**

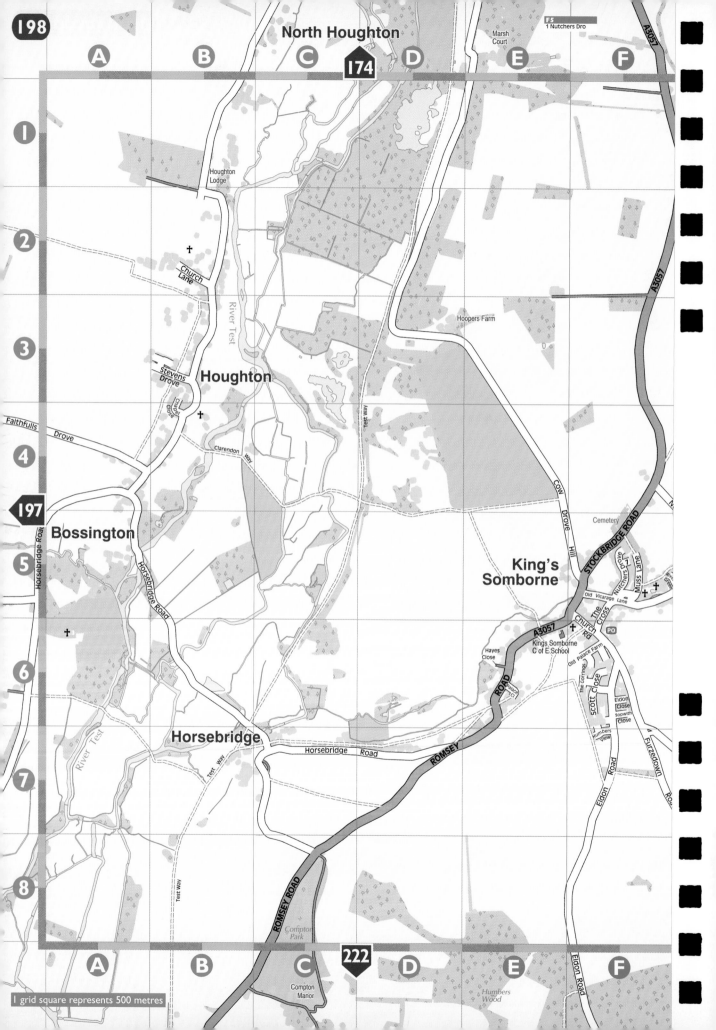

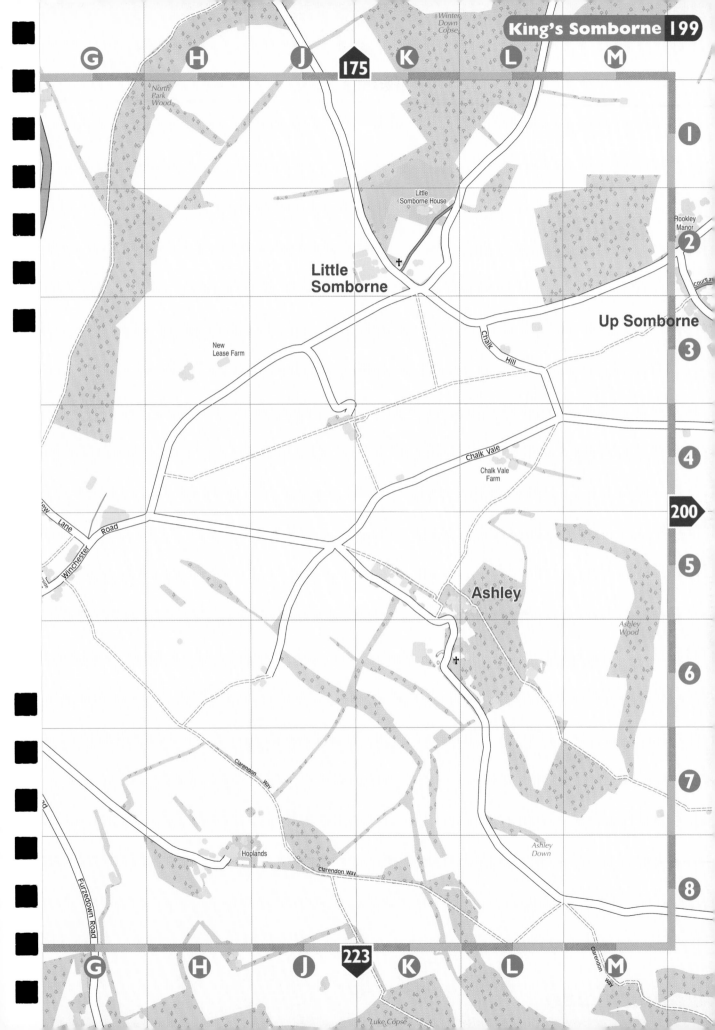

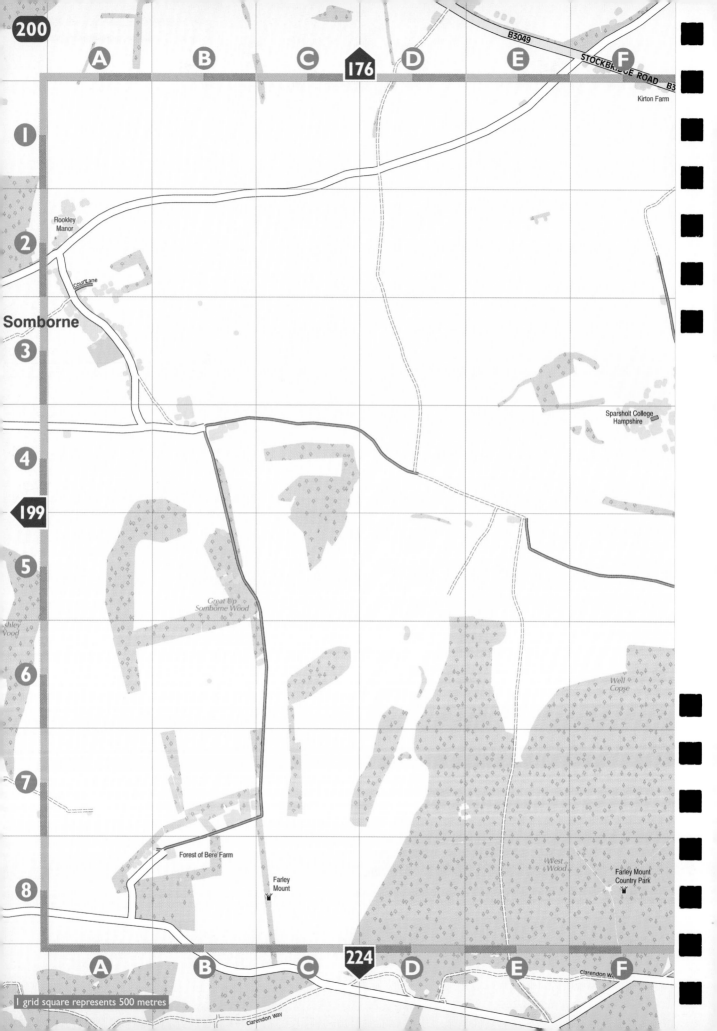

B3049

STOCKBRIDGE ROAD B3

A   B   C   176   D   E   F

Kirton Farm

1

Rookley
Manor

2

Court Lane

Somborne

3

Sparsholt College
Hampshire

4

199

5

Great Up
Somborne Wood

shley
Wood

6

Well
Copse

7

Forest of Bere Farm

West
Wood

Farley
Mount

Farley Mount
Country Park

8

A   B   C   224   D   E   Clarendon Way   F

Clarendon Way

1 grid square represents 500 metres

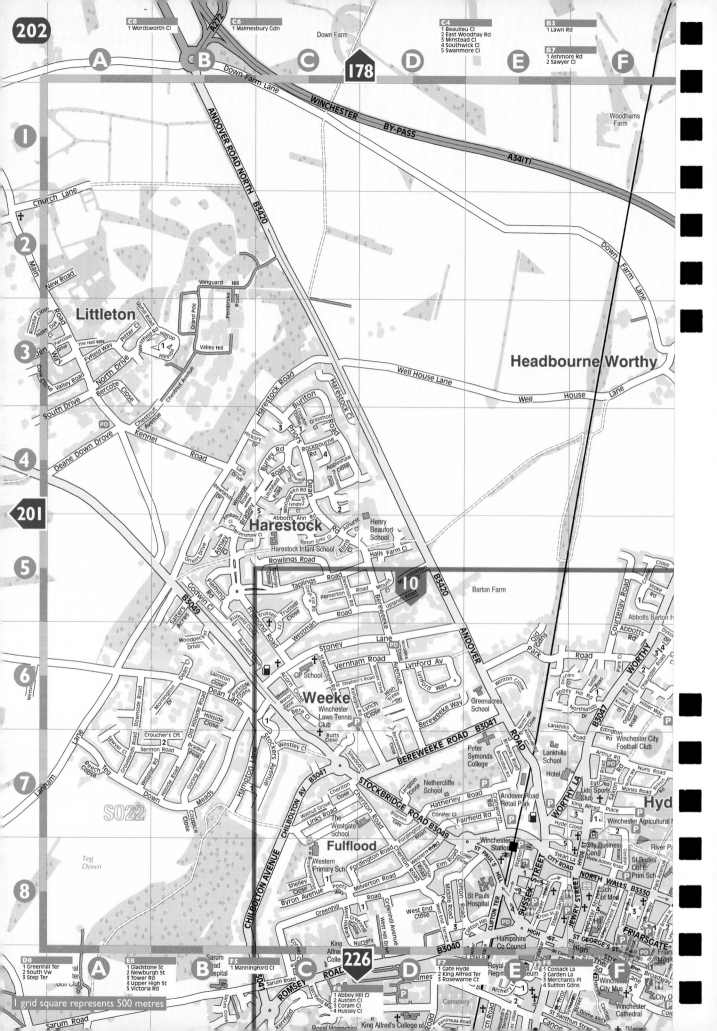

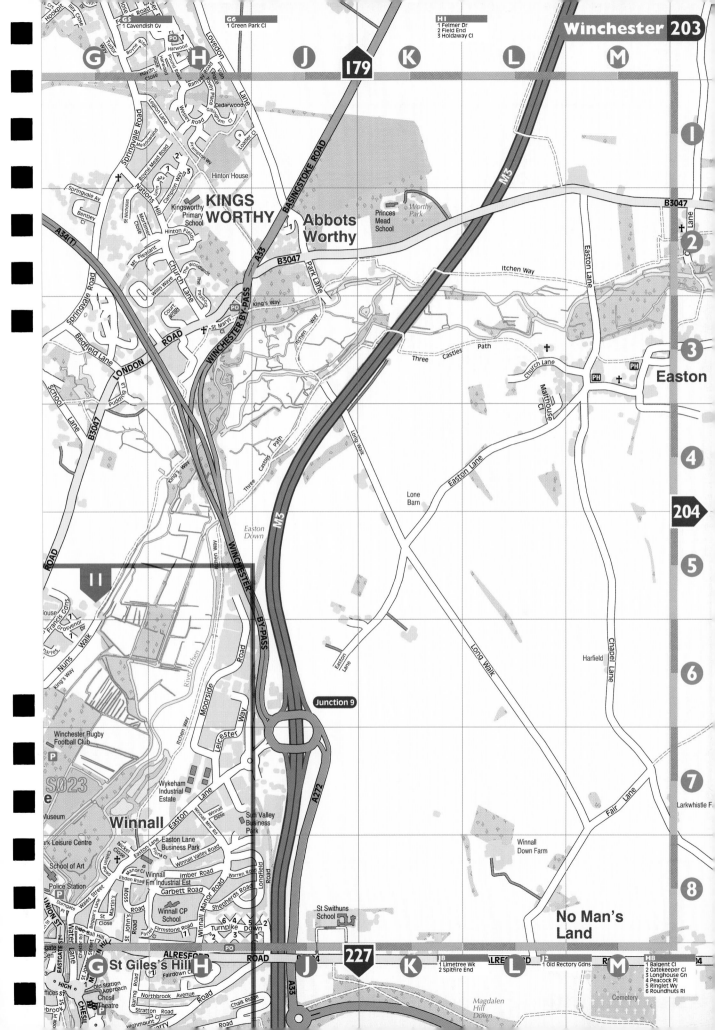

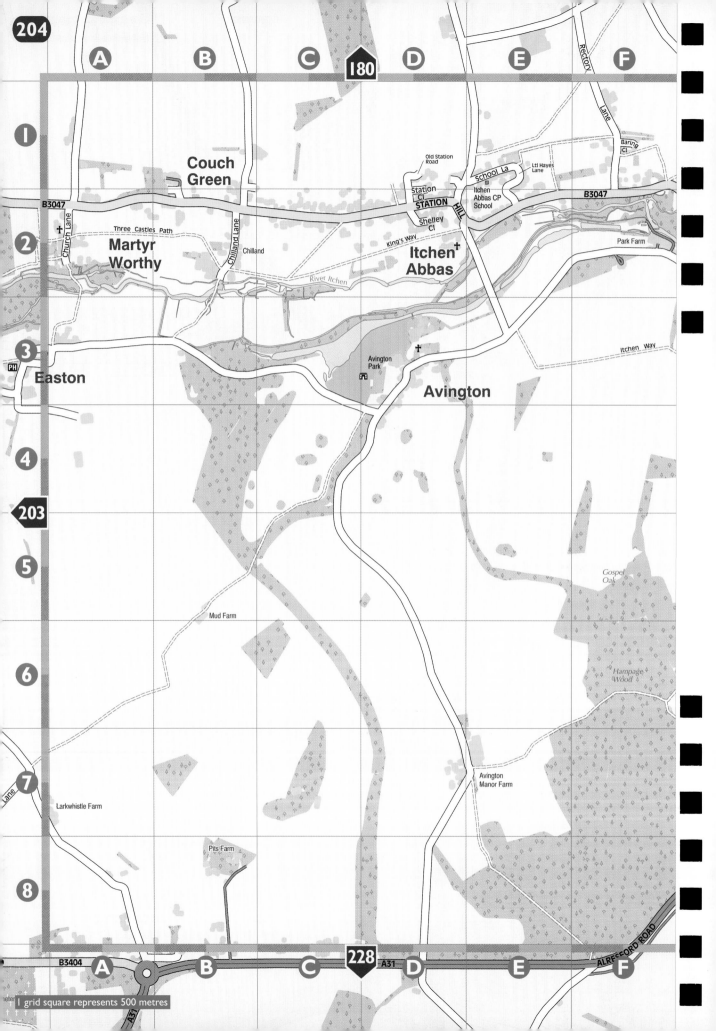

A B C **180** D E **Rectory Lane** F

I

Couch
Green

Old Station
Road

School La

Ltl Hayes
Lane

Baring
Cl

Station
Cl
STATION

Itchen
Abbas CP
School

B3047

B3047

2
Church Lane
Three Castles Path
Chilland Lane

**Martyr
Worthy**

Chilland

Shelley
Cl

King's Way

**Itchen†
Abbas**

HILL

Park Farm

River Itchen

3
PH
Easton

Avington
Park

†

Itchen Way

Avington

4

203

5
Gospel
Oak

Mud Farm

6
Hampage
Wood

7
Lane
Larkwhistle Farm

Avington
Manor Farm

Pits Farm

8

B3404 A B **228** A31 D E ALRESFORD ROAD F

A31

1 grid square represents 500 metres

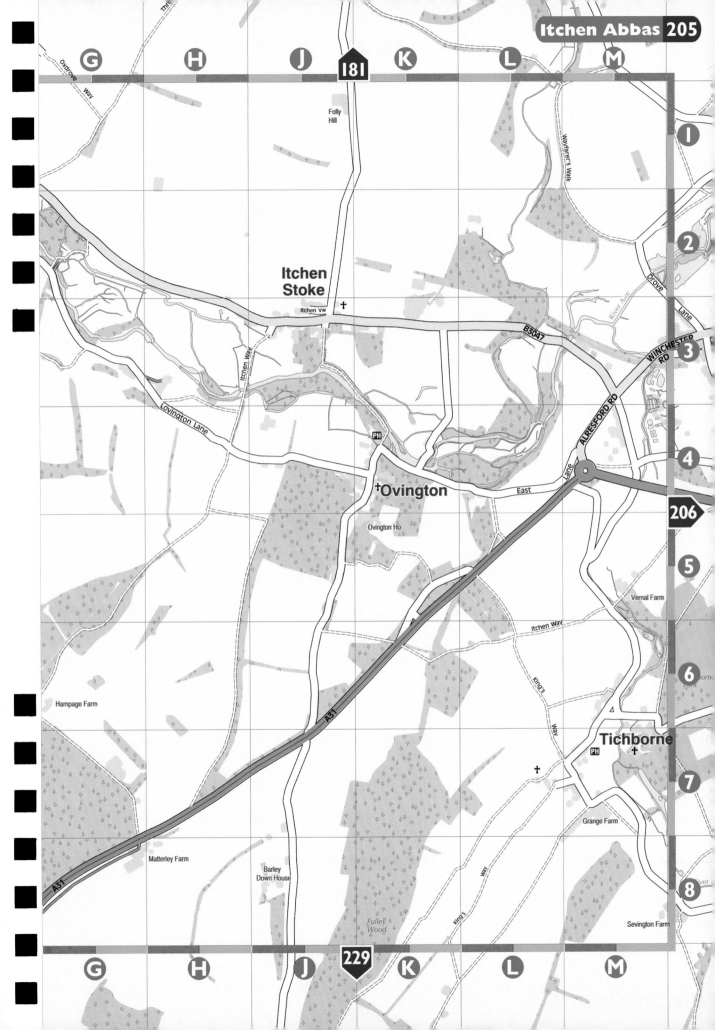

G H J **181** K L M

1
2
3
4
206
5
6
7
8

Oxdrove Way
Folly Hill
Wayfarer's Walk
Drove Lane
River Itchen
Itchen Stoke
Itchen Vw
B3047
WINCHESTER RD
Itchen Way
Lovington Lane
ALRESFORD RD
PH
Ovington
Ovington Ho
East Lane
Vernal Farm
Itchen Way
Hampage Farm
A31
King's Way
Tichborne
PH
Grange Farm
A31
Matterley Farm
Barley Down House
King's Way
Sevington Farm
Fulley Wood
River

G H J **229** K L M

A   **B**   **C**   **D**   **E**   **F**

C3
1 Carpenters
2 Ellingham Cl
3 Meadow Cl
4 Searles Cl

B4
1 Maple Cl
2 Robertson Rd

B3
1 Lovells Wk

A4
1 Watercress
  Meadow

182

1
2
3
4
5
6
7
8

S024

NEW ALRESFORD

Pinglestone Farm

Arle Cl
Arle Gdns
The Dean
Mallard Cl

Baytree Gallery

Candover Gallery

The George Yard

Old Alresford Pond

MILL HILL

THE SOKE

BROAD ST

Lady Well La

PH

M

WEST ST

EAST ST

West Hotel
PO

Brandy Mt

The Alresford Surg

Haig Rd

POUND HL

Perins County
Secondary
School

Station Ap

Nursery Road

Station Rd

Sun Lane

Watercress Line

B3047

B3047 THE AVENUE

WINCHESTER RD

De-Lucy Av

Bridge Rd

Grange Road

Roseberry Rd

Salisbury Rd

LIME Rd

Hawthorn Rd

BEECH Rd

Sun Lane

Western Court

Mill Lane

B3047

South Farm
Road

Ashburton Rd

South Road

Dorian Gv

Jesty Rd

Windsor Rd

Mervon Rd

Jacklyns Cl

JACKLYNS LANE

Elm Road

Oak Hill

Alresford County
Junior School

Beneden Gn

Sun Hill
Infant
School

Covey Wy

Perins Cl

Prospect Road

Prospect
Business
Cen

Linnets

Russell Rd

Culley VW

Beneden Gn

Lindley Gdns

Derwent Gdns

Sun Hill

Oak Hill

Crescent

Appledown

Tichborne
Down

Whitehill Lane

Hasted
Dr

Corfe
Cl

Fair VW

Paddock Wy

Shepherds Down

Spring Gdns

Spring Wy

Dover Cl

Orchard Cl

Bell Ho

205

A31

Tichborne   Down

A31

Alresford
Golf Club

Wayfarer's Walk

Appledown Lane

Scrubbs Lane

Vernal Farm

B3046

Tichborne
Park

Wayfarer's Walk

Scrubb Farm

Dark Lane

Cheriton La

Cheriton Lane

hborne

River Itchen

Itchen Way

Sevington Farm

Cheriton Mill

North End Lane

Bac Brear Lane

Middle Farm

230

C4
1 Arundel Cl
2 Buttermere Gdns
3 Carisbrooke Cl
4 Coniston Gv
5 Dickenson Wk
6 Ennerdale Gdns
7 Ulliswater Gv
8 Windermere Gdn
9 Witton Hl

North
End

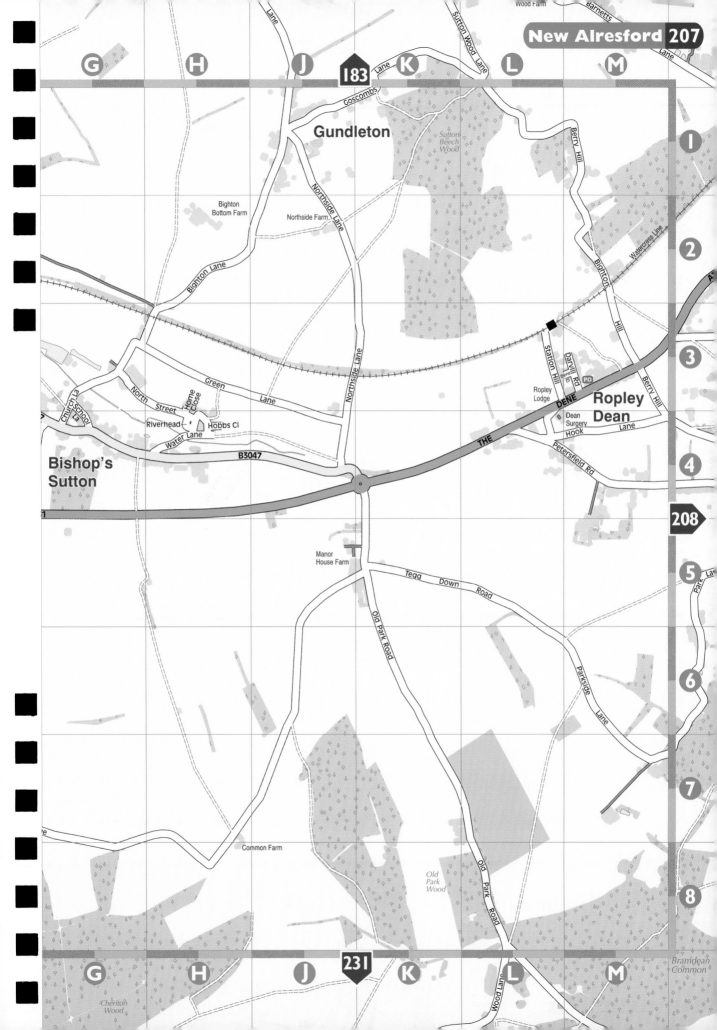

183

G H J K L M

I
2
3
208
4
5
6
7
8

Gundleton

Goscombs

Sutton
Wood Farm

Wood Farm

barnetts

Lane

Berry Hill

Watercress Line

Northside Lane

Bighton
Bottom Farm

Northside Farm

Sutton
Beech
Wood

Bighton Lane

Bighton Hill

Northside Lane

Berry Hill

Station Hill

Darvill Rd
Dene Cl

PO

Ropley
Lodge

Ropley
Dean

North Street

Green Lane

Home
Close

Church La

School

Riverhead

Hobbs Cl

THE DENE

Dean
Surgery

Hook Lane

Petersfield Rd

Water Lane

B3047

Bishop's
Sutton

Manor
House Farm

Tegg Down Road

Parkside Lane

Park La

Old Park Road

Common Farm

Old Park Wood

Old Park Road

Cheriton
Wood

Bramdean
Common

G H J K L M

231

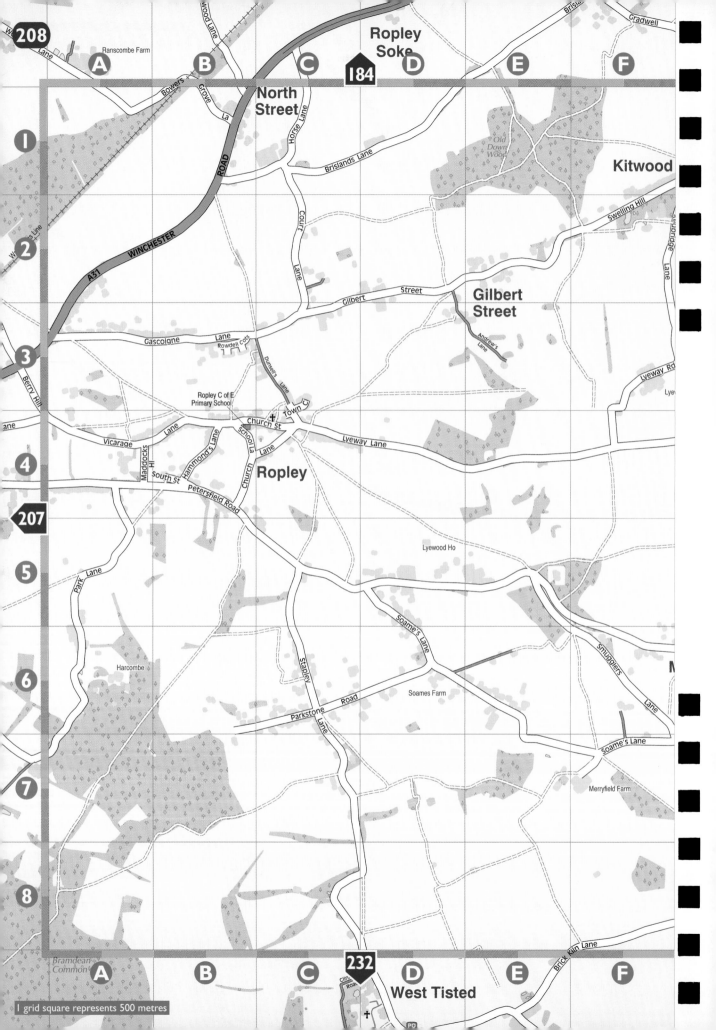

G H J **185** K L M

I

2

3

4

210

5

6

7

8

Hawthorn

Mary Lane

Newton Common

Plash Wood

Kitfield Farm

Hawthorn Road

Alton Lane

Lane

Kitwood Road

Kitwood Lane

Dogford Wood

Hawthorn Road

Rotherfield Park

Lyeway Lane

...way Farm

Winchester Wood

Ropley Road

Green Lane

Charlwood Lane

Plain Farm

Charlwood

Plaindell

A32

Monkwood

Petersfield Road

Hill Farm Road

Petersfield Road

Hill Farm Road

West Tisted Common

Brewers Lane

Woodside Farm

Reckste...

Brick Kiln Farm

Brick Kiln Lane

Lane End

233

Colemore Common

G H J **233** K L M

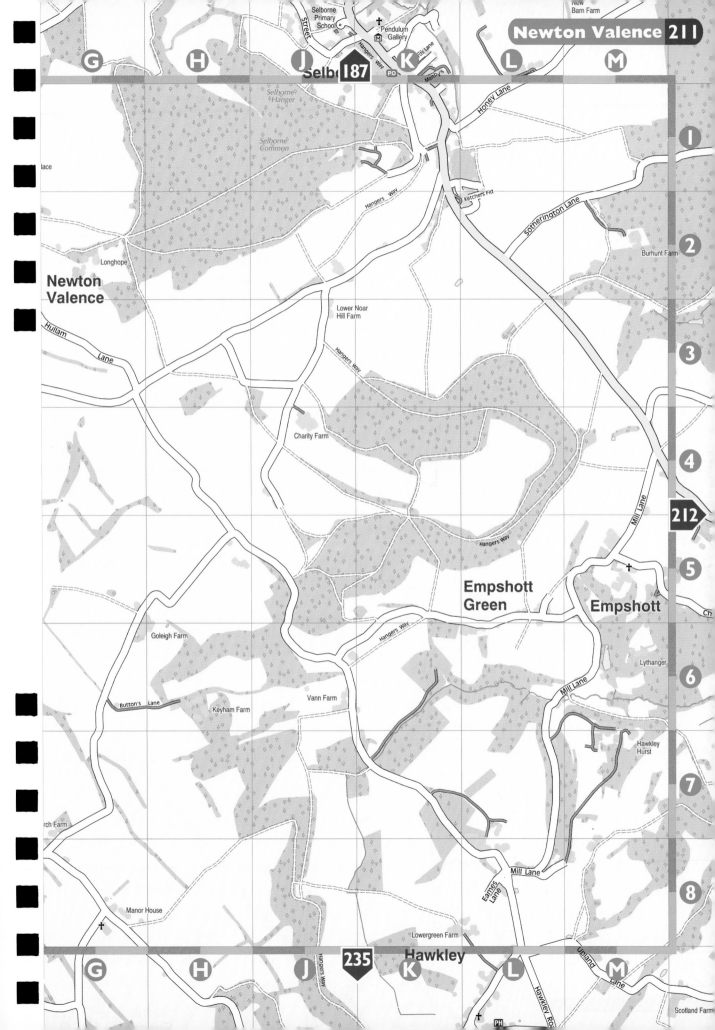

G H J K L M

Selborne
Primary
School

Pendulum
Gallery

Selbo 187
PO

New
Barn Farm

Honey Lane

1

Ketchers Fld

Sotherington Lane

Burhunt Farm 2

Longhope

Newton
Valence

Hullam
Lane

Lower Noar
Hill Farm

3

Hangers Way

Selborne
Hanger

Selborne
Common

Hangers Way

4

212

Charity Farm

Empshott
Green

Empshott 5

Hangers Way

Mill Lane

Ch

Lythanger 6

Goleigh Farm

Hangers Way

Button's Lane

Keyham Farm

Vann Farm

Mill Lane

Hawkley
Hurst

7

rch Farm

Eames
Lane

Mill Lane

8

Manor House

Lowergreen Farm

Hawkley Road

Upland
Lane

Hangers Way

235 Hawkley

G H J K L M

Scotland Farm

PH

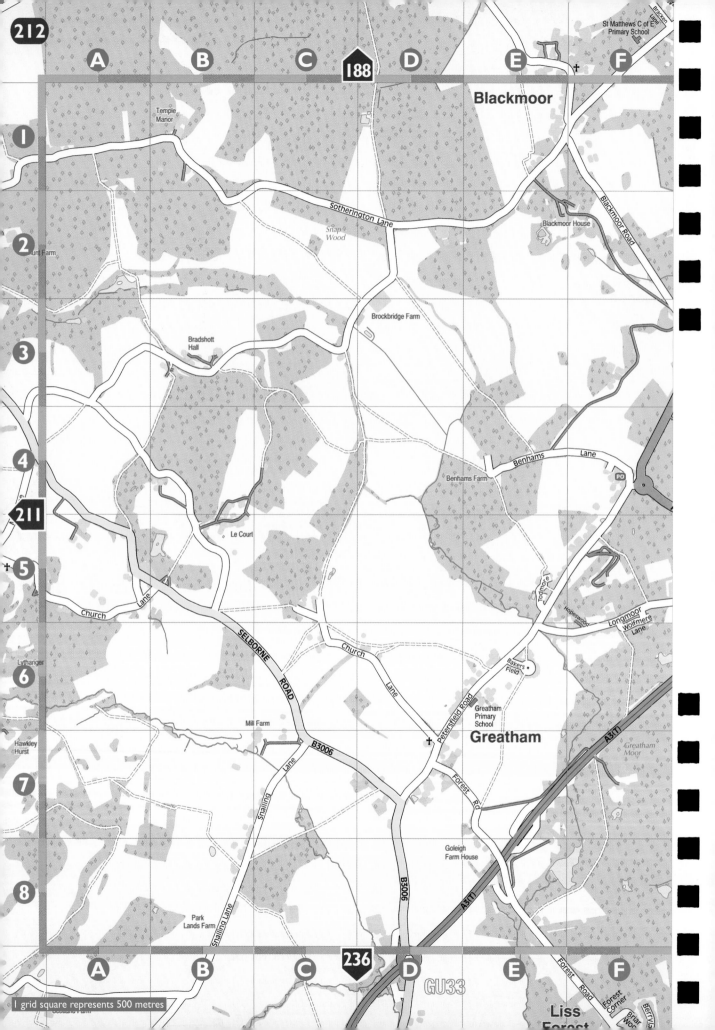

A B C 188 D E F

Blackmoor

St Matthews C of E
Primary School

1
Temple
Manor

Sotherington Lane

Snap
Wood

Blackmoor House

Blackmoor Road

2
Hunt Farm

Brockbridge Farm

3
Bradshott
Hall

4
Benhams Lane

Benhams Farm

PO

Le Court

Todmore

5

Church Lane

Hopeswood

Longmoor
Wolfmere
Lane

Lythanger

SELBORNE ROAD

Church Lane

Bakers
Field

6
Mill Farm

Greatham
Primary
School

Petersfield Road

Greatham

A3(T)

Greatham
Moor

Hawkley
Hurst

B3006

7
Snailing Lane

Forest Rd

8

Goleigh
Farm House

B3006

A3(T)

Park
Lands Farm

A B C 236 D GU33 E Forest Road F
Forest
Corner
Berry
Woo

Liss
Forest

I grid square represents 500 metres

189

214

G H J K L M

1
2
3
4
5
6
7
8

Liphook Road
Hollywater Road

Drift Rd

Cranmer Bottom

Linchborough Park

Brimstone Inclosure

Woolmer Forest

Forked Inclosure

PETERSFIELD ROAD
A325

Woolmer Pond

A325 WOOLMER ROAD

Longmoor Road

PORTSMOUTH ROAD

A3(T)

A3(T)

Road

Plumer Road

Railway Rd

French Rd

Kitchener Road

Methuen Rd

Roberts Rd

Warren Rd

Hunters Rd

Hamilton Rd

Longmoor Camp

White Avenue

Kimberley Rd

Baden Powell Rd

Union Rd

Pateson Rd

Pretoria

Ian Smuts Cl

Moor Road

Palmer's Ball

Longmoor Inclosure

Weavers Down

Queens Road

Sussex Border Path

The Wylds

A · B · C · 190 · D · E · F

213

238

E3
1 Allee Dr
2 Tylston Meadow

D4
1 Chalcraft Cl

A5
Bramshott
Court
1 Beechcroft Cl
2 Fairway Cl

A4
1 Longmoor Dr

Conford

Burgh Hill Road

HILL HOUSE HILL B3004

HEADLEY

Dryden Way

Tunbridge Lane

Bramshott Vale

Church Lane

Limes Close

Br

Hotel

A3(T)

Hunters Cha

Tunbridge Crs

Weyland Cl

ROAD B3004

B2171 ROAD

Forkedpond Inclosure

Hurst Close

Lark Rise

Avenue

Yeomans La

The

County Infant School

Liphook Junior School

Avenue Cl

Tower Road

Tower Rd

The Md

Meadow Wy

Meadow Cl

Malthouse Mdw

Calvecroft

Matthouse Mdw

LONDON

Longmoor Road

Forest Lane Close

Longmoor Road

Longmoor Road

Griggs Green

moor Road

Pines Road

Hazeldene Rd

Birchott Rd

Bohunt Community School

The Cv

Contour Gallery

Chappel Rd

Grenville

Chittie Mnr

PO

Old Thorns Golf & Country Club

Road

LIPHOOK

The Ship House Surgery

Court Cl

Field

Midhurst Rd

Newtown Road

Larch Cl

The Firs

Fletchers Fld

Newtown Road

Beaver Industrial Est

Bohunt Manor

Newtown

Foley Manor

Station Rd

Newtown Surg

Liphook Stn

Gunns Farm

Gunns Farm

PORTSMOUTH ROAD

Admers Crescent

Hollycombe Cl

Chittley

Forest Mere

B2070

Wheatsheaf Common

GU30

PORTSMOUTH RD

B2070

Home Park

Sussex

Border Path

Liphook Golf Club

Sussex Border

Shu

Border Path

A · B · C · 238 · D · E · F

E4
1 Childerstone Cl

E5
1 Shipley Ct

F3
1 Greenfield Cl

F4
1 Erles Rd

Hatch Farm

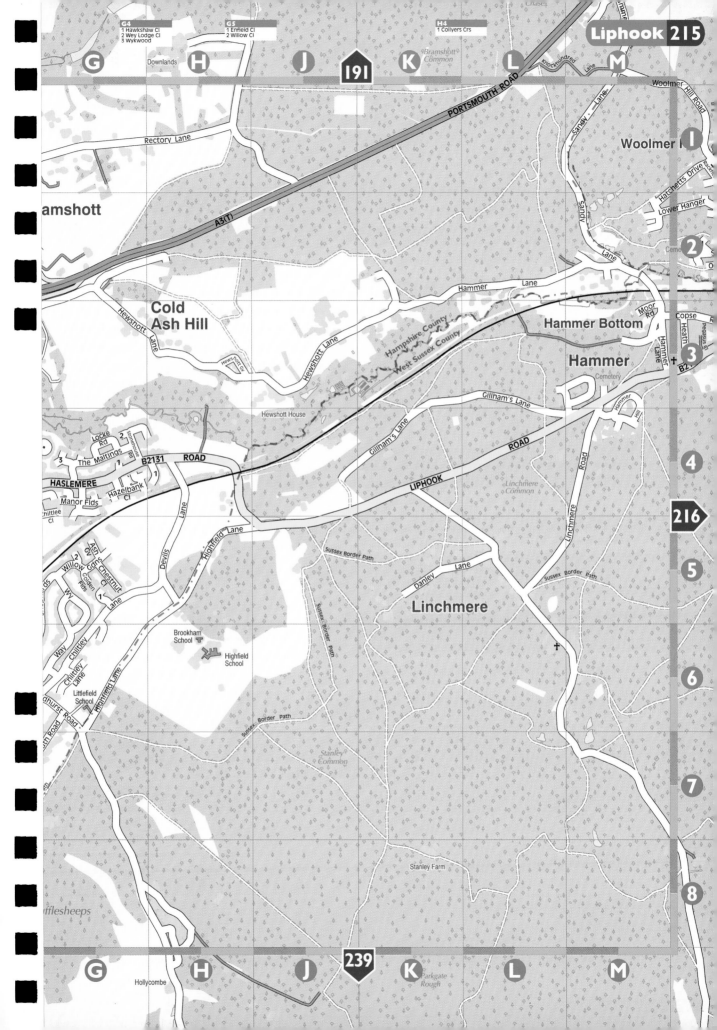

G4
1 Hawkshaw Cl
2 Wey Lodge Cl
3 Wykwood

G5
1 Enfield Cl
2 Willow Cl

H4
1 Collyers Crs

G Downlands **H** **J** **191** **K** Bramshott Common **L** **M** **I** Woolmer I

PORTSMOUTH ROAD

Woolmer Hill Road

Rectory Lane

Sandy Lane

Hatchetts Drive

Lower Hanger

A3(T)

amshott

Sandy Lane

2

Hammer Lane

Copse R

Cold Ash Hill

Hewshott Lane

Hampshire County

West Sussex County

Hammer Bottom

Moor Rd

Hammer Lane

Heath

Pegasus Ct

3

Hammer

B2

Hewshott Ln

Hews'ott Cv

Cemetery

+

Gillham's Lane

Hewshott House

Hammer Hill

Locke Rd

Stonehouse Rd

2

Gillham's Lane

LIPHOOK ROAD

Linchmere Road

4

The Maltings

B2131 **ROAD**

1

3

1

Hazelbank Cl

Linchmere Common

HASLEMERE

Manor Flds

Devils Lane

Highfield Lane

216

Chiltlee Cl

Sussex Border Path

5

Ash's Cv

Chestnut Lane

Danley Lane

Sussex Border Path

2

Willow Colden

1

Colden Flds

Way

Linchmere

+

Chiltley Way

Brookham School

Highfield School

Chiltley Lane

6

Littlefield School

Highfield Lane

Sussex Border Path

hurst Road

7

Stanley Common

8

Stanley Farm

ffleshheeps

G Hollycombe **H** **J** **239** **K** Parkgate Rough **L** **M**

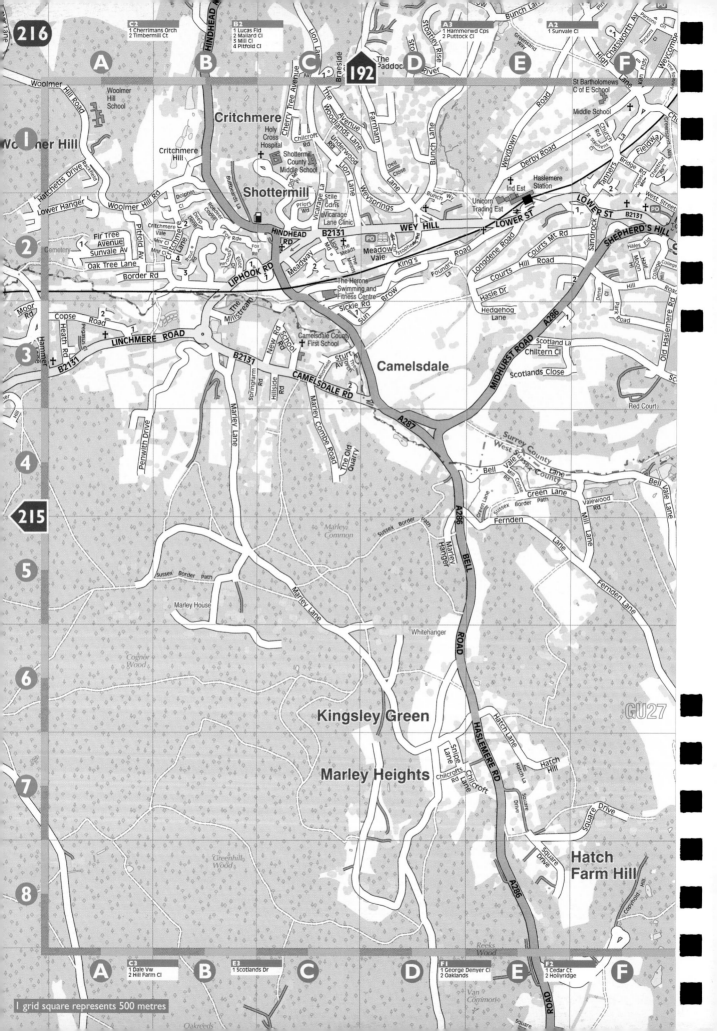

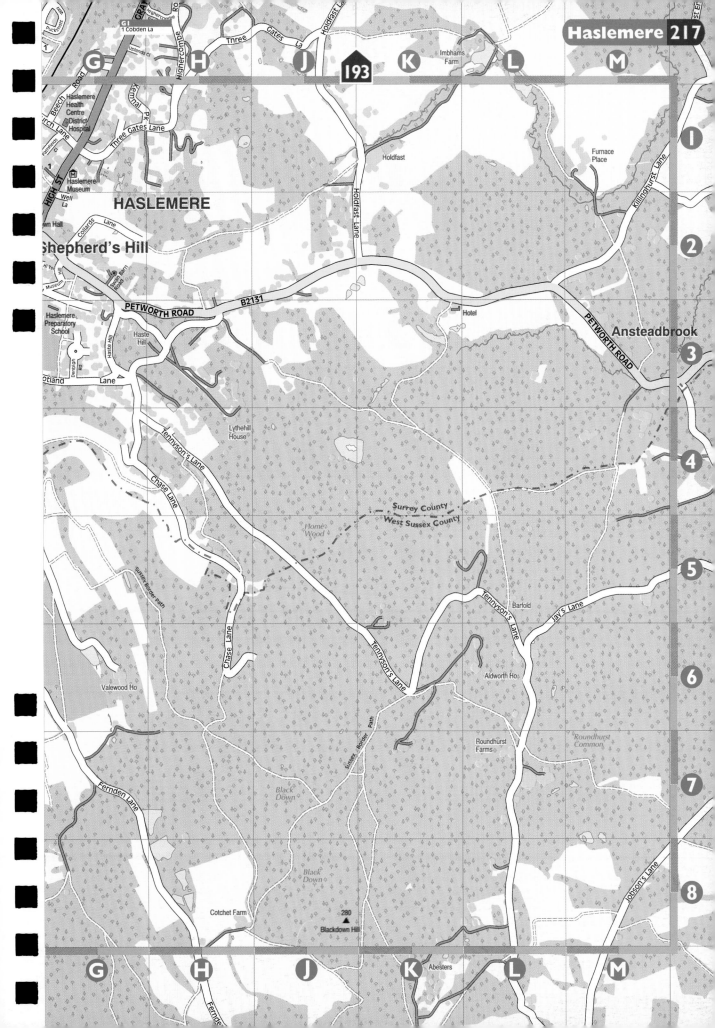

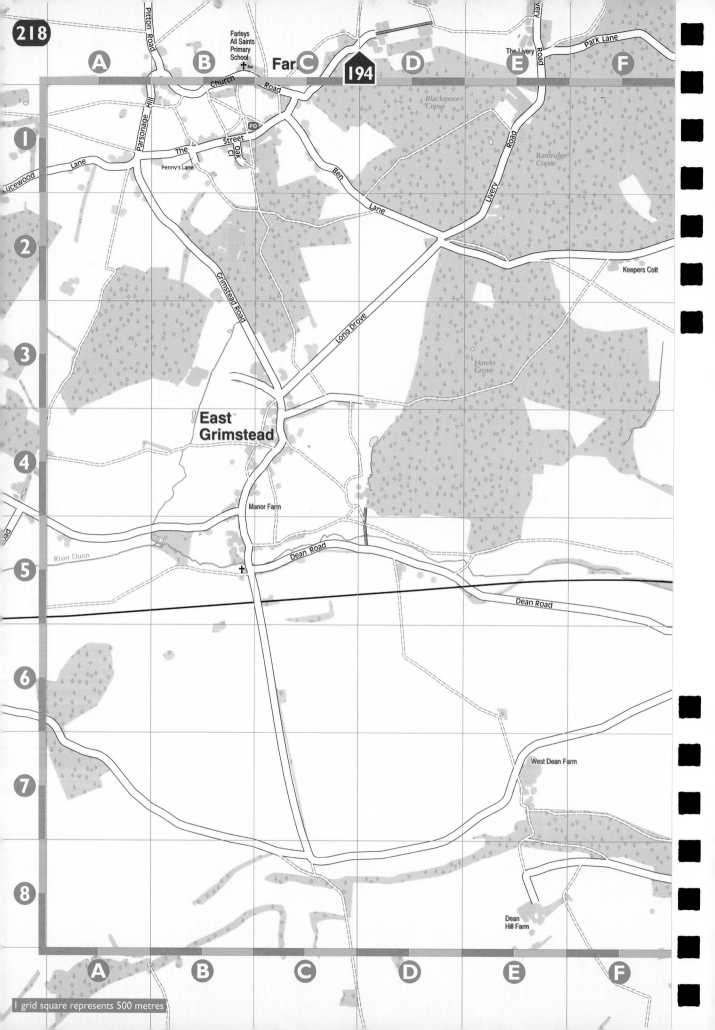

Pitton Road

Farleys
All Saints
Primary
School

Far C

194

The Livery

Road

Park Lane

Church Road

A

B

C

D

E

F

Blackmoor
Copse

Parsonage Hill

PO

Street

The

Oak

Penny's Lane

Lane

Lucewood

Lane

Ben

Lane

Livery Road

Barnridge
Copse

1

Grimstead Road

Long Drove

2

Keepers Cott

3

Hawks
Grove

**East
Grimstead**

4

Manor Farm

River Dunn

Dean Road

Dean Road

5

6

West Dean Farm

7

8

Dean
Hill Farm

A

B

C

D

E

F

I grid square represents 500 metres

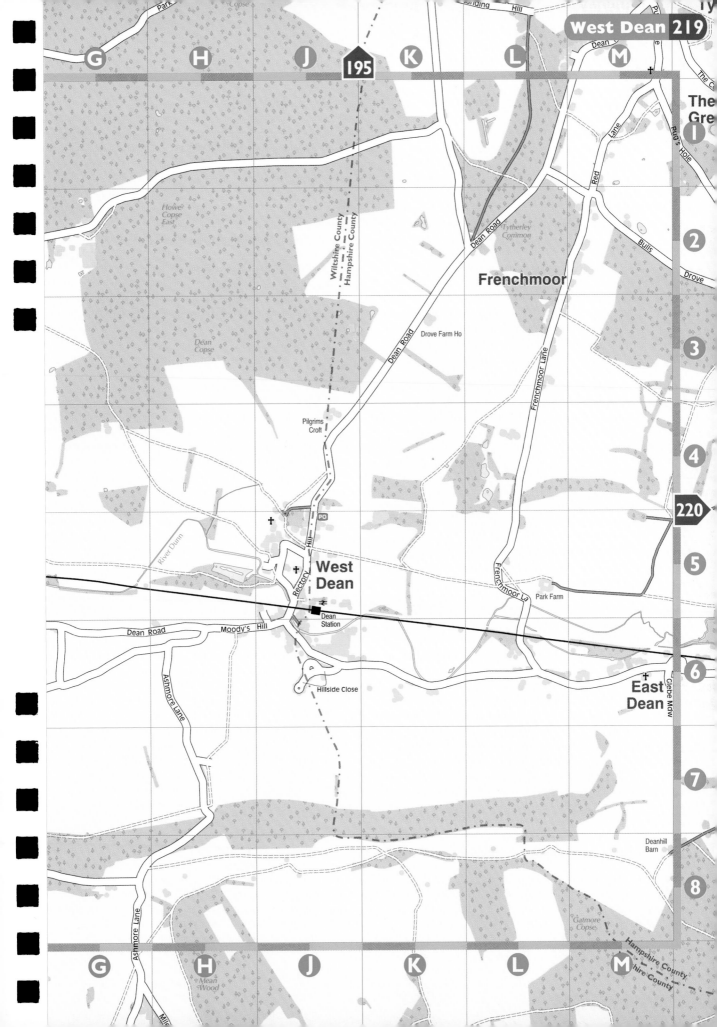

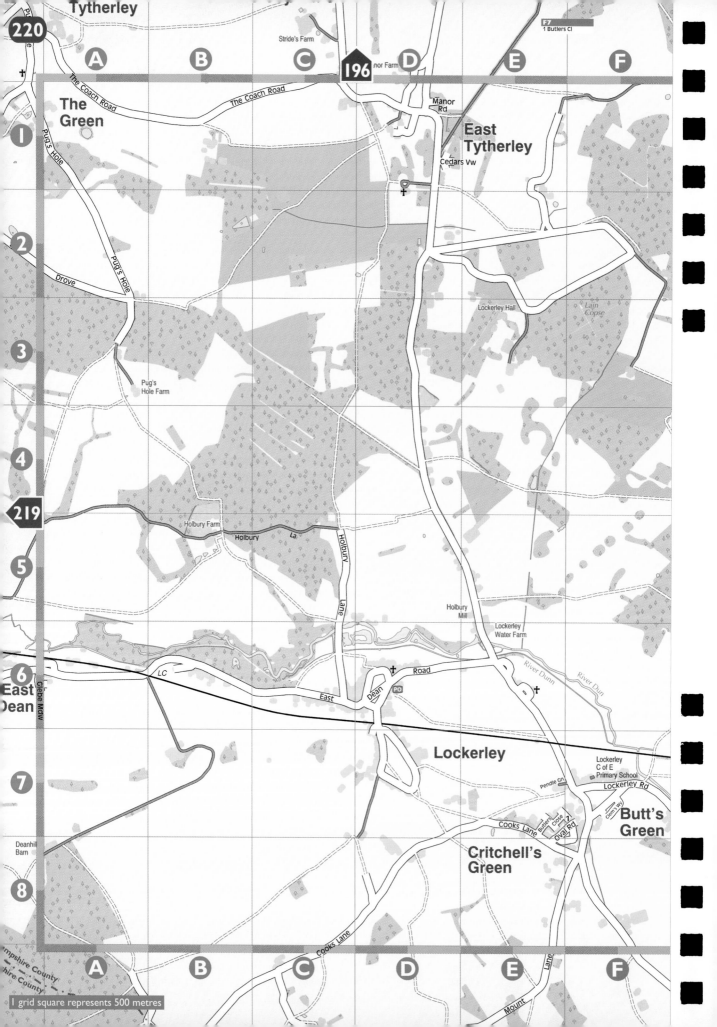

Tytherley

Stride's Farm

196

F7
1 Butlers Cl

The Coach Road

The Coach Road

The Green

East
Tytherley

Manor Farm

Manor
Rd

Cedars Vw

Pug's Hole

Drove

Lockerley Hall

Lain
Copse

3

Pug's
Hole Farm

4

219

Holbury Farm

Holbury   La

Holbury
Lane

Holbury
Mill

5

Lockerley
Water Farm

River Dunn

River Dun

6

East
Dean

Glebe Mdw

LC

East   Dean   Road

PO

Lockerley

7

Lockerley
C of E
Primary School

Pendle Gn

Lockerley Rd

Clem's Wy

Butlers
Close

Oval Rd

Butt's
Green

Deanhill
Barn

Cooks Lane

Critchell's
Green

8

ampshire County
hire County

Cooks Lane

Mount   Lane

197

222

Pittleworth

Bentley Farms

B3084

Back Lane

Spearywell Wood

River Test

Cadbury Fm

Oakley Fm

Test Way

Spearywell

Test Way

Oakley Rd

Mottisfont Abbey

Mottisfont Abbey Garden House & Estate (NT)

A3057

Keepers Lane

Benger's Lane

B3084

Mottisfont Club House

Hatt Lane

PO

Church Lane

Mottisfont

Hatt Hill

Church Lane

Stonym

LC

Dunbridge Station

Dunbridge

PH

Russell Dr

Mill Rise

River Dun

Lockerley Road

Canefield

DUNBRIDGE LANE

Monarch's Way

Kimbridge Lane

SP

River Test

Kimbridge

The LC

Kimbri

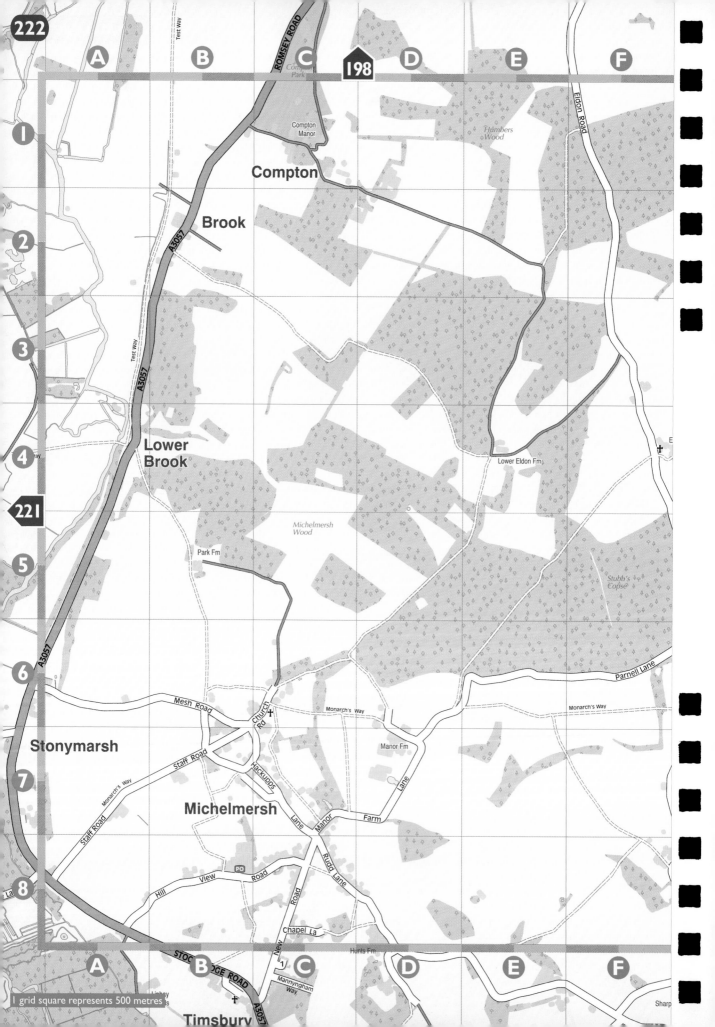

A B C 198 D E F

I

2

3

4

221

5

6

7

8

A B C D E F

Compton

Brook

Lower Brook

Stonymarsh

Michelmersh

Timsbury

ROMSEY ROAD

Compton Park

Compton Manor

Humbers Wood

Eldon Road

Test Way

A3057

A3057

A3057

Lower Eldon Fm

Michelmersh Wood

Park Fm

Stubb's Copse

Parnell Lane

Monarch's Way

Mesh Road

Church Rd

Monarch's Way

Manor Fm

Staff Road

Hackubbs Lane

Lane

Farm Lane

Manor Lane

Rudd Lane

Monarch's Way

PO

Hill View Road

New Road

chapel La

Hunts Fm

Mannyngham Way

STOCKBRIDGE ROAD

Sharp

1 grid square represents 500 metres

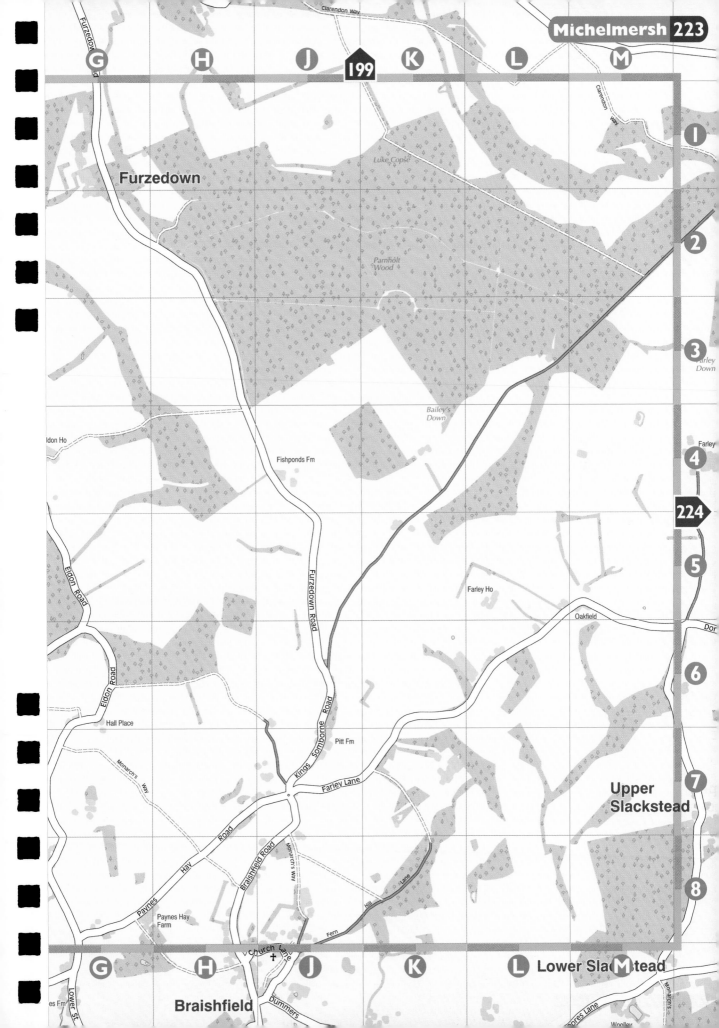

Farley Mount

A **B** **C** 200 **D** **E** **F**

Clarendon Way

Clarendon Way

Wood

Farley Mount
Country Park

Pitt
Down

Farley Mount Road

I

Mount
Down

2

3

Farley
Down

4 Farley Fm

Berrydown Farm

South
Lynch

Dores Lane

5

Southlynch
Plantn

Farley

6

Gudge
Copse

Merdon Manor Farm

Dores   Lane

7

ckstead

8

Dores   Lane

A Claypi **B** **C** **D** Home Farm **E** **F**

Hursley Park

I grid square represents 500 metres

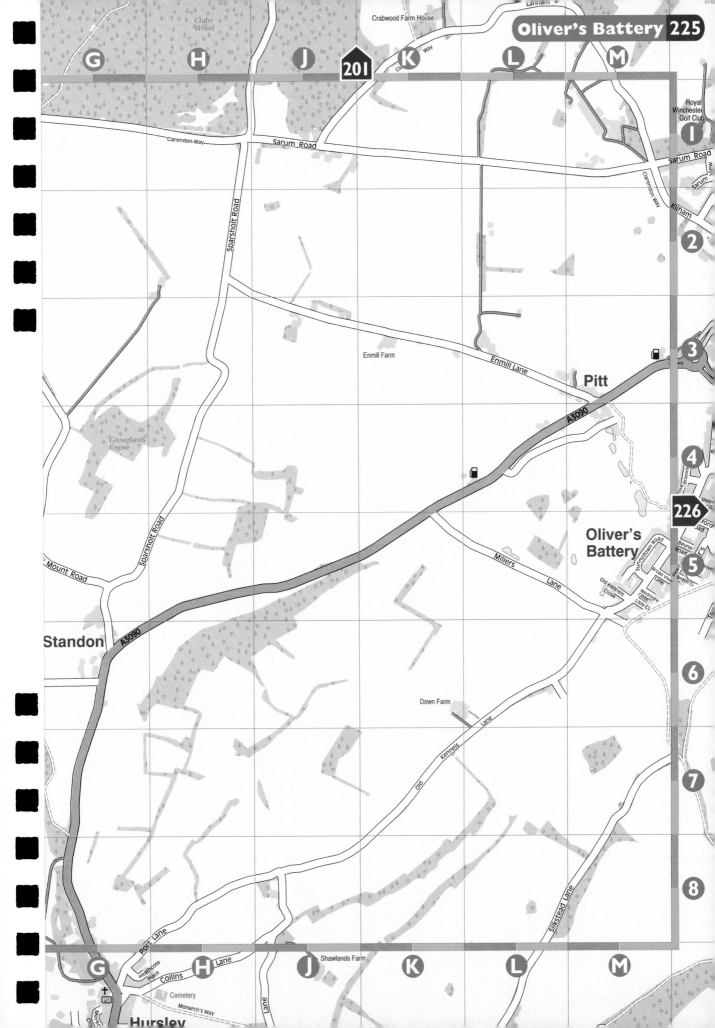

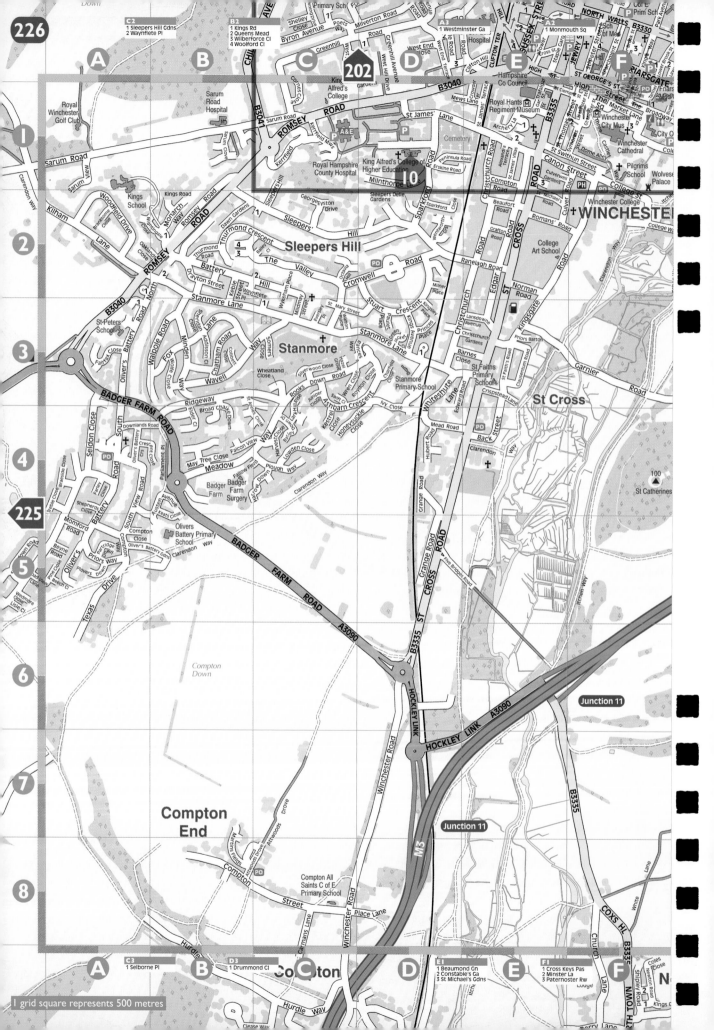

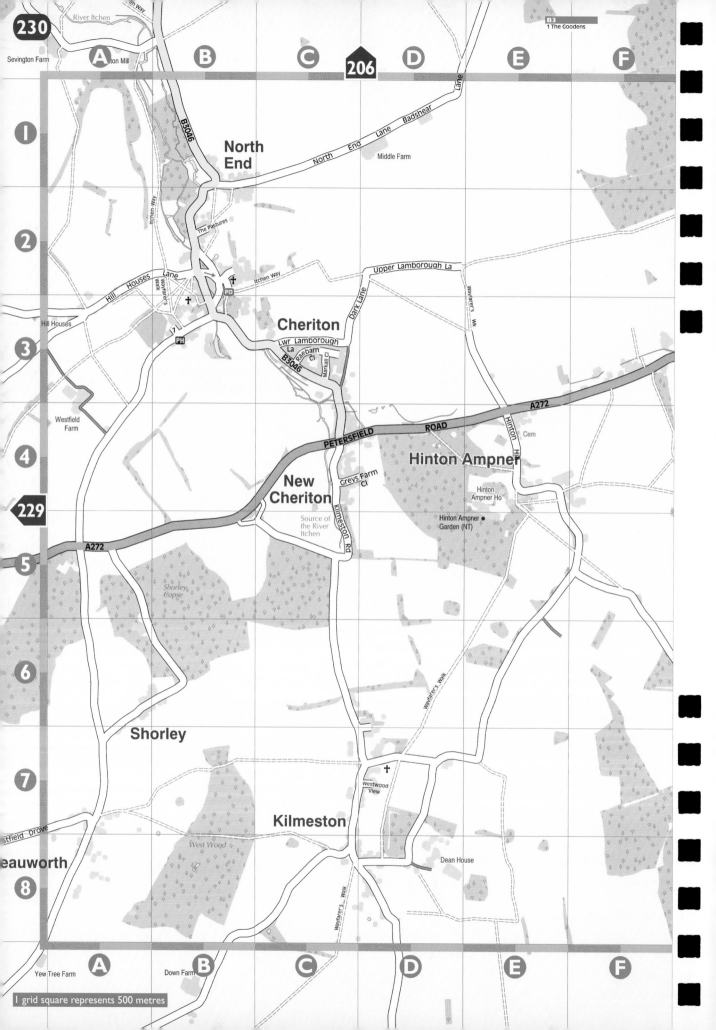

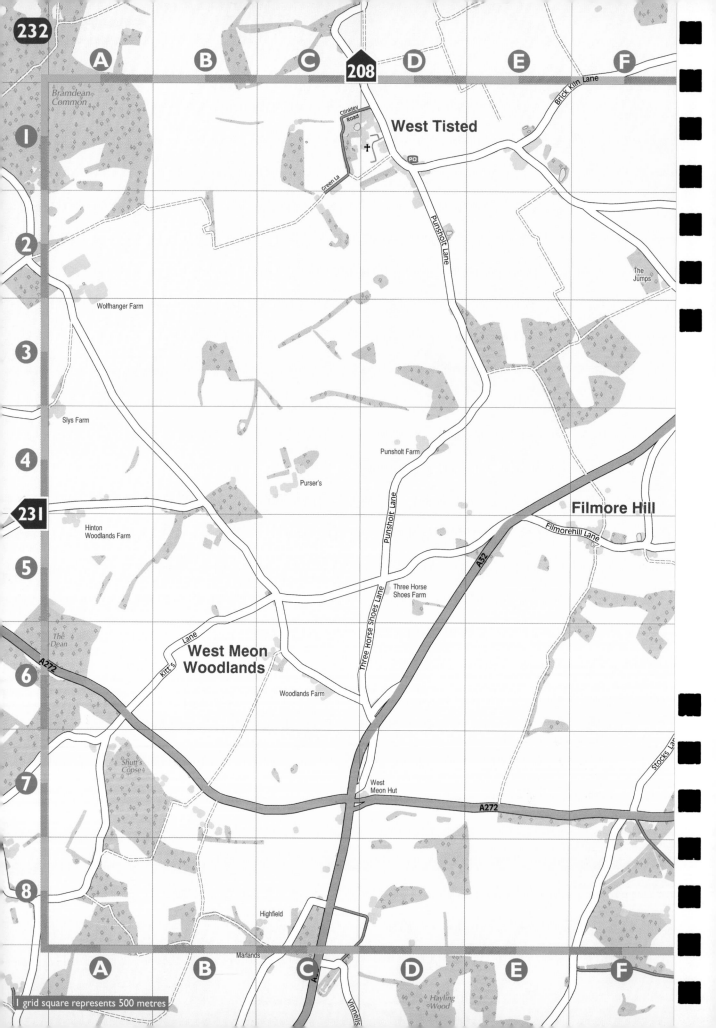

232

208

A   B   C   D   E   F

Brick Kiln Lane

Bramdean Common

West Tisted

Clinkley Road

PO

Green La

Punsholt Lane

The Jumps

Wolfhanger Farm

Slys Farm

Punsholt Farm

231

Filmore Hill

Filmorehill Lane

Hinton Woodlands Farm

Purser's

Punsholt Lane

A32

Three Horse Shoes Farm

Three Horse Shoes Lane

The Dean

A272

Lane

Kitt's

West Meon Woodlands

Woodlands Farm

Stocks Lane

Shutt's Copse

West Meon Hut

A272

Highfield

Marlands

Hayling Wood

Vinnells

A   B   C   D   E   F

1 grid square represents 500 metres

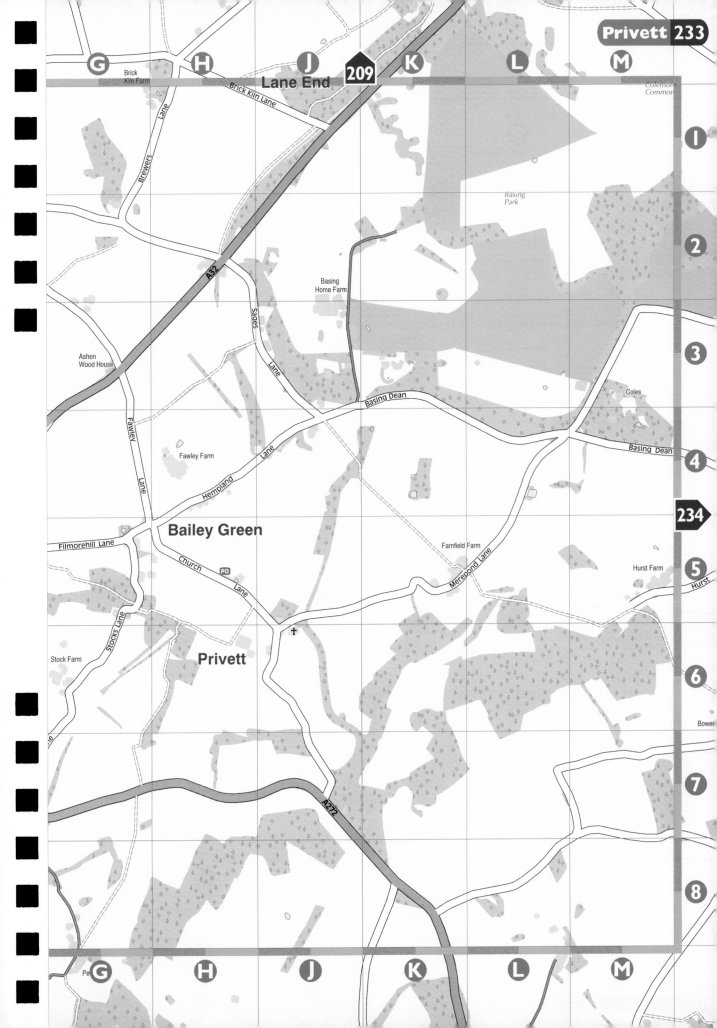

209

Lane End

G H J K L M

Brick Kiln Farm
Brick Kiln Lane

Colemore Common

Brewers Lane

Basing Park

A32

Sages Lane

Basing Home Farm

Ashen Wood House

Fawley Lane

Fawley Farm

Basing Dean

Coles

Basing Dean

Hempland Lane

Bailey Green

Filmorehill Lane

Church Lane

PO

Farnfield Farm

Merepond Lane

Hurst Farm

Hurst

Stocks Lane

Stock Farm

Privett

✝

Bower

A272

Pe

G H J K L M

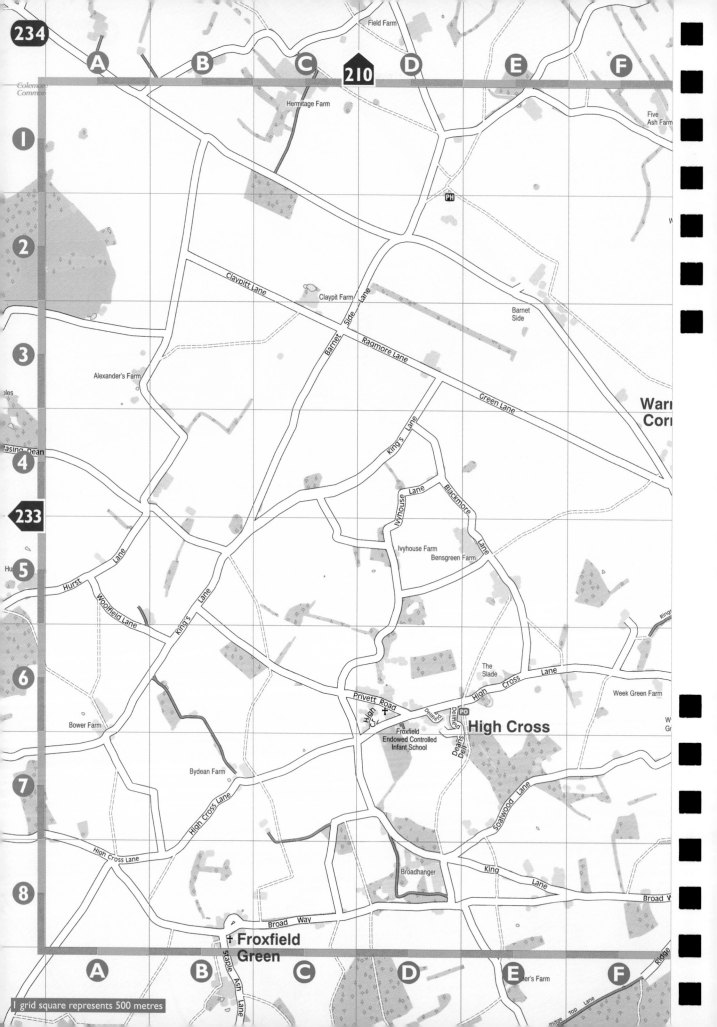

Colemore
Common

A **B** **C** 210 **D** **E** **F**

Field Farm

1

Hermitage Farm

PH

Five
Ash Farm

2

Claypitt Lane

Claypit Farm

Barnet
Side

Barnet Side Lane

Ragmore Lane

Barnet
Side

3

Alexander's Farm

bles

Green Lane

Warr
Corr

asing Dean

4

King's Lane

233

Ivyhouse Lane

Blackmore Lane

Ivyhouse Farm

Bensgreen Farm

Hu

5

Hurst Lane

Woolfield Lane

King's Lane

6

Bower Farm

The
Slade

High Cross Lane

Week Green Farm

W
Gr

Privett Road

High
Cr

Dellfield

Dellfield

PO

High Cross

Froxfield
Endowed Controlled
Infant School

Deans
Dell

7

Bydean Farm

High Cross Lane

Spalwood Lane

High Cross Lane

Broadhanger

King Lane

8

Broad Way

Froxfield
Green

Staple Ash Lane

er's Farm

Ridge

Ridge Top Lane

Broad W

A **B** **C** **D** **E** **F**

I grid square represents 500 metres

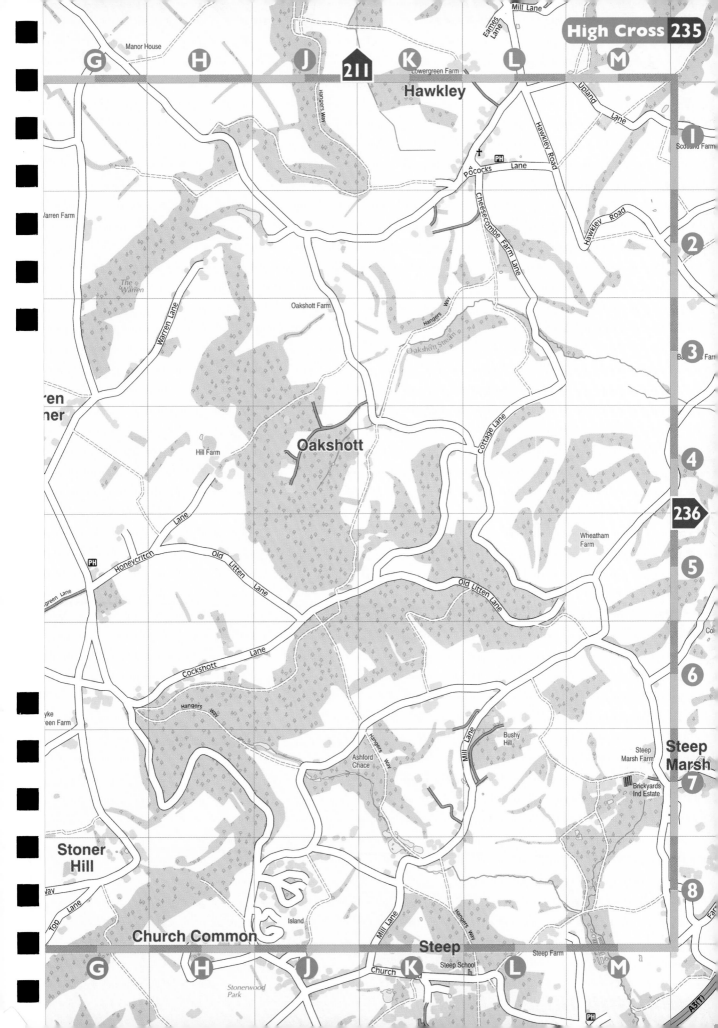

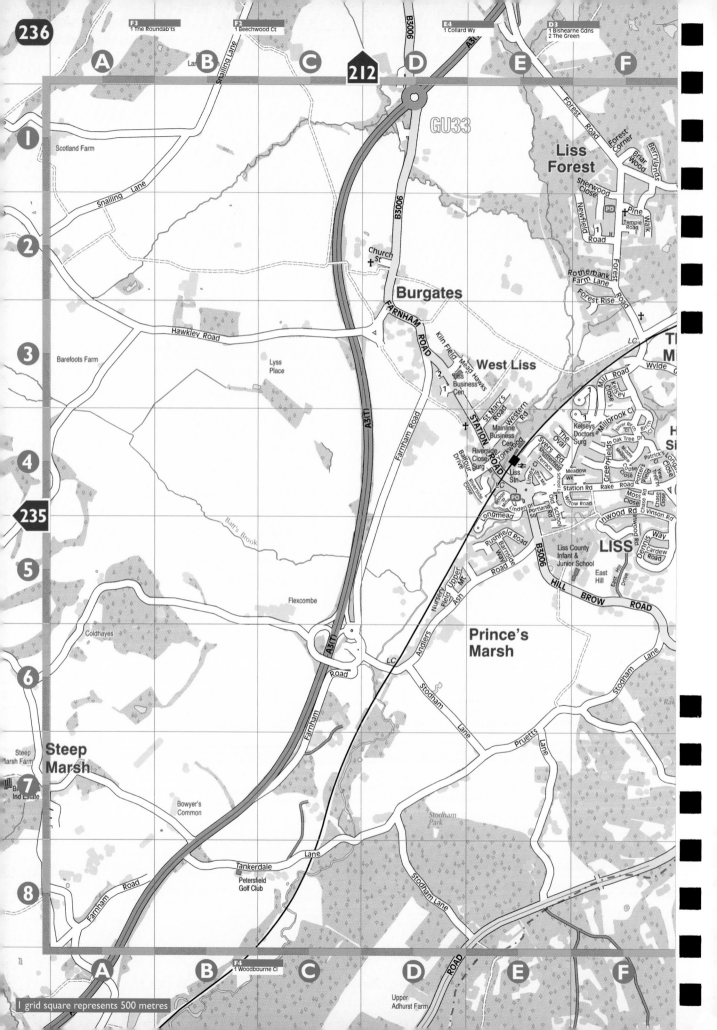

I

2

3

4

238

5

6

7

8

Warren Road

The Wylds

Mangers

Reeds Lane
Reeds Lane
Brewells Lane

Mint Road

Duckmead Lane

Palmers

Warren Road

Langley

Sussex Border Path

Langley Court

Rake Firs

Hampshire County
West Sussex County

Green Lane

Rake Road

The Point

Ciddy Hall

St   Patrick's   Lane

St Patrick's Lane

Rake C of E Controlled First School

B2070

ill de

Acre Barn Place
Highfield Gdns
The Ridings

Hatch   Lane

Primrose Lane

Rake

Bull Hill

PO

The Club House

Sandy Lane

Canhouse Lane

Goldring

Canhouse

East Liss

Woodlands Lane

Huntsbottom Lane

Hampshire County
West Sussex County
B2070

Sussex Border Path

e Common

Malvern Road
Plantation Road

Hill Brow

Combe Road

Knowles Meadow

Clayton Court

Sussex Border Path

Harting Combe

Tullecombe

Durford Woo

Rogate

A B C **214** D

Liphook Golf Club

I

Home Park

Border Path

Sussex

Ripsley House

Milland Lane

B2070

Hatch Farm

2

Chapel Common

Milland House

Upper Wardley

3

Maysleith

Wa

4

Maysleith Wood

Hollycomb School

Mill Farm

5

Mill Vale Meadows

Fernhurst Road

Stretton's Copse

Overland

Milland

6

Great Trippetts Farm

Chorley Common

Rake Road

Drakewls End

Pennels

Meade

Milland

Iping Road

Lyford Farm

Waldergrove Farm

Canhouse Lane

Rake Road

7

New Barn Farm

Cook's Pond Road

Bobbolds Farm

8

A **Trotten Marsh** B C D E F

Borden Wood

Stream

Kingsham Wood

Rol

G H J **215** K L M

fflesheeps

Hollycombe

Stanley Farm

Parkgate
Rough

I

2

Home
Farm

Minepit
Copse

3

Elmers
Marsh

rdley

Elmers
Copse

4

Northend Farm

Upper North
Park Farm

Linch Road

Woodmansgreen

5

Lambourne Lane

6

Inholms
Copse

Redford

7

Lambourne Lane

PO

Hurst
Farm

Titty Hill

Woolbeding
Common

8

Iping Road

Queen's
Corner

G H J K L M

 oins

Abbots Worthy 203 J2
Abbotstone 181 L6
Abbotts Ann 129 K5
Aldermaston 29 J1
Aldermaston Soke 30 C5
Aldermaston Wharf 17 M5
Aldershot 6 F1
Alton 164 D5
Amport 128 F3
Andover 9 J5
Andover Down 107 M8
Andwell 94 F3
Anna Valley 130 C3
Ansteadbrook 217 M3
Appleshaw 105 G2
Arborfield Garrison 35 K1
Arford 190 B2
Ash 101 K5
Ash Vale 101 K2
Ashe 89 K8
Ashford Hill 28 B7
Ashley 199 L5
Ashmansworth 63 L1
Avington 204 D3
Axford 139 H5
Axmansford 48 F1
Badshot Lea 123 M2
Bagmore 140 F2
Bagshot 20 C1
Bagshot 39 M5
Bailey Green 233 H5
Ball Hill 23 M5
Bar End 227 G2
Barford 169 H8
Barton Stacey 155 J2
Basingstoke 4 C6
Batt's Corner 168 A1
Baughurst 49 G1
Beacon Hill 192 A1
Beauworth 229 M8
Beech 163 M7
Beech Hill 32 F3
Beenham 17 J2
Beenham Stocks 17 L2
Bentley 144 B3
Bentworth 162 E3
Bidden 118 C1
Bighton 183 H7
Binley 63 L8
Binstead 166 D1
Bishop's Green 26 D5
Bishop's Sutton 207 G4
Black Dam 93 J5
Blackmoor 212 E1
Blacknest 167 J1
Blackwater 58 A4
Bordon 189 H5
Bossington 198 A5
Boundstone 146 E4
Bowling Alley 98 B8
Bradley 140 A8
Bramdean 231 H3
Bramley 51 K4
Bramley Corner 51 G5
Bramley Green 51 M6
Bramshill 54 E1
Bramshott 214 F2
Bransbury 132 F7
Brighton Hill 92 C8
Brimpton 28 B2
Brimpton Common 28 F6
Broad Layings 24 B7
Broad Oak 96 F4
Broadmere 115 J4
Brock's Green 46 D1
Brook 222 B2
Broughton 197 H2
Brown Candover 160 A5
Browninghill Green 49 J5
Bucks Horn Oak 145 K8
Buckskin 91 M4
Burgates 236 D2
Burghclere 45 J1
Burghclere Common 25 K7
Burghfield 19 M3
Burghfield Common 19 K6
Burghfield Hill 19 M5
Bury's Bank 26 B1
Buttermere 41 H1
Butt's Green 220 F7
Camberley 59 H1
Camelsdale 216 D3
Chandlers Green 53 J6
Charlton 106 D6
Charlwood 209 H5
Charter Alley 49 L8
Chawton 186 C1
Cheriton 230 C3
Chilbolton 153 M4
Chilbolton Down 176 D2
Chilcomb 227 L3
Chilton Candover 160 D3
Chineham 71 L5
Cholderton 126 B7
Church Common 235 G8
Church Crookham 98 E3
Church End 72 B2
Church Oakley 90 D6
Churt 169 J7
Chute Cadley 82 C1
Chute Standen 60 A8
Clanville 105 J1
Clarken Green 90 C6
Clatford Oakcuts 151 M4
Cliddesden 115 L1
Cold Ash 14 F1
Cold Ash Hill 215 H3
Cole Henley 87 J5
Colemore 210 C6
College Town 38 B8
Colt Hill 96 E5
Colthrop 15 L5
Combe 42 A2
Compton 123 J7
Compton 222 B1
Compton End 226 B7
Conford 214 C1
Cottonworth 153 K4

Couch Green 204 B1
Court Corner 50 A5
Cove 78 B2
Cranbourne 92 E6
Crawley 177 G6
Crawley Hill 59 H3
Cricket Hill 57 H3
Critchell's Green 220 E8
Critchmere 216 B1
Crockham Heath 24 C2
Crondall 121 H1
Crookham 27 L3
Crookham Village 98 B2
Crosswater 169 H4
Crossways 169 H7
Crowthorne 37 J4
Crux Easton 63 M3
Cuckoo's Corner 143 K8
Cufaude 71 K1
Daneshill 5 M2
Darby Green 57 K2
Deadwater 189 L5
Dean 201 K5
Deane 89 M7
Deepcut 79 M2
Dipley 54 D8
Dippenhall 122 A6
Dockenfield 168 C2
Dogmersfield 97 M2
Donnington 13 G2
Dora's Green 121 M3
Dry Hill 184 D3
Dummer 114 C7
Dunbridge 221 H7
Dunley 64 F8
Earlstone Common 25 J8
East Anton 107 H4
East Aston 133 J1
East Cholderton 128 C2
East Dean 219 M6
East End 43 K1
East Fields 3 G6
East Green 145 H2
East Grimstead 218 B4
East Liss 237 G5
East Oakley 91 H6
East Stratton 158 F4
East Tisted 210 B3
East Tytherley 220 E1
East Winterslow 170 E8
East Woodhay 43 H1
East Worldham 165 K7
Easton 203 M3
Eastrop 5 J9
Ecchinswell 46 D5
Egbury 86 B2
Egypt 156 C3
Ellisfield 116 A8
Elmers Marsh 239 K3
Elvetham 76 A3
Empshott 211 M5
Empshott Green 211 L5
Enborne 12 C8
Enborne Row 24 E4
Enham Alamein 107 H1
Eversley 35 L7
Eversley Centre 36 A8
Eversley Cross 36 C8
Ewshot 98 F8
Faberstown 81 G7
Faccombe 42 A7
Fair Oak 48 B1
Fair Oak Green 52 A2
Farleigh Wallop 115 K6
Farley 194 C8
Farley Hill 35 G3
Farnborough 78 D5
Farnborough Green 78 F3
Farnborough Park 79 G5
Farnborough Street 78 F3
Farnham 123 G7
Filmore Hill 232 F4
Finchampstead 36 A5
Firsdown 194 A1
Fleet 76 F7
Folly Hill 122 D3
Forton 132 E4
Fosbury 40 C7
Four Houses Corner 19 H8
Four Marks 185 H6
Fox Lane 58 C7
Foxdown 89 H6
Freefolk 110 D2
Frenchmoor 219 L2
Frensham 168 E1
Frimley 59 K6
Frimley Green 79 J1
Frimley Ridge 59 K5
Frithend 167 M5
Frogmore 57 L2
Froxfield Green 234 B8
Fulflood 10 B6
Fullerton 153 H5
Furzedown 223 G1
Fyfield 104 D6
Gilbert Street 208 E2
Gobley Hole 115 H8
Golden Pot 142 C5
Goldfinch Bottom 26 F3
Goodworth Clatford 130 E7
Goose Hill 27 L5
Gore End 23 L4
Grateley 127 M7
Grayshott 191 L5
Grayswood 193 K7
Great Shoddesden 103 M2
Greatham 212 E7
Green Cross 169 L7
Greenham 13 M8
Greywell 95 K5
Griggs Green 214 C4
Gundleton 207 J1
Hale 123 G3
Ham 41 M5
Hammer 215 M3
Hammer Bottom 215 L3
Hamstead Marshall 23 M1
Hannington 67 L4

Harestock 202 B5
Hartfordbridge 55 L8
Hartley Mauditt 187 K3
Hartley Wespall 53 C7
Hartley Wintney 75 K2
Haslemere 217 G2
Hatch 94 B3
Hatch Farm Hill 216 F8
Hatch Warren 114 F2
Hatherden 83 H7
Hatt Hill 221 J7
Hattingley 184 B1
Haughurst Hill 28 F7
Hawkley 235 K1
Hawley 58 B5
Hawley Lane 78 E1
Hawthorn 209 H1
Hazeley 54 D5
Hazeley Bottom 54 F7
Hazeley Lea 54 E5
Headbourne Worthy 202 E3
Headley 27 H7
Headley 190 A3
Headley Down 190 E4
Hearn 190 E1
Heath End 23 K7
Heath End 29 J7
Heath End 123 C1
Heath Green 183 M1
Heather Row 95 J2
Heatherside 59 M4
Heckfield 53 M2
Hell Corner 22 E3
Henley 40 D5
Herriard 116 E7
High Cross 234 E6
Highclere 44 C3
Highclere Street 44 A5
Hill Brow 237 H6
Hill Side 236 F4
Hillside 96 F6
Hindhead 192 C4
Hinton Ampner 230 D4
Hog Hatch 122 C2
Hollington 43 M4
Hollington Cross 44 A5
Hollywater 189 L7
Holt 74 C7
Holt End 162 F5
Holt Pound 146 A4
Holybourne 165 H1
Hook 74 A7
Horsebridge 198 B7
Houghton 198 B3
Hound Green 54 B5
Houndmills 92 D1
Hunton 156 F4
Hurstbourne Priors 109 H6
Hurstbourne Tarrant 84 D1
Hyde 11 H5
Hyde End 28 B4
Ibthorpe 62 B8
Ibworth 68 E6
Inhurst 28 F8
Inkpen 21 M3
Inkpen Common 22 C3
Isington 144 D7
Itchen Abbas 204 D2
Itchen Stoke 205 J2
Kempshott 91 M7
Kiff Green 16 E2
Kilmeston 230 C7
Kimbridge 221 K8
Kimpton 104 A6
King's Furlong 92 D4
King's Somborne 198 E5
Kings Worthy 203 H2
Kingsclere 47 H7
Kingsclere Woodlands 27 K8
Kingsley 166 F7
Kingsley Green 216 C6
Kitwood 208 F1
Knights Enham 106 F3
Lane End 169 G1
Lane End 229 H8
Lane End 233 J1
Langley 237 L2
Lasham 141 J6
Latchmere Green 50 F3
Laverstoke 111 H3
Leckford 153 J8
Linchmere 215 K5
Lindford 189 L4
Linkenholt 42 A7
Liphook 214 D5
Liss 236 F5
Liss Forest 236 E1
Litchfield 65 H8
Little Ann 129 M4
Little Hoddington 118 B3
Little London 50 C5
Little London 84 C8
Little Sandhurst 37 K6
Little Shoddesden 104 B2
Little Somborne 199 J2
Littledown 41 J8
Littleton 202 A3
Lockerley 220 D7
Long Park 177 K8
Long Sutton 119 K5
Longparish 133 G2
Longstock 174 D1
Lower Bourne 147 H2
Lower Brook 222 A4
Lower Bullington 155 M1
Lower Chute 82 A1
Lower Common 35 J7
Lower Common 140 A2
Lower Farringdon 186 C5
Lower Froyle 144 B3
Lower Green 21 L3
Lower Padworth 18 A3
Lower Wield 162 A2
Ludgershall 80 F5
Lyde Green 73 J1
Lynch 88 D3
Lynch Hill 110 C3
Maplederwell 94 D5

Marley Heights 216 C7
Marsh Benham 12 A5
Martyr Worthy 204 A2
Mattingley 54 A8
Medstead 184 D2
Micheldever 158 A5
Micheldever Station 136 A6
Michelmersh 222 B7
Middle Bourne 146 F2
Middle Wallop 150 D8
Middle Winterslow 194 F1
Middleton 132 F3
Midgham 16 B5
Midgham Green 16 E3
Miles's Green 15 M1
Mill Green 27 J5
Mill Lane 97 M7
Milland 238 D6
Millbridge 147 G7
Monk Sherborne 70 A2
Monkwood 208 F6
Montgomery Lines 100 F4
Monxton 129 H3
Moor Park 123 L7
Morestead 227 L8
Mortimer 31 K2
Mortimer West End 31 G4
Mottisfont 221 K6
Mullenspond 104 D8
Murrell Green 74 D5
Mytchett 79 H5
Mytchett Place 79 K6
Nash's Green 141 H1
Nately Scures 95 H1
Neatham 165 K2
Nether Wallop 173 G3
Netherton 42 C8
New Alresford 206 B2
New Cheriton 230 C4
Newbury 2 C4
Newfound 91 G5
Newnham 73 J8
Newton Stacey 154 D3
Newton Tony 148 A3
Newton Valence 211 G2
Newtown 25 L4
Newtown 164 C6
Newtown 214 E6
No Man's Land 203 L8
North Camp 100 E2
North End 23 J6
North End 230 B1
North Houghton 174 C8
North Oakley 67 K7
North Street 208 C1
North Tidworth 102 F1
North Town 101 H5
North Waltham 113 K6
North Warnborough 96 B4
Northbrook 157 L4
Northington 159 L8
Nutcombe 192 A6
Nutley 139 H3
Oakhanger 188 C4
Oakley 90 F7
Oakridge 4 E3
Oakshott 235 J4
Odiham 96 D6
Old Alresford 182 B7
Old Basing 93 M2
Old Burghclere 45 H8
Oliver's Battery 225 M5
Over Wallop 150 C6
Overton 112 A1
Ovington 205 K4
Owlsmoor 38 A6
Oxenwood 40 A5
Padworth 18 B7
Padworth Common 30 C2
Palestine 149 K2
Pamber End 50 A7
Pamber Green 50 B4
Pamber Heath 30 A6
Pardown 114 A2
Passfield 190 C7
Penton Corner 105 M7
Penton Grafton 105 K5
Penton Mewsey 105 M4
Penwood 44 C1
Perham Down 103 H1
Pheonix Green 74 F4
Picket Piece 107 M6
Pitt 225 M3
Plastow Green 47 K1
Pondtail 77 J8
Popham 137 K4
Popley 71 G7
Potbridge 74 F8
Pound Green 49 G5
Pound Street 44 F1
Powntley Copse 142 C3
Preston Candover 139 H8
Prince's Marsh 236 E6
Privett 233 H6
Pyott's Hill 71 M7
Quarley 127 M4
Queen's Corner 239 H8
Quidhampton 89 G7
Racedown 127 K2
Rafborough 78 B5
Ragged Appleshaw 105 H2
Rake 237 K4
Ramsdell 69 K1
Ravenswood Village
    Settlement 37 H2
Red Rice 130 B8
Redenham 104 F1
Redford 239 K7
Riseley 33 M5
Rivar 20 C8
Ropley 208 C4
Ropley Dean 207 M3
Ropley Soke 184 D8
Rotherwick 73 K3
Rotten Green 76 C3
Rowledge 146 C5
Runfold 123 M5

Rushmoor 169 M1
Salters Heath 50 C8
Sandhurst 37 L7
Sandy Cross 124 C4
Sarson 129 G2
Seale 124 E4
Selborne 187 J8
Shalbourne 20 C5
Shalden 141 M8
Shalden Green 141 M4
Shaw 13 L3
Shepherd's Hill 216 F2
Sherborne St John 70 C5
Sherfield on Loddon 52 D8
Shipton Bellinger 126 C1
Shorley 230 A7
Shortfield Common 146 E6
Shortheath 146 E2
Shortheath 188 D2
Shottermill 216 B2
Silchester 30 E8
Skinners Green 12 E8
Sladen Green 63 L7
Sleaford 167 K7
Sleepers Hill 226 C2
Smannell 107 K2
Soldridge 184 D6
South Farnborough 79 G7
South Ham 92 C5
South Tidworth 102 E4
South Town 184 D3
South View 4 E4
South Warnborough 118 F5
South Wonston 178 B3
Southington 111 L1
Southrope 141 H2
Southwood 77 L5
Spanish Green 52 E5
Sparsholt 201 H5
Spearywell 221 J5
Speen 12 F3
Spreakley 146 E8
St Cross 226 E3
St Giles's Hill 11 K8
St Mary Bourne 85 M7
Standford 189 M6
Standon 224 F6
Stanford End 33 H5
Stanmore 226 C3
Steep Marsh 235 M7
Steventon 113 G4
Stockbridge 174 E5
Stockcross 12 C3
Stoke 85 H4
Stoke Charity 156 F5
Stoner Hill 235 C8
Stony Batter 196 B8
Stony Heath 49 G7
Stonymarsh 221 M7
Stratfield Mortimer 32 A3
Stratfield Saye 32 E8
Stratfield Turgis 52 F4
Stroud Green 3 G7
Sulhampstead Abbots 19 J4
Sulhampstead
    Bannister Upper End 19 G3
Sulhamstead 18 E2
Sutton Scotney 156 C4
Swallowfield 34 A2
Swampton 85 L5
Swarraton 181 L1
Sydmonton 46 A8
Tadley 49 M1
Tangley 82 D2
Thatcham 14 F4
The Bourne 146 F2
The Butts 164 D6
The Common 194 F2
The Dene 62 E8
The Green 220 A1
The Mint 236 F3
The Mount 44 C1
The Ridges 36 E4
The Sands 124 B6
The Straits 166 F6
Three Ashes 51 G1
Thruxton 104 C8
Tichborne 205 M7
Tilford Common 147 L7
Tilford Reeds 147 L5
Tilly Down 104 F1
Titcomb 22 B1
Titty Hill 239 H8
Tongham 124 C2
Tot Hill 25 H7
Totford 159 M8
Towns End 48 D6
Trapshill 22 B4
Trash Green 19 K1
Tufton 110 A6
Tullecombe 237 K8
Tunworth 117 H2
Turgis Green 52 F5
Turner's Green 15 L1
Ufton Green 18 E3
Ufton Nervet 19 G4
Up Green 56 B2
Up Nately 95 G4
Up Somborne 199 M3
Upper Bucklebury 15 M2
Upper Bullington 134 B8
Upper Clatford 130 D4
Upper Common 139 L1
Upper Enham 84 A8
Upper Farringdon 186 E5
Upper Froyle 143 M6
Upper Green 22 A5
Upper Hale 122 E2
Upper Slackstead 223 M7
Upper Wardley 238 F3
Upper Wield 161 L6
Upper Woolhampton 16 E4
Upper Wootton 69 H6
Upton 61 L5
Upton Grey 117 M3
Vernham Bank 60 F2
Vernham Dean 61 G2
Vernham Row 40 E8

Vernham Street	41 J8	West End	146 C8	West Worldham	187 K1	Wildhern	83 K6	Woodcott	64 C6
Wadwick	86 B2	West End	184 A4	Weston Colley	157 K4	Wildmoor	72 D3	Woodhouse	107 H1
Wanborough	125 L2	West End Green	32 A3	Weston Corbett	117 L6	Wilsom	164 F4	Woodmancott	137 K7
Wardley	238 F4	West Fields	2 B5	Weston Patrick	117 M6	Wimble Hill	121 K6	Woodmansgreen	239 J5
Warnborough Green	96 A4	West Green	74 E3	Weybourne	6 C8	Winchester	11 G9	Woodspeen	12 D1
Warren Corner	121 M1	West Ham	92 C3	Weyhill	105 H6	Winchester	226 F2	Woolhampton	16 F6
Warren Corner	234 F3	West Heath	49 K7	Wheat Hold	48 B2	Winchfield	75 H6	Woolmer Hill	215 M1
Wash Common	25 G3	West Heath	78 B3	Wheatley	166 F3	Winchfield Hurst	75 K8	Woolton Hill	44 B1
Wash Water	24 E5	West Liss	236 E3	Wherwell	153 K2	Winklebury	92 A2	Wootton St Lawrence	91 J1
Wasing	29 G3	West Meon Woodlands	232 B6	Whitchurch	110 B3	Winnall	11 L6	Worting	91 M3
Water End	95 G2	West Stratton	158 D3	Whitehall	96 E2	Winslade	116 E3	Wrecclesham	146 C3
Weeke	10 B4	West Tisted	232 D1	Whitehill	189 H7	Wivelrod	163 H7	Wyck	165 M4
Well	120 B6	West Tytherley	196 C3	Whitehouse Green	19 K2	Wolverton	48 C7	Yateley	57 C2
West Dean	219 J5	West Winterslow	194 C3	Whitway	45 G4	Wolverton Common	48 D5	York Town	58 D4
West Down	153 L6	West Woodhay	22 F5	Wick Hill	36 D2	Wonston	156 E5		

USING THE STREET INDEX

Street names are listed alphabetically. Each street name is followed by its postal town or area locality, the Postcode District, the page number, and the reference to the square in which the name is found.

Abbottswood Cl *TADY* RG26 .... 49 L1 🔢

Some entries are followed by a number in a blue box. This number indicates the location of the street within the referenced grid square. The full street name is listed at the side of the map page.

GENERAL ABBREVIATIONS

ACC	ACCESS	CUTT	CUTTINGS	HOL	HOLLOW
ALY	ALLEY	CV	COVE	HOSP	HOSPITAL
AP	APPROACH	CYN	CANYON	HRB	HARBOUR
AR	ARCADE	DEPT	DEPARTMENT	HTH	HEATH
ASS	ASSOCIATION	DL	DALE	HTS	HEIGHTS
AV	AVENUE	DM	DAM	HVN	HAVEN
BCH	BEACH	DR	DRIVE	HWY	HIGHWAY
BLDS	BUILDINGS	DRO	DROVE	IMP	IMPERIAL
BND	BEND	DRY	DRIVEWAY	IN	INLET
BNK	BANK	DWGS	DWELLINGS	IND EST	INDUSTRIAL ESTATE
BR	BRIDGE	E	EAST	INF	INFIRMARY
BRK	BROOK	EMB	EMBANKMENT	INFO	INFORMATION
BTM	BOTTOM	EMBY	EMBASSY	INT	INTERCHANGE
BUS	BUSINESS	ESP	ESPLANADE	IS	ISLAND
BVD	BOULEVARD	EST	ESTATE	JCT	JUNCTION
BY	BYPASS	EX	EXCHANGE	JTY	JETTY
CATH	CATHEDRAL	EXPY	EXPRESSWAY	KG	KING
CEM	CEMETERY	EXT	EXTENSION	KNL	KNOLL
CEN	CENTRE	F/O	FLYOVER	L	LAKE
CFT	CROFT	FC	FOOTBALL CLUB	LA	LANE
CH	CHURCH	FK	FORK	LDG	LODGE
CHA	CHASE	FLD	FIELD	LGT	LIGHT
CHYD	CHURCHYARD	FLDS	FIELDS	LK	LOCK
CIR	CIRCLE	FLS	FALLS	LKS	LAKES
CIRC	CIRCUS	FLS	FLATS	LNDG	LANDING
CL	CLOSE	FM	FARM	LTL	LITTLE
CLFS	CLIFFS	FT	FORT	LWR	LOWER
CMP	CAMP	FWY	FREEWAY	MAG	MAGISTRATE
CNR	CORNER	FY	FERRY	MAN	MANSIONS
CO	COUNTY	GA	GATE	MD	MEAD
COLL	COLLEGE	GAL	GALLERY	MDW	MEADOWS
COM	COMMON	GDN	GARDEN	MEM	MEMORIAL
COMM	COMMISSION	GDNS	GARDENS	MKT	MARKET
CON	CONVENT	GLD	GLADE	MKTS	MARKETS
COT	COTTAGE	GLN	GLEN	ML	MALL
COTS	COTTAGES	GN	GREEN	ML	MILL
CP	CAPE	GND	GROUND	MNR	MANOR
CPS	COPSE	GRA	GRANGE	MS	MEWS
CR	CREEK	GRG	GARAGE	MSN	MISSION
CREM	CREMATORIUM	GT	GREAT	MT	MOUNT
CRS	CRESCENT	GTWY	GATEWAY	MTN	MOUNTAIN
CSWY	CAUSEWAY	GV	GROVE	MTS	MOUNTAINS
CT	COURT	HGR	HIGHER	MUS	MUSEUM
CTRL	CENTRAL	HL	HILL	MWY	MOTORWAY
CTS	COURTS	HLS	HILLS	N	NORTH
CTYD	COURTYARD	HO	HOUSE	NE	NORTH EAST

NW	NORTH WEST	SKWY	SKYWAY
O/P	OVERPASS	SMT	SUMMIT
OFF	OFFICE	SOC	SOCIETY
ORCH	ORCHARD	SP	SPUR
OV	OVAL	SPR	SPRING
PAL	PALACE	SQ	SQUARE
PAS	PASSAGE	ST	STREET
PAV	PAVILION	STN	STATION
PDE	PARADE	STR	STREAM
PH	PUBLIC HOUSE	STRD	STRAND
PK	PARK	SW	SOUTH WEST
PKWY	PARKWAY	TDG	TRADING
PL	PLACE	TER	TERRACE
PLN	PLAIN	THWY	THROUGHWAY
PLNS	PLAINS	TNL	TUNNEL
PLZ	PLAZA	TOLL	TOLLWAY
POL	POLICE STATION	TPK	TURNPIKE
PR	PRINCE	TR	TRACK
PREC	PRECINCT	TRL	TRAIL
PREP	PREPARATORY	TWR	TOWER
PRIM	PRIMARY	U/P	UNDERPASS
PROM	PROMENADE	UNI	UNIVERSITY
PRS	PRINCESS	UPR	UPPER
PRT	PORT	V	VALE
PT	POINT	VA	VALLEY
PTH	PATH	VIAD	VIADUCT
PZ	PIAZZA	VIL	VILLA
QD	QUADRANT	VIS	VISTA
QU	QUEEN	VLG	VILLAGE
QY	QUAY	VLS	VILLAS
R	RIVER	VW	VIEW
RBT	ROUNDABOUT	W	WEST
RD	ROAD	WD	WOOD
RDG	RIDGE	WHF	WHARF
REP	REPUBLIC	WK	WALK
RES	RESERVOIR	WKS	WALKS
RFC	RUGBY FOOTBALL CLUB	WLS	WELLS
RI	RISE	WY	WAY
RP	RAMP	YD	YARD
RW	ROW	YHA	YOUTH HOSTEL
S	SOUTH		
SCH	SCHOOL		
SE	SOUTH EAST		
SER	SERVICE AREA		
SH	SHORE		
SHOP	SHOPPING		

POSTCODE TOWNS AND AREA ABBREVIATIONS

ALDT	Aldershot	CBLY	Camberley	HASM	Haslemere
ALTN	Alton	CHIN	Chineham	HTWY	Hartley Wintney
AMSY	Amesbury	CHOB/PIR	Chobham/Pirbright	HUNG	Hungerford/Lambourn
AND	Andover	CWTH	Crowthorne	KEMP	Kempshott
ASC	Ascot	DEAN	Deane-Oakley	KSCL	Kingsclere/Rural Newbury
ASHV	Ash Vale	EPSF	Petersfield east	LIPH	Liphook
BAGS	Bagshot	EWKG	Wokingham east	LISS	Liss
BFOR	Bracknell Forest/Windlesham	FARN	Farnborough	LTWR	Lightwater
BLKW	Blackwater	FLET	Fleet	MARL	Marlborough
BOR	Bordon	FNM	Farnham	MFD/CHID	Milford/Chiddingfold
BPWT	Bishop's Waltham	FRIM	Frimley	MIDH	Midhurst
BSTK	Basingstoke	GSHT	Grayshott	NALR	New Alresford

NTHA	Thatcham north	RWIN	Rural Winchester
NTID	North Tidworth	SHST	Sandhurst
NWBY	Newbury	STHA	Thatcham south
ODIM	Odiham	STOK	Stockbridge
OVTN	Overton/Rural Basingstoke	TADY	Tadley
PSF	Petersfield	THLE	Theale/Rural Reading
RAND	Rural Andover	WHCH	Whitchurch
RDGW	Reading west	WHIT	Whitley/Arborfield
RFNM	Rural Farnham	WINC	Winchester
RGUW	Rural Guildford west	WINW	Winchester west
ROMY	Romsey	YTLY	Yateley
RSAL	Rural Salisbury		

A

Abbatt Cl *RAND* SP11	81 G6	Academy Cl *CBLY* GU15	39 H8	Aghemund Cl *CHIN* RG24	71 K5 🔢	Aldermaston Rd South		Alice Rd *ALDT* GU11	7 G2
Abbetts La *CBLY* GU15	58 E5	Accentors Cl *ALTN* GU34	164 E2	Agra Rd *NTID* SP9	102 B4	BSTK RG21	4 A4	Alison Cl *FARN* GU14	78 C5
Abbey Cl *NWBY* RG14	2 F9	Acheulian Cl *FNM* GU9	146 F1 🔢	Agravaine Cl *AND* SP10	106 F5 🔢	Alderney Av *KEMP* RG22	115 G1	THLE RG7	19 J7 🔢
Abbey Hill Cl *WINC* SO23	11 G3	Achilles Cl *CHIN* RG24	71 L4	Agricola Wy *STHA* RG19	15 J6	Alder Rd *BOR* GU35	190 E2	Alison Dr *CBLY* GU15	59 J3
Abbey Hill Rd *WINC* SO23	10 F3	Ackender Rd *ALTN* GU34	164 D5	Aintree Cl *NWBY* RG14	3 J8	Aldershot Rd *ASHV* GU12	101 J7	Alison Wy *ALDT* GU11	6 C2
Abbey Pk *THLE* RG7	19 J5	Ackrells Md *SHST* GU47	37 J7 🔢	Aircraft Esp *FARN* GU14	78 F7 🔢	FLET GU13	76 F8	Allden Av *ASHV* GU12	7 L7
Abbey Rd *ALTN* GU34	163 H8	Acorn Cl *WINW* SO22	10 A3	Aird Cl *KSCL* RG20	24 B8	FLET GU13	98 E4	Allee Dr *LIPH* GU30	214 E3 🔢
CHIN RG24	4 C2	Acorn Dr *NTHA* RG18	15 G3	Ajax Cl *CHIN* RG24	71 L4	Alderwood *CHIN* RG24	71 L5	Allenby Rd *CBLY* GU15	58 D2
Abbey St *FNM* GU9	122 F1	Acorn Keep *FNM* GU9	100 A8	Alamein Rd *ALDT* GU11	7 G1	Alder Wood Dr *HTWY* RG27	74 A6	Allen Cl *ALTN* GU34	164 F3
Abbey Wy *FARN* GU14	78 F4	Acorn Rd *BLKW* GU17	57 L3 🔢	RAND SP11	107 G1	Aldrin Cl *AND* SP10	106 D5	BSTK RG21	92 E5
Abbots Cl *FLET* GU13	76 F7	Acre Pth *AND* SP10	9 K5	Alanbrooke Cl *HTWY* RG27	75 H2	Aldrin Pl *FARN* GU14	78 A4	Allendale Cl *SHST* GU47	37 K6 🔢
Abbot's Ride *FNM* GU9	123 H8	Adam Cl *TADY* RG26	29 H7	Alanbrooke Rd *ALDT* GU11	101 G2	Aldwick Cl *FARN* GU14	78 D2	WHCH RG28	110 C4
Abbots Rd *NWBY* RG14	2 F7	Adampur Rd *NTID* SP9	102 B4	Albany Cl *FLET* GU13	77 G8	Aldworth Crs *KEMP* RG22	92 D4	Allnutt Av *BSTK* RG21	5 H8
THLE RG7	19 J5 🔢	Adams Dr *FLET* GU13	77 G7	Albany Pk *FRIM* GU16	58 F7	Aldworth Gdns *CWTH* RG45	37 K3	All Saints Crs *FARN* GU14	58 B7
Abbott Cl *KEMP* RG22	92 B6	Adams Park Rd *FNM* GU9	123 G4	Albany Rd *AND* SP10	8 C4	Alencon Link *BSTK* RG21	4 D7	Alma Cl *ASHV* GU12	101 G5
Abbotts Ann Rd *WINW* SO22	202 C5	Adams Wy *ALTN* GU34	164 F4	FLET GU13	76 F8	Alexander Rd *OVTN* RG25	111 M1	Alma La *FNM* GU9	122 F1
RAND SP11	129 H3	Addiscombe Rd *CWTH* RG45	37 M4	Albert Rd *ALDT* GU11	7 H2 🔢	STHA RG19	15 H6	Alma Rd *BOR* GU35	189 K5
Abbotts Cl *NTID* SP9	102 D1	Addison Gdns *ODIM* RG29	96 D5	ALTN GU34	164 D6	Alexandra Av *CBLY* GU15	58 D3	BOR GU35	190 F3
RAND SP11	129 M4	Addison Rd *FRIM* GU16	59 H8	CBLY GU15	58 F3 🔢	Alexandra Ct *FARN* GU14	78 F7 🔢	Alma Wy *FNM* GU9	123 G1
WINC SO23	11 G2	Addison Cl *WINW* SO22	226 B3	CWTH RG45	37 L3	BOR GU35	189 J5	Almond Av *NWBY* RG14	13 K5
Abbotts HI *RAND* SP11	129 M5	Adelaide Cl *RAND* SP11	103 J1 🔢	FARN GU14	78 F6	Alexandra Rd *ALDT* GU11	6 B3	Almond Cl *CHIN* RG24	93 M2
Abbotts Rd *NTID* SP9	102 D1	Adelaide Rd *AND* SP10	9 J5	FLET GU13	76 E7	ALTN GU34	164 E3	FARN GU14	78 D1
WINC SO23	11 H2	Adey's Cl *NWBY* RG14	3 G7	NWBY RG14	2 D3	AND SP10	8 F5	Almond Dr *NTHA* RG18	15 G4
Abbottswood Cl *TADY* RG26	49 L1 🔢	Adlington Pl *FARN* GU14	79 H6 🔢	Albert St *FLET* GU13	76 E7	ASHV GU12	101 J7	Almswood Rd *TADY* RG26	29 K8
Abex Rd *NWBY* RG14	3 K4	Admers Crs *LIPH* GU30	214 F6	Albion Rd *SHST* GU47	57 L1	BSTK RG21	4 B8	The Aloes *FLET* GU13	77 G8
Abingdon Rd *SHST* GU47	37 M8	Admirals Wy *AND* SP10	107 J8	Alcot Cl *CWTH* RG45	37 L4	FARN GU14	78 F6	Alphington Av *FRIM* GU16	59 J7
Above Town *RAND* SP11	130 D4	Admiralty Wy *CBLY* GU15	58 C4	Alderbrook Cl *CWTH* RG45	37 H4	Alexandra Ter *WINC* SO23	10 E9	Alphington Gn *FRIM* GU16	59 J7
Acacia Av *SHST* GU47	38 A7	Adrian Cl *HTWY* RG27	75 J3	Alder Cl *ALTN* GU34	164 D3	Alexandria Rd *RWIN* SO21	156 C3	Alpine Cl *FARN* GU14	78 A5
		Adwood Ct *STHA* RG19	15 H5	ASHV GU12	101 K1 🔢	Alfonso Cl *ASHV* GU12	7 K5	Alpine Ct *KEMP* RG22	91 M5
		Aelmas Mich Dro *RAND* SP11	105 G7 🔢	Alder Gld *THLE* RG7	19 J5	Alfred Rd *FNM* GU9	122 F7	Alpine Rd *BOR* GU35	189 J7
		Aerospace Bvd *ALDT* GU11	100 D1	Alder Gv *YTLY* GU46	56 F5 🔢	Alfriston Rd *FRIM* GU16	79 M1		
		FARN GU14	100 C1	Aldermaston Rd *TADY* RG26	50 A3				

Alresford Dro RWIN SO21 178 E3
Alresford Rd NALR SO24 205 M4
RWIN SO21 227 L1
WINC SO23 11 L8
Alston Ms STHA RG19 14 F6
Altona Gdns AND SP10 106 E5
Alton La ALTN GU34 185 G8
Alton Ride BLKW GU17 57 M2
Alton Rd FLET GU13 77 H7
NFNM GU10 146 A1
ODIM RG29 119 G4
Alverstoke Gdns ALDT GU11 6 B4
Alwin Pl FNM GU9 122 F1 1
Amazon Cl BSTK RG21 4 A9
Ambarrow Crs SHST GU47 37 J7
Ambarrow La CWTH RG45 37 G6
Amber Cl BOR GU35 189 K6 1
Amber Gdns AND SP10 8 B5
Amber Hl CBLY GU15 59 L4 1
Amberley Cl NWBY RG14 2 C1
Amberley Gra ALDT GU11 6 C5
Amberwood Dr CBLY GU15 59 J1
Ambleside Cl FARN GU14 78 B4
FRIM GU16 79 K6
Ambleside Crs FNM GU9 122 D2 1
Ambrose Rd TADY RG26 29 L8
Amery Hl ALTN GU34 164 E4
Amery St ALTN GU34 164 E5
Amesbury Rd RAND SP11 104 F7
Amherst Rd BOR GU35 189 H2
Ampere Rd NWBY RG14 3 G3
Amport Cl CHIN RG24 71 M8 1
WINW SO22 202 B5
Ancells Rd FARN GU14 77 G3
Anchor Meadow FARN GU14 78 C4
Anchor Rd KSCL RG20 47 J6
Anchor Yd BSTK RG21 4 F9
Andeferas Rd AND SP10 106 E5
Anders Rd RWIN SO21 178 D4
Andlers Ash Rd LISS GU33 236 D6
Andover Dro KSCL RG20 24 E4
Andover La RAND SP11 103 M1
Andover Rd BLKW GU17 57 M2
DEAN RG23 90 C7
WINW SO22 10 F3
KSCL RG20 24 E6
NWBY RG14 25 H1
OVTN RG25 89 M8
RAND SP11 80 F6
RAND SP11 129 K2
RWIN SO21 136 A6
Andover Rd North WINW SO22 202 B1
Andover Wy ALDT GU11 7 H8
FNM GU9 7 H8
Andrewartha Rd FARN GU14 79 H6 2
Andrews Cl FLET GU13 98 F2
Andrew's La NALR SO24 208 E3
ODIM RG29 119 L5
Andrews Rd FARN GU14 78 B3
Andwell La HTWY RG27 94 F2
Angel Ct NWBY RG14 2 E2
Angel Md THLE RG7 16 F6
Angel Mdw ODIM RG29 96 D5
Anglesey Av FARN GU14 78 C1
Anglesey Cl AND SP10 130 F3
CHIN RG24 71 H6
Anglesey Rd ASHV GU12 7 L3
Angora Wy FARN GU14 77 G4
Annandale Dr NFNM GU10 147 G3
Anne Armstrong Cl ALDT GU11 101 G3
Annes Wy FLET GU13 99 G2
Annettes Cft FLET GU13 98 D4 1
Annett's La HUNG RG17 20 C1
Ansell Rd FRIM GU16 59 H8
Anstey Cl BSTK RG21 92 F6
Anstey La ALTN GU34 142 E8
Anstey Mill Cl ALTN GU34 165 G3
Anstey Mill La ALTN GU34 165 G3
Anstey Pl THLE RG7 19 K5
Anstey Rd ALTN GU34 164 F4
Antar Cl BSTK RG21 4 A9
Anton Cl DEAN RG23 91 G7
Anton La RAND SP11 107 G2
Anton Mill Rd AND SP10 8 F8
Anton Rd AND SP10 9 G8
Antrim Cl KEMP RG22 92 A5 1
Anzio Cl ALDT GU11 6 F1
Apex Dr FRIM GU16 59 G7
Apollo Dr BOR GU35 189 K6
Apollo Ri FARN GU14 78 A4
Appelford Cl STHA RG19 15 G6
Appledore Ms FARN GU14 78 D1 1
Appledown Cl NALR SO24 206 C4
Appledown La NALR SO24 206 D5
Applegarth Cl BSTK RG21 93 H5
Applelands Cl NFNM GU10 146 D4
Appleshaw Cl WINW SO22 202 C4
Appleshaw Wy RAND SP11 103 J2
Appleton Cl STOK SO20 150 B7
Appleton Vw ALTN GU34 210 C3
Appletree Cl DEAN RG23 91 G8
Apple Tree Cl NWBY RG14 25 H1
Apple Tree Gv AND SP10 8 B2
Apple Tree Wy SHST GU47 38 A7
Apple Wy CHIN RG24 94 A3
Appley Dr CBLY GU15 58 E3
Approach Rd FNM GU9 122 F7
April Cl CBLY GU15 58 F6
Apsley Cl AND SP10 130 E1
Archangel Wy NTHA RG18 15 J4
Archery Flds ODIM RG29 96 E5
Archery La WINC SO23 10 E8
Archery Ri ALTN GU34 164 D6
Arcot Rd NTID SP9 102 C5
Ardglen Rd WHCH RG28 110 A3
Ardrossan Av CBLY GU15 59 K3 1
Ardwell Cl CWTH RG45 37 H3
Arena La ALDT GU11 100 B4
Arenal Dr CWTH RG45 37 L5
Arford Common BOR GU35 190 C2
Arford Rd BOR GU35 190 C2
Argente Cl FARN GU14 77 G4 1
Argyle Cl BOR GU35 189 J6
Argyle Rd NWBY RG14 2 D6
Ariel Rd FARN GU14 78 D6
Arkle Av STHA RG19 14 C5
Arkwright Cl KSCL RG20 44 C2
Arle Cl NALR SO24 206 B2
Arle Gdns NALR SO24 206 C2
Arlington Ter ALDT GU11 6 D2
Arlott Dr BSTK RG21 4 F4
Armitage Dr FRIM GU16 59 J7
Armstrong Cl RWIN SO21 178 D4
Armstrong Ml FARN GU14 78 A4
Armstrong Ri AND SP10 106 D5
Armstrong Rd CHIN RG24 5 L4
Armstrong Wy FARN GU14 77 L7
Arne Cl KEMP RG22 115 J1 1
Arnett Av EWKG RG40 36 E1
Arnhem Cl ALDT GU11 7 H1
Arnhem Rd NWBY RG14 3 H4
Arran Cl DEAN RG23 90 F6
Arrow La HTWY RG27 75 G1
Arrow Rd FARN GU14 78 C6
Arrow Smith Wy STHA RG19 15 J6 1
Arthur Cl FNM GU9 122 E7 1
Arthur Rd FNM GU9 122 F7
NWBY RG14 2 B6
WINC SO23 11 G4
Arthur St ALDT GU11 7 G3
Artillery Rd ALDT GU11 7 G1 1
Artists Wy AND SP10 8 E1
Arundel Cl FLET GU13 77 G8
LIPH GU30 190 A8 1
NALR SO24 206 C4 1
Arundel Gdns DEAN RG23 92 A1
Arundel Rd CBLY GU15 59 M4
Arwood Av TADY RG26 30 A7 1
Ascension Cl CHIN RG24 71 H7
Ascot Cl ALTN GU34 164 F6
NWBY RG14 3 J9
Ascot Ct ALDT GU11 6 F3
Ashbarn Crs WINW SO22 226 C3
Ashbourne Cl ASHV GU12 101 M5
Ashbourne Wy STHA RG19 14 E5
Ashburton Cl NALR SO24 206 B3
Ashburton Rd NALR SO24 206 B3
Ashbury Dr FARN GU14 58 D7
Ashbury Rd BOR GU35 189 J6
Ash Church Rd ASHV GU12 101 L6
Ash Cl ASHV GU12 101 L5
BLKW GU17 57 M3
NTID SP9 102 F1
Ashdale Pk EWKG RG40 36 F1
Ashdell Rd ALTN GU34 164 F5
Ashdene Crs ASHV GU12 101 K5
Ashdene Rd ASHV GU12 101 K5
Ashdown Av FARN GU14 79 H6
Ashdown Ter NTID SP9 102 E3
Ashfield CHIN RG24 71 L5
Ashfield Gn YTLY GU46 57 G3
Ashfield Rd AND SP10 8 A4
Ashfields RWIN SO21 155 J2
Ashford Hill Rd STHA RG19 27 G6
Ash Ga NTHA RG18 15 J4
Ash Green La East ASHV GU12 101 M8
Ash Green La West ASHV GU12 101 J8
Ash Green Rd ASHV GU12 101 M7
Ash Gv CHIN RG24 94 B2
KSCL RG20 47 G6
LIPH GU30 215 G5
Ash Hill Rd ASHV GU12 101 L5
Ash La TADY RG26 29 H7
TADY RG26 51 G3
THLE RG7 19 K4
Ashlawn Gdns AND SP10 9 J8
Ashlea HTWY RG27 74 A6
Ashley Cl FRIM GU16 79 K2
WINW SO22 202 B5
NFNM GU10 121 J1
Ashley Dr BLKW GU17 57 M4
Ashley Dro MARL SN8 40 C4
Ashley Rd ALTN GU34 162 E3
FARN GU14 79 G4
Ash Lodge Cl ASHV GU12 101 K7
Ash Lodge Dr ASHV GU12 101 K7
Ashman Rd STHA RG19 15 J5
Ashmead BOR GU35 189 J5
Ashmoor La CHIN RG24 94 D2
Ashmore Green Rd NTHA RG18 14 D1
Ashmore Rd WINW SO22 202 B7 1
Ashridge FARN GU14 78 C1
Ash Rd ASHV GU12 7 L5
KSCL RG20 26 C5
Ash St ASHV GU12 101 K6
Ash Tree Cl DEAN RG23 90 F8
FARN GU14 77 M5 1
HASM GU27 193 J7 1
Ash Tree Gv KSCL RG20 23 L1
Ash Tree Rd AND SP10 106 B8
Ashurst Cl WINW SO22 202 C5
TADY RG26 29 K8 1
Ashurst Rd ASHV GU12 101 J4
Ashwell Av CBLY GU15 59 J2
Ashwood Dr NWBY RG14 3 M2
Ashwood Wy DEAN RG23 92 C1
Ashworth Dr STHA RG19 14 F6 1
Aspen Cl BOR GU35 189 J7
Aspen Gdns HTWY RG27 74 A6 1
Aspin Wy BLKW GU17 57 K6
Aster Rd KEMP RG22 114 F1
Astor Crs RAND SP11 80 D6
Atbara Rd FLET GU13 98 E3
Athlone Cl RAND SP11 84 A8
Atholl Ct AND SP10 106 F5
Atholl Rd BOR GU35 189 J7
Atrebatti Rd SHST GU47 37 M7
Attenborough Cl FARN GU14 77 G5
Attfield Cl ASHV GU12 101 J7
Attlee Gdns FLET GU13 98 E4
Attwood Cl BSTK RG21 4 A9
BSTK RG21 92 E4
Attwoods Dro RWIN SO21 226 C8
Auchinleck Wy ALDT GU11 6 B2
Auckland Cl NTID SP9 102 F2
Auclum Cl THLE RG7 19 L6
Auclum La THLE RG7 19 L6
Audley Cl NWBY RG14 14 A3
Augustine Wy AND SP10 106 C5 1
Augustus Dr DEAN RG23 92 B1
Augustus Gdns CBLY GU15 59 M3 1
Auklet Cl KEMP RG22 114 E1
Austen Av WINW SO22 226 B5
Austen Cl WINC SO23 11 H2
Austen Gv KEMP RG22 92 B6
Austen Rd FARN GU14 78 D2
Aveley La FNM GU9 146 E1
Avenue Cl AND SP10 8 D5
LIPH GU30 214 E4
Avenue Rd ALTN GU34 141 K4
FARN GU14 79 G4
FLET GU13 76 E6
WINW SO22 10 D6
GSHT GU26 192 A5
Avenue Sucy CBLY GU15 58 D4
The Avenue ALDT GU11 7 K7
AND SP10 8 D5
CBLY GU15 58 E4
CWTH RG45 37 K3
FLET GU13 76 D7
GSHT GU26 192 A5
HASM GU27 216 C1
LIPH GU30 214 D4
NALR SO24 206 A3
NFNM GU10 146 B5
NTID SP9 102 D4
OVTN RG25 115 J5
RAND SP11 83 K6
RWIN SO21 133 H5
THLE RG7 31 L3
Avery Cl EWKG RG40 36 C2
Avocet Crs SHST GU47 38 A8
Avon Cl ASHV GU12 101 J7
FARN GU14 78 B1
Avondale ASHV GU12 101 J1
Avondale Rd ALDT GU11 7 H5
FLET GU13 76 F6
Avon Rd DEAN RG23 91 G7
FNM GU9 122 F7
NTID SP9 102 D3
Avonway NWBY RG14 3 M1
Avon Wy THLE RG7 18 B2
Award Rd FLET GU13 98 E3
Ayesgarth FLET GU13 99 G3
Ayjay Cl ALDT GU11 7 G7
Aylesford Wy STHA RG19 15 K6
Aylesham Wy YTLY GU46 56 E2
Ayling Cl FNM GU9 6 D7
Ayling Hl ALDT GU11 6 C4
Ayling La ALDT GU11 6 D5
Aylings Cl DEAN RG23 92 A4
Aylward's Dr ALTN GU34 186 B5
Aylwards Wy STOK SO20 172 E3
Aylwin Cl BSTK RG21 92 F6 1
Ayres La KSCL RG20 25 J8
Ayrshire Gdns FARN GU14 77 G4
Azalea Av BOR GU35 189 M3
Azalea Dr HASM GU27 192 C8 1
Azalea Gdns FLET GU13 99 G3
Azalea Wy CBLY GU15 59 L2

B

Babbs Md FNM GU9 122 D6
Babs Flds NFNM GU10 144 F3
Bach Cl KEMP RG22 115 J1
Back La HUNG RG17 22 C1
NFNM GU10 145 L8
OVTN RG25 141 J3
RAND SP11 61 G2
RAND SP11 105 H1
ROMY SO51 221 J3
THLE RG7 17 K2
THLE RG7 28 E5
THLE RG7 30 F4
Back St WINC SO23 226 E4
Bacon Cl SHST GU47 58 A2 1
Bacon La NFNM GU10 168 F4
Baden Powell Rd LISS GU33 213 H6
Badger Cl ALTN GU34 185 H5
Badger Farm Rd WINW SO22 226 A3
Badger's Bank CHIN RG24 71 L8
Badgers Cl FLET GU13 76 E8
Badgers Copse CBLY GU15 59 H5
Badgers Gld THLE RG7 19 K6
Badgers Holt YTLY GU46 56 E3 1
Badgers Sett CWTH RG45 37 J3 1
Badger Wy NFNM GU10 99 G8
Badgerwood Dr FRIM GU16 59 G6
Badshear La NALR SO24 230 D1
Badshot Lea Rd FNM GU9 123 K3
Badshot Pk FNM GU9 123 K2
Bagmore La OVTN RG25 140 D3
Bagnols Wy NWBY RG14 2 A6
Bagwell La ODIM RG29 97 H1
Baigent Cl WINC SO23 11 L7
Bailey Cl FRIM GU16 59 G8
WINW SO22 226 C2
Baileys Cl BLKW GU17 57 L4
Baily Av NTHA RG18 14 E4
Bain Av CBLY GU15 58 E7
Baird Av KEMP RG22 92 D6
Baird Rd FARN GU14 78 F2
Bakers Fld LISS GU33 212 E6
Baldreys FNM GU9 122 D8
Balfour Crs NWBY RG14 24 F3
Balfour Dr LISS GU33 236 D4
Balintore Ct SHST GU47 58 A1 1
Balksbury Hl RAND SP11 130 C3
Balksbury Rd RAND SP11 130 D3
Ball & Wicket La FNM GU9 122 F1
Ballantyne Rd FARN GU14 78 D2
Ballard Cl KEMP RG22 92 B5
Ballard Rd CBLY GU15 39 K8
Balliol Wy SHST GU47 38 B7
Balloon Rd FARN GU14 78 E6
Balmoral Cl ALTN GU34 164 C5
Balmoral Crs FNM GU9 122 E2 1
Balmoral Dr FRIM GU16 59 H8
Balmoral Rd AND SP10 9 G5
ASHV GU12 101 K4
Balmoral Wy KEMP RG22 114 F1
Bamber La ALTN GU34 144 A4
Banbury Cl FRIM GU16 79 K1 1
Bank Rd ALDT GU11 101 G3
Bank Side EWKG RG40 36 C2
Bankside FNM GU9 6 C8
Bannister Gdns HTWY RG27 36 B8 1
YTLY GU46 57 J3 1
Bannister Pl THLE RG7 28 C2 1
Bannister Rd THLE RG7 19 J6
Baptist Hl RAND SP11 85 L6
Barbara Cl FLET GU13 99 G2
Barbel Av BSTK RG21 5 K7
Barberry Cl FLET GU13 98 F2
Barberry Wy BLKW GU17 58 C5
Barbour Cl ODIM RG29 119 H1
Barcelona Cl AND SP10 9 K3
Bardsley Dr FNM GU9 122 D8
Bardwell Cl KEMP RG22 92 B4
The Baredown HTWY RG27 95 J1
Bar End Rd WINC SO23 227 G3
Barfield Cl WINC SO23 227 G2
Barfield Rd NTHA RG18 14 D4
Barford Cl FLET GU13 77 J8
Barge Cl ALDT GU11 101 H3
Barge La THLE RG7 33 K3
Baring Cl RWIN SO21 158 F4
RWIN SO21 204 F1
Baring Rd WINC SO23 11 K9
Barker Cl WHIT RG2 35 H1
Barkis Md SHST GU47 38 B6 1
Barley Down Dr WINW SO22 226 C4
Barley Mow Cl HTWY RG27 75 L8
Barley Mow Hl BOR GU35 190 C2
Barley Wy FARN GU14 77 G3
Barlows La AND SP10 130 E3
Barlows Rd TADY RG26 49 L1
Barnard Cl FRIM GU16 59 J8
Barn Cl CBLY GU15 59 H2
Barn Close La KSCL RG20 43 L8
Barn Crs NWBY RG14 25 G1
Barncroft FNM GU9 122 F7 1
RAND SP11 104 F3
Barnes Cl FARN GU14 79 G4
WINC SO23 226 D3
Barnes Rd FRIM GU16 59 H8
Barnet Side La PSF GU32 234 C3
Barnetts Wood La NALR SO24 183 M8
Barnfield YTLY GU46 57 G3 1
Barnfield Cl ALTN GU34 144 B4 1
Barnfield Ri AND SP10 8 C9
Barn La ALTN GU34 184 E7
DEAN RG23 90 F8
Barn Meadow Cl FLET GU13 98 E5
Barn Owl Wy THLE RG7 19 L5
Barnside Wy LISS GU33 236 E5
Barnsley Cl FRIM GU16 79 L7
The Barns OVTN RG25 114 C8
Baroda Rd NTID SP9 102 B4
Barossa Rd CBLY GU15 59 G1
Barracane Dr CWTH RG45 37 L4
Barrack Rd ALDT GU11 6 E2
Barracks Rd STHA RG19 26 C4
Barra Cl DEAN RG23 90 F6
Barrie Rd FNM GU9 122 D1
Barron Pl CHIN RG24 70 A8
Barrow Hl RAND SP11 130 D8
Barry Wy KEMP RG22 115 J1
Bartholomew Cl HASM GU27 193 G8 1
Bartholomew St NWBY RG14 2 D6
Bartlemy Cl NWBY RG14 2 A9
Bartlemy Rd NWBY RG14 2 A9
Bartley Wy HTWY RG27 74 B8
Bartok Cl KEMP RG22 92 D7
Barton Cl ALDT GU11 6 A3
AND SP10 106 C5 2
Barton Dro RWIN SO21 155 M4
Barton's Dr YTLY GU46 57 G4
Bartons La CHIN RG24 71 M8
Bartons Wy FARN GU14 77 M1
Barwell Cl CWTH RG45 37 J4
Basingbourne Cl FLET GU13 98 F2
Basingbourne Rd FLET GU13 98 E3
Basing Dean ALTN GU34 233 K3
Basing Dr ALDT GU11 7 H8
Basing Rd CHIN RG24 5 M6
Basingstoke Rd ALTN GU34 164 A5
HTWY RG27 53 J2
KSCL RG20 47 K6
RWIN SO21 179 M4
TADY RG26 69 K3
THLE RG7 17 K7
WINC SO23 203 J2
Basing Vw BSTK RG21 5 H6
Bassenthwaite Gdns
BOR GU35 189 J3 1
Bassett Cl FRIM GU16 59 H8
Bat & Ball La FNM GU9 146 D2
NFNM GU10 146 D3
Batchelor Dr CHIN RG24 94 B3
Batchelors Barn Rd AND SP10 9 L4
Bath Rd CBLY GU15 58 F2
NTHA RG18 14 C4
NWBY RG14 13 G3
THLE RG7 16 C6
Batsford RAND SP11 85 L6
Battens Av OVTN RG25 89 G8
Battery End NWBY RG14 25 G2
Battery Hl WINW SO22 226 B2
Battle Cl NWBY RG14 13 G4
Battle Rd NWBY RG14 24 F2
Baughurst Rd TADY RG26 29 H8
THLE RG7 30 D2
Baverstocks ALTN GU34 164 F2
The Baxendales NWBY RG14 3 J8
Bayfield Av FRIM GU16 59 H6
Bayford Cl FARN GU14 58 D7
Baynard Cl BSTK RG21 5 G4
Baywood Cl FARN GU14 77 M3 1
Bazaar Rd NTID SP9 102 B3
Beach's Crs TADY RG26 50 D5
Beacon Cl NFNM GU10 146 D3
Beacon Hill Ct GSHT GU26 192 A2
Beacon Hill Rd FLET GU13 99 G4
GSHT GU26 191 M2
Beacon Rd FARN GU14 78 E8
Beaconsfield Rd BSTK RG21 93 G4
Beale's Cl AND SP10 9 K5
Beales La NFNM GU10 146 C1
Bealeswood La NFNM GU10 168 B2
Beal's Pightle TADY RG26 69 L1
Beam Hollow FNM GU9 122 F1 2
Beancroft Rd STHA RG19 15 G6
Bear Hl KSCL RG20 47 H7
Bear La FNM GU9 122 E5
NWBY RG14 2 E4
Bearwood FLET GU13 76 F7
Beauclerk Gn HTWY RG27 75 H7
Beaufighter Rd FARN GU14 78 D8
Beaufort Rd FLET GU13 99 G1
FNM GU9 122 F5
BOR GU35 189 J3
WINC SO23 226 E2
Beaufront Cl CBLY GU15 59 K1
Beaufront Rd CBLY GU15 59 K1
Beaulieu Cl WINW SO22 202 C4 1
Beaulieu Ct AND SP10 107 H6 2
Beaulieu Gdns BLKW GU17 57 M3
Beaumaris Cl AND SP10 8 D9
Beaumaris Pde FRIM GU16 59 J8
Beaumond Gn WINC SO23 10 F8
Beaumont Gv ALDT GU11 6 B2 1
Beaurepaire Cl TADY RG26 51 J5
Beaver La YTLY GU46 57 H3
Beavers Cl ALTN GU34 164 D4
FNM GU9 122 D6
TADY RG26 29 J7
Beavers Hl FNM GU9 122 C6
Beavers Ms BOR GU35 189 K4 1
Beavers Rd FNM GU9 122 D6
Beckett Cl DEAN RG23 91 M3
Beckett Rd AND SP10 8 D4
Beck Gdns FNM GU9 122 D2 2
Beddington Ct CHIN RG24 71 M7 1
Bede Dr AND SP10 106 C5
Bedfield La WINC SO23 203 G3
Bedford Av FRIM GU16 79 J3
Bedford Cl BOR GU35 189 J7 1
NWBY RG14 24 F3 1
Bedford Crs FRIM GU16 79 H2
Bedford La FRIM GU16 79 J2
Beecham Berry KEMP RG22 115 J1
Beech Av CBLY GU15 59 G4
NFNM GU10 146 F3
Beechbrook Av YTLY GU46 57 G3
Beech Cl WINW SO22 226 A5
OVTN RG25 89 G6
RAND SP11 104 D8
STOK SO20 151 G4
TADY RG26 51 M6 1
TLHT RG30 19 L4
Beech Copse WINW SO22 202 A7
Beechcrest Vw HTWY RG27 74 A6 2
Beechcroft Cl LIPH GU30 214 A5 1
Beechcroft Cottages
STOK SO20 197 G2
Beech Dr BLKW GU17 58 A4
The Beeches ASHV GU12 79 J7 1
KEMP RG22 115 J2
Beechfield AMSY SP4 148 A2
Beech Gv RAND SP11 153 L2
Beech Hanger AMSY SP4 126 C7
Beech Hanger End GSHT GU26 191 L5
Beech Hl BOR GU35 190 E4
Beech Hill Rd BOR GU35 190 C2
NTID SP9 102 F1
THLE RG7 33 H2
Beeching Cl ASHV GU12 101 L5
Beechlands Rd ALTN GU34 185 G4
Beech La GSHT GU26 191 L4
Beechnut Dr BLKW GU17 57 L2
Beechnut Rd ASHV GU12 7 H3
Beech Ride FLET GU13 98 E1
SHST GU47 37 L8
Beech Rd FARN GU14 78 E1
FRIM GU16 79 J2
HASM GU27 217 G1
KSCL RG20 26 D6
NALR SO24 206 C3
Beech Tree Cl DEAN RG23 90 F8
Beech Tree Dr FNM GU9 123 K3
Beech Tree Wk ROMY SO51 197 H5
Beech Wk STHA RG19 15 H6
Beech Wy DEAN RG23 92 B1
Beechwood Cl FLET GU13 98 D2
KEMP RG22 115 H2
Beechwood Ct LISS GU33 236 F2 1
Beechwood Rd ALTN GU34 164 C6
Beethoven Rd KEMP RG22 92 D8
Beeton's Av ASHV GU12 101 K4
Beggar's La WINC SO23 11 J7
Beggarwood La DEAN RG23 114 F3
KEMP RG22 115 J2
Begonia Cl KEMP RG22 114 F1
Belaga Cl STOK SO20 150 F3
Beldham Rd NFNM GU10 146 C1
Belgrave Ct BLKW GU17 58 A5
Belland Dr ALDT GU11 6 B3
Bell Cl FARN GU14 78 F2
Bellever Hl CBLY GU15 59 H3
Bellevue WHCH RG28 110 B3
Belle Vue Cl ASHV GU12 7 M2
Belle Vue Rd AND SP10 9 J8
ASHV GU12 7 L2
CHIN RG24 94 A2
Bellew Rd FRIM GU16 79 L2
Bell Holt NWBY RG14 24 F3
Bell House NALR SO24 206 C4
Bellingham Cl CBLY GU15 59 M4
Bell La BLKW GU17 57 M3
HUNG RG17 22 A5
NFNM GU10 146 B5
OVTN RG25 140 C2
Bell Meadow Rd HTWY RG27 74 A7
Bell Rd AND SP10 9 L6
CHIN RG24 5 L5
HASM GU27 216 D5
Bell St RAND SP11 80 F6
WHCH RG28 110 B3
Bell Vale La HASM GU27 216 E4
Belmont Cl AND SP10 9 K8
FARN GU14 78 C1
Belmont Hts KEMP RG22 115 H3
Belmont Ms CBLY GU15 58 F5
Belmont Rd AND SP10 9 J8
CBLY GU15 58 F4
CWTH RG45 37 L2
Belsize Rd FARN GU14 78 F7 2
Belstone Ms FARN GU14 78 D1 2
Belton Rd CBLY GU15 59 H3
Belvedere Cl FLET GU13 76 B7 1
Belvedere Ct BLKW GU17 58 A5 1
Belvedere Dr NWBY RG14 2 E9
Belvedere Gdns CHIN RG24 71 M4 1
Belvedere Rd FARN GU14 78 F6 1
Belvoir Cl FRIM GU16 59 J7
Bembridge Ct CWTH RG45 37 H4 1

Ben - Bur 243

Beneden Gn NALR SO24 206 C3
Benenden Gn NALR SO24 206 C4
Benett Cl NWBY RG14 13 J3
Benett Gdns NWBY RG14 13 J3
Benger's La ROMY SO51 221 J6
Benham Cha KSCL RG20 12 B3
Benham Dro STOK SO20 172 C2
Benham Hl NTHA RG18 14 D4
Benham La THLE RG7 34 A5
Benhams La LISS GU33 212 E4
Benin Rd RAND SP11 103 J2
Ben La RSAL SP5 218 C1
Bennet Cl ALTN GU34 164 D4
BSTK RG21 5 H4
Bennett Ct CBLY GU15 58 F3 2
Bennett's Hl TLHT RG30 19 L1
Benson Rd CWTH RG45 37 J3
Benta Cl STOK SO20 150 F3
Bentley Cl WINC SO23 203 G2
Bentley Copse CBLY GU15 59 L4 2
Bentley Wy RSAL SP5 195 G3
Bent St STOK SO20 172 D2
Benwell Cl ODIM RG29 96 B8
Bercote Cl WINW SO22 202 A3
Bere Cl WINW SO22 10 A3
Bere Hl WHCH RG28 110 B2
Bere Hill Cl WHCH RG28 110 C2
Bere Hill Crs AND SP10 9 L7
Berehurst ALTN GU34 164 D6
Beresford Cl AND SP10 130 F3 1
FRIM GU16 79 J2
Bereweeke Av WINW SO22 10 C1
Bereweeke Cl WINW SO22 10 C4
Bereweeke Rd WINW SO22 10 C4
Bereweeke Wy WINW SO22 10 D3
Berewyk Cl KEMP RG22 114 F1 1
Berkeley Cl FLET GU13 77 G7 1
Berkeley Crs FRIM GU16 59 K8
Berkeley Dr KEMP RG22 92 E8
Berkeley Rd NWBY RG14 2 C5
Berkshire Circular Routes
HUNG RG17 21 H3
KSCL RG20 12 D8
THLE RG7 18 B2
THLE RG7 31 L4
Berkshire Corpse Rd
ALDT GU11 100 B1
Berkshire Dr STHA RG19 15 K6
Berkshire Rd CBLY GU15 39 J8
Bermuda Cl CHIN RG24 71 H7
Bernard Av ALTN GU34 185 G6
Bernersh Cl SHST GU47 37 M7 1
Bernstein Rd KEMP RG22 92 B8
Berrybank SHST GU47 58 B2
Berrydown La OVTN RG25 112 B1
OVTN RG25 140 B4
Berry Hl NALR SO24 207 M3
Berrylands LISS GU33 236 F1
Berrywood La NALR SO24 162 A2
Berwyn Cl KEMP RG22 91 M5
Bessemer Rd BSTK RG21 92 E6
Beta Rd FARN GU14 78 C3
Bethel Cl FNM GU9 123 G2
Bethel La FNM GU9 123 G2
Betjeman Wk YTLY GU46 56 E4
Betteridge Rd STHA RG19 15 J6
Beveren Cl FARN GU14 77 G4
Beverley Cl ASHV GU12 101 J7
BSTK RG21 93 G7
CBLY GU15 59 M2
NTHA RG18 14 F4
Beverley Crs FARN GU14 78 C5
The Bevers THLE RG7 31 K2
Bexmoor CHIN RG24 93 M2
Bexmoor Wy CHIN RG24 93 M2
Beyne Rd WINW SO22 226 A5
Bible Flds OVTN RG25 114 B8
Bicester Cl WHCH RG28 110 B3
Bicknell Rd FRIM GU16 59 H6
Bidden Rd ODIM RG29 95 M6
OVTN RG25 118 A3
Biddesden La RAND SP11 81 G6
Bideford Cl FARN GU14 78 D1
Bighton Dean La NALR SO24 183 J7
Bighton Hl NALR SO24 207 M2
Bighton La NALR SO24 207 H2
Bighton Rd ALTN GU34 184 B3
Bilbao Ct AND SP10 107 J7
Billing Av EWKG RG40 36 B2
Billington Wy NTHA RG18 14 F2
Binfields Cl CHIN RG24 71 L7
Bingley Cl ALTN GU34 164 D4
Binley Bottom RAND SP11 85 K3
Binstead Rd ALTN GU34 145 J8
NFNM GU10 145 K8
Binsted Dr BLKW GU17 58 A3
Binton La NFNM GU10 124 B6
Birch Av FLET GU13 76 E7
STOK SO20 151 G4
Birch Cl CBLY GU15 39 H8
BOR GU35 189 K6
LISS GU33 236 F4
NFNM GU10 146 D4
Birch Dr BLKW GU17 58 A5
Birches Crest KEMP RG22 115 J2
The Birches BLKW GU17 57 L3
FARN GU14 78 A4
Birchett Rd ALDT GU11 6 E2
FARN GU14 78 B3
Birchfields CBLY GU15 58 F4 1
Birch Gv HTWY RG27 74 A6
BOR GU35 189 J7
STOK SO20 154 A6
Birchland Cl THLE RG7 31 H2
Birch La THLE RG7 31 J3
Bircholt Rd LIPH GU30 214 A4
Birch Rd EWKG RG40 36 D1
BOR GU35 190 E2
TADY RG26 29 H6
THLE RG7 19 J5
Birch Side CWTH RG45 37 J2
Birchview Cl YTLY GU46 56 F4
Birch Wy ASHV GU12 101 K1
Birchwood CHIN RG24 71 L5 1
Birchwood Rd NWBY RG14 3 M1
Birdhaven NFNM GU10 146 D3
Birds La THLE RG7 16 B5
Birdwood Rd CBLY GU15 58 C2
Birinus Rd WINC SO23 11 H5
Birkbeck Pl SHST GU47 38 B7
Birkenholme Cl BOR GU35 190 F4
Bishearne Gdns LISS GU33 236 D3 1
Bishops Cl FLET GU13 98 F1
NTID SP9 102 E4
TADY RG26 29 K7
Bishop's Md FNM GU9 122 E6
Bishops Rd FNM GU9 122 E2
Bishop Sumner Dr FNM GU9 122 F2 1
Bishop's Vw ALTN GU34 184 E6
Bishop's Wy AND SP10 8 E4
Bishopswood La TADY RG26 29 H7
Bishopswood Rd TADY RG26 29 J7
Bitham La HUNG RG17 20 E3
Bittern Cl KEMP RG22 91 L8
SHST GU47 38 A8
Blackberry Cl ALTN GU34 185 H5
Blackberry La ALTN GU34 185 H6
Blackberry Wk CHIN RG24 5 M4
Blackbird Cl KEMP RG22 91 L8
SHST GU47 38 A8
THLE RG7 19 L5 1
Blackbird Ct AND SP10 107 G6 1
Blackbushes Rd HTWY RG27 76 D2
Blackcap Pl SHST GU47 38 B8
Blackdown Cl KEMP RG22 91 M5
Blackdown Rd FRIM GU16 79 M1
Blackdown Wy STHA RG19 14 F6
Blackheath Rd FNM GU9 122 D1
Blacklands Rd THLE RG7 15 M3
Blackman Gdns ALDT GU11 7 H6
Blackmoor Rd LISS GU33 212 F2
Blackmore La MARL SN8 80 E3
PSF GU32 234 D4
Blacknest Rd ALTN GU34 145 H6
Black Pond La NFNM GU10 146 F2
Blackstocks La HTWY RG27 95 G3
Blackstone Cl FARN GU14 78 A2
Blackthorn Cl RWIN SO21 178 B4
Blackthorn Crs FARN GU14 58 C8
Blackthorn Dr NTHA RG18 15 G3
Blackthorne Cl BOR GU35 189 K5 1
Blackthorn Wy DEAN RG23 92 B2
Blackwater Cl ASHV GU12 101 K7 1
BSTK RG21 5 H8
DEAN RG23 91 G7 1
Blackwater Vw EWKG RG40 36 D6
Blackwater Wy ASHV GU12 7 M6
Blackwell Rd RWIN SO21 178 B6
Blagdon Cl STHA RG19 14 A8 1
Blaire Pk YTLY GU46 36 E8
Blair Rd BSTK RG21 92 F5
Blaise Cl FARN GU14 79 G5
Blake Cl CWTH RG45 37 M4
ODIM RG29 96 B8 1
Blake's La TADY RG26 29 L7
Blakes Ride YTLY GU46 56 E2
Bland's Cl THLE RG7 19 J6
Blanket St ALTN GU34 165 L8
Bledlow Cl NWBY RG14 25 G3 1
Blendon Dr AND SP10 8 A3
Blenheim Cl ALTN GU34 164 F5 1
ALTN GU34 185 G5
NFNM GU10 124 B1 1
Blenheim Ct FARN GU14 79 G6
Blenheim Crs FNM GU9 122 D2
Blenheim Pk ALDT GU11 100 F1
Blenheim Rd ALDT GU11 100 F1
CHIN RG24 94 B3
NWBY RG14 2 C4
Blighton La NFNM GU10 124 A6
Bliss Cl KEMP RG22 92 D7
Bloomsbury Wy BLKW GU17 57 M5
Bloswood Dr WHCH RG28 110 A3
Bloswood La WHCH RG28 86 E8
Blue Ball Hl WINC SO23 11 J7
Bluebell Dr THLE RG7 19 J5
Bluebell Rd BOR GU35 189 M3
Bluebell Wy NTHA RG18 15 G3
Bluecoats NTHA RG18 15 G4
Bluethroat Cl SHST GU47 38 B8 1
Bluff Cove ALDT GU11 100 F5 1
Blunden Cl BSTK RG21 92 E7
Blunden Rd FARN GU14 78 C3
Blyth Av STHA RG19 15 H6
Blythwood Dr FRIM GU16 59 G6
Boames La KSCL RG20 24 C3
Boar's Br TADY RG26 50 D6
Bodin Gdns NWBY RG14 13 K8
Bodmin Cl KEMP RG22 92 A5
STHA RG19 14 F6
Bofors Rd FARN GU14 78 D8
Bogmoor Cl ALTN GU34 185 G6
Boldrewood THLE RG7 19 J6 1
Bolingbroke Wy STHA RG19 15 J5
Bolle Rd ALTN GU34 164 C6
Bolley Av BOR GU35 189 G3
Bolton Crs KEMP RG22 92 D5
Bond Cl CHIN RG24 5 M1
Bone La NWBY RG14 3 H4
Bonemill La KSCL RG20 13 G6
Bonhams Cl ALTN GU34 165 K1
Bonners Fld NFNM GU10 144 F3
Boon Wy DEAN RG23 90 F6
Borden Gates AND SP10 9 H7
Border Rd HASM GU27 216 A2
Borderside YTLY GU46 56 D2
Bordon Cl TADY RG26 29 K8
The Boreen BOR GU35 190 E3
Borkum Cl AND SP10 106 E5
Borman Wy RWIN SO21 178 D4
Borodin Cl KEMP RG22 92 E8
The Borough FNM GU9 122 E6
NFNM GU10 121 H2
Borovere Cl ALTN GU34 164 D6
Borovere Gdns ALTN GU34 164 D6
Borovere La ALTN GU34 164 D6
Borsberry Cl AND SP10 9 K4
Boscawen Wy STHA RG19 15 K5 1
Boscobel Rd WINW SO22 10 E4
Bostock Cl RWIN SO21 201 J5
Botany Cl STHA RG19 15 J5 1
Botany Hl NFNM GU10 124 A7
Botisdone Cl RAND SP11 61 G2
Bottle La HTWY RG27 53 M8
Boulters Rd ASHV GU12 7 H3
Boundary Rd FARN GU14 77 M7
GSHT GU26 192 A5
NFNM GU10 168 A2
NWBY RG14 3 H5
Boundstone Cl NFNM GU10 146 E3 1
Boundstone Rd NFNM GU10 146 C4
Bounty Ri BSTK RG21 92 F4
Bounty Rd BSTK RG21 92 F4
Bourley La NFNM GU10 99 J6
Bourley Rd FLET GU13 99 H4
Bourne Arch NTHA RG18 14 E4
Bourne Ct ALDT GU11 6 E5
AND SP10 9 L1
Bourne Dene NFNM GU10 146 D3
Bourne Fld CHIN RG24 70 D4
Bourne Firs NFNM GU10 147 G3
Bourne Gv NFNM GU10 147 H1
Bourne Grove Cl FNM GU9 147 H1
Bourne Grove Dr NFNM GU10 147 H1
Bourne La NTID SP9 126 E1
Bourne Meadow RAND SP11 85 M7
Bourne Mill Rbt FNM GU9 123 H5
Bournemouth Rd RAND SP11 149 K3
Bourne Rd NTID SP9 102 E2
STHA RG19 14 E4
The Bourne FLET GU13 98 F2
Bowcott Hl BOR GU35 190 C3
Bow Dr HTWY RG27 52 C8
Bowenhurst Gdns FLET GU13 98 F4
Bowenhurst Rd FLET GU13 98 F3
Bowenhust La NFNM GU10 98 B5
Bower Rd NFNM GU10 146 D3
Bowers Grove La ALTN GU34 208 B1
Bowers La RAND SP11 60 F1
Bowes Rd STHA RG19 15 G6
Bow Fld HTWY RG27 74 B7
Bow Gdns HTWY RG27 52 C8 1
Bow Gv HTWY RG27 52 C7
Bowling Court Gn FRIM GU16 79 H1
Bowling Green Dr HTWY RG27 73 L7 1
Bowling Green Rd NTHA RG18 14 D3
Bowman Ct CWTH RG45 37 H4
Bowman Rd CHIN RG24 71 L4
Bowmonts Rd TADY RG26 30 A8
Bow St ALTN GU34 164 D6
Boxall's Gv ALDT GU11 6 E6
Boxall's La ALDT GU11 6 F7
FNM GU9 6 D6
Boyce Cl KEMP RG22 92 B8
Boyne Mead Rd WINC SO23 203 G1
Boyne Ri WINC SO23 179 G8
Boyneswood Cl ALTN GU34 185 H4
Boyneswood La ALTN GU34 185 G4
Boyneswood Rd ALTN GU34 185 H4
Brabon Rd FARN GU14 78 C3
Bracebridge CBLY GU15 58 D3
Bracher Cl AND SP10 9 J4
Bracken Bank CHIN RG24 71 L8 1
Brackenbury AND SP10 8 A3
Brackendale Cl FRIM GU16 59 H5
Brackendale Rd CBLY GU15 59 G4
Brackendene ASHV GU12 101 M5
Bracken La BOR GU35 188 F8
YTLY GU46 56 D2
The Brackens CWTH RG45 37 K1
KEMP RG22 115 H2 1
Bracken Wy THLE RG7 19 K6 1
Bracklesham Cl FARN GU14 78 D1
Brackley Av HTWY RG27 75 H2
Brackley Wy KEMP RG22 92 B7
Bracknell Cl CBLY GU15 39 J7
Bracknell La HTWY RG27 75 H1
Bracknell Rd CBLY GU15 39 K6
CWTH RG45 37 M3
Bradbury Cl WHCH RG28 110 A3 1
Bradley-Moore Sq NTHA RG18 15 H3
Bradley Peak WINW SO22 202 B7
Bradley Rd WINW SO22 202 B5
Bradwell Cl AND SP10 106 C5
Braemar Cl FRIM GU16 59 J7
Braemar Dr DEAN RG23 90 F6
Braemore Cl STHA RG19 15 G7
Braeside Cl WINW SO22 226 A4
HASM GU27 192 C8
Brahms Rd KEMP RG22 92 D8
Brake Rd FARN GU14 78 B7
Bramble Bank FRIM GU16 79 K2
Bramblegate CWTH RG45 37 K2
Bramble Hl NALR SO24 206 C3
Brambles Cl ALTN GU34 185 G6
ASHV GU12 101 L7
The Brambles CWTH RG45 37 G2
NWBY RG14 13 H8
Brambleton Av FNM GU9 146 E1
Bramble Wy CHIN RG24 94 B2
Bramblewood Pl FLET GU13 76 D7
Brambling Cl KEMP RG22 114 E1 1
Bramblys Cl BSTK RG21 4 D9
Bramblys Dr BSTK RG21 4 C9
Bramcote CBLY GU15 59 M3
Bramdown Hts KEMP RG22 115 G2
Bramley Cl ALTN GU34 164 F4 1
Bramley Green Rd TADY RG26 51 M6
Bramley Gv CWTH RG45 37 G3
Bramley La BLKW GU17 57 L3
TADY RG26 51 L4
Bramley Rd CBLY GU15 58 E6 1
HTWY RG27 52 C7
TADY RG26 50 C7
THLE RG7 30 E7
Bramley Wk BOR GU35 189 G6
Bramling Av YTLY GU46 56 E2
Brammpton Gdns KEMP RG22 115 G3
Bramshaw Cl WINW SO22 202 B5
Bramshot Dr FLET GU13 76 F6
Bramshot La FARN GU14 77 K3
Bramshott Dr HTWY RG27 74 A7
Bramshott Rd FARN GU14 77 K7
Bramwell Cl STHA RG19 15 J6 2
Brancaster Av AND SP10 106 C5 3
Brandon Cl ALTN GU34 164 C4
Brandon Rd FLET GU13 98 D3
Brandy Mt NALR SO24 206 C2
Branksome Av STOK SO20 153 M5
Branksome Cl CBLY GU15 59 H2 1
WINW SO22 226 A2
STOK SO20 153 L5
Branksome Hill Rd SHST GU47 58 B1
Branksome Park Rd CBLY GU15 59 H2
Branksomewood Rd FLET GU13 76 D7
Branson Rd BOR GU35 189 K5
Branton Cl KEMP RG22 92 B5
Brassey Rd WINW SO22 10 E4
Braunfels Wk KSCL RG20 2 A6
NWBY RG14 2 A5
Braye Cl SHST GU47 37 M7 2
Breachfield KSCL RG20 45 J1
Breach La HTWY RG27 52 D8
RAND SP11 60 A8
Brecon Cl FARN GU14 78 A1
The Breech CBLY GU15 58 B1
Bremen Gdns AND SP10 106 E6
Brendon Rd FARN GU14 78 A1
Brent Cl STHA RG19 15 G6
Bret Harte Rd FRIM GU16 59 H7
Brewells La LISS GU33 237 K2
Brewer Cl KEMP RG22 92 B5
Brewers Cl FARN GU14 78 D3
Brewers La NALR SO24 209 J7
Brewery Common THLE RG7 31 L2
Brewhouse La HTWY RG27 75 J2 1
Briar La ALTN GU34 185 H5
Briarlea Rd THLE RG7 31 J2
Briars Cl FARN GU14 78 A5
The Briars ASHV GU12 101 L7
Briar Wy TADY RG26 29 M8
Briar Wd LISS GU33 236 F1
Briarwood Dr EWKG RG40 36 B2 1
Brickfields Cl CHIN RG24 71 M8 2
Brickiln La ALTN GU34 185 L2
Brick Kiln La ALTN GU34 164 B4
NALR SO24 232 E1
Brick La FLET GU13 76 F6
Bricksbury Hl FNM GU9 122 F1
Bridge End CBLY GU15 58 D8
Bridgefield FNM GU9 123 G6
Bridgemead FRIM GU16 59 G8
Bridge Mdw LISS GU33 236 E4
Bridge Rd ALDT GU11 6 F5
CBLY GU15 58 E5
FARN GU14 78 C4
HASM GU27 216 F1
NALR SO24 206 A3
ODIM RG29 96 D4
The Bridges THLE RG7 30 F3
Bridge St AND SP10 9 H6
NWBY RG14 2 E4
OVTN RG25 88 F8
WINC SO23 11 J8 1
Bridgetts La RWIN SO21 180 A6
Bridge Wk YTLY GU46 57 G1
Bridle Cl ALTN GU34 210 C3
GSHT GU26 191 K5
Bridle Ct ALDT GU11 6 B2
Briff La THLE RG7 15 L2
Brighton Rd ALDT GU11 7 K6
Brighton Wy KEMP RG22 92 C7
Brightstone La ALTN GU34 185 M6
Brightwells Rd FNM GU9 122 F6 1
Brimpton Rd THLE RG7 16 B7
THLE RG7 17 G3
Brindle Cl ALDT GU11 7 G7
Brinksway FLET GU13 76 F8
Brinn's La BLKW GU17 57 M3
Brisbane Cl RAND SP11 103 J1 1
Brislands La ALTN GU34 208 C1
Bristow Rd CBLY GU15 58 E5
Britannia Cl BOR GU35 189 L5 1
Britten Cl ASHV GU12 101 L6
Broadacres FLET GU13 76 C8 1
Broad Chalke Down
WINW SO22 226 B4
Broadhalfpenny La TADY RG26 29 M7
Broad Ha'penny NFNM GU10 146 D3
Broadhurst FARN GU14 77 M4
Broadhurst Gv CHIN RG24 93 L1
Broadlands FARN GU14 79 H6 2
FRIM GU16 59 J8
Broad La THLE RG7 15 L2
Broad Leaze HTWY RG27 73 M6 1
Broadmead FARN GU14 78 A5
Broadmeadow End NTHA RG18 15 J5
Broadoak TADY RG26 30 A8 1
Broad Oak La ODIM RG29 96 F5
Broad Rd RAND SP11 129 G5
Broad St NALR SO24 206 C2
Broadview Cl ALTN GU34 166 D1
Broad View La WINW SO22 225 M5
Broad Wk FRIM GU16 59 H6
Broad Wy FARN GU14 78 D8
PSF GU32 234 C8
THLE RG7 33 G5
Broadway STHA RG19 15 G5
WHCH RG28 110 C4
The Broadway SHST GU47 57 L1
WINC SO23 11 H8
Broadwell Rd NFNM GU10 146 C2
Brocas Dr BSTK RG21 5 H4
Brocas Rd THLE RG7 19 J7
Brockenhurst Dr YTLY GU46 57 G3 2
Brockenhurst Rd ALDT GU11 7 G5
Brockham Hill La ALTN GU34 142 F5
Brockhurst Ldg FNM GU9 146 E1
Brocklands YTLY GU46 56 E4 1
Brockwood Bottom
NALR SO24 231 K7
Broken Wy KSCL RG20 25 L6
Bromelia Cl TADY RG26 51 L4
Brook Av FNM GU9 6 D7
Brook Cl FLET GU13 76 F8
SHST GU47 38 B7
Brooke Cl WINC SO23 179 G8
Brookers Cnr CWTH RG45 37 M3
Brookers Rw CWTH RG45 37 M2
Brookfield Cl CHIN RG24 71 M5 1
Brookfield Rd ASHV GU12 101 H6
Brook Gdns FARN GU14 78 C6
Brook Gn TADY RG26 30 A8
Brookhouse Rd FARN GU14 78 C5
Brooklands ALDT GU11 6 B3 1
Brooklands Cl FNM GU9 123 G1
NFNM GU10 145 G3 1
Brooklands Wy FNM GU9 6 A8
Brookley Cl NFNM GU10 123 L5
Brookly Gdns FLET GU13 77 G6
Brook Rd CBLY GU15 58 E4
Brooksby Cl BLKW GU17 57 L3 2
Brooks Cl WHCH RG28 110 C4
Brookside FNM GU9 122 F2 2
SHST GU47 57 M1
Brooks Rd NTHA RG18 15 H4
The Brook NALR SO24 182 C8
Brookvale Cl BSTK RG21 4 C8
Brookway NWBY RG14 14 B5
RAND SP11 130 B4
Brookwood Rd FARN GU14 79 G4
Broom Acres FLET GU13 98 E2
SHST GU47 37 L8
Broom Cl BLKW GU17 58 B4 1
Broome Cl YTLY GU46 56 F1
Broomfield La NFNM GU10 146 D7
Broomfield Rd BOR GU35 189 G6
Broomhill NFNM GU10 99 G8
Broomhill Rd FARN GU14 78 A3
Broomleaf Cnr FNM GU9 123 G6 1
Broomleaf Rd FNM GU9 123 G6
Broomrigg Rd FLET GU13 76 C6
Broomwood Wy NFNM GU10 146 F2
Brougham Pl FNM GU9 122 E1
Broughton Ms FRIM GU16 59 J7 1
Broughton Rd STOK SO20 173 K6
Brown Cft HTWY RG27 73 L7
Browning Cl CBLY GU15 59 M4
CHIN RG24 5 G1
NTHA RG18 14 F4
Browning Dr WINW SO22 10 B6
Browning Rd FLET GU13 98 D5
Browns Cl TADY RG26 51 K4
Brownsfield Rd NTHA RG18 14 F5
Brownsover Rd FARN GU14 77 M4
Browns Wk NFNM GU10 146 C3
Broxhead Farm Rd BOR GU35 167 K8
Brtten Rd KEMP RG22 92 D8
Bruan Rd NWBY RG14 13 J8
Brummell Rd NWBY RG14 2 A1
Brunel Cl RWIN SO21 136 A6
Brunel Rd BSTK RG21 92 D2
Brunswick Rd FRIM GU16 79 M2
Bruntile Cl FARN GU14 79 G7
Bryanstone Cl FLET GU13 98 F2
Bryce Gdns ALDT GU11 7 K8
Bryces La NALR SO24 159 M5
Brydes Rd RAND SP11 80 E6
Bryn Rd NFNM GU10 146 C1 1
Buchanan Dr EWKG RG40 36 B1
Buchanan Sq STHA RG19 15 H7
The Buchan CBLY GU15 39 K8
Buckby La BSTK RG21 5 K7
Buckfast Cl CHIN RG24 70 F7
Buckholt Rd STOK SO20 196 F2
Buckhurst Rd FRIM GU16 79 J2
Buckingham Cl ALTN GU34 164 C5 1
Buckingham Rd NWBY RG14 2 B7
Buckland Av KEMP RG22 92 C7
Buckland Cl FARN GU14 78 F1
Buckskin La KEMP RG22 91 M6
Buddlesgate RWIN SO21 156 C5
Budd's Cl BSTK RG21 4 C9
Budds La BOR GU35 189 H4
Buffbeards La HASM GU27 216 B1
Buffins Rd ODIM RG29 96 B6
Bugkingham Wy FRIM GU16 59 J8
Bulbery RAND SP11 129 L5
Bulford Rd NTID SP9 102 A7
NTID SP9 102 D8
Bull Dro WINC SO23 227 G3
Buller Ct FARN GU14 78 F7 4
Buller Rd ALDT GU11 100 E4
Bullers Rd FNM GU9 123 H2
Bullfinch Cl SHST GU47 38 B8 2
Bull Hl LISS GU33 237 K4
Bullington La RWIN SO21 155 K1
Bull La THLE RG7 33 L5
Bulls Down Cl HTWY RG27 52 B7
Bulls Dro RSAL SP5 219 M2
Bulpits Hl RAND SP11 61 H2
Bunces La THLE RG7 19 K6
Bunch La HASM GU27 216 D1
Bunch Wy HASM GU27 216 D2
Bungalow Rd FARN GU14 78 E6
Bungler's Hl THLE RG7 34 E2
Bunkers Hl NWBY RG14 24 F3 2
Bunnian Pl BSTK RG21 4 F6
Bunting Cl KEMP RG22 114 E1
Bunting Ms KEMP RG22 114 F1 2
Buntings ALTN GU34 164 E2
Burchell Rd NWBY RG14 13 H3
Burdens Heath NTHA RG18 15 K1
Burdock Cl RAND SP11 130 E8
THLE RG7 19 L6
Burfield KSCL RG20 44 B3
Burford Rd CBLY GU15 58 E4 1
Burgess Cl ODIM RG29 96 B6 1
Burgess La KSCL RG20 22 F3
Burgess Rd BSTK RG21 4 D5
Burghead Cl SHST GU47 58 A1 2
Burgh Hill Rd LIPH GU30 214 C1
Burgoyne Rd CBLY GU15 59 K2
Buriton Rd WINW SO22 202 C4
Burkal Dr AND SP10 106 F4
Burleigh Rd FRIM GU16 59 G8
Burley La OVTN RG25 112 C7
Burley Rd WINW SO22 202 C4
Burley Wy BLKW GU17 57 M2
Burlington Ct BLKW GU17 57 M5
Burnaby Cl KEMP RG22 92 B5
Burne Cl RWIN SO21 178 C6
Burne-Jones Dr SHST GU47 58 A2
Burnett Cl WINW SO22 202 B6
Burney Bit TADY RG26 30 B8
Burnham Rd TADY RG26 29 J6
Burnhams Cl AND SP10 106 F5
Burnley Cl TADY RG26 49 L1
Burnmoor Meadow
EWKG RG40 36 B6
Burnsall Cl FARN GU14 78 E2
Burns Av FLET GU13 99 G2
Burns Cl CHIN RG24 5 H2
FARN GU14 78 C2
RWIN SO21 178 D4
Burnt Hill Rd NFNM GU10 146 F2
Burnt Hill Wy NFNM GU10 146 E3
Burrell Rd FRIM GU16 58 F8
Burr La MARL SN8 20 B6
Burrowfields KEMP RG22 115 G3 1

Burrow Rd RWIN SO21 .... 201 H7
Burrwood Gdns ALDT GU12 .... 101 K4
Burton's Gdns CHIN RG24 .... 94 A1
Burydown Cl OVTN RG25 .... 113 L7
Buryfields ODIM RG29 .... 96 D6
Bury Hill Cl RAND SP11 .... 130 C4
Bury Rd DEAN RG23 .... 92 C2
Bury's Bank Rd STHA RG19 .... 15 H8
  STHA RG19 .... 26 A1
Bushnells Dr KSCL RG20 .... 47 H6
Bushywarren La OVTN RG25 .... 116 E7
Busk Crs FARN GU14 .... 78 C5
Busket La WINC SO23 .... 11 H8
Butler Cl KEMP RG22 .... 92 B4
Butler Rd CWTH RG45 .... 37 L2
Butlers Cl ROMY SO51 .... 220 F7
Butson Cl NWBY RG14 .... 2 A4
Butt Cl RAND SP11 .... 80 D5
Buttercup Cl BOR GU35 .... 189 M3
Buttercup Pl NTHA RG18 .... 15 G4
Butterfield CBLY GU15 .... 58 E4
Buttermer Cl NFNM GU10 .... 146 B1
Buttermere Cl FARN GU14 .... 78 B4
  BOR GU35 .... 189 J3
Buttermere Dr KEMP RG22 .... 91 M7
Buttermere Gdns
  NALR SO24 .... 206 C2
Button's La ALTN GU34 .... 211 G6
Butts Meadow HTWY RG27 .... 73 M7
Butts Ms ALTN GU34 .... 164 D6
Butts Rd ALTN GU34 .... 164 D7
The Butts THLE RG7 .... 30 E8
Butt St RAND SP11 .... 80 D6
The Butty BSTK RG21 .... 5 K7
Byes La THLE RG7 .... 50 L1
Byeways KSCL RG20 .... 44 B3
Byfields Rd KSCL RG20 .... 47 H6
By Pass Rd RWIN SO21 .... 156 A4
Byrd Gdns KEMP RG22 .... 115 H1
Byron Av FRIM GU16 .... 59 L5
  WINC SO22 .... 10 A7
Byron Cl CHIN RG24 .... 71 H7
  FLET GU13 .... 76 F8
  NWBY RG14 .... 25 J1
  RAND SP11 .... 80 E6
  YTLY GU46 .... 56 E4
Byron Dr CWTH RG45 .... 37 L5
Byways YTLY GU46 .... 56 E3
Byworth Cl FNM GU9 .... 122 C6
Byworth Rd FNM GU9 .... 122 C6

C

Cabrol Rd FARN GU14 .... 78 D3
Cabul Rd NTID SP9 .... 102 C3
Cadet Wy FLET GU13 .... 99 G4
Cadnam Cl ALDT GU11 .... 7 J8
  DEAN RG23 .... 91 G6
Cadogen Rd ALDT GU11 .... 101 G1
Caerleon Cl GSHT GU26 .... 191 M2
Caerleon Dr AND SP10 .... 106 F4
Caernarvon FRIM GU16 .... 59 J8
Caernarvon Cl DEAN RG23 .... 92 B5
Caesar Ct ALDT GU11 .... 6 B2
Caesar Rd AND SP10 .... 107 G5
Caesar's Camp Rd CBLY GU15 .... 39 K8
Caesar's Cl CBLY GU15 .... 39 K8
Caesar's Wy WHCH RG28 .... 110 A2
Cairn Cl FRIM GU16 .... 59 L5
Cairngorm Cl KEMP RG22 .... 92 A4
Cairngorm Pl FARN GU14 .... 78 B1
Cairngorm Rd STHA RG19 .... 15 G6
Caithness Cl DEAN RG23 .... 90 F6
Caker's La ALTN GU34 .... 165 J6
Caker Stream Rd ALTN GU34 .... 165 G4
Calard Dr NTHA RG18 .... 14 D3
Calcott Pk YTLY GU46 .... 56 F2
Calder Ct AND SP10 .... 107 H6
Calender Cl ALTN GU34 .... 164 E6
Calleva Cl KEMP RG22 .... 115 G1
Calshot Wy FRIM GU16 .... 79 K1
Calthorpe Rd FLET GU13 .... 76 D6
  HTWY RG27 .... 76 D5
Calton Gdns ALDT GU11 .... 7 J8
Calvecroft LIPH GU30 .... 214 F4
Calvert Cl ASHV GU12 .... 7 M4
Calvin Cl CBLY GU15 .... 59 L4
Camberry Cl BSTK RG21 .... 93 H5
Cambrian Cl CBLY GU15 .... 58 E3
Cambrian Rd FARN GU14 .... 78 A1
Cambrian Wy KEMP RG22 .... 92 A5
Cambridge Rd ALDT GU11 .... 6 C2
  CWTH RG45 .... 37 M4
  SHST GU47 .... 38 B7
Cambridge Rd East
  FARN GU14 .... 78 F7
Cambridge Rd West FARN GU14 .. 78 F7
Camden Wk FLET GU13 .... 77 H7
Camelot Cl AND SP10 .... 106 F6
Camelsdale Rd HASM GU27 .... 216 C3
Camel Wy FARN GU14 .... 78 D8
Cameron Rd ALDT GU11 .... 101 G1
Camfield Cl BSTK RG21 .... 93 H5
Camlea Cl BSTK RG21 .... 93 H5
Camomile Dr RAND SP11 .... 80 E6
Campbell Cl ALDT GU11 .... 7 H8
  FLET GU13 .... 76 D7
  RAND SP11 .... 149 K1
  YTLY GU46 .... 57 J2
Campbell Pl FRIM GU16 .... 59 J5
Campbell Rd ALDT GU11 .... 100 D5
  RWIN SO21 .... 133 H6
  TADY RG26 .... 52 A6
Camp Farm Rd ALDT GU11 .... 101 G3
Camp Hl NFNM GU10 .... 123 M8
Campion Cl BLKW GU17 .... 58 C5
  BOR GU35 .... 189 M4
Campion Wy HTWY RG27 .... 75 J7
  WINC SO22 .... 203 H2
Camp Rd FARN GU14 .... 78 F8
  BOR GU35 .... 189 J3
  THLE RG7 .... 18 F5
Campsie Cl KEMP RG22 .... 92 A4
Camrose Wy BSTK RG21 .... 93 H5

Camus Cl FLET GU13 .... 98 C3
Camwood Cl BSTK RG21 .... 93 H5
Canada Wy BOR GU35 .... 189 L3
Canal Cl ALDT GU11 .... 101 G3
  ODIM RG29 .... 96 B4
Canal View Rd NWBY RG14 .... 3 M4
Canberra Cl HTWY RG27 .... 56 D1
Canberra Wy FARN GU14 .... 78 C8
Candover Cl TADY RG26 .... 49 L1
Canes La BOR GU35 .... 189 L3
Canhouse La LISS GU33 .... 237 L5
Canning Rd ASHV GU12 .... 7 L2
Cannon Cl SHST GU47 .... 38 C8
Canons Cl NTID SP9 .... 102 E4
Canon's Ct KSCL RG20 .... 47 H6
Canon St WINC SO23 .... 10 F9
Cansfield End NWBY RG14.... 2 D5
Canterbury Cl KEMP RG22 .... 92 A8
Canterbury Rd ASHV GU12 .... 101 K5
  FARN GU14 .... 79 G6
Canute Rd ASHV GU12 .... 227 G2
Capper Rd CBLY GU15 .... 58 D1
Carbinswood La THLE RG7 .... 17 G4
Carbonel Cl DEAN RG23 .... 91 M3
Cardew Rd LISS GU33 .... 236 F5
Carfax Av ALTN GU10 .... 101 J8
Cargate Av ALDT GU11 .... 6 E3
Cargate Gv ALDT GU11 .... 6 D3
Cargate Hl ALDT GU11 .... 6 D3
Cargate Ter ALDT GU11 .... 6 D4
Carisbrooke FRIM GU16 .... 59 J8
Carisbrooke Cl DEAN RG23 .... 92 B2
  NALR SO24 .... 206 C4
Carleton Cl HTWY RG27 .... 73 L7
Carlinwark Dr CBLY GU15 .... 59 J1
Carlisle Cl DEAN RG23 .... 92 B2
Carlisle Rd NFNM GU10 .... 169 L1
Carlton Cl FRIM GU16 .... 59 L5
Carlton Crs FLET GU13 .... 99 G2
Carlyon Cl FARN GU14 .... 78 F4
  FRIM GU16 .... 79 J4
Carmarthen Cl FARN GU14 .... 78 C1
Carmichael Wy KEMP RG22 .... 92 B8
Carnegie Rd NWBY RG14 .... 2 F5
Carolina Pl EWKG RG40 .... 36 B1
Caroline Wy FRIM GU16 .... 59 J7
Carpenter Rd RWIN SO21 .... 133 H6
Carpenters NALR SO24 .... 206 C3
Carpenters Cl HTWY RG27 .... 52 C7
Carpenter's Down CHIN RG24 .. 71 H2
Carrick La YTLY GU46 .... 57 H2
Carrington Crs TADY RG26 .... 29 L8
Carrinton La ASHV GU12.... 79 J8
Carshalton Rd CBLY GU15 .... 39 K7
Cartersland LIPH GU30 .... 238 E5
Carter's Meadow AND SP10 .... 106 C6
Carters Wk FNM GU9 .... 100 A8
Carthagena RWIN SO21 .... 156 C4
Carthona Dr FLET GU13 .... 98 E1
Carvers Hl MARL SN8 .... 20 A6
Cary Cl NWBY RG14 .... 25 G2
Cassino Cl ALDT GU11 .... 7 G1
Castle Cl CBLY GU15 .... 59 J4
Castle Ct RAND SP11 .... 80 D5
Castlecraig Ct SHST GU47 .... 58 A1
Castle Gv NWBY RG14 .... 13 J3
Castle Hl FNM GU9 .... 122 E5
  THLE RG7 .... 34 F1
Castle La NWBY RG14 .... 13 H2
Castle Ri ODIM RG29 .... 96 B4
  WINC SO23 .... 179 H7
Castle Rd ALDT GU11 .... 100 B4
  BSTK RG21 .... 93 G5
  CBLY GU15 .... 59 H4
Castle St ALTN GU34 .... 184 D1
  FLET GU13 .... 98 E1
  FNM GU9 .... 122 E5
  RAND SP11 .... 80 D5
Castor Ct FLET GU13 .... 99 G3
  YTLY GU46 .... 56 E1
Caswall Ride YTLY GU46 .... 57 J3
Caswell Cl FARN GU14 .... 78 C2
Catesby Gdns YTLY GU46 .... 56 D3
Cathedral Vw WINC SO23 .... 227 G2
Catherine Rd NWBY RG14 .... 2 E6
Catkin Cl CHIN RG24 .... 71 L5
Cattle La RAND SP11 .... 129 M4
Caunter Rd NWBY RG14 .... 13 G4
The Causeway HTWY RG27 .... 53 M1
  RSAL SP5 .... 194 F2
  STOK SO20 .... 172 E2
Cavalier Cl CHIN RG24 .... 94 B2
  NWBY RG14 .... 13 M3
Cavalier Rd CHIN RG24 .... 94 B2
Cavalier Wy ALTN GU34 .... 164 C6
Cavalry Ct ALDT GU11 .... 6 B2
Cavan's Rd ALDT GU11 .... 100 F2
Cavel Ct CHIN RG24 .... 71 M8
Cavendish Ct BLKW GU17 .... 58 A5
  NWBY RG14 .... 14 B3
Cavendish Gv WINC SO23 .... 11 J1
Cavendish Rd ALDT GU11 .... 6 B2
  FLET GU13 .... 98 D3
Caves Farm Cl SHST GU47 .... 37 K8
Caxton Cl AND SP10 .... 106 B7
Cayman Cl FARN GU14 .... 71 H7
Cedar Av BLKW GU17 .... 58 A3
Cedar Cl ASHV GU12 .... 101 H8
  TADY RG26 .... 50 A2
  WINC SO23 .... 179 G8
Cedar Ct HASM GU27 .... 216 F2
Cedar Dr FLET GU13 .... 77 G8
  KSCL RG20 .... 47 H6
Cedar Gv STHA RG19 .... 14 F5
Cedar Mt NWBY RG14 .... 13 J8
Cedar Rd FARN GU14 .... 78 F5
Cedars SHST GU47 .... 38 C7
The Cedars FLET GU13 .... 77 G8
Cedars Vw RSAL SP5 .... 220 D1
Cedar Tree Cl DEAN RG23 .... 90 F8
Cedarway FNM GU9 .... 146 E1
Cedarwood WINC SO23 .... 203 H1
Celandine Cl CWTH RG45 .... 37 M2
Celandine Ct YTLY GU46 .... 56 E1
Celandine Gv NTHA RG18 .... 15 J5
Celtic Dr AND SP10 .... 8 C8

Cemetery Hl ODIM RG29 .... 96 D6
Cemetery La NWBY RG25 .... 118 A3
Cemetery Rd FLET GU13 .... 98 D1
Central Rd BOR GU35 .... 189 J2
Central St RAND SP11 .... 80 E6
Centre Dr CHIN RG24 .... 71 L7
Centre Terrace Rd FARN GU14 .... 78 D8
Centurion Cl SHST GU47 .... 38 A8
Centurion Wy KEMP RG22 .... 115 G2
Chaffers Cl ODIM RG29 .... 119 J6
Chaffinch Cl KEMP RG22 .... 91 M4
  SHST GU47 .... 38 B8
Chalcraft Cl LIPH GU30 .... 214 D4
Chalcrafts ALTN GU34 .... 164 F3
Chalet Hl BOR GU35 .... 189 K5
Chalfont Dr FARN GU14 .... 78 F6
Chalford Rd NWBY RG14 .... 2 A5
Chalk Cl ALTN GU34 .... 185 G6
Chalkcroft La RAND SP11 .... 105 L4
Chalk Hl STOK SO20 .... 199 J3
Chalkpit La RAND SP11 .... 129 J3
Chalk Pit La RSAL SP5 .... 196 A7
Chalk Rdg WINC SO23 .... 11 M9
Chalk V CHIN RG24 .... 94 B3
  STOK SO20 .... 199 L4
Chalky Copse HTWY RG27 .... 73 M6
Chalky Hl ALTN GU34 .... 183 M2
Chalky La HTWY RG27 .... 97 L5
Challenor Cl EWKG RG40 .... 36 C1
Challis Cl KEMP RG22 .... 92 B6
Challis Ct RAND SP11 .... 80 F4
Challoner Cl KEMP RG22 .... 92 B5
Chamber La NFNM GU10 .... 121 M8
Chambers Rd ASHV GU12 .... 101 L2
Chamomile Gdns FARN GU14 .... 77 M3
Champion Wy FLET GU13 .... 98 F3
Champney Cl BOR GU35 .... 189 H7
Chandler Rd BSTK RG21 .... 92 F6
Chandlers La YTLY GU46 .... 56 F1
Chandlers Rd ASHV GU12 .... 101 L4
Chandos Rd NWBY RG14 .... 13 J8
Chant Cl RAND SP11 .... 153 L2
Chantreys FLET GU13 .... 76 C8
Chantry Cl FNM GU9 .... 122 D6
Chantry Ms KEMP RG22 .... 115 L1
The Chantrys FNM GU9 .... 122 C6
Chantry St AND SP10 .... 9 H5
Chapel Cl OVTN RG25 .... 114 C7
  RAND SP11 .... 129 G2
  STOK SO20 .... 198 B3
Chapel Ct NTHA RG18 .... 15 H4
Chapel Gdns BOR GU35 .... 189 L3
Chapel Hl BSTK RG21 .... 4 D6
Chapel La FARN GU14 .... 58 C8
  RAND SP11 .... 80 D6
  RAND SP11 .... 85 H4
  RAND SP11 .... 107 G2
  RAND SP11 .... 128 A8
  ROMY SO51 .... 222 C3
  RWIN SO21 .... 203 M6
  STHA RG19 .... 28 C7
  STOK SO20 .... 197 G1
  TADY RG26 .... 48 C4
  THLE RG7 .... 30 C3
Chapel Md HTWY RG27 .... 36 B8
Chapel Pond Dr ODIM RG29 .... 96 B5
Chapel River Cl AND SP10 .... 8 B6
Chapel Rd CBLY GU15 .... 58 E3
  KSCL RG20 .... 12 B2
  NFNM GU10 .... 146 B5
Chapel Sq CBLY GU15 .... 58 C2
Chapel St FARN GU14 .... 79 G2
  NTHA RG18 .... 15 H5
  OVTN RG25 .... 113 K7
Chaplain's Hl CWTH RG45 .... 38 A4
Chapman Wk NTHA RG18.... 14 E4
Chappell Cl LIPH GU30 .... 214 F4
Chapter Ter HTWY RG27 .... 75 J2
Charfield Cl WINW SO22 .... 226 D3
Charlcot Cl WHCH RG28 .... 110 B5
Charlcot Farm WHCH RG28 .... 110 B5
Charldon Gn CHIN RG24 .... 71 M8
Charlecote Cl FARN GU14.... 79 G5
Charledown Cl OVTN RG25 .... 111 M1
Charledown Rd OVTN RG25.... 111 M1
Charles Cl HTWY RG27 .... 73 M7
  WINC SO23 .... 11 H2
Charles Richards Cl
  BSTK RG21 .... 92 F5
Charles St CBLY GU15 .... 58 F3
  KEMP RG22 .... 92 C4
  NWBY RG14 .... 25 G2
Charlock Cl NTHA RG18.... 15 H3
Charlotte Cl AND SP10 .... 107 J8
  FNM GU9 .... 100 A3
Charlton Cl SHST GU47 .... 38 A7
Charlton La THLE RG7 .... 33 M3
Charlton Pl NWBY RG14 .... 2 F2
Charlton Rd AND SP10 .... 8 D2
Charlwood La ALTN GU34 .... 209 H4
Charmwood Cl NWBY RG14 .... 13 J3
Charnwood Cl AND SP10 .... 9 K8
  KEMP RG22 .... 92 A4
Charter Rd NWBY RG14 .... 13 J8
Chart House Rd ASHV GU12.... 101 K1
Chartwell FNM GU9 .... 146 C2
  FRIM GU16 .... 59 J6
Chartwell Gdns ALDT GU11 .... 100 F1
Chase Cl LISS GU33 .... 236 F4
Chase Fld ALTN GU34 .... 186 C6
Chase La HASM GU27 .... 217 H4
Chase Rd BOR GU35 .... 189 L3
  LISS GU33 .... 236 F4
The Chase CWTH RG45 .... 37 K2
  FARN GU14 .... 79 G2
  NWBY RG14 .... 13 J1
Chatfield Cl FARN GU14 .... 78 F6
Chatham Rd WINW SO22 .... 226 B5
Chatsworth Av HASM GU27.... 192 F8
Chatsworth Dr AND SP10 .... 8 B7
Chatsworth Gn KEMP RG22.... 115 G2
Chatsworth Gv FNM GU9 .... 122 E2
Chatsworth Hts CBLY GU15.... 59 L1
Chatsworth Rd FARN GU14.... 79 H5
The Chatters THLE RG7 .... 34 F1
Chaucer Av ASHV GU12.... 7 K4
Chaucer Cl CHIN RG24.... 71 H7
  RWIN SO21 .... 178 D3

Chaucer Crs NWBY RG14 .... 13 H3
Chaucer Gv CBLY GU15 .... 59 G3
Chaucer Rd CWTH RG45 .... 37 L4
  FARN GU14 .... 78 C2
Chaundler Rd WINC SO23 .... 11 H3
Chauntsingers Rd ALTN GU34 .... 164 E4
Chawton Cl WINW SO22 .... 202 C4
Chawton End Cl ALTN GU34 .... 185 H4
Chawton Park Rd ALTN GU34 .... 164 A8
Cheap St NWBY RG14 .... 2 E4
Cheavley Cl AND SP10 .... 106 B8
Cheesecombe Farm La
  LISS GU33 .... 235 L2
Cheetah Rd FARN GU14 .... 78 E6
Chelwood Dr SHST GU47 .... 37 J7
Chequer La THLE RG7 .... 33 H6
Chequers La HTWY RG27 .... 56 B1
Chequers Rd BSTK RG21 .... 4 F8
Cherberry Cl FARN GU14 .... 77 G4
Cheriton Cl WINW SO22 .... 10 B5
  NWBY RG14 .... 3 G8
  TADY RG26 .... 49 L1
Cheriton La NALR SO24 .... 206 E8
Cheriton Rd WINW SO22 .... 10 C5
Cheriton Wy BLKW GU17 .... 58 A3
Cherrimans Orch
  HASM GU27 .... 216 C2
Cherry Cl HTWY RG27 .... 74 A6
  NWBY RG14 .... 2 D1
  RWIN SO21 .... 178 C4
Cherryhill Gv ALDT GU11 .... 6 C4
Cherry Tree Av HASM GU27 .... 216 C1
  NTID SP9 .... 102 F1
Cherry Tree Cl FARN GU14 .... 77 M3
  SHST GU47 .... 38 A7
Cherry Tree Rd AND SP10 .... 8 C2
  NFNM GU10 .... 146 B5
Cherryway ALTN GU34 .... 164 D3
Cherrywood Rd FARN GU14 .... 78 D1
Chervil Wy THLE RG7 .... 19 L6
Chesil St WINC SO23 .... 11 J9
Chesilton Crs FLET GU13 .... 98 F4
Chester Cl ASHV GU12 .... 101 L6
  WINC SO23 .... 11 J8
Chesterfield Rd BSTK RG21 .... 93 H5
Chester Pl BSTK RG21 .... 92 F4
Chester Rd ASHV GU12 .... 101 L5
  WINC SO23 .... 11 J8
Chesters Rd CBLY GU15 .... 59 L3
Chesterton Rd NTHA RG18.... 14 F3
Chester Wy NFNM GU10 .... 124 C2
Chestnut Av AND SP10 .... 130 E3
  ASHV GU12 .... 124 B1
  CBLY GU15 .... 59 K2
  FNM GU9 .... 122 D8
  WINW SO22 .... 202 A4
  HASM GU27 .... 216 F1
  NTID SP9 .... 102 E1
Chestnut Cl ALTN GU34 .... 164 D3
  BLKW GU17 .... 58 B3
  FARN GU14 .... 77 H4
  GSHT GU26 .... 191 L5
  LIPH GU30 .... 215 G5
Chestnut Ct ASHV GU12 .... 7 M2
  BOR GU35 .... 189 K6
Chestnut Crs NWBY RG14 .... 2 E1
  STOK SO20 .... 151 G4
Chestnut Dr TLHT RG30 .... 19 L4
Chestnut End BOR GU35 .... 190 C4
Chestnut Gv FLET GU13 .... 77 G6
Chestnut Rd FARN GU14 .... 78 D3
Chestnut Ter ALDT GU11 .... 6 A3
Cheswell Gdns FLET GU13 .... 98 D2
Chetwode Pl ALDT GU11 .... 7 K7
Chetwode Ter ALDT GU11 .... 6 A3
Cheviot Cl CBLY GU15 .... 59 M4
  FARN GU14 .... 78 B1
  KEMP RG22 .... 92 A5
  NWBY RG14 .... 24 F3
Cheviot Dr FARN GU14 .... 77 G4
Cheviot Rd SHST GU47 .... 37 J7
Cheyne Wy FARN GU14 .... 78 C1
Chichester Cl AND SP10 .... 8 A4
Chichester Pl KEMP RG22 .... 92 D6
Chichester Rd ASHV GU12 .... 101 K5
Chilbolton Av WINW SO22 .... 10 A6
Chilcomb La RWIN SO21 .... 227 K3
  WINC SO23 .... 227 G1
Chilcroft La HASM GU27 .... 216 E7
Chilcroft Rd HASM GU27 .... 216 D7
Chilcrofts Rd HASM GU27 .... 216 D7
Childerstone Cl LIPH GU30 .... 214 E4
Chilham Cl FRIM GU16 .... 59 J8
Chillandham La RWIN SO21 .... 180 B5
Chilland La RWIN SO21 .... 204 B2
Chillingham Wy CBLY GU15 .... 58 F4
Chiltern Av FARN GU14 .... 78 A4
Chiltern Cl FARN GU14 .... 77 M4
  FLET GU13 .... 99 G3
  HASM GU27 .... 216 E3
  NWBY RG14 .... 24 F3
Chiltern Rd SHST GU47 .... 37 J7
Chiltern Wy KEMP RG22 .... 91 M5
Chiltlee Cl LIPH GU30 .... 214 F5
Chiltlee Mnr LIPH GU30 .... 214 F4
Chiltley La LIPH GU30 .... 215 G6
Chiltley Wy LIPH GU30 .... 214 F6
Chilton Rdg KEMP RG22 .... 115 G3
Chineham La CHIN RG24 .... 5 H2
  CHIN RG24 .... 70 F6
Chineham Park Ct CHIN RG24 .... 5 J1
The Chine NFNM GU10 .... 146 B1
Chingford Av FARN GU14 .... 78 F3
Chinnock Cl FLET GU13 .... 98 E1
Chivers Cl KEMP RG22 .... 92 A5
Chivers Dr EWKG RG40 .... 36 B1
Chobham Rd WINW SO22 .... 59 H6
Cholderton Rd AMSY SP4 .... 126 D7
  RAND SP11 .... 127 J3
Cholsey Cl STHA RG19 .... 15 J5
Chopin Rd KEMP RG22 .... 92 C8
Chrismas Av ASHV GU12 .... 7 K4
Chrismas Pl ASHV GU12 .... 7 K4
Christchurch Cl FLET GU13 .... 98 E4
Christchurch Dr BLKW GU17 .... 57 M2
Christchurch Gdns WINC SO23 .. 226 D3
Christchurch Rd WINC SO23 .... 226 D3

Christie Hts NWBY RG14 .... 13 L8
Christie Wk YTLY GU46 .... 56 F4
Christine Cl ASHV GU12 .... 101 J7
Christmas Hl RWIN SO21 .... 156 B6
Christopher Ct NWBY RG14 .... 3 H6
Christy Ct TADY RG26 .... 49 M1
Church Av FARN GU14 .... 78 F3
Church Bank Rd RWIN SO21 .... 158 A3
Church Barns Farm THLE RG7 .... 32 A3
Church Brook TADY RG26 .... 49 K2
Church Cir FARN GU14 .... 78 F7
Church Cl AND SP10 .... 9 J5
  HASM GU27 .... 193 J6
  KSCL RG20 .... 24 B2
Church Farm Cl OVTN RG25 .... 113 K6
Churchfields BOR GU35 .... 167 G7
Church Flds AND SP10 .... 190 B3
Church Ga STHA RG19 .... 15 G5
Church Gv FLET GU13 .... 76 D7
Church Hams EWKG RG40 .... 36 A2
Church Hl ALDT GU11 .... 7 J5
  ASHV GU12 .... 7 J4
  CBLY GU15 .... 59 H3
  STOK SO20 .... 172 F3
Churchill Av ASHV GU12 .... 7 J5
  ODIM RG29 .... 96 B7
Churchill Cl ALTN GU34 .... 164 E6
  ALTN GU34 .... 185 G5
  HTWY RG27 .... 75 G2
  ODIM RG29 .... 96 C8
  TADY RG26 .... 50 A1
  WINC SO23 .... 179 G7
Churchill Crs FARN GU14 .... 58 E8
  BOR GU35 .... 190 C4
Churchill Wy AND SP10 .... 9 L2
  BSTK RG21 .... 4 E7
Churchill Wy East BSTK RG21 .... 5 H7
Churchill Wy West AND SP10 .... 8 A1
  BSTK RG21 .... 4 A8
  KEMP RG22 .... 92 C3
Church Lands TADY RG26.... 51 J5
Church La ALTN GU34 .... 162 E6
  ALTN GU34 .... 165 H1
  ASHV GU12 .... 101 L6
  CHIN RG24 .... 94 A2
  DEAN RG23 .... 91 M4
  EWKG RG40 .... 36 E3
  FARN GU14 .... 78 B4
  WINW SO22 .... 201 M2
  GSHT GU26 .... 191 M5
  HASM GU27 .... 216 F1
  HTWY RG27 .... 53 M2
  HTWY RG27 .... 75 J4
  HUNG RG17 .... 42 A2
  KSCL RG20 .... 24 A8
  KSCL RG20 .... 45 K1
  BOR GU35 .... 190 A2
  LIPH GU30 .... 214 E2
  LISS GU33 .... 212 C6
  LISS GU33 .... 212 A5
  MARL SN8 .... 41 H2
  NALR SO24 .... 207 H4
  NALR SO24 .... 208 D3
  NALR SO24 .... 231 H4
  NFNM GU10 .... 122 A1
  NFNM GU10 .... 144 F2
  NFNM GU10 .... 146 B5
  NFNM GU10 .... 146 C1
  NWBY RG14 .... 13 G4
  OVTN RG25 .... 115 M1
  OVTN RG25 .... 116 A7
  RAND SP11 .... 40 F8
  RAND SP11 .... 80 D6
  RAND SP11 .... 130 F7
  ROMY SO51 .... 221 L6
  RWIN SO21 .... 201 H5
  RWIN SO21 .... 203 L3
  RWIN SO21 .... 204 A2
  RWIN SO21 .... 226 F8
  STHA RG19 .... 15 G5
  STOK SO20 .... 172 F3
  STOK SO20 .... 198 B2
  TADY RG26 .... 48 A6
  THLE RG7 .... 18 E4
  THLE RG7 .... 28 C2
  THLE RG7 .... 31 H7
  THLE RG7 .... 35 G2
  WINC SO23 .... 203 H2
Church La East ALDT GU11 .... 6 F4
Church La West ALDT GU11 .... 6 D4
Church Mdw NTID SP9 .... 102 D8
Church Pth ASHV GU12 .... 101 K5
Church Rd ALDT GU11 .... 7 J6
  ALTN GU34 .... 186 D5
  CBLY GU15 .... 58 C1
  FLET GU13 .... 76 D6
  FRIM GU16 .... 59 G8
  HASM GU27 .... 216 F1
  KSCL RG20 .... 12 B5
  LIPH GU30 .... 214 F2
  MARL SN8 .... 20 E6
  NWBY RG14 .... 13 K3
  OVTN RG25 .... 88 F8
  OVTN RG25 .... 113 K7
  ROMY SO51 .... 222 C6
  RSAL SP5 .... 218 B1
  SHST GU47 .... 37 J7
  SHST GU47 .... 38 A7
  STOK SO20 .... 174 C1
  STOK SO20 .... 198 F5
  TADY RG26 .... 30 B7
  TADY RG26 .... 49 L2
  THLE RG7 .... 29 M2
  THLE RG7 .... 29 K1
Church Rd East CWTH RG45 .... 37 L3
Church Rd West CWTH RG45 .... 37 L4
  FARN GU14 .... 78 F7
Church Sq BSTK RG21 .... 4 E8
Church St ALDT GU11 .... 6 C3
  ALTN GU34 .... 162 F4
  ALTN GU34 .... 164 E4
  BSTK RG21 .... 4 E8
  CWTH RG45 .... 37 L3
  LISS GU33 .... 236 D2
  NALR SO24 .... 208 B4

NFNM GU10 .... 121 H2
ODIM RG29 .... 96 C6
RAND SP11 .... 84 D1
RAND SP11 .... 153 M2
RWIN SO21 .... 157 M5
WHCH RG28 .... 110 B4
Church Vw ASHV GU12 .... 101 K6
HTWY RG27 .... 74 A7
HTWY RG27 .... 75 H3
ODIM RG29 .... 118 C5
THLE RG7 .... 17 K2
YTLY GU46 .... 57 C1
Churn Cl CHIN RG24 .... 94 A1
Churt Rd BOR GU35 .... 190 D1
NFNM GU10 .... 169 J8
Churt Wynde GSHT GU26 .... 192 A5
Chute Cswy RAND SP11 .... 60 A5
Cibbons Rd CHIN RG24 .... 71 L5
Circle Hill Rd CWTH RG45 .... 37 M3
City Rd WINC SO23 .... 10 F6
Clandon Ct FARN GU14 .... 79 G5
Clanfield Ride BLKW GU17 .... 58 A3
Clappers Farm Rd THLE RG7 .... 31 K8
Clapps Gate Rd TADY RG26 .... 30 B7
Clare Md NFNM GU10 .... 146 C5
Claremont Av CBLY GU15 .... 59 J3
Clarence Cl ASHV GU12 .... 7 K2
RAND SP11 .... 80 D6
Clarence Dr CBLY GU15 .... 59 L1
Clarence Rd FLET GU13 .... 76 E8
Clarendon Av AND SP10 .... 8 D8
Clarendon Ct BLKW GU17 .... 58 A5
Clarendon Gdns NWBY RG14.. .... 2 F2
Clarendon Wy RSAL SP5 .... 195 K2
STOK SO20 .... 196 E2
STOK SO20 .... 198 B4
STOK SO20 .... 224 B1
Clarewood Dr CBLY GU15 .... 59 H2
Clarke Crs CBLY GU15 .... 58 E3
Clarke's La RAND SP11 .... 82 E2
Clarks HI NFNM GU10 .... 121 M6
Claudius Cl AND SP10 .... 107 C4
Claudius Dr DEAN RG23 .... 92 B1
Clausentum Rd WINC SO23 .... 226 E3
Claycart Rd ALDT GU11 .... 100 A5
Claydon Gdns FARN GU14 .... 58 D7
Clay Hill Crs NWBY RG14 .... 14 A3
Clayhill Rd THLE RG7 .... 19 J5
Clay La THLE RG7 .... 17 J2
Claypitt La ALTN GU34 .... 234 B2
Clay's La ALTN GU34 .... 165 K7
Claythorpe Rd KEMP RG22 .... 92 A5
Clayton Barracks ALDT GU11 .... 101 C4
Clayton Cl HTWY RG27 .... 75 H3
Clayton Rd FARN GU14 .... 58 C7
Clemence Gdns WHCH RG28 .... 110 B3
Clements Cl ALTN GU34 .... 166 D1
Clem's Wy ROMY SO51 .... 220 F7
Clere Gdns CHIN RG24 .... 71 L6
Clerewater Pl STHA RG19 .... 14 D5
Clevedge Wy ODIM RG29 .... 96 B4
Clevedon Ct FARN GU14 .... 79 G5
FRIM GU16 .... 59 K8
Cleveland Cl BSTK RG21 .... 5 H5
Cleveland Gv NWBY RG14 .... 2 D3
Cleves La OVTN RG25 .... 118 A2
Clewborough Dr CBLY GU15 .... 59 L1
Cliddesden Ct BSTK RG21 .... 93 C6
Cliddesden La KEMP RG22 .... 115 C3
Cliddesden Rd BSTK RG21 .... 93 C6
Clifton Cl NFNM GU10 .... 146 D4
Clifton Gdns FRIM GU16 .... 79 J2
Clifton HI WINW SO22 .... 10 E7
Clifton Rd WINW SO22 .... 10 E7
NWBY RG14 .... 2 A5
Clifton Ter BSTK RG21 .... 4 F6
WINW SO22 .... 10 E7
Clinkley Rd NALR SO24 .... 232 C1
Clitheroe Rd FARN GU14 .... 57 J7
Clive Rd ASHV GU12 .... 7 L4
Clockhouse Rd FARN GU14 .... 78 F4
The Cloisters FRIM GU16 .... 59 G7
The Close FNM GU9 .... 123 C7
FRIM GU16 .... 58 F8
NTHA RG18 .... 14 E4
RAND SP11 .... 83 H6
SHST GU47 .... 38 B8
TADY RG26 .... 70 A2
THLE RG7 .... 19 K5
Closeworth Rd FARN GU14 .... 79 H8
Clough La RSAL SP5 .... 194 E1
Clouston Rd FARN GU14 .... 78 C3
Clovelly Dr GSHT GU26 .... 191 M1
Clovelly Rd GSHT GU26 .... 191 M2
Cloverbank WINC SO23 .... 179 G6
Clover Cl BOR GU35 .... 189 M3
Clover Fld CHIN RG24 .... 5 M3
Clover Gdns RAND SP11 .... 80 E6
Clover La YTLY GU46 .... 56 D2
Clubhouse Rd ALDT GU11 .... 100 C2
Club La CWTH RG45 .... 38 A3
NTID SP9 .... 102 D4
Clumps Rd NFNM GU10 .... 147 H4
Coach HI RAND SP11 .... 82 A4
Coach House Cl FRIM GU16 .... 59 H5
Coach House Gdns FLET GU13 .... 76 F5
Coachman's Ct NWBY RG14 .... 13 L3
Coachways AND SP10 .... 9 G8
Coate Dr RWIN SO21 .... 178 G5
Coates Cl KEMP RG22 .... 92 E7
Cobbets Rdg NFNM GU10 .... 123 M7
Cobbett Cl WINW SO22 .... 226 B3
Cobbett Gn KEMP RG22 .... 92 D6
Cobbett's La BLKW GU17 .... 57 J4
YTLY GU46 .... 57 J3
Cobbetts Wy FNM GU9 .... 146 C2
Cobden La HASM GU27 .... 217 G1
Cochrane Cl STHA RG19 .... 15 H5
Cock-a-dobby SHST GU47 .... 37 K7
Cockshott La PSF GU32 .... 235 H6
Cody Cl ASHV GU12 .... 101 J3
Cody Rd FARN GU14 .... 78 C5
Coe Cl ALDT GU11 .... 6 E3
Cokenor Wd NFNM GU10 .... 146 D4
Coker Cl WINW SO22 .... 10 M5
Colbeck FLET GU13 .... 99 G4
Colbred Cnr FARN GU14 .... 77 H4

Colden La NALR SO24 .... 182 D7
Coldharbour OVTN RG25 .... 113 K7
Cold Harbour La FARN GU14 .... 58 C8
Colebrook Pl WINC SO23 .... 11 J9
Colebrook St WINC SO23 .... 11 H9
Colebrook Wy AND SP10 .... 106 F4
Cole Cl AND SP10 .... 106 F4
Coleford Bridge Rd
FRIM GU16 .... 79 H4
Coleford Cl FRIM GU16 .... 79 J5
Coleford Paddocks
FRIM GU16 .... 79 J4
Coleman Cl BSTK RG21 .... 5 H5
Coleman Rd ASHV GU12 .... 7 L4
Colenzo Dr AND SP10 .... 9 K2
Coleridge Av YTLY GU46 .... 57 H3
Coleridge Cl CWTH RG45 .... 37 M4
Coleson Hill Rd NFNM GU10 .... 146 C3
Coleville Rd FARN GU14 .... 78 C3
Coley La STOK SO20 .... 153 L4
Collards La HASM GU27 .... 217 G2
Collard Wy LISS GU33 .... 236 E4
Collaroy Rd NTHA RG18 .... 14 F1
College Cl CBLY GU15 .... 39 G8
College Crs SHST GU47 .... 38 B8
College Gdns FNM GU9 .... 122 E6
College HI HASM GU27 .... 216 F2
College Hill Ter HASM GU27 .... 216 F2
College La OVTN RG25 .... 140 A2
College Piece THLE RG7 .... 31 J2
College Ride BAGS GU19 .... 39 M6
CBLY GU15 .... 59 G1
College Rd ASHV GU12 .... 101 K5
BSTK RG21 .... 4 B7
SHST GU47 .... 58 B1
College St WINC SO23 .... 11 G9
Collier Cl FARN GU14 .... 78 A3
Collingwood FARN GU14 .... 79 H6
Collingwood Grange Cl
CBLY GU15 .... 39 L8
Collingwood Ri CBLY GU15 .... 59 K1
Collins Cl AND SP10 .... 106 D5
NWBY RG14 .... 3 J1
Collins Gdns ASHV GU12 .... 101 L5
Collyers Crs LIPH GU30 .... 215 H4
Colne Valley Wy WHCH RG28 .... 111 G3
Colne Wy ASHV GU12 .... 101 K7
BSTK RG21 .... 5 J8
Colson Rd WINC SO23 .... 11 K6
Colthrop La STHA RG19 .... 15 L6
Coltsfoot Cl THLE RG7 .... 19 L5
Coltsfoot Pl HTWY RG27 .... 74 B6
Colts Foot Rd BOR GU35 .... 189 M3
Columbia Ct EWKG RG40 .... 36 B1
Columbine Rd KEMP RG22 .... 91 M8
Columbus Dr FARN GU14 .... 77 M5
Columbus Wy AND SP10 .... 107 K8
Colwyn Cl YTLY GU46 .... 56 F2
Colyer Cl KEMP RG22 .... 92 B5
Combe La FARN GU14 .... 78 D2
Combe Ri NFNM GU10 .... 147 G3
Combe Rd LISS GU33 .... 237 G7
Comfrey Cl FARN GU14 .... 77 M3
Commercial Rd ASHV GU12 .... 7 K5
Common HI ALTN GU34 .... 184 C2
Common Rd STHA RG19 .... 27 H8
The Common RSAL SP5 .... 195 F4
Compass Fld HTWY RG27 .... 74 A7
Complins ALTN GU34 .... 165 G2
Compound Rd FARN GU14 .... 78 D6
Compton Cl FLET GU13 .... 99 G3
WINW SO22 .... 226 A5
HTWY RG27 .... 74 A8
SHST GU47 .... 37 M7
Compton Rd FLET GU13 .... 99 G3
WINC SO23 .... 10 E9
Compton St RWIN SO21 .... 226 B8
Compton Wy WINW SO22 .... 226 A5
NFNM GU10 .... 123 K6
Conde Wy BOR GU35 .... 189 J6
Condor Rd FARN GU14 .... 78 E6
Congreve Cl THLE RG7 .... 29 J1
Conholt HI RAND SP11 .... 60 E3
Conholt La RAND SP11 .... 61 G5
Conholt Rd AND SP10 .... 130 F3
Conifer Cl FLET GU13 .... 98 E3
WINW SO22 .... 10 D5
BOR GU35 .... 189 H7
TADY RG26 .... 29 H7
Conifer Crest NWBY RG14 .... 24 F4
Conifer Dr CBLY GU15 .... 59 K2
The Conifers CWTH RG45 .... 37 K1
Coniston Cl CBLY GU15 .... 59 M5
FARN GU14 .... 78 B1
STHA RG19 .... 14 D5
Coniston Dr FNM GU9 .... 122 D2
Coniston Gv NALR SO24 .... 206 C4
Coniston Rd KEMP RG22 .... 92 A7
BOR GU35 .... 189 H3
Coniston Wy FLET GU13 .... 98 D3
Connaught Barracks
ALDT GU11 .... 101 G2
Connaught Cl BOR GU35 .... 189 J6
YTLY GU46 .... 56 E2
Connaught Rd ASHV GU12 .... 7 K2
BAGS GU19 .... 39 M5
CBLY GU15 .... 59 J3
FLET GU13 .... 76 F8
NWBY RG14 .... 3 G4
RWIN SO21 .... 178 B6
Connop Wy FRIM GU16 .... 59 J5
Consort Dr CBLY GU15 .... 59 M1
Constable Cl BSTK RG21 .... 93 J3
Constable Cl AND SP10 .... 9 G3
Constable's Ga WINC SO23 .... 10 E1
Constantine Wy KEMP RG22 .... 114 F2
Constant Rd FARN GU14 .... 77 K6
Conway Dr FARN GU14 .... 78 A3
NTHA RG18 .... 14 E3
Cookham Cl SHST GU47 .... 37 M1
Cook's Pond Rd LIPH GU30 .... 238 D3
Coolarne Ri CBLY GU15 .... 59 K2
Coolers Farm STOK SO20 .... 197 H2
Coombe Cl FRIM GU16 .... 59 G8
Coombe Ct NTHA RG18 .... 15 H1
Coombe Dr FLET GU13 .... 77 H7

Coombehurst Dr BSTK RG21 .... 93 G6
Coombe Rd YTLY GU46 .... 56 E1
Coombe Sq STHA RG19 .... 15 H5
The Cooperage ALTN GU34 .... 164 D5
Coopers Cl RWIN SO21 .... 178 C6
Coopers Ct TADY RG26 .... 51 L5
Coopers La NTHA RG18 .... 14 F4
Coopers's HI HTWY RG27 .... 56 A5
Coopers La TADY RG26 .... 51 K5
Cope Hall La NWBY RG14 .... 24 L1
Copes La HTWY RG27 .... 54 D1
Copland Rd KEMP RG22 .... 92 B8
Copnor Cl KSCL RG20 .... 23 M8
Copped Hall Dr CBLY GU15 .... 59 M2
Copped Hall Wy CBLY GU15 .... 59 M2
Copperfield Av SHST GU47 .... 38 B6
Coppice Cl FNM GU9 .... 6 B9
WINW SO22 .... 202 B7
NWBY RG14 .... 3 C9
TADY RG26 .... 29 C8
Coppice Gdns CWTH RG45 .... 37 J3
YTLY GU46 .... 56 F3
Coppice Ms DEAN RG23 .... 92 B2
Coppice Rd KSCL RG20 .... 47 K6
Copse Av FNM GU9 .... 6 A7
Copse Cl CBLY GU15 .... 59 K3
LISS GU33 .... 236 F4
Copse End CBLY GU15 .... 59 J2
Copse La NALR SO24 .... 159 K5
ODIM RG29 .... 119 J3
Copse Rd HASM GU27 .... 216 A3
OVTN RG25 .... 89 C6
The Copse DEAN RG23 .... 114 C5
FARN GU14 .... 78 A5
NFNM GU10 .... 146 C4
TADY RG26 .... 29 K8
Copse View Cl CHIN RG24 .... 71 M4
Copse Wy EWKG RG40 .... 36 B1
NFNM GU10 .... 146 C4
Copyhold HI HASM GU27 .... 216 F8
Coram Cl WINC SO23 .... 11 H1
Cordale Rd BSTK RG21 .... 92 F5
Cordelia Gdns ASHV GU12 .... 79 J8
Corderoy Cl STHA RG19 .... 15 J6
Cordwalles Rd CBLY GU15 .... 39 J8
Corfe Cl NALR SO24 .... 206 B4
Corfe Gdns FRIM GU16 .... 59 J7
Corfield Cl EWKG RG40 .... 36 B5
Corfe Wy FARN GU14 .... 79 H7
Coriander Cl FARN GU14 .... 77 M4
Corinthian Cl AND SP10 .... 107 C4
KEMP RG22 .... 115 H1
Cormorant Pl SHST GU47 .... 38 B8
Cornbunting Cl KEMP RG22 .... 115 H1
Cornelia Cl FARN GU14 .... 78 A5
Cornes Cl WINW SO22 .... 10 A7
Cornfields AND SP10 .... 9 K9
YTLY GU46 .... 56 E4
The Cornfields HASM GU27 .... 115 H1
Cornflower Wy RAND SP11 .... 80 E7
Cornish Cl KEMP RG22 .... 92 B5
Cornwall Cl CBLY GU15 .... 59 J1
Cornwall Rd BOR GU35 .... 189 J7
Coronation Cl KSCL RG20 .... 45 J1
ODIM RG29 .... 96 E5
Coronation Rd ALDT GU11 .... 7 H7
BSTK RG21 .... 5 H5
RAND SP11 .... 80 F6
YTLY GU46 .... 57 G1
Correlli Rd KEMP RG22 .... 92 E8
Corringway FLET GU13 .... 99 G2
Corry Rd GSHT GU26 .... 191 M2
Corsham Wy CWTH RG45 .... 37 L2
Corunna Main AND SP10 .... 9 K3
Cossack La WINC SO23 .... 11 H7
Coster Cl NWBY RG14 .... 13 G3
Cotswold Cl FARN GU14 .... 78 B1
KEMP RG22 .... 92 A4
Cotswold Rd SHST GU47 .... 37 J7
Cottage Gdns FARN GU14 .... 78 C4
Cottage Gn HTWY RG27 .... 75 J3
SP11 .... 130 E4
Cottage La LISS GU33 .... 235 L4
Cottage Rd STOK SO20 .... 150 B8
Cottington Cl KSCL RG20 .... 47 K6
Cottle Cl BSTK RG21 .... 92 F4
Council Rd BSTK RG21 .... 93 G4
Court Cl LIPH GU30 .... 214 E5
Court Gdns CBLY GU15 .... 59 G3
Courtlands Rd NWBY RG14 .... 3 G8
Court La ALTN GU34 .... 208 C2
STOK SO20 .... 200 F4
Courtmoor Av FLET GU13 .... 98 E1
Court Rd ALDT GU11 .... 6 F1
WINC SO23 .... 203 H3
Courts Hill Rd HASM GU27 .... 216 F2
Courts Mount Rd HASM GU27 .... 216 F2
Coventry Cl KEMP RG22 .... 92 A8
Cove Rd FARN GU14 .... 77 G5
Coverts Cl FNM GU9 .... 123 H4
The Covert FARN GU14 .... 58 B8
Covey Cl FARN GU14 .... 58 D8
Covey Rd NALR SO24 .... 206 A4
Cowdown La RAND SP11 .... 131 J5
Cowdray Pk ALTN GU34 .... 164 E6
Cowdrey Cl BSTK RG21 .... 5 H3
Cowdrey Hts CHIN RG24 .... 5 L6
Cow Drove HI STOK SO20 .... 198 G4
Cowfold La HTWY RG27 .... 73 M2
Cow La RAND SP11 .... 104 A5
Cowslade NWBY RG14 .... 13 G3
Cowley Dr RWIN SO21 .... 178 C6
Cowslip Bank CHIN RG24 .... 93 L1
Cowslip Crs NTHA RG18 .... 15 G4
Cowslip Cr BOR GU35 .... 189 M4
Coxbridge Farm FNM GU9 .... 122 C7
Coxbridge Mdw FNM GU9 .... 122 C7
Coxeter Rd NWBY RG14 .... 2 A1
Coxgreen SHST GU47 .... 58 A2
Coxheath Rd FLET GU13 .... 98 C3
Coxmoor Cl FLET GU13 .... 99 H3
Coxs HI RWIN SO21 .... 226 F8
Cox's La MARL SN8 .... 20 C5
THLE RG7 .... 16 A5
Crabs HI TADY RG26 .... 48 M2

Crabtree Gdns BOR GU35 .... 190 B3
Crabtree La BOR GU35 .... 190 B3
NFNM GU10 .... 169 K6
Crabtree Rd CBLY GU15 .... 58 E6
Crake Pl SHST GU47 .... 38 A4
Cramptons ALTN GU34 .... 163 M6
Cranbourne La BSTK RG21 .... 92 E6
Cranbrook Ct FLET GU13 .... 76 F3
Crane Cl SHST GU47 .... 38 A4
Cranesfield CHIN RG24 .... 70 D4
Cranes Rd CHIN RG24 .... 70 D4
Cranford Av FLET GU13 .... 98 D3
Cranford Dr ALTN GU34 .... 165 H2
Cranford Park Dr YTLY GU46 .... 57 G2
Cranleigh Ct FARN GU14 .... 78 C4
Cranmore Cl ALDT GU11 .... 6 A4
Cranmore Gdns ALDT GU11 .... 6 A4
Cranmore La ALDT GU11 .... 6 A4
Cranmore Rd FRIM GU16 .... 79 J4
Cranworth Rd WINW SO22 .... 10 E5
Craven Cl NFNM GU10 .... 146 C2
Craven Dene NWBY RG14 .... 3 L2
Craven Rd HUNG RG17 .... 21 L2
NWBY RG14 .... 2 A5
Crawford Gdns CBLY GU15 .... 58 E3
Crawford Pl NWBY RG14 .... 2 D3
Crawlboys La RAND SP11 .... 80 E5
Crawley Dr CBLY GU15 .... 59 J3
Crawley HI CBLY GU15 .... 59 J3
Crawley Rdg CBLY GU15 .... 59 J3
Crawley Wood Cl CBLY GU15 .... 59 J3
Crawts Rd OVTN RG25 .... 111 M1
Craydown La STOK SO20 .... 150 D6
Credon Cl FARN GU14 .... 78 B3
Crerar Cl FARN GU14 .... 78 A5
Crescent Cl WINW SO22 .... 226 A4
Crescent La ALTN GU34 .... 101 L3
The Crescent ALTN GU34 .... 185 G4
FARN GU14 .... 78 B8
FLET GU13 .... 98 B2
FNM GU9 .... 100 A8
RAND SP11 .... 84 D1
RAND SP11 .... 130 E7
RAND SP11 .... 130 D4
THLE RG7 .... 17 M1
THLE RG7 .... 31 K2
Cress Gdns AND SP10 .... 8 E8
Cresswell Rd NWBY RG14 .... 3 M1
Cricket Cl RWIN SO21 .... 177 G6
Cricketers KSCL RG20 .... 12 B2
Cricketers Wy AND SP10 .... 107 C5
Cricket Field Gv CWTH RG45 .... 38 K4
Cricket HI EWKG RG40 .... 36 C6
Cricket Hill La BLKW GU17 .... 57 G3
YTLY GU46 .... 57 H3
Cricket La BOR GU35 .... 147 C2
Crimea Rd ALDT GU11 .... 7 G2
Cripley Rd FARN GU14 .... 78 B3
Crispstead La WINC SO23 .... 226 E3
Critchmere HI HASM GU27 .... 216 B1
Critchmere La HASM GU27 .... 216 B2
Critchmere V HASM GU27 .... 216 A2
Crockett La BOR GU35 .... 189 L3
Crockford La CHIN RG24 .... 71 K4
Crocus Md NTHA RG18 .... 15 H4
Croft Av ASHV GU12 .... 9 H8
Crofter's Cl SHST GU47 .... 37 K8
Crofters Meadow CHIN RG24 .... 71 L8
Croft Gdns AND SP10 .... 9 H9
Croft La NFNM GU10 .... 121 H3
NWBY RG14 .... 2 B2
YTLY GU46 .... 57 G1
Croft Rd ALDT GU11 .... 7 H6
DEAN RG23 .... 90 F6
NWBY RG14 .... 2 D9
THLE RG7 .... 31 J2
The Crofts KEMP RG22 .... 115 H2
The Croft AMSY SP4 .... 148 A2
Croft Wy FRIM GU16 .... 59 J7
Cromwell Cl CHIN RG24 .... 94 A2
Cromwell Rd BSTK RG21 .... 4 D5
CBLY GU15 .... 59 G1
WINW SO22 .... 226 C2
NWBY RG14 .... 13 M3
Cromwell Wy FARN GU14 .... 78 E1
Crondall Ct CBLY GU15 .... 58 E4
Crondall End YTLY GU46 .... 56 F1
Crondall La NFNM GU10 .... 121 M6
Crondall Rd NFNM GU10 .... 98 B5
NFNM GU10 .... 145 K1
Crookham Cl TADY RG26 .... 49 L2
Crookham Reach FLET GU13 .... 98 D5
Crookham Rd FLET GU13 .... 98 D2
Crooksbury Rd NFNM GU10 .... 125 L5
Cropmark Wy KEMP RG22 .... 115 G1
Cropper Cl STHA RG19 .... 15 K5
Crosby Gdns YTLY GU46 .... 56 D1
Crosby HI Dr CBLY GU15 .... 59 J1
Crosby Wy FNM GU9 .... 122 D7
Cross & Pillory La ALTN GU34 .... 164 E5
Crossborough HI BSTK RG21 .... 93 H4
Cross Gdns FRIM GU16 .... 79 J2
Cross Keys Pas WINC SO23 .... 11 H8
Cross La AND SP10 .... 8 E4
FRIM GU16 .... 79 J2
KSCL RG20 .... 43 M8
Cross Rd ASHV GU12 .... 101 L5
FARN GU14 .... 78 F8
Cross St ALDT GU11 .... 6 E2
BSTK RG21 .... 5 H3
FARN GU14 .... 78 F8
WINC SO23 .... 11 G8
The Cross STOK SO20 .... 198 F5
Crosswater La NFNM GU10 .... 169 J2
Crossways ASHV GU12 .... 7 K4
NFNM GU10 .... 169 H7
The Crossways AND SP10 .... 8 F4
Croucher's Cft WINW SO22 .... 202 A7
Crowder Ter WINW SO22 .... 10 E8
Crowfield Dr STHA RG19 .... 14 E5
Crowley Dr ALTN GU34 .... 164 F5
Crown Acre Cl STHA RG19 .... 14 F5
Crown Dr FNM GU9 .... 123 K3
Crownfields ODIM RG29 .... 96 C6
Crown Gdns FLET GU13 .... 77 G8

Crown La CHIN RG24 .... 93 M2
FNM GU9 .... 123 K3
HTWY RG27 .... 73 H8
RAND SP11 .... 80 D6
Crown Pl SHST GU47 .... 38 B7
Crows La ALTN GU34 .... 186 D5
Crowthorne Rd SHST GU47 .... 37 L8
Croyde Cl FARN GU14 .... 78 D2
Croye Cl AND SP10 .... 8 C5
Cruikshank Lea SHST GU47 .... 58 B2
Cuckoo Cl OVTN RG25 .... 113 K7
Cufaude La TADY RG26 .... 71 L2
Cuffelle Cl CHIN RG24 .... 71 M5
Cullen Cl YTLY GU46 .... 56 F3
Culley Vw NALR SO24 .... 206 C4
Culverlands Crs ASHV GU12 .... 101 J5
Culver Rd BSTK RG21 .... 13 J8
NWBY RG14 .... 13 J8
SHST GU47 .... 38 A7
WINC SO23 .... 226 E2
Culverwell Gdns WINC SO23 .... 10 E3
Cumberland Av KEMP RG22 .... 92 D7
Cumberland Rd CBLY GU15 .... 59 M4
Cumbria Ct FARN GU14 .... 79 H3
Cundell Wy WINC SO23 .... 179 G7
Cunnington Rd FARN GU14 .... 79 H1
Curlew Cl KEMP RG22 .... 91 M7
STHA RG19 .... 14 F5
Curlews ALTN GU34 .... 164 E2
Curleys Wy THLE RG7 .... 34 A2
Curling Wy NWBY RG14 .... 3 K1
Curly Bridge Cl FARN GU14 .... 58 C8
Curtis Cl CBLY GU15 .... 59 M1
BOR GU35 .... 190 B2
Curtis La BOR GU35 .... 190 B2
Curtis Rd ALTN GU34 .... 164 F6
Curzon Dr FLET GU13 .... 98 F3
Cusden Dr AND SP10 .... 9 G1
Cuthbert Rd ASHV GU12 .... 101 L2
Cutting HI HUNG RG17 .... 20 D4
Cutts Rd ALDT GU11 .... 101 C1
Cuxhaven Wy AND SP10 .... 106 E5
Cygnet Cl STHA RG19 .... 14 E5
Cypress FARN GU14 .... 58 C7
Cypress Dr FLET GU13 .... 77 H7
Cypress Gv ASHV GU12 .... 101 J1
RAND SP11 .... 130 B1
Cypress Rd BOR GU35 .... 188 F5
Cypress Wy GSHT GU26 .... 192 A6
Cyprus Rd KEMP RG22 .... 115 H3
Cyril Vokins Rd NWBY RG14 .... 14 B6

D

Dacre Cl AND SP10 .... 106 C5
Daffodil Cl KEMP RG22 .... 91 M8
Dahlia Cl KEMP RG22 .... 91 M8
Dairy Gate Rd FARN GU14 .... 78 E8
Dalby Crs NWBY RG14 .... 3 H9
Dale Cl WINW SO22 .... 201 M3
NFNM GU10 .... 146 C1
Dale Gdns SHST GU47 .... 37 K8
Dale Vw HASM GU27 .... 216 C3
Dalewood KEMP RG22 .... 91 M6
Dalley Ct SHST GU47 .... 58 A1
Damsel La OVTN RG25 .... 139 J5
Damsel Pth BSTK RG21 .... 5 K8
Dancers Meadow CHIN RG24 .... 70 E5
Dances Cl AND SP10 .... 9 J3
Dances La WHCH RG28 .... 110 B2
Danebury Rd KEMP RG22 .... 115 G2
Danegeld Cl AND SP10 .... 107 C4
Danehurst Pl AND SP10 .... 106 B8
Daneshill Dr CHIN RG24 .... 71 L8
Danes Rd WINC SO23 .... 11 G4
Dankworth Rd KEMP RG22 .... 92 B8
Danley La HASM GU27 .... 215 K5
Danvers Cl STHA RG19 .... 15 G6
Danvers Dr FLET GU13 .... 98 C4
Daphne Dr FLET GU13 .... 98 D5
Darby Green La BLKW GU17 .... 57 J3
Darby Green Rd BLKW GU17 .... 57 K3
Dare's La NFNM GU10 .... 98 D3
Dark La CHIN RG24 .... 70 D5
NALR SO24 .... 206 C6
NALR SO24 .... 230 C3
RGUW GU3 .... 125 L4
Darleydale Cl SHST GU47 .... 38 A6
Darlington Rd BSTK RG21 .... 4 D4
Darracott Cl CBLY GU15 .... 59 L1
Darset Av FLET GU13 .... 76 F6
Dart Cl EWKG RG40 .... 36 C1
NTHA RG18 .... 14 E3
Dart Ct AND SP10 .... 107 H6
Dart Rd FARN GU14 .... 78 A3
Darvill Rd NALR SO24 .... 207 H3
Darvills La FNM GU9 .... 122 F6
Darwin Gv ALDT GU11 .... 100 F5
Dashwood Cl ALTN GU34 .... 164 C6
Dasna Rd NTID SP9 .... 102 C1
Daunch Cl NTID SP9 .... 102 C1
Dauntless Rd THLE RG7 .... 19 L5
Dauntsey Dro RAND SP11 .... 104 F6
Dauntsey La RAND SP11 .... 104 F3
Davis Gdns SHST GU47 .... 58 B1
Davy Cl KEMP RG22 .... 92 D3
Dawnay Rd CBLY GU15 .... 38 D8
Dawn Gdns WINW SO22 .... 226 A2
Dawsmere Cl CBLY GU15 .... 59 M3
Dawson Rd RWIN SO21 .... 133 H5
Deacon Rd RAND SP11 .... 104 B6
Deadbrook La ASHV GU12 .... 101 H5
Deadmans La STHA RG19 .... 25 L2
Deadmoor La KSCL RG20 .... 25 G2
Dean Cl WINW SO22 .... 202 A4
Deane Down Dro WINW SO22 .... 202 A4
Deane's Cl BSTK RG21 .... 5 C5
Dean La WINW SO22 .... 201 K5
Dean Ri RAND SP11 .... 84 E1
Dean Rd RSAL SP5 .... 218 C5
Deans Cl NTID SP9 .... 102 E4
Deans Dell PSF GU32 .... 234 D1
Deanswood Rd TADY RG26 .... 29 K8
The Dean NALR SO24 .... 206 B2
Decouttere Cl FLET GU13 .... 98 D5

Deedman Cl ASHV GU12 101 K6 1
Deep Dene HASM GU27 216 B2
Deepdene NFNM GU10 147 G2
Deep La BSTK RG21 4 A8
Deep Well Dr CBLY GU15 59 H3
Deer Rock Rd CBLY GU15 59 J1
Defiant Rd FARN GU14 78 C8
Delibes Rd KEMP RG22 92 E8
Delius Cl KEMP RG22 92 D7
Dellands OVTN RG25 111 M1
Dellands La OVTN RG25 88 E8
Dell Cl HASM GU27 216 D1
Dellfield DEAN RG23 91 G5
PSF GU32 234 D6
Dell Gv FRIM GU16 59 J6
Dell Rd AND SP10 8 E2
EWKG RG40 36 D5
WINC SO23 227 G2
The Dell FNM GU9 122 F1
KSCL RG20 47 J6
RAND SP11 61 H2
RAND SP11 128 A7
YTLY GU46 56 F3
De-Lucy Av NALR SO24 206 A3
Delville Cl FARN GU14 78 A5
De Montfort Rd NWBY RG14 13 G3
Denbigh Rd HASM GU27 217 G3
Dene Cl HASM GU27 216 F2
BOR GU35 189 J6 2
NALR SO24 207 L3
NFNM GU10 147 G2
Dene Ct AND SP10 9 J7
Dene La NFNM GU10 147 G2
Dene La West NFNM GU10 147 G3
Dene Rd AND SP10 9 J7
FARN GU14 78 C5
The Dene NALR SO24 207 L4
Dene Wk NFNM GU10 147 H2
Dene Wy NWBY RG14 13 J3
Denham Cl WINC SO23 10 F3
Denham Ct WINC SO23 11 G2
Denham Dr KEMP RG22 92 B6
YTLY GU46 57 H3 1
Denman Cl FLET GU13 77 H7
Denmark Rd NWBY RG14 3 G4
Denmark Sq ASHV GU12 7 M1
Denmark St ASHV GU12 7 M1
Denmead Rd TADY RG26 29 L8
Denning Cl FLET GU13 98 D1
Dennistoun Cl CBLY GU15 59 G3 1
Dennis Wy LISS GU33 236 F5
Denton Cl STHA RG19 14 F6
Denton Wy FRIM GU16 59 G6
Deptford La ODIM RG29 95 M5
Derby Flds ODIM RG29 96 B2
Derby Rd HASM GU27 216 E1
NWBY RG14 2 D7
Derry Cl ASHV GU12 101 J3
Derry Rd FARN GU14 58 C7
Derwent Av ASHV GU12 101 J4
Derwent Cl FARN GU14 78 A4
FNM GU9 122 D2
BOR GU35 189 J3 1
Derwent Gdns NALR SO24 206 C4
Derwent Rd KEMP RG22 91 M7
STHA RG19 14 D5
Devenish Rd WINW SO22 10 B1
Dever Cl RWIN SO21 157 M5
Dever Wy DEAN RG23 91 G7
The Devil's Hwy CWTH RG45 37 H3
Devils La LIPH GU30 215 H5
Devon Cl FARN GU14 77 G4
SHST GU47 58 A1
Devon Rd ALDT GU11 100 B1
BOR GU35 189 J5
Devonshire Dr CBLY GU15 59 J1
Devonshire Pl ALDT GU11 6 C4
BSTK RG21 92 F4
Deweys La RAND SP11 80 E6
Dewpond Wk CHIN RG24 71 L8
Dexter Wy FARN GU14 77 G4 3
Diamond Hl CBLY GU15 59 G1
Diamond Rdg CBLY GU15 59 G1
Diamond Wy FARN GU14 78 B8
Diana Cl KEMP RG22 92 D5
Dibley Cl KEMP RG22 92 B5
Dickens La CHIN RG24 93 M4
OVTN RG25 93 L6
Dickenson Wk NALR SO24 206 C4 1
Dickens Wy YTLY GU46 56 F4
Dicker's La ALTN GU34 164 F4
Dickson Rd RAND SP11 129 M1
Digby Rd NWBY RG14 2 B1
Dilly La HTWY RG27 75 H4
Dines Cl RAND SP11 84 C1
Dingley Wy FARN GU14 78 D8
Dinorben Av FLET GU13 98 D1
Dinorben Beeches FLET GU13 98 D1
Dinorben Cl FLET GU13 98 E1
Dippenhall Rd NFNM GU10 121 L6
Dippenhall St NFNM GU10 121 J2
The Dittons EWKG RG40 36 C2 1
Divers Cl ALTN GU34 164 E2
Dixon Rd HTWY RG27 52 A8
Dixons La STOK SO20 197 G1
Dockenfield St NFNM GU10 167 L1
Doctors Dro RAND SP11 84 C1
Dogflud Wy FNM GU9 122 F5
Dolly Bottom RAND SP11 63 J8
Dollis Dr FNM GU9 123 G5 1
Dollis Gn TADY RG26 51 L5
Dolman Rd NWBY RG14 2 E1
Dolomans La RAND SP11 84 C1
Dolphin Cl HASM GU27 216 B2
Doman Rd CBLY GU15 58 D4
Dome Aly WINC SO23 11 G9
Dominica Cl CHIN RG24 71 H6
Domum Rd WINC SO23 227 G2
Donlan Dr FARN GU14 77 M7
Donnington Cl CBLY GU15 58 E4 4
Donnington Pk NWBY RG14 13 J2
Donnington Sq NWBY RG14 13 J3
Dora's Green La NFNM GU10 121 M2
Dorcas Ct CBLY GU15 58 E5 1
Dorchester Cl DEAN RG23 92 A3
Dorchester Rd HTWY RG27 73 M7
Dorchester Wy ODIM RG29 95 L4
Doreen Cl FARN GU14 58 A8
Dores La ROMY SO51 224 A6
RWIN SO21 224 B5
Dorian Gv NALR SO24 206 A4
Dormer Cl CWTH RG45 37 K3
NWBY RG14 59 H2
Dorrel Cl KEMP RG22 115 G2
Dorset Rd ASHV GU12 101 K3
Doswell Wy BSTK RG21 5 G5
Douai Cl FARN GU14 78 F4
Doublet Cl STHA RG19 14 D5
Doughty Wy AND SP10 107 K7
Douglas Gv NFNM GU10 146 F3
Douglas Ride KSCL RG20 24 B8
Douglas Rd RAND SP11 130 A1
Dove Cl AND SP10 107 G6 2
KEMP RG22 91 L7
Dovedale Cl SHST GU47 38 A6
Dover Cl DEAN RG23 92 C2
NALR SO24 206 C4
Doveton Wy NWBY RG14 3 H1
Dowden Gv ALTN GU34 164 E3
Dowding Ct CWTH RG45 37 M2 1
Down Farm La WINW SO22 178 B8
Down Ga NALR SO24 206 B4
Downing St FNM GU9 122 E6
Downlands Rd WINW SO22 226 A4
Downlands Wy RWIN SO21 178 C4
Down La OVTN RG25 94 F6
Down Rd RAND SP11 103 L5
Downside GSHT GU26 192 A1 1
Downside Rd WINW SO22 202 A6
Downsland Rd BSTK RG21 4 B9
Downs La MARL SN8 41 G3
Downs Rd RWIN SO21 178 B4
STOK SO20 150 B5
Down St OVTN RG25 114 C7
Downs Vw ALTN GU34 165 K1
Downsview Rd BOR GU35 190 F3
Downsview Wy RAND SP11 103 J2
Downs Wy ALTN GU34 164 C6
Downview Cl GSHT GU26 192 A2
Doyle Gdns YTLY GU46 56 F3 2
Dragonfly Dr CHIN RG24 71 L8 4
Dragoon Ct ALDT GU11 6 B2 2
Drake Av FRIM GU16 79 K7
Drake Cl EWKG RG40 36 B1
Drakeleys Fld LIPH GU30 238 E6
Draper Cl STHA RG19 15 G6
Drayman's Wy ALTN GU34 164 E5
Drayton St WINW SO22 226 B2
Drift Rd BOR GU35 189 G8
STOK SO20 154 E6
Driftway Rd HTWY RG27 74 B7
The Drive DEAN RG23 91 G7
FNM GU9 146 E1
NWBY RG14 2 B9
Drove Hl STOK SO20 153 M5
Drove La NALR SO24 205 M2
Drove Rd STOK SO20 153 M5
Drovers End FARN GU14 77 H4
Drovers Wy ASHV GU12 101 M7
FNM GU9 122 D2
The Drove AND SP10 8 B4
Droxford Crs TADY RG26 49 K1
Druce Wy STHA RG19 15 G5
Drummond Cl ALTN GU34 184 E6 1
WINW SO22 226 D3 1
Drury Cl WHCH RG28 109 J8
Drury La ALTN GU34 162 F3
THLE RG7 31 L4
Dryden Cl NTHA RG18 14 F3
Dryden Rd FARN GU14 78 C2
Dryden Wy LIPH GU30 214 D3
Duchess Cl ALTN GU34 164 D5 2
CWTH RG45 37 L1 1
Duchess of Kent Barracks
ALDT GU11 100 E5
Ducklands BOR GU35 189 K6 3
Duckmead La LISS GU33 237 G2
Ducks La STOK SO20 172 E2
Duddon Wy BSTK RG21 5 K8
Dudley Cl DEAN RG23 92 A3
BOR GU35 189 H7
Duke of Cornwall Av
CBLY GU15 39 G7
Dukes Cl ALTN GU34 164 C6
FNM GU9 122 D2 3
Dukes Md FLET GU13 76 C7
Dukes Pk ALDT GU11 101 G2
Duke's Ride CWTH RG45 37 J4
THLE RG7 30 E8
Duke St RWIN SO21 158 A5
Dukes Wd CWTH RG45 37 L3
Dumas Cl YTLY GU46 56 F3 3
Du Maurier Cl FLET GU13 98 D5
Dummer Down La OVTN RG25 138 A1
Dummer La RAND SP11 60 A8
Dump Rd FARN GU14 78 B7
Dunbar Rd FRIM GU16 79 J1
Dunbridge La ROMY SO51 221 K8
Duncan's Ct RAND SP11 104 D6
Dundaff Cl CBLY GU15 59 K3
Dunedin Cl NTID SP9 102 F2
Dungells Farm Cl YTLY GU46 57 G4 1
Dungells La YTLY GU46 56 F4
Dunhills La RAND SP11 84 B8
Dunkirt La RAND SP11 129 K5
Dunley's Hl ODIM RG29 96 B5
Dunmow Hl FLET GU13 76 F6
Dunmow Rd AND SP10 9 K8
Dunsell's La NALR SO24 208 C3
Dunsford Crs DEAN RG23 92 B1
Dunsmore Gdns YTLY GU46 56 D3
Dunstall Pk FARN GU14 78 D1
Dunstan Rd NTHA RG18 15 H4
Dunstan's Dro RAND SP11 62 B7
Durbidges STHA RG19 27 H8
Durham Rd SHST GU47 38 B6
Durham Wy KEMP RG22 92 A8 1
Durley Cl AND SP10 8 C7
Durnford Cl STOK SO20 153 M4
Durngate Pl WINC SO23 11 J7
Durngate Ter WINC SO23 11 J7
Durnsford Av FLET GU13 98 E1
Dyson Dr WINC SO23 11 H2
Dysons Cl NWBY RG14 2 B4

E

Eagle Cl ALTN GU34 164 E2
CWTH RG45 37 K1
KEMP RG22 91 L8 1
Eagle Rd FARN GU14 78 E6
KSCL RG20 26 D6
Eagles Nest SHST GU47 37 K7 2
Eames La LISS GU33 211 L8
Eardley Av AND SP10 8 A3
Earlsbourne FLET GU13 99 G4
Earls Gv CBLY GU15 59 H2
East Av FNM GU9 123 G2
Eastbrooke Rd ALTN GU34 164 F4
East Dean Rd ROMY SO51 220 C6
Eastern Av AND SP10 9 J7
Eastern La CWTH RG45 38 C4
Eastern Rd ASHV GU12 7 M2
BOR GU35 189 J2
Eastfield Av BSTK RG21 5 G8
Eastfield Cl AND SP10 9 L5
Eastfield Rd AND SP10 9 J5
Eastgate St WINC SO23 11 J8
East Gn BLKW GU17 57 M4
East Hl WINC SO23 227 G2
East Hill Dr LISS GU33 236 F5
East La NALR SO24 205 L4
Eastlyn Rd TADY RG26 30 B7
Eastmans Fld STOK SO20 153 M5
Eastmead FARN GU14 78 E4
Easton Common Hl RSAL SP5 195 H2
Easton La RWIN SO21 203 J6
WINC SO23 11 L6
East Portway AND SP10 106 B8
East Rd RWIN SO21 155 K1
Eastrop La BSTK RG21 5 G8
Eastrop Rbt BSTK RG21 5 G7
Eastrop Wy BSTK RG21 5 G7
East Station Rd ASHV GU12 7 G3
East St AND SP10 9 J6
FNM GU9 122 F6
NALR SO24 206 C2
East Woodhay Rd
WINW SO22 202 C4 2
Eaton Rd CBLY GU15 58 E4
Ebble Cl NTID SP9 102 E1
Ebden Rd WINC SO23 11 K6
Ecchinswell Rd KSCL RG20 47 G6
Echo Barn La NFNM GU10 146 B3
Eddeys Cl BOR GU35 190 E2 1
Eddeys La BOR GU35 190 E3
Eddy Rd ASHV GU12 7 J3
Edelweiss Cl RAND SP11 80 E7
Edgar Cl AND SP10 107 G4
Edgar Rd WINC SO23 226 E2
Edgbarrowhill Star CWTH RG45 37 K5
Edgbarrow Ri SHST GU47 37 K6
Edgcumbe Park Dr CWTH RG45 37 K3
Edgecombe La NWBY RG14 13 M3
Edgedale Cl CWTH RG45 37 L4 1
Edgehill Cl KEMP RG22 92 A5
Edgemoor Rd FRIM GU16 59 M5 1
Edgewood Cl CWTH RG45 37 K1 1
Edinburgh Rd WINC SO23 179 G7
Edington Rd WINC SO23 11 G3
Edney Cl FLET GU13 99 G2
Edric's Gn AMSY SP4 126 C7
Edward Av CBLY GU15 58 D3
Edward Rd ALTN GU34 164 F3
FNM GU9 146 F1
WINC SO23 226 D4
Edward St ALDT GU11 6 D2
Edwin Cl STHA RG19 15 J5
Eeklo Pl NWBY RG14 2 F8
Eelmoor Br ALDT GU11 99 M2
Eelmoor Plain Rd ALDT GU11 100 A4
Eelmoor Rd ALDT GU11 100 A3
FARN GU14 78 C6
Egbert Rd WINC SO23 11 G4
Egbury Rd RAND SP11 85 M6
Egerton Rd CBLY GU15 58 C2
SHST GU47 58 B2
Eggars Cl ALTN GU34 165 G4
Eggars Fld NFNM GU10 145 G3
Eggar's Hl ALDT GU11 6 E6
Eggleton Cl FLET GU13 98 D3 2
Eglinton Rd NFNM GU10 169 L2
Eland Rd ASHV GU12 7 L4
Elbe Wy AND SP10 106 E5
Elbow Cnr BSTK RG21 4 E8
Elderberry Bank CHIN RG24 71 L8
Elderberry Rd BOR GU35 189 M3
Elder Cl WINW SO22 226 B4
Eldergrove FARN GU14 79 H6 1
Eldon Cl STOK SO20 198 F6
Eldon Dr NFNM GU10 147 G3
Eldon Rd STOK SO20 198 F7
Eleanor Cl LIPH GU30 190 A8
Eleanor Cl RAND SP11 80 D6
Elgar Av CWTH RG45 37 L2
Elgar Cl KEMP RG22 92 D8
Elgin Rd BLKW GU17 57 H7
Elgin Wy FRIM GU16 79 J1
Eling Cl WINW SO22 202 C5
Eliot Cl CBLY GU15 59 L1
NTHA RG18 14 F3
Eliot Dr HASM GU27 216 B2
Elizabethan Ri OVTN RG25 113 K6
Elizabeth Av NWBY RG14 25 G1
Elizabeth Cl WINC SO23 179 G7
Elizabeth Dr FLET GU13 98 F3
Elizabeth Rd KEMP RG22 92 D4
Ellen Dr FARN GU14 77 H4
Ellen Gdns TADY RG26 51 K5
Elleray Ct ASHV GU12 101 K3
Elles Cl FARN GU14 78 E5
Elles Rd FARN GU14 78 B6
Ellingham Cl NALR SO24 206 C3 2
Ellington Cl RAND SP11 130 A1
Ellington Dr KEMP RG22 115 H1
Ellison Wy NFNM GU10 124 C1
Ellis Rd CWTH RG45 37 L2
Elm Bank YTLY GU46 56 F1 1
Elm Bank Rd AND SP10 9 H7
Elm Cl BOR GU35 189 K5
RAND SP11 81 G6
RAND SP11 104 C8
STOK SO20 151 G4
Elm Crs FNM GU9 123 G1
Elmcroft Cl FRIM GU16 79 J1 1
Elm Dr TLHT RG30 19 L3
Elm Farm Gv KSCL RG20 47 J6 1
Elm Gv FNM GU9 122 F1
KSCL RG20 47 J6
NTHA RG18 14 E3
Elm Grove Rd FARN GU14 78 E4
Elmhurst TADY RG26 49 L1
Elmhurst Rd NTHA RG18 14 D3
Elm La NFNM GU10 101 J8
Elm Pl ALDT GU11 7 J6
Elm Rd CHIN RG24 70 C6
FNM GU9 123 G1
WINW SO22 10 D6
NALR SO24 206 C3
OVTN RG25 89 G6
Elms Av STHA RG19 15 H5
Elmsleigh Rd FARN GU14 78 D4
Elms Rd ALDT GU11 6 F3
FLET GU13 77 H7
HTWY RG27 73 M6 3
The Elms AND SP10 8 F6
NFNM GU10 124 C1
Elm Vw ASHV GU12 101 L5
Elmwood Cl ALTN GU34 164 C6 1
Elmwood Wy DEAN RG23 92 B1
Elsenwood Crs CBLY GU15 59 K2
Elsenwood Dr CBLY GU15 59 K1
Elsley Cl FRIM GU16 79 J2
Elstead Rd NFNM GU10 124 D3
Elston Pl ASHV GU12 7 J5
Elston Rd ASHV GU12 7 J5
Elvetham Cl FLET GU13 76 E5
Elvetham La HTWY RG27 55 L8
Elvetham Pl HTWY RG27 76 D5
Elvetham Rd FLET GU13 76 C6
Ely Cl FRIM GU16 79 K1
Embleton Rd BOR GU35 190 E2 2
Emden Rd AND SP10 106 E5
Empress Av FARN GU14 78 E3
Empress Wy RAND SP11 80 E6
Enborne Gv NWBY RG14 2 B6
Enborne Pl NWBY RG14 2 B6
Enborne Rd KSCL RG20 12 F7
NWBY RG14 2 B6
Enborne St KSCL RG20 24 D4
Enborne Wy THLE RG7 28 C2
Enfield Cl LIPH GU30 215 G5 1
Enfield Rd ASHV GU12 101 L3
Enham La AND SP10 106 D5
Enmill La WINW SO22 225 L3
Ennerdale Cl KEMP RG22 92 A6
Ennerdale Gdns NALR SO24 206 C4 3
Ennerdale Gv FNM GU9 122 D2
Ennerdale Rd BOR GU35 189 J3
Ennerdale Wy STHA RG19 14 D5 2
Enterprise Wy STHA RG19 15 K6
Epsom Cl CBLY GU15 38 F8
Epsom Crs NWBY RG14 3 H8
Epsom Down ALTN GU34 164 E6
Epts Rd FARN GU14 78 D8
Equine Wy NWBY RG14 25 L1
Equinox Wy NWBY RG14 25 L1
Erleigh Dene NWBY RG14 2 C8
Erles Rd LIPH GU30 214 F4 1
Ernest Cl NFNM GU10 146 E2
Erskine Cl TADY RG26 30 C7
Erskine Rd WINW SO22 10 D9
Esher Cl KEMP RG22 92 C7
Esher Rd CBLY GU15 39 K7
Eskdale Wy CBLY GU15 59 M4
Essex Cl FRIM GU16 79 K1
Essex Rd BSTK RG21 4 D8
BOR GU35 189 J4
Essex St NWBY RG14 25 G1
Ethelbert Dr AND SP10 106 C5 1
Eton Cl KEMP RG22 114 F2
Eton Pl FNM GU9 122 E1
Etps Rd FARN GU14 78 E8
Etwall RAND SP11 127 M4
Europa Cl TADY RG26 51 L5
Euskirchen Wy KEMP RG22 92 B3
Evans Cl STOK SO20 150 A6
Eveley Cl BOR GU35 189 G8
Evelyn Av ALDT GU11 7 H6
Evelyn Woods Rd ALDT GU11 100 F1
Evenlode Wy SHST GU47 37 M8
Everest Rd CBLY GU15 39 G8
CWTH RG45 37 L2
Evergreen Rd FRIM GU16 59 J6
Eversfield Cl AND SP10 8 E5
Eversley Pl WINW SO22 226 C3
Eversley St HTWY RG27 35 K7
Evesham Wk SHST GU47 37 M7
Evingar Gdns WHCH RG28 110 B2
Evingar Rd WHCH RG28 110 B2
Evreux Cl STHA RG19 15 J6 1
Ewhurst Rd TADY RG26 69 H1
Ewins Cl ASHV GU12 101 K6
Ewshot La FLET GU13 98 E5
Exbury Wy AND SP10 8 C7
Exeter Cl KEMP RG22 115 G1
Exeter Gdns YTLY GU46 56 E1
Exeter Rd ASHV GU12 101 K5
Exhibition Rd FARN GU14 78 D8
Exmoor Cl KEMP RG22 92 A5
Exmoor Rd STHA RG19 14 F5
Express Wy NWBY RG14 14 B6

F

Fairacre KSCL RG20 24 C8
Fair Cl WHCH RG28 110 B4
Fairclose Dr WINW SO22 202 A3
Fairdown Cl WINC SO23 11 M8
Fairfax Cl WINW SO22 226 A3
Fairfax Ms FARN GU14 79 G6 1
Fairfax Pl NWBY RG14 14 B3 1
Fairfax Rd FARN GU14 78 E1
Fairfield WHCH RG28 110 B2
Fairfield Dr FRIM GU16 59 H5
Fairfield Gn ALTN GU34 185 H5
Fairfield Rd WINW SO22 10 D5
Fairfields Rd BSTK RG21 93 G5
The Fairfield FNM GU9 122 F6
Fairholme Gdns FNM GU9 122 F7 2
Fairland Cl FLET GU13 77 G8
Fair La RWIN SO21 203 M7
Fairlawn Rd TADY RG26 50 A1
Fairlight Gdns ALTN GU34 185 H5 1
Fairmead Cl SHST GU47 58 B1
Fairmile FLET GU13 98 F2
Fair Oak La THLE RG7 52 B1
Fairoak Wy TADY RG26 29 G7
Fairthorne Ri CHIN RG24 94 B3 1
Fair Vw NALR SO24 206 B4
Fairview Gdns FNM GU9 123 G2
Fairview Meadow DEAN RG23 91 G8
Fairview Rd ASHV GU12 101 L5
BOR GU35 190 E3
Fairway Cl LIPH GU30 214 A5 2
Fairway Hts CBLY GU15 59 L2
Fairways GSHT GU26 191 L2
RAND SP11 105 G6
The Fairway FARN GU14 77 L8
FNM GU9 123 G1 1
FRIM GU16 59 K5
BOR GU35 189 G7
Faithfulls Dro STOK SO20 197 M4
Fakenham Wy SHST GU47 38 A7
Falaise Cl ALDT GU11 7 G1
Falaise Rd STOK SO20 150 F4
Falcon Cl KEMP RG22 91 L7
NTID SP9 102 E1
Falcon Coppice KSCL RG20 24 C8 1
Falcon Flds TADY RG26 29 L6
Falcon House Gdns KSCL RG20 24 B8
Falcon Vw WINW SO22 226 B4
Falcon Wy YTLY GU46 56 E2 1
Falkland Dr NWBY RG14 2 C9
Falkland Garth NWBY RG14 25 G1
Falkland Rd CHIN RG24 71 H6 1
NWBY RG14 25 G2
Falkner Rd FNM GU9 122 D6
Falkners Cl FARN GU14 77 H4
Fallowfield FARN GU14 77 H4 2
Fallow Fld WINW SO22 226 B4
Fallowfield YTLY GU46 56 E1
Falmouth Cl CBLY GU15 59 K4
Falmouth Wy STHA RG19 15 J5
Fannys La THLE RG7 15 L1
Fantails ALTN GU34 164 E2
Faraday Cl WHIT RG2 35 H1 1
Faraday Rd CHIN RG24 5 K2
FARN GU14 78 F2
NWBY RG14 3 G3
Farcrosse Cl SHST GU47 37 M8
Fareham Dr YTLY GU46 56 E1 1
Faringdon Cl SHST GU47 37 M7
Farleigh La OVTN RG25 114 F7
Farleigh Ri BSTK RG21 93 H6
Farleigh Rd OVTN RG25 115 K4
Farley Cl WINW SO22 226 A4
Farley La ROMY SO51 223 J7
Farley Mount Rd RWIN SO21 224 F2
Farley St STOK SO20 172 E2
Farm Cl CWTH RG45 37 M1
YTLY GU46 57 G3
Farm Dr FARN GU14 77 G4
Farm Ground Cl HTWY RG27 74 B7 1
Farmhouse Wy FLET GU13 98 D3
Farm La NFNM GU10 121 H3
Farm Rd ASHV GU12 101 H5
FRIM GU16 59 H6
RAND SP11 129 M2
Farm Vw YTLY GU46 57 G3
Farm View Dr CHIN RG24 71 M5
Farm Wk ASHV GU12 101 M8
Farnborough Rd ALDT GU11 100 A7
FARN GU14 78 E8
FNM GU9 100 A8
Farnborough St FARN GU14 79 G3
Farnham By-pass FNM GU9 122 C8
Farnham La HASM GU27 192 D7
Farnham Park Cl FNM GU9 122 E2
Farnham Rd FLET GU13 77 J7
BOR GU35 189 J2
LISS GU33 236 D4
ODIM RG29 96 F5
PSF GU32 236 A8
Faroe Cl CHIN RG24 71 J7
Farrell Cl CBLY GU15 58 F5
Farriers Cl TADY RG26 51 L5
Farrier's Fld OVTN RG25 115 M8
Farringdon Wy TADY RG26 49 L1
Farrs Av AND SP10 9 K8
Farthing Flds BOR GU35 190 B3
Faversham Rd SHST GU47 38 A7 2
Fawconer Rd KSCL RG20 47 J6
Fawley La ALTN GU34 233 G4
RWIN SO21 227 L8
Fayrewood Cha KEMP RG22 115 G1 2
Feathers La BSTK RG21 4 F9
Felbridge Cl FRIM GU16 59 J6
Feld Wy CHIN RG24 93 M1
Fellows Rd FARN GU14 79 G7
Felmer Dr WINC SO23 203 H1 1
Fennel Cl CHIN RG24 71 M3
FARN GU14 77 L4
NWBY RG14 14 A3
Ferbies FLET GU13 98 F2
Ferguson Cl BSTK RG21 92 F6
Fernbank EWKG RG40 36 A1 1
Fernbrae Cl NFNM GU10 146 E6
Fern Cl CWTH RG45 37 L1
FRIM GU16 59 M5
Ferncote Rd BOR GU35 189 K5 2
Ferndale Ct STHA RG19 15 G5
Ferndale Gdns HTWY RG27 73 M6 4
Ferndale Rd AND SP10 8 C3
FLET GU13 98 E3
Fernden La HASM GU27 216 E5
Ferndown Gdns FARN GU14 78 B4 1
Fern Dr FLET GU13 98 D2
Ferney Cl ALTN GU34 186 C1
Ferney La ALTN GU34 161 L8
Fernhill Cl FARN GU14 58 B7
FNM GU9 122 E2
Fernhill Dr FNM GU9 122 E2
Fernhill La FARN GU14 58 C7
FNM GU9 122 E1

Fern Hill La *ROMY* SO51 .... 223 J8
Fernhill Rd *BLKW* GU17 .... 58 B6
   FARN GU14 .... 78 B1
Fernhill Wk *FARN* GU14 .... 58 C7 2
Fernhurst Rd *LIPH* GU30 .... 238 E5
Fernlea *BOR* GU35 .... 189 G7
Fernleigh Ri *FRIM* GU16 .... 79 M1
Ferrell Fld *HTWY* RG27 .... 73 L7
Fiddlers Fld *SHST* GU34 .... 142 A8
Field Cl *THLE* RG7 .... 19 L6
Field End *FNM* GU9 .... 123 J4
   WINC SO23 .... 203 H1 2
Fielders Ct *ALTN* GU34 .... 164 E5
The Fielders *HTWY* RG27 .... 36 B8
Fieldfare Av *YTLY* GU46 .... 56 D2
Field Gate Dr *KSCL* RG20 .... 47 H6
Fielding Gdns *CWTH* RG45 ...... 37 K4
Fielding Rd *SHST* GU47 .... 58 B2
Field La *FRIM* GU16 .... 59 H7
Field Pl *LIPH* GU30 .... 214 E5
Field Rd *FARN* GU14 .... 58 C7
Field Stores Ap *ALDT* GU11 ... 100 F5
Fieldway *FLET* GU13 .... 76 C8 3
   HASM GU27 .... 216 F1
Field Wy *NFNM* GU10 .... 124 C1
   ASHV GU12 .... 101 H6
Fie Yard Rd *FARN* GU14 .... 78 D6
Fifield La *NFNM* GU10 .... 146 F6
Fifth Rd *NWBY* RG14 .... 2 A8
Fifth St *STHA* RG19 .... 26 C3
Filmorehill La *ALTN* GU34 ...... 232 E5
Fincham End Dr *CWTH* RG45 .. 37 J4 4
Finchampstead Rd
   EWKG RG40 .... 36 D1 5
Finch Cl *TADY* RG26 .... 49 M1 6
Finches Gn *ALTN* GU34 .... 164 E5
Finch Wy *THLE* RG7 .... 19 L5
Findhorn Cl *SHST* GU47 ...... 58 A1 7
The Findings *FARN* GU14 .... 58 B8
Fingle Dr *YTLY* GU46 .... 57 G1
Finkley Rd *RAND* SP11 .... 107 L3
Fintry Pl *FARN* GU14 .... 78 B1 8
Fiona Cl *WINC* SO23 .... 11 L6
Fir Acre Rd *ASHV* GU12 .... 101 K2
Fir Cl *FLET* GU13 .... 76 E8
Fir Dr *BLKW* GU17 .... 58 A5
Firecrest Rd *KEMP* RG22 .... 114 C2
Fire Station Rd *ALDT* GU11 .... 100 E5
Fire Thorn Cl *FLET* GU13 .... 98 E2
Firfield Rd *FNM* GU9 .... 146 D1
Firglen Dr *YTLY* GU46 .... 57 G1
Fir Gv *BOR* GU35 .... 189 G7
Firgrove Ct *FNM* GU9 .... 122 F7 9
Firgrove Hl *FNM* GU9 .... 122 F7
Firgrove Pde *FARN* GU14 ...... 78 E4 10
Firgrove Rd *FARN* GU14 .... 78 E4
   BOR GU35 .... 189 G7
   YTLY GU46 .... 56 E2
Firlands Av *CBLY* GU15 .... 59 G3 11
Firmstone Rd *WINC* SO23 .... 11 L7
Firs Cl *EWKG* RG40 .... 36 C1
   FARN GU14 .... 78 F6
Firs Crs *WINC* SO23 .... 178 F8
Fir's End *THLE* RG7 .... 19 K6
Firs La *ODIM* RG29 .... 96 B6
First Av *THLE* RG7 .... 29 M6
The Firs *LIPH* GU30 .... 214 E5
   NTHA RG18 .... 14 E4
First St *STHA* RG19 .... 26 D3
Firs Wy *DEAN* RG23 .... 92 A1
   WHCH RG28 .... 110 B3
Firth Cl *THLE* RG7 .... 30 E8 12
Fir Tree Av *HASM* GU27 .... 216 A2
Firtree Cl *SHST* GU47 .... 37 J8
Fir Tree La *NWBY* RG14 .... 14 B4
Firtree Wy *FLET* GU13 .... 77 G8
Firway *CSHT* GU26 .... 191 H3
Firwood Dr *CBLY* GU15 .... 58 F3
Fisherman's La *THLE* RG7 ...... 29 K1
Fishermen's Cl *ALDT* GU11 .... 101 H4
Fiske Cl *KEMP* RG22 .... 92 B4
Fitzroy Rd *FLET* GU13 .... 76 C7
Five Acres Cl *BOR* GU35 .... 189 L3 13
Five Ash Rd *ALTN* GU34 .... 184 F4
Five Bells La *STOK* SO20 ...... 172 D3
Five Bridges *WINC* SO23 ...... 226 D5
Fivefields Cl *WINC* SO23 .... 11 L9
Fivefields Rd *WINC* SO23 .... 11 M9
Flag Staff Rd *STHA* RG19 .... 15 H7
The Flashett *RSAL* SP5 .... 195 G2
The Flats *BLKW* GU17 .... 57 L4
Flaxfield Ct *BSTK* RG21 .... 4 D8
Flaxfield Rd *BSTK* RG21 .... 4 D8
Flecker Cl *NTHA* RG18 .... 14 F3 14
Fleet Hl *EWKG* RG40 .... 35 M6
Fleet La *EWKG* RG40 .... 35 L6
Fleet Rd *ALDT* GU11 .... 99 L2
   FARN GU14 .... 77 M4
   FLET GU13 .... 76 E7
   HTWY RG27 .... 75 M3
Fleetwood Cl *NWBY* RG14 ...... 14 A3
Fleming Cl *FARN* GU14 .... 79 G2
   RAND SP11 .... 80 E6
   WHIT RG2 .... 35 H1
Fleming Rd *WINC* SO23 .... 202 B5
   NWBY RG14 .... 3 G3
Flensburg Cl *AND* SP10 .... 106 C5
Fletcher Cl *BSTK* RG21 .... 92 E4
Fletchers Fld *LIPH* GU30 ...... 214 E5
Flexford Cl *KSCL* RG20 .... 44 C3
Flint Cl *AND* SP10 .... 8 B9
Flint La *RAND* SP11 .... 82 C2
The Flood *RSAL* SP5 .... 194 E1
Floral Wy *AND* SP10 .... 8 C8
   NTHA RG18 .... 15 G3
   RAND SP11 .... 8 A9
Floreat Gdns *NWBY* RG14 .... 2 A7
Florence Cl *YTLY* GU46 .... 56 F2 15
Florence Ct *AND* SP10 .... 107 G5
Florence Portal Cl *WHCH* RG28.. 111 C3
   SHST GU47 .... 58 B1
Florence Wy *CHIN* RG24 .... 70 B8
Focus Wy *AND* SP10 .... 107 J7
Foden Rd *ALDT* GU11 .... 6 F3

Fokerham Rd *STHA* RG19 .... 15 J6
Folly Cl *FLET* GU13 .... 98 F1
Folly Hi *FNM* GU9 .... 122 D3
Folly La *TADY* RG26 .... 52 A4
   THLE RG7 .... 19 J3
Folly La North *FNM* GU9 .... 122 E1
Folly La South *FNM* GU9 .. 122 D2 16
Folly Rd *HUNG* RG17 .... 21 M2
The Folly *NWBY* RG14 .... 3 G8
Fontwell Dr *ALTN* GU34 .... 164 E6
Fontwell Rd *NWBY* RG14 .... 3 M8
Forbes Cha *SHST* GU47 .... 58 A1
Forbes Rd *WINC* SO23 .... 179 G8
Forbury La *HUNG* RG17 .... 22 E1
Fordington Gv *BLKW* GU17 ...... 57 M4
Fordington Rd *WINW* SO22 ...... 10 C6
Ford La *NFNM* GU10 .... 146 E2
   ODIM RG29 .... 118 F1
   THLE RG7 .... 34 D4
The Forehead *THLE* RG7 .... 32 C4
Foreman Pk *ASHV* GU12 .... 101 K6
Foreman Rd *ASHV* GU12 .... 101 L7
Forest Cl *TADY* RG26 .... 29 H7
Forest Cnr *LISS* GU33 .... 236 F1
Forestdale *CSHT* GU26 .... 192 A5
Forest Dean *FARN* GU14 .... 77 H4
   NTID SP9 .... 102 F1 17
Forest End *FLET* GU13 .... 98 C2
Forest End Rd *SHST* GU47 ...... 37 J8
Foresters Wy *CWTH* RG45 ...... 38 C1
Forest Gld *NFNM* GU10 .... 146 A5
Forest Hills *CBLY* GU15 .... 58 E4
Forest La *BOR* GU35 .... 189 M2
   RAND SP11 .... 131 L2
   TADY RG26 .... 50 A2
Forest Lane Cl *LIPH* GU30 .... 214 D4
Forest Ri *LISS* GU33 .... 236 F2
Forest Rd *CWTH* RG45 .... 37 M3
   BOR GU35 .... 189 J7
   LISS GU33 .... 236 E1
Forge Cl *FNM* GU9 .... 123 G5
   TADY RG26 .... 51 M6
Forge La *ALDT* GU11 .... 100 C2
Forge Rd *BOR* GU35 .... 166 F8
Forth Cl *FARN* GU14 .... 78 A2
Fortrose Cl *SHST* GU47 ...... 58 A1 18
Fosseway *CWTH* RG45 .... 37 J3 19
Fossewood Dr *CBLY* GU15 .... 58 F3
Foul La *ALTN* GU34 .... 184 E1
Foundry La *HASM* GU27 .... 216 D2
Foundry Rd *RAND* SP11 .... 130 B4
Fountains Cl *CHIN* RG24 .... 70 F7
Four Acre Coppice
   HTWY RG27 .... 74 B6 2
   HTWY RG27 .... 74 B7 2
Four Lanes Cl *CHIN* RG24 ...... 71 M5
Four Oaks *KSCL* RG20 .... 44 C2
Fowler Av *FARN* GU14 .... 78 E6
Fowler Rd *FARN* GU14 .... 78 E6
Fowler's Rd *ALDT* GU11 .... 100 F3
Foxborough *THLE* RG7 .... 34 E2
Fox Cl *THLE* RG7 .... 19 K5
Foxcote *EWKG* RG40 .... 36 D1
Foxcotte Cl *AND* SP10 .... 106 C6
Foxcotte La *RAND* SP11 .... 106 A6
Fox Cft *FLET* GU13 .... 98 F3
Foxdown *OVTN* RG25 .... 88 F6
Foxdown Cl *CBLY* GU15 .... 58 F3
Fox Dr *YTLY* GU46 .... 57 G1
Foxglove Cl *KEMP* RG22 .... 114 F1
Foxglove Dr *BOR* GU35 .... 189 K6 2
Foxglove Wy *NTHA* RG18 .... 15 H3
Fox Heath *FARN* GU14 .... 77 M5
Foxhill Crs *CBLY* GU15 .... 39 L8
Fox Hills La *ASHV* GU12 .... 101 M5
Foxhunter Wy *STHA* RG19 .. 14 C5 20
Foxhurst Rd *ASHV* GU12 ...... 101 K3
Fox La *DEAN* RG23 .... 91 H5
   WINW SO22 .... 226 B3
   HTWY RG27 .... 36 C3
Foxley Cl *BLKW* GU17 .... 57 M3
Foxmoor Cl *DEAN* RG23 .... 91 G5
Fox Rd *HASM* GU27 .... 216 B2
   NFNM GU10 .... 146 F2
Foxwood *FARN* GU14 .... 77 H5 2
Fox Yd *FNM* GU9 .... 122 E6 2
Foye La *FLET* GU13 .... 99 G3
Foyle Pk *BSTK* RG21 .... 93 G6
Frampton Wy *WINC* SO23 .... 203 H1
France Hill Dr *CBLY* GU15 ...... 58 F3
Frances Rd *BSTK* RG21 .... 92 F4
The Frances *NTHA* RG18 .... 15 G4
Francis Gdns *WINC* SO23 .... 11 J2
Franklin Av *HTWY* RG27 ...... 75 G1 2
   TADY RG26 .... 29 K7
Fraser Cl *AND* SP10 .... 94 B2
Fraser Md *SHST* GU47 .... 58 B2
Fraser Rd *WINC* SO23 .... 179 G8
Frederick St *ALDT* GU11 .... 6 E2
Freelands Dr *FLET* GU13 .... 98 D3
Freemantle Cl *BSTK* RG21 .... 5 J7
French Gdns *BLKW* GU17 .... 58 A4
Frenchmoor La *RSAL* SP5 .... 219 L5
French Rd *LISS* GU33 .... 213 J5
Frensham Av *FLET* GU13 .... 77 H7
Frensham Cl *YTLY* GU46 .... 56 F2
Frensham Ct *NFNM* GU10 .... 146 E4
Frensham Heights Rd
   NFNM GU10 .... 146 D2
Frensham Rd *BOR* GU35 ...... 189 M6
Frensham Rd *CWTH* RG45 ...... 37 L1
   FNM GU9 .... 147 G1
   NFNM GU10 .... 147 G4
Frensham V *NFNM* GU10 ...... 146 F4
Frere Av *FLET* GU13 .... 98 D1
Frescade Crs *BSTK* RG21 .... 92 F5
Freshwood Dr *YTLY* GU46 ...... 56 F4
Friarsgate *WINC* SO23 .... 11 H7
Friars Rd *NWBY* RG14 .... 2 E9
Friend Av *ASHV* GU12 .... 7 M4
Friesian Cl *FARN* GU14 .... 77 G2
Frimley Green Rd *FRIM* GU16 .. 59 H8
Frimley Grove Gdns *FRIM* GU16 .. 59 G7

Frimley Hall Dr *CBLY* GU15 ...... 59 J2
Frimley High St *FRIM* GU16 .. 59 G7 1
   FRIM GU16 .... 59 G8 2
Frimley Rd *ASHV* GU12 .... 79 K8
   CBLY GU15 .... 58 E4
   FRIM GU16 .... 58 F7
Frith End Rd *ALTN* GU34 ...... 145 J8
   BOR GU35 .... 167 L4
Frith Hill Rd *FRIM* GU16 .... 59 M7
Frithmead Cl *BSTK* RG21 .... 92 F6
Frodsham Wy *SHST* GU47 .. 38 B6 2
Frog La *HTWY* RG27 .... 73 J1
   OVTN RG25 .... 94 E3
   TADY RG26 .... 50 E3
Frogmore Gv *BLKW* GU17 ...... 57 M4
Frogmore Park Dr *BLKW* GU17.. 58 A4
Frogmore Rd *BLKW* GU17 ...... 57 M4
Frogs Hole *KSCL* RG20 .... 47 H6
Frome Cl *BSTK* RG21 .... 5 J7
   DEAN RG23 .... 91 H7
   FARN GU14 .... 78 A2
Fromond Rd *WINW* SO22 ...... 202 B5
Fromont Dr *STHA* RG19 .... 15 G5
Froud Cl *HTWY* RG27 .... 73 L8 3
Frouds La *THLE* RG7 .... 17 J6
Froxfield Cl *WINC* SO23 .... 202 C4
Froyle La *ODIM* RG29 .... 118 F5
Fry's La *YTLY* GU46 .... 57 H1
Fugelmere Rd *FLET* GU13 ...... 77 H8
Fulbrook Wy *ODIM* RG29 .... 96 C3
Fuller Cl *STHA* RG19 .... 15 J6
Fullers La *KSCL* RG20 .... 43 L1
Fullers Rd *NFNM* GU10 .... 146 A4
Fullers V *BOR* GU35 .... 190 C1
Fullerton Rd *RAND* SP11 ...... 130 B8
Fullerton Wy *TADY* RG26 .... 49 M1
Fulmar Cl *KEMP* RG22 .... 114 E1
Furley Cl *WINC* SO23 .... 11 K7
Furse Cl *CBLY* GU15 .... 59 L4
Furse Hill Rd *NTID* SP9 .... 102 E3
Further Vell-Mead *FLET* GU13.. 98 D4
Furze Cl *ASHV* GU12 .... 101 K1
Furzedown La *RAND* SP11 .... 128 D3
Furzedown Rd *STOK* SO20 .... 198 F7
Furze Dr *RAND* SP11 .... 103 J2
Furze Hill Crs *CWTH* RG45 ...... 37 M4
Furze Hill Rd *BOR* GU35 .... 190 F4
Furzen La *OVTN* RG25 .... 140 A1
Furze Rd *TADY* RG26 .... 29 J6
Furze Vale Rd *BOR* GU35 ...... 190 E4
Fuzzy Dro *KEMP* RG22 .... 91 H7
Fyfield Cl *BLKW* GU17 .... 58 A3
Fyfield La *RAND* SP11 .... 104 F6
Fyfield Rd *RAND* SP11 .... 104 F6
   STHA RG19 .... 15 G6
Fyfield Wy *WINW* SO22 .... 202 A3
   RAND SP11 .... 103 J2
Fylingdales *STHA* RG19 .... 14 F6
Fylingdales Cl *KEMP* RG22 ...... 91 M5

G

Gables Cl *ASHV* GU12 .... 101 K3
   FARN GU14 .... 78 D4
Gables Rd *FLET* GU13 .... 98 E4
Gables Wy *STHA* RG19 .... 15 L6
Gabriel Dr *CBLY* GU15 .... 59 L4
The Gabriels *NWBY* RG14 ...... 25 G2
Gaffney Cl *ALDT* GU11 .... 101 L1
Gage Cl *CHIN* RG24 .... 93 L1
Gainsborough Cl *CBLY* GU15 .. 59 J1 3
   FARN GU14 .... 79 G6 2
Gainsborough Rd *BSTK* RG21 .. 93 H6
Galahad Cl *AND* SP10 .... 106 F6
Gallaghers Md *AND* SP10 ...... 106 A8
Galley La *STHA* RG19 .... 27 G7
The Gallop *YTLY* GU46 .... 57 G1
Galloway Cl *FARN* GU14 .... 77 H4
   KEMP RG22 .... 92 A5
Gallwey Rd *ALDT* GU11 .... 100 E5
Gally Hill Rd *FLET* GU13 .... 98 E4
Gander Dr *CHIN* RG24 .... 70 B8
Gangbridge La *RAND* SP11 ...... 85 J5
Gannet Cl *KEMP* RG22 .... 114 E1
Garbett Rd *WINC* SO23 .... 11 L7
Garbetts Wy *NFNM* GU10 ...... 124 B2
Garden Cl *FARN* GU14 .... 78 B6
   HTWY RG27 .... 73 L7 2
   KSCL RG20 .... 47 H6 2
   OVTN RG25 .... 139 G7
Garden Close La *NWBY* RG14.. 25 G4
Gardeners Gn *NTID* SP9 .... 126 C1
Gardener's Hill Rd *NFNM* GU10.. 146 E4
Garden La *WINC* SO23 .... 11 H7
The Gardens *NFNM* GU10 ...... 124 C1
Garfield Rd *CBLY* GU15 .... 58 F3
Garford Crs *NWBY* RG14 .... 13 G8
Garlands Cl *THLE* RG7 .... 19 K6
Garnet Fld *YTLY* GU46 .... 56 D3
Garnet Rd *BOR* GU35 .... 189 K6
Garnier Rd *WINC* SO23 .... 226 F3
Garrett Cl *KSCL* RG20 .... 47 H5
Garrick Wy *FRIM* GU16 .... 79 H2
Garston Mede *STOK* SO20 .... 153 M4
Gar St *WINC* SO23 .... 10 F8
Garth Cl *FNM* GU9 .... 146 D1 2
Garth Rd *THLE* RG7 .... 31 K3
The Garth *ASHV* GU12 .... 101 J7
   FARN GU14 .... 79 G4
Gascoigne La *NALR* SO24 ...... 208 A3
Gaskell Cl *ALTN* GU34 .... 165 H4
Gaston La *ALTN* GU34 .... 186 D5
   ODIM RG29 .... 118 E2
Gate Hyde *WINC* SO23 .... 11 G5 2
Gatekeeper Cl *WINC* SO23 ...... 11 M7
The Gates *FARN* GU14 .... 77 H4
Gauvain Cl *ALTN* GU34 .... 164 E6
Gawaine Cl *AND* SP10 .... 106 F4 2
Gaywood Dr *NWBY* RG14 .... 3 M4
Geale's Crs *ALTN* GU34 .... 164 F4
Genoa Cl *AND* SP10 .... 107 G5
Gentles La *LIPH* GU30 .... 190 D7
George Denyer Cl
   HASM GU27 .... 216 F1 2
George Eyston Dr *WINW* SO22..226 C2
George Gdns *ALDT* GU11 .... 7 K7

Georgeham Rd *SHST* GU47 .. 38 A6 2
George Rd *FLET* GU13 .... 77 G7
George St *BSTK* RG21 .... 4 B8
   KSCL RG20 .... 47 H6
George Yd *AND* SP10 .... 9 J6
The George Yd *NALR* SO24 .... 206 C2
Georgia Cl *AND* SP10 .... 8 B9
Georgia Gdns *TADY* RG26 ...... 30 B8
Georgian Cl *CBLY* GU15 .... 59 H1
Gerald Sq *ALTN* GU34 .... 164 F2
German Rd *TADY* RG26 .... 51 M6
Gershwin Rd *KEMP* RG22 ...... 92 B8
Gibbet La *CBLY* GU15 .... 59 K1
Gibbons Cl *SHST* GU47 .... 57 M1
Gibbs Cl *EWKG* RG40 .... 36 B2
Gibbs' *BOR* GU35 .... 188 F2
Gibbs Wy *YTLY* GU46 .... 56 E4
Gid La *ALTN* GU34 .... 144 A5
Giffard Dr *FARN* GU14 .... 78 C2
Giffards Meadow *FNM* GU9 .. 123 H7
Gilbard Ct *FRIM* GU16 .... 71 M5 2
Gilbert Rd *FRIM* GU16 .... 58 F7
Gilbert's Gn *NTID* SP9 .... 126 D1 2
Gilberts Mead Cl *RAND* SP11.. 130 A4 4
Gilbert St *NALR* SO24 .... 208 C3
Gilbert White Wy *ALTN* GU34.. 164 E3
Giles Rd *TADY* RG26 .... 29 M8
Gillham's La *HASM* GU27 ...... 215 K4
Gillian Av *ASHV* GU12 .... 7 L5
Gillian Cl *ASHV* GU12 .... 7 L5
Gillies Dr *CHIN* RG24 .... 70 B8
Gillingham Cl *WINC* SO23 .... 203 H1
Gilroy Cl *NWBY* RG14 .... 24 F2
Girton Cl *SHST* GU47 .... 58 B7
Gisbourne Cl *NTID* SP9 .... 102 F2 2
Glade Cl *CHIN* RG24 .... 71 L6
The Glade *FNM* GU9 .... 123 G5
   FRIM GU16 .... 79 J6
   NFNM GU10 .... 145 L7
   NWBY RG14 .... 13 J8 2
Gladiator Wy *FARN* GU14 .... 78 D8
Gladstone Cl *WINC* SO23 .... 10 F6
Glaisdale *STHA* RG19 .... 14 F6
Glamis Cl *DEAN* RG23 .... 90 F6
   FRIM GU16 .... 79 J1
Glastonbury Cl *CHIN* RG24 .... 4 D1
Glaston Hill Rd *HTWY* RG27 .... 35 L8
Glayshers Hl *BOR* GU35 ...... 190 D2
Glebe Cl *ALTN* GU34 .... 163 G2
   OVTN RG25 .... 114 C7
   TADY RG26 .... 49 M1
Glebe Ct *FLET* GU13 .... 76 E7
Glebe Flds *ALTN* GU34 .... 163 G2
Glebefields *NWBY* RG14 ...... 13 L3 2
Glebeland Rd *CBLY* GU15 .... 58 C4
Glebelands *RAND* SP11 .... 131 G6
   STHA RG19 .... 14 F5
Glebe La *DEAN* RG23 .... 91 M4
   HTWY RG27 .... 75 J3
   KSCL RG20 .... 12 B3
   NFNM GU10 .... 169 M3
Glebe Meadow *OVTN* RG25 .... 88 F8 2
   RSAL SP5 .... 219 M6
Glebe Rd *FARN* GU14 .... 78 C3
   BOR GU35 .... 190 B3
   NFNM GU10 .... 121 J2
Glenavon Gdns *YTLY* GU46 .. 57 G4 2
Glen Cl *AND* SP10 .... 8 C5
Glencoe Cl *FRIM* GU16 .... 59 J8
Glendale Av *NWBY* RG14 .... 24 F3
Glendale Pk *FLET* GU13 .... 76 B6
Glendale Rd *TADY* RG26 .... 29 K7
Gleneagles Dr *FARN* GU14 ...... 77 M5
Glenfield Cl *RSAL* SP5 .... 195 G2 2
Glenhurst Cl *BLKW* GU17 .... 58 B4 2
Glen Innes *SHST* GU47 .... 38 C7
Glenlea Cl *CSHT* GU26 .... 192 B7
Glenlea Hollow *CSHT* GU26 .. 192 B6
Glenmore Cl *FRIM* GU16 .... 15 G6 3
Glenmount Rd *FRIM* GU16 ...... 79 K6
Glen Rd *FLET* GU13 .... 76 E8
   CSHT GU26 .... 191 M2
The Glen *TADY* RG26 .... 30 B7
Glenville Gdns *CSHT* GU26 .... 192 B4
Globe Farm La *BLKW* GU17 ...... 57 L3
Glorney Md *FNM* GU9 .... 6 E2
Gloucester Cl *ALTN* GU34 ...... 184 F6
   FRIM GU16 .... 79 H2
Gloucester Dr *KEMP* RG22 .... 115 C1
Gloucester Rd *ALDT* GU11 .... 7 J7
   NWBY RG14 .... 2 B5
Glynswood *CBLY* GU15 .... 59 J5
   NFNM GU10 .... 146 D4
Goatacre Rd *ALTN* GU34 .... 184 B3
Goat La *BSTK* RG21 .... 5 C8
Goch Wy *AND* SP10 .... 106 D6
Goddard Dr *THLE* RG7 .... 16 C5
Goddards Cl *HTWY* RG27 .... 52 C8 2
Goddards Firs *DEAN* RG23 ...... 91 H8
Goddards La *CBLY* GU15 .... 58 E5
Goddards Md *AND* SP10 .... 8 D7
Goddard Sq *AND* SP10 .... 107 G6
Godwin Cl *WINW* SO22 .... 202 B5
Goldcrest Cl *YTLY* GU46 .... 56 E2
Golden Flds *LIPH* GU30 .... 215 G5
Goldfinch Wy *RWIN* SO21 ...... 178 D3
Goldhill *NFNM* GU10 .... 146 F2
Golding Cl *STHA* RG19 .... 15 J3 2
Gold La *ALDT* GU11 .... 101 H4
Goldney Rd *CBLY* GU15 .... 59 J4
Goldsmith Cl *NTHA* RG18 .... 14 F3
Goldsmith Wy *CWTH* RG45 ...... 37 L4
Goldwell Dr *NWBY* RG14 .... 2 C2
Golf Dr *CBLY* GU15 .... 59 J4
Golf La *BOR* GU35 .... 189 G7
Golf Links Av *CSHT* GU26 ...... 191 L2
Gondreville Gdns *FLET* GU13 .. 98 D4
Gong Hl *NFNM* GU10 .... 147 G6
Gong Hi *NFNM* GU10 .... 147 G4
Goodden Crs *FARN* GU14 .... 78 C6
The Goodens *NALR* SO24 .... 230 B3 2
Goodman Cl *BSTK* RG21 .... 92 E4
Goodwood Cl *ALTN* GU34 ...... 164 E6
   CBLY GU15 .... 38 F8
   THLE RG7 .... 19 J6

Goodwood Pl *FARN* GU14 ...... 79 H5 2
Goodwood Wy *NWBY* RG14 ...... 3 K8
Goodwyns Cl *NTID* SP9 .... 126 C1 2
Goodyers *ALTN* GU34 .... 164 F5
Goose Gn *HTWY* RG27 .... 75 H5
Goose Green Wy *STHA* RG19 .. 15 H5 2
Goose La *HTWY* RG27 .... 73 M6
Gordon Av *CBLY* GU15 .... 58 E4
   FLET GU13 .... 99 G2
   WINC SO23 .... 227 H2
Gordon Cl *BSTK* RG21 .... 5 H5
Gordon Crs *CBLY* GU15 .... 58 E4
Gordon Rd *ALDT* GU11 .... 6 F3
   CBLY GU15 .... 58 E4
   CWTH RG45 .... 38 A5
   FARN GU14 .... 79 G8
   NTHA RG18 .... 14 D3
   NWBY RG14 .... 3 G3
   WINC SO23 .... 11 H5
Gordon Wk *YTLY* GU46 .... 57 H3
Gore End Rd *KSCL* RG20 .... 23 L5
Goring Rd *WINW* SO22 .... 202 B7
Goring La *THLE* RG7 .... 19 J7
The Gorrings *STOK* SO20 ...... 198 F6
Gorse Cl *FNM* GU9 .... 146 D2
Gorsedown Cl *BOR* GU35 .... 189 G7 2
Gorselands *NWBY* RG14 .... 25 G3
   TADY RG26 .... 29 M8
   YTLY GU46 .... 56 F4
Gorselands Cl *ASHV* GU12 .... 101 K3
   BOR GU35 .... 190 F4 2
Gorse La *NFNM* GU10 .... 146 D2
Gorse Ride North *EWKG* RG40.. 36 B1
Gorse Ride South *EWKG* RG40.. 36 B1
Gorse Rd *FRIM* GU16 .... 59 H6
Gorseway *FLET* GU13 .... 98 F1
Gort Cl *ALDT* GU11 .... 101 H1
Goscombs La *NALR* SO24 ...... 207 J1
Goslings Cft *ALTN* GU34 ...... 187 K7
Gough Rd *FLET* GU13 .... 76 D6
Gould Cl *RAND* SP11 .... 80 D6
Government House Rd
   ALDT GU11 .... 100 D1
Government Rd *ALDT* GU11 .... 101 H4
Governor's Rd *CBLY* GU15 ...... 58 D4
Gower Cl *BSTK* RG21 .... 4 E4
Gower Crs *HTWY* RG27 .... 74 A7 2
Gower Pk *SHST* GU47 .... 58 A1
Grace Bennett Cl *FARN* GU14.. 78 D1 2
Gracemere Crs *KEMP* RG22 .. 114 C1
Grace Sq *AND* SP10 .... 107 H6
Gracious St *ALTN* GU34 .... 187 J8
Gradwell La *ALTN* GU34 .... 144 F4
Grafton Cl *BOR* GU35 .... 189 K6
Grafton Rd *WINC* SO23 .... 226 E2
Grafton Wy *KEMP* RG22 .... 92 C4
Grainger Cl *KEMP* RG22 .... 92 D7
Grammarsham La *OVTN* RG25.. 115 L6
Grampian Rd *SHST* GU47 .... 37 J6
Grampian Wy *KEMP* RG22 ...... 92 A5
Granada Pl *AND* SP10 .... 9 M3
Granby End *THLE* RG7 .... 19 L5 2
Grand Av *CBLY* GU15 .... 58 F2
Grand Pde *WINW* SO22 .... 202 B3
Grand Trunk Rd *NTID* SP9 .... 102 B4
Grange Av *CWTH* RG45 .... 37 L2
Grange Cl *RAND* SP11 .... 104 D6
Grange Farm Rd *ASHV* GU12.. 101 L5
Grange La *HTWY* RG27 .... 75 G3
Grange Rd *ASHV* GU12 .... 101 L7
   CBLY GU15 .... 59 H3
   FARN GU14 .... 78 E1
   FLET GU13 .... 98 E3
   NALR SO24 .... 206 B3
   NFNM GU10 .... 124 B2
   NFNM GU10 .... 147 L8
   WINC SO23 .... 226 D4
The Grange *NWBY* RG14 .... 24 F3
Grantham Cl *SHST* GU47 ...... 38 B7 2
Grantley Dr *FLET* GU13 .... 98 E1
Grant Rd *CWTH* RG45 .... 37 M5
Grasmere Cl *BOR* GU35 ...... 189 J3 2
Grasmere Rd *FARN* GU14 .... 78 B5
   FNM GU9 .... 122 D2
Graspan Rd *RAND* SP11 .... 81 G7
Grassington Pl *STHA* RG19 ...... 15 G5
Grassmead *STHA* RG19 .... 15 H6
Grateley Dro *RAND* SP11 ...... 127 L7
   RAND SP11 .... 128 C6
Grateley Rd *AMSY* SP4 .... 126 C7
Gratton Cl *RWIN* SO21 .... 156 C4
Gravel Cl *NALR* SO24 .... 160 B4
Gravel Hl *KSCL* RG20 .... 12 B3
Gravel Hill Rd *NFNM* GU10 .... 145 J4
Gravel La *ALTN* GU34 .... 184 D7
   RWIN SO21 .... 155 J2
Gravelly Cl *KSCL* RG20 .... 23 K5
   TADY RG26 .... 29 G8
Gravel Rd *FARN* GU14 .... 79 G8
   FLET GU13 .... 99 G2
   FNM GU9 .... 122 E1
Grays Cl *HASM* GU27 .... 193 H8
Grayshot Dr *BLKW* GU17 ...... 57 M3 2
Grayshott Cl *WINW* SO22 ...... 202 C4
Grayshott Laurels
   BOR GU35 .... 189 M3 2
Grayshott Rd *BOR* GU35 ...... 190 F3
Grayswood Dr *FRIM* GU16 ...... 79 K7
Grayswood Rd *HASM* GU27 .. 193 H8
Great Austins *FNM* GU9 .... 123 G8
Great Binfields Crs *CHIN* RG24.. 71 L8
Great Binfields Rd *CHIN* RG24.. 93 L1
Greatfield Cl *FARN* GU14 .... 58 D8
Greatfield Rd *FARN* GU14 .... 58 D8
Great Field Rd *WINW* SO22 ...... 10 F7
Great La *WHCH* RG28 .... 110 B3
Great Minster St *WINC* SO23 .. 10 F8
Great Oaks Cha *CHIN* RG24 .. 71 K6 2
Great Sheldons Coppice
   HTWY RG27 .... 73 M6
Grebe Cl *ALTN* GU34 .... 164 D2 2
   KEMP RG22 .... 114 E1
Green Acre *ALDT* GU11 .... 6 D4
Greenacre *KSCL* RG20 .... 47 J6 2
Greenacres *KSCL* RG20 .... 24 B8
   BOR GU35 .... 189 L4 2
   NFNM GU10 .... 123 H6

RWIN SO21 155 H2
Greenbirch Cl KEMP RG22 114 E1
Greenbury Cl DEAN RG23 92 B3
Green Cl NALR SO24 182 C7
RWIN SO21 178 D4
Greencroft FARN GU14 78 E4 [2]
Green Cross La NFNM GU10 169 K7
Green Dro RAND SP11 84 A6
Green End YTLY GU46 57 G1 [1]
Greenfield Cl LIPH GU30 214 F3 [1]
Greenfield Rd FNM GU9 146 C1
Greenfields LISS GU33 236 F4
RAND SP11 84 B8 [1]
Greenfields Av ALTN GU34 164 D4
Greenfield Wy CWTH RG45 37 K1
Green Finch Cl CWTH RG45 37 J2 [1]
Green Glades FLET GU13 98 E3
Greenham Rd NWBY RG14 2 F6
Greenhanger NFNM GU10 169 J8
Greenhaven YTLY GU46 56 E3
Greenhaven Cl AND SP10 9 L6 [1]
Greenhill Av WINW SO22 10 C7
Green Hill Cl CBLY GU15 59 M2
Greenhill Cl FNM GU9 146 D1 [2]
WINW SO22 10 C7
Green Hill Rd CBLY GU15 59 M2
Greenhill Rd FNM GU9 123 G8
WINW SO22 10 B7
Greenhill Ter WINW SO22 10 C7
Greenhill Wy FNM GU9 146 D1
Green Jacket Cl WINW SO22 226 D3
Greenlands KSCL RG20 24 B7
Greenlands Rd CBLY GU15 58 E7
KSCL RG20 47 J6
NWBY RG14 3 G9
Green La ALTN GU34 184 E8
ALTN GU34 209 H4
BLKW GU17 57 L4
BLKW GU17 58 B4
FNM GU9 6 D9
FNM GU9 122 D8
HASM GU27 216 E4
HTWY RG27 75 H3
NALR SO24 207 H3
NALR SO24 232 C2
NFNM GU10 168 B2
NFNM GU10 169 J8
NWBY RG14 2 B5
OVTN RG25 115 M8
PSF GU32 234 E3
RAND SP11 129 H3
SHST GU47 57 M1
STHA RG19 14 F5
TADY RG26 50 B4
THLE RG7 18 F6
THLE RG7 32 C8
YTLY GU46 56 E1
Green Lane Cl CBLY GU15 58 F1
Greenleas FRIM GU16 59 H6
Greenleas Cl YTLY GU46 56 F1
Green Leys FLET GU13 98 E4
Green Meadows La
RAND SP11 130 F6
Green Park Cl WINC SO23 11 J2
Greensand Wy FNM GU9 123 H6
GSHT GU26 192 D6
HASM GU27 216 F1
Greenside CWTH RG45 37 J3
Green Springs NFNM GU10 121 J1
Green Stile ALTN GU34 184 D2
Green St BOR GU35 166 C8
The Green AND SP10 106 D6 [1]
FNM GU9 122 F2
FNM GU9 123 K3
FRIM GU16 79 J2
LISS GU33 236 D3 [2]
NFNM GU10 124 B7
OVTN RG25 89 G8
TADY RG26 49 M2
WHCH RG28 110 C3
Green Wy ASHV GU12 101 H5
Greenway HTWY RG27 52 C8
Greenways FLET GU13 98 E2
KSCL RG20 24 B7
SHST GU47 37 L7
Greenwich Wy AND SP10 106 F6
Greenwood Dr CHIN RG24 71 L4 [1]
Greenwood Rd CWTH RG45 37 K2
Greenwoods WHCH RG28 110 B2
Gregory Cl BSTK RG21 5 H3
Greig Rd KEMP RG22 92 D7
Grenadier Rd ASHV GU12 101 L4
Grenadiers Wy FARN GU14 77 M5 [2]
Grensell Cl HTWY RG27 36 B8 [3]
Grenville Cl LIPH GU30 214 F4
Grenville Dr FLET GU13 98 D1
Grenville Gdns FRIM GU16 79 H2
Gresham Wy FRIM GU16 79 H2
Gresley Rd BSTK RG21 5 K5
CHIN RG24 5 K4
Greyberry Copse Rd
STHA RG19 14 A8
Greyhound Cl ASHV GU12 101 J7
Greyhound La OVTN RG25 111 M1
Greys Ct ALDT GU11 6 A2 [1]
Greys Farm Cl NALR SO24 230 C4
Greystead Pk NFNM GU10 146 B2
Greystoke Ct CWTH RG45 37 K4
Greywell Cl TADY RG26 29 K8 [2]
Greywell Rd CHIN RG24 94 C3
HTWY RG27 95 H4
Grieve Cl NFNM GU10 124 B1
Griffin Wy South HTWY RG27 74 A5
Griffiths Cl STHA RG19 15 J6
Griffon Cl FARN GU14 78 A5
Grimstead Rd RSAL SP5 218 B2
Grindle Cl NTHA RG18 14 F3
Grosvenor Cl KEMP RG22 115 G3 [2]
Grosvenor Ct BLKW GU17 58 A5
Grosvenor Dr WINC SO23 11 J2
Grosvenor Rd ALDT GU11 6 E2
ALTN GU34 184 D6
Grove Cl BSTK RG21 93 H5
EWKG RG40 37 H1
Grove Cross Rd FRIM GU16 59 G7
Grove End Rd FNM GU9 146 E1
Grovefields Av FRIM GU16 59 G7
Groveland Rd NWBY RG14 13 G3
Grovelands NFNM GU10 147 H1
Grovelands Rd WINW SO22 202 A7
Grove Rd ALTN GU34 164 E6
ASHV GU12 101 K4
BSTK RG21 93 H6
CBLY GU15 59 H3
FLET GU13 57 G4
GSHT GU26 191 M2
NWBY RG14 13 G3
Groves Cl RWIN SO21 178 B4
Groves Lea THLE RG7 31 J2
The Grove ALDT GU11 6 F3
FARN GU14 79 G7
FRIM GU16 59 G7
LIPH GU30 214 E4
NTHA RG18 15 G4
RAND SP11 105 L4
Guernsey Cl CHIN RG24 71 H6
Guernsey Dr FARN GU14 77 G4
Guildford Rd ALDT GU11 7 L7
FLET GU13 77 H7
FNM GU9 123 G5
FRIM GU16 79 K3
NFNM GU10 123 K4
Guildford Rd East FARN GU14 78 F7
Guildford Rd West FARN GU14 78 F7
Guillemont Flds FARN GU14 77 M3
Guinea Ct CHIN RG24 71 M5 [3]
Gulley Rd FARN GU14 78 D8
Gun Hl ALDT GU11 100 E5
Gunners La RWIN SO21 159 M2
Gunns Farm LIPH GU30 214 F6
Gunville Hl RSAL SP5 195 H2
Gunville Rd RSAL SP5 195 G2
Gurdons ALTN GU34 164 C7
Guttridge La TADY RG26 29 K8
Gwyn Cl NWBY RG14 13 J8

H

Hacks La RWIN SO21 177 G5
Hackupps La ROMY SO51 222 B7
Hackwood Cl AND SP10 8 B7
Hackwood La OVTN RG25 116 A2
Hackwood Rd BSTK RG21 93 H5
Hackwood Road Rbt
BSTK RG21 93 H5
Hadleigh Pl BSTK RG21 4 D8
Hadleys NFNM GU10 146 B5
Hadrian Rd AND SP10 107 G5
Hadrians Wy DEAN RG23 92 B1 [2]
Hagley Rd FLET GU13 76 D6
Haig La FLET GU13 99 G3
Haig Rd AND SP10 8 C4
ASHV GU12 7 K3
CBLY GU15 58 C2
NALR SO24 206 C2
Hailsham Cl SHST GU47 38 A7 [3]
Hailstone Rd BSTK RG21 4 E2
Haining Gdns FRIM GU16 79 K5
Halcyon Dr RAND SP11 104 D8
Hale House La NFNM GU10 169 K7
Hale Pl FNM GU9 123 H3
Hale Reeds FNM GU9 123 G2
Hale Rd FNM GU9 123 G5
Hales Fld HASM GU27 216 F2
Hale Wy FRIM GU16 59 G7
Half Moon Hl HASM GU27 216 F2
Halifax Cl AND SP10 8 E3
FARN GU14 78 C5
Halifax Pl NTHA RG18 14 F4 [1]
Halifax Wy FARN GU14 100 C1
Halimote Rd ALDT GU11 6 F3
Hall Cl CBLY GU15 59 H2
Hall Farm Crs YTLY GU46 56 F3
Halliday Cl BSTK RG21 92 F6
Hall La ALTN GU34 187 H6
YTLY GU46 56 F3
Hallmark Cl SHST GU47 38 B8
Hall Rd ALTN GU34 164 F2
FARN GU14 78 E6
Halls Farm Cl WINW SO22 202 D5
The Hall Wy WINW SO22 202 A3
Halters End GSHT GU26 191 K5
The Halters NWBY RG14 25 L1 [1]
Halton Rd RAND SP11 103 J1
Hamble Av BLKW GU17 58 A3
Hamble Cl DEAN RG23 91 G7 [2]
Hamble Ct BSTK RG21 5 K8
Hambledon Cl WINW SO22 202 C4
Hamble Dr TADY RG26 30 A8
Hambleton Cl CBLY GU15 59 L5
Hamborne Ga NWBY RG14 13 G7
Ham Br STHA RG19 14 B5
Hambridge La NWBY RG14 14 B6
Hambridge Rd NWBY RG14 3 J5
Hamburg Cl AND SP10 106 E5 [1]
Hamdens NWBY RG14 24 F2
Hamelyn Rd BSTK RG21 92 F4
Hamesmoor Rd FRIM GU16 79 H4
Hamesmoor Wy FRIM GU16 79 J4
Hamilton Cl BOR GU35 189 L4
NWBY RG14 2 F9
Hamilton Rd FLET GU13 99 G2 [1]
LISS GU33 213 J6
Ham La TADY RG26 48 E4
Hamlash La NFNM GU10 146 F7
Hammer Hl HASM GU27 215 M4
Hammer La GSHT GU26 191 M8
HASM GU27 215 M3
LIPH GU30 215 K2
Hammersley Rd ALDT GU11 100 E1
Hammerwood Copse
HASM GU27 216 A3 [1]
Hammond Cl STHA RG19 15 H6
Hammond Rd BSTK RG21 92 F5 [2]
Hammonds Heath THLE RG7 31 L2
Hammond's La NALR SO24 208 B4
Hampshire Cl ASHV GU12 7 M7
KEMP RG22 91 M5
Hampshire Rd CBLY GU15 39 J8
BOR GU35 189 J4
Hampton Cl FLET GU13 98 F4
Hampton La WINW SO22 202 B7
Hampton Rd FNM GU9 122 D3
NWBY RG14 2 D7
Ham Rd HUNG RG17 20 D5
Hanbury Wy CBLY GU15 58 F5
Hancombe Rd SHST GU47 37 K6
Handcroft Cl NFNM GU10 98 C8
Handel Cl KEMP RG22 92 D7
Handford La YTLY GU46 57 G4
Hangerfield Cl YTLY GU46 56 F3
Hanger Rd TADY RG26 29 J7
Hangers Wy ALTN GU34 164 F4
The Hanger BOR GU35 190 B1
Hanmore Rd CHIN RG24 71 K6
Hannam's Farm NFNM GU10 121 H2 [1]
Hanningtons Wy THLE RG7 19 M5
Hanover Cl AND SP10 8 B8
FRIM GU16 59 H7
Hanover Dr FARN GU14 77 H4
Hanover Gdns BSTK RG21 92 F6
FARN GU14 78 B2
Hanson Cl CBLY GU15 59 L1
Hanson Rd AND SP10 8 D3
Harbour Cl FARN GU14 58 D8
Harcourt Rd CBLY GU15 58 E3
Hardings La HTWY RG27 75 J2 [3]
Hardy Av YTLY GU46 56 F4
Hardy Cl NTHA RG18 14 F3 [2]
Hardyfair Cl RAND SP11 105 J6
Hardy Gn CWTH RG45 37 L4
Hardy La BSTK RG21 92 E4
Hardys Fld KSCL RG20 47 H5
Harebell Cl HTWY RG27 75 J1 [1]
Harebell Dr NTHA RG18 15 H4
Harebell Gdns HTWY RG27 75 J1
Hare's La HTWY RG27 55 K8
Harestock Cl WINW SO22 202 C3
Harestock Rd WINW SO22 202 C4
Harfield Cl HTWY RG27 73 M7 [2]
Harlech Cl DEAN RG23 92 B3
Harlech Rd BLKW GU17 58 A4 [1]
Harlington Wy FLET GU13 76 D8
Harmsworth Rd TADY RG26 29 L8 [1]
Harold Gdns ALTN GU34 164 F3
Harpdon Pde YTLY GU46 57 G1 [2]
Harper's Rd ASHV GU12 101 M6
Harpton Cl YTLY GU46 57 G1
Harrington Cl NWBY RG14 14 A3
Harris Hl KEMP RG22 115 G1
Harroway RAND SP11 108 F3
WHCH RG28 87 G7
Harroway La RAND SP11 105 M6
Harrow Down WINW SO22 226 C4
Harrow Wy AND SP10 8 A2
OVTN RG25 90 A5
RAND SP11 105 M6
The Harrow Wy KEMP RG22 92 D7
Hart Cl FARN GU14 58 B8
Hartford Bridge Flats
HTWY RG27 55 M7
Hartford Ct HTWY RG27 75 H2 [1]
Hartford Ri CBLY GU15 59 G2
Hartford Rd HTWY RG27 75 H2
Hartland Pl FARN GU14 78 D2 [2]
Hartley Cl BLKW GU17 57 L3
Hartley Gdns TADY RG26 49 L1
Hartley La HTWY RG27 52 E6
Hartley Meadow
WHCH RG28 110 A3 [2]
Hartleys THLE RG7 30 D8
Hartmead Rd STHA RG19 15 H5
Harts Hill Rd NTHA RG18 15 H4
Hartshill Rd TADY RG26 29 J8
Harts La KSCL RG20 45 H2
THLE RG7 18 E3
Hartsleaf Cl FLET GU13 76 E8 [1]
Harts Leap Cl SHST GU47 37 K7
Harts Leap Rd SHST GU47 37 J7
Hartswood CHIN RG24 71 K6
The Hart FNM GU9 122 E6
Harvard Rd SHST GU47 38 C7
Harvest Cl WINW SO22 226 C4
YTLY GU46 56 E4
Harvest Crs FARN GU14 77 G3
Harvest Gn NWBY RG14 2 B8
Harvest Wy CHIN RG24 71 L8
Harvey Rd FARN GU14 77 M3
Harveys Fld OVTN RG25 88 F8
Harwood Pl WINC SO23 179 H8
Harwood Ri KSCL RG20 24 C7
Hasle Dr HASM GU27 216 E3
Haslemere Cl FRIM GU16 59 M5 [2]
Haslemere Rd HASM GU27 216 E6
LIPH GU30 215 G4
Hastards La ALTN GU34 187 K8
Hasted Dr NALR SO24 206 B4
Haste Hl HASM GU27 217 G3
Hastings Cl DEAN RG23 92 A3
FRIM GU16 79 K1
Hatchbury La RAND SP11 61 H2
Hatch Cl THLE RG7 16 F1
The Hatches FNM GU9 122 C8
FRIM GU16 79 J2
Hatchet La RAND SP11 83 H7
Hatchetts Dr HASM GU27 215 M2
Hatchgate Cl NTHA RG18 14 F2
Hatchgate Md HTWY RG27 73 M6 [3]
Hatch Hl HASM GU27 216 E7
Hatch La CHIN RG24 94 A3
HASM GU27 216 E6
LISS GU33 237 H4
THLE RG7 16 F2
Hatch Ride CWTH RG45 37 L1
Hatchwarren Gdns
KEMP RG22 115 K1 [1]
Hatch Warren La KEMP RG22 92 E7
Hatchwarren La KEMP RG22 115 H1
Hatfield Ct CBLY GU15 58 E3 [1]
Hatfield Gdns FARN GU14 79 H5 [2]
Hathaway Gdns CHIN RG24 5 H1
Hatherley Rd WINW SO22 10 D5
Hatherwood YTLY GU46 57 J3 [3]
Hatern Pl AND SP10 106 E6 [1]
Hattingley Rd ALTN GU34 184 B1
Hatt La ROMY SO51 221 K6
Haughurst Hl STHA RG19 28 E8
Haven Wy FNM GU9 123 G4
Haweswater Cl BOR GU35 189 J3
Hawk Cl KEMP RG22 91 L8 [2]
Hawker Rd ASHV GU12 101 J3
Hawkes Cl HTWY RG27 75 H1
Hawkfield La BSTK RG21 92 F5
Hawkins Gv FLET GU13 98 C2
Hawkins Wy FLET GU13 77 H8 [1]
Hawkley Dr TADY RG26 49 M1
Hawkley Rd LISS GU33 235 L1
Hawkshaw Cl LIPH GU30 215 G4 [1]
Hawkswood Av FRIM GU16 59 J6
Hawksworth Rd THLE RG7 19 L5
Hawkwell FLET GU13 99 G4
Hawley Gn BLKW GU17 58 B5
Hawley La FARN GU14 58 E8
Hawley Rd BLKW GU17 58 B5
Hawthorn Cl ASHV GU12 101 H8 [1]
NALR SO24 206 C3
RWIN SO21 158 A6
Hawthorne Cl RAND SP11 128 A8 [1]
Hawthorne Crs BLKW GU17 58 B4
Hawthorn La ALTN GU34 185 J8
NFNM GU10 146 C5
Hawthorn Ri HTWY RG27 74 A6 [3]
Hawthorn Rd ALTN GU34 185 G8
FRIM GU16 59 J6
NTID SP9 102 E1
NWBY RG14 2 E1
Hawthorns ALTN GU34 164 D3
The Hawthorns TADY RG26 29 H8 [1]
Hawthorn Wy DEAN RG23 92 B2
Haydn Cl WINC SO23 179 G8
Haydn Rd KEMP RG22 92 C8
Haydock Cl ALTN GU34 164 E6
Hay Down La RAND SP11 128 D3
Hayes Cl STOK SO20 198 E6
Hayley La ODIM RG29 119 G3
Haywarden Pl HTWY RG27 75 J1
The Haywards NTHA RG18 15 G4
Haywood Dr FLET GU13 98 F1
Hazel Av FARN GU14 78 C6
Hazelbank EWKG RG40 36 A2
Hazelbank Cl LIPH GU30 215 G4
Hazel Cl DEAN RG23 91 G7
RAND SP11 8 B9
TLHT RG30 19 L3
Hazel Coppice HTWY RG27 74 A6 [4]
Hazeldene CHIN RG24 71 L6 [1]
Hazeldene Rd LIPH GU30 214 A4
Hazeley Cl HTWY RG27 75 H1
Hazel Gn TADY RG26 29 G7 [1]
Hazel Gv WINW SO22 226 C3
GSHT GU26 192 B7
NTHA RG18 15 G3
Hazell Rd FNM GU9 122 C6
Hazel Rd ALTN GU34 185 H5 [2]
ASHV GU12 124 F1
FRIM GU16 79 K6
Hazelwood Cl DEAN RG23 92 C1
Hazelwood Dr DEAN RG23 92 C1
Hazely Cl HTWY RG27 75 H1
Headington Cl KEMP RG22 92 C8 [1]
Headley Flds BOR GU35 190 B4
Headley Hill Rd BOR GU35 190 C3
Headley La LIPH GU30 190 B6
Headley Rd GSHT GU26 191 J4
BOR GU35 189 M3
LIPH GU30 214 D2
Headmore La ALTN GU34 185 K7
Heads La HUNG RG17 22 D3
Heardman Cl STHA RG19 15 J6
Hearmon Cl YTLY GU46 57 G2
Hearn V BOR GU35 190 D1
Hearsey Gdns BLKW GU17 57 L2
Heath Cl FNM GU9 122 F1 [3]
GSHT GU26 191 M1
Heathcote Rd ASHV GU12 101 L5
CBLY GU15 59 G3
BOR GU35 189 K5
Heath End Rd TADY RG26 29 H7
Heather Cl ALDT GU11 6 A3
ASHV GU12 101 L3 [1]
EWKG RG40 36 B1 [4]
FNM GU9 146 C2 [1]
BOR GU35 189 G7
Heatherdale Rd CBLY GU15 58 F4
Heatherdene Av CWTH RG45 37 H4
Heather Dr AND SP10 8 F3
FLET GU13 98 E3
BOR GU35 189 L3
NTHA RG18 15 G3
TADY RG26 29 J6
Heather Gdns FARN GU14 78 B6 [1]
Heather Gv HTWY RG27 75 H1
Heather La HTWY RG27 95 H3
Heatherley Cl CBLY GU15 58 E3 [2]
Heatherley Rd CBLY GU15 58 E3
Heather Md FRIM GU16 59 J6
Heathermount Dr CWTH RG45 37 J2
Heather Row La HTWY RG27 95 J3
Heatherway CWTH RG45 37 K3
Heather Wy GSHT GU26 192 C4
KEMP RG22 114 F1
Heathfield Ct FLET GU13 98 D1
Heathfield Rd KEMP RG22 115 J1
Heath Green La ALTN GU34 183 M1
Heath Hl NFNM GU10 168 B5
Heath Hill Rd North CWTH RG45 37 L3
Heath Hill Rd South CWTH RG45 37 L3
Heathlands KSCL RG20 24 D8
TADY RG26 29 H7 [1]
Heathland St ALDT GU11 6 F2
Heath La FNM GU9 122 F1
MARL SN8 41 H1
NFNM GU10 121 J2
NTHA RG18 14 F3
Heathman St STOK SO20 172 F2
Heath Ride CWTH RG45 37 G4
EWKG RG40 36 E2
Heath Ri CBLY GU15 59 G3
Heath Rd HASM GU27 216 A3
TADY RG26 30 B7
Heathrow Copse TADY RG26 29 G8
Heathside La GSHT GU26 192 A2 [1]
Heathside Pk CBLY GU15 59 M1
Heath V AND SP10 9 J7
Heathvale Bridge Rd
ASHV GU12 101 K2
Heathview HTWY RG27 74 B6 [3]
Heathway CBLY GU15 59 G3
Heathway Cl CBLY GU15 59 G3
Heathwood Cl YTLY GU46 57 G1 [3]
Heathyfields Rd FNM GU9 122 C2
Hebden Cl STHA RG19 14 F7
Heddon Wk FARN GU14 78 D1 [2]
Hedge End Rd AND SP10 9 K8
Hedgehog La HASM GU27 216 E3
The Hedgerows CHIN RG24 71 M8
Hedges Cl NTID SP9 126 C1
Hedges Md AND SP10 8 E8
Hedgeway NWBY RG14 3 K1
Heenan Cl FRIM GU16 79 H1
Hei-Lin Wy RAND SP11 80 D6
Hele Cl BSTK RG21 92 F6
Helen Ct FARN GU14 78 E4 [3]
Helford Ct AND SP10 107 H6 [9]
Helksham Cl SHST GU47 38 A7 [2]
Hempland La ALTN GU34 233 H4
Hendon Rd BOR GU35 189 K6 [5]
Hendren Sq AND SP10 107 H6 [10]
Hengest Cl AND SP10 106 C5 [5]
Henley Cl FARN GU14 58 B8
Henley Dr FRIM GU16 79 H1
Henley Gdns YTLY GU46 57 G3
The Henrys NTHA RG18 15 G4
Henshaw Crs NWBY RG14 13 G8
Henwick Cl NTHA RG18 14 D2
Henwick La NTHA RG18 14 D3
Hepplewhite Cl TADY RG26 29 H7
Hepplewhite Dr KEMP RG22 114 F1
Hepworth Cl AND SP10 9 H2
Hepworth Cft SHST GU47 58 B2 [1]
Herbert Rd FLET GU13 76 D7
Herbs End FARN GU14 77 M3
Hereford Cl ODIM RG29 96 B6 [2]
Hereford La FNM GU9 122 E2
Hereford Md FARN GU14 77 G4 [1]
Hereford Rd DEAN RG23 92 B3
Herewood Cl NWBY RG14 2 C1
Heritage Pk DEAN RG23 115 G3
Hermes Cl FLET GU13 77 H7
Hermitage Cl FARN GU14 79 G7 [1]
FRIM GU16 59 J7
Hermits Cl THLE RG7 19 L5
Heron Cl ALTN GU34 164 E2
FLET GU13 99 H3
FRIM GU16 79 J4
Herondale HASM GU27 216 B2
Heron Pk CHIN RG24 71 L7
Herons Ri AND SP10 9 K9
Heron Wy KEMP RG22 91 L8
STHA RG19 14 E5
THLE RG7 17 L5
Heron Wood Rd ASHV GU12 7 M6
Herretts Gdns ASHV GU12 7 M4
Herrett St ASHV GU12 7 L5
Herriard Wy TADY RG26 49 L1 [2]
Herrick Cl FRIM GU16 59 M5
Herriot Ct YTLY GU46 56 F4
Hewshott Gv LIPH GU30 215 H3
Hewshott La LIPH GU30 215 G3
Hexham Cl SHST GU47 38 A6
Heywood Dr BAGS GU19 39 M6
Hibiscus Gv BOR GU35 189 K6 [5]
Hickory Dr WINW SO22 202 B4
Hicks La BLKW GU17 57 L3
Hides Cl WHCH RG28 110 B4
Highams Cl KSCL RG20 47 J6
High Beeches FRIM GU16 59 G6
Highbury Crs CBLY GU15 59 K1
Highbury Gv HASM GU27 192 F8 [1]
Highbury Rd RAND SP11 130 C4
Highclere Dr CBLY GU15 59 K1
Highclere Rd ASHV GU12 7 L5
Highcliffe Rd WINC SO23 227 G2
High Cross PSF GU32 234 D6
High Cross La PSF GU32 234 A8
Highdown FLET GU13 76 F6
Highdowns KEMP RG22 115 H2
High Dr KEMP RG22 92 B6
Highercombe Rd HASM GU27 193 H8
Higher Md CHIN RG24 71 L8
Highfield Av ALDT GU11 6 F6
NWBY RG14 2 E5
Highfield Cha BSTK RG21 4 B8
Highfield Cl ALDT GU11 7 G6
FARN GU14 78 C4
FNM GU9 146 E1 [1]
Highfield Crs GSHT GU26 192 B4
RSAL SP5 194 E2
Highfield Gdns ALDT GU11 6 F6
LISS GU33 237 G4
Highfield La LIPH GU30 215 G6
RGUW GU3 125 K5
Highfield Pth FARN GU14 78 C4
Highfield Rd FARN GU14 78 C4
NWBY RG14 2 D9
Highgate La FARN GU14 78 F3
Highgrove FARN GU14 78 E1 [2]
Highland Dr DEAN RG23 90 F6
FARN GU14 77 G5
Highland Rd ASHV GU12 7 L2
CBLY GU15 39 H8
Highlands Cl FNM GU9 146 E1
Highlands Rd AND SP10 9 M6
FNM GU9 122 F1
KEMP RG22 91 M5
High La HASM GU27 192 F8
Highmoors CHIN RG24 71 K5
Highmount Cl WINC SO23 11 K9
High Park Rd FNM GU9 122 E5
High Pitfold GSHT GU26 192 A7
Highridge ALTN GU34 164 C5
High St ALDT GU11 6 E1
ALTN GU34 164 E5
ALTN GU34 184 E1
AND SP10 9 H5
ASHV GU12 7 H3
CBLY GU15 59 G2
CWTH RG45 37 M4
FARN GU14 78 F8
HASM GU27 217 G2
HTWY RG27 75 J2
BOR GU35 189 J5
BOR GU35 190 B3
NFNM GU10 146 B5
NTID SP9 102 D8
ODIM RG29 96 C6
OVTN RG25 88 F8
RAND SP11 80 D6

RAND SP11 .... 128 A7
SHST GU47 .... 37 J8
STHA RG19 .... 15 C5
STOK SO20 .... 172 F3
STOK SO20 .... 174 D5
STOK SO20 .... 197 K2
WINC SO23 .... 10 F7
High Thicket Rd NFNM GU10 .... 168 A4
High Trees Dr WINW SO22 .... 10 C3
High View Cl FARN GU14 .... 78 D4
Highview Crs CBLY GU15 .... 39 J7
High View Rd FARN GU14 .... 78 D4
Highway CWTH RG45 .... 37 K3
Highwood Cl NWBY RG14 .... 13 C3
　YTLY GU46 .... 56 F4
Highwood Rdg KEMP RG22 .... 115 G2
Hilary Dr CWTH RG45 .... 37 L2
Hilden Wy WINW SO22 .... 201 M3
Hilder Gdns FARN GU14 .... 79 G5
Hilfield BLKW GU17 .... 57 J3
Hilland Ri BOR GU35 .... 190 C4
Hillary Cl FNM GU9 .... 122 E8
　FNM GU9 .... 146 F1
Hill Barn La RWIN SO21 .... 155 M2
Hillbrook Ri FNM GU9 .... 122 D2
Hill Brow Rd LISS GU33 .... 236 E5
Hillbury Av AND SP10 .... 8 D8
Hill Cl FARN GU14 .... 78 D4
Hill Ct FARN GU14 .... 58 C7
Hillcrest FLET GU13 .... 76 F5
Hillcrest Cl DEAN RG23 .... 92 A2
Hill Crest Dr NFNM GU10 .... 146 C2
Hillcrest Rd CBLY GU15 .... 59 L1
Hill Farm La HASM GU27 .... 216 C3
Hillgarth GSHT GU26 .... 192 A3
Hill House Hl LIPH GU30 .... 214 C1
Hillhouse La STHA RG19 .... 27 K7
Hill Houses La NALR SO24 .... 230 A3
Hillier Wy WINC SO23 .... 11 H3
Hill Meadow OVTN RG25 .... 88 F6
Hill Rd DEAN RG23 .... 90 F7
　FNM GU9 .... 123 G1
　GSHT GU26 .... 191 M5
　GSHT GU26 .... 191 M2
　HASM GU27 .... 216 F2
　NWBY RG14 .... 2 A2
　RWIN SO21 .... 133 G6
Hillsborough Cl FARN GU14 .... 58 B8
Hillsborough Pk CBLY GU15 .... 59 M3
Hill School NFNM GU10 .... 146 C1
Hillside CBLY GU15 .... 58 C1
　WINW SO22 .... 202 B3
　RAND SP11 .... 129 L4
　TADY RG26 .... 49 C4
　THLE RG7 .... 19 M5
Hillside Cl ALTN GU34 .... 164 E3
　FLET GU13 .... 98 B2
　WINW SO22 .... 202 B6
　BOR GU35 .... 190 D2
　RSAL SP5 .... 219 J6
Hillside Ct AND SP10 .... 8 E6
Hillside Crs FRIM GU16 .... 79 J1
Hillside La ALTN GU34 .... 123 C1
Hillside Rd ALDT GU11 .... 6 D6
　ASHV GU12 .... 101 L5
　FNM GU9 .... 6 B8
　WINW SO22 .... 202 B7
　HASM GU27 .... 216 C3
　NFNM GU10 .... 146 E5
　ODIM RG29 .... 96 E7
Hilltop WINW SO22 .... 202 B3
Hilltop Rd OVTN RG25 .... 89 G6
Hilltop Vw YTLY GU46 .... 56 E3
Hill View FNM GU9 .... 122 C6
　KEMP RG22 .... 92 D5
　ROMY SO51 .... 222 B8
Hinaidi Wy FARN GU14 .... 78 C8
Hindell Cl FARN GU14 .... 58 D8
Hindhead Rd HASM GU27 .... 192 B8
Hinstock Cl FARN GU14 .... 78 D5
Hinton Cl CWTH RG45 .... 37 L1
　TADY RG26 .... 49 L1
Hinton Dr CWTH RG45 .... 37 L1
Hinton Flds WINC SO23 .... 203 H2
Hinton Hl NALR SO24 .... 230 E4
Hinwood Cl STOK SO20 .... 197 G1
Hirst Copse RAND SP11 .... 85 M6
Hitches La FLET GU13 .... 98 B1
H Jones Crs ALDT GU11 .... 100 F5
Hobbs Cl NALR SO24 .... 207 H4
Hobbs Sq AND SP10 .... 107 H6
Hockford La THLE RG7 .... 28 D5
Hockley Link RWIN SO21 .... 226 D7
Hogarth Cl BSTK RG21 .... 93 K4
　SHST GU47 .... 58 B2
Hogarth Ct AND SP10 .... 8 E2
Hoghatch La FNM GU9 .... 122 D2
Hogwood La EWKG RG40 .... 35 K2
Holbeche Cl YTLY GU46 .... 56 D3
Holbein Cl BSTK RG21 .... 93 J5
Holborne Cl NWBY RG14 .... 24 F3
Holbrook Cl FNM GU9 .... 6 D6
Holbrook Wy ALDT GU11 .... 7 G7
Holbury La RSAL SP5 .... 220 B5
Holdaway Cl WINC SO23 .... 203 H1
Holder Rd ASHV GU12 .... 101 K7
Holdfast La HASM GU27 .... 193 J8
Holding La NALR SO24 .... 229 K6
Hole La NFNM GU10 .... 120 F7
Holland Cl FNM GU9 .... 123 H7
Holland Dr AND SP10 .... 106 C5
Holland Gdns FLET GU13 .... 76 F8
The Hollands STHA RG19 .... 15 H5
The Hollies NWBY RG14 .... 25 G3
Hollington La KSCL RG20 .... 43 M4
Hollow La BOR GU35 .... 190 B2
Hollowshot La KSCL RG20 .... 47 H7
　TADY RG26 .... 47 M8
The Hollow STOK SO20 .... 197 H4
Holly Av FRIM GU16 .... 59 L5
Hollybrook Pk BOR GU35 .... 189 K5
Hollybush La ALDT GU11 .... 79 H8
　HTWY RG27 .... 36 B8
　TADY RG26 .... 49 J6

THLE RG7 .... 19 J6
Hollybush Ride EWKG RG40 .... 36 F3
Holly Cl ALDT GU12 .... 7 K2
　FARN GU14 .... 78 D4
　BOR GU35 .... 190 F3
　TADY RG26 .... 51 M6
Hollycombe Cl LIPH GU30 .... 214 F6
Holly Dr CHIN RG24 .... 94 B2
Hollyfields Cl CBLY GU15 .... 58 E3
Holly Hedge Cl FRIM GU16 .... 59 H6
Holly Hedge Rd FRIM GU16 .... 59 H6
Hollyhock Cl KEMP RG22 .... 91 M8
Holly La THLE RG7 .... 30 E8
Hollyridge HASM GU27 .... 216 F2
Holly Rd ASHV GU12 .... 7 K2
　FARN GU14 .... 78 C4
Hollytree Gdns FRIM GU16 .... 59 G8
Hollytrees FLET GU13 .... 98 D3
Hollywater Rd LIPH GU30 .... 189 L8
Holly Wy BLKW GU17 .... 58 A4
Holmbrook Cl FARN GU14 .... 77 M4
Holmbury Av CWTH RG45 .... 37 K5
Holmdene THLE RG7 .... 19 L5
Holme Cl CWTH RG45 .... 37 K1
Holmes Cl KEMP RG22 .... 115 H2
Holmes Ct AND SP10 .... 8 C3
Holm Oak Cl WINW SO22 .... 201 M3
Holst Cl KEMP RG22 .... 115 K1
Holt Cl FARN GU14 .... 78 F1
Holt Cottages STHA RG19 .... 28 E8
Holt End La ALTN GU34 .... 162 D6
　ALTN GU34 .... 162 F4
Holt La HTWY RG27 .... 96 B1
　RAND SP11 .... 61 G8
　TADY RG26 .... 48 C4
Holt Pound La NFNM GU10 .... 145 M3
Holt Wy HTWY RG27 .... 74 B6
Holtwood Rd KSCL RG20 .... 23 L2
Holy Barn Cl KEMP RG22 .... 91 M7
Holyhook Cl CWTH RG45 .... 37 K2
Holywell Cl FARN GU14 .... 78 F1
Holywell Ct STHA RG19 .... 15 G5
Home Cl NALR SO24 .... 161 M6
　NALR SO24 .... 207 H3
Home Farm Cl FARN GU14 .... 79 C2
Home Farm Gdns AND SP10 .... 106 C5
Home Farm Rd HTWY RG27 .... 76 A1
Home La RWIN SO21 .... 201 H5
Homelea Cl FARN GU14 .... 58 E8
Homeleigh Crs ASHV GU12 .... 79 K8
Home Md OVTN RG25 .... 113 J7
Home Mead Cl NWBY RG14 .... 13 H8
Home Park Rd YTLY GU46 .... 56 F7
Homestead Rd ALTN GU34 .... 184 C3
Homesteads Rd KEMP RG22 .... 91 M7
Hone Hl SHST GU47 .... 57 L1
Honeybottom Rd TADY RG26 .... 29 L7
Honeycritch La PSF GU32 .... 235 G5
Honey La ALTN GU34 .... 211 L1
Honeysuckle Cl CWTH RG45 .... 37 K1
　WINW SO22 .... 226 C1
　KEMP RG22 .... 91 M8
　YTLY GU46 .... 56 D2
Honeysuckle La BOR GU35 .... 190 E3
Honister Gdns FLET GU13 .... 77 H6
Hook La NALR SO24 .... 207 M4
　TADY RG26 .... 48 E2
　TADY RG26 .... 68 F8
Hookpit Farm La WINC SO23 .... 179 G8
Hook Rd HTWY RG27 .... 73 M3
　HTWY RG27 .... 95 M1
　KSCL RG20 .... 47 K6
　ODIM RG29 .... 95 L4
　ODIM RG29 .... 96 B3
Hookstile La FNM GU9 .... 122 F7
Hookwood La RAND SP11 .... 81 M4
Hoopersmead OVTN RG25 .... 115 M1
Hoopers Cl DEAN RG23 .... 91 C7
Hope Fountain CBLY GU15 .... 59 J4
Hope Grant's Rd ALDT GU11 .... 100 D4
Hope La FNM GU9 .... 122 E2
Hopeman Cl SHST GU47 .... 58 A1
Hopeswood LISS GU33 .... 212 E5
Hopfield Rd HTWY RG27 .... 75 H3
Hop Gdn FLET GU13 .... 98 D4
Hop Garden Rd HTWY RG27 .... 73 L7
Hopkinson Wy AND SP10 .... 106 A7
Hopton Garth CHIN RG24 .... 71 M7
Hopwood Cl NWBY RG14 .... 3 L1
Hormer Cl SHST GU47 .... 38 A7
Hornbeam Cl FARN GU14 .... 77 M3
　RWIN SO21 .... 178 D4
　SHST GU47 .... 38 A7
Hornbeam Pl HTWY RG27 .... 74 A6
Horne Rd STHA RG19 .... 15 G6
Horn Rd FARN GU14 .... 78 B3
Horsebridge Rd STOK SO20 .... 197 K4
Horse La ALTN GU34 .... 208 C1
Horseshoe Bend GSHT GU26 .... 191 K5
Horseshoe Cl CBLY GU15 .... 39 J8
　BOR GU35 .... 189 K5
　THLE RG7 .... 19 K5
Horseshoe Crs CBLY GU15 .... 39 J8
Horseshoe End NWBY RG14 .... 25 L1
Horseshoe La ASHV GU12 .... 101 K2
　RAND SP11 .... 62 C8
Horsham Rd SHST GU47 .... 38 A7
Horwood Gdns BSTK RG21 .... 92 E6
Hose Hl THLE RG7 .... 19 K1
Hosketts La STOK SO20 .... 172 D3
Hospital Hl ALDT GU11 .... 100 D5
Hospital Rd ALDT GU11 .... 100 D5
Hostel Rd FARN GU14 .... 78 E8
Hound Green Cl HTWY RG27 .... 54 A5
Houndmills Rd BSTK RG21 .... 92 D2
Houseman Rd FARN GU14 .... 78 C2
Howard Cl FLET GU13 .... 77 H7
Howard Cole Wy ALDT GU11 .... 6 A2
Howard Rd BSTK RG21 .... 93 H5
　NWBY RG14 .... 2 A7
Howard's La ALTN GU34 .... 165 H1
Howes Gdns FLET GU13 .... 98 D2
The Howe FARN GU14 .... 77 L7
Hubbard Rd BSTK RG21 .... 4 A4
Hubert Rd WINC SO23 .... 226 D4
Huddington Gld HTWY RG27 .... 56 D3

Hudsons Meadow HTWY RG27 .... 54 A5
Huish La OVTN RG25 .... 94 A6
Hulbert Wy KEMP RG22 .... 92 B6
Hulfords La HTWY RG27 .... 55 K7
Hullam La ALTN GU34 .... 211 G3
Humber Cl NTHA RG18 .... 14 E3
Humber La NTID SP9 .... 102 C4
Humberstone Rd AND SP10 .... 9 H8
Humbers Vw STOK SO20 .... 198 F7
Humber Wy SHST GU47 .... 38 A3
Hungerford Cl SHST GU47 .... 37 M8
Hungerford La AND SP10 .... 106 C2
　RAND SP11 .... 60 D6
Hungerford Rd MARL SN8 .... 40 F2
Hunnels Cl FLET GU13 .... 98 D5
Hunt Cl RWIN SO21 .... 178 D4
Hunter Rd FARN GU14 .... 78 C5
Hunters Cha LIPH GU30 .... 214 E5
Hunters Cl DEAN RG23 .... 91 G5
Hunters Hl THLE RG7 .... 19 J5
Hunters Rd LISS GU33 .... 213 J4
Huntingdon House Dr
　GSHT GU26 .... 192 B7
Huntingford Cl GSHT GU26 .... 191 M1
Hunton Down La RWIN SO21 .... 156 F4
Hunton La RWIN SO21 .... 156 E4
Huntsbottom La LISS GU33 .... 237 G5
Hunts Cl HTWY RG27 .... 74 B7
Huntsman's Ms FRIM GU16 .... 79 J5
Huntsmead NALR SO24 .... 164 F5
Huntsmoor Rd TADY RG26 .... 29 J8
Hurdle Wy RWIN SO21 .... 226 B8
Hurland La BOR GU35 .... 190 C4
Hurlands Cl FNM GU9 .... 123 J4
Hurlands Pl FNM GU9 .... 123 J4
Hurricane Wy FARN GU14 .... 100 C1
Hurst Cl LIPH GU30 .... 214 D3
Hurst La ALTN GU34 .... 234 A5
Hurstmere Cl GSHT GU26 .... 192 A5
Hurst Rd ALDT GU11 .... 100 F5
　FARN GU14 .... 58 E8
The Hurst HTWY RG27 .... 75 L7
Hussar Cl ALDT GU11 .... 6 A2
Hussell La ALTN GU34 .... 184 E1
Hussey Cl WINC SO23 .... 11 H2
Hussey's La ALTN GU34 .... 144 B3
Hutton Cl NWBY RG14 .... 3 C1
Hutton Rd ASHV GU12 .... 101 K2
Hutton Sq AND SP10 .... 107 H6
Hyacinth Cl KEMP RG22 .... 91 M8
Hyde Abbey Rd WINC SO23 .... 11 C6
Hyde Church La WINC SO23 .... 11 G5
Hyde Cl WINC SO23 .... 10 F5
Hyde End La STHA RG19 .... 28 A3
Hyde La KSCL RG20 .... 46 D2
Hyde St WINC SO23 .... 11 G5
Hydes Platt THLE RG7 .... 30 E8
Hyson Crs RAND SP11 .... 81 J8

I

Iberian Wy CBLY GU15 .... 59 K2
Ibworth La TADY RG26 .... 68 A5
Icknield Wy AND SP10 .... 107 G3
Ilex Cl TADY RG26 .... 30 B7
　WINC SO23 .... 179 G8
　YTLY GU46 .... 56 F2
Ilkley Wy STHA RG19 .... 14 F6
Imadene Crs BOR GU35 .... 189 L4
Imber Rd WINC SO23 .... 11 L6
Imjin Cl ALDT GU11 .... 100 E5
Impstone Rd TADY RG26 .... 30 C7
Imran Ct ASHV GU12 .... 7 J5
Ingle Dell CBLY GU15 .... 59 G4
Ingle Gln EWKG RG40 .... 36 D1
Ingles Edge HUNG RG17 .... 22 A4
Inglewood Av CBLY GU15 .... 59 M4
Inglewood Dr KEMP RG22 .... 115 G2
Inhams Rd ALTN GU34 .... 165 J2
Inhams Wy THLE RG7 .... 30 D8
Inhurst La STHA RG19 .... 28 F7
Inhurst Wy TADY RG26 .... 29 J7
Inkpen Gdns CHIN RG24 .... 71 M8
Innisfail Gdns ALDT GU11 .... 6 C5
Institute Rd ALDT GU11 .... 7 L5
Instow Gdns FARN GU14 .... 78 D1
Inval Hl HASM GU27 .... 192 F8
Inverness Wy SHST GU47 .... 58 A1
Invincible Rd FARN GU14 .... 78 D6
Inwood Rd LISS GU33 .... 236 F5
Iping Rd LIPH GU30 .... 238 G6
Ipoh Cl STOK SO20 .... 150 F3
Iris Cl KEMP RG22 .... 114 F1
Irvine Dr FARN GU14 .... 58 B8
Irwell Cl BSTK RG21 .... 5 J8
Isington La ALTN GU34 .... 144 D5
Isington Rd ALTN GU34 .... 144 C3
Isis Wy SHST GU47 .... 38 A3
Island Farm Rd THLE RG7 .... 19 H7
Itchel La ALTN GU34 .... 144 D5
Itchen Cl DEAN RG23 .... 91 G7
　AND SP10 .... 9 M1
Itchen Vw NALR SO24 .... 205 J3
Itchen Wy NALR SO24 .... 206 A8
　RWIN SO21 .... 203 J3
　RWIN SO21 .... 204 F3
　WINC SO23 .... 11 M1
Ivanhoe Rd EWKG RG40 .... 35 K2
Ivar Gdns CHIN RG24 .... 71 M8
Ively Rd FARN GU14 .... 77 M7
Ives Cl YTLY GU46 .... 56 E1
Ivy Cl WINW SO22 .... 226 D3
Ivy Down La DEAN RG23 .... 90 D5
Ivyhole Hl HTWY RG27 .... 56 A8
Ivyhouse La PSF GU32 .... 234 D5
Ivy La FNM GU9 .... 122 E6
Ivy Rd ASHV GU12 .... 101 H6

J

Jacaranda Rd BOR GU35 .... 189 J6
Jackdaw Cl KEMP RG22 .... 91 L8
Jacklyns Cl NALR SO24 .... 206 B4

Jacklyns La NALR SO24 .... 206 B4
Jacob Rd CBLY GU15 .... 58 D1
Jagdalik Rd NTID SP9 .... 102 D4
Jaguar Rd FARN GU14 .... 78 E6
James Cl BSTK RG21 .... 5 C3
James Rd ALDT GU11 .... 101 G1
　CBLY GU15 .... 58 E6
James Wy CBLY GU15 .... 58 E6
Jamrud Rd NTID SP9 .... 102 C3
Jan Smuts Cl LISS GU33 .... 213 J7
Jaques's La THLE RG7 .... 19 J6
Jardine Sq AND SP10 .... 107 H6
Jarvis Cl HTWY RG27 .... 36 B8
Jasmine Cl KEMP RG22 .... 92 A8
Jasmine Wy BOR GU35 .... 189 K6
Jays Cl KEMP RG22 .... 92 F7
Jay's La HASM GU27 .... 217 L5
Jays Nest Cl BLKW GU17 .... 58 A4
Jedburgh Cl STHA RG19 .... 15 J5
Jefferson Rd BSTK RG21 .... 4 F3
Jenkins' Hill London Rd
　BAGS GU19 .... 39 M7
Jenner Wy ALTN GU34 .... 164 F2
Jennie Green La ALTN GU34 .... 162 D6
Jenny's Wk YTLY GU46 .... 57 H2
Jenson Gdns AND SP10 .... 8 C6
Jerome Cnr CWTH RG45 .... 37 M5
Jersey Brow Rd FARN GU14 .... 78 D6
Jersey Cl CHIN RG24 .... 71 H6
　FARN GU14 .... 77 C4
Jesmond Dene NWBY RG14 .... 2 C7
Jesse Cl BLKW GU17 .... 57 J3
Jessett Dr FLET GU13 .... 98 D4
Jesty Rd NALR SO24 .... 206 A4
Jewry St WINC SO23 .... 11 G7
Jibbs Meadow TADY RG26 .... 51 L5
Jobson Cl WHCH RG28 .... 110 B3
Jobson's La HASM GU27 .... 217 M8
John Cl ALDT GU11 .... 6 A5
John Hunt Cl STHA RG19 .... 15 J6
John Morgan Cl HTWY RG27 .... 73 M6
　HTWY RG27 .... 74 A5
Johnson Dr EWKG RG40 .... 36 E1
Johnson Wy FLET GU13 .... 98 E2
Jonathan Hl KSCL RG20 .... 25 L5
Jordan's La THLE RG7 .... 19 J6
Jouldings La HTWY RG27 .... 35 C4
Joule Rd AND SP10 .... 106 A7
　BSTK RG21 .... 4 B4
Joy's La STOK SO20 .... 153 M4
Jubilee Cl FARN GU14 .... 77 M4
　TADY RG26 .... 30 B7
Jubilee Dr ASHV GU12 .... 101 K2
Jubilee Hall Rd FARN GU14 .... 78 F4
Jubilee La GSHT GU26 .... 191 M5
　NFNM GU10 .... 146 D3
Jubilee Rd ALDT GU11 .... 7 H7
　BSTK RG21 .... 93 C4
　EWKG RG40 .... 36 C5
　FRIM GU16 .... 79 K6
　NWBY RG14 .... 3 C6
Julius Cl CHIN RG24 .... 70 B8
Jumps Rd NFNM GU10 .... 169 H5
Junction Rd AND SP10 .... 8 E3
Junction Ter NWBY RG14 .... 3 J5
June Dr DEAN RG23 .... 92 A3
Juniper Cl CHIN RG24 .... 71 M4
　WINW SO22 .... 226 C3
　BOR GU35 .... 188 F6
Juniper Rd FARN GU14 .... 77 M3
Justice Cl STHA RG19 .... 15 J6
Jutland Crs AND SP10 .... 106 E4

K

Karachi Cl NTID SP9 .... 102 D1
Kathleen Cl BSTK RG21 .... 92 F6
Kay Crs BOR GU35 .... 190 D2
Keable Rd NFNM GU10 .... 146 C1
Keats Cl CHIN RG24 .... 71 H7
　WINW SO22 .... 226 B4
　RWIN SO21 .... 178 C4
Keats Wy CWTH RG45 .... 37 L1
　YTLY GU46 .... 56 E4
Keble St WINW SO22 .... 226 B2
Keble Wy SHST GU47 .... 38 B6
Keeper's Hl RAND SP11 .... 128 F3
Keepers La ROMY SO51 .... 221 H6
Keeps Md KSCL RG20 .... 47 H5
Keighley Cl STHA RG19 .... 14 F6
Keith Lucas Rd FARN GU14 .... 78 C6
Kellynch Cl ALTN GU34 .... 164 D4
Kellys Wk AND SP10 .... 8 C3
Kelsey Av EWKG RG40 .... 36 B2
Kelsey Cl LISS GU33 .... 236 F3
Kelsey Gv YTLY GU46 .... 57 H3
Kelvin Cl WHIT RG2 .... 35 H1
Kelvin Hl KEMP RG22 .... 92 D6
Kelvin Rd NWBY RG14 .... 3 G2
Kemmel Rd RAND SP11 .... 103 H1
Kemmitt Wy AND SP10 .... 8 C9
Kemnal Pk HASM GU27 .... 193 G8
Kempshott Gdns KEMP RG22 .... 91 M4
Kempshott Gv KEMP RG22 .... 91 M4
Kempshott La KEMP RG22 .... 91 M7
Kempton Cl ALTN GU34 .... 164 E6
　NWBY RG14 .... 3 K8
Kempton Ct FARN GU14 .... 78 B4
Kendal Cl FARN GU14 .... 78 B4
　NTHA RG18 .... 14 C2
Kendal Gdns KEMP RG22 .... 92 A7
Kendrick Rd FLET GU13 .... 77 H6
Kenilworth Crs FLET GU13 .... 77 H6
Kenilworth Rd DEAN RG23 .... 92 A2
　FARN GU14 .... 77 M3
Kenley Rd BOR GU35 .... 190 E3
Kenmore Cl FLET GU13 .... 99 C3
　FRIM GU16 .... 59 L8
Kennedy Cl NWBY RG14 .... 25 C2
Kennel La NFNM GU10 .... 146 F6
Kennel Mdw WINW SO22 .... 202 A4
Kennels La FARN GU14 .... 77 L5
Kennet Cl ASHV GU12 .... 101 K7
　BSTK RG21 .... 5 C8
　FARN GU14 .... 78 A2

STHA RG19 .... 15 H5
Kennet Pl THLE RG7 .... 19 L5
Kennet Rd NTID SP9 .... 102 C2
　NWBY RG14 .... 2 D5
Kennet Side NWBY RG14 .... 3 J4
Kennet Wy DEAN RG23 .... 91 G3
Kentigern Dr CWTH RG45 .... 38 B3
Kenton Cl FRIM GU16 .... 59 J6
Kent Rd FLET GU13 .... 77 G7
　BOR GU35 .... 189 J6
Kenwith Av FLET GU13 .... 77 H7
Kenyons Yd AND SP10 .... 8 C5
Keogh Barracks FRIM GU16 .... 79 K8
Keogh Cl FRIM GU16 .... 79 K8
Kerchers Fld OVTN RG25 .... 111 M1
Kerfield Wy HTWY RG27 .... 74 A7
Kerrfield WINW SO22 .... 10 A8
Kerrfield Ms WINW SO22 .... 10 A8
Kerry Cl FARN GU14 .... 77 G3
Kersey Crs NWBY RG14 .... 13 H5
Kersley Crs ODIM RG29 .... 96 B3
Kestrel Cl WINW SO22 .... 226 C4
　NFNM GU10 .... 122 A1
　NTID SP9 .... 102 F1
　STHA RG19 .... 14 E5
Kestrel Rd FARN GU14 .... 78 E6
　KEMP RG22 .... 91 L7
Kestrel Wy THLE RG7 .... 19 L4
Keswick Cl CBLY GU15 .... 59 M4
Ketchers Fld ALTN GU34 .... 211 L2
Ketelbey Ri KEMP RG22 .... 115 L1
Kevin Cl KSCL RG20 .... 47 H1
Kevins Dr YTLY GU46 .... 57 H1
Kevins Gv FLET GU13 .... 77 G7
Kew Wk AND SP10 .... 8 C7
Keynes Cl FLET GU13 .... 99 C4
Keynsham Wy SHST GU47 .... 38 A6
Kiel Dr AND SP10 .... 106 E4
Kildare Rd BOR GU35 .... 189 J4
Kilham La WINW SO22 .... 226 A2
Killinghurst La HASM GU27 .... 217 M2
Kilmarlin Gdns FRIM GU16 .... 59 J7
Kilmeston Rd NALR SO24 .... 230 C4
Kilmore Dr CBLY GU15 .... 59 L4
Kilmuir Cl SHST GU47 .... 58 A1
Kiln Fld LISS GU33 .... 236 E5
Kiln Flds HASM GU27 .... 192 F8
Kiln Gdns HTWY RG27 .... 75 H2
Kiln Hl THLE RG7 .... 34 E1
Kiln La NALR SO24 .... 182 C1
　NFNM GU10 .... 146 F2
　TADY RG26 .... 69 M3
　THLE RG7 .... 31 M3
Kiln Ride EWKG RG40 .... 36 D2
Kiln Ride Extension EWKG RG40 .... 36 D2
Kiln Rd CHIN RG24 .... 70 D5
　NWBY RG14 .... 13 M3
Kiln Wy ALDT GU11 .... 7 G7
　GSHT GU26 .... 191 H3
Kimball Rd KEMP RG22 .... 92 E6
Kimber Cl CHIN RG24 .... 71 L6
Kimberley FLET GU13 .... 99 C4
Kimberley Cl AND SP10 .... 106 C6
Kimberley Rd KEMP RG22 .... 92 D5
　LISS GU33 .... 213 L1
Kimbers Dr NWBY RG14 .... 12 F3
Kimbers La FARN GU14 .... 123 C5
　TADY RG26 .... 50 A3
King Alfred Pl WINC SO23 .... 11 C5
King Alfred Ter WINC SO23 .... 11 C5
King Arthur's Wy AND SP10 .... 106 F5
Kingfisher Cl FARN GU14 .... 77 M2
　FLET GU13 .... 98 C5
　KEMP RG22 .... 91 L7
　BOR GU35 .... 189 K6
　THLE RG7 .... 17 M5
Kingfisher Dr YTLY GU46 .... 56 E2
Kingfishers NTID SP9 .... 126 D1
Kingfisher Wk ASHV GU12 .... 101 J5
King George Rd AND SP10 .... 8 C7
King John Rd KSCL RG20 .... 47 J6
King Johns Rd ODIM RG29 .... 96 B4
King La PSF GU32 .... 234 E4
　STOK SO20 .... 150 A2
Kings Av WINW SO22 .... 226 D3
　NFNM GU10 .... 101 H8
Kingsbridge Hl THLE RG7 .... 33 K2
Kingsbridge Rd NWBY RG14 .... 2 A7
Kingsclear Pk CBLY GU15 .... 59 C4
　DEAN RG23 .... 69 K6
　OVTN RG25 .... 88 F7
Kings Cl WINC SO23 .... 179 C1
King's Ct NFNM GU10 .... 101 J8
King's Crs CBLY GU15 .... 38 F8
Kings Elms RWIN SO21 .... 155 J3
Kings Furlong Dr BSTK RG21 .... 92 E5
Kingsgate Rd WINC SO23 .... 226 B3
King's Hl ALTN GU34 .... 163 J8
Kings Keep FLET GU13 .... 98 F2
　SHST GU47 .... 37 L7
Kingsland Gra NWBY RG14 .... 13 H8
Kingsland Rd ALTN GU34 .... 164 D5
Kings La NFNM GU10 .... 146 D2
　PSF GU32 .... 234 B6
　RWIN SO21 .... 227 L2
Kingsley Av CBLY GU15 .... 58 F4
　NWBY RG14 .... 13 L2
Kingsley Cl CWTH RG45 .... 37 L5
　NWBY RG14 .... 13 L2
Kingsley Pk WHCH RG28 .... 110 B3
Kingsley Pl WINW SO22 .... 226 D3
Kingsley Rd FARN GU14 .... 78 C2
　HTWY RG27 .... 35 M8
Kingsmead ALTN GU34 .... 164 E5
　FARN GU14 .... 78 E4
　FRIM GU16 .... 79 H1
　RAND SP11 .... 130 D3
Kings Meadow AND SP10 .... 9 J8
　OVTN RG25 .... 88 F9
Kingsmill Rd BSTK RG21 .... 92 F6
Kings Orch DEAN RG23 .... 91 C4
Kings Paddock RSAL SP5 .... 194 D3
Kings Pightle CHIN RG24 .... 71 L5
King's Ride CBLY GU15 .... 39 C7
King's Ride Rd ALDT GU11 .... 6 D3
　ALTN GU34 .... 164 C6
　CWTH RG45 .... 37 L4
　FLET GU13 .... 77 G7

WINW SO22 226 B2 1
HASM GU27 216 D2
KEMP RG22 92 D5
NWBY RG14 2 F5
RAND SP11 107 G1
THLE RG7 30 D7
Kings Rd West NWBY RG14 2 F5
Kings Somborne Rd
ROMY SO51 223 J7
Kingston Cl AND SP10 8 D9
Kingston La THLE RG7 18 F2
Kingston Rd CBLY GU15 39 K8
MARL SN8 20 B6
King St ODIM RG29 96 D5
THLE RG7 31 K2
Kings Wk WHCH RG28 110 B3
Kingsway ALDT GU11 6 C6
BLKW GU17 58 B4
King's Wy NALR SO24 205 L6
RWIN SO21 204 D2
RWIN SO21 228 C4
RWIN SO21 228 F2
WINC SO23 11 H4
Kingswood Firs GSHT GU26 191 M6
Kingswood La GSHT GU26 191 M6
Kingswood Ri ALTN GU34 184 E6
King's Yd AND SP10 9 J5
Kintbury Rd HUNG RG17 22 C2
Kintyre Cl DEAN RG23 90 F6
Kipling Cl NTHA RG18 14 F3
YTLY GU46 56 F4 1
Kipling Wk KEMP RG22 92 D5
Kirkee Rd NTID SP9 102 D3
Kirkham Cl SHST GU47 38 A6 3
Kirk Knoll BOR GU35 190 C3
Kirkwood Crs THLE RG7 19 J5 2
Kitchener Rd ALDT GU11 101 G2
LISS GU33 213 H6
Kitcombe La ALTN GU34 186 A7
Kitt's La NALR SO24 232 B6
NFNM GU10 169 J8
Kitwood La ALTN GU34 209 H1
Kitwood Rd ALTN GU34 209 G1
Knapp La TADY RG26 50 A2
Knight Cl FLET GU13 98 B2
WINC SO23 11 G3
Knightsbridge Dr STHA RG19 26 E5
Knightsbridge Rd CBLY GU15 59 H1
RAND SP11 107 H1
Knights La KSCL RG20 23 M5
Knights Lea KSCL RG20 23 L5
Knights Rd FNM GU9 6 A9
Knight St BSTK RG21 92 E4
Knights Wy ALTN GU34 164 C5
CBLY GU15 59 M4
Knockhundred La GSHT GU26 191 L8
Knockwood La STOK SO20 172 D1
Knoll Cl FLET GU13 76 F6
Knoll Rd CBLY GU15 59 G2
FLET GU13 76 F6
Knollys' Rd ALDT GU11 100 C5
THLE RG7 30 C7
Knott La THLE RG7 17 L4
Knowle Crs KSCL RG20 47 J6
Knowles Av CWTH RG45 37 J4
Knowles Meadow LISS GU33 237 G7
The Knowlings WHCH RG28 110 C4
Knox Cl FLET GU13 98 C3
Kohat Cl NTID SP9 102 C1
Kohat Ct ALDT GU11 6 C2
Kohima Cl ALDT GU11 7 H1
Komat Rd NTID SP9 102 D3
Krooner Rd CBLY GU15 58 E5
Kynegils Rd WINW SO22 10 B3

L

Laburnum Cl ALDT GU11 6 E3 1
Laburnum Gv NWBY RG14 2 E1
Laburnum Pas ALDT GU11 6 E3 2
Laburnum Rd ALDT GU11 6 E3
FNM GU9 6 A8 1
The Laburnums BLKW GU17 57 L3
Laburnum Wy DEAN RG23 92 C2
Ladwell Cl NWBY RG14 25 G3
Lady Diana Ct RAND SP11 80 E6
Ladygate Dr GSHT GU26 191 K5
Lady Godley Cl NTID SP9 102 D3
Lady Jane Wk RAND SP11 80 E6 1
Ladysmith Pl BOR GU35 189 H3
Ladywell La NALR SO24 206 C1
Ladywood Av FARN GU14 77 M4
Laffan's Rd ALDT GU11 100 C3
ODIM RG29 96 C8
Laffan Tr ALDT GU11 99 M2
Lahore Cl NTID SP9 102 D1
Lahore Rd NTID SP9 102 D1
Lainston Cl WINW SO22 202 B6
Lake Dr BOR GU35 189 K5
Lake End Wy CWTH RG45 37 K4
Lakeland Dr FRIM GU16 59 H7
Lakelands TADY RG26 29 G7 2
Lake La NFNM GU10 168 B2
Lake Rd FRIM GU16 79 K2
Laker Sq AND SP10 107 H6
Lakeside Cl AND SP10 106 C6
ASHV GU12 101 J4
Lakeside Ct FARN GU14 77 G5
Lakeside Dr HTWY RG27 55 G4
Lakeside Gdns FARN GU14 78 A1
Lakeside Rd ALDT GU11 100 D1
ASHV GU12 101 J4
The Lake Side BLKW GU17 58 A4
Lamb Cl AND SP10 9 L6
NTHA RG18 14 F3
Lambdens Hl THLE RG7 18 B1
Lambdens Wk TADY RG26 29 L8 2
Lambdown Ap RAND SP11 103 H2
Lambdown Ter RAND SP11 103 G1
Lambert Crs BLKW GU17 57 M4
Lamborne Cl SHST GU47 37 K7
Lambourne Cl RAND SP11 104 D8
RWIN SO21 201 H5
Lambourne La LIPH GU30 239 G5
Lambourne Wy NFNM GU10 124 B1
RAND SP11 104 D8
Lambourn Rd KSCL RG20 12 F2
Lambourn Valley Wy
NWBY RG14 2 B4
Lambs Rw CHIN RG24 93 L1
Lamden Wy THLE RG7 19 L5
Lamerton Rd BOR GU35 189 H4
Lamp Acres NWBY RG14 13 L3
Lampard La NFNM GU10 169 G6
Lampards Cl HTWY RG27 73 L2
Lanark Cl FRIM GU16 59 H6 1
Lancaster Av FNM GU9 122 F8
Lancaster Cl AND SP10 8 E2
ASHV GU12 101 J3
NTHA RG18 14 F4
Lancaster Dr CBLY GU15 59 G2 1
Lancaster Rd BSTK RG21 4 C5
FARN GU14 78 E7
Lancaster Wy FARN GU14 78 F1
Lancer Ct ALDT GU11 6 A2
Landale Cl RAND SP11 107 G1
Landseer Cl BSTK RG21 93 J5
SHST GU47 58 B2
Landseer Ct AND SP10 8 F2
Lands End La BOR GU35 189 K3
Lane End TADY RG26 51 L6
Laneswood THLE RG7 31 H3
The Lane TADY RG26 29 L8
Langdale Cl FARN GU14 78 B4 3
Langdon Cl CBLY GU15 59 M4
Langham Rd ALTN GU34 164 D5
Langley Cl FLET GU13 98 E4
Langley Dr CBLY GU15 59 G2
Langton Cl WINW SO22 10 C5
Langton Dr BOR GU35 190 D1
Lanham La WINW SO22 201 L8
Lankhills Rd WINC SO23 10 F3
Lansdowne Av AND SP10 8 D8
WINC SO23 226 E3
Lansdowne Rd ALDT GU11 6 E3
ALTN GU34 164 F3
FRIM GU16 59 K8
Lansley Rd BSTK RG21 4 E2
Lapin La KEMP RG22 115 G3
Lapwing Ri WHCH RG28 110 A2
Larch Cl CBLY GU15 39 H7
LIPH GU30 214 E5
NWBY RG14 13 H5
STOK SO20 151 G4
TLHT RG30 19 L4
WINC SO23 179 G8
Larch Dr AND SP10 130 B1
KSCL RG20 47 J6
Larchfield Rd FLET GU13 98 F1
Larch Rd BOR GU35 190 E2
Larch Wy FARN GU14 77 M5
Larchwood CHIN RG24 71 L5 2
Larchwood Gld CBLY GU15 59 K1
Larg Dr WINW SO22 202 B4
Lark Cl AND SP10 107 G6
KEMP RG22 91 L8
NTID SP9 102 E1
Larkfield CHIN RG24 71 L5
Larkfield Rd FNM GU9 122 C5
Lark Hill Ri WINW SO22 226 C4
Lark Ri LIPH GU30 214 D3
Larks Barrow Hl WHCH RG28 87 H6
Larkspur Cl ALDT GU11 6 F7
Larkspur Gdns NTHA RG18 15 J4
Larkswood Cl SHST GU47 37 K7 3
Larkswood Dr CWTH RG45 37 L3
Larkwhistle Farm Rd
RWIN SO21 136 C7
Larmer Cl FLET GU13 98 D7
Larwood Sq AND SP10 107 H6 13
Lascombe La RGUW GU3 125 K4
Latchwood La NFNM GU10 147 G3
Latham Av FRIM GU16 59 H6
Laud Cl NWBY RG14 14 A3
Lauder Cl FRIM GU16 59 H6
Lauderdale FARN GU14 78 A5 2
Launcelot Cl AND SP10 106 F5
Laundry La CBLY GU15 59 H8
HTWY RG27 54 A3
Laurel Cl CBLY GU15 59 G4
FARN GU14 77 M5
ODIM RG29 96 B5
Laurel Gdns ALDT GU11 6 F7
Laurel Gv NFNM GU10 146 C3
The Laurels AND SP10 8 D3
BSTK RG21 5 H5
FLET GU13 76 F7
FNM GU9 6 C7
Laurence Ct RAND SP11 80 E6
Lavell's La THLE RG7 31 M8
Lavender Gdns BOR GU35 189 J5 1
Lavender La NFNM GU10 146 C4
Lavender Rd KEMP RG22 114 F1
Laverstoke La OVTN RG25 111 H8
WHCH RG28 111 H3
Lawday Link FNM GU9 122 D1
Lawday Pl FNM GU9 122 D1 1
Lawday Place La FNM GU9 122 D1
Lawford Crs YTLY GU46 57 G2
Lawn Rd WINW SO22 202 B3 1
The Lawns FARN GU14 78 B5
Lawn St WINC SO23 11 H7
Lawrence Cl AND SP10 8 E1
CHIN RG24 71 H7
Lawrencedale Ct BSTK RG21 4 B9
Lawrence Houses RAND SP11 128 A7
Lawrence Rd FLET GU13 76 E8
Lawrences La NTHA RG18 15 G2
Lawrence Wy CBLY GU15 58 C4
Laws Ter ALDT GU11 7 J1
Lay Fld HTWY RG27 73 L7
Lea Cl ASHV GU12 101 K7
BSTK RG21 5 K7
FNM GU9 6 F9
Lea Ct FNM GU9 6 D7
Lea Cft CWTH RG45 37 L2
Leaden Vere ODIM RG29 119 J4
Lea Rd CBLY GU15 58 E6
Lea Springs FLET GU13 98 C1
The Lea FLET GU13 98 C1
Lea Wy ASHV GU12 101 J5
Leawood Rd FLET GU13 98 C1 1
Le Borowe FLET GU13 98 D4
Leckford La STOK SO20 175 G1
Lee Ct ALDT GU11 7 J5
Lee Rd ALDT GU11 6 A2
Lefroy Av BSTK RG21 5 G4
Lefroy's Fld NFNM GU10 98 C8
Legion Cl FLET GU13 98 D3
Legge Crs ALDT GU11 6 A3 1
Legion La WINC SO23 203 H1
Lehar Cl KEMP RG22 92 C8
Leicester Pl AND SP10 9 G6
Leicester Wy WINC SO23 11 M4
Leigh Cl AND SP10 9 L7
Leigh Fld THLE RG7 31 J2
Leigh Gdns AND SP10 9 L7
Leigh La FNM GU9 123 H8
Leigh Rd AND SP10 9 L7
Leipzig Barracks FLET GU13 99 G6
Leipzig Rd FLET GU13 99 G5
Leith Cl CWTH RG45 37 K1
Le Marchant Rd FRIM GU16 59 J5
Lemon Gv BOR GU35 189 H7
Lena Cl RAND SP11 80 D6
Lendore Rd FRIM GU16 59 G8
Lennel Gdns FLET GU13 99 H2
Lennon Wy KEMP RG22 115 H1
Lenten St ALTN GU34 164 D5
Leonard Cl FRIM GU16 59 G8
Leopold Av FARN GU14 78 E3
Leslie Southern Ct NWBY RG14 3 G2
Lestock Wy FLET GU13 77 H7
Levell Ct RAND SP11 80 E6 2
Levern Dr FNM GU9 122 F2 3
Levignen Cl FLET GU13 98 C3
Lewis Cl BSTK RG21 5 H4
Lewisham Wy SHST GU47 38 A7
Ley Rd FARN GU14 58 D8
Leys Gdns NWBY RG14 2 D2
Leyside CWTH RG45 37 K3
Leyton Wy RAND SP11 8 C9
Library Rd FARN GU14 78 E6
Lickfolds Rd NFNM GU10 146 B6
Liddell Cl EWKG RG40 36 B5
Lightfoot Gv BSTK RG21 93 G6
Lightsfield DEAN RG23 91 G6
Lilac Cl BOR GU35 189 J6
Lilac Wy DEAN RG23 92 C2
Lille Barracks ALDT GU11 79 G8
Lillywhite Crs AND SP10 107 G3 2
Lily Cl KEMP RG22 114 F1
Limbrey Hl OVTN RG25 118 A3
Lime Av ALTN GU34 164 D3
CBLY GU15 59 K2
Lime Cl NWBY RG14 3 M2
Limecroft YTLY GU46 56 F3
Lime Dr FARN GU14 77 G4 3
Lime Gv ALTN GU34 164 D3
Limekiln Rd RAND SP11 82 A3
Lime Rd NALR SO24 206 C3
Limes Av KSCL RG20 45 K1
Limes Cl LIPH GU30 214 F1
LISS GU33 236 E4
Limes Rd FARN GU14 77 M3
The Limes TADY RG26 52 A6
Lime St ALDT GU11 6 D2
Limetree Av KSCL RG20 44 E6
Limetree Wk WINC SO23 11 M7
Lime Tree Wy CHIN RG24 71 K5
Linchmere Rd HASM GU27 215 M5
Linch Rd HASM GU27 239 K5
Lincoln Cl ASHV GU12 101 K3
CBLY GU15 59 L4
KEMP RG22 115 G1
Lincoln Gn ALTN GU34 164 D6
Lincoln Rd FARN GU14 78 D7
Linden Av CHIN RG24 94 A3
ODIM RG29 96 E4
Linden Cl NWBY RG14 2 C1
RAND SP11 80 F6
Linden Ct CBLY GU15 59 J1
Linden Dr LISS GU33 236 E4
Linden Rd BOR GU35 190 E3
The Lindens FNM GU9 123 G7
Lindford Cha BOR GU35 189 L3
Lindford Rd BOR GU35 189 K2
Lindford Wey BOR GU35 189 L3
Lindley Gdns NALR SO24 206 C4
Lindum Dene ALDT GU11 6 E4
The Lines KSCL RG20 47 J5
Ling Crs BOR GU35 190 E2
Lingen Cl AND SP10 106 E5 2
Lingfield Cl CHIN RG24 94 B3
Lingfield Rd NWBY RG14 3 J9
Lingmala Gv FLET GU13 99 G3 2
Link Rd ALTN GU34 164 F2
FARN GU14 78 A8
KSCL RG20 47 K6
NWBY RG14 2 E6
Linkside East GSHT GU26 191 L1
Linkside North GSHT GU26 191 L1
Linkside South GSHT GU26 191 M2
Linkside West GSHT GU26 191 L1
Links Rd WINW SO22 10 A5
The Links BOR GU35 189 G7
Links Wy FARN GU14 77 M5
The Link AND SP10 106 B8
YTLY GU46 56 F1
Linkway CBLY GU15 58 F4
CWTH RG45 37 J3
FLET GU13 98 E2
Link Wy NTHA RG18 14 E4
DEAN RG23 91 G7
Linnet Cl KEMP RG22 91 M6
Linnets Rd NALR SO24 206 B4
Linnets Wy ALTN GU34 164 E3
Linsford La FRIM GU16 79 J5
Linstead Rd FARN GU14 58 B8
Linsted La BOR GU35 190 A1
Linsted Cl TADY RG26 49 M1
Linton Dr AND SP10 8 F2
Lion & Lamb Wy FNM GU9 122 E6
Lion Cl OVTN RG25 111 M1
Lion La GSHT GU26 192 C7
Lion Md HASM GU27 216 C2
Lion Rd FARN GU14 78 E6
Lions Fld BOR GU35 188 C4
Lion Wy FLET GU13 99 G3
Liphook Rd HASM GU27 215 K4
BOR GU35 189 L3
BOR GU35 189 H8
BOR GU35 190 B5
Lipscombe Cl NWBY RG14 2 A5
Lipscombe Ri ALTN GU34 164 E3
Liskeard Dr FARN GU14 78 D2 3
Lisle Cl WINW SO22 225 M5
NWBY RG14 13 J3
Lismoyne Cl FLET GU13 76 E6 1
Lister Rd KEMP RG22 92 C8
Litchfield Cl AND SP10 106 C5
Litchfield Rd WINW SO22 202 C4
Little Aldershot La STHA RG19 28 F6
Little Austins Rd FNM GU9 123 G8
Little Barn Pl LISS GU33 237 G4
Little Basing CHIN RG24 93 L1
Little Copse AND SP10 8 C9
FLET GU13 98 E1
YTLY GU46 56 F1
Little Copse Cha CHIN RG24 71 K6
Little Dean La OVTN RG25 118 D3
Little Drove Rd STOK SO20 153 M5
Little Fallow CHIN RG24 71 L8
Littlefield Cl ASHV GU12 101 K7
Littlefield Gdns ASHV GU12 101 K7
Littlefield Rd ALTN GU34 164 F4
Little Frith EWKG RG40 36 F2
Little Green La FNM GU9 146 C1
Little Hayes La RWIN SO21 204 E1
Little Hoddington Cl
OVTN RG25 118 B3
Little Knowle Hl KSCL RG20 47 L4
STHA RG19 48 A2
Little La THLE RG7 15 M2
Little London Rd THLE RG7 50 D2
Little Md MARL SN8 20 C6
Little Minster St WINC SO23 11 G8
Little Moor SHST GU47 37 M7
Little Paddock CBLY GU15 39 K8
Little Thurbans Cl FNM GU9 146 D2
Littleton La RWIN SO21 201 J6
Little Vigo YTLY GU46 56 E4
Little Wellington St ALDT GU11 6 F2
Littleworth Rd NFNM GU10 124 C7
Litton Gdns DEAN RG23 91 G7
Livery Rd RSAL SP5 194 D3
Livia Cl AND SP10 107 G4
Livingstone Rd NWBY RG14 3 G5
Llangar Gv CWTH RG45 37 K3
Lloyd's La TADY RG26 68 F3
Loader Cl WINC SO23 203 H1
Locke Cl RAND SP11 149 K1
Lockerley Rd ROMY SO51 220 F7
Locke Rd LIPH GU30 215 G4
Locke's Dro RAND SP11 61 K8
Lockram La THLE RG7 19 M7
Lock Rd ALDT GU11 101 G3
Locksbridge La TADY RG26 51 J6
Lockside Ct THLE RG7 17 M5 2
Lock's La RWIN SO21 201 J5
Lockwood Cl FARN GU14 58 B8
Loddon Cl CBLY GU15 59 K2
Loddon Dr BSTK RG21 5 J8
Loddon Rd FARN GU14 78 A2
Loddon Wy ASHV GU12 101 K7
Lodge Cl AND SP10 8 C5
Lodge Dr RAND SP11 105 J6
Lodge Gv YTLY GU46 57 J2
Lodge Hill Cl NFNM GU10 147 G2
Lodge Hill Rd NFNM GU10 147 G2
Lodge La RAND SP11 82 A5
Lodsworth FARN GU14 78 A5 3
Loggon Rd BSTK RG21 92 F7
Loman Rd FRIM GU16 79 K5
Lomond Cl DEAN RG23 90 F7
Londlandes FLET GU13 98 D4
London Rd ALTN GU34 165 G3
AND SP10 9 K6
BLKW GU17 58 B4
BSTK RG21 4 F9
CBLY GU15 58 F2
CHIN RG24 94 A4
HTWY RG27 75 H3 2
HTWY RG27 94 F1
LIPH GU30 214 F4
NWBY RG14 2 E2
ODIM RG29 96 D5
OVTN RG25 111 L1
RAND SP11 107 L8
STHA RG19 15 H5
STOK SO20 174 F4
WHCH RG28 110 D3
WINC SO23 203 G4
London St AND SP10 9 J6
WHCH RG28 110 B3
Longacre ASHV GU12 101 K6
NWBY RG14 13 G8
Longacre Cl LISS GU33 236 F4
Longacre Ri CHIN RG24 71 K6 2
Long Barrow Cl RWIN SO21 178 D3
Long Beech Dr FARN GU14 77 M5
Long Bottom RAND SP11 81 L5
Long Br FNM GU9 122 F6
Longbridge Cl HTWY RG27 52 D7
Longbridge Rd TADY RG26 51 L5 2
Long Copse Cha CHIN RG24 71 K6
Longcroft NFNM GU10 144 F3
Longcroft Rd KSCL RG20 47 H5
STHA RG19 15 H6
Long Cross Hl BOR GU35 190 B3
Long Cross La KEMP RG22 114 F2
Longdene Rd HASM GU27 216 E2
Longdown FLET GU13 98 E2
Longdown Cl NFNM GU10 146 F2
Longdown Rd NFNM GU10 146 E3
SHST GU47 37 K7
Long Dro RSAL SP5 218 C3
Longfield Cl FARN GU14 58 D8
OVTN RG25 113 K7
Longfield Rd ASHV GU12 101 K6
WINC SO23 203 J8
Longford Cl CBLY GU15 59 G4 1
Long Garden Wk FNM GU9 122 E6 3
Long Garden Wk East
FNM GU9 122 E6 4
Long Garden Wk West
FNM GU9 122 E6 5
Long Garden Wy FNM GU9 122 E6
Long Gv TADY RG26 29 G6
THLE RG7 15 L3
Long Hl NFNM GU10 124 B7
Longhope Dr NFNM GU10 146 D2
Longhouse Gn WINC SO23 11 M7
Long La CHIN RG24 71 M6
NWBY RG14 13 M1
ODIM RG29 96 E8
Longleat Sq FARN GU14 79 H5 3
Long Leaze RAND SP11 85 H4
Longley Rd FNM GU9 123 G7
Longmead FLET GU13 98 F2
KSCL RG20 24 C7
LISS GU33 236 E5
Longmeadow FRIM GU16 59 J5
Long Mickle SHST GU47 37 K7
Longmoor Dr LIPH GU30 214 A4 1
Longmoor La THLE RG7 31 K1
Longmoor Rd BSTK RG21 92 F4
LIPH GU30 213 M4
LISS GU33 212 F6
Longparish Rd RAND SP11 153 M1
WHCH RG28 109 J7
The Long Rd NFNM GU10 146 C5
Longroden La OVTN RG25 117 G1
Longs Ct WHCH RG28 110 B3 3
Longstock Cl AND SP10 8 C7 1
CHIN RG24 72 A4
Longstock Rd RAND SP11 152 E4
Long Wk RWIN SO21 203 J4
Longwater La EWKG RG40 36 B6
Longwater Rd EWKG RG40 36 C6
HTWY RG27 36 C8
Lordsfield Gdns OVTN RG25 88 E8
Lordswood THLE RG7 30 D8
Lorraine Rd CBLY GU15 39 J8
Louisburg Rd BOR GU35 189 J2
Loundyes Cl NTHA RG18 14 E4
Lovedon La WINC SO23 179 H8
Lovegroves CHIN RG24 71 M5
Love La AND SP10 9 J7
KSCL RG20 47 J6
NWBY RG14 13 J2
ODIM RG29 96 C7
Lovell Cl RAND SP11 128 C1
RWIN SO21 178 D4
Lovells Wk NALR SO24 206 B3 1
Loveridge Cl AND SP10 107 G4
BSTK RG21 92 F6
Lovers La NFNM GU10 168 F1
Love's Cl THLE RG7 19 J5
Loves Wd THLE RG7 31 J3
Lovington La RWIN SO21 205 H4
Lowa Cl NTID SP9 102 D3
Lowa Rd NTID SP9 102 C2
Lowden Cl WINW SO22 226 C4
Lower Broadmoor Rd
CWTH RG45 38 A4
Lower Brook St BSTK RG21 4 A8
WINC SO23 11 H7
Lower Canes YTLY GU46 56 D2
Lower Chestnut Dr BSTK RG21 92 E5
Lower Church La FNM GU9 122 E6 3
Lower Church Rd SHST GU47 37 H7
Lower Common HTWY RG27 35 H7
Lower Evingar Rd WHCH RG28 110 B3
Lower Farm Ct STHA RG19 14 C7
Lower Farnham Rd ALDT GU11 7 J7
Lower Hanger HASM GU27 215 M2
Lower Lamborough La
NALR SO24 230 C3
Lower Moor YTLY GU46 57 G3 3
Lower Neatham Mill La
ALTN GU34 165 K2
Lower Nelson St ALDT GU11 6 E1
Lower Newport Rd ASHV GU12 7 M5
Lower Paice La ALTN GU34 184 B4
Lower Pool Rd HTWY RG27 55 G4
Lower Rd HASM GU27 193 J6
RWIN SO21 178 B4
RWIN SO21 178 E4
Lower Sandhurst Rd
EWKG RG40 36 D6
Lower South Vw FNM GU9 122 F5
Lower St HASM GU27 216 E2
Lower Terrace Rd FARN GU14 78 D8
Lower Turk St ALTN GU34 164 E5
Lower Wy STHA RG19 14 C5
Lower Weybourne La FNM GU9 6 C9
Lower Wokingham Rd
EWKG RG40 37 G2
Lower Wote St BSTK RG21 4 F7
Loweswater Gdns BOR GU35 189 J3
Lowicks Rd NFNM GU10 169 L2
Lowlands Rd BLKW GU17 57 M4
KEMP RG22 91 M5
Low La FNM GU9 7 G9
Lowry Cl SHST GU47 58 A2
Lowry Ct AND SP10 8 F2
Loxwood Av FLET GU13 98 D1
Loyalty La CHIN RG24 94 A2
Lubeck Dr AND SP10 106 E5
Lucas Cl YTLY GU46 57 G3
Lucas Fld HASM GU27 216 B2 1
Ludgershall Rd NTID SP9 102 E1
Ludlow Cl DEAN RG23 92 B3
FRIM GU16 79 K1
NWBY RG14 14 B4 2
Ludlow Gdns DEAN RG23 92 C3
Ludshott Gv BOR GU35 190 E3
Luke Rd ALDT GU11 6 A5
Luke Rd East ALDT GU11 6 B5
Lulworth Cl FARN GU14 78 D1
Lundy Cl CHIN RG24 71 J7
Lune Cl BSTK RG21 5 J8
Lune Ct AND SP10 9 M1 2
Lupin Cl BAGS GU19 39 M7
KEMP RG22 91 M8
Lutyens Cl CHIN RG24 71 L8
Lyall Pl FNM GU9 122 E1
Lych Gate Cl SHST GU47 37 J8
Lyde Cl BSTK RG21 91 G7
Lydford Cl FARN GU14 78 D1 6
FRIM GU16 79 K1 2
Lye Copse Av FARN GU14 58 E8
Lyeway La NALR SO24 208 C4
Lyeway Rd ALTN GU34 208 F3
Lyford Rd BSTK RG21 4 F5
Lymington Av YTLY GU46 56 F3
Lymington Bottom ALTN GU34 185 G6

Lymington Bottom Rd
ALTN GU34 184 F4
Lymington Cl ALTN GU34 184 F6
KEMP RG22 115 G2
Lymington Ri ALTN GU34 185 G6
Lynchborough Rd LIPH GU30 190 A8
Lynch Cl WINW SO22 10 C3
Lynchford La FARN GU14 79 H7
Lynchford Rd ALDT GU11 78 F8
FARN GU14 78 F8 1
Lynch Hl WHCH RG28 110 B3
Lynch Hill Pk WHCH RG28 110 C3
Lynch Rd FNM GU9 123 G6
The Lynch MARL SN8 20 C6
OVTN RG25 88 D8
WHCH RG28 110 C3
Lyndale Dr FLET GU13 77 J7
Lyndford Ter FLET GU13 98 E1
Lyndhurst Av ALDT GU11 7 J9
BLKW GU17 57 M2
Lyndhurst Cl WINW SO22 202 C4
Lyndhurst Dr KEMP RG22 115 H2
Lyndsey Cl FARN GU14 77 L4
Lyneham Rd CWTH RG45 37 L3
Lynford Av WINW SO22 10 C2
Lynford Wy WINW SO22 10 D2
Lynn Wy FARN GU14 78 C1
WINC SO23 203 H2
Lynton Cl FNM GU9 146 D1
Lynton Meadow STOK SO20 153 M4 1
Lynton Rd BOR GU35 189 J5
Lynwood Cl BOR GU35 189 M3 4
Lynwood Dr AND SP10 8 D6
FRIM GU16 79 K5
Lynwood Gdns HTWY RG27 73 M7
Lyon Cl STHA RG19 15 J6
Lyon Rd CWTH RG45 37 M2
Lyon Wy FRIM GU16 58 F7
Lysander Wy FARN GU14 78 E7
Lysons Av ASHV GU12 79 J8
Lysons Rd ALDT GU11 6 F3
Lytton Rd BSTK RG21 5 H8

M

Mabbs La HTWY RG27 75 H4
Macadam Wy AND SP10 106 A7
Maccullum Rd RAND SP11 84 A8
Macdonald Rd FNM GU9 122 E1
Macrae Rd YTLY GU46 56 F2
Maddocks Hl NALR SO24 208 A4
Madeira Cl CHIN RG24 71 J7
Madeley Rd FLET GU13 99 G2
Madox Brown End SHST
GU47 58 B2 2
Madrid Rd AND SP10 9 M3
Magazine Rd FARN GU14 78 A8
Magdalene Rd SHST GU47 38 C6
Magdalen Hl WINC SO23 11 J8
Magnolia Cl AND SP10 8 C7
SHST GU47 38 A7 7
Magnolia Wy FLET GU13 98 F1
Magnus Dr KEMP RG22 115 G1
Magpie Cl KEMP RG22 91 L8
BOR GU35 189 K6 5
NFNM GU10 99 G8 1
STHA RG19 14 E5
Maguire Dr FRIM GU16 59 M5
Mahler Cl KEMP RG22 92 E8 1
Maida Rd ALDT GU11 100 E4
Maidenthorn La OVTN RG25 113 L7
Main Gate Rd FARN GU14 78 E6
Main Rd WINW SO22 201 M2
TADY RG26 50 A2
Mainstone Cl FRIM GU16 79 M1 1
Main St STHA RG19 26 D3
Maitland Rd FARN GU14 78 E8
Maitlands Cl NFNM GU10 124 B2
Majendie Cl NWBY RG14 13 G3 3
Majestic Rd KEMP RG22 114 F3
Majorca Av AND SP10 9 L2
Maldive Rd CHIN RG24 71 J7
Malham Gdns KEMP RG22 115 C3
Malham Rd STHA RG19 14 F5
Mallard Cl AND SP10 107 G6
ASHV GU12 101 J6
HASM GU27 216 B2 2
KEMP RG22 114 E1
NALR SO24 206 C2
Mallard Ct NWBY RG14 2 C4
Mallards ALTN GU34 164 E3
Mallard Wy THLE RG7 17 L5
YTLY GU46 56 E2 2
Mallow Cl BOR GU35 189 M3 3
The Mall NTID SP9 102 A4
Malmesbury Gdns WINW SO22 10 A3
Malmsbury Rd BOR GU35 189 J6
Malpass Rd RWIN SO21 178 B6
Malshanger La DEAN RG23 90 F5
Malta Cl CHIN RG24 71 H7
Maltby's ALTN GU34 187 K8
Malthouse Cl FLET GU13 98 D3
RWIN SO21 203 L3
Malthouse La NALR SO24 183 H7
TADY RG26 50 A2
Malt House La RAND SP11 107 H1
Malthouse Mdw LIPH GU30 214 F4
Malthouse Ms ALTN GU34 165 H2 1
Maltings Cl ALTN GU34 164 E6
The Maltings LIPH GU30 215 G4
TADY RG26 51 L6
Malvern Cl KEMP RG22 91 M5
Malvern Ct NWBY RG14 2 D7
Malvern Rd BLKW GU17 57 J7
FARN GU14 78 A1
LISS GU33 237 G6
Mandora Rd ALDT GU11 100 E4
Manfield Rd ASHV GU12 101 K6
Manica Cl BOR GU35 189 J5 2
Manley Bridge Rd NFNM GU10 146 B4
Manley James Cl ODIM RG29 96 D5 1
Mann Cl WHCH RG28 110 C4
Manningford Cl WINC SO23 11 H1
Manor Bridge Ct NTID SP9 102 E1
Manor Cl ALTN GU34 164 F2
HASM GU27 216 B2
KEMP RG22 114 F2
NFNM GU10 124 C1
NTID SP9 126 D1
RAND SP11 129 M5
WINC SO23 11 K6
Manor Copse AND SP10 107 G3
Manor Ct FLET GU13 98 F4
Manor Farm Cl ASHV GU12 101 J7 1
Manor Farm La ROMY SO51 222 C7
Manor Flds LIPH GU30 215 G4
Manor Gdns NFNM GU10 147 G3
Manor La CHIN RG24 94 A2
NTHA RG18 14 B4
STHA RG19 28 A1
Manor Park Dr EWKG RG40 36 B2 2
EWKG RG40 36 A2 1
YTLY GU46 57 G3
Manor Pl NWBY RG14 13 G3
Manor Ri RAND SP11 130 D4
Manor Rd ALDT GU11 6 D5
ALTN GU34 164 F2
AND SP10 8 E3
ASHV GU12 101 J7
CHIN RG24 70 D5
FARN GU14 79 G5
FNM GU9 123 H4
NFNM GU10 101 J8
RSAL SP5 220 D1
Manorside Cl NFNM GU10 101 J8 1
Manor Wk ASHV GU12 7 G4
Manse La TADY RG26 50 A2
Mansell Dr NWBY RG14 24 F3
Mansfield Rd KEMP RG22 92 D6
Man's Hl THLE RG7 19 M5
Mansion Dr HTWY RG27 55 G4
Maple Cl ALTN GU34 164 E3 2
ASHV GU12 101 J1
BLKW GU17 57 M3
NALR SO24 206 B4 1
SHST GU47 37 J7
STOK SO20 151 G4
Maple Crs BSTK RG21 4 E3
NWBY RG14 2 E1
RAND SP11 81 G6
Maple Dr CWTH RG45 37 M1 1
WINC SO23 179 G8
Maple Gdns YTLY GU46 57 G3
Maple Gv TADY RG26 29 L8
Maplehurst Cha KEMP RG22 115 G2
Maple Leaf Cl FARN GU14 78 C5 1
Maple Leaf Dr BOR GU35 189 J4
Maple Wk ASHV GU12 7 M6
Maple Wy BOR GU35 190 E2
Marchant Cl STHA RG19 26 A1 1
Marchant Rd AND SP10 8 D7
March Cl AND SP10 9 K3
Marconi Rd NWBY RG14 3 G2
Mardale CBLY GU15 59 M4
Mareth Cl ALDT GU11 7 H1
Margaret Rd KEMP RG22 92 C4
Margha Rd NTID SP9 102 D2
Marigold Cl CWTH RG45 37 J1
KEMP RG22 91 M8
Mariners Cl TADY RG26 50 A2
Marino Wy EWKG RG40 35 K2
Marjoram Cl FARN GU14 77 L4 1
Markall Cl NALR SO24 230 C3
Market La WINC SO23 11 G8
Market Pl BSTK RG21 4 F9
Market Sq ALTN GU34 164 E5
Market St ALTN GU34 164 E5
NWBY RG14 2 E5
WINC SO23 11 G8
Markham Ct CBLY GU15 59 G2 2
Markson Rd RWIN SO21 178 B4
Marlborough Cl FLET GU13 77 J8
Marlborough Gdns
DEAN RG23 91 G6 1
Marlborough Ri CBLY GU15 59 H2
Marlborough St AND SP10 9 H4
Marlborough Vw FARN GU14 77 M3
Marley Combe Rd HASM GU27 216 C3
Marley Hanger HASM GU27 216 D5
Marley La HASM GU27 216 B3
Marlowe Cl CHIN RG24 5 H1
The Marlowes NWBY RG14 13 J8
Marl's La CHIN RG24 71 G4
Marrowbrook Cl FARN GU14 78 D5
Marrowbrook La FARN GU14 78 C6
Marsden Ct WHCH RG28 111 H2 1
Marshall Cl FARN GU14 78 C1
Marshall Gdns BSTK RG21 4 F4
Marshall Rd SHST GU47 58 A1
Marshalls Ct NWBY RG14 13 G3 4
Marsh Cl BOR GU35 189 L5
Marshcourt CHIN RG24 71 L8
Marsh La HTWY RG27 56 B3
NWBY RG14 2 E3
Marsh Rd NTHA RG18 15 H4
Marston Dr FARN GU14 78 E1
NWBY RG14 14 A3
Marston Rd FNM GU9 122 C6
Marsum Cl AND SP10 106 E4 1
Martel Cl CBLY GU15 59 M1
Martin Cl BSTK RG21 5 H3
NTID SP9 102 F2
Martindale Av CBLY GU15 59 M5
Martingale Ct ALDT GU11 6 B2 3
Martins Cl ALTN GU34 164 F3
BLKW GU17 58 A4
Martins Flds RWIN SO21 226 B7
Martins La STOK SO20 154 A4
The Martins STHA RG19 15 J6
Martins Wd CHIN RG24 71 L5 3
Martin Wy AND SP10 107 G6 3
FRIM GU16 59 H7
Maryland EWKG RG40 36 A1
Mary La ALTN GU34 185 L8
OVTN RG25 113 K6
Masefield Rd NTHA RG18 14 F4
Maskell Wy FARN GU14 77 M5
Mason Cl YTLY GU46 57 H3 2
Mason Pl SHST GU47 37 J8
Mason Rd FARN GU14 78 B2
Mason Wy ALDT GU11 7 G7
Mathias Wk KEMP RG22 115 J2
Matilda Dr KEMP RG22 115 G1 3
Matthew Rd FNM GU9 6 A5
Matthews Cl STHA RG19 14 E5 2
Matthews Rd CBLY GU15 38 F8
Matthews Wy DEAN RG23 91 H7
Mattock Wy CHIN RG24 71 L5
Maultway Cl CBLY GU15 39 L8 1
Maultway Crs CBLY GU15 39 L8
Maultway North CBLY GU15 39 L7
The Maultway CBLY GU15 39 L8
Mavins Rd FNM GU9 123 G8
Maw Cl KEMP RG22 92 E8 2
Maxine Cl SHST GU47 37 L7
Maybrick Cl SHST GU47 37 J7
Maybrook CHIN RG24 71 L4
Maybury Cl FRIM GU16 59 G8
May Cl CHIN RG24 94 B2
BOR GU35 190 B4
SHST GU47 38 A8
May Crs ASHV GU12 101 H7
Mayfair Dr NWBY RG14 2 A7
Mayfield NFNM GU10 146 C5
Mayfield Cl FNM GU9 7 G9
NTID SP9 126 C1
Mayfield Ct HTWY RG27 36 A8
Mayfield Rdg DEAN RG23 115 G3
Mayfield Rd CBLY GU15 58 E7 1
FARN GU14 78 C1
Mayflower Cl CHIN RG24 71 K6
Mayflower Dr YTLY GU46 56 D1
Mayflower Rd BOR GU35 189 H7 1
Maynard Cl NTHA RG18 14 F3
Maynard's Wd CHIN RG24 71 K6
Mayors La NWBY RG14 2 E5
Mayow Cl STHA RG19 15 J6
May Pl BSTK RG21 4 F9
May Tree Cl WINW SO22 226 B4
May Tree Rd AND SP10 8 B3
Maywood Dr CBLY GU15 59 L1
Mccartney Wk KEMP RG22 115 H1
Mcfauld Wy WHCH RG28 110 B4
Mcgrigor Barracks ALDT GU11 100 E5
Mckay Cl ALDT GU11 100 F5
Mc Naughton Cl FARN GU14 77 M5
Mead Cl AND SP10 8 E7
Meade Rd RAND SP11 80 F6
Meadham La OVTN RG25 67 G5
Mead Hawks LISS GU33 236 D3
Mead La FNM GU9 122 E7
Meadow Cl ASHV GU12 79 J7
BLKW GU17 58 A4
LIPH GU30 214 F4
NALR SO24 206 C3 3
STHA RG19 14 F5
Meadow Dr RAND SP11 130 E8
Meadow Gate Rd FARN GU14 78 C7
Meadowland CHIN RG24 71 K5
WINC SO23 203 G1
Meadow La HTWY RG27 75 H2
Meadow Pound WHCH RG28 110 C3 1
Meadowridge KEMP RG22 115 H3
Meadow Ri OVTN RG25 113 L7 2
Meadow Rd BSTK RG21 92 F7
FARN GU14 78 E1
NWBY RG14 2 D9
The Meadows HTWY RG27 52 C7
NFNM GU10 169 J7
Meadowsweet Cl NTHA RG18 15 H4
Meadow V HASM GU27 216 D2
Meadow Vw FLET GU13 98 D3 3
BOR GU35 189 K5
WHCH RG28 110 A3
Meadow Wk LISS GU33 236 E4
Meadow Wy AND SP10 8 A5
ASHV GU12 101 J5
BLKW GU17 57 M3
WINW SO22 226 B4
LIPH GU30 214 F3
NFNM GU10 146 C5
Mead Rd AND SP10 8 E7
GSHT GU26 192 C4
WINC SO23 226 D4
The Meads HASM GU27 216 C2
The Mead CHIN RG24 94 A2
LIPH GU30 214 E3
LISS GU33 236 E4
Meadway FRIM GU16 59 J6
HASM GU27 216 C2
Mede Cl OVTN RG25 112 A1
Medina Gdns DEAN RG23 91 G7 3
Medlar Dr BLKW GU17 58 C5
Medonte Cl FLET GU13 77 G8 1
Medstead Rd ALTN GU34 163 K7
Medway Av DEAN RG23 91 G6
Medway Cl NTHA RG18 14 E3
Medway Ct AND SP10 107 H6
BSTK RG21 5 K8
Medway Dr FARN GU14 78 B1
Meerut Rd NTID SP9 102 D2
Meitner Cl TADY RG26 51 L4
Meldrum Cl NWBY RG14 24 F2 1
Melford Gdns KEMP RG22 91 M6
Meliot Ri AND SP10 106 F4
Melrose Av FARN GU14 77 M3
Melrose Cl BOR GU35 189 J6 3
Melville Av FRIM GU16 59 J7
Membury Cl FRIM GU16 79 K1 3
Memorial Rd HTWY RG27 73 M8
Mendip Cl KEMP RG22 91 M5
Mendip Rd FARN GU14 78 B1
Menin Wy FNM GU9 123 G7
Meon Cl FARN GU14 78 A2
TADY RG26 29 K7
Meon Rd DEAN RG23 91 G7
Mercer Cl KEMP RG22 92 B4
Merchants Pl WINC SO23 11 H7
Mercia Av AND SP10 106 C5
Mercury Cl BOR GU35 189 L5 2
Merepond La ALTN GU34 233 K5
Merivale FLET GU13 76 C8
Merlin Cl AND SP10 106 F5
Merlin Md KEMP RG22 114 E2
Merlin Rd ALTN GU34 185 G6
FARN GU14 78 E6
Merlins Cl FNM GU9 122 F7 4
Merlin Wy FARN GU14 78 A5
Merriatt Cl BSTK RG21 93 G6
Merrileas Gdns KEMP RG22 91 M8
Merron Cl YTLY GU46 56 F3 4
Merrydown La CHIN RG24 71 M6 1
Merryfield CHIN RG24 71 K5
Merryman Dr CWTH RG45 37 J2
Merrywood Pk CBLY GU15 59 J4
Mersey Wy NTHA RG18 14 E3
Merton Cl SHST GU47 38 C6
Merton Rd BSTK RG21 4 B5
Meryon Rd NALR SO24 206 B4
Mesh Rd ROMY SO51 222 B6
Meteor Wy FARN GU14 78 D7
Methuen Rd LISS GU33 213 H5
Meudon Av FARN GU14 78 E5
Mews La WINW SO22 10 D8
The Mews TADY RG26 52 A6
Meyrick Dr NWBY RG14 24 F3
Michaelmas Cl YTLY GU46 57 G4
Micheldever Cl WHCH RG28 110 C5
Micheldever Rd AND SP10 9 K6
WHCH RG28 110 C4
Mickle Hl SHST GU47 37 K7
Middle Av FNM GU9 123 G8
Middle Bourne La NFNM GU10 146 E2
Middle Brook St WINC SO23 11 H7
Middle Church La FNM GU9 122 E6 7
Middle Cl CBLY GU15 59 M2
NWBY RG14 25 G1
Middlefield FNM GU9 146 D1
Middle Gordon Rd CBLY GU15 58 F3
Middle Hl ALDT GU11 6 F1
Middle Md HTWY RG27 73 M7 3
Middle Meadow LISS GU33 236 F4
Middlemoor Rd FRIM GU16 59 H8
Middle Old Pk FNM GU9 122 C4
Middle Rd WINW SO22 10 D6
Middleton Ct NWBY RG14 14 B3
Middleton Gdns BSTK RG21 4 F4
FARN GU14 78 B2
Middleton Rd CBLY GU15 59 H2
RSAL SP5 194 E1
The Middleway RAND SP11 108 A8
Midhurst Rd HASM GU27 216 E3
LIPH GU30 214 F5
Midlane Cl BSTK RG21 92 F6
Mike Hawthorn Dr FNM GU9 122 F5 1
Milden Cl FRIM GU16 79 K2
Milden Gdns FRIM GU16 79 K2
Mildmay Ct ODIM RG29 96 D6
Mildmay St WINW SO22 226 C3
Miles Rd ASHV GU12 101 L5
Milkhouse Rd KSCL RG20 12 A2
Milkingpen La CHIN RG24 94 A1
Milland La LIPH GU30 238 D2
Milland Rd LIPH GU30 238 E6
WINC SO23 227 G2
Millard Cl BSTK RG21 4 B3
Millbridge Rd YTLY GU46 36 E8
Millbrook Cl LISS GU33 236 F4
Mill Chase Rd BOR GU35 189 K5
Mill Cl HASM GU27 216 B2 3
Mill Copse Rd HASM GU27 216 E4
Mill Cnr FARN GU14 77 H3 1
Millers La WINW SO22 225 L5
Millers Rd TADY RG26 29 L8
Millgreen La STHA RG19 27 J6
Mill Hl NALR SO24 206 C1
Millins Cl SHST GU47 38 A7
Mill La ALTN GU34 165 G4
HASM GU27 216 F4
HTWY RG27 73 G1
KSCL RG20 46 D4
BOR GU35 189 M4
LISS GU33 211 L8
MARL SN8 20 C4
NALR SO24 206 F3
NFNM GU10 168 E1
NWBY RG14 2 F4
ODIM RG29 96 A3
PSF GU32 235 K8
RAND SP11 133 H3
RSAL SP5 171 G8
TADY RG26 52 B5
THLE RG7 17 M5
THLE RG7 52 B3
YTLY GU46 37 G8
Millmere YTLY GU46 57 G1
Mill Reef Cl STHA RG19 14 C5
Mill Ri ROMY SO51 221 J8
Mill Rd CHIN RG24 70 B8
LISS GU33 236 F3
Mill Stream FNM GU9 6 B9
Millstream Cl AND SP10 8 F9
The Millstream HASM GU27 216 B3
Mill Vale Mdw LIPH GU30 238 E5
Millway Cl AND SP10 8 C6
Millway Rd AND SP10 8 C5
Milner Pl WINW SO22 226 D2
Milnthorpe La WINW SO22 10 C9
The Milsons STOK SO20 174 E6
Milton Av AND SP10 8 B3
Milton Cl CHIN RG24 5 H1
Milverton Rd WINW SO22 10 C6
Mimosa Cl BOR GU35 189 M3
Minchens La TADY RG26 51 K5
Minden Cl AND SP10 106 E5 3
CHIN RG24 71 K6 3
Minden Wy WINW SO22 226 B3
Minehurst Rd FRIM GU16 79 J4
Minerva Rd FARN GU14 78 E7
Ministry Rd STHA RG19 26 D3
Minley Cl FARN GU14 78 B4
Minley Gv FARN GU14 77 G5 1
Minley Rd FARN GU14 57 H7
Minstead Cl WINW SO22 202 C4 3
TADY RG26 49 L2
Minstead Dr YTLY GU46 56 F3
Minster La WINC SO23 11 G8
Mint Rd LISS GU33 237 G2
Mistletoe Rd YTLY GU46 57 G4
Mitcham Rd CBLY GU15 39 K7
Mitchell Av HTWY RG27 75 H3
Mitchell Cl AND SP10 106 A7
Mitchell Gdns KEMP RG22 115 H1 1
Mitford Rd NALR SO24 206 A3
Moat Cl TADY RG26 51 K4
Moffatts Cl SHST GU47 37 K8
Mole Cl FARN GU14 78 A2
Momford Rd WINW SO22 226 A5
Monachus La HTWY RG27 75 J1
Monarch Cl KEMP RG22 114 F2
Monarch's Wy ROMY SO51 221 L8
RSAL SP5 196 B3
STOK SO20 196 E2
Monarch Wy WINW SO22 226 B2
Mongers Piece CHIN RG24 71 M4
Monier Williams Rd
RWIN SO21 133 G5
Monks Cl FARN GU14 78 F4
NTID SP9 102 D1
Monkshanger FNM GU9 123 H6
Monk Sherborne Rd TADY RG26 69 J1
Monks La NWBY RG14 25 H1
Monks Ri FLET GU13 76 C7 1
Monks Rd WINC SO23 11 G5
Monk's Wk NFNM GU10 147 J1
Monks' Well NFNM GU10 123 M8
Monkswood Cl NWBY RG14 25 G1 3
Monks Wood Crs TADY RG26 49 L1 3
Monkton La FNM GU9 123 H3
Monktons La THLE RG7 31 M3
Monmouth Sq WINW SO22 226 A2 1
Mons Barracks ALDT GU11 100 F3
Mons Cl ALDT GU11 101 H1
Montacute Cl FARN GU14 79 G4 1
Montacute Dr STHA RG19 15 J6 3
Montague Cl CBLY GU15 58 E3 4
Montague Pl BSTK RG21 93 G5 1
Montague Ter NWBY RG14 2 E9
Monteagle La YTLY GU46 56 D2
Montgomery Cl SHST GU47 37 L8 1
Montgomery Rd FARN GU14 78 C5
NWBY RG14 2 A9
Montrose Cl FLET GU13 77 G8
FRIM GU16 59 H6 2
BOR GU35 189 J7
Montserrat Pl CHIN RG24 71 H6 2
Montserrat Rd CHIN RG24 71 H6
Monument Cha BOR GU35 189 K7
Monument Cl NWBY RG14 25 G1 2
Monxton Rd RAND SP11 128 B7
RAND SP11 129 L1
Moody's Hl RSAL SP5 219 H6
Moons Hl NFNM GU10 146 E6
Moor Cl EWKG RG40 36 B1
BOR GU35 189 G5
SHST GU47 38 B7
Moor Court La RWIN SO21 201 G5
Moorcroft Cl RWIN SO21 156 C5
Moore Cl AND SP10 9 H2
FLET GU13 98 F3
NFNM GU10 101 J8 2
Moore Rd FLET GU13 98 F3
Moorfield HASM GU27 216 C3
Moorfoot Gdns KEMP RG22 92 A5
Moorhams Av KEMP RG22 114 F2
The Moorings BSTK RG21 5 K7
Moorlands Cl FLET GU13 77 G8 2
GSHT GU26 192 B4
Moorlands Rd CBLY GU15 58 D4
Moor Park La NFNM GU10 123 J5
Moor Park Wy FNM GU9 123 J6
Moor Rd FARN GU14 58 D8
FRIM GU16 59 J8
HASM GU27 215 M3
LISS GU33 213 G7
Moorside Cl FARN GU14 58 D7
Moorside Rd WINC SO23 11 M3
The Moors NFNM GU10 124 C1 1
STHA RG19 15 G6
Moor Vw CHIN RG24 94 A1
Moot Cl AND SP10 107 G4
Moray Av SHST GU47 58 A1
Moreland Cl ALTN GU34 164 E6
Morestead Rd RWIN SO21 227 G3
Moreton Cl FLET GU13 98 E4
NFNM GU10 169 H7
Morgaston Rd TADY RG26 70 E1
Morland Rd ALDT GU11 7 H8
Morland's Rd ALDT GU11 101 G3
Morley Cl YTLY GU46 56 E3
Morley Rd BSTK RG21 92 F7
FNM GU9 122 F7
Mornington Cl AND SP10 130 F3 2
TADY RG26 29 G7
Mornington Dr WINW SO22 202 B6
Mornington Rd BOR GU35 188 F6
Morris Rd FARN GU14 79 G8
Morris St HTWY RG27 73 K8
Morse Rd KEMP RG22 92 D4
Mortimer Cl HTWY RG27 75 G4 1
WINC SO23 203 G2
Mortimer Gdns TADY RG26 49 M1
Mortimer La BSTK RG21 4 D8
THLE RG7 32 A8
THLE RG7 32 A1
Morton Cl FRIM GU16 79 J1
Morval Cl FARN GU14 78 B4
Moselle Cl FARN GU14 78 A3
Moss Cl LISS GU33 236 F4
Moss Rd WINC SO23 11 K7
Moulsham Copse La YTLY GU46 56 E1
Moulsham La YTLY GU46 56 E1
Moulshay La HTWY RG27 72 B3
Mountbatten Cl NWBY RG14 13 M3 2
Mountbatten Ct WINW SO22 10 C1
Mountbatten Pl WINC SO23 179 H8 1
Mountbatten Ri SHST GU47 37 J7
Mount Carmel Rd RAND SP11 149 J3
Mount Cl WINW SO22 10 C1
KSCL RG20 44 C2
NWBY RG14 2 E8
Mounters La ALTN GU34 164 C7
Mount Hermon Rd RAND SP11 149 K2
Mount Pleasant FNM GU9 122 D6
HTWY RG27 75 J2
SHST GU47 37 K7 4
TADY RG26 29 K8
WINC SO23 203 G2
Mount Pleasant Rd ALTN GU34 164 E6
ASHV GU12 7 J2
BOR GU35 189 L3
Mount Rd KSCL RG20 44 C1
NTHA RG18 15 G4
Mountsom's La ALTN GU34 186 E4
The Mount FLET GU13 76 F6
HASM GU27 193 J6
BOR GU35 190 D2
Mount Vw ALDT GU11 6 E4

Mourne Cl *KEMP* RG22 .... 92 A4
Mozart Cl *KEMP* RG22 .... 92 D8
Mud La *HTWY* RG27 .... 35 J2
Mulberry Cl *ASHV* GU12 .... 101 K4
CWTH RG45 .... 37 M4
SHST GU47 .... 38 A8 ③
Mulberry Ct *ALTN* GU34 .... 185 H5
Mulberry Wy *CHIN* RG24 .... 71 L5
Mulfords Hl *TADY* RG26 .... 29 L7
Mulgrave Rd *FRIM* GU16 .... 59 J6 ⑥
Mull Cl *DEAN* RG23 .... 90 F6
Mullins Cl *BSTK* RG21 .... 4 F2
Mulroy Dr *CBLY* GU15 .... 59 K2
Munday's Boro *RGUW* GU3 .... 125 K4
Munday's Boro Rd
RGUW GU3 .... 125 K4 ①
Munkle Marsh *STHA* RG19 .... 15 K5 ③
Munnings Cl *BSTK* RG21 .... 93 J5
Munnings Dr *SHST* GU47 .... 58 A2
Murray Cl *AND* SP10 .... 130 E3
Murray Rd *FARN* GU14 .... 78 C5
Murray's Rd *ALDT* GU11 .... 101 G3
Murrell Green Rd *HTWY* RG27 .... 74 D3
Murrell Rd *ASHV* GU12 .... 101 K5
Murrells La *CBLY* GU15 .... 58 E5
Muscott Cl *NTID* SP9 .... 126 C1 ③
Museum Hl *HASM* GU27 .... 217 G2
Musgrave Cl *KEMP* RG22 .... 92 C8 ⑥
Musgrove Gdns *ALTN* GU34 .... 164 D4
Musket Copse *CHIN* RG24 .... 93 M2
Muss La *STOK* SO20 .... 198 F5
Myland Cl *BSTK* RG21 .... 5 G3
Mylen Rd *AND* SP10 .... 8 D4
Myrtle Cl *THLE* RG7 .... 19 M5
Myrtle Dr *BLKW* GU17 .... 58 A4
Mytchett Heath *FRIM* GU16 .... 79 K5
Mytchett Lake Rd *FRIM* GU16 .... 79 K6
Mytchett Place Rd *FRIM* GU16 .... 79 K5
Mytchett Rd *FRIM* GU16 .... 79 J4

N

Nadder Rd *NTID* SP9 .... 102 E2
Naini Tal Rd *NTID* SP9 .... 102 D1
Nairn Cl *FRIM* GU16 .... 59 H6 ⑧
Napier Cl *ALDT* GU11 .... 101 H1 ③
CWTH RG45 .... 37 M4
NTID SP9 .... 102 F2
Napier Dr *CBLY* GU15 .... 59 K1
Napier Rd *CWTH* RG45 .... 37 M4
Napoleon Av *FARN* GU14 .... 78 E2
Napoleon Dr *DEAN* RG23 .... 92 B1
Naseby Ri *NWBY* RG14 .... 14 A3
Nash Cl *BSTK* RG21 .... 5 C4
FARN GU14 .... 78 C4
Nash Mdw *ODIM* RG29 .... 118 D4
Nately Rd *OVTN* RG25 .... 95 J5
Nations Hl *WINC* SO23 .... 203 C1
The Naylors *THLE* RG7 .... 34 A2
Neath Rd *BSTK* RG21 .... 5 J7
Nelson Cl *ASHV* GU12 .... 7 K3
FNM GU9 .... 100 A8
STOK SO20 .... 174 C5
WINC SO23 .... 11 L9
Nelson St *ALDT* GU11 .... 6 C1
Nelson Wy *CBLY* GU15 .... 58 C4
Nene Ct *AND* SP10 .... 107 H6 ⑩
Nepaul Rd *NTID* SP9 .... 102 D1
Neptune Rd *BOR* GU35 .... 189 K6 ⑩
Nestor Cl *AND* SP10 .... 8 E2
Netherfield Cl *ALTN* GU34 .... 164 D4
Netherhouse Moor
FLET GU13 .... 98 C1 ③
Netley St *FARN* GU14 .... 78 E4
Nettlebeds La *NALR* SO24 .... 183 G6
Neuvic Wy *WHCH* RG28 .... 110 C4
Nevada Cl *FARN* GU14 .... 78 A5 ⑩
Neville Cl *AND* SP10 .... 9 K4
BSTK RG21 .... 93 G6
Neville Dr *STHA* RG19 .... 15 H5
Neville Duke Rd *FARN* GU14 .... 58 C4
Newall Rd *RAND* SP11 .... 129 M1
Newark Rd *BLKW* GU17 .... 57 H7
New Barn Cl *FLET* GU13 .... 98 C1 ③
RAND SP11 .... 164 E6
Newbold Rd *NWBY* RG14 .... 13 G3 ⑩
Newbolt Cl *NTHA* RG18 .... 14 F3
Newburgh St *WINC* SO23 .... 10 F6 ⑩
Newbury Rd *AND* SP10 .... 106 F5
KSCL SO20 .... 47 H5
RAND SP11 .... 107 G1
WHCH RG28 .... 87 J7
Newbury St *AND* SP10 .... 9 G3
WHCH RG28 .... 110 B3
Newchurch Rd *TADY* RG26 .... 29 K7
Newcomb Cl *AND* SP10 .... 130 E3
Newcome Rd *FNM* GU9 .... 6 A8
New Crs *RAND* SP11 .... 80 D7
New Dawn Cl *FARN* GU14 .... 78 A5
New Dro *RAND* SP11 .... 80 D7
New Farm Rd *NALR* SO24 .... 206 A3
RWIN SO21 .... 158 E5
Newfield Av *FARN* GU14 .... 78 B2
Newfield Rd *ASHV* GU12 .... 101 K2
LISS GU33 .... 236 E4
New House La *RAND* SP11 .... 104 F1
Newlands *FLET* GU13 .... 98 F2
Newlands Cl *YTLY* GU46 .... 57 G3
Newlands Dr *ASHV* GU12 .... 101 L4
Newlands Rd *FRIM* GU16 .... 59 J5
New La *STOK* SO20 .... 198 F4
Newman La *ALTN* GU34 .... 165 G3
Newmans Ct *FNM* GU9 .... 122 D2
New Mill La *CHIN* RG24 .... 71 H4
New Mill Rd *HTWY* RG27 .... 35 H6
Newnham La *CHIN* RG24 .... 71 H6
HTWY RG27 .... 73 H7
Newnham Pk *HTWY* RG27 .... 73 L8 ②
Newnham Rd *HTWY* RG27 .... 73 J8
New Odiham Rd *ALTN* GU34 .... 164 C4
New Paddock La *ALTN* GU34 .... 165 H2
Newport Cl *NWBY* RG14 .... 3 H2
Newport Rd *ASHV* GU12 .... 7 K4

NWBY RG14 .... 3 H1
New Rd *BLKW* GU17 .... 58 B4
BSTK RG21 .... 4 F9
CWTH RG45 .... 37 M3
FLET GU13 .... 99 G2
HASM GU27 .... 216 C3
HTWY RG27 .... 56 B1
HTWY RG27 .... 73 M7
HTWY RG27 .... 75 H2
BOR GU35 .... 189 H7
NFNM GU10 .... 124 C2
NWBY RG14 .... 3 G7
ODIM RG29 .... 96 B4
RWIN SO21 .... 136 A6
SHST GU47 .... 37 K8
STOK SO20 .... 150 B8
TADY RG26 .... 49 K1
TADY RG26 .... 50 B5
New Road Hl *THLE* RG7 .... 16 E5
New St *AND* SP10 .... 9 J4
BSTK RG21 .... 4 E9
STOK SO20 .... 174 E6
THLE RG7 .... 32 D8
Newton La *ALTN* GU34 .... 186 D8
Newton Rd *FARN* GU14 .... 79 G2
Newton Wy *NFNM* GU10 .... 124 B1
Newtown *TADY* RG26 .... 29 K7
Newtown Cl *AND* SP10 .... 8 D6
Newtown Rd *LIPH* GU30 .... 214 D3
NWBY RG14 .... 2 E8
SHST GU47 .... 37 L8
New Wokingham Rd
CWTH RG45 .... 37 K2
Nickel Cl *WINC* SO23 .... 11 K6
Nideggan Cl *STHA* RG19 .... 15 C5
Nightingale Cl *FARN* GU14 .... 77 M2
WINW SO22 .... 226 A2
Nightingale Dr *FRIM* GU16 .... 79 K5 ③
Nightingale Gdns *CHIN* RG24 .... 70 B8
HTWY RG27 .... 73 M7
SHST GU47 .... 37 L8
Nightingale La *THLE* RG7 .... 32 A2
Nightingale Ri *OVTN* RG25 .... 112 A1
Nightingale Rd *ASHV* GU12 .... 101 M5
BOR GU35 .... 189 K6 ③
The Nightingales *NWBY* RG14 .... 2 F9
Nightjar Cl *NFNM* GU10 .... 99 G8
Nine Mile Ride *EWKG* RG40 .... 36 A2
Norden Cl *BSTK* RG21 .... 4 F5
Norlands *NTHA* RG18 .... 14 F3
Norman Cl *BOR* GU35 .... 189 K5 ③
Norman Court La *RAND* SP11 .... 130 E4
Normandy St *ALTN* GU34 .... 164 E4
Norman Rd *WINC* SO23 .... 226 E2
Normanton Rd *BSTK* RG21 .... 4 F2
Normay Ri *NWBY* RG14 .... 24 F3
Normoor Rd *THLE* RG7 .... 19 J7
Norn Hl *BSTK* RG21 .... 5 H5
Norn Hill Cl *BSTK* RG21 .... 5 H5
Norris Br *FARN* GU14 .... 77 K8
Norris Cl *BOR* GU35 .... 189 G7
Norris Hill Rd *FLET* GU13 .... 99 J1
Northanger Cl *ALTN* GU34 .... 164 D4
North Av *FNM* GU9 .... 123 G5
Northbrook Av *WINC* SO23 .... 11 K8
Northbrook Cl *WINC* SO23 .... 11 L8
Northbrook Rd *ALDT* GU11 .... 7 G5
Northbrook St *NWBY* RG14 .... 2 E5
North Cl *ASHV* GU12 .... 7 M4
FARN GU14 .... 58 D8
Northcote Rd *ASHV* GU12 .... 101 K1
FARN GU14 .... 78 B2
Northcroft La *NWBY* RG14 .... 2 C6
North Downs Wy *NFNM* GU10 .... 123 K6
RGUW GU3 .... 125 G3
North Dr *WINW* SO22 .... 202 A3
THLE RG7 .... 19 G1
North End La *NALR* SO24 .... 230 C1
Northern Av *AND* SP10 .... 9 H3
NWBY RG14 .... 13 K2
North Farm Rd *FARN* GU14 .... 58 B8
Northfield Cl *ASHV* GU12 .... 7 M3
FLET GU13 .... 99 G2 ②
Northfield La *ALTN* GU34 .... 164 B8
Northfield Rd *FLET* GU13 .... 99 G2
NTHA RG18 .... 14 E4
North Fryerne *YTLY* GU46 .... 37 L8
Northgate Dr *CBLY* GU15 .... 59 K1
Northgate La *OVTN* RG25 .... 116 A7
North Gate Rd *FARN* GU14 .... 78 F6
North Hill Cl *WINW* SO22 .... 10 F3
Northington Rd *RWIN* SO21 .... 181 G7
Northlands Dr *WINC* SO23 .... 11 G3
North La *ALDT* GU11 .... 101 G5
RSAL SP5 .... 195 M8
Northmead *FARN* GU14 .... 78 E4
North Pde *BOR* GU35 .... 189 H2
North Rd *ALDT* GU11 .... 101 G1
ASHV GU12 .... 101 J4
WINC SO23 .... 179 G8
Northside La *NALR* SO24 .... 207 J1
North St *KSCL* SO20 .... 47 J6
NALR SO24 .... 207 G3
Northumberland Rd
BOR GU35 .... 189 J4
North View Rd *TADY* RG26 .... 50 A1
North Walls *WINC* SO23 .... 11 J7
North Warnborough St
ODIM RG29 .... 96 A5
North Wy *AND* SP10 .... 107 K6
Northway *NTHA* RG18 .... 14 F3
NWBY RG14 .... 3 G6
Northwood Dr *NWBY* RG14 .... 3 H2
Norton Cl *NWBY* RG14 .... 24 F2 ②
Norton Ride *CHIN* RG24 .... 93 L1
Norton Rd *CBLY* GU15 .... 59 M4
THLE RG7 .... 33 M6
Norwich Av *CBLY* GU15 .... 59 H5
Novello Cl *KEMP* RG22 .... 115 J1
Nuffield Dr *SHST* GU47 .... 38 C7
Nuffield Rd *WHIT* RG2 .... 35 J1
Nugee Ct *CWTH* RG45 .... 37 L3 ⑩
Nuns Rd *WINC* SO23 .... 11 H4
Nuns Wk *WINC* SO23 .... 11 H4

Nursery Cl *CHIN* RG24 .... 71 M5 ⑩
FLET GU13 .... 77 J8
FRIM GU16 .... 79 J1
HTWY RG27 .... 73 M6 ②
Nursery Fld *LISS* GU33 .... 236 D5
Nursery Gdns *WINW* SO22 .... 10 B1
Nursery Rd *ALTN* GU34 .... 164 F4
NALR SO24 .... 206 C3
Nutbane La *RAND* SP11 .... 105 L1
Nutbean La *THLE* RG7 .... 34 C3
Nutbourne *FNM* GU9 .... 6 B7
Nutchers Dro *RAND* SP11 .... 198 F5 ③
Nutcombe La *GSHT* GU26 .... 192 B7
Nuthatch Cl *NFNM* GU10 .... 122 A1
Nutley Cl *BOR* GU35 .... 189 J6 ②
YTLY GU46 .... 57 G3
Nutley La *OVTN* RG25 .... 114 E7
Nutmeg Ct *FARN* GU14 .... 77 M3 ⑩
Nutshell La *FNM* GU9 .... 122 F2

O

Oak Av *SHST* GU47 .... 38 A7
Oak Bank *AND* SP10 .... 9 H8
Oak Cl *DEAN* RG23 .... 91 G7
NTID SP9 .... 102 F1
OVTN RG25 .... 111 M1
RSAL SP5 .... 218 B1
STOK SO20 .... 151 G4
Oak Dr *NWBY* RG14 .... 2 C6
Oakdene *ALTN* GU34 .... 164 D3
THLE RG7 .... 19 K5
Oak Dr *THLE* RG7 .... 19 J6
Oaken Copse *CBLY* GU15 .... 59 M1
FLET GU13 .... 99 G4
Oaken Copse Crs *FARN* GU14 .... 78 E1
Oak End Wy *THLE* RG7 .... 17 M4
Oaken Gv *NWBY* RG14 .... 13 G8
Oak Farm Cl *BLKW* GU17 .... 57 M3
Oakfield Rd *BLKW* GU17 .... 58 B4
TADY RG26 .... 30 B7
Oakfields Cl *KSCL* SO20 .... 46 C4
Oak Grove Crs *CBLY* GU15 .... 58 C2
Oak Hanger Cl *HTWY* RG27 .... 74 A7 ⑩
Oakhanger Rd *BOR* GU35 .... 188 F3
Oak Hl *NALR* SO24 .... 206 C3
Oakhill Rd *BOR* GU35 .... 190 E3
Oakhurst *GSHT* GU26 .... 192 A5
Oakland Av *FNM* GU9 .... 6 A7
Oakland Rd *WHCH* RG28 .... 110 B3
Oaklands *HASM* GU27 .... 216 F1 ②
RWIN SO21 .... 178 C4
YTLY GU46 .... 57 G2
Oaklands *WINW* SO22 .... 226 A2
Oaklands La *CWTH* RG45 .... 37 K2
Oaklands Rd *DEAN* RG23 .... 92 B2
Oaklea *ASHV* GU12 .... 101 K3
Oaklea Dr *HTWY* RG27 .... 35 H6
Oaklea Gdns *TADY* RG26 .... 52 A6
Oakley Dr *FLET* GU13 .... 76 F8
Oakley La *DEAN* RG23 .... 91 G6
Oakley Rd *CBLY* GU15 .... 58 E4
BOR GU35 .... 189 J3
NWBY RG14 .... 3 L1
ROMY SO51 .... 221 K6
TADY RG26 .... 67 L5
Oakmead *TADY* RG26 .... 51 K4
Oakridge Rd *BSTK* RG21 .... 4 B3
Oak Rd *FARN* GU14 .... 78 F5
The Oaks *ALTN* GU34 .... 184 F1
FLET GU13 .... 76 C7
TADY RG26 .... 29 K8
YTLY GU46 .... 57 G3
Oak Tree Cl *ASHV* GU12 .... 7 M6
LISS GU33 .... 236 F4
Oak Tree La *HASM* GU27 .... 216 A2
Oak Tree Rd *BOR* GU35 .... 189 H7
RG19 .... 15 H6
Oaktrees *ASHV* GU12 .... 101 J7
FNM GU9 .... 122 E2 ③
Oak Tree Vw *FNM* GU9 .... 123 G2
Oaktree Wy *SHST* GU47 .... 37 K7
Oakway *ASHV* GU12 .... 101 H8
NFNM GU10 .... 144 F4
Oakway Dr *FRIM* GU16 .... 59 H7
Oakwood *NALR* SO24 .... 206 C5
Oakwood Cl *RGUW* RG24 .... 71 L5
FLET GU13 .... 98 F4
Oasthouse Dr *FARN* GU14 .... 77 H4
Oast House La *FNM* GU9 .... 123 G3
Oast La *ALDT* GU11 .... 7 G7
Oban Cl *DEAN* RG23 .... 90 F6
O'bee Gdns *TADY* RG26 .... 29 H7
Obelisk Wy *CBLY* GU15 .... 58 F2
Oberursel Wy *ALDT* GU11 .... 6 D1 ⑩
Ochil Cl *KEMP* RG22 .... 92 A5
O'connor Rd *ALDT* GU11 .... 101 G1
Octavia Hl *WINW* SO22 .... 226 C2
Octavian Cl *KEMP* RG22 .... 115 G1
Oddfellows Rd *NWBY* RG14 .... 2 D5
Odette Gdns *TADY* RG26 .... 29 L7
Odiham Rd *HTWY* RG27 .... 34 A7
HTWY RG27 .... 96 F1
NFNM GU10 .... 98 E8
THLE RG7 .... 33 M5
Officers Rw *TADY* RG26 .... 52 A6
Oglander Rd *WINC* SO23 .... 11 H3
O'gorman Av *FARN* GU14 .... 78 E6
Okingham Cl *SHST* GU47 .... 38 A7 ③
Olaf Cl *AND* SP10 .... 107 G4 ⑧
Old Acre Rd *ALTN* GU34 .... 164 D6
Old Barn La *NFNM* GU10 .... 169 L6
Old Barn Rd *OVTN* RG25 .... 113 K7 ⑩
Old Bath Rd *NWBY* RG14 .... 2 B1
Oldberg Gdns *KEMP* RG22 .... 92 E8 ③
Old Bisley Rd *FRIM* GU16 .... 59 K6
Old Brickfield Rd *ALDT* GU11 .... 7 G7
Oldbury Cl *FRIM* GU16 .... 59 J8 ③
Old Church La *FNM* GU9 .... 147 G1
Old Coach Rd *NTID* SP9 .... 103 G8
Old Common Rd *BSTK* RG21 .... 93 J4
Old Common Wy *RAND* SP11 .... 80 E6

Old Compton La *FNM* GU9 .... 123 H7
Oldcorne Hollow *HTWY* RG27 .... 56 D3
Old Cove Rd *FARN* GU14 .... 77 M5
Old Cross Tree Wy *ASHV* GU12 .... 101 M8
Old Dean Rd *CBLY* GU15 .... 59 G1
Old Down Cl *KEMP* RG22 .... 91 M7
Olde Farm Dr *BLKW* GU17 .... 57 L3
Old English Dr *AND* SP10 .... 106 E4
Old Farm Pl *ASHV* GU12 .... 101 J4
Old Farnham La *FNM* GU9 .... 122 F8
NFNM GU10 .... 121 K7
Oldfield Vw *HTWY* RG27 .... 75 H3 ③
Old Frensham Rd *NFNM* GU10 .... 147 G2
Old Gdns *WINW* SO22 .... 10 F2
Old Green La *CBLY* GU15 .... 58 F1
Old Guildford Rd *FARN* GU14 .... 79 L3
Old Haslemere Rd *HASM* GU27 .... 216 F3
Old Heath Wy *FNM* GU9 .... 122 F1 ③
The Old Hl *RAND* SP11 .... 153 L2 ⑩
Old Kempshott La *KEMP* RG22 .... 91 M5
Old Kennels Cl *WINW* SO22 .... 225 M5
Old Kennels La *RWIN* SO21 .... 225 K7
Old Kiln Cl *NFNM* GU10 .... 169 J6
Old Kiln La *NFNM* GU10 .... 169 J6
Old La *ALDT* GU11 .... 6 E7
ASHV GU12 .... 101 H5
NFNM GU10 .... 168 B4
STHA RG19 .... 28 B7
Old Litten La *PSF* GU32 .... 235 H5
Old London Rd *STOK* SO20 .... 174 F5
Old Micheldever Rd
RAND SP11 .... 131 M3
Old Mill Pl *HASM* GU27 .... 216 C1
Old Newtown Rd *NWBY* RG14 .... 2 D7 ⑩
Old Odiham Rd *ALTN* GU34 .... 142 C5
The Old Orch *FNM* GU9 .... 122 C8
ODIM RG29 .... 118 C4
Old Palace Farm *STOK* SO20 .... 198 F6
Old Park Cl *FNM* GU9 .... 122 D2
Old Park La *FNM* GU9 .... 122 C1
Old Park Rd *NALR* SO24 .... 207 K5
Old Pasture Rd *FRIM* GU16 .... 59 J5
Old Pharmacy Ct *CWTH* RG45 .... 37 M4 ⑧
Old Pond Cl *FRIM* GU16 .... 58 E7
Old Portsmouth Rd *CBLY* GU15 .... 59 K4
Old Potbridge Rd *HTWY* RG27 .... 74 F7
The Old Quarry *HASM* GU27 .... 216 C4
Old Reading Rd *BSTK* RG21 .... 5 G7
Old Rectory Dr *ASHV* GU12 .... 101 M4
Old Rectory Gdns *FARN* GU14 .... 79 G4 ⑧
WINC SO23 .... 203 J2 ②
Old Salisbury Rd *RAND* SP11 .... 130 A3
Old Sawmill La *CWTH* RG45 .... 37 M2
The Old Sawmills *HUNG* RG17 .... 22 B2
Old School Cl *ASHV* GU12 .... 101 K5
FLET GU13 .... 76 F7 ⑩
HTWY RG27 .... 75 J2 ②
Old School La *YTLY* GU46 .... 56 F7
LISS GU33 .... 236 E4
Old School Rd *HTWY* RG27 .... 73 K8
Old Station Ap *WINC* SO23 .... 11 K8
Old Station Rd *RWIN* SO21 .... 204 D1
Old Station Wy *BOR* GU35 .... 188 F3
Old Stockbridge Rd
RAND SP11 .... 150 A2
STOK SO20 .... 150 F3
Old Stoke Rd *RWIN* SO21 .... 178 F2
Old Vicarage La *STOK* SO20 .... 198 F5
Old Vyne La *TADY* RG26 .... 49 J7
Old Welmore *YTLY* GU46 .... 57 H3
Old Winton Rd *AND* SP10 .... 9 J7
Old Wokingham Rd *CWTH* RG45 .... 37 M1
Oldwood Cha *FARN* GU14 .... 77 L5
Old Worting Rd *KEMP* RG22 .... 92 B4
Oleander Cl *CWTH* RG45 .... 37 J1
Olive Gv *RAND* SP11 .... 149 K3
Oliver Ri *ALTN* GU34 .... 164 E4
Oliver's Battery Crs
WINW SO22 .... 226 A4
Oliver's Battery Gdns
WINW SO22 .... 226 A5
Oliver's Battery Rd North
WINW SO22 .... 226 A3
Oliver's Battery Rd South
WINW SO22 .... 226 A5
Olivers Cl *TADY* RG26 .... 51 M6
Oliver's La *TADY* RG26 .... 51 M4
Oliver's Wk *CHIN* RG24 .... 93 L1
Omega *KEMP* RG22 .... 165 G5
Omer's Ri *THLE* RG7 .... 19 K5
Onslow Cl *CHIN* RG24 .... 71 K7
Openfields *BOR* GU35 .... 190 B2
Orange Gv *RAND* SP11 .... 149 K3
Orange La *STOK* SO20 .... 150 B6
Orbit Cl *EWKG* RG40 .... 36 C2
Orchard Cl *ASHV* GU12 .... 101 K3
FARN GU14 .... 58 C7
FNM GU9 .... 6 F9
NALR SO24 .... 206 C4
NWBY RG14 .... 15 M3
RWIN SO21 .... 178 A5
THLE RG7 .... 16 F6
Orchard End *NFNM* GU10 .... 146 C5
Orchardene *NWBY* RG14 .... 3 H2
Orchard Gdns *ALDT* GU11 .... 7 K6
Orchard Ga *SHST* GU47 .... 37 K8
Orchard La *ALTN* GU34 .... 164 F4
Orchard Rd *AND* SP10 .... 8 C3
FARN GU14 .... 78 D4
FNM GU9 .... 6 F9
KEMP RG22 .... 92 B4
RWIN SO21 .... 178 A5
THLE RG7 .... 31 L3
Orchard Wy *ALDT* GU11 .... 7 H5
CBLY GU15 .... 58 E6
Orchid Dr *RAND* SP11 .... 80 E7
Ordnance Rd *ALDT* GU11 .... 7 H1
NTID SP9 .... 102 E2
Oregon Wk *EWKG* RG40 .... 36 A1 ⑩
Oriel Hl *CBLY* GU15 .... 59 G4
Orient Dr *WINW* SO22 .... 202 B5
Orkney Cl *CHIN* RG24 .... 71 J7
Orwell Cl *FARN* GU14 .... 78 B1

Osborne Cl *ALTN* GU34 .... 164 C5
BSTK RG21 .... 4 C5
Osborne Dr *FLET* GU13 .... 99 G1
Osborne Rd *AND* SP10 .... 8 F6
FARN GU14 .... 78 F8
Osborn Cl *FNM* GU9 .... 123 G4
Osborn Wy *HTWY* RG27 .... 74 A8
Osler Cl *TADY* RG26 .... 51 L5
Osnaburgh Hl *CBLY* GU15 .... 58 E3
Osprey Cl *KEMP* RG22 .... 91 L7
Osprey Rd *KEMP* RG22 .... 91 L7
Otterbourne Crs *TADY* RG26 .... 49 L2
Otter Cl *CWTH* RG45 .... 37 K1
Ouse Ct *AND* SP10 .... 107 H6
Oval Rd *ROMY* SO51 .... 220 E8
The Oval *LISS* GU33 .... 236 E4
Overbridge Sq *NWBY* RG14 .... 3 M8
Overdale Ri *FRIM* GU16 .... 59 H5
Overdale Wk *BOR* GU35 .... 189 J7
Overlord Cl *CBLY* GU15 .... 38 F8 ⑩
Overton Cl *ALDT* GU11 .... 7 J9
Overton Rd *RWIN* SO21 .... 136 A6
Owen Rd *NWBY* RG14 .... 13 L2
Owen's Rd *WINW* SO22 .... 10 E4
Owlsmoor Rd *SHST* GU47 .... 38 A8
Ox Dro *RAND* SP11 .... 103 L6
RAND SP11 .... 107 M6
RWIN SO21 .... 178 E4
Ox Drove Ri *RAND* SP11 .... 108 A5
Oxdrove Wy *NALR* SO24 .... 160 C6
OVTN RG25 .... 161 J2
RWIN SO21 .... 159 J1
Oxenden Ct *NFNM* GU10 .... 101 H8 ②
Oxenden Rd *NFNM* GU10 .... 101 H8
Oxford Rd *FARN* GU14 .... 78 F7
NWBY RG14 .... 2 D1
RWIN SO21 .... 156 B5
SHST GU47 .... 38 B6
Oxford St *NWBY* RG14 .... 2 D2
Oxlease La *OVTN* RG25 .... 140 D1
Oyster Cl *KEMP* RG22 .... 114 F1

P

Packenham Rd *BSTK* RG21 .... 92 E4
Pack La *DEAN* RG23 .... 91 G5
KEMP RG22 .... 91 M6
Packway *FNM* GU9 .... 147 G3
Paddock Cl *CBLY* GU15 .... 59 J4
RWIN SO21 .... 178 D4 ②
Paddock Ct *HTWY* RG27 .... 75 H3 ②
Paddock Fld *STOK* SO20 .... 154 A3
Paddockfields *CHIN* RG24 .... 94 A1
Paddock Rd *KEMP* RG22 .... 92 C5
NWBY RG14 .... 2 D8
The Paddock *CWTH* RG45 .... 37 K2
GSHT GU26 .... 191 K4 ②
HASM GU27 .... 192 D8
HTWY RG27 .... 75 J1
KSCL RG20 .... 47 H6
BOR GU35 .... 190 B3
NWBY RG14 .... 3 K5
WINC SO23 .... 203 H2
Paddock Wy *HASM* GU27 .... 193 K6
LIPH GU30 .... 214 E2
NALR SO24 .... 206 B4
Padwick Cl *BSTK* RG21 .... 92 E4
Padworth La *THLE* RG7 .... 18 B5
Padworth Rd *THLE* RG7 .... 19 H8
Paget Cl *CBLY* GU15 .... 59 L1
Paice La *ALTN* GU34 .... 184 D4
Paices Hl *THLE* RG7 .... 29 K4
Painters Pightle *HTWY* RG27 .... 73 L7
Palace Cl *STOK* SO20 .... 198 E6
Palace Ga *ODIM* RG29 .... 96 C5
Pale La *HTWY* RG27 .... 76 A4
Palestine Rd *RAND* SP11 .... 149 J2
Palmer Cl *BSTK* RG21 .... 5 G2
Palmer Dr *AND* SP10 .... 107 J8 ②
Palmer's La *THLE* RG7 .... 19 K6
Palmerston Cl *FARN* GU14 .... 78 A5 ③
Palm Hall Cl *WINC* SO23 .... 11 L8
Pamber Heath Rd *TADY* RG26 .... 30 A8
Pamber Rd *THLE* RG7 .... 30 D7
Pankridge St *NFNM* GU10 .... 121 J1
Pannells *NFNM* GU10 .... 147 G3
Pan's Gdns *CBLY* GU15 .... 59 J4
Pantile Dr *HTWY* RG27 .... 74 E7
Pantings La *KSCL* RG20 .... 44 C2
Papermakers *OVTN* RG25 .... 112 A1
Paper Mill La *ALTN* GU34 .... 164 F4
The Parade *NWBY* RG14 .... 29 L7 ②
Paradise Wy *THLE* RG7 .... 16 F1
Parchment St *WINC* SO23 .... 11 G7
Pardown *DEAN* RG23 .... 114 A1
Parfitts Cl *FNM* GU9 .... 122 D6
Parish Cl *ASHV* GU12 .... 101 L7
FNM GU9 .... 122 D2
Parish Rd *FARN* GU14 .... 78 E8
Park Av *CBLY* GU15 .... 58 F4
CHIN RG24 .... 94 A3
NTHA RG18 .... 15 G4
WINC SO23 .... 11 H6
Park Cl *DEAN* RG23 .... 90 F6
HASM GU27 .... 193 J7
BOR GU35 .... 167 H7
NFNM GU10 .... 145 K6
WINC SO23 .... 11 G2
Park Close Rd *ALTN* GU34 .... 164 F3
Park Dro *STOK* SO20 .... 150 D4
Park End *NWBY* RG14 .... 3 K5
Parkfields *YTLY* GU46 .... 57 G3
Park Gdns *BSTK* RG21 .... 93 J5
Park Hl *FLET* GU13 .... 98 E4
Parkhill Cl *BLKW* GU17 .... 58 A4
Parkhill Rd *BLKW* GU17 .... 58 A4
Parkhouse Rd *NTID* SP9 .... 126 C1
Parkhurst Flds *NFNM* GU10 .... 169 J7
Parkway Gv *FNM* GU9 .... 6 C6
Park La *ALTN* GU34 .... 144 B4
CBLY GU15 .... 58 F3 ③
CHIN RG24 .... 94 A3
EWKG RG40 .... 35 K5
MFD/CHID GU8 .... 193 H1
NALR SO24 .... 208 A3
NTHA RG18 .... 15 G3

RAND SP11 .... 127 M4
RSAL SP5 .... 194 F8
RWIN SO21 .... 203 J2
THLE RG7 .... 31 M6
Park Pl FLET GU13 .... 98 E3
Park Rd ALDT GU11 .... 7 H7
CBLY GU15 .... 58 F5
FARN GU14 .... 79 H7
FNM GU9 .... 123 G4
WINW SO22 .... 10 E2
HASM GU27 .... 216 F2
NTID SP9 .... 102 E2
SHST GU47 .... 57 M1
Park Rw FNM GU9 .... 122 E5
Parkside FNM GU9 .... 122 F2
Parkside La NALR SO24 .... 207 M6
Parkside Rd BSTK RG21 .... 93 H5
NTHA RG18 .... 15 G3
Parkside Gdns WINW SO22 .... 202 B6
Parkstone Dr CBLY GU15 .... 58 F4
Parkstone Rd NALR SO24 .... 208 C6
Park St CBLY GU15 .... 58 F2
BOR GU35 .... 189 J5
NWBY RG14 .... 2 E2
Parkview Cl AND SP10 .... 8 C1
Parkway CBLY GU15 .... 58 F5
CWTH RG45 .... 37 K3
Parkwood Cl CHIN RG24 .... 71 L4 9
Parliament Pl WINW SO22 .... 226 B4
Parnell La ROMY SO51 .... 222 F6
Parsonage Cl ALTN GU34 .... 186 D5
Parsonage Hl RSAL SP5 .... 218 A1
Parsonage Wy FRIM GU16 .... 59 H7
Parsons Cl FLET GU13 .... 98 E3
HASM GU27 .... 192 F6
NWBY RG14 .... 2 A5
WHIT RG2 .... 35 K1
Parsons Fld SHST GU47 .... 37 L8
Parsons Gn HASM GU27 .... 192 F8
Parsons La GSHT GU26 .... 191 M2
Part La THLE RG7 .... 33 M5
Partridge Av YTLY GU46 .... 56 F2
Partridge Cl FRIM GU16 .... 59 H7
NFNM GU10 .... 99 G8 2
RWIN SO21 .... 155 J1
Partridge Down WINW SO22 .... 226 A5
Partridge Gn ALTN GU34 .... 164 E3
Paschal Rd CBLY GU15 .... 39 J8
Passfield Rd LIPH GU30 .... 190 B8
The Pastures NALR SO24 .... 230 B2
WINC SO23 .... 179 C7
Paternoster Rw WINC SO23 .... 11 H8
Paterson Cl FRIM GU16 .... 59 M5 9
KEMP RG22 .... 115 H1
Paterson Rd LISS GU33 .... 213 H6
Pathfields Cl HASM GU27 .... 217 G1
The Pathfinders FARN GU14 .... 77 M5 9
Patrick's Cl LISS GU33 .... 236 F4
Patten Av YTLY GU46 .... 56 F3
Pattinson Crs RAND SP11 .... 129 H1
Paul Cl ALDT GU11 .... 6 B5
Paulet Pl CHIN RG24 .... 94 A2
WINW SO22 .... 226 D3
Paul's Fld HTWY RG27 .... 36 D3
Pavilion Rd ALDT GU11 .... 6 A3
ALDT GU11 .... 99 M2
The Pavilions End CBLY GU15 .... 59 C5 2
Pavy Cl STHA RG19 .... 15 J6
Pawley Cl NFNM GU10 .... 124 C1
Pawmers Md FLET GU13 .... 98 C5
Pax Hl NFNM GU10 .... 144 E4
Paxton Cl KEMP RG22 .... 115 G1 2
Paynes Cl STHA RG19 .... 27 H8
STOK SO20 .... 197 G1
Paynesdown Rd STHA RG19 .... 14 E5
Paynes Hay Rd ROMY SO51 .... 223 E8
Paynes La STOK SO20 .... 197 G1
Peabody Rd FARN GU14 .... 79 G7
Peachey Dr STHA RG19 .... 15 J6
Peach Gv RAND SP11 .... 149 K3
Peach Tree Cl FARN GU14 .... 78 D1
Peacock Pl WINC SO23 .... 11 M7
Peakfield NFNM GU10 .... 168 F1
Pearman Dr AND SP10 .... 107 J8
Pear Tree Av FLET GU13 .... 76 E6 2
Pear Tree Cl BOR GU35 .... 189 L4
Pear Tree La NFNM GU10 .... 146 C5
NWBY RG14 .... 13 M3
Pear Tree Rd BOR GU35 .... 189 L3
Peatmoor Cl FLET GU13 .... 76 D6
Peat Moor Cl FLET GU13 .... 76 D6 9
Pebble Hl HUNG RG17 .... 22 E1
Peddlars Gv YTLY GU46 .... 57 H2
Peel Av FRIM GU16 .... 79 K1
Peel Ct HTWY RG27 .... 75 H2 2
Peel Gdns KSCL RG20 .... 47 H5
Pegasus Av ASHV GU12 .... 101 H5
Pegasus Cl HASM GU27 .... 216 A3
STHA RG19 .... 14 D4
Pegasus Rd FARN GU14 .... 78 C1 2
FARN GU14 .... 78 E6
Peggotty Pl SHST GU47 .... 38 B6 3
Pelham Cl CHIN RG24 .... 94 A3
BOR GU35 .... 189 J7
Pelham Pl NFNM GU10 .... 146 D4 9
Pelican Cl AND SP10 .... 9 J3
Pelican La NWBY RG14 .... 2 E2
Pelican Rd TADY RG26 .... 30 B6
Pelton Rd BSTK RG21 .... 4 B6
Pembroke Broadway
CBLY GU15 .... 58 F3
Pembroke Ct THLE RG7 .... 19 M5
Pembroke Rd DEAN RG23 .... 92 A3 2
WINW SO22 .... 202 B3
NWBY RG14 .... 2 D3
Pemerton Rd BSTK RG21 .... 5 H4
WINW SO22 .... 10 B1
Pen Cl AND SP10 .... 9 M6
Pendennis Cl DEAN RG23 .... 92 A4
Pendle Gn ROMY SO51 .... 220 E7
Penfold Cft FNM GU9 .... 123 J4
Pengilly Rd FNM GU9 .... 122 E6
Peninsula Rd WINW SO22 .... 10 D9
Pennefather's Rd ALDT GU11 .... 100 C5
Pennels Cl LIPH GU30 .... 238 C6
Pennine Wy FARN GU14 .... 78 A1
KEMP RG22 .... 92 B5

Penn Rd NWBY RG14 .... 13 G3
Penns Wd FARN GU14 .... 79 G7
Penns Yd FNM GU9 .... 122 E6 2
Penny La STOK SO20 .... 174 F7
Penny's Hatch KSCL RG20 .... 47 K6
Penrhyn Cl ASHV GU12 .... 7 G4
Penrith Rd BSTK RG21 .... 4 C9
Penrose Cl NWBY RG14 .... 13 J3
Penryn Dr BOR GU35 .... 190 F3 9
Pensford Cl CWTH RG45 .... 37 L1
Penshurst Ri FRIM GU16 .... 59 J8
Pentland Cl KEMP RG22 .... 92 A5
Penton La AND SP11 .... 105 L2
Penwith Dr HASM GU27 .... 216 A4
Penwood Hts KSCL RG20 .... 24 D8
Penwood Rd KSCL RG20 .... 24 F5
Peperham Rd HASM GU27 .... 192 F5
Perham Crs RAND SP11 .... 80 F6
Perins Cl NALR SO24 .... 206 A4
Periwinkle Cl BOR GU35 .... 189 M3 2
Perowne St ALDT GU11 .... 6 C2
Perring Av FARN GU14 .... 58 B8
Perring Rd FARN GU14 .... 78 D6
Perry Dr FLET GU13 .... 76 E6
Perryhill Dr SHST GU47 .... 37 J7
Perry Wy FNM GU9 .... 122 E1
BOR GU35 .... 190 C4
Pershore Rd CHIN RG24 .... 71 G7
Perth Cl RAND SP11 .... 103 J1
Peterhouse Cl SHST GU47 .... 38 C6
Petersfield Cl RAND SP11 .... 72 A4 9
Petersfield Rd BOR GU35 .... 189 H7 2
LISS GU33 .... 213 G3
NALR SO24 .... 207 L4
NALR SO24 .... 230 C4
RWIN SO21 .... 227 M2
RWIN SO23 .... 11 L9
Petrel Cft KEMP RG22 .... 91 M8 2
Petty's Brook Rd CHIN RG24 .... 71 L4
Petunia Cl KEMP RG22 .... 91 M8
Petworth Cl FRIM GU16 .... 59 J8 2
KEMP RG22 .... 115 G2 2
Petworth Rd HASM GU27 .... 217 G3
Pevensey Wy FRIM GU16 .... 59 K8
Pheaben's Fld TADY RG26 .... 51 K5 9
Pheasant Cl KEMP RG22 .... 91 L8
NTID SP9 .... 102 F2 2
RWIN SO21 .... 155 J1
Pheasant Copse FLET GU13 .... 76 C6
Pheby Rd KEMP RG22 .... 92 C6
Philips Crs BOR GU35 .... 190 C3
Phillips Cl BOR GU35 .... 190 C3
NFNM GU10 .... 101 H8
Phoenix Ct HTWY RG27 .... 75 G4
KSCL RG20 .... 47 J6
Phoenix Park Ter BSTK RG21 .... 4 E6
Phoenix Ter HTWY RG27 .... 75 G4
Pickaxe La ODIM RG29 .... 118 E8
Picketts Hl BOR GU35 .... 167 M7
Picket Twenty RAND SP11 .... 107 K8
Pickford St ALDT GU11 .... 7 G2
Picton Cl CBLY GU15 .... 59 M1
Picton Rd AND SP10 .... 130 E3
Pierrefondes Av FARN GU14 .... 78 D3
Pigeon Cl TADY RG26 .... 51 M6
Pigeonhouse Fld RWIN SO21 .. 156 B4 9
Pigeons Farm Rd STHA RG19 .... 26 A1
Pike Cl ALDT GU11 .... 7 K1
Pike St NWBY RG14 .... 3 H1
Pilcot Rd HTWY RG27 .... 98 A2
Pilgrims Cl FNM GU9 .... 122 D8
Pilgrims Ga WINW SO22 .... 10 C5
Pilgrims Vw ASHV GU12 .... 101 M8
Pilgrims Wy AND SP10 .... 9 L2
BOR GU35 .... 190 B3 9
Pimpernel Pl NTHA RG18 .... 15 J4 9
Pimpernel Wy CHIN RG24 .... 93 L1
Pinchcut THLE RG7 .... 19 K5
Pinchington La NWBY RG14 .... 25 K1 9
Pindar Pl NWBY RG14 .... 14 B3 9
Pine Av CBLY GU15 .... 59 G4
Pine Bank GSHT GU26 .... 192 B4
Pine Cl ASHV GU12 .... 101 K2
CBLY GU15 .... 58 B1
WINW SO22 .... 226 A5
RWIN SO21 .... 178 D4
STOK SO20 .... 151 G4
Pine Dr BLKW GU17 .... 58 B5
EWKG RG40 .... 36 D1
THLE RG7 .... 31 J2
Pinefields Cl CWTH RG45 .... 37 L3 2
Pine Gv FLET GU13 .... 99 G3
NFNM GU10 .... 147 H2
Pinehill Ri SHST GU47 .... 37 L8
Pinehill Rd CWTH RG45 .... 37 L4
BOR GU35 .... 189 K6
Pinehurst TADY RG26 .... 49 L1
Pinehurst Av FARN GU14 .... 78 E6
Pine Mount Rd CBLY GU15 .... 59 G4
Pine Rdg NWBY RG14 .... 13 M3
Pine Ridge Dr NFNM GU10... 146 E6 2
Pine Ridge Rd THLE RG7 .... 19 K6
Pine Rd ALTN GU34 .... 185 H5
Pines Rd FLET GU13 .... 76 E6
LIPH GU30 .... 214 B4
The Pines AND SP10 .... 8 C4
CBLY GU15 .... 59 J1
Pine Vw BOR GU35 .... 190 E2
Pine View Cl FNM GU9 .... 123 K3
HASM GU27 .... 192 F8
Pine Wk LISS GU33 .... 236 F2
Pinewood Av CWTH RG45 .... 37 K4 2
Pinewood Cl SHST GU47 .... 37 J8
TADY RG26 .... 29 G7
Pinewood Crs FARN GU14 .... 77 M3 2
Pinewood Dr KSCL RG20 .... 25 K6
Pinewood Gdns BAGS GU19 .... 39 M5
Pinewood Hl FLET GU13 .... 76 F6
Pinewood Pk FARN GU14 .... 77 M1
Pinkerton Rd KEMP RG22 .... 92 B6
Pinks La TADY RG26 .... 29 H7
Pinnell Cl KEMP RG22 .... 114 F2
Pintail Cl KEMP RG22 .... 114 E1 2
Pipers Cft FLET GU13 .... 98 F4 2
Pipers La STHA RG19 .... 15 J7
Pipers Patch FARN GU14 .... 78 E4 2
Pipers Wy STHA RG19 .... 15 K6

Pipit Cl STHA RG19 .... 14 E5
Pipsons Cl YTLY GU46 .... 57 G2
Pirbright Rd FARN GU14 .... 78 F5
Pitcairn Cl CHIN RG24 .... 71 H6
Pitfield La THLE RG7 .... 31 M4
Pitfold Av HASM GU27 .... 216 A2
Pitfold Cl HASM GU27 .... 216 B2 2
Pither Rd ODIM RG29 .... 96 B8
Pitman Cl KEMP RG22 .... 92 A6
Pittard Rd BSTK RG21 .... 92 E5
Pitter Cl WINW SO22 .... 202 A3
Pitt La NFNM GU10 .... 168 D2
Pitton Rd RSAL SP5 .... 194 D8
Pitts La AND SP10 .... 9 G8
Pitt Wy FARN GU14 .... 78 C3
Pit Wk AMSY SP4 .... 148 C1
Place La RWIN SO21 .... 226 C6
Plantation Rd AND SP10 .... 8 C6
LISS GU33 .... 237 G6
NTID SP9 .... 102 E3
TADY RG26 .... 29 H6
The Plantation RSAL SP5 .... 194 D3
Plantation Wy BOR GU35 .... 188 F8
Plassey Rd NTID SP9 .... 102 D1
Pleasant Hl TADY RG26 .... 29 L8
Plough Gdns STOK SO20 .... 197 G2
Plough La NFNM GU10 .... 146 B5
Plough Rd YTLY GU46 .... 57 H1
Plough Wy WINW SO22 .... 226 C4
Plover Cl AND SP10 .... 107 G6 2
KEMP RG22 .... 91 M7
Plovers Down WINW SO22 .... 226 A5
Plovers Wy ALTN GU34 .... 164 F2
Plumer Rd LISS GU33 .... 213 H5
Plumpton Rd NWBY RG14 .... 3 J8
Plumpton Wy ALTN GU34 .... 164 E6 2
Poachers Fld ODIM RG29 .... 118 F5
Pococks La LISS GU33 .... 235 L1
Poets Wy WINW SO22 .... 10 B6
Poffley Pl STHA RG19 .... 15 K5 2
Poland La ODIM RG29 .... 96 D7
Polden Cl FARN GU14 .... 78 B1
Polkerris Wy FLET GU13 .... 99 G4 2
Pollard Gv CBLY GU15 .... 59 M4 2
Polmear Cl FLET GU13 .... 99 G4
Pond Cl NWBY RG14 .... 25 C1
OVTN RG25 .... 111 M2
Pond Cft YTLY GU46 .... 57 H2
Pond La NFNM GU10 .... 168 F4 2
Pond Rd FARN GU14 .... 78 E6
BOR GU35 .... 190 D4
TADY RG26 .... 51 M6
Pondtail Cl FLET GU13 .... 77 H8
Pondtail Gdns FLET GU13 .... 77 H8
Pondtail Rd FLET GU13 .... 77 H8
Pondview Cl FLET GU13 .... 77 H6
Pookies La ALTN GU34 .... 166 A7
Pool Rd ALDT GU11 .... 7 K8
HTWY RG27 .... 75 H1
Poors Farm Rd CHIN RG24 .... 72 D8
Popes Cl HASM GU27 .... 216 F1
Popes Md HASM GU27 .... 216 F1
Popham La OVTN RG25 .... 113 K8
Poplar Cl FRIM GU16 .... 79 K5
HTWY RG27 .... 52 C7
TADY RG26 .... 29 G8
Poplar Pl NWBY RG14 .... 13 K3
Poplars Cl FARN GU14 .... 77 M3
Poplar Wk FNM GU9 .... 123 G1
Popley Wy CHIN RG24 .... 71 J3
Poppy Dr NTHA RG18 .... 15 J4
Poppy Flds CHIN RG24 .... 71 M8
Poppyhills Rd CBLY GU15 .... 39 J8
Porchester Cl AND SP10 .... 106 C5
Porchester Rd NWBY RG14 .... 2 E8
Porlock Cl STHA RG19 .... 15 G6 2
Portacre Ri BSTK RG21 .... 92 E5
Portal Cl RAND SP11 .... 130 A1
Portal Rd WINC SO23 .... 227 G2
Porter Cl ODIM RG29 .... 96 B8 2
Porter End KEMP RG22 .... 92 E7
Porters Cl AND SP10 .... 8 B3
OVTN RG25 .... 114 C7
Portesbery Rd CBLY GU15 .... 59 G2
Portesbery Hill Dr CBLY GU15 ... 59 G1
Portiswood Cl TADY RG26 .... 30 A8 2
Portland Dr FLET GU13 .... 98 E4
Portland Gv ALDT GU11 .... 9 G5
Portland Sq LISS GU33 .... 236 E4
Portsmouth Cl CBLY GU15 .... 59 K2
FRIM GU16 .... 59 H5
LIPH GU30 .... 213 L5
LIPH GU30 .... 214 B7
Portway TADY RG26 .... 29 G7
THLE RG7 .... 33 M6
Portway Pl AND SP10 .... 8 A5
Portway Pl DEAN RG23 .... 92 A3
Portway Rd AND SP10 .... 8 A5
Post Horn La HTWY RG27 .... 73 K7
Posting House Ms NWBY RG14 ... 2 B7
Post Office La OVTN RG25 .... 114 C7
TLHT RG30 .... 19 M3
Post Office Rd HUNG RG17 .... 22 B4
Potbridge Rd ODIM RG29 .... 74 B8
Pot La CHIN RG24 .... 72 E8
Potley Hill Rd YTLY GU46 .... 57 J3
Potteries La FRIM GU16 .... 79 J5
The Potteries FARN GU14 .... 78 A2
Potters Crs ASHV GU12 .... 101 L5
Potters Fld LISS GU33 .... 236 F4
Potters Ga FNM GU9 .... 122 D6
Potters La HTWY RG27 .... 52 E5
Pottery Dro STOK SO20 .... 149 M6
Pottery La HUNG RG17 .... 22 A3
NFNM GU10 .... 146 C2 2
Poultons Cl OVTN RG25 .... 111 M2
Poultons Rd OVTN RG25 .... 111 M1
Pound Cl ALTN GU34 .... 164 F3 2
Pound Hl NALR SO24 .... 206 A7
Pound La KSCL RG20 .... 45 H2
NWBY RG14 .... 13 G4
STHA RG19 .... 14 D5
Pound Meadow HTWY RG27 .... 52 D8
Pound Rd ASHV GU12 .... 7 H3
OVTN RG25 .... 112 A1

STOK SO20 .... 150 B6
WINC SO23 .... 179 H8
Pound St NWBY RG14 .... 2 D6
Poveys Md KSCL RG20 .... 47 K6
Poyle Rd NFNM GU10 .... 124 D1
Poynings Crs BSTK RG21 .... 93 H6
Poynters Cl AND SP10 .... 8 F1
Poyntz Rd OVTN RG25 .... 111 M1
Prentice Cl FARN GU14 .... 58 E8 2
Preston Pl NWBY RG14 .... 14 A3 2
Prestwick La HASM GU27 .... 193 K6
Pretoria Cl LISS GU33 .... 213 H6
Pretoria Rd RAND SP11 .... 81 G7
Priestley Rd BSTK RG21 .... 92 D1
Primrose Dr HTWY RG27 .... 75 H1
Primrose Gdns FARN GU14 .... 78 B5 2
KEMP RG22 .... 115 G3
Primrose La LISS GU33 .... 237 J4
Primrose Rd RAND SP11 .... 80 E6
Primrose Wy SHST GU47 .... 37 L7
Primula Rd BOR GU35 .... 189 K5 2
Prince Charles Cl RAND SP11 .... 80 E6
Prince Charles Crs FARN GU14 ... 58 E8
Prince Dr SHST GU47 .... 37 K7
Prince Hold Rd STHA RG19 .... 14 D5
Prince's Av ALDT GU11 .... 100 F3
Princes Cl BOR GU35 .... 189 H7
Princess Av KEMP RG22 .... 92 D5
Princess Dr ALTN GU34 .... 164 C5
Princess Mary Gdns RAND SP11 ... 80 E6
Priestley Rd BSTK RG21 .... 92 D1
Princes' Crs KEMP RG22 .... 92 D5
Princes Wy CBLY GU15 .... 58 F3
Princes Wy ALDT GU11 .... 6 E1
Prinstead Cl WINC SO23 .... 227 G2 2
Prior Croft Cl CBLY GU15 .... 59 K4
Prior End CBLY GU15 .... 59 K3
Prior Rd CBLY GU15 .... 59 L4
Priors Barton WINC SO23 .... 226 E3
Priors Cl FARN GU14 .... 58 E8
KSCL RG20 .... 47 J6 2
Priors Dean Rd WINW SO22 .... 202 C4
Priors Keep FLET GU13 .... 77 H8
Prior's La BLKW GU17 .... 57 K3
Priors Rd TADY RG26 .... 29 K7
Priors Wy WINW SO22 .... 226 A5
Priors Wd CWTH RG45 .... 37 G4
HASM GU27 .... 216 C2
Priory Cl FLET GU13 .... 76 C8
Priory Gdns CHIN RG24 .... 94 A1
Priory La HTWY RG27 .... 75 H4
WINC SO23 .... 147 G8
WHCH RG28 .... 110 F1
Priory Pl NWBY RG14 .... 25 L2
Priory Rd NWBY RG14 .... 2 L8
Priory St FARN GU14 .... 79 H8
Pritchard Cl STHA RG19 .... 26 A1 2
Privet La RAND SP11 .... 104 E4
Privet Rd BOR GU35 .... 189 M3
Privett Cl CHIN RG24 .... 71 M8
Privett Rd PSF GU32 .... 234 C6
Propeller Rd FARN GU14 .... 78 E6
Prospect Av FARN GU14 .... 78 E2
Prospect Pl NWBY RG14 .... 2 E7
Prospect Rd ASHV GU12 .... 101 K3
FARN GU14 .... 78 D4
BSTK RG21 .... 4 A4
NFNM GU10 .... 146 B5
Provident Wy BSTK RG21 .... 4 E7
Pruetts La LISS GU33 .... 236 F4
Puckridge Gate Rd ALDT GU11 ... 100 A2
Puckridge Hill Rd ALDT GU11 ... 100 B3
Puckshott Wy HASM GU27 .... 193 G8
Pudding La WINC SO23 .... 203 G4
Puffers Wy NWBY RG14 .... 2 A5
Puffin Cl KEMP RG22 .... 114 E2
Pug's Hole RSAL SP5 .... 195 M8
Punshott La NALR SO24 .... 232 D5
Purbrook Rd TADY RG26 .... 29 K8
Purcell Cl KEMP RG22 .... 92 E7
Purcell Rd CWTH RG45 .... 37 L1
Purley Wy FRIM GU16 .... 59 H8
Purmerend Cl FARN GU14 .... 77 M3 2
Puttenham Hl RGUW GU3 .... 125 M3
Puttenham La MFD/CHID GU8 . 125 M7
Puttenham Rd CHIN RG24 .... 71 M5
NFNM GU10 .... 124 E4
Puttock Cl HASM GU27 .... 216 A3 2
Pyestock Crs FARN GU14 .... 77 M4 2
Pyotts Copse CHIN RG24 .... 71 M7
Pyotts Ct CHIN RG24 .... 71 M7
Pyotts Hl CHIN RG24 .... 71 M7

NWBY RG14 .... 3 G6
ODIM RG29 .... 96 B5 2
WHCH RG28 .... 110 C5
Queen St FRIM GU16 .... 7 M1
Queensway FRIM GU16 .... 79 K1
Queenwood Rd STOK SO20 .... 197 G2
Quennells Hl NFNM GU10 .... 146 B2
Quilter Rd KEMP RG22 .... 92 B8
Quince Tree Wy HTWY RG27 .... 74 A7

R

Rack Cl AND SP10 .... 9 J5
Rack Close Rd ALTN GU34 .... 164 D5
Rackfield HASM GU27 .... 216 A1
Rackstraw Rd SHST GU47 .... 38 A7
SHST GU47 .... 58 A1
Radar Rd FARN GU14 .... 78 A7
Radcliffe Cl FRIM GU16 .... 79 J1
Radford Cl FNM GU9 .... 123 H3
Radford Gdns BSTK RG21 .... 92 E6
Radical Ride EWKG RG40 .... 36 C1
Raeburn Cl NALR SO24 .... 230 C3
Raeburn Wy SHST GU47 .... 38 A7
Rae Rd FARN GU14 .... 78 E7
Raf Gate Rd FARN GU14 .... 78 E7 2
Ragdale THLE RG7 .... 19 K5
Raghill THLE RG7 .... 30 A2
Raglan Cl ASHV GU12 .... 7 J4
FRIM GU16 .... 59 J8
Ragmore La PSF GU32 .... 234 D3
Railside THLE RG7 .... 17 J6
Railway Rd LISS GU33 .... 213 J5
NWBY RG14 .... 3 G5
Rainbow Cl CHIN RG24 .... 94 B3
Rainham Cl KEMP RG22 .... 114 E1
Rakemakers ALTN GU34 .... 165 J1 2
LISS GU33 .... 236 F4
Raleigh Wy CBLY GU15 .... 59 J5
Ram Aly STHA RG19 .... 27 M8
Ramblers Md RAND SP11 .... 105 L5 2
Ramillies Cl ALDT GU11 .... 101 H1
The Ramparts AND SP10 .... 8 C9
Rampton Rd WHCH RG28 .... 110 C4
Rampton's Meadow TADY RG26... 50 A1
Ramsay Cl CBLY GU15 .... 39 L8 2
Ramsay Rd WINC SO23 .... 203 H1
Ramsdell Cl TADY RG26 .... 49 L1
Ramsdell Rd TADY RG26 .... 48 B7
TADY RG26 .... 51 G1
Ramsholt Cl OVTN RG25 .... 113 K7 2
Rances Wy WINW SO22 .... 226 D3
Randolph Dr FARN GU14 .... 77 M5
Ranelagh Rd WINC SO23 .... 226 D2
Range Ride CBLY GU15 .... 58 C1
Range Rd EWKG RG40 .... 36 C1
FARN GU14 .... 77 M7
Range Vw SHST GU47 .... 38 B8
Rankine Cl FNM GU9 .... 6 F9
Rapallo Cl FARN GU14 .... 78 F4 2
Raphael Cl BSTK RG21 .... 93 J5
Rapley Cl CBLY GU15 .... 39 J8
Ratcliffe Rd FARN GU14 .... 58 C8
Ravel Cl KEMP RG22 .... 92 D7
Ravelin Cl NFNM GU10 .... 121 J5 2
Raven Cl NTID SP9 .... 102 F2
YTLY GU46 .... 56 E2 2
Raven Rd HTWY RG27 .... 73 M7
Ravens Cft HTWY RG27 .... 74 B7 2
Raven Sq ALTN GU34 .... 164 E2
Ravenswood Av CWTH RG45 .... 37 H3
Ravenswood Dr CBLY GU15 .... 59 K3
Ravensworth Rd THLE RG7 .... 31 H2
Rawlings Rd HTWY RG27 .... 74 A8
Rawlinson Rd CBLY GU15 .... 58 C2
Rayleigh Rd BSTK RG21 .... 4 D8
Reading Rd BLKW GU17 .... 57 L4
CHIN RG24 .... 5 J1
CHIN RG24 .... 71 K6
EWKG RG40 .... 35 J4
FARN GU14 .... 79 H8
HTWY RG27 .... 36 A8
HTWY RG27 .... 52 C8
HTWY RG27 .... 54 B8
HTWY RG27 .... 56 C1
HTWY RG27 .... 73 M6 2
HTWY RG27 .... 74 A6
THLE RG7 .... 19 J8
THLE RG7 .... 30 C3
TLHT RG30 .... 19 M4
YTLY GU46 .... 56 D1
Reading Rd North FLET GU13 .... 76 F7
Reading Rd South FLET GU13 .... 98 F1
Read's Fld ALTN GU34 .... 185 G6
Rebecca Cl FLET GU13 .... 98 D5
Recreation Cl FARN GU14 .... 58 C7 2
Recreation Rd AND SP10 .... 9 K4
NFNM GU10 .... 146 B5
ODIM RG29 .... 96 B6
RAND SP11 .... 80 E6
THLE RG7 .... 19 K6
Rectory Cl NWBY RG14 .... 2 C7
SHST GU47 .... 37 J8 2
TADY RG26 .... 49 M2
Rectory Hl RSAL SP5 .... 195 M7
RSAL SP5 .... 219 J5
Rectory La LIPH GU30 .... 215 G1
NFNM GU10 .... 145 G4
RWIN SO21 .... 180 F8
STOK SO20 .... 197 G2
TADY RG26 .... 47 M8
Rectory Pl RAND SP11 .... 105 J6
Rectory Rd DEAN RG23 .... 90 D7
FARN GU14 .... 78 F4
HTWY RG27 .... 73 M8
THLE RG7 .... 30 C1
Reculver Wy AND SP10 .... 106 C5
Redan Gdns ASHV GU12 .... 7 J2
Redan Rd ASHV GU12 .... 7 J2
Redbridge Dr AND SP10 .... 8 B4
Redbridge La ALTN GU34 .... 208 F2
CHIN RG24 .... 5 M8

Redcrest Gdns *CBLY* GU15 ..... 59 J3
Redenham Dro *RAND* SP11 ..... 81 M8
Redfield Ct *NWBY* RG14 ..... 3 M2
Redfields La *NFNM* GU10 ..... 98 D7
Redgauntlet *EWKG* RG40 ..... 36 B2 🔢
Redhearne Flds *NFNM* GU10 ..... 169 H6
Red Hl *ALTN* GU34 ..... 185 G3
  HTWY RG27 ..... 54 D7
  KSCL RG20 ..... 63 M2
  RAND SP11 ..... 63 H6
Redlands La *NFNM* GU10 ..... 121 J1
Red La *BOR* GU35 ..... 190 E1
  OVTN RG25 ..... 140 B4
  RSAL SP5 ..... 219 M1
  THLE RG7 ..... 30 A3
Redmayne *CBLY* GU15 ..... 59 M4 🔢
Red Post La *RAND* SP11 ..... 105 K8
Red Rice Rd *RAND* SP11 ..... 130 B7
Redvers Buller Rd *ALDT* GU11 ..... 100 F1
Redwing Cl *KEMP* RG22 ..... 114 C1
Redwood La *ALTN* GU34 ..... 162 F8
Redwoods Wy *FLET* GU13 ..... 99 G4
Reed Cl *ALDT* GU11 ..... 101 G2
Reeds La *LISS* GU33 ..... 237 J2
The Reeds Rd *NFNM* GU10 ..... 147 G7
Rees Rd *RWIN* SO21 ..... 178 B6
Reeves Rd *ASHV* GU12 ..... 7 J3
Regent Cl *FLET* GU13 ..... 76 F8
Regents Pl *SHST* GU47 ..... 37 M8
Regent St *FLET* GU13 ..... 76 F8
Regent Wy *FRIM* GU16 ..... 59 J7
Regiment Cl *FARN* GU14 ..... 77 M5 🔢
Regnum Dr *NWBY* RG14 ..... 13 J8
Reith Wy *AND* SP10 ..... 106 A7
Rembrandt Cl *BSTK* RG21 ..... 93 J5
Remembrance Gdns
  CHIN RG24 ..... 71 L6 🔢
Remembrance Rd *NWBY* RG14 ..... 2 A6
Renoir Cl *BSTK* RG21 ..... 93 J5
Renown Wy *CHIN* RG24 ..... 71 L4 🔢
Reservoir Rd *FARN* GU14 ..... 78 A7
Restormel Cl *DEAN* RG23 ..... 92 A2
Reuben's Crs *TADY* RG26 ..... 49 L1
Revelstoke Av *FARN* GU14 ..... 78 E2
Rewlands Dr *WINW* SO22 ..... 202 B4
Reynards Cl *TADY* RG26 ..... 29 L8
Reynolds Cl *BSTK* RG21 ..... 93 J4
Reynolds Gn *SHST* GU47 ..... 58 A2 🔢
Reyntiens Vw *ODIM* RG29 ..... 96 D5 🔢
Rhine Banks *FARN* GU14 ..... 78 A3
Rhododendron Rd *FRIM* GU16 ..... 59 L8
Ribble Pl *FARN* GU14 ..... 78 B2
Ribble Wy *BSTK* RG21 ..... 5 J8
Richard Cl *FLET* GU13 ..... 98 D1
Richards Cl *ASHV* GU12 ..... 101 K3 🔢
Richborough Dr *AND* SP10 ..... 106 B5
Richmond Cl *FARN* GU14 ..... 78 A5
  FLET GU13 ..... 98 E2
  FRIM GU16 ..... 59 L7
  BOR GU35 ..... 189 J7 🔢
Richmond Rd *BSTK* RG21 ..... 4 D5
  SHST GU47 ..... 38 B8
Riddings La *STHA* RG19 ..... 27 M6
Rideway Cl *CBLY* GU15 ..... 58 F8
Ridge Cl *KEMP* RG22 ..... 115 H3
Ridge La *HTWY* RG27 ..... 73 K6
Ridge Moor Cl *GSHT* GU26 ..... 192 B3
Ridges Cl *RAND* SP11 ..... 84 C8 🔢
Ridgeway *WINW* SO22 ..... 226 B3
Ridgeway Hill Rd *NFNM* GU9 ..... 122 F8
Ridgeway Rd *FNM* GU9 ..... 146 F1
The Ridgeway *ALTN* GU34 ..... 164 E6
The Ridings *FRIM* GU16 ..... 59 L5
  LISS GU33 ..... 237 G4
Ridley Cl *FLET* GU13 ..... 98 E1
Ridleys Piece *ODIM* RG29 ..... 118 F4
Rifle Wy *FARN* GU14 ..... 77 M5 🔢
Riley La *CHIN* RG24 ..... 94 A1
Riley Rd *RWIN* SO21 ..... 178 D6
Rimbault Cl *ALDT* GU11 ..... 101 G1 🔢
Rimes's La *TADY* RG26 ..... 49 J2
Ringlet Wy *WINC* SO23 ..... 11 M7
Ringsgreen La *PSF* GU32 ..... 234 F5
Ringshall Gdns *TADY* RG26 ..... 51 K5
Ringway East *CHIN* RG24 ..... 5 K3
Ringway North *CHIN* RG24 ..... 92 D1
Ringway South *BSTK* RG21 ..... 93 H5
Ringway West *DEAN* RG23 ..... 92 D1
  KEMP RG22 ..... 92 D4
Ringwood Rd *BLKW* GU17 ..... 57 M2 🔢
  FARN GU14 ..... 78 F1
Ripon Cl *BLKW* GU17 ..... 57 J7
Ripplesmore Cl *SHST* GU47 ..... 37 L8 🔢
The Rise *CWTH* RG45 ..... 37 J3
  EWKG RG40 ..... 35 K6
Rivar Rd *MARL* SN8 ..... 20 B6
River Cl *ALTN* GU34 ..... 185 G6
Riverdale *NFNM* GU10 ..... 146 B1
Riverhead *NALR* SO24 ..... 207 H4
River La *FNM* GU9 ..... 146 B1
Rivermead Rd *CBLY* GU15 ..... 58 E6
Rivermede *BOR* GU35 ..... 189 K4
River Pde *AND* SP10 ..... 9 L1 🔢
River Pk *NWBY* RG14 ..... 3 M3
River Rd *YTLY* GU46 ..... 56 E1
Rivers Cl *FARN* GU14 ..... 79 H7
Riverside Cl *CHIN* RG24 ..... 94 A1
  FARN GU14 ..... 78 C3
  LISS GU33 ..... 236 E4
  OVTN RG25 ..... 89 C8
Riverside Gn *STOK* SO20 ..... 198 F5
Riverside Wy *CBLY* GU15 ..... 58 D5
River View *LISS* GU33 ..... 153 L4
River Wy *AND* SP10 ..... 9 K1
Robert Mays Rd *ODIM* RG29 ..... 96 B6 🔢
Roberts Cl *WINC* SO23 ..... 179 G7
Robertsfield *STHA* RG19 ..... 14 C5
Robertson Cl *NWBY* RG14 ..... 13 L8 🔢
Robertson Rd *FARN* GU14 ..... 206 B4 🔢
Robertson Wy *ASHV* GU12 ..... 101 J7
Roberts Rd *ASHV* GU12 ..... 7 J3
  CBLY GU15 ..... 58 D2
  LISS GU33 ..... 213 H6
  RAND SP11 ..... 80 D7

  ..... 133 J8
Robert Wy *FRIM* GU16 ..... 79 J5
Robin Cl *ALTN* GU34 ..... 164 F2
  ASHV GU12 ..... 101 J2
  KEMP RG22 ..... 91 M8
  THLE RG7 ..... 19 L5 🔢
Robin Hill Dr *CBLY* GU15 ..... 59 K5
Robin Hood Cl *FARN* GU14 ..... 78 D1
Robin La *SHST* GU47 ..... 37 M8
Robins Cl *NWBY* RG14 ..... 25 J1
Robins Grove Crs *YTLY* GU46 ..... 56 E2
Robins Hl *HUNG* RG17 ..... 22 B2
Robinson Cl *BOR* GU35 ..... 189 K6
Robin Wy *AND* SP10 ..... 107 G6
Rochester Cl *KEMP* RG22 ..... 92 A8 🔢
Rochester Gv *FLET* GU13 ..... 76 E8
Rochford Rd *BSTK* RG21 ..... 4 C8
Rockbourne Rd *WINW* SO22 ..... 202 C4
Rockdale Dr *GSHT* GU26 ..... 192 A5 🔢
The Rockery *FARN* GU14 ..... 78 A5
Rocket Rd *FARN* GU14 ..... 78 A7
Rockfield Wy *SHST* GU47 ..... 38 A8 🔢
Rock Gdns *ALDT* GU11 ..... 6 C3
Rockingham Rd *NWBY* RG14 ..... 2 C5
Rockmoor La *RAND* SP11 ..... 41 J6
Rodfield La *RWIN* SO21 ..... 229 G5
Roding Cl *BSTK* RG21 ..... 5 J8
Rodmel Ct *FARN* GU14 ..... 79 H7
Roebuts Cl *NWBY* RG14 ..... 13 J8
Roedeer Copse *HASM* GU27 ..... 216 B2
Roe Downs Rd *ALTN* GU34 ..... 184 E2
Roentgen Rd *CHIN* RG24 ..... 5 M4
Rogers Ct *ALTN* GU34 ..... 164 E4
Rokeby Cl *NWBY* RG14 ..... 25 K1
Roke La *ODIM* RG29 ..... 96 F8
Rokes Pl *YTLY* GU46 ..... 56 D2
Roman Ride *CWTH* RG45 ..... 37 G3
Roman Rd *DEAN* RG23 ..... 92 A3
  STOK SO20 ..... 174 C5
Romans Fld *THLE* RG7 ..... 30 E7 🔢
Romans Ga *THLE* RG7 ..... 30 C7
Romans' Rd *WINC* SO23 ..... 226 E2
Roman Wy *AND* SP10 ..... 107 G4
  DEAN RG23 ..... 91 M3
  FNM GU9 ..... 123 H4
  NTHA RG18 ..... 14 D4
  RWIN SO21 ..... 133 K8
The Romany *FARN* GU14 ..... 77 K7
Romayne Cl *FARN* GU14 ..... 78 D3
Romney Rd *FARN* GU14 ..... 78 B7
Romsey Cl *ALDT* GU11 ..... 7 K9
  BLKW GU17 ..... 57 M2 🔢
  CHIN RG24 ..... 70 F7
Romsey Rd *WINW* SO22 ..... 10 C8
  RAND SP11 ..... 131 H8
  STOK SO20 ..... 172 C1
  STOK SO20 ..... 197 G3
  STOK SO20 ..... 198 D7
Rookery La *STOK* SO20 ..... 197 H2
The Rookery *WHCH* RG28 ..... 110 B3 🔢
Rook La *RWIN* SO21 ..... 157 M5
Rooksbury Rd *AND* SP10 ..... 8 D8
Rooksdown Av *CHIN* RG24 ..... 70 B8
Rooksdown La *CHIN* RG24 ..... 70 B7
Rooks Down Rd *WINW* SO22 ..... 226 C3
Rooksfield *KSCL* RG20 ..... 26 D6
Rooksnest La *HUNG* RG17 ..... 22 D3
Rookswood *ALTN* GU34 ..... 164 E3
  KSCL RG20 ..... 26 D6
Rookswood Cl *HTWY* RG27 ..... 74 A7 🔢
Rookswood Av *SHST* GU47 ..... 38 B7
Rookwood La *ALTN* GU34 ..... 184 B6
Rope Wk *STHA* RG19 ..... 14 F5
Ropley Cl *TADY* RG26 ..... 49 K1
Ropley Rd *ALTN* GU34 ..... 209 L3
Rorkes Drift *FRIM* GU16 ..... 79 J4
Rosary Gdns *YTLY* GU46 ..... 57 G2 🔢
Rose Bay Gdns *HTWY* RG27 ..... 74 B6 🔢
Roseberry Cl *KEMP* RG22 ..... 115 G3
Rosebery Rd *NALR* SO24 ..... 206 B3
Rose Cl *KEMP* RG22 ..... 92 A8
Rosedale *ASHV* GU12 ..... 7 J2
Rosedale Gdns *STHA* RG19 ..... 14 F6
Rosedene Gdns *FLET* GU13 ..... 76 E6
Rosedene La *SHST* GU47 ..... 58 B1 🔢
Rose Gdns *FARN* GU14 ..... 78 A5
Rosehip Wy *CHIN* RG24 ..... 93 L1
Rose Hodson Pl *DEAN* RG23 ..... 92 B1
Rosemary Av *ASHV* GU12 ..... 79 K8
Rosemary Cl *FARN* GU14 ..... 78 A3
Rosemary Dr *TADY* RG26 ..... 49 L2
Rosemary Gdns *BLKW* GU17 ..... 57 M3
Rosemary La *BLKW* GU17 ..... 57 M2
  NFNM GU10 ..... 146 B4
Rose Wk *FLET* GU13 ..... 76 E6
Rosewarne Cl *WINC* SO23 ..... 10 F1
Rosewood Rd *BOR* GU35 ..... 189 M3
Rosier Cl *STHA* RG19 ..... 15 J6
Ross Cl *BSTK* RG21 ..... 92 F6 🔢
Rossini Cl *KEMP* RG22 ..... 92 D8
Rossmore Gdns *ALDT* GU11 ..... 6 B4
Rothay Ct *BSTK* RG21 ..... 5 J8
Rotherbank Farm La
  LISS GU33 ..... 236 E2
Rother Cl *SHST* GU47 ..... 37 M8
Rother Rd *FARN* GU14 ..... 78 B2
Rotherwick La *HTWY* RG27 ..... 53 G8
Rotherwick Rd *TADY* RG26 ..... 49 L1
Rotten Green Rd *HTWY* RG27 ..... 76 D2
Rotten Hl *OVTN* RG25 ..... 111 K2
The Roundabouts *LISS* GU33 ..... 236 F3 🔢
Roundaway La *RAND* SP11 ..... 82 D6
Round Cl *YTLY* GU46 ..... 57 J3
Round End *NWBY* RG14 ..... 25 K1
Roundfield *THLE* RG7 ..... 15 L2 🔢
Roundhuts Ri *WINC* SO23 ..... 11 M7
Roundmead Rd *BSTK* RG21 ..... 4 C9
Roundway *CBLY* GU15 ..... 59 M2
Roundway Cl *CBLY* GU15 ..... 59 M2
Roundway Ct *AND* SP10 ..... 8 C5
Rounton Rd *FLET* GU13 ..... 98 F1
Rowan Cha *NFNM* GU10 ..... 146 D3 🔢
Rowan Cl *CBLY* GU15 ..... 39 J8
  FLET GU13 ..... 77 H7
  RWIN SO21 ..... 178 D4
Rowan Dl *FLET* GU13 ..... 98 E3
Rowan Dr *CWTH* RG45 ..... 37 M1

  NWBY RG14 ..... 13 K3
Rowan Rd *TADY* RG26 ..... 49 M1
Rowans Cl *FARN* GU14 ..... 58 B7
Rowanside Cl *BOR* GU35 ..... 190 F4
The Rowans *GSHT* GU26 ..... 192 A6 🔢
Rowan Wy *TLHT* RG30 ..... 19 L4
Rowcroft Cl *ASHV* GU12 ..... 101 K2
Rowcroft Rd *WHIT* RG2 ..... 35 J1
Rowdell Cottages *NALR* SO24 ..... 208 B3
Rowhill Av *ALDT* GU11 ..... 6 C5
Rowhill Crs *ALDT* GU11 ..... 6 C6
Rowhills Cl *FNM* GU9 ..... 6 C6
Rowland's La *THLE* RG7 ..... 30 F3
Rowlings Rd *WINW* SO22 ..... 202 C5
Roxbee Cox Rd *FARN* GU14 ..... 77 K7
Roxburgh Cl *CBLY* GU15 ..... 59 M4
Roxburghe Cl *BOR* GU35 ..... 189 J6
Royal Cl *DEAN* RG23 ..... 114 F3
Royale Cl *ALDT* GU11 ..... 7 K6 🔢
Royce Cl *AND* SP10 ..... 106 A7
Roydon Cl *WINW* SO22 ..... 226 C3
Rozelle Cl *WINW* SO22 ..... 201 M3
Rubens Cl *BSTK* RG21 ..... 93 J4
Rudd Hall Ri *CBLY* GU15 ..... 59 G5
Rudd La *ROMY* SO51 ..... 222 C8
Rudland Cl *STHA* RG19 ..... 15 G6
Ruffield Cl *WINW* SO22 ..... 202 B5
Rufford Cl *FLET* GU13 ..... 98 F2
Rugby Cl *SHST* GU47 ..... 38 B7 🔢
Rune Dr *AND* SP10 ..... 106 E4
Runwick La *NFNM* GU10 ..... 122 A7
Rupert Rd *NWBY* RG14 ..... 13 J8
Rushden Wy *FNM* GU9 ..... 123 G1
The Rushes *BSTK* RG21 ..... 5 K8
Rushfield Rd *LISS* GU33 ..... 236 E5
Rushmoor Cl *FLET* GU13 ..... 98 F1
Rushmoor Rd *ALDT* GU11 ..... 100 B5
Ruskin Cl *BSTK* RG21 ..... 93 J5
Ruskin Ct *CWTH* RG45 ..... 37 J4 🔢
Russell Cl *BLKW* GU17 ..... 58 A3 🔢
Russell Dr *ROMY* SO51 ..... 221 J8
Russell Rd *NWBY* RG14 ..... 2 B5
  WINC SO23 ..... 11 H3
Russet Cl *NALR* SO24 ..... 206 B4
  NFNM GU10 ..... 124 B1
Russet Gdns *CBLY* GU15 ..... 59 C5
Russet Gld *ALDT* GU11 ..... 6 A4
  FNM GU9 ..... 100 A8
  THLE RG7 ..... 19 L6
Russett Rd *ALTN* GU34 ..... 164 F5
Russetts Dr *FLET* GU13 ..... 76 F8
Rustic Gln *FLET* GU13 ..... 98 E3
Ruth Cl *FARN* GU14 ..... 77 M3
Rutherford Rd *CHIN* RG24 ..... 5 J2
Rutland Cl *ALDT* GU11 ..... 100 D5
Ryan Mt *SHST* GU47 ..... 37 K8
Rydal Cl *FARN* GU14 ..... 78 A5 🔢
  BOR GU35 ..... 189 J3
Rydal Dr *FLET* GU13 ..... 98 D3
  STHA RG19 ..... 14 D5
Ryebeck Rd *FLET* GU13 ..... 98 F3
Rye Cl *FARN* GU14 ..... 77 H3
  FARN GU14 ..... 78 B2
Rye Cft *FLET* GU13 ..... 98 D4
Ryecroft Gdns *BLKW* GU17 ..... 58 B4 🔢
Ryeland Cl *FARN* GU14 ..... 77 H3 🔢
Ryelaw Rd *FLET* GU13 ..... 98 F3
Ryle Rd *FNM* GU9 ..... 122 E8
Ryon Cl *AND* SP10 ..... 106 F4
Ryves Av *YTLY* GU46 ..... 56 D3

S

Sabre Ct *ALDT* GU11 ..... 6 B2
Saddleback Rd *CBLY* GU15 ..... 39 H8
Saddleback Wy *FARN* GU14 ..... 77 G4
Saddlers Cl *RWIN* SO21 ..... 156 B4
Saddlers Scarp *GSHT* GU26 ..... 191 K4
Saddlewood *CBLY* GU15 ..... 58 F4
Sadlers Rd *HUNG* RG17 ..... 21 J2
Saffron Cl *CHIN* RG24 ..... 71 L4
  NWBY RG14 ..... 2 B3
Sagecroft Rd *NTHA* RG18 ..... 14 F3
Sages La *PSF* GU32 ..... 233 H3
Sainfoin La *DEAN* RG23 ..... 91 G8
Sainsbury Cl *AND* SP10 ..... 8 E8
St Andrews Cl *CWTH* RG45 ..... 37 J2
St Andrew's Rd *KEMP* RG22 ..... 92 C5
  BOR GU35 ..... 189 G6
  NTID SP9 ..... 102 D2
St Andrew's Wy *FRIM* GU16 ..... 79 J1
St Annes Cl *WINW* SO22 ..... 226 B3
St Ann's Cl *AND* SP10 ..... 8 F7
  AND SP10 ..... 9 G7 🔢
St Aubins Cl *ALTN* GU34 ..... 185 G6
St Augustine's Cl *ASHV* GU12 ..... 7 M3
St Barbara's Cl *TADY* RG26 ..... 52 A4
St Benedict's Cl *ALDT* GU11 ..... 6 C4
St Catherine's Hl *THLE* RG7 ..... 31 H3
St Catherines Rd *FRIM* GU16 ..... 59 K7
  WINC SO23 ..... 227 G1
St Christophers Cl *ASHV* GU12 ..... 7 L1
  KEMP RG22 ..... 92 B5 🔢
St Christophers Pl *FARN* GU14 ..... 78 C5 🔢
St Christopher's Rd *FARN* GU14 ..... 78 D5 🔢
  HASM GU27 ..... 216 D2
St Clement St *WINC* SO23 ..... 10 F8
St Cross Rd *FNM* GU9 ..... 122 F5 🔢
  WINW SO22 ..... 226 E2 🔢
St David's Cl *FARN* GU14 ..... 58 C8
St David's Rd *KEMP* RG22 ..... 92 D5
  NWBY RG14 ..... 2 D5
St Donats Pl *NWBY* RG14 ..... 2 F6
St Faith's Rd *WINC* SO23 ..... 226 E2
St Gabriels Lea *CHIN* RG24 ..... 71 M5
St George's Av *NWBY* RG14 ..... 2 B4
St George's Cl *FNM* GU9 ..... 123 L2 🔢
St George's Rd *ASHV* GU12 ..... 7 G4
  CBLY GU15 ..... 59 G2
  FNM GU9 ..... 123 L2 🔢

  FNM GU9 ..... 123 G7
  NFNM GU10 ..... 123 L4
  NTID SP9 ..... 102 D2
St George's Rd East *ASHV* GU12 ..... 7 H3
St George's St *WINC* SO23 ..... 11 G7
St Giles *WINC* SO23 ..... 11 G7
St Helens Crs *SHST* GU47 ..... 37 L8 🔢
St Hubert Rd *AND* SP10 ..... 8 D6
St James' Av *FNM* GU9 ..... 123 G4
St James' La *WINC* SO22 ..... 10 D8
St James Rd *FLET* GU13 ..... 76 E8
St James Ter *FNM* GU9 ..... 122 F5
  WINC SO22 ..... 10 E8
St James' Vls *WINC* SO23 ..... 10 E8
St John Cl *TADY* RG26 ..... 51 M6
St Johns Cl *HTWY* RG27 ..... 74 A7 🔢
St Johns Gv *FNM* GU9 ..... 146 E1
St John's Piece *DEAN* RG23 ..... 91 G8
St John's Rd *AND* SP10 ..... 9 J4
  DEAN RG23 ..... 91 G6
  FARN GU14 ..... 78 B4
  FNM GU9 ..... 122 E8
  HTWY RG27 ..... 75 J3
  NWBY RG14 ..... 2 F7
  SHST GU47 ..... 57 L1
  STHA RG19 ..... 14 F5
  THLE RG7 ..... 31 K3
  WINC SO23 ..... 11 K7
St John's St *WINC* SO23 ..... 11 J8
St Joseph's Crs *CHIN* RG24 ..... 71 L6 🔢
St Joseph's Rd *ALDT* GU11 ..... 6 F4
  ASHV GU12 ..... 7 G4
St Just Cl *AMSY* SP4 ..... 148 A3
St Lawrence Rd *ALTN* GU34 ..... 164 E4
St Leonards Rd *RAND* SP11 ..... 128 A7 🔢
St Leonard's Av *CHIN* RG24 ..... 71 M5
St Marks Cl *FARN* GU14 ..... 78 F7 🔢
  STHA RG19 ..... 14 F5
St Marks Pl *FNM* GU9 ..... 122 E1 🔢
St Martin's Cl *WINC* SO23 ..... 11 K7
St Mary's Av *TADY* RG26 ..... 52 A6
St Marys Cl *ALTN* GU34 ..... 164 E6
  SHST GU47 ..... 37 M8
  WINC SO23 ..... 203 H3
St Mary's Ct *BSTK* RG21 ..... 5 C8
St Mary's Meadow
  RAND SP11 ..... 129 M4 🔢
St Mary's Rd *ASHV* GU12 ..... 101 K3
  CBLY GU15 ..... 58 F2 🔢
  HTWY RG27 ..... 75 H3
  KSCL RG20 ..... 47 J8
  LISS GU33 ..... 236 E4
  NWBY RG14 ..... 2 F2
  THLE RG7 ..... 31 K3
St Mary St *WINW* SO22 ..... 226 E2
St Mary's Wy *THLE* RG7 ..... 19 M5 🔢
St Matthews Rd *WINW* SO22 ..... 10 B2
St Michaels Av *NTID* SP9 ..... 102 D3
St Michaels Cl *FLET* GU13 ..... 77 H8
  OVTN RG25 ..... 113 K7
St Michael's La *THLE* RG7 ..... 19 L5
St Michael's Rd *ASHV* GU12 ..... 7 H4
  CBLY GU15 ..... 58 E3 🔢
  FARN GU14 ..... 78 E2
  KEMP RG22 ..... 92 B5
  NWBY RG14 ..... 2 C6
  SHST GU47 ..... 37 J8
  WINC SO22 ..... 226 E2
St Neot's Rd *HTWY* RG27 ..... 55 J1
St Nicholas *WINC* SO23 ..... 203 G2
St Nicholas Cl *FLET* GU13 ..... 76 E7
  RAND SP11 ..... 81 G6 🔢
St Nicholas Ct *KEMP* RG22 ..... 92 E8
St Nicholas' Rd *NWBY* RG14 ..... 2 D5
St Omer Barracks *ALDT* GU11 ..... 101 G3
St Patricks Av *NTID* SP9 ..... 102 C3
St Patrick's La *LISS* GU33 ..... 237 H3
St Patrick's Rd *KEMP* RG22 ..... 92 D5
St Pauls Cl *NFNM* GU10 ..... 124 C1 🔢
St Paul's Hl *WINW* SO22 ..... 10 E6
St Paul's Rd *NFNM* GU10 ..... 146 C2
St Peters Cl *NTID* SP9 ..... 126 D1
St Peter's Gdns *NFNM* GU10 ..... 146 C2 🔢
  YTLY GU46 ..... 57 G2
St Peters Md *ASHV* GU12 ..... 101 L6
St Peter's Pk *ALDT* GU11 ..... 6 A5 🔢
St Peter's Rd *KEMP* RG22 ..... 92 E8
St Peter St *WINC* SO23 ..... 11 G7
St Peter's Wy *FRIM* GU16 ..... 79 J1
St Richards Rd *NWBY* RG14 ..... 13 L3
St Stephens Cl *HASM* GU27 ..... 216 F1
St Stephen's Rd *WINC* SO23 ..... 10 F9
St Swithun St *WINC* SO23 ..... 11 F9
St Thomas Cl *AND* SP10 ..... 106 D5
  BSTK RG21 ..... 4 D4
St Thomas St *WINC* SO23 ..... 10 F9
Salamanca *CWTH* RG45 ..... 37 H3 🔢
Salcombe Rd *NWBY* RG14 ..... 2 A7
Salcot Rd *WINC* SO23 ..... 11 G3
Salerno Cl *ALDT* GU11 ..... 6 F1
Salesian Vw *FARN* GU14 ..... 79 H8
Salisbury Cl *ALTN* GU34 ..... 164 F6
  ODIM RG29 ..... 96 B6 🔢
Salisbury Gdns *KEMP* RG22 ..... 92 B4
Salisbury Gv *FRIM* GU16 ..... 79 K5
Salisbury La *STOK* SO20 ..... 150 B7
Salisbury Rd *AND* SP10 ..... 8 B9
  ASHV GU12 ..... 101 K6
  BLKW GU17 ..... 57 M3 🔢
  FARN GU14 ..... 78 B4
  NALR SO24 ..... 206 B3
  NTID SP9 ..... 126 D3
  RAND SP11 ..... 129 M7
  RAND SP11 ..... 149 K2
  RAND SP11 ..... 151 J2
  STOK SO20 ..... 196 F1
Salisbury Ter *FRIM* GU16 ..... 79 K5
Salmond Rd *RAND* SP11 ..... 106 A8
Salmons Rd *ODIM* RG29 ..... 96 B6
Salters Acres *WINW* SO22 ..... 202 B6
Salters Heath Rd *TADY* RG26 ..... 70 A2
Saltram Rd *FARN* GU14 ..... 79 H6
Samarkand *CBLY* GU15 ..... 59 L4
Sam Whites Hl *HASM* GU27 ..... 130 D4 🔢
San Carlos Ap *ALDT* GU11 ..... 7 K1
Sandbanks Dr *KEMP* RG22 ..... 115 G1 🔢

Sandford Cl *KSCL* RG20 ..... 47 L6
Sandford Ct *ALDT* GU11 ..... 6 B3
Sandford Rd *ALDT* GU11 ..... 6 D2 🔢
  FNM GU9 ..... 122 E1
  TADY RG26 ..... 29 K8
Sandheath Rd *GSHT* GU26 ..... 191 M1
Sand Hl *FARN* GU14 ..... 78 E1
Sandhurst La *BLKW* GU17 ..... 57 L2
Sandhurst Rd *CWTH* RG45 ..... 37 L5
  YTLY GU46 ..... 57 H2
Sandleford Ri *NWBY* RG14 ..... 25 K1
Sandown Cl *ALTN* GU34 ..... 164 F6 🔢
  BLKW GU17 ..... 58 A3
Sandown Crs *ALDT* GU11 ..... 7 C8
Sandown Dr *FRIM* GU16 ..... 59 G6
Sandown Wy *NWBY* RG14 ..... 3 J8
Sandpiper Wy *KEMP* RG22 ..... 114 C1
Sandpit Hl *KSCL* RG20 ..... 24 F5
Sandpit La *THLE* RG7 ..... 8 A8
Sandringham Cl *ALTN* GU34 ..... 164 C5 🔢
Sandringham Wy *FRIM* GU16 ..... 59 J8
Sandrock *HASM* GU27 ..... 216 F2
Sandrock Hill Rd *NFNM* GU10 ..... 146 C2
Sands Rd *NFNM* GU10 ..... 124 A6
  NFNM GU10 ..... 123 M6
The Sands *BOR* GU35 ..... 188 F6
Sandy Hill Rd *FNM* GU9 ..... 122 D1
Sandy La *CBLY* GU15 ..... 59 H8
  FARN GU14 ..... 77 M2
  FLET GU13 ..... 98 F4
  GSHT GU26 ..... 192 C6
  HASM GU27 ..... 193 H7
  HASM GU27 ..... 215 M1
  HTWY RG27 ..... 75 J3
  LISS GU33 ..... 237 K5
  NALR SO24 ..... 146 F7
  NFNM GU10 ..... 169 K2
  SHST GU47 ..... 37 J7
  TADY RG26 ..... 30 A8
Sandys Cl *KEMP* RG22 ..... 92 D5
Sandys Rd *KEMP* RG22 ..... 92 D4
Sankey La *FARN* GU14 ..... 77 J4
Santina Cl *FNM* GU9 ..... 100 A8
Saor Ms *AND* SP10 ..... 8 F4
Sapley La *OVTN* RG25 ..... 111 M1
Sarah Wy *FARN* GU14 ..... 78 E4
Sargood Cl *STHA* RG19 ..... 15 H6 🔢
Sarisbury Cl *TADY* RG26 ..... 29 K8
Sarson Cl *RAND* SP11 ..... 129 G2
Sarson La *RAND* SP11 ..... 129 G1
Sarum Cl *WINW* SO22 ..... 226 B1
  NTID SP9 ..... 102 C8
  STOK SO20 ..... 150 C8
Sarum Hl *BSTK* RG21 ..... 4 D9
Sarum Rd *WINW* SO22 ..... 10 A8
  WINW SO22 ..... 225 J1
  TADY RG26 ..... 29 K7
Sarum Vw *WINW* SO22 ..... 226 A2
Saunton Gdns *FARN* GU14 ..... 78 D2 🔢
Savile Crs *BOR* GU35 ..... 189 J5
Saville Gdns *CBLY* GU15 ..... 59 L3
Savoy Cl *AND* SP10 ..... 9 J6
Savoy Gv *BLKW* GU17 ..... 58 A5
Sawyer Cl *WINW* SO22 ..... 202 B7 🔢
Saxby Cl *THLE* RG7 ..... 19 L5
Saxon Cl *STHA* RG19 ..... 14 D5 🔢
Saxon Cft *FNM* GU9 ..... 122 F7 🔢
Saxon Leas *RSAL* SP5 ..... 194 F2
Saxon Rd *WINC* SO23 ..... 11 G5
Saxon Wy *AND* SP10 ..... 106 E4
  CHIN RG24 ..... 93 L1
Sayers Cl *FRIM* GU16 ..... 79 H1
  NWBY RG14 ..... 13 L3
Sbac Tr *ALDT* GU11 ..... 100 B2
Scarlatti Rd *KEMP* RG22 ..... 92 E8
Scarlet Oaks *CBLY* GU15 ..... 59 H5
Scarlett's Rd *ALDT* GU11 ..... 100 D5
School Cl *RAND* SP11 ..... 61 H3
School Flds *BOR* GU35 ..... 167 G7
School Hl *CWTH* RG45 ..... 38 A4
  NFNM GU10 ..... 124 E4
  NFNM GU10 ..... 146 C2
  SHST GU47 ..... 37 K7
School La *LISS* GU33 ..... 236 E4
  NALR SO24 ..... 207 G3
  NALR SO24 ..... 208 B4
  NFNM GU10 ..... 145 G3
  NFNM GU10 ..... 147 G2
  RGUW GU3 ..... 125 M4
  RWIN SO21 ..... 204 E1
  STOK SO20 ..... 150 E8
  STOK SO20 ..... 196 F1
  THLE RG7 ..... 19 J6
  THLE RG7 ..... 30 E7
  THLE RG7 ..... 34 B5
  WINC SO23 ..... 203 G3
  YTLY GU46 ..... 56 E2
School Rd *GSHT* GU26 ..... 191 L5
  HASM GU27 ..... 216 C3
  BOR GU35 ..... 189 J4
  NFNM GU10 ..... 146 B5
  THLE RG7 ..... 18 C7
  THLE RG7 ..... 34 B4
  TLHT RG30 ..... 19 M2
Schroeder Cl *BSTK* RG21 ..... 92 F6
Schubert Rd *KEMP* RG22 ..... 92 D8
Scotland Cl *ASHV* GU12 ..... 101 K3
Scotland Farm Rd *ASHV* GU12 ..... 101 K3
Scotland Hl *SHST* GU47 ..... 37 K8
Scotland La *HASM* GU27 ..... 216 E3
Scotlands Cl *HASM* GU27 ..... 216 E3
Scotlands Dr *HASM* GU27 ..... 216 E3 🔢
Scotney Rd *BSTK* RG21 ..... 4 E3
Scott Cl *STOK* SO20 ..... 198 F6
Scott's Ct *FARN* GU14 ..... 78 E1
Scrivens Md *STHA* RG19 ..... 15 J5
Scrubbs La *NALR* SO24 ..... 206 F5
Scures Rd *HTWY* RG27 ..... 73 L7
Seafire Wy *FARN* GU14 ..... 100 B1
Seagull Cl *KEMP* RG22 ..... 91 L8 🔢
Seale La *NFNM* GU10 ..... 124 A4
  RGUW GU3 ..... 125 J4
Seale Rd *MFD/CHID* GU8 ..... 124 C8
Seal Rd *BSTK* RG21 ..... 4 F8
Searing Wy *TADY* RG26 ..... 29 K7
Searle Rd *FNM* GU9 ..... 122 F8
Searles Cl *NALR* SO24 ..... 206 C3 🔢
Searl's La *HTWY* RG27 ..... 74 A4

Seaton Rd *CBLY* GU15 .... 58 E3
Sebastopol Rd *ALDT* GU11 .... 7 G2
Second Av *THLE* RG7 .... 29 M6
Second St *STHA* RG19 .... 26 C4
Sedgefield Rd *NWBY* RG14 .... 15 H4
Sedge Gv *NTHA* RG18 .... 15 H4
Sedgemoor Rd *FARN* GU14 .... 78 E1
Seebys Oak *SHST* GU47 .... 58 B2
Sek Kong Cl *STOK* SP10 .... 150 F4
Selborne Av *ALDT* GU11 .... 7 J8
Selborne Cl *BLKW* GU17 .... 57 M2
    HTWY RG27 .... 74 A7
Selborne Gdns *FNM* GU9 .... 146 D1
Selborne Pl *WINW* SO22 .... 226 C3
Selborne Rd *ALTN* GU34 .... 164 F8
    LISS GU33 .... 212 B6
Selborne Wy *BOR* GU35 .... 188 F6
Seldon Cl *WINW* SO22 .... 226 A4
Selwyn Dr *YTLY* GU46 .... 56 F2
Seremban Cl *STOK* SO20 .... 150 F3
Sermon Rd *WINW* SO22 .... 202 A7
Seton Dr *HTWY* RG27 .... 73 L8
The Sett *YTLY* GU46 .... 56 E3
Seventh St *STHA* RG19 .... 26 C3
The Severals *CHIN* GU24 .... 70 D5
Severn Cl *NTHA* RG18 .... 14 E4
    SHST GU47 .... 37 M8
Severn Ct *AND* SP10 .... 9 M1
Severn Gdns *DEAN* RG23 .... 91 C7
Severn Rd *FARN* GU14 .... 78 B2
Severn Wy *BSTK* RG21 .... 5 K3
Seville Crs *AND* SP10 .... 9 L3
Seymour Dr *CBLY* GU15 .... 39 L8
Seymour Rd *KEMP* RG22 .... 92 B6
    BOR GU35 .... 190 F4
Shady Nook *FNM* GU9 .... 122 F8
Shaftesbury Mt *BLKW* GU17 .... 57 M5
Shakespeare Av *AND* SP10 .... 8 A3
Shakespeare Gdns
    FARN GU14 .... 78 A3
    NTHA RG18 .... 14 F4
Shakespeare Rd *CHIN* GU24 .... 5 G1
    NTHA RG18 .... 14 F4
Shalbourne Ri *CBLY* GU15 .... 59 G3
Shalden Rd *ASHV* GU12 .... 7 L5
Shaldon Wy *FLET* GU13 .... 76 E3
Shamrock Cl *FRIM* GU16 .... 59 G8
Shanklin Ct *ASHV* GU12 .... 7 K4
Shannon Ct *AND* SP10 .... 9 M1
Shaw Cl *AND* SP10 .... 106 B8
Shaw Farm Rd *NWBY* RG14 .... 13 L3
Shawfield La *ASHV* GU12 .... 101 J6
Shawfield Rd *ASHV* GU12 .... 101 J7
Shaw Hl *MARL* SN8 .... 80 A4
    NWBY RG14 .... 13 L3
Shaw La *TADY* RG26 .... 49 J2
Shaw Pk *CWTH* RG45 .... 37 L5
Shaw Pightle *HTWY* RG27 .... 73 L7
Shaw Rd *NWBY* RG14 .... 3 G1
Sheep Dro *STOK* SO20 .... 172 C4
Sheep Fair Cl *AND* SP10 .... 9 L5
Sheephatch La *NFNM* GU10 .... 147 L3
Sheephouse *FNM* GU9 .... 122 F8
Sheepwash La *KSCL* RG20 .... 25 K6
    TADY RG26 .... 69 J2
Sheerlands Rd *EWKG* RG40 .... 35 H2
Sheffield Cl *FARN* GU14 .... 78 C4
Sheldon's La *HTWY* RG27 .... 73 M7
Sheldon's Rd *HTWY* RG27 .... 73 M7
Shelley Cl *CHIN* GU24 .... 5 H1
    FLET GU13 .... 76 F8
    WINW SO22 .... 10 A6
    RWIN SO21 .... 204 D2
Shelley Ct *CBLY* GU15 .... 58 F3
Shelley Rd *NTHA* RG18 .... 14 F4
Shelleys La *ALTN* GU34 .... 165 K7
Shelley Wk *YTLY* GU46 .... 56 F2
Shell La *ALTN* GU34 .... 210 A5
Shelly Ri *FARN* GU14 .... 78 C2
Shepherds Cl *WINW* SO22 .... 226 A4
Shepherds Down *NALR* SO24 .... 206 B4
Shepherd's Hl *HASM* GU27 .... 216 F2
Shepherds Ri *RAND* SP11 .... 61 H3
Shepherds Rd *WINC* SO23 .... 11 M7
Shepherds Rw *AND* SP10 .... 9 L6
Shepherds Spring La *AND* SP10 .... 9 H4
Shepherds Wk *FARN* GU14 .... 78 B1
Shepherds Wy *CWTH* RG45 .... 37 H5
    LIPH GU30 .... 215 G5
    NFNM GU10 .... 147 M4
Sheppard Cl *WHCH* RG28 .... 110 B4
Sheppard Rd *BSTK* RG21 .... 92 F6
Sheraton Av *KEMP* RG22 .... 115 G1
Sheraton Cl *BLKW* GU17 .... 57 M5
Sherborne Rd *BSTK* RG21 .... 4 C4
    CHIN GU24 .... 70 E6
    FARN GU14 .... 79 G8
Sherbrooke Cl *WINC* SO23 .... 179 H7
Sherfield Rd *TADY* RG26 .... 51 L5
Sheridan Cl *WINW* SO22 .... 226 B3
Sheridan Crs *TADY* RG26 .... 29 H7
Sheridan Rd *FRIM* GU16 .... 59 G8
Sherlock Lea *HTWY* RG27 .... 56 B1
Sherrardmead *NWBY* RG14 .... 13 L3
Sherwin Crs *FARN* GU14 .... 58 L8
Sherwood Cl *KEMP* RG22 .... 115 H2
    LISS GU33 .... 236 F1
Shetland Cl *CHIN* GU24 .... 71 H7
Shetland Wy *FARN* GU14 .... 77 G4
Ship Aly *FARN* GU14 .... 78 F2
Ship La *FARN* GU14 .... 78 F2
Shipley Ct *LIPH* GU30 .... 214 E5
Shipton Wy *KEMP* RG22 .... 92 B6
Shire Av *FARN* GU14 .... 77 H5
Shire Ct *ALDT* GU11 .... 6 A2
Shires Wy *YTLY* GU46 .... 37 G8
Shoddesden La *RAND* SP11 .... 80 F8
    RAND SP11 .... 104 B2
Shoe La *ALDT* GU11 .... 100 D2
Shooters Wy *BSTK* RG21 .... 5 G4
Shop La *NWBY* RG14 .... 13 J2
Short Dale Rd *ALDT* GU11 .... 7 K9
Shortfield Rd *NFNM* GU10 .... 146 F7
Shortheath Crest *FNM* GU9 .... 146 E7
Shortheath La *THLE* RG7 .... 19 G5
Shortheath Rd *FNM* GU9 .... 146 D2
Short La *RAND* SP11 .... 105 M7
Short St *ALDT* GU11 .... 6 E1
    RAND SP11 .... 80 E6

Shotterfield Ter *LISS* GU33 .... 236 E4
Shotters La *ALTN* GU34 .... 210 E2
The Shrave *ALTN* GU34 .... 185 K4
Shrivenham Cl *SHST* GU47 .... 38 A8
The Shrubbery *FARN* GU14 .... 78 A5
Shrubs La *NFNM* GU10 .... 146 C4
Shyshack La *TADY* RG26 .... 29 H7
Sian Cl *FLET* GU13 .... 99 G3
Sibelius Cl *KEMP* RG22 .... 115 K1
Sickle Rd *HASM* GU27 .... 216 C3
Sickles Rd *BOR* GU35 .... 167 G6
Sidbury Circular Rd *NTID* SP9 .... 102 C1
Sidestrand Rd *ALDT* GU11 .... 100 B1
    NWBY RG14 .... 13 G8
The Sidings *ALDT* GU11 .... 100 F5
Sidlaw Cl *KEMP* RG22 .... 91 M5
Sidlaws Rd *FARN* GU14 .... 78 A1
Sidmouth Rd *AND* SP10 .... 9 M5
Silchester Cl *AND* SP10 .... 8 C1
Silchester Rd *TADY* RG26 .... 29 L7
    TADY RG26 .... 50 D3
    TADY RG26 .... 51 G5
Silk Mill La *OVTN* RG25 .... 88 E8
Silkweavers Rd *AND* SP10 .... 9 J4
Silver Birch Cl *FLET* GU13 .... 98 E3
    LISS GU33 .... 236 F4
Silver Birch Rd *AND* SP10 .... 8 C3
Silverdale *FLET* GU13 .... 98 F2
Silverdale Rd *TADY* RG26 .... 29 K7
Silver Dr *FRIM* GU16 .... 59 M5
Silverglades *YTLY* GU46 .... 56 F4
Silver Hl *SHST* GU47 .... 38 B8
    WINC SO23 .... 11 H8
Silver La *THLE* RG7 .... 18 D8
Silver Park Cl *FLET* GU13 .... 99 G2
Silverwood Cl *WINW* SO22 .... 226 C3
Silverwood Dr *CBLY* GU15 .... 59 K1
Silvester Cl *BSTK* RG21 .... 5 H4
Silvester Wy *FLET* GU13 .... 98 D4
Silwood Cl *WINW* SO22 .... 10 B4
Simmondstone La *NFNM* GU10 .... 169 G6
Simms Farm La *THLE* RG7 .... 31 J4
Simms Cl *TADY* RG26 .... 52 A6
Sine Cl *FARN* GU14 .... 58 E8
Sinhurst Rd *CBLY* GU15 .... 58 E4
Six Acre La *HUNG* RG17 .... 20 C2
Sixth St *STHA* RG19 .... 26 C3
Skates La *TADY* RG26 .... 50 A3
Skew Rd *RAND* SP11 .... 128 A5
Skilman Dr *STHA* RG19 .... 15 J5
Skinner's Green La *KSCL* RG20 .... 24 C2
Skippetts La East *BSTK* RG21 .... 93 H6
Skippetts La West *BSTK* RG21 .... 93 G6
Skippons Cl *NWBY* RG14 .... 24 F2
Skylark Ri *WHCH* RG28 .... 110 A2
Skyllings *NWBY* RG14 .... 3 J2
Sleepers Delle Gdns
    WINW SO22 .... 226 D2
Sleepers' Hl *WINW* SO22 .... 226 B1
    WINW SO22 .... 226 C2
Sleepers Hill Gdns
    WINW SO22 .... 226 C2
Slessor Cl *RAND* SP11 .... 130 A1
Slim Cl *ALDT* GU11 .... 101 H1
Slim Rd *CBLY* GU15 .... 58 E1
Smallfield Dr *HTWY* RG27 .... 74 B7
Smallridge *KSCL* RG20 .... 24 F4
Smannell Rd *RAND* SP11 .... 107 J4
Smay Down La *MARL* SN8 .... 40 A4
Smeaton Rd *ALDT* GU11 .... 106 A6
Smithfield La *BOR* GU35 .... 168 B6
Smith's Md *OVTN* RG25 .... 113 L7
Smithy Cl *ALTN* GU34 .... 165 J1
Smithy La *BOR* GU35 .... 168 B6
The Smithy *TADY* RG26 .... 51 L5
Smugglers La *NALR* SO24 .... 208 F2
Smugglers' Wy *NFNM* GU10 .... 124 B8
Snailing La *LISS* GU33 .... 212 C7
    LISS GU33 .... 236 A2
Snailslynch *FNM* GU9 .... 123 G6
Snake La *KSCL* RG20 .... 12 D2
Snipe La *HASM* GU27 .... 216 D1
Snoddington Rd *RAND* SP11 .... 127 J1
Snode Hl *ALTN* GU34 .... 163 M5
Snowdon Cl *STHA* RG19 .... 15 G6
Snowdon Rd *FARN* GU14 .... 78 B1
Snowdrop Cl *KEMP* RG22 .... 91 M8
Snowdrop Copse *NTHA* RG18 .... 15 J4
Soalwood La *PSF* GU32 .... 234 E7
Soame's La *NALR* SO24 .... 208 D5
Sobers Sq *AND* SP10 .... 107 H5
Soke Hl *ALTN* GU34 .... 184 D8
Soke The *THLE* RG7 .... 30 C6
The Soke *NALR* SO24 .... 206 C1
Solartron Rd *FARN* GU14 .... 78 D5
Solby's Rd *BSTK* RG21 .... 4 C8
Soldiers Ri *EWKG* RG40 .... 37 G1
Soldridge Rd *ALTN* GU34 .... 184 D5
Solent Dr *KEMP* RG22 .... 115 G1
Somborne Park Rd *STOK* SO20 .... 175 H7
Somers Cl *WINW* SO22 .... 226 C3
Somerset Av *BOR* GU35 .... 189 J5
Somerset Rd *FARN* GU14 .... 78 F7
Somerton Gv *STHA* RG19 .... 14 F6
Somerville Crs *YTLY* GU46 .... 57 H2
Somerville Rd *WINC* SO23 .... 179 H7
Somme Rd *RAND* SP11 .... 80 C8
Sonning Cl *KEMP* RG22 .... 114 E1
Sonninge Cl *SHST* GU47 .... 38 A8
Soper Gv *BSTK* RG21 .... 4 E5
Sopwith Cl *STOK* SO20 .... 198 F6
Sopwith Pk *AND* SP10 .... 106 A7
Sorrel Cl *NWBY* RG14 .... 13 J8
    THLE RG7 .... 19 L5
Sorrell's Cl *CHIN* GU24 .... 71 L5
Sotherington La *ALTN* GU34 .... 211 L2
Southampton Cl *BLKW* GU17 .... 57 M2
Southampton St *FARN* GU14 .... 78 E8
South Atlantic Dr *ALDT* GU11 .... 100 F5
South Av *FARN* GU14 .... 78 E6
South Beta Rd *FARN* GU14 .... 78 E6
Southbrook Pl *RWIN* SO21 .... 157 M5
Southby Dr *FLET* GU13 .... 77 G7
South Cl *NALR* SO24 .... 206 A3
Southcote Dr *CBLY* GU15 .... 59 K3

Southdown Rd *STHA* RG19 .... 14 C4
    TADY RG26 .... 29 K7
Southdowns *NALR* SO24 .... 182 C7
South Downs Wy *NALR* SO24 .... 229 J4
South Dr *WINW* SO22 .... 201 M4
    NTID SP9 .... 102 D4
South Gv *FARN* GU14 .... 77 H4
South Hl *WINC* SO23 .... 19 G1
South End Rd *AND* SP10 .... 9 H8
Southend *NTHA* RG18 .... 14 F2
Southend Rd *BSTK* RG21 .... 4 C8
Southern Haye *HTWY* RG27 .... 75 H3
Southern Rd *BSTK* RG21 .... 93 G4
    CBLY GU15 .... 58 F2
    BOR GU35 .... 189 J2
Southern Wy *FARN* GU14 .... 78 A5
Southgate St *WINC* SO23 .... 10 F8
South Ham Rd *KEMP* RG22 .... 92 D4
South Hurst *BOR* GU35 .... 189 J7
Southington Cl *OVTN* RG25 .... 88 D8
Southington La *OVTN* RG25 .... 88 E8
Southlands *CHIN* GU24 .... 71 K5
Southlands Cl *ASHV* GU12 .... 101 K7
Southlands Rd *ASHV* GU12 .... 101 K7
South Meadow *CWTH* RG45 .... 38 A5
Southmead Rd *ALDT* GU11 .... 7 G5
South Rdg *ODIM* RG29 .... 96 D6
South Rd *ASHV* GU12 .... 101 J4
    CWTH RG45 .... 38 B5
    KSCL RG20 .... 47 K6
    LIPH GU30 .... 214 F7
    NALR SO24 .... 206 A3
    STOK SO20 .... 197 H5
Southrope Gn *OVTN* RG25 .... 141 H1
Southside Rd *RAND* SP11 .... 133 C3
South St *AND* SP10 .... 9 H8
    FARN GU14 .... 79 H7
    FNM GU9 .... 122 F6
    NALR SO24 .... 208 A4
South Town Rd *ALTN* GU34 .... 184 E2
South Vw *WINW* SO22 .... 10 D7
South View Cl *RWIN* SO21 .... 156 C5
South View Cottages
    WHCH RG28 .... 110 F1
Southview Gdns *AND* SP10 .... 9 J7
Southview Ri *ALTN* GU34 .... 164 D5
South View Rd *WINW* SO22 .... 226 A5
Southview Rd *BOR* GU35 .... 190 E3
South View Ter *RAND* SP11 .... 85 M8
South Wk *ASHV* GU12 .... 7 M1
Southwark Cl *YTLY* GU46 .... 56 F2
South Wy *AND* SP10 .... 107 K6
Southway *CBLY* GU15 .... 58 E4
Southwell Park Rd *CBLY* GU15 .... 58 E3
Southwick Cl *WINW* SO22 .... 202 C4
Southwood Gdns *THLE* RG7 .... 19 K5
Southwood La *FARN* GU14 .... 77 K5
Southwood Rd *ALTN* GU34 .... 142 A8
    FARN GU14 .... 57 H7
    FARN GU14 .... 78 B4
Sovereign Dr *CBLY* GU15 .... 59 L1
Sowcroft La *ODIM* RG29 .... 142 F3
Spackman Ct *STHA* RG19 .... 15 G6
Spain La *ALTN* GU34 .... 140 D5
Sparkford Cl *WINW* SO22 .... 226 D2
Sparkford Rd *WINW* SO22 .... 226 D2
Sparrowhawk Cl *NFNM* GU10 .... 99 G8
Sparsholt Rd *RWIN* SO21 .... 225 G5
Sparvells *HTWY* RG27 .... 36 B8
Spats La *BOR* GU35 .... 168 C8
Speckled Wood Rd *CHIN* GU24 .... 71 G7
Speedwell Wy *NTHA* RG18 .... 15 J4
Speen Hill Cl *NWBY* RG14 .... 2 B2
Speen La *NWBY* RG14 .... 2 B2
Speen Lodge Ct *NWBY* RG14 .... 2 A1
Speen Pl *NWBY* RG14 .... 2 A1
Spencer Cl *ALTN* GU34 .... 185 G5
    FLET GU13 .... 99 H3
    FRIM GU16 .... 79 H7
Spencer Rd *NWBY* RG14 .... 25 C2
Spenser Cl *ALTN* GU34 .... 164 F3
Sperrin Cl *KEMP* RG22 .... 92 A5
Spicers *ALTN* GU34 .... 164 F5
Spiers Cl *TADY* RG26 .... 30 A8
Spiers La *NALR* SO24 .... 160 D5
The Spinney *CBLY* GU15 .... 59 M2
    FLET GU13 .... 76 C8
    CSHT GU26 .... 191 K4
    HASM GU27 .... 192 F8
    HTWY RG27 .... 73 M6
    NALR SO24 .... 231 H3
    YTLY GU46 .... 56 F1
Spitalfields Rd *ALTN* GU34 .... 164 E4
Spitalhatch *ALTN* GU34 .... 165 C5
Spitfire End *WINC* SO23 .... 203 J8
Spitfire Wy *FARN* GU14 .... 78 B8
Spoil La *NFNM* GU10 .... 124 C1
Spokane Cl *ALDT* GU11 .... 6 D5
Sprat's Hatch La *HTWY* RG27 .... 97 K1
    ODIM RG29 .... 97 J3
Spray Leaze *RAND* SP11 .... 81 G6
Spray Rd *MARL* SN8 .... 21 H5
Spriggs Cl *STHA* RG19 .... 15 G6
Spring Cl *CHIN* GU24 .... 70 C5
Springcross Av *BLKW* GU17 .... 58 A4
Springfarm Rd *HASM* GU27 .... 216 B3
Springfield *DEAN* RG23 .... 91 G6
Springfield Av *HTWY* RG27 .... 75 H1
Springfield Cl *AND* SP10 .... 107 J8
Springfield La *FLET* GU13 .... 76 D7
    NWBY RG14 .... 13 K8
Springfield Rd *ASHV* GU12 .... 101 K3
    CBLY GU15 .... 59 K3
    TADY RG26 .... 30 B7
Spring Gdns *CBLY* GU15 .... 59 K3
    FARN GU14 .... 78 D7
    NALR SO24 .... 206 A4
Spring Hill La *RAND* SP11 .... 85 L6
Spring La *FNM* GU9 .... 122 D1
    KSCL RG20 .... 45 J2
    THLE RG7 .... 29 M2
    THLE RG7 .... 31 K1
    THLE RG7 .... 33 L3
Spring La West *FNM* GU9 .... 122 C7
Spring Ms *AND* SP10 .... 9 J3

    FRIM GU16 .... 59 H6
Stirling Wy *FARN* GU14 .... 100 A1
    NTHA RG18 .... 14 F4
Stirrup Pightle *NWBY* RG14 .... 25 L1
Stoatley Hollow *HASM* GU27 .... 192 D8
Stoatley Ri *HASM* GU27 .... 192 D8
Stockbridge Dr *ALDT* GU11 .... 7 K9
Stockbridge Rd *WINW* SO22 .... 10 C5
    RAND SP11 .... 151 M5
    RWIN SO21 .... 156 B4
    RWIN SO21 .... 176 B8
    STOK SO20 .... 198 F5
Stockbridge Wy *YTLY* GU46 .... 57 G4
Stocker Cl *BSTK* RG21 .... 92 F6
Stockers Av *WINW* SO22 .... 10 A3
Stocks La *ALTN* GU34 .... 232 F7
Stockton Av *FLET* GU13 .... 76 E6
Stockton Pk *FLET* GU13 .... 76 E6
Stockwood Ri *CBLY* GU15 .... 59 J3
Stockwood Wy *FNM* GU9 .... 6 D7
Stodham La *EPSF* GU31 .... 236 D8
    LISS GU33 .... 236 D5
Stoke Charity Rd *RWIN* SO21 .... 178 F5
Stoke Hl *RAND* SP11 .... 85 G5
Stoke Hills *FNM* GU9 .... 122 F5
Stoke La *RAND* SP11 .... 84 F3
Stoken La *HTWY* RG27 .... 74 E1
Stoke Rd *RAND* SP11 .... 84 E8
    WINC SO23 .... 11 H1
Stokes La *STHA* RG19 .... 28 F7
Stone Cl *AND* SP10 .... 8 C9
    RSAL SP5 .... 194 F2
Stone Copse *NTHA* RG18 .... 14 B1
Stonedene Cl *BOR* GU35 .... 190 E4
Stonegate *CBLY* GU15 .... 59 M2
Stonehill Pk *BOR* GU35 .... 190 E4
Stonehill Rd *BOR* GU35 .... 190 F4
Stonehouse Ri *FRIM* GU16 .... 59 H7
Stonehouse Rd *LIPH* GU30 .... 215 G4
Stoneleigh Ct *FRIM* GU16 .... 59 J7
Stone St *ASHV* GU12 .... 7 M5
Stoney Bottom *CSHT* GU26 .... 191 H5
Stoney Cl *YTLY* GU46 .... 57 G4
Stoney Cross *RAND* SP11 .... 80 E6
Stoneyfield *THLE* RG7 .... 17 K2
Stoneyfields *FNM* GU9 .... 123 H7
Stoney La *ALTN* GU34 .... 185 G4
    WINW SO22 .... 10 A2
    NWBY RG14 .... 14 A2
    STHA RG19 .... 15 H5
Stookes Wy *YTLY* GU46 .... 56 F4
Stourhead Cl *AND* SP10 .... 8 B7
    FARN GU14 .... 79 G4
Stour Rd *DEAN* RG23 .... 91 G7
Stovold's Wy *ALDT* GU11 .... 6 C5
Stratfield Av *TADY* RG26 .... 49 L1
Stratfield Rd *BSTK* RG21 .... 4 E2
Stratfield Saye Rd *TADY* RG26 .... 51 M3
Stratford Rd *ASHV* GU12 .... 79 J8
Strathfield Rd *AND* SP10 .... 130 E3
Stratton Cl *RWIN* SO21 .... 158 F4
Stratton La *RWIN* SO21 .... 159 H7
Stratton Rd *BSTK* RG21 .... 92 F4
    WINC SO23 .... 11 K9
Stratton Wk *FARN* GU14 .... 78 D1
Strauss Rd *KEMP* RG22 .... 92 B8
Stravinsky Rd *KEMP* RG22 .... 92 B8
Strawberry Flds *TADY* RG26 .... 51 L5
Strawberry Hl *NWBY* RG14 .... 2 A2
Stream Farm Cl *NFNM* GU10 .... 147 G1
Streamside *FLET* GU13 .... 76 E3
Stream Valley Rd *NFNM* GU10 .... 146 F2
Street End *HTWY* RG27 .... 76 A4
The Street *ALTN* GU34 .... 166 D1
    CHIN GU24 .... 93 M2
    FLET GU13 .... 98 C3
    HTWY RG27 .... 73 K3
    NFNM GU10 .... 124 C3
    NFNM GU10 .... 146 B2
    NFNM GU10 .... 168 A1
    NFNM GU10 .... 168 B2
    ODIM RG29 .... 95 L5
    ODIM RG29 .... 119 J5
    RGUW GU3 .... 125 L4
    RSAL SP5 .... 194 C2
    RSAL SP5 .... 218 B1
    TADY RG26 .... 51 J6
    THLE RG7 .... 29 K1
    THLE RG7 .... 31 J3
    THLE RG7 .... 33 M2
Streetway Rd *RAND* SP11 .... 149 K2
Strettons Copse *LIPH* GU30 .... 238 E5
Strokins Rd *KSCL* RG20 .... 47 J5
Stroud Cl *CHIN* GU24 .... 71 K6
Stroud La *HTWY* RG27 .... 98 B3
Stroudley Rd *CHIN* GU24 .... 5 M3
Strouds Meadow *NTHA* RG18 .... 14 F1
The Strouds *THLE* RG7 .... 17 J2
Stuart Cl *FARN* GU14 .... 78 D3
Stuart Crs *WINW* SO22 .... 226 B3
Stuart Rd *NWBY* RG14 .... 24 F2
Stubbington Av *BOR* GU35 .... 189 H7
Stubbs Ct *AND* SP10 .... 8 B7
Stubbs Court Ct *AND* SP10 .... 8 B7
Stubbs Folly *SHST* GU47 .... 58 A1
Stubbs Moor Rd *FARN* GU14 .... 78 C3
Stubbs Rd *BSTK* RG21 .... 93 H6
Stukeley Rd *BSTK* RG21 .... 92 E4
Sturdee Cl *FRIM* GU16 .... 59 H7
Sturt Av *HASM* GU27 .... 216 D4
Sturt Rd *FNM* GU9 .... 122 L1
    FRIM GU16 .... 79 J3
    HASM GU27 .... 216 D4
Suffield La *RGUW* GU3 .... 125 J8
Suffolk Rd *AND* SP10 .... 8 F7
Sulhamstead Hl *THLE* RG7 .... 18 F2
Sulhamstead Rd *THLE* RG7 .... 18 F2
Sullivan Cl *FARN* GU14 .... 78 E4
Sullivan Rd *CBLY* GU15 .... 58 D3
    KEMP RG22 .... 92 D7
Summer Down La *DEAN* RG23 .... 90 D3
Summerfield La *NFNM* GU10 .... 146 D6
Summerfields *CHIN* GU24 .... 71 M4
Summer Gdns *CBLY* GU15 .... 59 M5
Summit Av *FARN* GU14 .... 77 M5
Summit Cl *EWKG* RG40 .... 36 C2
Sumner Rd *FNM* GU9 .... 122 F5

Sun Brow HASM GU27 216 C3
Sunbury Cl BOR GU35 189 K5
Sunderland Pl NTHA RG18 14 F4 2
Sunflower Cl KEMP RG22 114 F1 3
Sun Gdns THLE RG7 19 K7
Sun Hill Crs NALR SO24 206 C4
Sun La NALR SO24 206 C4
THLE RG7 33 L6
Sunley Cl NWBY RG14 25 G2
Sunnybank RAND SP11 129 K2
Sunnybank Rd FARN GU14 78 A2
Sunnydell La FNM GU9 146 D2
Sunnydown Rd WINW SO22 225 M5
Sunny Hill Rd ALDT GU11 100 A6
Sunny Md DEAN RG23 91 G8
Sunnyside FLET GU13 76 D6
Sunnyside Cl AND SP10 106 C6
Sunnyside Rd BOR GU35 190 F4
Sun Ray Est SHST GU47 37 J8
Sunvale Av HASM GU27 216 A2
Sunvale Cl HASM GU27 216 A2 1
Surbiton Rd CBLY GU15 39 K7
Surrey Av CBLY GU15 58 D4
Sussex Border Pth
HASM GU27 217 J7
LIPH GU30 214 E8
LISS GU33 237 L2
Sussex Gdns FARN GU14 77 G4
Sussex St WINC SO23 10 F7
Sutherland Cl BOR GU35 189 J7
Sutherlands NWBY RG14 25 H1 1
Sutton Fld BOR GU35 189 H7
Sutton Gdns WINC SO23 11 G7
Sutton Rd BSTK RG21 4 E4
CBLY GU15 39 K7
NWBY RG14 13 G3
Sutton Wood La NALR SO24 183 K8
Swains Cl TADY RG26 29 L8
Swains Rd TADY RG26 29 L8
Swaledale Gdns FARN GU14 77 G4
Swale Rd FARN GU14 78 A2
Swallow Cl ALTN GU34 164 F2
KEMP RG22 91 L8
NTID SP9 102 E2
YTLY GU46 56 E2
Swallowfield Rd THLE RG7 34 D1
Swallowfields AND SP10 107 G6
Swan Barn Rd HASM GU27 217 G2
Swan Ct HTWY RG27 75 J2 5
Swan Dr THLE RG7 17 L5
Swan La SHST GU47 57 L2
WINC SO23 10 F6
Swan Ms ODIM RG29 96 B4 2
Swanmore Cl WINW SO22 202 C4 5
Swan St KSCL RG20 47 H7
Swan Wy FLET GU13 98 C1
Swedish Houses TADY RG26 49 M1
Sweetbriar CWTH RG45 37 K1 2
Sweetzer's Piece THLE RG7 31 H2
Swelling Hl ALTN GU34 208 F2
Swift Cl AND SP10 107 G6
WINW SO22 226 C3
Swift Rd FNM GU9 122 E1
Swift's Cl NFNM GU10 123 L7
Swingate Rd FNM GU9 122 F8
Swing Swang La CHIN RG24 5 L3
Swiss Cl NFNM GU10 146 C4
Switchback La NFNM GU10 146 C4 1
Swordfish Wy FARN GU14 100 B1
Sycamore Cl FRIM GU16 59 H7
NTID SP9 102 F2 3
SHST GU47 57 L1
TLHT RG30 19 L3
Sycamore Crs FLET GU13 98 D2
STOK SO20 151 G4
Sycamore Dr ASHV GU12 101 J1
FRIM GU16 59 H6
NFNM GU10 146 D2 1
WINC SO23 179 G8
Sycamore Ri NWBY RG14 13 M2
Sycamore Rd FARN GU14 78 F6
The Sycamores BLKW GU17 57 L3
FARN GU14 79 G5
Sycamore Wy DEAN RG23 91 J2
The Sydings NWBY RG14 13 G3
Sydney Cl CWTH RG45 37 M1
RAND SP11 103 J1 2
Sydney Rd BOR GU35 189 J5
Sydney Smith Av FARN GU14 78 E7
Syers Rd LISS GU33 236 E4
Sylvan Rdg SHST GU47 37 K7
Sylvan Wy FLET GU13 98 E3
Sylvester Cl NWBY RG14 13 H3 1
Symonds St WINC SO23 11 G9
Sympson Rd TADY RG26 30 A7
Syon Pl FARN GU14 79 G4 3

T

Tadham Pl STHA RG19 14 F6
Tadley Common Rd TADY RG26 29 M7
Tadley Hl TADY RG26 49 M1
Tadpole La NFNM GU10 99 G7
Taiping Rd STOK SO20 150 F4 1
Talbot Cl FRIM GU16 79 K4
NWBY RG14 13 H3
Talbot Rd FNM GU9 122 E8
Talgarth Dr FARN GU14 79 G6
Talisman Cl CWTH RG45 37 G3
Tallis Gdns KEMP RG22 92 D7
Talmey Cl CHIN RG24 71 K5
Tamar Dr DEAN RG23 91 G7
Tamarisk Cl KEMP RG22 115 H3 1
Tamarisk Ct NTHA RG18 15 J4
Tamworth Dr FARN GU14 77 G4
Tangier Ct ALDT GU11 6 C2
Tanglewood EWKG RG40 36 D1
Tangway CHIN RG24 71 L4
Tanhouse La ALTN GU34 164 D5
Tankerdale La PSF GU32 236 B8
Tanker Rd FARN GU14 78 E7
Tank Rd CBLY GU15 58 C3
Tanners Cl THLE RG7 19 J7
Tanners La HASM GU27 216 F1
Tanner St WINC SO23 11 H8
Tanners Wy DEAN RG23 91 G6
Taplings Cl WINW SO22 10 A1
Taplings Rd WINW SO22 10 A1
Taplin's Farm La HTWY RG27 75 K5
Tarbat Ct SHST GU47 38 A8 7
Tarn Cl FARN GU14 78 B6
Tarn La NWBY RG14 2 C9
Tarn Rd GSHT GU26 192 A5
Tarragon Cl FARN GU14 77 M4
Tarragon Wy THLE RG7 19 L5
Taskers Dr RAND SP11 130 B3
Tasmania Cl CHIN RG24 71 H6 3
Taverner Cl BSTK RG21 5 J4
Tavistock Gdns FARN GU14 78 E1
Tavistock Rd FLET GU13 76 C8 3
Tawny Gv ALTN GU34 184 F6
Tay Cl FARN GU14 78 B2
Taylor Dr TADY RG26 51 M6
Taylors La BOR GU35 189 L3
Teal Crs KEMP RG22 114 E1
Teasel Cl RAND SP11 80 E7
Tedder Cl RAND SP11 130 A1
Tees Cl FARN GU14 78 B2
Teg Down Meads WINW SO22 202 A7
Tegg Down Rd NALR SO24 207 K5
Tekels Av CBLY GU15 59 G4
Tekels Wy CBLY GU15 59 J5
Telconia Cl BOR GU35 190 F4 2
Telegraph La ALTN GU34 185 J5
Templar Ct SHST GU47 37 K8
Temple Rd LISS GU33 236 F2
Temple's Cl NFNM GU10 123 M7
Tenby Rd FRIM GU16 59 K8
Tennyson Rd NTHA RG18 14 F4
Tennyson's La HASM GU27 217 H4
Tennyson Wy KEMP RG22 92 D5 1
The Terrace CBLY GU15 58 C3
CWTH RG45 38 A3
Tesimond Dr YTLY GU46 56 D3
Test Ri STOK SO20 153 M5
Test Rd WHCH RG28 110 B4
Test Wy BSTK RG21 5 J8
MARL SN8 41 K4
RAND SP11 85 M7
RAND SP11 108 C4
ROMY SO51 221 K5
STOK SO20 153 L3
STOK SO20 175 G2
STOK SO20 198 B7
Tewkesbury Cl CHIN RG24 71 G7
Texas Dr WINW SO22 226 A6
Thackham's La HTWY RG27 74 E3
The Thakerays STHA RG19 15 G6 3
Thames Ct AND SP10 107 J6 1
BSTK RG21 5 J7
Thames Rd NTHA RG18 14 E3
Theal Cl SHST GU47 38 A8
Theale Rd TLHT RG30 19 L2
Theatre Rd FARN GU14 78 E8
Theobalds Wy FRIM GU16 59 M5
Thibet Rd SHST GU47 37 M8
Third St STHA RG19 26 C3
Thirlmere Cl FARN GU14 78 B4
BOR GU35 189 J3 3
Thirlmere Crs FLET GU13 98 D3 4
Thirsk Ct ASHV GU12 7 M1
Thirt Wy STOK SO20 154 B7
Thistledown Cl AND SP10 8 D3 1
Thompson Dr STHA RG19 15 H6 2
Thorburn Cha SHST GU47 58 B2 1
Thornbury Cl CWTH RG45 37 L3
Thorn Cl NFNM GU10 146 C4 2
Thorn Ct ALTN GU34 185 G6
Thorn Crs ALTN GU34 185 G6 2
Thorn Dr ALTN GU34 185 G6 3
Thorne Cl CWTH RG45 37 K1 3
Thorneley Rd KSCL RG20 47 J6 3
Thornfield STHA RG19 27 G5 1
Thornfield Gn BLKW GU17 58 C5
Thornford Rd STHA RG19 26 E4
Thornhill Rd ALDT GU11 101 G4
Thornhill Wy CHIN RG24 71 M4
Thorn La ALTN GU34 185 H6
Thorn Rd NFNM GU10 146 C3
Thornton End ALTN GU34 165 H2
Thornyhurst Rd FRIM GU16 79 K4
Thorold Rd FNM GU9 122 F5 3
Thorpe Gdns ALTN GU34 164 C4
Threadgill Wy NTID SP9 126 B1
Three Acre Rd NWBY RG14 13 J8
Three Castles Pth HTWY RG27 55 K3
NALR SO24 160 F8
NALR SO24 182 C1
ODIM RG29 95 L6
OVTN RG25 94 F7
RWIN SO21 181 H8
RWIN SO21 203 H4
Three Firs Wy THLE RG7 19 H7
Three Gates La HASM GU27 217 G1
Three Horse Shoes La
ALTN GU34 232 D6
Three Stiles Rd FNM GU9 122 C5
Threshers Cnr FARN GU14 77 H4 3
Throgmorton Rd YTLY GU46 56 D3
Thrush Cl THLE RG7 19 L5
Thuillier Rd RWIN SO21 133 H6
Thumwood CHIN RG24 71 L5 3
Thundery Hl NFNM GU10 124 C4
Thurbans Rd FNM GU9 146 D1 3
Thurmond Crs WINW SO22 226 B2
Thurmond Rd WINW SO22 226 B2
Thursley Rd NFNM GU10 169 M5
Thurston Pl BSTK RG21 92 E7
Thurstons ALTN GU34 166 D2
Thyme Cl CHIN RG24 71 M4
Thyme Ct FARN GU14 77 M3
Tiberius Cl DEAN RG23 92 B1
Tiberius Rd AND SP10 107 G5
Tichborne Cl BLKW GU17 58 A3 3
Tichborne Down NALR SO24 206 B5
Tichborne Pl ASHV GU12 7 L6
Tichbourne Cl FRIM GU16 59 J5
Tickenor Dr EWKG RG40 36 C1
Tidworth Rd RAND SP11 80 E6
Tigwells Fld ODIM RG29 118 F4
Tilbury's Cl BOR GU35 189 J5 3
Tile Barn Cl FARN GU14 78 D2
Tilford Rd FNM GU9 123 G7
GSHT GU26 192 C3
NFNM GU10 147 M5
Tilford St NFNM GU10 147 M5
Tilney Cl ALTN GU34 164 D4
Timber Bank FRIM GU16 79 K3
Timbercroft Cl ALTN GU34 184 F7
Timberlake Rd BSTK RG21 4 E8
Timberley Pl CWTH RG45 37 H4 2
Timbermill Ct HASM GU27 216 C2 2
Tindal Cl YTLY GU46 57 G2
Tintagel Cl AND SP10 106 F5
DEAN RG23 92 B2
Tintagel Dr FRIM GU16 59 J7
Tintern Cl CHIN RG24 4 B1
Tippet Gdns KEMP RG22 92 E8
Titchfield Cl TADY RG26 49 M1 3
Tithelands La NALR SO24 231 L4
Tithe Meadow KEMP RG22 115 H3 2
Tittymouse La RAND SP11 105 H6
Tiverton Rd DEAN RG23 92 B3
Toad La BLKW GU17 58 B4
Tobago Cl CHIN RG24 71 G7
Tobruk Cl RAND SP11 107 G1
Tobruk Rd RAND SP11 103 J2
Todmore LISS GU33 212 E5
Toledo Gv AND SP10 9 L2
Tollgate Cl DEAN RG23 91 G5
Tollgate Rd AND SP10 8 B2
Tollway CHIN RG24 71 M5
Tolpuddle Wy YTLY GU46 57 J3
Tomlin Cl STHA RG19 15 H6 3
Tomlins Av FRIM GU16 59 J6
Tomlins Cl TADY RG26 49 L1
Tomlinscote Wy FRIM GU16 59 K6
Tomlinson Dr EWKG RG40 36 D2
Tongham Mdw NFNM GU10 124 C1 3
Tongham Rd ASHV GU12 7 L6
NFNM GU10 123 M4
The Topiary CHIN RG24 71 M8
FARN GU14 78 B5
Toplady Pl FNM GU9 122 F1 5
Top Terrace Rd FARN GU14 78 D8
Torrington Cl BOR GU35 189 M3 7
Tor Rd FNM GU9 122 C6
Totford La NFNM GU10 125 H5
Totland Cl FARN GU14 78 D2
Tottenham Cl TADY RG26 51 L4
Tottenham Wk SHST GU47 38 A7
Totterdown THLE RG7 19 J7
Totters La HTWY RG27 74 E7
Tournai Cl ALDT GU11 101 H1
Tovey Pl WINC SO23 179 H8
Tower Cl AND SP10 106 C5
Tower Hl FARN GU14 78 D5
Tower Rd GSHT GU26 192 B4
LIPH GU30 214 E4
WINC SO23 10 F6
Towers Dr CWTH RG45 37 L4
Tower St ALTN GU34 164 D6
WINC SO23 10 F7
Town Cl NALR SO24 208 C4
Town Mill La WHCH RG28 110 C3
Townsend Cl BSTK RG21 4 B9
Townside Pl CBLY GU15 59 G2 3
Trafalgar Ct FNM GU9 122 E7
Trafalgar St WINC SO23 10 F8
Trafalgar Wy CBLY GU15 58 C4
STOK SO20 174 E6
Trafford Rd FRIM GU16 59 G8
Transport Rd FARN GU14 78 E7
Travis La SHST GU47 57 M1 1
Treble Cl WINW SO22 226 A4
Trebor Av FNM GU9 123 G7
Tredenham Cl FARN GU14 78 F8 2
Tree Av HASM GU27 192 C8
Treeside Dr FNM GU9 6 A8
Tree Tops Av CBLY GU15 39 K8
Trefoil Cl HTWY RG27 75 H1
Trefoil Dro NTHA RG18 15 J4
Tregolls Dr FARN GU14 78 F5
Trellis Dr CHIN RG24 71 M8
Tremayne Wk CBLY GU15 59 M4
Trenchard Rd RAND SP11 130 A1
Trent Cl FARN GU14 78 B2
Trent Ct AND SP10 9 M1 3
Trent Crs NTHA RG18 14 E3
Trenton Cl FRIM GU16 59 K6
Trent Wy BSTK RG21 5 K8
Tresham Crs YTLY GU46 56 D2 2
The Triangle NWBY RG14 25 L1
Trimmers Cl FNM GU9 122 F1 3
Trimmers Wd GSHT GU26 192 A2
Trinidad Cl CHIN RG24 71 G7
Trinity SHST GU47 38 B6
Trinity Flds FNM GU9 122 D2 3
Trinity Hl ALTN GU34 162 D8
FNM GU9 122 D2
Trinity Ri RAND SP11 105 L4
Trinity Rd ALTN GU34 162 D7
Trotwood Cl SHST GU47 38 B6 3
Trout Rd HASM GU27 216 B2
Trout Wk NWBY RG14 13 L3
Trowe's La THLE RG7 33 G4
Trunk Rd FARN GU14 77 M4
Trussell Cl WINW SO22 10 A1
Trussell Crs WINW SO22 10 A1
Trust Cl HTWY RG27 73 L7 3
Tubb's La KSCL RG20 44 C2
TADY RG26 49 M8
Tudor Cl GSHT GU26 192 A6
Tudor Dr YTLY GU46 57 G3 3
Tudor Rd NWBY RG14 2 F7
Tudor Wy FLET GU13 98 F4
WINC SO23 179 G8
Tulip Cl KEMP RG22 114 F1
Tulls La BOR GU35 190 A6
Tunball La MARL SN8 60 B1
Tunbridge Crs LIPH GU30 214 E3
Tunbridge La LIPH GU30 214 E2
Tunnel Rd FARN GU14 78 A7
Tunworth Ms TADY RG26 29 M8
Tunworth Rd OVTN RG25 94 D4
Turbary Gdns TADY RG26 29 L7
Turf Hill Rd CBLY GU15 39 J8
Turin Ct AND SP10 107 G4
Turk's La THLE RG7 31 J4
Turk St ALTN GU34 164 E5
Turner Cl BSTK RG21 93 K4
Turner Pl SHST GU47 58 A2
Turners Dr STHA RG19 15 H5
Turner's Green La HTWY RG27 76 B4
The Turnery STHA RG19 14 F5 3
Turnfields STHA RG19 15 G5
Turnpike Down WINC SO23 11 M7
Turnpike Rd NTHA RG18 14 B4
NWBY RG14 3 M1
Turnpike Wy DEAN RG23 90 F6
Turnstone End YTLY GU46 56 E2 1
Tweed Cl FARN GU14 78 B2
Tweedsmuir Cl FARN GU14 78 A5 7
KEMP RG22 92 A4
Twelve Acre Crs FARN GU14 78 A3 2
Tweseldown Rd FLET GU13 99 G4
Twisell Thorne FLET GU13 98 D4
Two Gate La OVTN RG25 112 A1
Two Gate Meadow OVTN RG25 89 G8
Two Rivers Wy NWBY RG14 3 M3
Twyford La NFNM GU10 146 E2
Tydehams NWBY RG14 25 H1
Tyfield CHIN RG24 70 D5
Tyler Dr WHIT RG2 35 H1
Tylney La HTWY RG27 73 J7
Tylston Meadow LIPH GU30 214 E3 2
Tyne Cl FARN GU14 78 B2
Tyne Ct AND SP10 107 J6 2
Tyne Wy NTHA RG18 14 E3
Tytherley Rd RSAL SP5 195 H2

U

Ullswater Av FARN GU14 78 B5
Ullswater Cl FNM GU9 122 D2 3
BOR GU35 189 J3
STHA RG19 14 D5
Ullswater Gv NALR SO24 206 C4 7
Underhill La FNM GU9 146 E1
Underwood Av ASHV GU12 101 H7
Underwood Rd HASM GU27 216 C1
Union Cl SHST GU47 38 B6
Union La KSCL RG20 47 J5
Union Ri LISS GU33 213 J6
Union Rd FNM GU9 122 F6
Union St FARN GU14 78 D4
WINC SO23 11 J7
Union Ter ALDT GU11 6 E2
Upfallow CHIN RG24 93 M1
Uphill Rd WINW SO22 202 A3
Upland La LISS GU33 235 M1
Upland Rd CBLY GU15 59 G1
Uplands Cl HASM GU27 193 G8
SHST GU47 37 L8 3
Uplands La ALTN GU34 184 F7
Uplands Rd FNM GU9 123 H7
WINW SO22 10 C1
Upnor Cl RAND SP11 103 J1
Upper Bourne La NFNM GU10 146 D3
Upper Bourne V NFNM GU10 146 D3 2
Upper Broadmoor Rd
CWTH RG45 37 M3
Upper Brook St WINC SO23 11 H7
Upper Charles St CBLY GU15 58 F2
Upper Chestnut Dr BSTK RG21 92 E5
Upper Chobham Rd CBLY GU15 59 L4
FRIM GU16 59 K5
Upper Church La FNM GU9 122 E6 3
Upper College Ride CBLY GU15 39 H8
Upper Dro AND SP10 106 B8
Upper Elms Rd ALDT GU11 6 E3
Upper Farm Rd DEAN RG23 90 F8
Upper Gordon Rd CBLY GU15 59 G3
Upper Grove Rd ALTN GU34 164 E6
Upper Hale Rd FNM GU9 122 E1
Upper High St WINW SO22 10 E6
Upper Lamborough La
NALR SO24 230 D2
Upper Lanham La NALR SO24 183 J1
Upper Mt HASM GU27 193 J7
LISS GU33 236 D5
Upper Neatham Mill La
ALTN GU34 165 H2
Upper Old Park La FNM GU9 122 C3
Upper Park Rd CBLY GU15 59 G3
Upper Pinewood Rd
ASHV GU12 101 M5
Upper St Michael's Rd
ALDT GU11 7 G5
Upper Sherborne Rd BSTK RG21 4 C2
Upper Soldridge Rd
ALTN GU34 184 C6
Upper South Vw FNM GU9 122 F5
Upper St FLET GU13 76 E7
Upper Terrace Rd FARN GU14 78 D8
Upper Union St ALDT GU11 6 D2
Upper Union Ter ALDT GU11 6 E2
Upper Verran Rd CBLY GU15 59 G5
Upper Wy FNM GU9 122 E8
Upper Weybourne La
FNM GU9 100 A8
Upron Field Cl KEMP RG22 115 G1
Up St OVTN RG25 113 K7
Upton Cl FARN GU14 79 G5 3
Upton Crs BSTK RG21 4 D3
Upton Grey Cl WINW SO22 202 C5
Upton Grey Rd OVTN RG25 95 J7
Urquhart Rd STHA RG19 15 G7

V

Vale Cl NFNM GU10 146 F4
Valencia Wy AND SP10 9 K3
Vale Rd ASHV GU12 101 K3
CBLY GU15 58 D4
WINC SO23 227 G2
The Vale DEAN RG23 90 F7
Vale View Dr THLE RG7 33 G3
Vale Wy WINC SO23 179 G7
Vale Wood Dr NFNM GU10 147 G4
Vale Wood La GSHT GU26 191 M4
Valewood Rd HASM GU27 216 F4
Valiant Wy FARN GU14 78 A8
Valley Hl WINW SO22 202 B3
Valley La FNM GU9 146 F1
Valley Md RAND SP11 130 B3
Valley Ri RAND SP11 130 D4
Valley Rd FRIM GU16 59 L8
WINW SO22 202 A3
NWBY RG14 2 A9
NWBY RG14 13 G8
THLE RG7 19 K5
Valley Side LIPH GU30 214 E3
The Valley WINW SO22 226 C2
Valley Vw SHST GU47 57 K1
Valley Wy TADY RG26 30 B7
Valmeade Cl HTWY RG27 74 A7 7
Valroy Cl CBLY GU15 59 G2
Vampire Wy FARN GU14 78 B8
Vanburgh Gdns KEMP RG22 115 G1
Van Dyck Cl BSTK RG21 93 K5
Vanguard Hl WINW SO22 202 B2
Vanners La KSCL RG20 24 A3
Varna Rd BOR GU35 189 K5
Varney Cl FARN GU14 78 B3
Vaughans ALTN GU34 164 F5
Vectis Cl ALTN GU34 185 G6
Velmead Cl FLET GU13 99 G1
Velmead Rd FLET GU13 98 F1
Venice Ct AND SP10 107 H5
Ventnor Ter ASHV GU12 7 J4
Verden Wy AND SP10 106 E5 3
Verdi Cl KEMP RG22 92 C8
Vermont Woods EWKG RG40 36 B1
Verner Cl BOR GU35 190 B4
The Verne FLET GU13 98 F3
Vernham Rd WINW SO22 10 B2
Veronica Cl KEMP RG22 114 F1
Veronica Dr FLET GU13 98 C3
Verran Rd CBLY GU15 59 G5
Vesey Cl FARN GU14 78 D3
Vespasian Gdns CHIN RG24 70 B8
Vespasian Rd AND SP10 107 G4
Vestry Cl AND SP10 8 F5
Vetch Flds HTWY RG27 74 B7
Viables La BSTK RG21 93 G7
Vian Pl WINC SO23 179 H8
Vicarage Cl EWKG RG40 36 C2 2
FNM GU9 147 G1
Vicarage Gdns FLET GU13 98 E4
GSHT GU26 191 M5
Vicarage Hl ALTN GU34 164 E5
FNM GU9 147 G1
HTWY RG27 75 J3
Vicarage La FNM GU9 122 F1
FNM GU9 122 E6
FNM GU9 147 G1
HASM GU27 216 C2
HTWY RG27 53 L7
NALR SO24 208 A4
YTLY GU46 56 F1
Vicarage Rd ALTN GU34 164 D6
BFOR GU20 39 M5
BLKW GU17 58 B4
YTLY GU46 56 F1
Vickers Rd ASHV GU12 101 J3
Victoria Av CBLY GU15 58 D3
Victoria Ct AND SP10 9 G6
Victoria Dr BLKW GU17 57 M4
Victoria Gdns NWBY RG14 2 F2
Victoria Hill Rd FLET GU13 76 D7
Victoria Rd ALDT GU11 6 F2
ALTN GU34 164 E4
FARN GU14 78 E4
FLET GU13 76 D7
FNM GU9 122 F6
SHST GU47 38 B7
THLE RG7 31 J2
WINC SO23 10 F5
Victoria Rd East ALTN GU34 164 F4
Victoria St BSTK RG21 4 E9
Victoria Tr ALDT GU11 100 A1
Victor Pl THLE RG7 16 F6
Victor Rd STHA RG19 15 H5
Victor Wy FARN GU14 77 M8
Victory Rbt BSTK RG21 4 D7
Vigo La YTLY GU46 56 F5
Vigo Rd AND SP10 9 L3
Viking Wy AND SP10 107 G4
Village St ALTN GU34 163 G3
STOK SO20 153 M4
The Village EWKG RG40 36 B5
Village Wy YTLY GU46 57 G1
Villiers Wy NWBY RG14 24 F2
Vincent Dr AND SP10 9 K6
Vincent Rd NTHA RG18 15 H4
Vindomis Cl ALTN GU34 165 J1
Vine Cl ALDT GU11 100 D2
NFNM GU10 146 D4
Vine House Cl FRIM GU16 79 K5 2
Vine St ALDT GU11 6 E3
Vine Tree Cl TADY RG26 50 A1
Vine Wy NFNM GU10 146 D3
Vinns La OVTN RG25 111 L1
Vinson Rd LISS GU33 236 F4
Violet Cl KEMP RG22 114 F1
Violet Gv NTHA RG18 15 H3
Violet La TADY RG26 48 F2
Virginia Gdns FARN GU14 78 F6
Vivaldi Cl KEMP RG22 115 K1
Vivian Cl FLET GU13 99 G2
Vivian Rd BSTK RG21 5 H3
Vulcan Wy FARN GU14 77 M8
SHST GU47 57 K1
Vyne Cl ALTN GU34 164 E3 3
Vyne Meadow CHIN RG24 70 E4
Vyne Rd BSTK RG21 4 E5
CHIN RG24 70 E4

W

Wade Rd CHIN RG24 5 M1
Wadham SHST GU47 38 C7
Wadwick Bottom RAND SP11 85 L5
Waggoners Wy GSHT GU26 191 K4
Waggoners Wells Rd
GSHT GU26 191 K6
Wagner Cl KEMP RG22 92 D8
Wagon La HTWY RG27 74 A6
Wakeford Cl TADY RG26 30 B7 2
Wakefords Copse FLET GU13 99 G5
Wakefords Pk FLET GU13 99 G5

Waldorf Hts BLKW GU17 58 A4
Wales St WINC SO23 11 J7
Walker's Rdg CBLY GU15 59 H3
Walldown Rd BOR GU35 189 J8
Walled Meadow AND SP10 9 K6
Waller Dr NWBY RG14 14 B3
Wallington Rd CBLY GU15 39 K7
Wallins Copse CHIN RG24 71 L6 [4]
Wallis Dr TADY RG26 52 A6
Wallis Rd BSTK RG21 93 G5
Wall La THLE RG7 30 F6
Wallop Dr KEMP RG22 114 F2
Wallop Dro STOK SO20 172 C4
Wallop Rd RAND SP11 150 A1
STOK SO20 149 M4
Walmer Cl CWTH RG45 37 M3
FRIM GU16 79 J1
Walnut Cl ALDT GU11 6 F6
ALTN GU34 164 E3
YTLY GU46 57 G4
Walnut Gv WINW SO22 10 B5
Walnut Tree Cl RWIN SO21 178 C4
Walnut Tree Rd AND SP10 8 E7
Walpole Rd WINW SO22 226 B3
Walrus Rd FARN GU14 78 A8
Waltham Cl SHST GU47 38 A7 [5]
Waltham Ct OVTN RG25 89 G8 [1]
Waltham La OVTN RG25 112 D4
Waltham Rd OVTN RG25 112 A1
Walton Pl WINW SO22 226 C3
Walton Wy NWBY RG14 3 J1
Walworth Rd RAND SP11 107 L6
Wanborough Hl RGUW GU3 125 M2
Wandle Cl ASHV GU12 101 K7
Wandsdyke Cl FRIM GU16 59 J8
Wansey Gdns NWBY RG14 14 A3
Wantage Rd SHST GU47 38 A8
Wapiti Wy FARN GU14 78 A8
Warbleton Rd CHIN RG24 71 M5 [5]
Warblington Cl TADY RG26 49 M1
Warbrook La HTWY RG27 35 K8
Ward Cl AND SP10 9 G1
Warehouse Rd STHA RG19 26 C3
Wargrove Dr SHST GU47 38 A8
The Warings THLE RG7 17 K1
Warner Ct AND SP10 8 F5
Warren Cl FLET GU13 99 G1
HTWY RG27 75 J3
BOR GU35 188 F6
SHST GU47 37 K8
THLE RG7 19 K6
Warren Cnr NFNM GU10 121 M1
Warren Dr RAND SP11 129 L5
Warren La EWKG RG40 36 A3
PSF GU32 235 H3
RWIN SO21 228 D8
Warren Ri FRIM GU16 59 H5
Warren Rd LISS GU33 213 J6
LISS GU33 236 F1
NWBY RG14 25 G2
WINC SO23 11 M6
The Warren ALDT GU11 6 D3
FNM GU9 6 A6
TADY RG26 29 K8
Warrington Ms ALDT GU11 6 A5 [2]
Warton Rd BSTK RG21 5 G5
Warwick Cl ALDT GU11 7 J6
CBLY GU15 59 L5
WINC SO23 11 G3
Warwick Dr NWBY RG14 3 H8
Warwick Rd ASHV GU12 79 J7
DEAN RG23 92 B2
FARN GU14 78 A8
Wasdale Cl SHST GU47 38 A6
Wash Brook HTWY RG27 73 M6 [9]
Washford La BOR GU35 189 L4
Wash Water KSCL RG20 24 D5
Wasing La THLE RG7 29 G2
Watchetts Dr CBLY GU15 58 F6
Watchetts Lake Cl CBLY GU15 59 G5 [2]
Watchetts Rd CBLY GU15 58 E5
Watch La WHCH RG28 87 M7
Watchmoor Rd CBLY GU15 58 D4
Watercress Meadow
NALR SO24 206 A4 [1]
Water End La CHIN RG24 94 E1
Waterhouse Md SHST GU47 58 A1 [7]
Wateridge Rd BSTK RG21 5 G2
Water La FARN GU14 78 D1
FNM GU9 123 J4
NALR SO24 207 H4
RAND SP11 130 E4
STHA RG19 25 M1
WINC SO23 11 J7
Waterlily Cl BSTK RG21 5 K8
Waterloo Av DEAN RG23 92 B1
Waterloo Cl CBLY GU15 59 L1
Waterloo Ct AND SP10 9 H6
Waterloo Rd ASHV GU12 7 J4
CWTH RG45 37 K4
Waterman Cl BOR GU35 189 L6
Watermills Cl AND SP10 8 F9
Water Rede FLET GU13 98 D5
Water Ridges DEAN RG23 91 G8
Waterside Cl BOR GU35 189 K4
Waterside Ct ALTN GU34 164 F4 [2]
FARN GU14 77 G5
Water Wy BSTK RG21 5 K7
Watery La AND SP10 9 K2
FLET GU13 98 D5
KSCL RG20 23 J3
Watley La RWIN SO21 201 J4
Watling End KEMP RG22 115 G1
Watson Acre AND SP10 8 C4
Watson Wy DEAN RG23 92 C1
Watt Cl AND SP10 106 B7
Watts Common Rd ALDT GU11 100 B1
Watts Rd FARN GU14 78 C3
Wavell Cl KEMP RG22 92 D6
Wavell Wy WINW SO22 226 B3
Waverley Av BSTK RG21 92 F6
FLET GU13 76 E5
Waverley Cl CBLY GU15 59 J4
ODIM RG29 96 E5
Waverley Dr ASHV GU12 101 K2
CBLY GU15 59 H3
RWIN SO21 178 D4
Waverley Gdns ASHV GU12 101 K2 [1]
Waverley La FNM GU9 123 M8
Waverley Rd FARN GU14 79 G5
The Waverleys NTHA RG18 15 G4 [1]
Wayfarer's Wk DEAN RG23 114 D5
KSCL RG20 42 E1
KSCL RG20 66 E2
NALR SO24 160 B4
NALR SO24 230 B2
RAND SP11 43 J4
Wayman Rd FARN GU14 58 B8
Waynflete La FNM GU9 122 C6
Waynflete Pl WINW SO22 226 C2 [2]
Ways End CBLY GU15 59 H4
Wayside Rd DEAN RG23 92 A3
Weapon Rd FARN GU14 78 E6
Weatherby Gdns HTWY RG27 75 J2 [6]
Weathermore La ALTN GU34 185 J6
Weavers Cl AND SP10 9 J4
Weavers Gdns NFNM GU10 146 C1 [3]
Webb Cl CHIN RG24 71 K6
Webbs Acre STHA RG19 15 J6
Webbs Farm Cl WHCH RG28 110 B5
Webbs La THLE RG7 17 L1
Webster Rd WINW SO22 202 A7
Wedman's La HTWY RG27 73 L1
Wedmore Cl WINW SO22 225 M5
Weeke Manor Cl WINW SO22 10 A3
Weir Av FARN GU14 78 D5
Weir Cl FARN GU14 78 D5
Weir Rd FARN GU14 77 K6
HTWY RG27 75 G4
The Weir WHCH RG28 110 B5
Welbeck Cl FARN GU14 78 C4
Weldon Cl FLET GU13 99 G3
Wella Rd KEMP RG22 92 E6
Wellburn Cl SHST GU47 57 L1
Well Cl CBLY GU15 58 E4
OVTN RG25 113 K7
Weller Dr CBLY GU15 58 F5
EWKG RG40 35 K2
Wellesley Cl ASHV GU12 101 J1
BAGS GU19 39 M5
Wellesley Dr CWTH RG45 37 H3
Wellesley Gdn FNM GU9 122 F1
Wellesley Rd ALDT GU11 100 A5
AND SP10 9 G9
FARN GU14 78 A8
NFNM GU10 169 L2
Well House La WINW SO22 202 D3
HTWY RG27 34 E5
Wellhouse Rd ALTN GU34 163 L6
Wellington Av ALDT GU11 6 F1
FLET GU13 77 G6
BOR GU35 189 H6
Wellington Cl NWBY RG14 13 M3 [3]
SHST GU47 37 M8
Wellington Crs TADY RG26 29 G7
Wellingtonia Av EWKG RG40 36 E4
Wellington La FNM GU9 123 G1
Wellington Rd AND SP10 8 E3
CWTH RG45 37 M4
SHST GU47 37 L8
Wellington St ALDT GU11 6 F1
Wellington Ter DEAN RG23 92 B1
SHST GU47 37 M8 [1]
Wellington Wy FARN GU14 100 A1
Well La ALTN GU34 120 A8
ALTN GU34 144 A2
HASM GU27 217 G2
Wellmans Meadow KSCL RG20 47 H5
Well Meadow NWBY RG14 13 L3
Well Rd NFNM GU10 121 H2
Wells Cottages FNM GU9 146 D1 [5]
Wells's La WHCH RG28 110 A4
Well St KSCL RG20 45 K4
Welsh La THLE RG7 33 K6
Welshman's Rd THLE RG7 30 E3
Welton Ct BSTK RG21 4 C7
Wendan Rd NWBY RG14 2 D9
Wendover Dr FRIM GU16 59 M5
Wenlock Wy STHA RG19 15 G6 [7]
Wensley Dr FLET GU13 76 F5 [2]
Wentworth Cl ASHV GU12 101 K1
CWTH RG45 37 J2
FNM GU9 6 C9
YTLY GU46 57 G3 [5]
Wentworth Ct NWBY RG14 3 G7
Wentworth Crs ASHV GU12 101 K2
Wentworth Gdns ALTN GU34 164 D4
Wentworth Gra WINW SO22 226 D2
Wesley Rd WINC SO23 203 H1
Wessex Av ODIM RG29 96 C7
Wessex Cl BSTK RG21 92 F5
Wessex Crs ODIM RG29 96 C7
Wessex Dr WINW SO22 10 C2
ODIM RG29 96 C7
Wessex Gdns AND SP10 8 F4
Wessex Pl FNM GU9 122 F7
Wessex Rd FARN GU14 78 C6
West Av FNM GU9 123 G2
Westbourne Rd SHST GU47 58 B1
West Brook Cl DEAN RG23 91 G8
Westbrooke Cl AND SP10 9 H6
Westbrooke Rd ALTN GU34 164 D5
Westburn ALTN GU34 144 B4
Westbury Av FLET GU13 77 J8
Westbury Cl CWTH RG45 37 L2
FLET GU13 77 H8
Westbury Gdns FLET GU13 77 J8
FNM GU9 123 H4 [2]
Westbury Wy ASHV GU12 7 L1
West Cl FNM GU9 123 G1
Westdean Ct BSTK RG21 4 B9
Westdeane Ct BSTK RG21 4 B9
West End TADY RG26 70 C3
West End Cl WINW SO22 10 D7
West End Gv FNM GU9 122 D6
West End La ALTN GU34 184 A4
NFNM GU10 146 B7
West End Rd THLE RG7 31 H3
West End Ter WINW SO22 10 D7
Westerdale STHA RG19 14 F5
Westerdale Dr FRIM GU16 59 L5
Western Av AND SP10 9 H7
NWBY RG14 2 E1
Western End NWBY RG14 2 A6 [1]
Western La ODIM RG29 96 C6
Western Rd ALDT GU11 6 B3
AND SP10 9 G6
WINW SO22 10 D6
BOR GU35 189 H2
LISS GU33 236 E4
Western Wy KEMP RG22 92 C6
West Field Cl TADY RG26 30 A8
Westfield Crs NTHA RG18 14 E4
Westfield Dro NALR SO24 229 M8
Westfield La NFNM GU10 146 B2
Westfield Rd BSTK RG21 93 H5
CBLY GU15 58 E6
WINW SO22 202 A3
NTHA RG18 14 D3
West Field Rd WINC SO23 179 H8
Westfield Wy NWBY RG14 2 A6
West Fryerne YTLY GU46 57 G1
Westgate Rd NWBY RG14 2 A6
Westglade FARN GU14 78 A4 [1]
West Gn YTLY GU46 56 E1
West Green Rd HTWY RG27 74 E2
West Ham Cl KEMP RG22 92 B4
West Ham La KEMP RG22 92 A4
West Heath Rd FARN GU14 78 C4
West Hill Dr WINW SO22 10 C7
West Hill Pk WINW SO22 10 B7
West Hill Rd North RWIN SO21 178 D3
West Hill Rd South RWIN SO21 178 D4
Westland NTHA RG18 14 E4 [1]
Westlands Rd NWBY RG14 2 F9
Westley Cl WINW SO22 10 A4
Westley La RWIN SO21 201 H4
Westlyn Rd TADY RG26 30 B7
Westman Rd WINW SO22 10 A2
Westmead FARN GU14 78 E5
Westmead Dr NWBY RG14 13 J8
West Meade LIPH GU30 238 E6
West Mills NWBY RG14 2 D4
Westminster Cl FLET GU13 76 F6 [1]
KEMP RG22 115 G1 [6]
Westminster Ga WINW SO22 226 A3 [1]
Westmorland Dr CBLY GU15 59 L5
Weston Ct RAND SP11 84 A8
Weston Down Rd RWIN SO21 157 K3
Weston La RSAL SP5 194 E3
Weston Rd OVTN RG25 117 M5
Westover Rd FLET GU13 77 G7
West Pk RAND SP11 105 G2
West Portway AND SP10 106 A6
Westray Cl BSTK RG21 5 J4
Westridge KSCL RG20 44 B4
West Rd CBLY GU15 59 G3
FARN GU14 58 D8
RWIN SO21 155 J1
Westside Cl KEMP RG22 92 C5 [1]
West St AND SP10 9 G5
FNM GU9 122 C7
HASM GU27 216 F2
KSCL RG20 45 H4
NALR SO24 206 C2
NWBY RG14 2 D3
ODIM RG29 96 B6
TADY RG26 30 A8
West View Dr STOK SO20 153 M5
Westview Rd WINW SO22 201 M6
West View Rd BOR GU35 190 F4
Westwood La RGUW GU3 125 L1
Westwood Rd NWBY RG14 3 H9
Westwood Vw NALR SO24 230 D7
Wetherby Gdns AND SP10 106 D6
FARN GU14 78 F8 [3]
Wey Bank ALTN GU34 145 H5
Weybank Cl FNM GU9 122 F5 [4]
Weybourne Rd FNM GU9 123 H3
Weybridge Md YTLY GU46 57 H1
Weybrook Ct TADY RG26 70 C4
Wey Cl ASHV GU12 101 K7
CBLY GU15 58 E3
Weycombe Rd HASM GU27 192 F8
Weydon Hill Cl FNM GU9 122 E8 [2]
Weydon Hill Rd FNM GU9 122 E8
Weydon La FNM GU9 122 D8
Weydon Mill La FNM GU9 122 E7
Weydown Rd HASM GU27 216 E1
Wey Hl HASM GU27 216 D2
Weyhill Cl TADY RG26 49 L1
Weyhill Gdns RAND SP11 105 J6
Weyhill Rd AND SP10 8 E6
RAND SP11 105 M7
Weyland Cl LIPH GU30 214 F3
Wey Lodge Cl LIPH GU30 215 G4 [2]
Weysprings HASM GU27 216 C1
Weysprings Cl BSTK RG21 5 J7
Weywood Cl FNM GU9 6 C8
Weywood La FNM GU9 6 B8
Wharfenden Wy FRIM GU16 79 J2
Wharf Hl WINC SO23 227 G2
Wharf Rd ASHV GU12 101 K4
FRIM GU16 79 J2
NWBY RG14 2 F4
Wharfside THLE RG7 17 M5
Wharf St NWBY RG14 2 E4
Wharf Wy FRIM GU16 79 J2
Wheatland Cl WINW SO22 226 C3
Wheatlands La NWBY RG14 24 E2
Wheatley La ALTN GU34 166 F1
Wheeler Cl THLE RG7 19 L5 [6]
WHCH RG28 110 C4
Wheeler Hl HTWY RG27 74 B7
Wheelers Green Wy STHA RG19 15 H6
Wheelwrights La GSHT GU26 191 K4
Whetstone Rd FARN GU14 77 M4
Whinchat Cl HTWY RG27 75 H1
Whin Holt FLET GU13 98 F2
Whins Cl CBLY GU15 58 E4
Whins Dr CBLY GU15 58 E4
Whistler Cl BSTK RG21 93 J5
Whistler Gv SHST GU47 58 A2
Whistlers La THLE RG7 30 E7
Whitby Cl FARN GU14 79 H7 [1]
Whitchurch Cl ALDT GU11 7 L9
White Acres Rd FRIM GU16 79 J4
White Av LISS GU33 213 H6
Whitebeams Gdns
FARN GU14 77 M5 [7]
White City CWTH RG45 38 A3
White Cottage Cl FNM GU9 123 G2
Whitedown ALTN GU34 164 D6
Whitedown La ALTN GU34 164 C6
Whitedown Rd TADY RG26 29 J8
White Farm La MARL SN8 41 G3
Whitehall Rd STOK SO20 175 M8
White Hart La BSTK RG21 5 G9
TADY RG26 49 K8
Whitehead Cl CHIN RG24 93 L1 [2]
White Hl KSCL RG20 45 G6
KSCL RG20 46 C5
ODIM RG29 120 A6
Whitehill Cl CBLY GU15 59 G1
Whitehill La NALR SO24 206 E4
Whitehill Rd BOR GU35 189 L7
White Horse La EWKG RG40 35 M3
White House Cl KEMP RG22 92 C6
White House Gdns YTLY GU46 56 F1 [2]
White House Wk FNM GU9 123 G1 [2]
Whitelands Rd NTHA RG18 14 F4
White La ASHV GU12 101 M7
NFNM GU10 124 F1
OVTN RG25 95 J6
RWIN SO21 226 F8
TADY RG26 90 B2
White Lion Wy YTLY GU46 57 G1
White Oak Wy RAND SP11 130 B4
White Post La NFNM GU10 146 D4
White Rd CBLY GU15 58 C2
White Rose La FNM GU9 146 E1
Whites Cl HTWY RG27 73 L7 [5]
White's Hl THLE RG7 19 H4
Whiteshoot STOK SO20 197 G1
Whiteshute La WINC SO23 226 D4
Whites Rd FARN GU14 79 H7
Whitestones KEMP RG22 115 H2 [3]
Whitethorn Cl ASHV GU12 101 L7
Whitewater Ri HTWY RG27 74 B6 [6]
Whitewater Rd ODIM RG29 96 B4
Whitewood CHIN RG24 71 L5
Whitfield Cl HASM GU27 192 F7 [1]
Whitfield Rd HASM GU27 192 F8
Whitlet Cl FNM GU9 122 E7 [2]
Whitley Rd YTLY GU46 57 G4
Whitley Wy FARN GU14 78 B7
Whitmarsh La CHIN RG24 72 A5
Whitmoor Vale Rd GSHT GU26 191 J1
Whitmore Cl SHST GU47 38 A8
Whitmore Gn FNM GU9 123 H2
Whitmore V GSHT GU26 191 J2
Whitmore Vale Rd GSHT GU26 191 L4
Whitney Rd CHIN RG24 5 L4
Whittle Cl EWKG RG40 36 B1
SHST GU47 37 K7 [5]
Whittle Crs FARN GU14 78 C1
Whittle Rd AND SP10 106 A7
Whitworth Rd WHIT RG2 35 K1
Whynot La AND SP10 8 D5
Whyte Av ASHV GU12 7 L7
Wicket Hl NFNM GU10 146 D2
Wickham Cl ALTN GU34 164 C6
FLET GU13 98 D3
TADY RG26 29 L8
Wickham Pl FLET GU13 98 D2
Wickham Rd CBLY GU15 39 H8
FLET GU13 98 D2
Wick Hill La EWKG RG40 36 D2
Wicklow Cl KEMP RG22 92 A5
Widgeons ALTN GU34 164 E3
Widmore Rd KEMP RG22 92 B6
Wield Rd ALTN GU34 162 A5
Wigan Rd FARN GU14 78 A8
Wights Wk KEMP RG22 115 G1 [7]
Wigmore Rd TADY RG26 29 J7
Wilberforce Cl WINW SO22 226 B2 [3]
Wild Briar EWKG RG40 36 C1
Wilderness Rd FRIM GU16 59 H6
Wilders Cl FRIM GU16 59 G5
Wild Herons HTWY RG27 74 B7 [5]
Wildmoor La HTWY RG27 72 B2
Wildwood Gdns YTLY GU46 56 F4
Wilfred Wy STHA RG19 15 J5
Willems Av ALDT GU11 6 D1
Will Hall Cl ALTN GU34 164 C6
William Cl STHA RG19 15 G6
William Farthing Cl ALDT GU11 6 E2
Williamson Cl HASM GU27 193 J7 [2]
RAND SP11 80 D6
Williams Wy FLET GU13 77 H7
William Wy ALTN GU34 164 F3 [2]
Willington Cl CBLY GU15 58 E2 [1]
Willis La ALTN GU34 185 J7
Willis Waye WINC SO23 203 H3
Willoughby Cl ALTN GU34 164 D4
Willoughby Wy DEAN RG23 92 C2
Willow Cl FRIM GU16 79 H4
BOR GU35 189 K5
LIPH GU30 215 G5 [2]
NWBY RG14 2 D8
TLHT RG30 19 L3
Willow Ct FRIM GU16 59 G7
Willow Crs FARN GU14 78 E1
Willowford YTLY GU46 57 G2
Willow Gdns LIPH GU30 215 G5
Willow Gv AND SP10 8 F7
Willow La BLKW GU17 58 A4
Willowmead Cl NWBY RG14 24 F3
Willow Pk ASHV GU12 101 J6
Willow Rd KSCL RG20 26 C6
LISS GU33 236 E4
TADY RG26 29 L8
Willows End SHST GU47 37 L8 [4]
The Willows AND SP10 8 E8
NFNM GU10 123 M4
Willow Wy ASHV GU12 101 H8
DEAN RG23 92 C1
FNM GU9 123 G2
HTWY RG27 52 C7
SHST GU47 37 J7
STOK SO20 151 G4
Wilmott Wy DEAN RG23 92 C2
Wilmot Wy CBLY GU15 59 J5
Wilsom Cl ALTN GU34 164 F5
Wilsom Rd ALTN GU34 165 G5
Wilson Rd ASHV GU12 7 M4
FARN GU14 78 C5 [3]
Wilsons Rd BOR GU35 190 E3
Wilton Ct FARN GU14 79 G5
Wilton Pl BSTK RG21 4 B8
Wilton Rd CBLY GU15 58 E5
Wiltshire Av CWTH RG45 37 L2
Wimbledon Cl CBLY GU15 39 J7
Wimbledon Rd CBLY GU15 39 J7
Wimbushes EWKG RG40 36 A2
Wincanton Cl ALTN GU34 164 F6
Winchcombe Cl FLET GU13 76 F7
Winchcombe Rd BSTK RG21 4 C9
NWBY RG14 2 F5
Winchester By-pass
RWIN SO21 156 A7
WINC SO23 203 H5
WINC SO23 203 H3
Winchester Gdns AND SP10 9 H9
Winchester Hl RWIN SO21 156 B5
Winchester Rd ALTN GU34 164 D7
ALTN GU34 185 H5
ASHV GU12 101 K5
BSTK RG21 92 F5
DEAN RG23 114 D4
KEMP RG22 114 F1
KSCL RG20 67 H1
NALR SO24 205 M3
NFNM GU10 169 L1
RAND SP11 130 F4
RAND SP11 154 B2
RWIN SO21 158 A7
STOK SO20 154 A3
STOK SO20 199 G5
WHCH RG28 110 B5
Winchester St AND SP10 9 J6
BSTK RG21 4 E9
FARN GU14 78 F8
OVTN RG25 89 G8
WHCH RG28 110 B4
Winchester Wy BLKW GU17 57 M2 [5]
Winchfield Ct HTWY RG27 75 M7 [1]
Windermere Av KEMP RG22 91 M6
Windermere Cl FARN GU14 78 B5 [2]
Windermere Gdns
NALR SO24 206 C4 [3]
Windermere Rd BOR GU35 189 J3
Windermere Wy FNM GU9 122 D2
STHA RG19 14 D5
Winding Wood Dr CBLY GU15 59 L4
Windmill Cnr THLE RG7 31 K2
Windmill Dr BOR GU35 190 E2
Windmill Flds ALTN GU34 185 G5
Windmill Hl ALTN GU34 164 F6
Windmill La RAND SP11 84 B1
THLE RG7 16 D3
Windmill Rd ASHV GU12 7 J3
THLE RG7 31 K2
Windrush Hts SHST GU47 37 L8 [5]
Windsor Cl ALTN GU34 164 C5 [3]
Windsor Crs FNM GU9 122 E2
Windsor Gdns ASHV GU12 101 J7 [2]
KEMP RG22 114 F2
Windsor Pk ALTN GU34 164 E6
Windsor Ride CBLY GU15 38 D8
EWKG RG40 36 D1
Windsor Ri NWBY RG14 3 J9
Windsor Rd ALTN GU34 185 G4
AND SP10 8 F5
FARN GU14 78 A8
BOR GU35 189 L3
NALR SO24 206 B4
Windsor Wk BOR GU35 189 L3
Windsor Wy ALDT GU11 7 G2
FRIM GU16 59 J8
Wingate Ct ALDT GU11 6 D1
Wingate Rd ODIM RG29 119 J5
Wings Cl FNM GU9 122 E2 [4]
Wings Rd FNM GU9 122 E2
Winklebury Wy DEAN RG23 92 A3
Winkworth La THLE RG7 29 M6
Winnall Cl WINC SO23 11 M5
Winnall Manor Rd WINC SO23 11 M7
Winnall Valley Rd WINC SO23 11 L6
Winslade Rd WINW SO22 202 B4
Winston Av TADY RG26 50 A1
Winston Cl FRIM GU16 79 J2
Winston Ri ALTN GU34 185 G5
Winston Wk NFNM GU10 146 F2 [1]
Winston Wy STHA RG19 14 C4
Winterdyne Ms AND SP10 8 E6
Winterthur Wy BSTK RG21 4 D7
Winterton Dr NWBY RG14 13 G3
Winton Cha AND SP10 107 J8
Winton Cl NTID SP9 102 E4
Winton Crs YTLY GU46 57 G3
Winton Hl STOK SO20 174 F5
Winton Rd ALDT GU11 6 E4
FNM GU9 123 G4 [1]
Wiremead La RAND SP11 128 F2
Wise's Firs THLE RG7 19 G5
Wishanger La BOR GU35 168 E6
Wishmoor Cl CBLY GU15 39 H8
Wishmoor Rd CBLY GU15 39 H8
Wisley Gdns FARN GU14 78 A6
Wisley Rd AND SP10 8 C7
Wistaria La YTLY GU46 56 F3
Wisteria Dr BOR GU35 189 J6
Witan Cl AND SP10 107 G4
Witan Ct WHCH RG28 110 A2
Wither Ri DEAN RG23 90 F6
Witherslack Cl BOR GU35 190 F4 [3]
The Withies RSAL SP5 195 M8 [1]
Withybed Wy NTHA RG18 15 H3
Wittmead Rd FRIM GU16 79 J4
Witton Hl NALR SO24 206 C4 [5]
Witt Rd RSAL SP5 195 G2
Wivelrod Rd ALTN GU34 163 H8
Winton Cl WINW SO22 10 E3
Woburn Av FARN GU14 79 G4
Woburn Cl FRIM GU16 59 K7
Wokingham Rd CWTH RG45 37 H5
Wolfe Cl WINW SO22 226 B3
Wolfe Rd ASHV GU12 7 K3
Wolfmere La LISS GU33 212 F6
Wolf's La ALTN GU34 164 D8
Wolseley Rd ALDT GU11 6 F3
Wolsingham Wy STHA RG19 15 G6 [3]
Wolversdene Cl AND SP10 9 L7
Wolversdene Gdns AND SP10 9 M7
Wolversdene Rd AND SP10 9 K7
AND SP10 9 M7 [1]
Wolverton La TADY RG26 48 C7
Wolverton Rd TADY RG26 48 B6
Wonston Cl RWIN SO21 156 C5

Wonston La *RWIN* SO21 .... 178 B1
Woodbine Cl *SHST* GU47 .... 57 L1
Woodbine La *KSCL* RG20 .... 25 J2
Woodbourne Farm *FNM* GU9 .... 6 B7
Woodbourne Cl *LISS* GU33 .... 236 F4 🖪
  YTLY GU46 .... 57 G2 🖪
Woodbridge Dr *CBLY* GU15 .... 59 C1
Woodbridge Rd *BLKW* GU17 .... 57 L3
Woodbury Rd *KEMP* RG22 .... 115 G2
Wood Cl *KEMP* RG22 .... 115 G2
Woodcock Cl *NTID* SP9 .... 102 E2 🖪
Woodcote Gn *FLET* GU13 .... 76 C8
Woodcote Rd *MARL* SN8 .... 40 F1
Woodcot Gdns *FARN* GU14 .... 78 A4 🖪
Woodcott Ter *ASHV* GU12 .... 7 L5
Woodcut Rd *NFNM* GU10 .... 146 C3
Wood End *CWTH* RG45 .... 37 J4
Woodend *FARN* GU14 .... 79 G5 🖪
Woodend Rd *FRIM* GU16 .... 79 M1
Woodfield *BOR* GU35 .... 167 G7
Woodfield Dr *WINW* SO22 .... 226 A2
Woodgarston Dr *KEMP* RG22 .... 114 F2
Woodgate *FARN* GU14 .... 77 H5 🖪
Woodgreen Rd *WINW* SO22 .... 202 C4
Wood Hill La *ODIM* RG29 .... 119 J4
Woodhouse La *STHA* RG19 .... 28 B5
Woodland Dr *NFNM* GU10 .... 146 E2
  RSAL SP5 .... 194 E1 🖪
  TADY RG26 .... 52 A6
Woodland Ri *FLET* GU13 .... 98 D3
Woodlands *CHIN* RG24 .... 71 M4 🖪
  CWTH RG45 .... 37 L5
  FLET GU13 .... 76 E6
  KSCL RG20 .... 44 D1
  OVTN RG25 .... 88 F8
  YTLY GU46 .... 57 G5
Woodlands Av *FNM* GU9 .... 6 C7
  THLE RG7 .... 19 K5
Woodlands Ct *ASHV* GU12 .... 101 K3 🖪
  FARN GU14 .... 58 B7
Woodlands Ct *SHST* GU47 .... 38 C7
Woodlands La *HASM* GU27 .... 216 C1
  LISS GU33 .... 237 G6
Woodlands Rd *CBLY* GU15 .... 58 E3
  FARN GU14 .... 78 A2
  TADY RG26 .... 29 G7

The Woodlands *BOR* GU35 .... 189 J7
  WINC SO23 .... 203 H2
Woodlands Wk *FARN* GU14 .... 58 B7
Woodlands Wy *AND* SP10 .... 9 L5
Wood La *FARN* GU14 .... 78 D5
  FLET GU13 .... 77 H7
  HTWY RG27 .... 95 H3
  NALR SO24 .... 231 J5
  NFNM GU10 .... 124 E4
  THLE RG7 .... 33 H3
Woodlane Cl *NALR* SO24 .... 231 J5
Woodlea Cl *WINW* SO22 .... 10 C2
Woodleigh *FLET* GU13 .... 76 F8
Woodman Cl *RWIN* SO21 .... 201 J6
Woodman La *RWIN* SO21 .... 201 K5
Woodman's La *THLE* RG7 .... 19 J5
Woodmere Cft *KEMP* RG22 .... 114 E1
Wood Moor *EWKG* RG40 .... 36 C6
Woodpecker Cl *KEMP* RG22 .... 91 L8
  BOR GU35 .... 189 J6
  NFNM GU10 .... 99 G8 🖪
Woodpecker Dr *WINW* SO22 .... 202 B6
Wood Rdg *NWBY* RG14 .... 25 H1
Wood Rd *CBLY* GU15 .... 58 E7
  FNM GU9 .... 122 F1
  GSHT GU26 .... 192 A2
Woodroffe Dr *KEMP* RG22 .... 92 B7
Woodside *BLKW* GU17 .... 57 M5
  CBLY GU15 .... 58 C1
  NWBY RG14 .... 25 G1
Woodside Cl *BOR* GU35 .... 189 J5
  THLE RG7 .... 15 M3
  THLE RG7 .... 31 K2 🖪
Woodside Crs *BOR* GU35 .... 189 J5 🖪
Woodside Gdns *CHIN* RG24 .... 71 L4
  FLET GU13 .... 77 H6
Woodside La *ALTN* GU34 .... 185 M4
Woodside Pk *BOR* GU35 .... 189 J5
Woodside Rd *ALDT* GU11 .... 100 C1
  FNM GU9 .... 6 A8
Woods La *OVTN* RG25 .... 115 L1
Woodstocks *FARN* GU14 .... 78 F2
Wood St *ASHV* GU12 .... 101 K2
Woodville Cl *BLKW* GU17 .... 57 L3
Woodway *CBLY* GU15 .... 58 E3 🖪
Wooldridge Crs *ODIM* RG29 .... 96 B8

Woolfield La *ALTN* GU34 .... 234 A5
Woolford Cl *WINW* SO22 .... 226 B2 🖪
Woolford Wy *DEAN* RG23 .... 92 C2
Wool Gv *AND* SP10 .... 9 L6
Woolhampton Hl *THLE* RG7 .... 16 F6
Woollards Rd *ASHV* GU12 .... 101 K4
Woolmead Rd *FNM* GU9 .... 122 F6
Woolmer Hill Rd *HASM* GU27 .... 215 M1
Woolmer La *LIPH* GU30 .... 190 F8
Woolmer St *LISS* GU33 .... 213 G5
Woolton Wy *BOR* GU35 .... 189 H6
Woolton Lodge Gdns
  KSCL RG20 .... 24 C6 🖪
Wooteys Wy *ALTN* GU34 .... 164 E3
Worcester Av *KEMP* RG22 .... 92 A8
Worcester Cl *FARN* GU14 .... 78 E1 🖪
Wordsworth Av *YTLY* GU46 .... 56 E4
Wordsworth Cl *CHIN* RG24 .... 5 C1
  WINW SO22 .... 10 B6
Wordsworth Rd *NTHA* RG18 .... 14 F4 🖪
Wordnam Hl *ALTN* GU34 .... 165 M7
Wormersley Rd *STHA* RG19 .... 26 A1
Worsley Rd *FRIM* GU16 .... 79 J1
Worthy La *WINC* SO23 .... 10 F5
Worthy Rd *WINC* SO23 .... 11 C3
Worting Rd *BSTK* RG21 .... 4 B9
  DEAN RG23 .... 91 K4
  KEMP RG22 .... 92 C4
Wote St *BSTK* RG21 .... 4 F9
Wouldham Cl *RAND* SP11 .... 103 J1
Wrecclesham Hl *NFNM* GU10 .... 146 B3
Wrecclesham Rd *FNM* GU9 .... 146 C1
Wrekin Cl *KEMP* RG22 .... 92 A5
The Wrekin *FARN* GU14 .... 79 H7
Wren Cl *ALTN* GU34 .... 164 F3
  WINW SO22 .... 226 C3
  THLE RG7 .... 19 L5 🖪
  YTLY GU46 .... 56 E2 🖪
Wren Ct *ASHV* GU12 .... 101 L5
Wren Wy *FARN* GU14 .... 78 C1
Wrights Cl *RWIN* SO21 .... 178 C4
Wurford Dr *STHA* RG19 .... 15 J5
Wychwood Cl *ASHV* GU12 .... 101 J6
Wychwood Pl *CBLY* GU15 .... 39 C7

Wyck La *ALTN* GU34 .... 165 M6
Wye Ct *AND* SP10 .... 9 M1
Wykeham Ct *ODIM* RG29 .... 96 C8
Wykeham Dr *DEAN* RG23 .... 91 M4
Wykeham Pl *WINW* SO22 .... 226 C3
Wykeham Rd *FNM* GU9 .... 122 F5 🖪
Wykwood *LIPH* GU30 .... 215 G4 🖪
Wylde Green La *LISS* GU33 .... 236 F3
Wylye Rd *NTID* SP9 .... 102 E1
Wymering Ct *FARN* GU14 .... 79 G5
Wyndham Cl *YTLY* GU46 .... 57 G1
Wyndham Rd *AND* SP10 .... 8 D8
  NWBY RG14 .... 14 A3
Wyndham St *ASHV* GU12 .... 7 J3
Wynfields *FRIM* GU16 .... 79 J5
Wynne Gdns *FLET* GU13 .... 99 G3
Wyvern Cl *ASHV* GU12 .... 101 J3 🖪

Y

Yale Cl *SHST* GU47 .... 38 C6
Yarmley La *RSAL* SP5 .... 194 E2
Yarnhams Cl *ALTN* GU34 .... 185 G6
Yateley Rd *YTLY* GU46 .... 57 J1
Yatesbury Cl *FNM* GU9 .... 146 C1
Yates Copse *NTHA* RG18 .... 14 B3
Yellowhammer Rd
  KEMP RG22 .... 114 E2
Yellowhammers *ALTN* GU34 .... 164 E2
Yeomans *HTWY* RG27 .... 56 B1
Yeomans Cl *FARN* GU14 .... 78 D3
  NFNM GU10 .... 101 J8
Yeomans La *KSCL* RG20 .... 25 K7
  LIPH GU30 .... 214 D4
Yeomans Pl *BOR* GU35 .... 190 B3 🖪
Yeomans Wy *CBLY* GU15 .... 59 H3
Yeovil Cl *FARN* GU14 .... 79 G7
Yeovil Rd *SHST* GU47 .... 38 D7
Yetminster Rd *FARN* GU14 .... 79 G7
Yew Cl *KSCL* RG20 .... 47 K6
Yew Ga *NWBY* RG14 .... 13 J2
Yew Tree Cl *DEAN* RG23 .... 91 G8
  FARN GU14 .... 77 M5 🖪
  RAND SP11 .... 130 F7

  RSAL SP5 .... 194 E2 🖪
  TADY RG26 .... 51 M6
Yew Tree La *OVTN* RG25 .... 113 K7
  RSAL SP5 .... 196 A5
Yew Tree Pl *LISS* GU33 .... 236 F4
Yew Tree Wk *FRIM* GU16 .... 59 H7
Yolland *LIPH* GU30 .... 122 F1
York Cl *KEMP* RG22 .... 92 A8
  BOR GU35 .... 189 J6
  NWBY RG14 .... 3 G6
York Crs *ALDT* GU11 .... 6 D4
York La *HTWY* RG27 .... 75 H3
York Ms *ALTN* GU34 .... 164 F4
York Pl *CBLY* GU15 .... 59 G1
York Rd *ALDT* GU11 .... 6 D4
  ASHV GU12 .... 101 K5
  CBLY GU15 .... 59 G1
  FARN GU14 .... 78 F7
  FNM GU9 .... 122 F8
  NWBY RG14 .... 3 G6
Yorktown Rd *SHST* GU47 .... 57 M1
York Wy *SHST* GU47 .... 37 K8
Yorkwood *LISS* GU33 .... 236 E4
Youlden Cl *CBLY* GU15 .... 59 K3
Youlden Dr *CBLY* GU15 .... 59 K3
Young Crs *STHA* RG19 .... 3 M9
Youngs Dr *ASHV* GU12 .... 101 J6
Youngs Paddock *RSAL* SP5 .... 194 F2 🖪
Youngs Rd *ALTN* GU34 .... 164 E4

Z

Zinnia Cl *KEMP* RG22 .... 114 F2
Zion Rd *RAND* SP11 .... 149 J3
Zouch Av *NTID* SP9 .... 102 D1
Zouch Cl *NTID* SP9 .... 102 D1
Zouch Farm Rd *NTID* SP9 .... 102 D1

Index - featured places

The AA - Fanum House
  BSTK RG21 .... 5 K6
Abbey Business Park
  FNM GU9 .... 123 K8
The Abbey School
  FNM GU9 .... 123 G7
Abbotsford Farm
  Business Centre
  ALTN GU34 .... 185 J5
Abbotts Ann Primary School
  RAND SP11 .... 129 L4
Abro Industrial Estate
  ALDT GU11 .... 101 G5
Adelaide Medical Centre
  AND SP10 .... 9 K5
AFC Newbury Football Ground
  NWBY RG14 .... 3 G3
Airborne Forces Museum
  ALDT GU11 .... 100 D3
Aldermaston C of E School
  THLE RG7 .... 29 J1
Aldershot & Farnham
  County Court
  ALDT GU11 .... 7 G2
Aldershot Health Centre
  ALDT GU11 .... 6 D1
Aldershot Military Historical
  Trust & Museum
  ALDT GU11 .... 100 F1
Aldershot Town Football Club
  ALDT GU11 .... 7 H2
Alexander House
  Business Centre
  ALDT GU11 .... 7 G2
Alexandra Surgery
  ALDT GU11 .... 6 D1
Allen Gallery
  ALTN GU34 .... 164 E5
All Hallows RC
  Secondary School
  FNM GU9 .... 6 C8
All Saints C of E First School
  NFNM GU10 .... 147 M5
All Saints C of E Junior School
  FLET GU13 .... 76 C8
All Saints Community
  Primary School
  WINC SO23 .... 227 G2
Alresford County
  Junior School
  NALR SO24 .... 206 C3
Alresford Golf Club
  NALR SO24 .... 206 B5
The Alresford Surgery
  NALR SO24 .... 206 C2
Alton Business Centre
  ALTN GU34 .... 165 G5
Alton College
  ALTN GU34 .... 164 E3
Alton Convent School
  ALTN GU34 .... 164 F2
Alton County Infant School
  ALTN GU34 .... 164 F4
Alton Health Centre
  ALTN GU34 .... 164 F4
Alton Rugby Club
  ALTN GU34 .... 164 F2
Alton Town Football Club
  ALTN GU34 .... 164 F3
Amery Hill Secondary School
  ALTN GU34 .... 164 E4
Amesbury School
  GSHT GU26 .... 192 B7

Amport C of E (aided)
  Primary School
  RAND SP11 .... 128 F3
Andover Football Club
  AND SP10 .... 106 B6
Andover Golf Club
  AND SP10 .... 9 H9
Andover Museum &
  the Museum of the Iron Age
  AND SP10 .... 9 J4
Andover Road Retail Park
  WINW SO22 .... 10 C3
Andrews Endowed
  Primary School
  ALTN GU34 .... 165 H2
Anstey County Junior School
  ALTN GU34 .... 164 E4
Anton County Infant School
  AND SP10 .... 9 C9
Anton County Junior School
  AND SP10 .... 9 C9
Anton Trading Estate
  AND SP10 .... 9 G8
The Anvil Concert Hall
  BSTK RG21 .... 4 E7
Appleshaw School
  RAND SP11 .... 105 C1
Arena Leisure Centre
  CBLY GU15 .... 58 E2
The Ark School
  THLE RG7 .... 18 C7
Army Golf Club
  ALDT GU11 .... 100 B2
Arnhem Barracks
  ALDT GU11 .... 100 D5
Arrow Industrial Estate
  FARN GU14 .... 78 C6
Ashdown Family &
  Health Centre
  NTID SP9 .... 102 E2
Ashford Hill Primary School
  STHA RG19 .... 28 B7
Ash Grange CP School
  ASHV GU12 .... 101 L6
Ash Manor School
  ASHV GU12 .... 101 J8
Ash Vale Health Centre
  ASHV GU12 .... 101 L4
Avington Park
  RWIN SO21 .... 204 D3
Badger Farm Surgery
  WINW SO22 .... 226 B4
Badgerswood Surgery
  BOR GU35 .... 190 A3
Badshot Lea County
  First School
  FNM GU9 .... 123 K2
Balksbury County
  Infant School
  AND SP10 .... 8 B7
Balksbury Industrial Estate
  RAND SP11 .... 130 D3
Bartley Wood Business Park
  HTWY RG27 .... 74 B8
Barton Industrial Estate
  NALR SO24 .... 161 L7
Barton Stacey C of E
  Primary School
  RWIN SO21 .... 133 K8
Basing County Infants School
  CHIN RG24 .... 94 A2
Basingstoke Business Centre
  KEMP RG22 .... 92 D6

Basingstoke College of
  Technology
  BSTK RG21 .... 4 C8
Basingstoke County Court
  BSTK RG21 .... 5 H7
Basingstoke & Deane
  Borough Council
  CHIN RG24 .... 5 L2
Basingstoke Ice Rink
  KEMP RG22 .... 92 C4
Basingstoke & North
  Hants Cricket Club
  BSTK RG21 .... 93 G5
Basingstoke Rugby Club
  KEMP RG22 .... 92 A7
Basingstoke Sports Centre
  BSTK RG21 .... 4 E7
Basingstoke Town Football Club
  KEMP RG22 .... 92 D6
Baytree Gallery
  NALR SO24 .... 206 B2
Beacon Hill County
  Primary School
  GSHT GU26 .... 191 M2
Beaumont County
  Junior School
  ALDT GU11 .... 6 C2
Beaver Industrial Estate
  LIPH GU30 .... 214 F5
Beech Down County
  Primary School
  KEMP RG22 .... 92 C8
Beechnut Industrial Estate
  ALDT GU11 .... 7 H3
Belle Vue County Infant School
  ASHV GU12 .... 7 L1
Benham Park
  KSCL RG20 .... 12 D4
Berkshire Business Centre
  STHA RG19 .... 15 K6
Berkshire County Council
  NWBY RG14 .... 2 E1
Berkshire County Council
  NWBY RG14 .... 2 B8
Berkshire County Council
  NWBY RG14 .... 2 D3
Bilton Industrial Estate
  CHIN RG24 .... 71 J7
Binsted C of E Primary School
  ALTN GU34 .... 166 C1
Binswood View
  Business Centre
  ALTN GU34 .... 188 C1
Bishop Challoner RC Secondary
  School
  KEMP RG22 .... 92 B5
Bishopswood Co Junior School
  TADY RG26 .... 29 L8
Bishopwood Co Infant School
  TADY RG26 .... 49 L1
Blackmoor Golf Club
  BOR GU35 .... 188 F7
Blackwater & Hawley
  Leisure Centre
  BLKW GU17 .... 58 A5
Blackwater Industrial Estate
  BLKW GU17 .... 58 B4
Blackwater Trading Estate
  ASHV GU12 .... 101 H8
Bladon Gallery
  RAND SP11 .... 62 D8
Blands Infant School
  THLE RG7 .... 19 J6

Bohunt Community School
  LIPH GU30 .... 214 E4
Bohunt Manor
  LIPH GU30 .... 214 E5
Bordon County Junior &
  Infant School
  BOR GU35 .... 189 H4
Bordon Trading Estate
  BOR GU35 .... 188 F3
Boundaries Surgery
  ALTN GU34 .... 185 H5
Bourne County First School
  NFNM GU10 .... 147 G1
Bourne Mill Industrial Estate
  FNM GU9 .... 123 H5
Bourne Tennis Club
  FNM GU9 .... 122 F8
Bramley C of E Primary School
  TADY RG26 .... 51 L4
Brick Kiln Industrial Estate
  TADY RG26 .... 29 M7
Brickyards Industrial Estate
  PSF GU32 .... 235 M7
Brighton Hill
  Community School
  KEMP RG22 .... 92 C7
Brimpton School
  THLE RG7 .... 28 C2
Bristow County First School
  CBLY GU15 .... 58 E6
Broadmoor County
  Primary School
  CWTH RG45 .... 38 A4
Broadmoor Hospital
  CWTH RG45 .... 38 A4
Brookham School
  LIPH GU30 .... 215 H6
Brookside Business Centre
  FNM GU9 .... 34 A2
The Brook Trading Estate
  ASHV GU12 .... 101 H5
Broughton County
  Primary School
  STOK SO20 .... 197 G1
Browning Barracks
  ALDT GU11 .... 100 D3
Broxhead Trading Estate
  BOR GU35 .... 189 L2
Bucklebury C of E
  Primary School
  THLE RG7 .... 15 M2
Burdwood Surgery
  STHA RG19 .... 15 H6
Burghclere CP School
  KSCL RG20 .... 45 K2
Burghfield Health Centre
  THLE RG7 .... 19 L5
Burnham Copse Junior School
  TADY RG26 .... 29 K7
Burnside Surgery
  FLET GU13 .... 76 F7
Buryfields Infant School
  ODIM RG29 .... 96 D6
Bury Hill
  RAND SP11 .... 130 C4
The Business Centre
  BSTK RG21 .... 5 G8
The Business Centre
  THLE RG7 .... 28 C2
The Butts County
  Primary School
  ALTN GU34 .... 164 C6

Calleva Roman
  Antiquity and Museum
  THLE RG7 .... 30 E7
Calthorpe Park School
  FLET GU13 .... 76 B8
Camberley County
  Infant School
  CBLY GU15 .... 58 E3
Camberley Cricket Club
  CBLY GU15 .... 59 G5
Camberley Health Centre
  CBLY GU15 .... 58 E5
Camberley Heath Golf Club
  CBLY GU15 .... 59 K4
Camberley Magistrates Court
  CBLY GU15 .... 59 G2
Camberley Rugby Football Club
  CBLY GU15 .... 58 F5
Camberley Town Football Club
  CBLY GU15 .... 58 E5
Cambridge Military Hospital
  ALDT GU11 .... 100 E5
Camelsdale County First School
  HASM GU27 .... 216 C3
Camp Road Industrial Estate
  FARN GU14 .... 79 G8
Candover Gallery
  NALR SO24 .... 206 C2
Carwarden House School
  CBLY GU15 .... 59 K5
Castledown
  Comprehensive School
  RAND SP11 .... 80 B7
Castle Hill Junior School
  DEAN RG23 .... 92 A3
Castle Industrial Park
  NWBY RG14 .... 13 M3
Castle Primary School
  RAND SP11 .... 80 F6
Castle School
  NWBY RG14 .... 13 J2
Cedars School
  THLE RG7 .... 29 K1
Central Estate
  ALDT GU11 .... 7 H2
Century Galleries
  HTWY RG27 .... 75 J2
Chalkridge School
  KEMP RG22 .... 92 D7
Chantry Centre
  Shopping Precinct
  AND SP10 .... 9 H5
Chapel House Gallery
  OVTN RG25 .... 114 C7
Charles Kingsley School
  HTWY RG27 .... 35 M8
Charlton Hill Surgery
  AND SP10 .... 8 D2
Charlton Road Health Centre
  AND SP10 .... 8 D2
Chase Community Hospital
  BOR GU35 .... 189 J6
Chawton Primary School
  ALTN GU34 .... 186 C1
Chesil Theatre
  WINC SO23 .... 11 J9
Cheswycks School
  FRIM GU16 .... 79 L3
Chineham Park Primary School
  CHIN RG24 .... 5 J2

Church Grange &
Bramblys Grange
Health Centre
BSTK RG21 .... 4 D9
Church Grange Lychpit Surgery
CHIN RG24 .... 93 L1
Church of England
Primary School
AND SP10 .... 9 J6
Church of England School
THLE RG7 .... 17 G4
City Business Centre
WINC SO23 .... 11 G5
City Offices
WINC SO23 .... 11 H8
Clarendon County
Junior & Infant School
NTID SP9 .... 102 E1
Clatford Primary School
RAND SP11 .... 130 F7
Clayton Barracks
ALDT GU11 .... 101 G4
The Clere Secondary School
KSCL RG20 .... 45 K1
Clewborough House
Preparatory School
CBLY GU15 .... 59 K2
Cliddesden Primary School
OVTN RG25 .... 115 M3
Clift Surgery
TADY RG26 .... 51 K4
The Clinic
FNM GU9 .... 122 F6
Club House
OVTN RG25 .... 114 D6
The Club House
LISS GU33 .... 237 K4
Coliseum Business Centre
CBLY GU15 .... 58 D5
College Art School
WINC SO23 .... 226 E2
Collingwood College
CBLY GU15 .... 39 K8
Coltwood Business Centre
ALDT GU11 .... 7 G2
The Community Hospital
ALTN GU34 .... 164 C1
Comprehensive
YTLY GU46 .... 56 F4
Compton All Saints C of E
Primary School
RWIN SO21 .... 226 C8
The Connaught School
ASHV GU12 .... 124 B1
Contour Gallery
LIPH GU30 .... 214 C4
Cordwalles County
Middle School
CBLY GU15 .... 39 J8
County Primary School
NTID SP9 .... 126 C1
Court Moor School
FLET GU13 .... 98 E1
Cove County Infant School
FARN GU14 .... 78 B2
Cove County Junior School
FARN GU14 .... 78 B3
Cove County Secondary School
FARN GU14 .... 78 B3
Cove Cricket Club
FARN GU14 .... 78 B4
Cove Manor County
Junior & Infant School
FARN GU14 .... 78 C2
Coxmoor Farm Light
Industrial Estate
NFNM GU10 .... 98 A6
Cranbourne Secondary School
BSTK RG21 .... 92 E5
Crawley Ridge First School
CBLY GU15 .... 59 J2
Cricklade College
AND SP10 .... 9 H4
Cricklade Theatre
AND SP10 .... 9 G4
Crondall CP School
NFNM GU10 .... 121 H2
Crookham C of E
Infants School
FLET GU13 .... 98 C4
Crookham County
Junior School
FLET GU13 .... 99 G4
Crowthorne Business Centre
CWTH RG45 .... 37 M1
Crowthorne C of E
Primary School
CWTH RG45 .... 37 L3
Curtis Museum
ALTN GU34 .... 164 E4
Daneshill East Industrial Estate
CHIN RG24 .... 5 L5
Daneshill Industrial Estate
CHIN RG24 .... 5 M4
Daneshill School
HTWY RG27 .... 53 J4
Deane's Almshouses
BSTK RG21 .... 93 G4
Dean Surgery
NALR SO24 .... 207 M4
Derry Down Health Clinic
RAND SP11 .... 85 M7
Diva Gallery
ODIM RG29 .... 96 D5
Dogmersfield C of E
Primary School
HTWY RG27 .... 97 M1
Donnington Castle
NWBY RG14 .... 13 H1
Douai School
THLE RG7 .... 17 G3
Dove House School
BSTK RG21 .... 4 F4
Dr Gregs Surgery
NTID SP9 .... 102 E2
Dunston Park School
NTHA RG18 .... 15 G4

Eagle House School
SHST GU47 .... 37 K6
East Barn Surgery
CHIN RG24 .... 71 L8
East Berkshire Golf Club
CWTH RG45 .... 37 H3
Eastfield House Surgery
NWBY RG14 .... 2 E6
Easton Lane Business Park
WINC SO23 .... 11 L6
Eccossis Hospital Products
RAND SP11 .... 104 F6
Edgebarrow School
CWTH RG45 .... 37 L5
Edgebarrow Sports Centre
CWTH RG45 .... 37 M5
Edgeborough School
NFNM GU10 .... 146 F5
Eggars School
ALTN GU34 .... 165 G2
Elliott Industrial Park
ASHV GU12 .... 101 H6
Elm House Surgery
NTID SP9 .... 102 D1
Elstree School
THLE RG7 .... 17 G4
Enborne C of E School
KSCL RG20 .... 24 B2
Enborne Lodge (Sch)
NWBY RG14 .... 24 E3
Enterprise Industrial Estate
ASHV GU12 .... 101 J1
Eversley Cricket Club
HTWY RG27 .... 36 C8
Evingar Industrial Estate
WHCH RG28 .... 110 A2
Fairfax Industrial Estate
ASHV GU12 .... 101 H6
Fairfields Primary School
BSTK RG21 .... 93 G4
Falkland CP School
NWBY RG14 .... 25 G2
Farleigh House Sch
OVTN RG25 .... 115 K6
Farleigh School
RAND SP11 .... 130 A8
Farley Hill Primary School
THLE RG7 .... 34 F3
Farleys All Saints
Primary School
RSAL SP5 .... 194 B8
Farmhouse Gallery
KSCL RG20 .... 44 E1
Farnborough Business Centre
FARN GU14 .... 78 C6
Farnborough College of
Technology
ASHV GU12 .... 7 H4
Farnborough College of
Technology
FARN GU14 .... 78 E8
Farnborough College of
Technology
FARN GU14 .... 78 F6
Farnborough Grange
County Junior School
FARN GU14 .... 58 C8
Farnborough Hill School
FARN GU14 .... 78 F3
Farnborough Recreation Centre
FARN GU14 .... 78 E5
Farnborough Rugby
Football Club
FARN GU14 .... 78 D2
Farnborough Town
Football Club
FARN GU14 .... 58 D8
Farnham Business Centre
FNM GU9 .... 122 E8
Farnham Business Centre
FNM GU9 .... 122 F5
Farnham Business Park
FNM GU9 .... 122 D7
Farnham Castle
FNM GU9 .... 122 F5
Farnham College
FNM GU9 .... 122 F7
Farnham Golf Club
NFNM GU10 .... 124 A6
Farnham Hospital
FNM GU9 .... 123 H5
Farnham Museum
FNM GU9 .... 122 E6
Farnham Retail Park
FNM GU9 .... 123 H5
Farringdon Industrial Centre
ALTN GU34 .... 186 B6
Farringdon Industrial Estate
ALTN GU34 .... 186 B6
Fernhill Comprehensive School
FARN GU14 .... 58 C7
Fernhill Primary School
FARN GU14 .... 58 C7
Finchampstead C of E
Primary School
EWKG RG40 .... 36 B5
Finchampstead Sports Club
EWKG RG40 .... 36 B5
Finns Industrial Park
NFNM GU10 .... 98 A6
Fir Tree CP School
NTHA RG18 .... 14 B4
Fleet Business Park
FLET GU13 .... 99 G5
Fleet Community Hospital
FLET GU13 .... 76 D6
Fleet Police Station
FLET GU13 .... 76 E8
Focus 303 Business Centre
AND SP10 .... 107 J7
Folly Hill County Infant School
FNM GU9 .... 122 D2
Forest Surgery
BOR GU35 .... 189 J5
Fort Hill School
DEAN RG23 .... 92 B2
Forthill Surgery
DEAN RG23 .... 92 B2

Fosters Business Park
HTWY RG27 .... 95 J1
France Hill School
CBLY GU15 .... 58 F6
Francis Bailey School
STHA RG19 .... 15 H5
Frensham C of E First School
NFNM GU10 .... 147 G8
Frensham Heights School
NFNM GU10 .... 146 D6
Frensham Pond Sailing Club
NFNM GU10 .... 168 F3
Friarsgate Medical Centre
WINC SO23 .... 11 H8
Frimley C of E First &
Middle School
FRIM GU16 .... 79 H1
Frimley Green Medical Centre
FRIM GU16 .... 79 J2
Frimley Park Hospital
FRIM GU16 .... 59 G6
Frogmore Community School
BLKW GU17 .... 57 J3
Frogmore County
Infant School
BLKW GU17 .... 57 L4
Frogmore Endowed
Controlled Infant School
PSF GU32 .... 234 D6
The Gallery
SHST GU47 .... 37 M8
Garlands County Junior School
THLE RG7 .... 19 K5
Garrison Theatre
NTID SP9 .... 102 C2
Gillies Health Centre
KEMP RG22 .... 92 C8
Global Adventure Sailing Club
FNM GU9 .... 122 E6
Golf Club Bungalow
ALTN GU34 .... 142 D7
Gorse Ride Junior School
EWKG RG40 .... 36 B1
The Grange Park
NALR SO24 .... 181 K3
Grateley Business Park
RAND SP11 .... 149 K1
Grateley Junior & Infant School
RAND SP11 .... 127 M8
Gratton Surgery
RWIN SO21 .... 156 B4
Grayshott Clinic
GSHT GU26 .... 191 L4
Grayshott Council Office
GSHT GU26 .... 192 A5
Grayshott Primary School
GSHT GU26 .... 191 L5
Grayshott Surgery
GSHT GU26 .... 192 A5
Grayswood C of E School
HASM GU27 .... 193 J6
Greatham Primary School
LISS GU33 .... 212 E6
Greenacres School
WINW SO22 .... 10 E3
Green Croft School
FARN GU14 .... 79 G2
Greenfields Junior School
HTWY RG27 .... 75 H3
Greenham Road Retail Park
NWBY RG14 .... 2 F6
Gresham Industrial Estate
ASHV GU12 .... 101 H6
Grey House Private School
HTWY RG27 .... 75 J2
Group Practice
NTID SP9 .... 102 E3
Grovebell Industrial Estate
NFNM GU10 .... 146 C1
Grove County Primary School
FRIM GU16 .... 59 H6
Guildford Road
Industrial Estate
FNM GU9 .... 123 G5
Guillemont County
Junior School
FARN GU14 .... 77 M1
Hackwood Ho
OVTN RG25 .... 93 J8
Hale County First &
Middle School
FNM GU9 .... 122 E1
The Hampshire Clinic
CHIN RG24 .... 5 M5
Hampshire County Council
BSTK RG21 .... 4 F8
Hampshire County Council
WINC SO23 .... 10 E7
Hampshire County Council -
Basing House
CHIN RG24 .... 93 M2
Hampshire County Council -
Chute House
BSTK RG21 .... 4 E7
Hampshire Golf Club
RAND SP11 .... 131 G5
Harestock Infant School
WINW SO22 .... 202 C5
Harriet Costello School
BSTK RG21 .... 5 H9
Harrow Way Community School
AND SP10 .... 8 B1
Hartley Park Farm
Business Centre
ALTN GU34 .... 187 J4
Hart Sports Centre
FLET GU13 .... 76 B8
Haslemere District Hospital
HASM GU27 .... 217 G1
Haslemere Health Centre
HASM GU27 .... 217 G1
Haslemere Museum
HASM GU27 .... 217 G1
Haslemere Preparatory School
HASM GU27 .... 217 G3

Hassocks Wood
Industrial Estate
CHIN RG24 .... 5 M3
Hatch Ride Primary School
CWTH RG45 .... 37 L1
Hatch Warren County
Infant School
KEMP RG22 .... 115 H1
Hatch Warren County
Junior School
KEMP RG22 .... 115 H1
Hatch Warren Retail Park
KEMP RG22 .... 114 F2
Hatch Warren Surgery
KEMP RG22 .... 114 F2
Hatherden C of E
Primary School
RAND SP11 .... 83 H7
Hawley CP School
BLKW GU17 .... 58 B5
Hawley Lane Industrial Estate
FARN GU14 .... 58 E8
Hawley Place School
BLKW GU17 .... 58 A7
The Hawthorns School
KEMP RG22 .... 92 B7
Haymarket Theatre
BSTK RG21 .... 4 E9
Headley Park Country Club
BOR GU35 .... 168 F3
Heath End County
Secondary School
FNM GU9 .... 123 H2
Heatherside Surgery
CBLY GU15 .... 59 M4
Heath Hill Surgery
CWTH RG45 .... 37 L4
Henry Beaufort School
WINW SO22 .... 202 D5
The Herons Swimming and
Fitness Centre
HASM GU27 .... 216 C2
Highclere Castle
KSCL RG20 .... 44 E6
Highfield School
LIPH GU30 .... 215 H6
Hindhead Golf Club
GSHT GU26 .... 191 L2
Hollycombe School
LIPH GU30 .... 238 F4
Holly Lodge CP School
ASHV GU12 .... 79 J8
Holly Tree Surgery
NFNM GU10 .... 146 D4
Holmwood Health Centre
TADY RG26 .... 29 K7
Holybourne Theatre
ALTN GU34 .... 165 H2
Holy Cross Hospital
HASM GU27 .... 216 C1
Home Farm School
THLE RG7 .... 17 G5
Hook County Junior School
HTWY RG27 .... 74 A7
Hook Infant School
HTWY RG27 .... 74 A7
The Hop Kiln
FNM GU9 .... 122 E7
Horris Hill Preparatory School
KSCL RG20 .... 25 H5
The Hospital
CBLY GU15 .... 38 D8
Houndmills Industrial Estate
BSTK RG21 .... 92 D1
Hurstbourne Tarrant School
RAND SP11 .... 84 D2
The Hurst Community School
TADY RG26 .... 29 C7
Ian Walker Odiham Gallery
ODIM RG29 .... 96 D5
Icknield School
AND SP10 .... 107 J6
Industrial Estate
DEAN RG23 .... 114 E4
Inhurst House School
STHA RG19 .... 28 F7
Inkpen Primary School
HUNG RG17 .... 22 A2
Itchen Abbas Cp School
RWIN SO21 .... 204 D1
Jenner House Surgery
FARN GU14 .... 78 B4
The Jigsaw School
FRIM GU16 .... 79 H5
John Hanson
Community School
AND SP10 .... 8 E6
John Hunt of Everest
Community School
CHIN RG24 .... 71 H7
John Rankin County
Infants School
NWBY RG14 .... 13 G8
John Rankin Junior
NWBY RG14 .... 13 G8
Kelseys Doctors Surgery
LISS GU33 .... 236 E4
Kempshott County
Infant School
KEMP RG22 .... 91 M8
Kempshott County
Junior School
KEMP RG22 .... 91 M8
Kennet Secondary School
STHA RG19 .... 15 H5
The Kerridge Industrial Estate
ALTN GU34 .... 164 F4
Kimpton Primary School
RAND SP11 .... 104 C1
King Alfred College
WINW SO22 .... 10 B8
King Alfreds College of Higher
Education
WINW SO22 .... 10 C9
The Kings Centre
ALDT GU11 .... 6 F1
Kingsclere Health Centre
KSCL RG20 .... 47 J6

Kingsclere Primary School
KSCL RG20 .... 47 J6
Kings Furlong Infant School
BSTK RG21 .... 92 E5
Kings Furlong Junior School
BSTK RG21 .... 92 E5
Kingsgrove Industrial Estate
FARN GU14 .... 78 D5
Kingsley Business Park
BOR GU35 .... 167 H7
Kings School
BSTK RG21 .... 4 D9
Kings School
WINW SO22 .... 226 A2
Kings Somborne C of E School
STOK SO20 .... 198 E6
Kingstons Industrial Estate
ASHV GU12 .... 101 H6
Kingsworthy Primary School
WINC SO23 .... 203 H2
Knights Enham Infants
Infant School
AND SP10 .... 106 F5
Knights Enham Junior School
AND SP10 .... 106 F5
Lakeside Business Park
SHST GU47 .... 57 K1
Lakeside Country Club
FRIM GU16 .... 79 K2
Lakeside County
Primary School
FRIM GU16 .... 59 J7
Lankhills School
WINC SO23 .... 10 F4
Leisure Centre
AND SP10 .... 9 H4
Lido Sports Club
WINC SO23 .... 11 G5
The Lilley Clinic
HUNG RG17 .... 20 E2
Limington House School
KEMP RG22 .... 92 C5
Linsford Business Park
FRIM GU16 .... 79 J5
Liphook County Infant School
LIPH GU30 .... 214 E4
Liphook Golf Club
LIPH GU30 .... 214 D8
Liphook Junior School
LIPH GU30 .... 214 D4
Liss Business Centre
LISS GU33 .... 236 D3
Liss County Infant &
Junior School
LISS GU33 .... 236 E5
Littlefield School
LIPH GU30 .... 215 G6
Lockerley C of E (a)
Primary School
ROMY SO51 .... 220 F7
Loddon Business Centre
CHIN RG24 .... 5 M4
London Road School
ODIM RG29 .... 96 D5
Longfellow Parade Clinic
CHIN RG24 .... 5 H1
Longparish School
RAND SP11 .... 133 G4
Longsutton Primary School
ODIM RG29 .... 119 J5
Lord Mayor Treloar College
Lower School
ALTN GU34 .... 144 A6
Lord Mayor Treloar College
Upper School
ALTN GU34 .... 165 G1
Lord Wandsworth College
ODIM RG29 .... 119 K6
Lorraine County First School
CBLY GU15 .... 39 K8
Ludgershall Health Centre
RAND SP11 .... 80 E6
Ludgershall Sports Club
RAND SP11 .... 80 D6
Lymington Farm
Industrial Estate
ALTN GU34 .... 184 F5
Lyndhurst School
CBLY GU15 .... 58 E3
Mainline Business Centre
LISS GU33 .... 236 E4
The Malls/the Walks
Shopping Centre
BSTK RG21 .... 4 F7
Manor Farm Business Centre
NFNM GU10 .... 124 C3
Manorfield Infant School
KEMP RG22 .... 115 K1
The Manse Health Centre
AND SP10 .... 9 J5
Mansfield Business Park
ALTN GU34 .... 184 F5
Maple Ridge School
BSTK RG21 .... 4 E4
Mark Way School
AND SP10 .... 9 M4
Marlborough County
Infant School
ALDT GU11 .... 100 F1
Marnel Infant &
Junior Schools
CHIN RG24 .... 71 H7
Marsh Farm Business Centre
NFNM GU10 .... 98 C7
Mayfield Avenue
Industrial Park
RAND SP11 .... 104 F6
Mayfield County
Junior & Infant School
FARN GU14 .... 78 D2
Mayfield School
ALTN GU34 .... 165 G3
Mayhill County Junior School
ODIM RG29 .... 96 D6
May's Bounty
BSTK RG21 .... 93 G5
The Meadow School
BOR GU35 .... 189 M4

Mecca Leisure Bingo and
  Social Club
  AND SP10 .... **9** G6
Medstead School
  ALTN GU34 .... **184** E2
Merton County Junior School
  CHIN RG24 .... **4** C1
Micheldever Primary School
  RWIN SO21 .... **157** M5
Middle Hill Health Clinic
  ALDT GU11 .... **100** D5
Milestone Transport Museum
  KEMP RG22 .... **92** B3
Mill Chase County
  Secondary School
  BOR GU35 .... **189** L5
Moor Park College
  NFNM GU10 .... **123** K7
More House School
  NFNM GU10 .... **146** F6
Morland Surgery
  TADY RG26 .... **49** L1
Mortimer Surgery
  THLE RG7 .... **31** J2
Mottisfont Abbey
  ROMY SO51 .... **221** L5
Mottisfont Club House
  ROMY SO51 .... **221** K6
Murrell Green Business Park
  HTWY RG27 .... **74** D6
Museum of Army Flying
  STOK SO20 .... **150** F5
Mylen Business Centre
  AND SP10 .... **8** D3
Mytchett County First School
  FRIM GU16 .... **79** J4
The Natural Health Centre
  NWBY RG14 .... **25** G2
Nethercliffe School
  WINW SO22 .... **10** D5
New Ashgate Gallery
  FNM GU9 .... **122** E6
Newbury Business Park
  NWBY RG14 .... **3** J2
Newbury College of Further
  Education
  NWBY RG14 .... **2** C1
Newbury District Council
  NWBY RG14 .... **3** G6
Newbury District Council
  WHCH RG28 .... **110** B2
Newbury District Hospital
  NWBY RG14 .... **2** D7
Newbury District
  Museum & Tourist Information
  Centre
  NWBY RG14 .... **2** F4
Newbury Retail Park
  NWBY RG14 .... **25** L1
Newbury Rugby
  Football Club Ltd
  NWBY RG14 .... **25** J2
Newbury Town Council
  NWBY RG14 .... **2** E4
The New Chineham Surgery
  CHIN RG24 .... **71** L6
New Greenham Park
  Leisure Centre
  STHA RG19 .... **26** D4
Newlands CP School
  YTLY GU46 .... **56** F9
Newport County Junior & Infant
  School
  ASHV GU12 .... **7** L4
New Scotland Hill CP School
  SHST GU47 .... **37** K6
New Street Football Club
  RAND SP11 .... **106** C3
New Street Medical Centre
  AND SP10 .... **9** K3
Newton Toney School
  AMSY SP4 .... **148** A3
Newtown Surgery
  LIPH GU30 .... **214** E6
Norman Court School
  RSAL SP5 .... **195** K6
The Norman Gate
  School (acorns)
  AND SP10 .... **9** M3
Northcroft Surgery
  NWBY RG14 .... **2** D4
North Farnborough
  County Infant School
  FARN GU14 .... **79** G4
North Hampshire Hospital
  CHIN RG24 .... **70** D8
North Hants Golf Club
  FARN GU14 .... **76** F4
North Lane Practice
  ASHV GU12 .... **101** H7
Northtown Trading Estate
  ASHV GU12 .... **101** H7
North Waltham
  Business Centre
  OVTN RG25 .... **114** A6
North Waltham School
  OVTN RG25 .... **113** K7
Oak Farm Community School
  FARN GU14 .... **78** D2
Oaklands County
  Junior & Infant School
  CWTH RG45 .... **37** K2
Oakley C of E Junior School
  DEAN RG23 .... **90** F7
Oakley County Infant School
  DEAN RG23 .... **90** F7
Oak Park Golf Club
  NFNM GU10 .... **121** K2
Oakridge County Junior School
  BSTK RG21 .... **4** C3
Oakwood School
  HTWY RG27 .... **75** J3
Odiham Castle
  ODIM RG29 .... **96** A4
Odiham Cottage Hospital
  ODIM RG29 .... **96** D6
The Odiham Health Centre
  ODIM RG29 .... **96** C5

Old Basing Surgery
  CHIN RG24 .... **94** A3
Old Thorns Golf &
  Country Club
  LIPH GU30 .... **214** A4
Olivers Battery Primary School
  WINW SO22 .... **226** B5
The Omni Business Centre
  ALTN GU34 .... **165** G5
Oriel Business Park
  ALTN GU34 .... **165** G5
Osborn Way Industrial Estate
  HTWY RG27 .... **73** M8
Our Ladys Preparatory School
  CWTH RG45 .... **37** K3
Overbridge Surgery
  KEMP RG22 .... **92** D4
Overton C of E Primary School
  OVTN RG25 .... **88** E7
Overton Gallery
  OVTN RG25 .... **88** F8
Overton Surgery
  OVTN RG25 .... **89** C8
Owlsmoor Primary School
  SHST GU47 .... **38** B7
Padworth College
  THLE RG7 .... **18** B7
Park House School
  NWBY RG14 .... **25** H2
Park Primary School
  ALDT GU11 .... **7** J7
Park View Infant School
  KEMP RG22 .... **92** B6
Park View Junior School
  KEMP RG22 .... **92** B5
Parsons Down Infant School
  STHA RG19 .... **14** E5
Parsons Down Junior School
  STHA RG19 .... **14** D5
Passfield Mill Business Park
  LIPH GU30 .... **190** A7
Pendulum Gallery
  ALTN GU34 .... **187** K8
Perins County
  Secondary School
  NALR SO24 .... **206** B3
Petersfield Golf Club
  PSF GU32 .... **236** B8
Peter Symonds College
  WINW SO22 .... **10** E4
The Pheasant Hotel
  AMSY SP4 .... **170** D6
Pierreponte School
  NFNM GU10 .... **147** H7
Pilgrims School
  WINC SO23 .... **11** H9
Pilgrims Way Infants School
  FNM GU9 .... **122** E8
Pinehill Surgery
  BOR GU35 .... **189** J6
Pineridge County First School
  CBLY GU15 .... **39** K7
Pinewood Infants School
  FARN GU14 .... **78** A1
Pipers Industrial Estate
  STHA RG19 .... **15** J7
Portesbery School
  CBLY GU15 .... **59** G2
Portway County Infants School
  AND SP10 .... **8** A4
Portway Junior School
  AND SP10 .... **106** B8
Potley Hill County
  Primary School
  BLKW GU17 .... **57** L3
Potters Gate Primary School
  FNM GU9 .... **122** D6
Preston Candover
  Primary School
  OVTN RG25 .... **139** G8
Preston Ho
  OVTN RG25 .... **139** G7
Princes Hall
  ALDT GU11 .... **6** E1
Princes Mead School
  RWIN SO21 .... **203** K2
Prior Heath School
  CBLY GU15 .... **59** K3
The Priory Primary School
  TADY RG26 .... **50** J7
Prospect Business Centre
  NALR SO24 .... **206** B4
Puttenham C of E School
  RGUW GU3 .... **125** L4
Queen Marys College
  BSTK RG21 .... **93** G5
Raceview Business Centre
  NWBY RG14 .... **3** H5
Rake C of E Controlled
  First School
  LISS GU33 .... **237** L3
Redfields Industrial Estate
  FLET GU13 .... **98** E5
Redfields Industrial Park
  FLET GU13 .... **98** D6
Retail Park
  NWBY RG14 .... **3** K3
Richard Aldworth
  Community School
  KEMP RG22 .... **92** C6
Richmond Surgery
  FLET GU13 .... **98** E2
Ridgeway School
  FNM GU9 .... **146** F1
Riverpark Industrial Estate
  NWBY RG14 .... **3** J3
River Park Leisure Centre
  WINC SO23 .... **11** H5
Riverside Business Park
  FNM GU9 .... **122** F5
Riverside Close Surgery
  LISS GU33 .... **236** D4
Riverside Park
  Industrial Estate
  FNM GU9 .... **123** G5
Riverwey Industrial Park
  ALTN GU34 .... **165** G4

Robert Mays School
  ODIM RG29 .... **96** B5
Romans Business Park
  FNM GU9 .... **123** G5
Roman Way Primary School
  AND SP10 .... **106** F4
Ropley C of E Primary School
  NALR SO24 .... **208** B3
Rowledge C of E First School
  NFNM GU10 .... **146** A5
Royal Army Medical Corps
  ALDT GU11 .... **101** G4
Royal Hampshire
  County Hospital
  WINW SO22 .... **10** B8
Royal Hampshire
  Regiment Museum
  WINC SO23 .... **10** F8
The Royal School
  HASM GU27 .... **192** D6
Royal Winchester Golf Club
  WINW SO22 .... **226** A1
Ruckstall County
  Primary School
  BSTK RG21 .... **93** J5
Rushmoor Borough Council
  FARN GU14 .... **78** E5
St Annes Catholic
  Primary School
  KEMP RG22 .... **92** C5
St Bartholomews C of E School
  HASM GU27 .... **192** F8
St Bartholomews (Joint School)
  NWBY RG14 .... **2** B7
St Bartholomews School
  NWBY RG14 .... **2** B8
St Bedes Catholic
  Primary School
  CHIN RG24 .... **70** F7
St Bedes C of E Primary School
  WINC SO23 .... **11** H6
St Benedicts Convent School
  RAND SP11 .... **105** M5
St Bernadettes RC
  Primary School
  FARN GU14 .... **78** D3
St Catherines School
  CBLY GU15 .... **58** F4
St Edmunds School
  CSHT GU26 .... **192** A5
St Faiths Primary School
  WINC SO23 .... **226** E3
St Gabriels School
  KSCL RG20 .... **25** L2
St Georges Industrial Estate
  CBLY GU15 .... **58** E5
St Georges University
  School of Medicine
  WINC SO23 .... **11** G7
St Johns C of E First School
  NFNM GU10 .... **169** H7
St Johns School
  BSTK RG21 .... **92** F5
St Johns School
  NWBY RG14 .... **2** D9
St Johns School
  THLE RG7 .... **31** K3
St John the Baptist RC
  Primary School
  AND SP10 .... **8** B6
St Josephs Gm RC
  Primary School
  ALDT GU11 .... **6** C1
St Josephs RC Primary School
  NWBY RG14 .... **3** H1
St Jospehs RC Junior School
  ALDT GU11 .... **6** F5
St Lawrence C of E (Controlled)
  Primary School
  ALTN GU34 .... **164** D4
St Marks C of E Primary School
  FARN GU14 .... **79** G8
St Marks Primary School
  KEMP RG22 .... **115** G2
St Martins East Woodhay C of E
  Primary School
  KSCL RG20 .... **43** K1
St Mary Bourne School
  RAND SP11 .... **85** L6
St Marys C of E Junior School
  CHIN RG24 .... **94** A2
St Marys C of E Junior School
  NTHA RG18 .... **15** G4
St Marys Primary School
  ALTN GU34 .... **163** G3
St Marys Primary School
  TLHT RG30 .... **19** M2
St Marys School
  THLE RG7 .... **32** A3
St Marys Surgery
  AND SP10 .... **9** J4
St Matthews C of E
  Primary School
  BOR GU35 .... **188** F8
St Michaels Abbey
  FARN GU14 .... **78** F3
St Michaels C of E Controlled
  Secondary School
  ALDT GU11 .... **7** J6
St Michaels C of E Infant School
  ALDT GU11 .... **7** H6
St Michaels C of E
  Primary School
  SHST GU47 .... **37** H8
St Michaels School
  KSCL RG20 .... **45** J2
St Neots Preparatory
  School Ltd
  HTWY RG27 .... **35** H8
St Nicholas C of E School
  NWBY RG14 .... **2** D6
St Nicholas School
  NFNM GU10 .... **98** D4
St Omer Barracks
  ALDT GU11 .... **101** G4
St Patricks RC School
  FARN GU14 .... **79** G4

St Pauls C of E First School
  NFNM GU10 .... **124** D1
St Pauls Hospital
  WINW SO22 .... **10** E6
St Peters C of E Middle School
  FNM GU9 .... **146** C2
St Peters Gm C of E School
  YTLY GU46 .... **57** G2
St Peters Junior School
  FARN GU14 .... **78** F4
St Peters School
  WINW SO22 .... **226** A3
St Polycarps RC
  Primary School
  FNM GU9 .... **123** G7
St Swithuns School
  RWIN SO21 .... **203** J8
St Thomas Infant School
  KSCL RG20 .... **24** B8
Salesian College
  FARN GU14 .... **79** G7
Sampson Business Park
  CBLY GU15 .... **58** E5
The Samuel Cody School
  FARN GU14 .... **100** E1
Sandford Springs Golf Club
  TADY RG26 .... **47** M6
Sandhurst College Town County
  Junior School
  SHST GU47 .... **38** B8
Sandhurst School
  SHST GU47 .... **38** A8
Sandhurst Sports Club
  SHST GU47 .... **57** M1
Sandhurst Surgery
  SHST GU47 .... **57** L1
Sandleford Hospital
  NWBY RG14 .... **13** K8
Sarum Road Hospital
  WINW SO22 .... **226** B1
Saxonwood School for the
  Handicapped
  DEAN RG23 .... **70** A8
Selborne Primary School
  ALTN GU34 .... **187** J8
Shalbourne C of E School
  MARL SN8 .... **20** B4
Shaw-cum-donnington School
  NWBY RG14 .... **13** K2
Shawfield County Infant School
  ASHV GU12 .... **101** K5
Shepherd Spring
  Medical Centre
  AND SP10 .... **107** G5
Shepherds Spring
  County Infants School
  AND SP10 .... **107** G5
Sherborne St John
  Primary School
  CHIN RG24 .... **70** D4
The Ship House Surgery
  LIPH GU30 .... **214** E5
Shottermill County
  Middle School
  HASM GU27 .... **216** C1
Silchester Primary School
  THLE RG7 .... **30** E7
The Sixth Form College
  FARN GU14 .... **78** E1
Smannell & Enham
  Primary School
  RAND SP11 .... **107** K1
South Farnborough
  County Junior School
  FARN GU14 .... **79** G6
South Farnborough
  Infant School
  FARN GU14 .... **79** G8
South Farnham Middle School
  FNM GU9 .... **123** H7
South Ham Medical Centre
  KEMP RG22 .... **92** B5
Southlea Surgery
  ALDT GU11 .... **7** H7
South Wonston Primary School
  RWIN SO21 .... **178** C4
Southwood Golf Club
  FARN GU14 .... **78** B6
Sparsholt College Hampshire
  RWIN SO21 .... **200** F4
Sparsholt Primary School
  RWIN SO21 .... **201** J5
Speenhamland Cp School
  NWBY RG14 .... **2** D1
Springlake Country Club
  ASHV GU12 .... **101** H4
Spurcroft Primary School
  STHA RG19 .... **15** G6
Staff College
  CBLY GU15 .... **58** F1
Stanmore Primary School
  WINW SO22 .... **226** D3
Station Industrial Estate
  FLET GU13 .... **77** G5
Station Road Surgery
  FARN GU14 .... **59** G8
Sterling Industrial Estate
  NWBY RG14 .... **3** G5
Stockbridge CP School
  STOK SO20 .... **174** F5
Stockcross School
  KSCL RG20 .... **12** B2
Stratfield Saye
  THLE RG7 .... **53** G1
Stubbs Industrial Estate
  ALDT GU11 .... **101** H3
Sun Hill Infant School
  NALR SO24 .... **206** C4
Sun Valley Business Park
  WINC SO23 .... **11** M5
Superstore
  BSTK RG21 .... **4** A8
Surrey Hampshire Borders
  Nhs Trust
  BSTK RG21 .... **5** G8
Swallowfield Medical Practice
  THLE RG7 .... **33** M1

Tadley CP School
  TADY RG26 .... **49** M2
Tadley Police Station
  TADY RG26 .... **29** L7
Talavera County Junior & Infant
  School
  ALDT GU11 .... **100** E5
Tavistock County Infant School
  FLET GU13 .... **76** C8
Tempus Business Centre
  BSTK RG21 .... **4** A4
Tennis Club
  FLET GU13 .... **98** E5
Testbourne Community School
  WHCH RG28 .... **110** C5
Test Valley County
  Secondary School
  STOK SO20 .... **174** C5
Thatcham Bowling Club
  NTHA RG18 .... **15** G4
Thatcham Health Centre
  NTHA RG18 .... **14** F4
Thatcham Town Council
  NTHA RG18 .... **14** F4
Thatcham Town Football Club
  STHA RG19 .... **15** J8
Thorneycroft Industrial Estate
  BSTK RG21 .... **4** A9
Thorngrove School
  KSCL RG20 .... **44** B1
Tidworth Garrison Golf Club
  NTID SP9 .... **102** B4
Tidworth Health Centre
  NTID SP9 .... **102** E2
Tomlinscote School
  FRIM GU16 .... **59** J6
Tower Hill CP School
  FARN GU14 .... **78** C5
Trinity School
  NWBY RG14 .... **13** L3
Tunworth Ho
  OVTN RG25 .... **94** C8
Tweseldown Infant School
  FLET GU13 .... **99** G4
Tylney Park Golf Club
  HTWY RG27 .... **73** J4
Ufton Nervet Parochial
  Primary School
  THLE RG7 .... **18** F4
Unicorn Trading Estate
  HASM GU27 .... **216** E1
Union Buildings Playschool
  ALDT GU11 .... **100** D5
Uplands CP School
  SHST GU47 .... **37** L8
Upton Grey Ho
  OVTN RG25 .... **117** M2
Vernham Dean School
  RAND SP11 .... **61** J3
Viables Industrial Estate
  KEMP RG22 .... **92** F7
Vicarage Lane Clinic
  HASM GU27 .... **216** C2
Vickers Business Centre
  CHIN RG24 .... **70** D8
Vigo County Infant School
  AND SP10 .... **9** M3
Vigo County Junior School
  AND SP10 .... **9** M3
Wallop CP School
  STOK SO20 .... **172** E1
Walsh C of E First &
  Middle School
  ASHV GU12 .... **101** J7
War Memorial Hospital
  AND SP10 .... **8** D1
Watchetts County
  Middle School
  CBLY GU15 .... **58** F6
Watermill Theatre
  STHA RG19 .... **26** C3
Watermill Theatre & Restaurant
  KSCL RG20 .... **12** E1
The Wavell School
  ALDT GU11 .... **100** E1
Waverley Abbey C of E School
  NFNM GU10 .... **147** M3
Weeke CP School
  WINW SO22 .... **10** A2
Weford County Infants School
  BOR GU35 .... **189** L4
Wellington Business Park
  CWTH RG45 .... **37** H4
Wellington College
  CWTH RG45 .... **37** K5
Wellington Shopping Centre
  ALDT GU11 .... **6** F2
Wellington Sports Centre
  CWTH RG45 .... **37** J4
Wellum House Dental
  Health Centre
  AND SP10 .... **9** J7
Wessex Bowl
  KEMP RG22 .... **92** B3
Wessex Downs Golf Club
  THLE RG7 .... **17** H4
West Berkshire Council
  NWBY RG14 .... **2** D5
West Berkshire District Council
  NWBY RG14 .... **2** D3
West Berkshire District Council
  NWBY RG14 .... **2** E5
West Berkshire District Council
  NWBY RG14 .... **2** E4
West Berkshire District Council
  NWBY RG14 .... **3** G2
Westend County Infant School
  ALDT GU11 .... **6** D3
Western Primary School
  WINW SO22 .... **10** B6
Westfield County Junior School
  YTLY GU46 .... **56** E3
The Westgate School
  WINW SO22 .... **10** C5
West March Business Centre
  AND SP10 .... **9** J1
West Point Business Park
  AND SP10 .... **106** A7

West Portway Industrial Estate
RAND SP11 .... 105 M7
West Suuex County Council
CBLY GU15 .... 58 E3
West Tytherley Primary School
RSAL SP5 .... 195 M8
Weybourne County
Infant School
FNM GU9 .... 6 A9
Weydon County
Secondary School
FNM GU9 .... 146 C1
Weydown Industrial Estate
HASM GU27 .... 216 E1
Weyford County Junior School
BOR GU35 .... 189 L4
Wherwell School
RAND SP11 .... 154 A1
Whitchurch C of E
Primary School
WHCH RG28 .... 110 C4
Whitchurch Medical Centre
WHCH RG28 .... 110 A4
Whitedown Special School
ALTN GU34 .... 164 D6

White Hart Gallery
OVTN RG25 .... 88 F8
White Hart Industrial Estate
BLKW GU17 .... 58 B3
Whitelands Park CP School
NTHA RG18 .... 14 F3
Whitewater C of E (Controlled)
Primary School
HTWY RG27 .... 73 K3
William Cobbett County
Junior School
FNM GU9 .... 6 B9
Willink Leisure Centre
THLE RG7 .... 19 J6
Willink School
THLE RG7 .... 19 J6
Willis Museum
BSTK RG21 .... 4 F9
Willowdene Play School
CHIN RG24 .... 71 L6
Winchcombe CP Infant School
NWBY RG14 .... 13 K3
Winchcombe Junior School
NWBY RG14 .... 2 E1

Winchester
Agricultural Museum
WINC SO23 .... 11 G5
Winchester City Museum
WINC SO23 .... 11 G8
Winchester College
WINC SO23 .... 226 F2
Winchester Lawn Tennis Club
WINW SO22 .... 10 B3
Winchester Recreation Centre
WINC SO23 .... 11 H6
Winchester Road
Industrial Estate
BSTK RG21 .... 92 E5
Winchester Rugby
Football Club
WINC SO23 .... 11 J4
Winchester School of Art
WINC SO23 .... 11 J6
Winklebury Infant School
DEAN RG23 .... 92 C2
Winklebury Junior School
DEAN RG23 .... 92 C2
Winklebury Medical Centre
DEAN RG23 .... 92 B2

Winnall CP School
WINC SO23 .... 11 L7
Winnall Farm Industrial Estate
WINC SO23 .... 11 K6
Winterslow Primary School
RSAL SP5 .... 194 E2
Winton Play School
AND SP10 .... 9 L4
The Winton School
AND SP10 .... 107 J8
Wispers School
HASM GU27 .... 192 F7
Wolverdene School
AND SP10 .... 9 K7
Wolvesey Palace
WINC SO23 .... 11 H9
Woodlea Primary School
BOR GU35 .... 189 J7
Woolmer Hill School
HASM GU27 .... 216 A1
Woolmer Surgery
BOR GU35 .... 189 J5

Woolton Hill County
Junior School
KSCL RG20 .... 44 B1
Worldham Park Golf Club
ALTN GU34 .... 165 H6
Worting County Infant School
DEAN RG23 .... 91 M4
Worting County Junior School
KEMP RG22 .... 92 A4
Wykeham Gallery
WINC SO23 .... 174 E5
Wykeham Industrial Estate
WINC SO23 .... 11 L4
Yateley County Infant School
YTLY GU46 .... 57 G2
Yateley Health Centre
YTLY GU46 .... 57 G2
Yateley Manor
Preparatory School
YTLY GU46 .... 57 G1
Yateley School
YTLY GU46 .... 56 F3
Youngs Industrial Estate
THLE RG7 .... 29 J4

Notes

Notes

Notes